Social Work and Social Welfare
An Introduction

Joseph Heffernan
University of Texas—Austin

Guy Shuttlesworth
University of Texas—Austin

Rosalie Ambrosino
University of Texas—Austin

Social Work and Social Welfare

An Introduction

Second Edition

West Publishing Company
St. Paul   New York   Los Angeles   San Francisco

COPYRIGHT © 1992 By WEST PUBLISHING COMPANY
COPYRIGHT © 1988 By WEST PUBLISHING COMPANY
50 W. Kellogg Boulevard
P.O. Box 64526
St. Paul, MN 55164-0526

Printed in the United States of America

99 98 97 96 95 94 93 92   8 7 6 5 4 3 2 1
Library of Congress Cataloging-in-Publication Data

Heffernan, Joseph.
    Social work and social welfare: an introduction/Joseph
Heffernan, Guy Shuttlesworth, Rosalie Ambrosino—2nd ed.
        p.   cm.
    Includes bibliographical references and index.
    ISBN 0-314-83693-4
    1. Social service—United States.   I. Shuttlesworth, Guy.
II. Ambrosino, Rosalie.   III. title.
HV91.H424   1991
361.3′2—dc20

∞

91-40
CIP
Rev.

Cover Image Harriet Chaprack Kapel, *Cityscape,* 1983. Watercolor on paper, 26″ × 40″.
                    © 1987 Harriet Chaprack Kapel
Text Design David Farr, Imagesmythe, Inc.
Cover Design K. M. Weber
Copyediting Sharon Sharp
Artwork Rolin Graphics and Alice Thiede
Composition Parkwood Composition
Index E. Virginia Hobbs

Photo Credits

ii © Michael Dwyer/Stock Boston; **0** © Susan Lapides/Design Conceptions; **13** © Joel Gordon; **18** © Kent Reno/Jeroboam; **33** © Michael Weissbrot and family/Stock Boston; **45** © Susan Lapides/Design Conceptions; **54** © Gale Zucker/Stock Boston; **64** © Joel Gordon; **80** © Ulrike Welsch/Photo Edit; **95** © Joel Gordon; **100** © James Holland/Stock Boston; **112** © Joel Gordon; **151** © Jeffrey W. Myers/Stock Boston; **157** © Tom Ferentz/Jeroboam; **199** © Jeff Albertson/Stock Boston; **205** Courtesy of the National Committee for Prevention of Child Abuse; **207** © Frank Siteman/Stock Boston; **215** © Kathy Sloane/Jeroboam; **233** © Susan Lapides/Design Conceptions; **255** © Bohdan Hrynewych/Stock Boston; **261** © Jane Scherr/Jeroboam; **278** © George Bellerose/Stock Boston; **286** © Irene Kane/Jeroboam; **300** © Jim Whittmer/Stock Boston; **329** © George Bellerose/Stock Boston; **340** © Susan Lapides/Design Conceptions; **346** © Susan Lapides/Design Conceptions; **366** © Joel Gordon; **382** © Michael Dwyer/Stock Boston; **391** © Susan Lapides/Design Conceptions; **400** © Ron Delany/Jeroboam; **405** © Susan Lapides/Design Conceptions; **417** © Don Melandry/Jeroboam; **418** © Lionel Delevingne/Stock Boston; **432** © Olof Källström; **441** © Joel Gordon; **444** © Rhoda Sidney/Stock Boston; **453** © Jane Scherr/Jeroboam.

to our students

Contents

Chapter 3
A Systems/Ecological Perspective to Understanding Social Work and Social Welfare 49

Part II
Fields of Practice and Populations Served 81

Chapter 4
Poverty and Income Security 83

Chapter 7
The Needs of Children, Youth, and Families 179

Chapter 8
Services to Children, Youth, and Families 213

Chapter 11
Social Work in Rural Settings 297

Chapter 12
Old Age: Issues, Problems, and Services 315

Preface

This book is about the many social welfare issues facing the United States today and the diverse roles that social work professionals play in responding to those issues. Approaches to social welfare have changed over the decades; however, the problems to which the social work profession responds have remained. This does not occur because the profession has been ineffective, but because as society advances, so do the standards of ways that we address social issues. Thomas Merton has suggested that in a community of saints, sin needs to be redefined—so too, with social problems and social responses. There is a rhythm of social responses to social welfare problems. At this time, poverty, homelessness, AIDS, substance abuse, child abuse and neglect, and inadequacies of health care stand high on the social agenda. At other times, these problems are barely perceived as problems at all, while other problems demand the limelight and receive the bulk of public attention. It is our intent that this text will help students develop a frame of reference for understanding social welfare and an approach to addressing social issues which will serve them well in times of commitment and retrenchment.

This is a collaborative work among three colleagues. Where consensus was possible we sought it; where it was not possible we sought to identify the diverse views that exist about the established wisdom of social work. Each of us contributed the perspectives of our own education: sociology, education, and psychology in the case of Ambrosino; sociology and history in the case of Shuttlesworth; political science and economics in the case of Heffernan; and social work for all three authors. The text is interdisciplinary in this sense, but it is disciplined by the continuity and the certainty of unresolved social problems to which social work skills are relevant.

Four "referent" groups played an important role in strengthening this book: our families, our students, our colleagues in Austin, and our colleagues in the profession. We owe our gratitude to our families—Bob, Megan, Will, Jean, and Linda—for their support and understanding when the book took priority over them. We also thank our colleagues at the University of Texas School of Social Work for their critique and for assuming tasks for us at times when we were trying to meet deadlines: Julie Cunniff, Joyce Hunter, Kelly Larson, Kathy Selber, Michelle Vinet, Rosemarie Penzerro, and Karen Knox.

We also personally thank the diverse group of reviewers whose comments significantly contributed to the quality of this second edition: Richard Enos, University of North Texas; Susan E. Dawson, Utah State University; Steven L. McMurtry, Arizona State University; Carl S. Wilks, University of Tennessee; Kenneth W. Green, Southeast Missouri State University; Ronald H. Ozaki, University of Nebraska at Lincoln; Gust William Mitchell, University of Maryland; Stephen C. Anderson, University of Oklahoma; Charlene A. Urwin, Texas Christian University; Ernest W. Kachingwe, Kearney State College, Nebraska; John L. Erlich, California State University, Sacramento; and Margaret Elbow, Texas Tech University. We very much appreciate the excellent guidance they provided to us in making revisions from the first edition.

The referent group of greatest relevance has been our students. Their comments in classes over our collective sixty years of teaching helped us to shape our views of what they wanted and needed to know to become better social workers and citizens in our complex society. We especially appreciate their critique of the first edition and their enthusiastic suggestions for changes. We have incorporated many of their ideas into this second edition.

Last but not least, we express our gratitude to our acquisition's editor, Tom LaMarre, for his persistence and encouragement in the book preparation and publication, and his executive assistant, Bernice Carlin. Also, many thanks to the production guidance and abilities of Jayne Lindesmith of West Publishing Company and to all those who helped with this publication along the way.

We hope that some students using this text will be persuaded, or have their choices reinforced, to join the social work profession. We urge those students considering a career in social work to talk with their course instructors about the BSW degree. We also recommend that they visit social agencies and complete some volunteer experience in conjunction with this course. Most importantly, however, we hope this book in some way contributes to the social conscience of students no matter what career they choose and encourages students to recognize social work as a dynamic, challenging profession.

Rosalie Ambrosino
Joe Heffernan
Guy Shuttlesworth

Social Work and Social Welfare
An Introduction

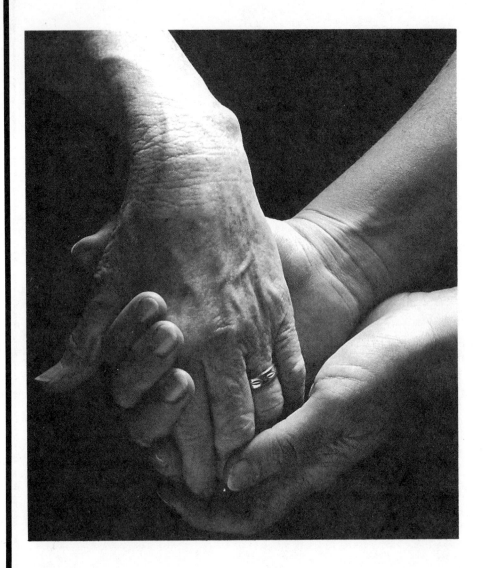

Part
I

Introduction

This opening section introduces the reader to the nature of social welfare and social work: what social welfare encompasses and what social workers who function in social welfare settings do. Also provided are historical and theoretical contexts that can be used as a framework for understanding subsequent chapters in the book.

Chapter 1, "Social Work: A Helping Profession," examines social welfare as a broad system intended to maintain the well-being of individuals within a society. The roles and functions of social work professionals who work within the social welfare system also are explored. This chapter portrays the social welfare system and the profession of social work as challenging and dynamic arenas for those interested in careers in this helping profession.

Chapter 2, "Social Welfare, Past and Present," discusses the historical context of social welfare and social work. Selected historical welfare policies that have influenced the structure and format of our contemporary social welfare institutions are examined, and the evolution of social work as a profession is explored.

Chapter 3, "A Systems/Ecological Perspective to Understanding Social Work and Social Welfare," provides a theoretical framework for subsequent chapters. The social work profession's use of systems theory and an ecological perspective for viewing individuals within the broader context of their environment is explained. This framework is discussed from an individual perspective, a family perspective, and a broad societal perspective to help the reader see how this framework can be used at all levels by social work practitioners. An introduction to the problem-solving approach, a generalist social work approach that incorporates the systems/ecological framework, also is provided.

These chapters lay the groundwork for content addressed in the remaining chapters of the book. A systems/ecological framework and problem-solving approach provide the context for understanding the functions that social workers play in intervening in all settings and with all populations discussed in Section II. The methods of social work presented in Section III incorporate the systems/ecological framework and the problem-solving approach. Finally, the special issues faced by the social welfare system and social work practitioners discussed in Section IV can be understood from a systems/ecological framework and addressed using the problem-solving approach.

Social Work: A Helping Profession

Carla Boyle, a social worker who serves as case manager for the Lowell family, has called a meeting of social workers from the agencies who are providing the family with support services. Tony Jones, a school social worker, has been working with the school system to make special arrangements for Charles Lowell (a six-year-old) to receive math tutoring. Eloise Morales, a social worker with the Department of Human Services Child Protection Service Unit, is providing counseling services for Mr. and Mrs. Lowell, who have been abusive parents to Charles and his younger sister, Amy (age three).

Jan Nevil, a social worker at Bigtown Day Care Center, has been working on arrangements for Amy to receive special care at the center, while Ida Smith, a social worker for the local Family Service Association, is coordinating efforts with the employment agency to secure employment for Mr. Lowell. Carla Boyle has called this meeting so each of the social workers involved with the Lowell family can report on his or her progress with the family. At the conclusion of their meeting they will agree on a plan for continuing work with the Lowells.

The situation just described represents only a few of the broad and diverse activities that encompass social work practice. Social workers are employed by a wide variety of local, state, and federal agencies as professionals who engage clients in seeking solutions to problems. The aim of this book is to provide the reader with an understanding of the goals and objectives of professional social work practice, the nature of the profession, and the types of problems that social workers help their clients resolve. Social work practice demands from its practitioners the utmost in intellect, creativity, skill, and knowledge. It is an exciting, challenging profession. Students who have the aptitude and desire to prepare for a career in the helping professions may find social work well suited to their needs and interests.

In this chapter, we examine the professional culture, activities, knowledge base, and skills incorporated into social work practice. The broader field of social welfare, of which professional social work practice is the major discipline, also is reviewed. But first, we examine why people have unresolved problems and why they need professional assistance in seeking solutions to them.

WHY DO PEOPLE HAVE PROBLEMS?

No one is free from problems, and what may be a problem for one person is not necessarily viewed that way by another. For example, some people are very meticulous in their dress and spend hours putting their hair, clothing, and adornments in order so that their public appearance will reflect perfection in personal grooming. Others appear to place little emphasis on personal appearance. Decision making for some individuals comes only with great difficulty, whereas others seem to have little trouble making choices.

Social workers deal with problems that inhibit optimal functioning for individuals and groups, or those that result in dysfunctional behavior. Poverty, marital conflict, parent–child relationship problems, delinquency, abuse and neglect, substance abuse, and mental/emotional stress are among the many problems that professional social workers help people address.

Why do individuals develop problems so great that outside assistance is needed? That question may not be answered simply! Obviously, no rational person plans to have debilitating problems. No child plans to spend a life in poverty, nor does an adolescent choose a life of mental illness. What newly married couple, much in love and looking forward to the future together, plans for marital disharmony, family violence, or divorce? Why, then, do these problems emerge? Why do some individuals experience happy, satisfying marriages, whereas others move from marriage to marriage without finding satisfaction? Why are some people prosperous and readily move up the occupational and income ladders, whereas others remain deeply enmeshed in poverty? A matter of personal choice? Of course not! Problems of social functioning result from a mix of many factors. Briefly, we need to examine the factors that contribute to adaptation.

Genetics and Heredity

From the biological standpoint, people are born with many of the physiological characteristics of their ancestors. Some people have a tendency to be tall, others short; some lean, others heavy; some physically attractive, others less attractive; and so on. Undoubtedly. many people have greater intellectual potential than others; some are more agile, others less so. To a certain degree these characteristics affect their adaptation and, indeed, opportunities throughout life. For example, regardless of skill or ability, it is virtually impossible for a 5'6" young man to become a professional basketball player, or for an overweight young woman to be selected Miss America. Regardless of desire or skill, opportunity is affected by physical characteristics. The reader is encouraged to think of other examples where genetic and/or hereditary factors might impose limitations on social behavior or opportunities.

Socialization

Whatever limits may be imposed by heredity, individuals develop as social beings through the process of **socialization**. Social behavior is learned behavior acquired through interacting with other human beings. Parents are the primary source of early socialization experiences. Family culture has a significant impact on the development of values, priorities, and role prescriptions. Families, of course, are not the only source of our social development. Neighbors, play-mates, and acquaintances from school and other community institutions also play a part. Lower-income parents and wealthy ones socialize their children in very different ways, because resources and problem-solving opportunities vary so much. Thus, as children develop, their behaviors are shaped by the particular learning opportunities available to them. The thoughts people have and the mental attitudes they develop are as much a product of learning as are the skills they develop. Children who grow up in dysfunctional families often learn inappropriate techniques of problem solving.

Environmental Factors

Geography, climate, and resources all affect quality of life and opportunities available for satisfactory growth and development. These factors vary through-out the land. Added to this are the economic and political forces that largely determine the availability of opportunities and resources around which people seek to organize their lives. Smog-infested, polluted areas contribute to a variety of health problems. Unpredictable economic trends may result in many workers losing their jobs. Discrimination limits opportunities for career development and impedes adequate employment. The environment is a major element in the opportunity structure. It can serve as a stimulus for producing life's satisfactions or become a major source of the problems people experience.

The Opportunity Structure

Obviously, genetics and heredity, socialization, and environmental factors are important in understanding why people have problems. All of the factors shape an individual's **opportunity structure**, that is, the accessibility of opportunities for an individual within that individual's environment. For example, a person may have physical traits and characteristics that are valued by society, a good educational background, a stable and supportive family, work-oriented values, and a desire to work yet have no job because of a recession or depression. In spite of suitable preparation, this person may remain unemployed for some time, with all the problems associated with lack of income. Or, we might consider an individual who was born into a poor family, was abused as a child, did not receive the encouragement or incentives to complete school, and had poorly developed social skills because of inadequate parenting. Even if jobs were plentiful, this person would not be able to compete except for the lowest-paying positions, if at all.

Other illustrations relate to genetic endowment. Gender, race and minority status often result in discrimination and unequal treatment in both job opportunities and the amount of remuneration a person will receive on the job. Women, blacks, and Hispanics, for example, are not afforded equal opportunity in the job market even when all other factors are equal.

SOCIAL WORK DEFINED

Social workers are all too often identified as "welfare" workers, which, in the minds of many, links them primarily to public assistance. Obviously, this is a false premise, since social workers engage in practice in a wide range of service areas. **Social welfare** is the provision of institutional programs for the needy. **Social work,** on the other hand, is one of the professions that is instrumental in administering planned change activities prescribed by our social welfare institutions.

We must keep in mind, too, that the opportunity structure consists not only of what is available in the environment but also of inner resources such as cognitive development and personality structure. Furthermore, many problems that individuals, families, and groups experience result from the way society is organized and the limited choices that are available to some people.

Because social workers are actively involved in wide-ranging tasks, devising a specific, all-inclusive definition of *social work* is difficult. For example, Box 1–1 lists some of the roles played by social workers today. Unfortunately, this has resulted in definitions that are so general that they fail to relate appropriately all of the activities encompassed by the profession. In an attempt to define the field of social work, Pincus and Minahan (1973) offer the following:

> Social work is concerned with the interactions between people and their social environment which affect the ability of people to accomplish their life tasks, alleviate distress, and realize their aspirations and values. (p. 9)

Pincus and Minahan's definition is clear with regard to the goals of the profession. Perhaps a more widely accepted definition is the one offered by the **National Association of Social Workers (NASW).** This definition states that social work is

> the professional activity of helping individuals, groups or communities enhance or restore their capacity for social functioning and creating societal conditions favorable to that goal. (NASW 1973, 4)

Broadly interpreted, these definitions are similar. Social work is viewed as an activity that seeks to remediate human problems by helping individuals, groups, or communities engage resources that will alleviate those problems. In addition, social work is concerned with enabling clients to develop capacities and strengths that will improve their social functioning. As these definitions indicate, social work is an active, "doing" profession that brings about positive change in problem situations through problem solving or prevention. The social work profession is also committed to effecting changes in societal values and policies that limit or prohibit the free and full participation of any individuals. Social workers have a professional responsibility to work for changes in discriminatory or otherwise restrictive practices that limit opportunities and prevent maximal social functioning.

Box 1–1   Roles For Social Workers

○ Outreach worker: A social worker who identifies and detects individuals, groups or communities who are having difficulty (in crisis) or are in danger of becoming vulnerable (at risk) works as an outreach worker.

○ Broker: The social worker who steers people toward existing services that may be of service to them is called a broker in the same way that a stockbroker steers prospective buyers toward stocks which may be useful to them.

○ Advocate: A social worker who fights for the rights and dignity of people in need of help advocates their cause.

○ Evaluator: A social worker who gathers information, assesses problems and makes decisions for action is, among other things, an evaluator.

○ Mobilizer: A social worker who assembles, energizes and organizes existing or new groups takes the role of mobilizer. This is most often a community organization role, although not always.

○ Teacher: A social worker whose main task is to convey and impart information and knowledge and to develop skills is a teacher. This role may or may not be played in a formal classroom situation.

○ Behavior changer: A social worker who works to bring about change in behavior patterns, habits and perception of individuals or groups is a behavior changer.

○ Consultant: A social worker who works with other workers or other agencies to help them increase their skills and solve client's problems is a consultant.

○ Community planner: A social worker who works with neighborhood groups, agencies, community agents or government in the development of community programs is called a community planner.

○ Data manager: A social worker who collects, classifies and analyzes data generated within the welfare environment is a data manager. This role may be performed by a supervisor, administrator, or it may be carried out by a clerical person with the necessary skills.

○ Administrator: A social worker who manages an agency, a facility, or a small unit is operating in the role of administrator.

○ Care giver: A social worker who provides ongoing care—physical, custodial, financial—for whatever reason is acting as a care giver.

Source: From Betty J. Piccard. *An Introduction to Social Work: A Primer*, 4th ed., pp. 27–28. Homewood, Ill.: The Dorsey Press, 1988. Reprinted with permission of Wadsworth, Inc.

THE EARLY YEARS

Professional social work developed slowly over the years as a result of efforts to refine and improve its knowledge and skill base. As discussed further in Chapter 2, the early administration of relief to the needy was accomplished by a wide variety of individuals: overseers of the poor, friends and neighbors, church members, the clergy, philanthropists, and friendly visitors, among others. As early as 1814 in Scotland, the Reverend Thomas Chalmers expressed concern over wasteful and inefficient approaches used by relief programs and sought to encourage the development of a more humane and effective system for providing services and support. Chalmers emphasized the need for a more personalized involvement with the needy. He devised a system wherein his parish was divided into districts, with a deacon assigned to investigate each case in order to determine the causes of problems. If the resultant analysis indicated that self-sufficiency was not possible, an attempt was made to engage family, friends, neighbors, or wealthy citizens to provide the necessary assistance for the needy. As a last resort, the congregation was asked to provide assistance (Pumphrey and Pumphrey 1961).

Later, in the United States, the Association for Improving the Conditions of the Poor (New York City) and the Charity Organization Society (Buffalo, New York City, and Philadelphia) used similar approaches when organizing activities to help the poor. The **Charity Organization Society (COS)** had a profound effect on establishing social work as a specialized practice. The COS promoted "scientific philanthropy," emphasizing that charity was more than almsgiving and had as its "long-run goal . . . to restore the recipient of charity to the dignity of as much self-sufficiency and responsibility as he could manage" (Leiby 1978, 111–12). Furthermore, the COS stressed the importance of individual assessment and a coordinated plan of service. The COS was the first relief organization to pay personnel to investigate requests for assistance and to refer eligible applicants to one or more existing agencies for intensive aid and supervision. Special emphasis was given to "following up" on the recipients of assistance, and efforts were made to secure someone to establish friendly relationships with them (Leiby 1978, 112–35).

Just as "friendly visiting" was encouraged, attention was also given to data collection and assessment. It was believed that a more structured, informed, and skillful approach would increase efficiency, discourage dependence on charity, lead to personal development and self-sufficiency, and reduce the practice of providing relief for chronic beggars.

The settlement house movement also emerged as a viable means for providing a variety of community services and advocacy for the poor and disenfranchised during the late 1800s. Perhaps the most noteworthy of the settlements was Hull House, established in 1889 by Jane Addams, a pioneer social worker. The success of this venture was immediate, and the programs offered by Hull House captured the imagination of both philanthropic helpers and the needy. The settlements maintained a strong family focus, provided socialization experiences, and, through advocacy efforts, sought to influence the community to correct the dismal social conditions under which the poor were living.

This structured approach to managing charitable efforts quickly resulted in the need for trained workers. Mary Richmond, a major contributor to the COS movement (and considered by many to be the founder of the professional social work movement), inaugurated the first training program for social workers at the New York School of Applied Philanthropy, the forerunner of schools of social work. Richmond also formulated the concept and base for **social casework,** a practice method designed to "develop personality through adjustments consciously effected, individual by individual, between men and their environment" (Richmond 1922, 9). She also maintained a keen interest in personality and family development and stressed the environmental influence within which interpersonal interactions transpired. Believing that environmental factors were significant contributors to personal as well as family dysfunctions, she maintained a strong interest in social reform that would promote a better quality of life for individuals (Leiby 1978, 124). Richmond was convinced that this task should be included in the social worker's sphere of responsibility. In her classic work, *Social Diagnosis* (1917), she laid the framework for social casework practice. Under the impetus provided by Richmond, Jane Addams, and other early social work pioneers, a profession was born.

Schools of social work began to emerge along the Eastern Seaboard and in larger cities of the Midwest, emphasizing direct social work practice (casework). Many were influenced by newly developing psychological perspectives, most notably those of Sigmund Freud and Otto Rank. Schools adopting Freudian psychology were more prevalent and became identified as "diagnostic" schools. Schools incorporating Rankian theory were known as "functional" schools. Shaping of curriculum around psychological theories increased the scientific knowledge base for social work practice.

By the late 1920s, **social group work** had gained visibility as a method of social intervention, rather than "treatment" per se. Learning and social development were believed to be enhanced through structured group interactions. This technique soon became popular in settlement houses and in work with street gangs, organized recreational clubs, and residents of institutions. Social group work became well entrenched as a viable helping method and later was adopted as a social work method.

Community organization had its roots in the New York Society for the Prevention of Pauperism, the Association for Improving Conditions of the Poor, and the Charity Organization Society. It became prominent as a resource development method by the late 1930s. Dealing largely with community development and stressing the importance of citizen participation and environmental change, community organizers plied their skills in identifying unmet human needs and working toward the development of community resources to meet those needs. Skills in needs assessment, planning, public relations, organizing, influencing, and resource development were among the prerequisites for community organizers.

By the 1950s, social casework, group work, and community organization were all considered methods of social work practice. In 1955, the various associations established to promote and develop each separate method merged and became known as the National Association of Social Workers (NASW).

NASW continues to serve as the main professional organization for social workers today, with over 100,000 members. NASW seeks to promote quality in practice, stimulates political participation and social action, maintains standards of eligibility for membership in the association, and publishes several journals, including *Social Work*. Each state has an NASW chapter with a designated headquarters, and local membership units are active in all major cities.

UNDERPINNINGS OF THE PROFESSION

Social work practice is based on values, knowledge of human behavior, practice skills, and planned change. Each of these attributes is important to professional social workers.

Values

Social workers are committed to the dignity, worth, and value of all human beings, regardless of social class, race, color, creed, gender, or age. The value of human life transcends all other values, and the best interest of human beings merits a humane and helpful response from society. People with problems, regardless of the nature of those problems, are not to be judged, condemned, or demeaned. Social workers emphasize that nonjudgmental attitudes are essential for maintaining clients' dignity and privacy, and that clients must be accepted as they are, with no strings attached. Furthermore, clients (or the **client system,** which may include more than one individual, such as a family or a group of retarded adults) have the right to autonomy, that is, the right to determine courses of action that will affect their lives. Likewise, groups and communities hold these fundamental rights.

Knowledge

Social work practice is derived from theories of human behavior as well as experimental knowledge related to practice. Research is an integrally important contributor to understanding individual, group, and community behavior. Research also is a method of identifying more effective interventive techniques. Students of social work are expected to have an understanding of the life cycle, as well as personality development, social dysfunction, developmental processes, group dynamics, effects of discrimination, social policy formulation, research methods, and community environments. Schools of social work encourage students to become familiar with a wide range of social and behavioral science theories that serve as a basis for understanding how client systems adapt and cope with problems and how theory guides planned social intervention. This knowledge undergirds the social worker's practice competence.

Practice Skills

Social workers are familiar with techniques related to direct practice with individuals (casework) and groups (group work), as well as communities (community organization). Organizing, planning, and administration also are included as areas of specialization for many social work practitioners. Research skills are essential for evaluating practice effectiveness, too.

Planned Change

Professional social work intervention is based on a process of planned change. Change is indicated when client systems present dysfunctional problems that go unresolved. Planned change is an orderly approach to problem solving and is based on problem assessment, knowledge of the client system's capacity for change, and focused intervention. The social worker functions as a change agent in this process. Planned change is characterized by purpose and a greater likelihood of predictable outcomes derived from the change effort. Box 1–2 presents a statement of the purpose of social work formulated by social workers.

These underpinnings of the profession (values, knowledge, practice skills, and planned change) are discussed in greater detail in Chapters 13 through 16.

SOCIAL WORK METHODS

Social workers are committed to the process of planned change. In their role, they become agents of change, who focus on improving the conditions that adversely affect the functioning of clients (or client systems). Change efforts may be geared toward assisting individuals, groups, or communities (or all three), and appropriate methods of intervention for achieving problem solutions are engaged. Practice methods incorporate social work values, principles, and techniques in

1. helping people obtain resources;
2. conducting counseling and psychotherapy with individuals or groups;
3. helping communities or groups provide or improve social and health services, and
4. participating in relevant legislative processes that affect the quality of life for all citizens.

A variety of social work practice methods exist, as discussed in the following sections and described more extensively in Part III.

Direct Practice with Individuals and Families

When the social worker's effort is focused on working directly with individuals or families, the process is called **direct practice** (casework). This type of method is geared toward helping individuals and families identify solutions to personal or other problems related to difficulty in social functioning. In many instances, problems related to social inadequacy, emotional conflict, interpersonal loss, social stress, or the lack of familiarity with resources create dysfunction for individuals. Practitioners are skilled in assessment and know how to intervene

Box 1–2 Working Statement on the Purpose of Social Work

The purpose of social work is to promote or restore a mutually beneficial interaction between individuals and society in order to improve the quality of life for everyone. Social workers hold the following beliefs:

○ The environment (social, physical, organizational) should provide the opportunity and resources for the maximum realization of the potential and aspirations of all individuals, and should provide for their common human needs and for the alleviation of distress and suffering.
○ Individuals should contribute as effectively as they can to their own well-being and to the social welfare of others in their immediate environment as well as to the collective society.
○ Transactions between individuals and others in their environment should enhance the dignity, individuality, and self-determination of everyone. People should be treated humanely and with justice.

Clients of social workers may be an individual, a family, a group, a community, or an organization.

Objectives
Social workers focus on person-and-environment in interaction. To carry out their purpose, they work with people to achieve the following objectives:

○ Help people enlarge their competence and increase their problem-solving and coping abilities.
○ Help people obtain resources.
○ Make organizations responsive to people.
○ Facilitate interaction between individuals and others in their environment.
○ Influence social and environmental policy.

To achieve these objectives, social workers work with other people. At different times, the target of change varies—it may be the client, others in the environment, or both.

Source: Copyright, 1990, National Association of Social Workers, Inc. Reprinted with permission.

strategically in providing assistance for those problems. Direct practice is often considered to be therapeutic in nature.

Direct Practice with Groups (Group Work)

Group work techniques seek to enrich the lives of individuals through planned group experiences. Group work stresses the value of self-development through

Social workers take on many roles in working with people. Here, an elderly woman in a nursing home receives counseling to help her adjust to her new residence and cope with her health problems.

structured interaction with other group members. This process is based on theories of group dynamics and encourages personal growth through active participation as a group member. Groups may be natural (already formed), such as street gangs, or formed purposefully at the group work setting, such as support groups. In either instance, the value of participation, democratic goal setting, freedom of expression, acceptance, and the development of positive attitudes through sharing is stressed. Group work generally is not considered therapeutic, and it should not be confused with group therapy, which also utilizes group processes. Group therapy is designed to be therapeutic in that it seeks to alter or diminish dysfunctional behavior through the dynamic use of group interaction. Members of therapeutic groups often share common emotionally distressing experiences (e.g., a group of recent divorcées) and through focused discussion develop options for more adaptive behaviors.

Community Organization

Social workers who practice at the community level utilize techniques of community organization to promote change. Recognizing that citizen awareness and support are vital to the development of resources in generating a more healthy and constructive environment for all citizens, community organizers work with established organizations within the community such as Lions and Kiwanis clubs, city governments, welfare organizations, the Junior League, political groups, social action groups, and other citizens' organizations in order to gain support for needed services and to secure funding for their maintenance. Social workers who intervene at this level may be employed by city governments, planning agencies, councils of social agencies, or related community agencies.

Social Work Research

Although all social workers use research, many social workers specialize in social work research. This serves to increase both the knowledge base of practice and the effectiveness of intervention. Research also provides an empirical base upon which more focused policy formulation may be designed. Social research is essential in the process of establishing a scientific framework for solving problems and refining social work practice methods. Evaluative research enables agencies as well as practitioners to gain a better understanding of the effectiveness of efforts designed to meet goals and objectives around which practice efforts are focused. Competent social work practitioners keep abreast of the professional research and utilize research findings in their practice.

Social Work Administration and Planning

Administration and planning is a social work method that seeks to maximize the effective use of agency resources in problem solving. Administrators must be skilled in organizing, planning, and mangement techniques, as well as having knowledge about social work practice. Many social agency administrators begin their careers as direct practitioners, subsequently become supervisors, and then move into administrative roles. Social planning also is seen as a social work role, which is discussed in Chapter 15.

SOCIAL WORK: PROFESSIONAL ISSUES

Social work, like professional fields such as nursing and public administration, has experienced resistance in being acknowledged as a profession. To the extent that this is an important question, one really needs to ask, what are the characteristics of a profession?

Ernest Greenwood (1957) suggests that a profession is identified by the following characteristics:

1. A systematic body of theory
2. Professional authority
3. Sanction of the community
4. A regulative code of ethics
5. A professional culture

The attributes outlined by Greenwood have long characterized social work, which has emerged as one of the more significant helping professions. For example, education for social work practice is predicated on the foundations of social and behavioral sciences, as well as theory and knowledge produced by social work research and years of experimental practice. The social worker's authority is acknowledged by the community and clients who are involved with the profession. Authority presumes the social worker's expertise, including assessment capabilities as well as knowledge about appropriate interventions designed to alleviate problems. Community sanction for social work practice has become more evident within recent years through state laws requiring registration, certification, or licensing of social workers. The National Association of Social Workers has established a code of ethics (Box 1–3) for its members, and a strong professional culture has developed and is expressed through the state and national associations (such as NASW) of social work practitioners. The increasing number of social workers engaged in private practice also contributes to the recognition of social work's professional status. All evidence suggests that social work meets the standards identified by Greenwald for professional status.

Box 1–3   Code of Ethics,
National Association of Social Workers

Preamble
This code is intended to serve as a guide to the everyday conduct of members of the social work profession and as a basis for the adjudication of issues in ethics when the conduct of social workers is alleged to deviate from the standards expressed or implied in this code. It represents standards of ethical behavior for social workers in professional relationships with those served, with colleagues, with employers, with other individuals and professions, and with the community and society as a whole. It also embodies standards of ethical behavior governing individual conduct to the extent that such conduct is associated with an individual's status and identity as a social worker.

This code is based on the fundamental values of the social work profession that include the worth, dignity, and uniqueness of all persons as well as their rights and opportunities. It is also based on the nature of social work, which fosters conditions that promote these values.

In subscribing to and abiding by this code, the social worker is expected to view ethical responsibility in as inclusive a context as each situation demands and within which ethical judgement is required. The social worker is expected to take into consideration all the principles in this code that have a bearing upon any situation in which ethical judgement is to be exercised and professional invervention or conduct is planned. The course of action that the social worker chooses is expected to be consistent with the spirit as well as the letter of this code.

In itself, this code does not represent a set of rules that will prescribe all the behaviors of social workers in all the complexities of professional life. Rather, it offers general principles to guide conduct, and the judicious appraisal of conduct, in situations that have ethical implications. It provides the basis for making judgements about ethical actions before and after they occur. Frequently, the particular situation determines the ethical principles

continued on next page

that apply and the manner of their application. In such cases, not only the particular ethical principles are taken into immediate consideration, but also the entire code and its spirit. Specific applications of ethical principles must be judged within the context in which they are being considered. Ethical behavior in a given situation must satisfy not only the judgement of the individual social worker, but also the judgement of an unbiased jury of professional peers.

This code should not be used as an instrument to deprive any social worker of the opportunity or freedom to practice with complete professional integrity; nor should any disciplinary action be taken on the basis of this code without maximum provision for safeguarding the rights of the social worker affected.

The ethical behavior of social workers results not from edict, but from a personal commitment of the individual. This code is offered to affirm the will and zeal of all social workers to be ethical and to act ethically in all that they do as social workers.

The following codified ethical principles should guide social workers in the various roles and relationships and at the various levels of responsibility in which they function professionally. These principles also serve as a basis for the adjudication by the National Association of Social Workers of issues in ethics.

In subscribing to this code, social workers are required to cooperate in its implementation and abide by any disciplinary rulings based on it. They should also take adequate measures to discourage, prevent, expose, and correct the unethical conduct of colleagues. Finally, social workers should be equally ready to defend and assist colleagues unjustly charged with unethical conduct.

Summary of Major Principles

I. The Social Worker's Conduct and Comportment as a Social Worker
Propriety. The social worker should maintain high standards of personal conduct in the capacity or identity as social worker.
Competence and Professional Development. The social worker should strive to become and remain proficient in professional practice and the performance of professional functions.
Service. The social worker should regard as primary the service obligation of the social work profession.
Integrity. The social worker should act in accordance with the highest standards of professional integrity.
Scholarship and Research. The social worker engaged in study and research should be guided by the conventions of scholarly inquiry.

II. The Social Worker's Ethical Responsibility to Clients
Primacy of Clients' Interests. The social worker's primary responsibility is to clients.
Rights and Prerogatives of Clients. The social worker should make every effort to foster maximum self-determination on the part of clients.
Confidentiality and Privacy. The social worker should respect the privacy of clients and hold in confidence all information obtained in the course of professional service.
Fees. When setting fees, the social worker should ensure that they are

continued on next page

fair, reasonable, considerate, and commensurate with the service performed and with due regard for the clients' ability to pay.

III. The Social Worker's Ethical Responsibility to Colleagues
Respect, Fairness, and Courtesy. The social worker should treat colleagues with respect, courtesy, fairness, and good faith.
Dealing with Colleagues' Clients. The social worker has the responsibility to relate to the clients of colleagues with full professional consideration.

IV. The Social Worker's Ethical Responsibility to Employers and Employing Organizations
Commitments to Employing Organizations. The social worker should adhere to commitments made to the employing organizations.

V. The Social Worker's Ethical Responsibility to the Social Work Profession
Maintaining the Integrity of the Profession. The social worker should uphold and advance the values, ethics, knowledge, and mission of the profession.
Community Service. The social worker should assist the profession in making social services available to the general public.
Development of Knowledge. The social worker should take responsibility for identifying, developing, and fully utilizing knowledge for professional practice.

VI. The Social Worker's Ethical Responsibility to Society
Promoting the General Welfare. The social worker should promote the general welfare of society.

Source: Copyright 1980, National Association of Social Workers, Inc., NASW Code of Ethics. Reprinted with permission.

THE SOCIAL AGENCY

The majority of social workers perform their professional functions through the auspices of a social agency. **Social agencies** are organizations that have been formed by communities to address social problems experienced by a significant number of citizens. Agencies may be *public* (funded by taxes), *voluntary* (funded through contributions), or, in increasing numbers, proprietary (profit-oriented). The typical social agency is headed by a board of directors of local citizens. It meets regularly to review the agency's activities and to establish policy that governs agency services. Many larger agencies have an administrator who has sole responsibility for supervising the agency's activities. In many smaller agencies, the administrator also may be involved in assisting clients with their problems.

Agencies are community resources that stand ready to assist in resolving problems that make day-by-day functioning difficult. Social workers are employed to carry out the mission of the agency. Many agencies do not charge fees for the services they provide. In some instances, however, agencies employ a "sliding-fee scale" and adjust the fee to the client's ability to pay. All clients, regardless of ability to pay, are afforded the same quality of service.

Typically, agencies cooperate in meeting human needs. Referrals are often made when clients have problems that can be resolved more effectively by

Social workers completing BSW degrees receive training both to become generalist practitioners and to work in a diversity of settings. Here a BSW student completing his field practicum at a hospice program talks with two clients that have cancer.

another agency. Interagency coordination is a helpful process, maximizing community resources to bring about problem resolution.

EDUCATION AND LEVELS OF SOCIAL WORK PRACTICE

Professional social workers are involved in assisting clients with a large variety of problems. As a consequence, the nature and degree of skills necessary for effective problem resolution vary with the complexities of the problems encountered. Recognizing that professional competence is a right clients have in seeking assistance, regardless of how difficult their problems might be, the social work profession has established three differing levels of practice for meeting these divergent needs. The profession has also established the **Council on Social Work Education (CSWE).**

Bachelor of Social Work

The entry level for professional social work practice is the baccalaureate (BSW) degree. Social work practitioners entering practice at this level must complete the educational requirements of an undergraduate social work program accredited by the Council on Social Work Education. Currently, in the United States, there are 363 (CSWE, 1989) accredited BSW programs. Although professional social work educational programs offered by colleges and universities may vary, CSWE mandates that each must provide basic education in human growth and behavior, social policy, research, practice methods, and culturally divergent groups as a minimum requirement for meeting accreditation standards. All students who graduate from an accredited BSW program must complete 480 clock hours of field experience in a social work or related setting under the supervision of a social work practitioner. Students are placed in settings such as senior citizens' centers, battered women's shelters, child welfare agencies, residential treatment centers, juvenile and adult probation programs, public schools, health clinics, hospitals, industries, and mental health agencies.

The educational curriculum for baccalaureate-level practice is developed around the generalist method of practice. Typically, the generalist practitioner is knowledgeable about the systems/ecological approach (see Chapter 3 for a complete discussion) to practice and is skillful in problem assessment, interviewing, resource development, case management, use of community resources, establishment of intervention objectives with clients, and problem solving. Baer and Federico (1978) have outlined **competencies**, skills necessary to perform certain functions, that undergird social work practice at the BSW level:

1. *Identify and assess situations where the relationship between people and social institutions needs to be initiated, enhanced, restored, protected, or terminated.*

2. *Develop and implement a plan for improving the well-being of people based on problem assessment and the exploration of obtainable goals and available options.*

3. *Enhance the problem-solving, coping and developmental capacities of people.*

4. *Link people with systems that provide them with resources, services, and opportunities.*

5. *Intervene effectively on behalf of populations most vulnerable and discriminated against.*

6. *Promote the effective and humane operation of the systems that provide people with services, resources and opportunities.*

7. *Actively participate with others in creating new, modified, or improved service, resource, opportunity systems that are more equitable, just, and responsive to consumers of services, and work with others to eliminate those systems that are unjust.*

8. *Evaluate the extent to which the objectives of intervention were achieved.*

9. *Continually evaluate one's own professional growth and development through assessment of practice behaviors and skills.*

10. *Contribute to the improvement of service delivery by adding to the knowledge base of the profession as appropriate and by supporting and upholding the standards and ethics of the profession. (pp. 86–89)*

Entry-level social workers are employed by agencies offering a wide spectrum of services. As direct practice workers, they may perform professional activities as eligibility workers for state human resources departments; work with children and families as protective services (protecting children from abuse and neglect) workers; serve as youth or adult probation workers; work in institutional care agencies that provide services for children or adults, especially the aged; engage in school social work; act as program workers or planners for areawide agencies on aging; work in mental health outreach centers or institutions; serve as family assistance workers in industry; or perform their professional tasks in many other agencies providing human services. It is not uncommon for baccalaureate-level professionals with experience and demonstrated competence to be promoted to supervisory and administrative positions.

Social work professionals at the BSW level of practice are eligible for full membership in the NASW. The professional activities they perform in helping clients resolve problems are challenging and rewarding. Many social workers prefer to practice at this level throughout their careers. For others, an advanced degree in social work is desirable and opens up areas of practice that are not typically in the domain of the baccalaureate (BSW) practitioner. For those who have completed their undergraduate social work education from an accredited college or university, advanced standing may be granted by the school of social work to which they apply. Although not all graduate schools accept advanced-standing students, the CSWE provides a listing of those that do. Advanced-standing students, when admitted to a graduate program, are able to shorten the time required to secure the masters degree without diluting the quality of their educational experience. Advanced practice in social work is predicated upon the master's degree in social work (MSW).

Master of Social Work (Advanced Practice)

Approximately ninety-seven (CSWE, 1989) colleges and universities have accredited graduate schools of social work. Students in these programs are engaged in an educational curriculum that is more specialized than the BSW curriculum. Students may specialize in direct services (casework or group work), community organization, administration, planning, or research. All students master a common core of basic knowledge, including human growth and behavior, social policy, research, and practice methods related to their area of specialization. Many graduate programs also offer fields of specialization, such as social work with the aged, child welfare, medical social work, industrial social work, mental health, or social work with the developmentally disabled. The two-year master's degree program (MSW) is balanced between classroom learning and clinical (field) practice. Graduates seek employment in such specialized settings as Veterans Administration hospitals, family and children's service agencies, counseling centers, and related settings that require specialized professional education.

Doctorate in Social Work

Professional social workers interested in social work education, highly advanced clinical practice, research, planning, or administration often seek advanced study in programs offering the Doctor of Social Work (DSW) or the Doctor of Philosophy in Social Work (PhD). A number of graduate schools of social work offer education at this level. Students admitted tend to be seasoned social work practitioners, although this is not a prerequisite for admission to all schools. Education at this level stresses research, advanced clinical practice, advanced theory, administration, and social policy. Graduates usually seek employment on the faculty of schools of social work or in the administration of social welfare agencies, or with increasing frequency, in private clinical practice.

SOCIAL WORK CAREERS

The number of employed social service workers grew rapidly from 95,000 in 1960 to approximately 350,000 in 1989. However, with federal funding reductions, the rate of growth of new jobs in social work has decreased. Based on current federal and state funding, it is unlikely that the rate of growth will increase dramatically in the near future. However, this should not discourage students interested in a social work career. New positions are being created in addition to the vacancies created through attrition. Some fields of practice with a vast potential for growth are beginning to emerge. For example, the fields of aging and substance abuse are experiencing a great need for professional social workers.

Social work is an ideal profession for individuals interested in working with people and solving problems. These are the heart of the social work profession. Positions in a wide variety of areas continue to attract social workers at all levels of practice, such as child welfare, health, corrections, mental retardation, family counseling, substance abuse, minority relations, and public assistance programs.

Wages in social work usually are adequate, and increases are based on skill and experience. Baccalaureate-level workers typically earn less than the more specialized master's degree workers. Entrance salaries may range from $15,000 to $25,000 per year, depending on experience, degree, location, and agency sponsorship. A few social workers earn upwards of $75,000 after extensive experience. Mobility often is a valuable asset to the worker looking for an initial social work job. Rural areas often experience shortages of workers, whereas some metropolitan areas have a tighter employment market. Employment vacancies often are listed with college placement services, state employment commissions, professional associations, state agencies, or local newspapers.

SUMMARY

In this chapter, we have reviewed briefly the history of the development of social work, examined the practice base of the profession, identified the practice methods employed by social workers, discussed the professional attributes of the profession, and defined *social work*. When we move to specific social problem areas, the activities of social workers who work in those problem areas are presented in greater detail. First, however, we briefly review the development of the social welfare institution.

KEY TERMS

Charity Organization Society (COS)   opportunity structure
client system   social agencies
community organization   social casework
competencies   social group work
Council on Social Work   social welfare
   Education (CSWE)   social work
direct practice   social worker
National Association of Social   socialization
   Workers (NASW)

DISCUSSION QUESTIONS

1. What factors contribute to the problems that people experience?

2. Define *social work*. What are the goals of social work practice?

3. Trace the development of social work as a profession. What events do you feel were most important in the development of the profession?

4. Differentiate among the various methods of social work practice. How are the methods similar? Different?

5. What are the underpinnings of the profession? How do they relate to social work practice?

6. Identify the levels of professional social work practice. How do these practice levels relate to professional education for social work practice?

7. Describe the competencies that undergird baccalaureate social work practice.

REFERENCES

Baer, Betty L., and Ronald Federico. 1978. *Educating the baccalaureate social worker.* Cambridge: Ballinger.

Council on Social Work Education. 1989. *Colleges and universities with accredited social work degree programs.* Washington, D.C.: Author.

Greenwood, Ernest. 1957. Attributes of a profession. *Social Work* 2 (3): 44–45.

Leiby, James. 1978. *A history of social welfare and social work in the United States.* New York: Columbia University Press.

National Association of Social Workers. 1973. *Standards for social service manpower.* New York: Author.

Piccard, Betty J. 1988. *An introduction to social work: A primer.* Homewood, Ill.: Dorsey.

Pincus, Allen, and Anne Minihan. 1973. *Social work practice: Model and method.* Itasca, Ill.: Peacock.

Pumphrey, Ralph E., and Muriel W. Pumphrey. 1961. *The heritage of American social work.* New York: Columbia University Press.

Richmond, Mary. 1917. *Social diagnosis.* New York: Russell Sage.

——— 1922. *What is social casework?* New York: Russell Sage.

U.S. Department of Labor. 1982. *Occupational outlook handbook, 1982–83.* Washington, D.C.: GPO.

U.S. Department of Labor. 1986. *Occupational outlook handbook, 1986–87.* Washington, D.C.: GPO.

Zastrow, Charles. 1986. *Introduction to social welfare institutions.* 3d ed. Chicago: Dorsey.

SUGGESTED FURTHER READINGS

Bell, Winfred. 1987. *Comtemporary social work practice.* 2d ed. New York: Macmillan.

Compton, Beulah R., and Burt Galaway. 1975. *Social work processes.* Homewood, Ill.: Dorsey.

Epstein, Laura. 1980. *Helping people: The task-centered approach.* St. Louis: Mosby.

Howell, Joseph J. 1972. *Hard living on Clay Street.* New York: Association Press.

Klein, Alan F. 1972. *Effective groupwork.* New York: Association Press.

National Association of Social Workers. 1981. *NASW standards for the classification of social work practice: Policy statement 4.* Silver Springs, Md.: NASW Task Force on Sector Classification.

Slavin, Simon. 1978. *Social administration,* New York: Haworth.

Tripodi, Tony, Phillip Fellin, Irwin Epstein, and Roger Lind. 1972. *Social workers at work.* Itasca, Ill.: Peacock.

Wells, Carolyn C. 1989. *Social work: Day to day.* 2d ed. New York: Longman.

Social Welfare, Past and Present

*D*ecisions about who is needy and how the needy are to be helped bear on economic development, political organization, social stability, and family integrity. Social welfare programs involve a redistribution of resources from the haves to the have nots. U.S. policymakers have been reluctant to do that, holding instead to a faith in laissez faire practices and individualism, valuing the private economy over the public one, and emphasizing individual choice over the collective choices.

Social welfare goals tend to polarize Americans because conflicting ideologies lead to different decisions about priorities for funding of programs. For example, programs for old people or children vie with programs meant to encourage work among employable people. In addition, social welfare goals—for example, ones regarding the elderly or children—may conflict with traditions of self-help among family members and, consequently, lead to programs that discourage acceptance of needed help (Axinn & Levin 1975, 1).

Obviously, no consensus exists regarding the nature, focus, and development of social policy or the responsibility—if any—that the government has in developing programs to assist those in need. The following discussion identifies some of the more salient factors related to developing a comprehensive approach to social welfare in the United States. But first, a few basic questions are in order: What is social welfare? Who gets it? Who pays for it? Does it create dependency? Why is our social welfare system organized as it is? *Social welfare* (which we define in Chapter 1) in our society long has been a matter of dispute and controversy. Often the controversy surrounding the topic of social welfare results from a misunderstanding of the policies that govern social welfare as well as misinformation about people who are entitled to receive benefits. Welfare clients often are viewed as ne'er-do-wells who are too lazy to work and are willing to live off the labor of others. Others identify them as victims of a rapidly changing society who lack necessary employment skills. Some view poverty, mental illness, unemployment, broken homes, lack of income in old age, and related problems as matters of personal failure or personal neglect. It is understandable, then, that people who hold divergent views would have different opinions about the nature of social welfare programs and the people served by them.

Determining who is in need has always been a problem in our society. This is particularly true in relation to providing assistance for those who are poor but appear to be able to work. This concern has resulted in analyses that are often incorrect and ill-founded. Does it seem reasonable to assume that individuals who are poor choose a life of poverty? Why, then, does the problem persist? Assessments which conclude that the poor have elected such a lifestyle, are lazy, or lack motivation often fail to consider how changing social systems contribute to outcomes that result in poverty for a substantial portion of the population. Frequently, a distinction is made between the needy poor and the undeserving poor. Many individuals are more accepting of the needs of the aged, disabled, and chronically ill than those of seemingly able-bodied persons. In this chapter we examine selected historical welfare policies that have influenced the structure and format of our contemporary social welfare institutions.

A DEFINITION OF SOCIAL WELFARE

What is social welfare? We briefly defined it in Chapter 1, but definitions invariably reflect the definer's knowledge and value base. A broad definition of what constitutes social welfare may well include all organized social responses that promote the social well-being of a population. This definition would include, at least, education, health, rehabilitation, protective services for adults and children, public assistance, social insurance, bilingual education, services for the physically and mentally disabled, job-training programs, marriage counseling, psychotherapy, pregnancy counseling, adoption, and a myriad of related activities designed to promote social well-being. Perhaps the most widely accepted definition of social welfare is provided in the *Encyclopedia of Social Work,* which states:

> *Social welfare is an organized effort to insure a basic standard of decency in relation to the physical and mental well-being of the citizenry. . . . [It] is characterized by a large complex of interlocking preventive and protective laws and organizations designed to provide at the least, universal access to the mainstream of society. . . . [It involves] the everpresent, active assistance to individuals and groups to facilitate their attaining and maintaining a respectable lifestyle. (p. 1503).*

Social welfare denotes the full range of organized activities of public and voluntary agencies that seek to prevent, alleviate, or contribute to the solution of a selected set of social problems. The length and breadth of that list of social welfare problems are dependent on one's taste for specificity. By convention, social welfare problems are those problems associated with the attainment of a socially accepted minimum standard of living. Social welfare programs are designed, presumably, to ensure that the specified standard is, in fact, available to selected populations within a nation. In some instances, the standard is provided directly by the agency to the client, whereas in others the agency is structured to help recipients achieve the standard by their own effort. The standards sought are by no means uniform for those in similar life circumstances; for example, those designated for a widowed mother and child are not the same as those identified for an unmarried mother and child. In some instances, the difference reflects a conscious social choice by policymakers, whereas in others, the differences reflect accidents of history and/or geography. Rather than one social welfare program, the United States has, in fact, thousands.

As Wilensky and Lebeaux (1965) point out, social welfare programs may be of an institutional or a residual nature. **Institutional programs** are traditional, first-line efforts that, along with the marketplace and family, are designed to meet the expected needs of individuals and families. The ultimate utility of institutional programs is their ability to anticipate needs before they occur. A good example would be the U.S. social insurance program. We know that as people grow old, they are much more likely to retire from the work force. On the other hand, they must have income to meet food, clothing, shelter, health, and recreational needs throughout life. Social insurance (an institutional program) is designed to provide minimal incomes for retirees, thus making the transition from work to retirement less traumatic and more secure.

By contrast, **residual programs** are established after a need has been identified and when the "normal" institutions of society have failed to meet those needs. Thus, residual programs are reactive—that is, they develop as a reaction to unmet needs. Unlike institutional programs, which are designed to be permanent, residual programs are expected to withdraw as soon as the normal institutional structures of society are functioning well enough to meet needs. Relief programs developed during the Great Depression, as discussed later in this chapter, are a good example of residual programs. At that time of economic downturn, many people lost their jobs and, as a consequence, their incomes. Residual programs such as those enabled by the Federal Emergency Relief Act (FERA) provided jobs, assistance, and related forms of relief to the unemployed. Once the economy was on an even footing, the FERA programs were dissolved.

Occasionally, residual programs become institutional in nature. This happens when a need persists in spite of economic upturns or when a redefintion of needs or the liberalization of eligibility requirements occurs. Public assistance, which is described later, is a case in point.

THE VALUE BASE OF SOCIAL WELFARE

Any discussion of social welfare and/or of its development of social welfare organizations would be incomplete without identifying the value context within which they occur. **Values** are assumptions, convictions, or beliefs about the way people should behave and the principles that should govern behavior. In as much as values are beliefs, they may vary with socialization experiences. Many values are dominant and are supported by the majority of the population. For example, life is viewed as sacred, and taking another's life is viewed as a criminal offense by rich and poor alike. On the other hand, support of capital punishment is a value around which our society is divided.

The history of the development of social welfare reflects differences in values as they relate to social responsibility for making provisions for the needy. Values, however, are not the sole determinant of social policy. Availability of resources, coupled with economic, religious, and political influences, results in an evolving policy of social responsibility for the disadvantaged. One dominant value that has guided our social welfare system development is humanitarianism, which is derived from our Judeo-Christian background. The social application of humanitarianism, however, often is obscured by the need to find the most efficient and effective way to help the needy.

As noted earlier, our society also is influenced largely by the economic doctrine of **laissez faire,** which stresses limited government involvement, individualism, and motivation. Government welfare programs are viewed as a threat to those cherished ends. Problems of the poor and the disenfranchised are perceived as a matter of personal failure that only would be perpetuated by government welfare programs. Social responsibility for the needy, from the laissez-faire point of view, would be carried out through volunteerism aimed at encouraging the needy to become self-sufficient. Work is considered the only justifiable means of self-maintenance, since it contributes to the productive effort of society.

Other values maintain that we all are members of society and, by virtue of that membership, are entitled to share in its productive effort. This belief argues that people become poor or needy as a result of inefficient social institutions. For example, the continually changing economic system results in layoffs, unemployment, obsolescent jobs, and transiency. Individuals do not cause these conditions—rather, they are victimized by them. Minority group members may suffer from inferior educational resources, limited (and usually menial) job opportunities, poor housing, and less-than-adequate health resources. No thoughtful analysis would lay blame for these conditions on minority group members but would clearly identify institutional discrimination as the causal factor.

When considering these two value positions, the reader can readily understand that there are wide variations regarding societal responsibility for the needy. In our discussion of the historical influences that have converged to shape our present social welfare structure, the reader should look for value positions that have contributed to social policy formulation.

OUR ENGLISH HERITAGE

In England, prior to the period of mercantilism, care for the poor was primarily a function of the church. By extending themselves through charitable efforts to those in need, parishioners fulfilled a required sacred function. The resources of the church usually were sufficient to provide the relief that was made available to the poor. The feudal system itself provided a structure that met the needs of most of the population. The only significant government legislation that existed during this time was passed as a result of the so-called Black Death—bubonic plague—which began in 1348 and resulted in the death of approximately two-thirds of the English population within two years. In 1349, King Edward III mandated the Statute of Laborers Act, which made it mandatory that all able-bodied persons accept any type of employment within their parish. Furthermore, it laid the groundwork for residency requirements, which later became an intrinsic part of American social welfare legislation, by forbidding able-bodied persons from leaving their parish.

Some 150 years later, with the breakdown of the feudal system and the division of the church during the Reformation, organized religious efforts no longer could provide for the increasing numbers of poor. Without the church or the fuedal manor to rely on in times of need, the poor were left to their own means of survival. This often meant malnutrition, transiency, poor health, broken families, and even death.

Many of the poor found their way into cities where they were unwanted. Employment was always a problem, since most of the poor were illiterate, and their skills generally were related to agricultural backgrounds. Many turned to begging. Local officials were pressed to find suitable solutions for the problem. As Europe struggled with the transition from an agricultural society to an industrial one, the numbers of dislodged persons increased. National practices differed, but in England, legislation originated in parishes throughout the country to deal with problems of the homeless, the poor, and dependent children.

Overseers were appointed by magistrates to assume responsibility for the poor residing in the various parishes. The overseer assessed the needs of the poor and made judicious responses to those needs. The role played by overseers was important, since it usually was their judgment alone that determined the fate of the poor.

Analyses of the situation invariably led to the conclusion that problems were of an individual nature and likely resulted from the economic transition. Unfortunately, legislation often had punitive overtones, which added to the burden of the poor and left them hopelessly entwined in impoverished conditions with little opportunity to find a way out. In response to these alarming conditions, the Elizabethan **Poor Law** [Liz 43] was passed in 1601. This legislation is significant in that it attempted to codify earlier legislation and establish a national policy for the poor. The Poor Law established "categories" of assistance, a practice found in our current social welfare legislation.

The first of two categories was designed for individuals considered to be "worthy," since there was little doubt that their impoverishment was not a fraudulent attempt to secure assistance. These included the aged, the chronically ill, the disabled, and orphaned children. Those eligible typically were placed in almshouses (poorhouses), where the physically able assisted the ill and disabled. This practice was referred to as **indoor relief**, since it provided services to the poor by placing them in institutions. In some instances, children were placed with families and often were required to work for their keep.

The second category included the able-bodied poor. Here, programs were less humane. Some of the able bodied were placed in prisons, others were sent to workhouses, and many were indentured to local factories or farms as slave laborers. Unlike the worthy poor, the able-bodied poor were assumed to be malingerers or ne'er-do-wells who lacked the motivation to secure employment. The treatment they received was designed to serve as a deterrent to others, as well as to punish them for their transiency and idleness.

This act was to be of crucial significance because it established the guiding philosophy of public assistance legislation in England until 1834 and in the

United States until 1935. The important aspects of the law (Axinn & Levin 1975, 10) in relation to U.S. policies toward the poor are the establishment of

1. clear government responsibility for those in need;
2. government authority to force people to work;
3. government enforcement of family responsibility;
4. responsibility to be exercised at the local level;
5. residence requirements.

The Elizabethan Poor Law was enacted less out of altruism and concern for the poor than as an orderly process of standardizing the way in which they were to be managed. It established a precedent for subsequent social legislation in the United Kingdom as well as the United States.

The Poor Law Reform Act of 1834 was passed as a reaction to concerns that the Poor Law of 1601 was not being implemented as intended and that liberalized supervision of the programs for the poor had served as a disincentive for work and had, in effect, created dependency on the program. The Poor Law Reform Act mandated that all forms of "out-door" relief (assistance provided to one in one's home) be abolished and that the full intention of the provisions of the Poor Law of 1601 be rigidly enforced. Furthermore, it established "the principle of least eligibility," which prescribed that no assistance be provided in an amount that rendered the recipient better off than the lowest-paid worker. This principle also served as a basic tenet of early American social welfare legislation.

SPEENHAMLAND

Although the Poor Law remained the dominant legislation under which services to the poor were administered, attempts were made to create labor laws that would serve as an incentive for the poor to engage in employment. One such effort took the form of "minimum wage" legislation and was enacted in Speenhamland in 1795. Motivated by a desire to induce large numbers of the poor into the labor market, the Speenhamland Act provided for the payment of minimum wages to workers and their families. Wages were adjusted according to family size, thereby assuring minimally adequate income even for the largest of families. Employers were encouraged to pay minimum wages, and where this was not possible, the government made up the difference. It was anticipated that business would be stimulated to produce more commodities through the added incentives provided by the government subsidy, which, in turn, would create a need for more workers. Unfortunately, the effect of the subsidy program was to drive wages down, and employers then turned to the government to make up the difference.

The Speenhamland Act was not designed specifically to be a social welfare reform measure, although it did have implications for the working poor, the unemployed, and the impoverished. In effect, it was a work incentive program. Although important symbolically, the Speenhamland Act had little impact. Ultimately rejected by employers, it proved expensive for the government and was never applied uniformly. It did establish the principle of government subsidy for private employers, a practice that is relatively wide-spread in our society today.

SOCIAL WELFARE IN COLONIAL AMERICA

Early American settlers brought a religious heritage that emphasized charity and the mutual interdependence of people. They also brought with them the heritage of the English Poor Law. America, in the early days, was a land of vast natural resources, and settlers found it essential to work hard in order to survive. When neighbors became needy through illness or death, church members usually were quick to respond. No formal government network for providing assistance existed on any significant basis. Later, as the population increased, many colonies passed laws requiring that immigrants demonstrate their ability to sustain themselves, or in the absence of such ability, sponsors were required to pledge support for new arrivals. Transients were "warned out" and often returned to their place of residence (Federico 1938, 98). In some instances, the homeless and unemployed were returned to England. Times were difficult, the Puritan work ethic was embedded deeply, and with little surplus to redistribute to those in need, assistance often was inadequate. The practice of posting names of habitual paupers at the town house was a routine procedure in many towns and villages.

It is difficult to obtain reliable estimates of the magnitude of public welfare in colonial America. One important fact was that the presence of the indentured servant system rekindled in this country a replica of feudal welfare. In the indentured system of the middle colonies and the slavery system of the southern colonies, there was a clear lack of freedom for the pauper class. Often overlooked, however, was the existence of a set of harsh laws—reasonably enforced up until the time of independence—that required masters to meet the basic survival needs of servants and slaves. (Almost half of all colonists came to the country as indentured servants.) Ironically, as the economy matured from plantation to artisan and became preindustrial in character, economic uncertainty also increased. Consequently, public relief was the largest expenditure in the public budgets of most major cities at the time of the American Revolution.

Concomitantly, a rigid restraint of the Poor Law philosophy was thoroughly consistent with the fact that the colonial economy was one of extreme scarcity. Colonial law stressed the provision of indoor relief, where paupers could be conveniently segregated within almshouses and put to tasks that at least paid for their meager keep. The apprenticeship of children reflected a belief in family controls for children and stressed work and training for productive employment. Also, the deification of the work ethic and the belief that pauperism was a visible symbol of sin permitted a harsh response to those in need, as a means of saving their souls.

CHANGING PATTERNS AFTER THE REVOLUTION

Between the American Revolution and the Civil War, several broad patterns of welfare emerged, all of which were thoroughly consistent with the basic tenets of the Elizabethan Poor Law. The American separation of church and state forced a severance of the connection between parish and local welfare office. Nevertheless, many states—most, in fact—retained a religious connection, with the requirement that at least one member of the welfare board must be a "licensed preacher." Local governments accepted grudgingly the role of welfare caretaker and adopted rigid residency requirements.

The most important shift in this period was from indoor to **outdoor relief**. Outdoor aid, with its reliance on in-kind aid and work-relief projects, was most adaptable to the volatile economics of the first half of the nineteenth century. This led some to see early American welfare as principally an instrument for the regulation of the supply of labor. The contrary evidence, that it essentially is a fiscal choice, stems from the observation that the shift to outdoor relief occurred within places of both labor shortage and labor surplus.

Another significant movement before the Civil War was the shift away from public sector to private sector welfare, or voluntary welfare. The responsibility for welfare therefore was left to charitable institutions rather than remaining a public concern.

CARING FOR THE URBAN POOR

As the new nation grew, cities began to appear on the eastern seaboard. With immigrants arriving regularly, jobs often were difficult to find, and a large population of displaced poor began to emerge. Persons interested in those less fortunate sought avenues for meeting the needs of the poor. Although attaching the poor to subsistence-level employment usually was the goal, there was concern over assuring that basic needs were met until income could be derived through employment. Although almshouses often were used to care for the chronic poor, outdoor relief found increased acceptance as a suitable way of caring for the poor. Outdoor relief was a practice of providing cash assistance to persons who remained in their own homes. Differing segments of the population found cause for alarm in the practices of both indoor and outdoor relief.

One of the earlier major organizations to seek solutions to problems of poverty was the New York Society for the Prevention of Pauperism, established in 1817. This society sought to identify and remedy the causes of poverty. Following the precedent established by Thomas Chalmers in England, the society divided the city into districts and assigned "friendly visitors" to each district to assess and respond to the needs of the poor (Friedlander & Apte 1974, 21). Later, in 1843, the Association for Improving the Conditions of the Poor was established in New York City to coordinate relief efforts for the unemployed. One significant technique introduced by the association was the requirement that relief could not be disbursed until the individual's needs were assessed so that agencies providing relief could do so more effectively.

Perhaps the most effective relief organization for the poor was Buffalo's Charity Organization Society (COS). A private organization modeled after London's COS, it was founded by wealthy citizens who embraced the work ethic yet had compassion for the deserving poor. The COS sought to add efficiency and economy to programs serving the poor, as well as to organize charities in

Many social workers in the early 1900s worked with poor immigrants in urban areas like this tenement section on the lower East Side in New York City.

an effort to prevent duplication of services and reduce dependency on charitable efforts. Like the Association for Improving Conditions of the Poor, which preceded it, the COS emphasized the necessity for assessing the condition of the poor and added the dimension of engaging "friendly visitors" with clients in an effort to provide guidance, rehabilitation, and assistance in preparing for self-sufficiency. The COS had little sympathy for chronic beggars and viewed them essentially as hopeless derelicts.

CARING FOR SPECIFIC POPULATIONS

During these early years, many other private charities emerged to address special problem areas, such as the Orphan's Home Movement, which provided institutional care for children left alone as the result of the death of their parents. Other institutional services began to appear throughout the country to provide care for the deaf, blind, and mentally ill. These services largely were sponsored by state or local governments. There was often grave concern regarding the treatment received by inmates. Dorothea Dix, a philanthropist and social reformer, traveled the United States observing the care provided for the "insane" and was appalled by horrid conditions and inhumane care (Axinn & Levin 1975). Dix sought to convince President Franklin Pierce to allocate federal and land-grant monies for the purpose of establishing federal institutions to care for the mentally ill. Her plea was blocked by Congress, who believed such matters to be the states' responsibility. Resources allocated for institutional care by states were limited. The results were poor conditions and limited treatment.

Toward the latter part of the nineteenth century, a number of states developed centralized agencies following the precedent by state boards of charities, agencies that had been organized in several states to oversee the activities of charitable institutions. State charity agencies sought to ensure a better quality of care for institutional inmates, as well as to seek greater efficiency and economy in the provision of poor relief. With the federal government assuming only limited responsibility for selected groups (veterans, for example), state agencies became the primary public resource for addressing the problems of the poor and debilitated (Leiby 1978, 130–131).

A new wave of immigrants from southern Europe entering this country in the late 1800s and early 1900s further added to the burden of unemployment, homelessness, and poverty. Reacting to the problems experienced by immigrants in coping with the new culture, Jane Addams, a social worker, was instrumental in anchoring the settlement house movement as a resource for dealing with problems of assimilation and in preparing immigrants to live in a new society. Education was emphasized for adults and children alike. In Chicago, Hull House, established by Addams in 1869, sparked the initiative for similar movements in other cities. It also sought needed social reforms to improve the quality of life and opportunity structure for all new citizens. By addressing the problems of poor housing, low wages, child labor, and disease, Hull House and other settlement houses became major social action agencies.

During the 1800s more clearly defined parameters of public versus private welfare programs were established. Public welfare benefit programs relied on taxation for funding. Private welfare programs were funded through the voluntary contributions of individuals or philanthropic organizations. No clearly defined limits determined what types of benefits would be offered by either public of private (voluntary) agencies. As a result, services often overlapped. Public agencies were administered by government agencies at the local, state, or federal levels. Private agencies often had religious or philanthropic sponsorship or received contributions from citizens.

Following World War I, the nation entered a period of great social change and prosperity. The economy was improving, and the nation experienced a sense of euphoria. In 1929 this euphoria ended with the economic downturn that led to the Great Depression. In short order, conditions were grave. Businesses considered to be stable ceased their production, banks declared bankruptcy, and thousands of workers lost their jobs. Although this nation had experienced recessions and depressions before, none was quite as devastating to the economic security of Americans as the Great Depression.

THE NEW DEAL

Today, it is difficult for us to comprehend the effects the Great Depression had on Americans. Savings were lost as banks collapsed, and many were left penniless, homeless, and without resources as unemployment increased. Jobs became scarce, and the unemployed had nowhere to turn. Organized charities quickly exhausted their limited resources. Pessimism and despair were rampant, and many experienced a sense of hopelessness. Unemployment insurance was nonexistent, and no federal guarantees existed for monies lost in bank failures. The economic disaster produced a state of chaos never experienced before on American soil. As conditions worsened, homes were lost through foreclosed mortgages.

State and local governments responded to the extent that resources permitted; however, many of the poor states lacked resources to provide relief even of a temporary nature. In the state of New York, an Emergency Relief Act was passed providing public employment, in-kind relief (food, clothing, and shelter), and limited cash benefits. This act later served as a model for federal relief programs.

Following the earlier constitutional interpretation by President Pierce, the Hoover administration reinforced the position that federal involvement in relief programs was not mandatory but rather a matter that should be delegated to the states. Although sympathetic with those victimized by the Depression, President Hoover was convinced that the most effective solution to the Depression and its consequences was to provide incentives for business to regain its footing, expand, and provide jobs for the jobless.

The critical nature of the Depression was manifested in starvation, deprivation, and the suffering of millions of Americans and required an immediate response. Under these conditions, Franklin Delano Roosevelt, the former governor of New York, was elected president in 1932.

One of President Roosevelt's initial actions was to institute emergency legislation that provided assistance for the jobless and poor. Not only did this legislation mark the first time the federal government engaged itself directly in providing relief, it also invoked an interpretation of the health and welfare provisions of the constitution that established a historical precedent. The result mandated the federal government to assume health and welfare responsibility for its citizens. The statement was clear: citizens were first and foremost citizens of the United States and, second, residents of specific states. This policy opened the door for later federal legislation in the areas of civil rights, fair employment practices, school busing, public assistance, and a variety of other social programs.

One of the first attempts to provide relief for depression victims was the Federal Emergency Relief Act. Modeled after the New York Emergency Relief Act, it provided food, clothing, and shelter allowances for the homeless and displaced. In a cooperative relationship with states, the federal government made monies available to states to administer the relief programs. States were responsible for establishing agencies for that purpose and also were required to contribute state funds, where possible, for the purpose of broadening the resource base available to those in need. This established the precedent for "matching grants," which later became an integral requirement for public assistance programs.

Additional federal emergency legislation was enacted to provide public employment for the unemployed. In 1935 the Works Progress Administration (WPA) was created to provide public service jobs. Although resisted by private contractors, the WPA ultimately employed approximately 8 million workers over the duration of the Depression. States and local governments identified needed projects and supplied necessary materials for laborers, who were paid by the WPA. Many public schools, streets, parks, post office buildings, state college buildings, and related public projects were constructed under the auspices of the WPA. It was anticipated that as the private business sector expanded, WPA workers would secure employment in the private sector.

Youth programs also were established. Perhaps the most noteworthy was the Civilian Conservation Corps, which was designed to protect natural resources and to improve and develop public recreational areas. Primarily a forest camp activity, the CCC provided young men between the ages of seventeen and twenty-three with jobs, food, clothing, and shelter. Wages were nominal (around twenty-five dollars per month), and the major portion of the wages (twenty dollars per month) was conscripted and sent home to help support families. Many national parks were improved and developed by CCC labor. The National Youth Administration was also established under the WPA and provided work-study assistance to high school and college youth as an incentive to remain in school. In addition, the NYA provided part-time jobs for out-of-school students to learn job skills and increase their employability (Friedlander & Apte 1974, 113).

Low-interest loans to farmers and small business operators also were extended through FERA programs as a means of enabling those activities to survive and become sources of employment for the unemployed.

In retrospect, it is clear that the Depression legislation was designed to be temporary in nature and had as its main focus the creation of work activities that enabled individuals to earn their income rather than become objects of charity. It also was anticipated that the private economic business sector would prosper and emergency relief employment would no longer be needed.

The Depression legislation offered a temporary solution to the crisis generated by the Great Depression. The jobless found jobs, the hungry were fed, and the homeless were given shelter. Perhaps of more importance, the nation felt the full impact of system changes. The issue of blaming poverty on idleness and laziness was put to rest at least temporarily.

THE SOCIAL SECURITY ACT

The **Social Security Act** was passed by Congress and signed into law by President Roosevelt on August 14, 1935. Even today this act remains the most significant piece of social legislation yet enacted in the United States. It also paved the way for greater federal involvement in health and welfare. The act reflected a realization that our economic system was subject to vacillations that would invariably leave many people without resources due to unemployment in an ever-shifting economic marketplace. It also acknowledged that older adults needed income security as an incentive to retire. This act was designed to be a permanent resource system administered by the federal government. The provisions of the act were outlined under three major categories. Chapter 4 covers these categories in greater depth. Briefly, the provisions of the act were social insurance, public assistance, and health and welfare services.

Social Insurance

Social insurance, commonly referred to as **Social Security,** consisted of two important benefit programs. The first (and most widely known) consisted of three categories: Old Age, Survivors, and Disability Insurance (OASDI; see Chapter 4). These programs were based on taxes deducted from employees' wages and matched by employer contributions. Eligibility was based on participation earned through employment. The second type of insurance program was unemployment insurance, with the funds contributed by employers. The purpose of the unemployment benefit program was to provide a source of income security for covered workers who had lost their jobs.

Benefits derived from these programs were considered to be a matter of right in that the recipients and their employers had paid "premiums" for the benefits they would receive. In many ways, social insurance was similar to private insurance, where entitlement to benefits is directly related to beneficiary participation through contributions.

Public Assistance

Public assistance was based on "need" and was not established as a right earned through employment. This program was administered by states with monies made available by states and matched by the federal government (matching grants). Public assistance consisted of three categories: Old Age Assistance, Aid to Dependent Children, and Aid to the Blind. In 1955, the category of Aid to the Permanently and Totally Disabled was added. Benefits under each of these categories were invariably low and varied among the states according to each state's willingness to "match" federal funds. Eligibility requirements were rigid and rigorously enforced. Participation further was based on a "means" test, a test that required applicants to demonstrate that they were hopelessly without resources. The private lives of recipients were opened to the scrutiny of welfare workers in an attempt to minimize fraud and to assure that benefit levels did not exceed budgeted needs. Perhaps the most controversial assistance program was Aid to Dependent Children. This program made limited funds available to mothers with dependent children where no man was present in the home. Since benefit levels were adjusted for family size (to a maximum of four children), there was concern that promiscuity and illegitimacy would be rewarded by increasing benefits as the family size increased. Rigid cohabitation policies were instituted mandating that mothers guilty of cohabitation would lose their grant funds entirely. Since most ADC recipients were able-bodied, there was also concern that welfare payments provided a disincentive for meeting their needs through gainful employment. In many ways, ADC recipients were treated as the "unworthy" poor and, as a consequence, were often dealt with in a punitive manner.

Public assistance generally is referred to as *welfare* by the public. Since benefits are based on impoverishment and not earned through employment, participation in the program carries a stigma of personal imprudence, ineptness, or failure.

Health and Welfare Services

Programs authorized under **health and welfare services** provided for maternal and child care services, vocational rehabilitation, public health, and services for physically impaired children. The provision of services was emphasized. Services authorized under this title are discussed more fully in chapters 6, 7, 8, and 10.

In the ensuing years, amendments to the Social Security Act extended each of these titles and included more people in their coverage. Social insurance later added health insurance (Medicare), and a health assistance program (Medicaid) was instituted for public assistance recipients. The ADC assistance category was redefined as Aid to Families with Dependent Children (AFDC) to allow states to provide assistance to families under limited circumstances when an employable unemployed man was in the home (AFDC-UP/AFDC-Unemployed Parent). Only a few states adopted the AFDC-UP provisions. As requirements for participation in these programs became less stringent in the 1960s and 1970s, welfare rolls increased dramatically.

SOCIAL WELFARE: THE POST–SOCIAL SECURITY ERA

Establishing well-focused comprehensive social welfare programs in the United States has been problematic because of differing values, vacillations of the economy, and fluctuations in resources available to meet the needs of an expanding population. The period since passage of the Social Security Act has been tumultuous, with three wars, a long-standing cold war (now coming to an end), and periods of economic upswings as well as recessions and depressions. Unemployment has varied from 12 percent of the work force in 1979 to 6.1 percent in 1990. Among other things, the divorce rate has increased dramatically since the 1940s, single-parent families are more common, the population is growing older, and diseases have become more costly to treat. All of these factors affect how the government will respond to social needs. In the following paragraphs we discuss some of the more significant governmental attempts to address the need for support services.

The Great Society Programs

Attempts to broaden the activities of government in securing the rights of citizens and providing for personal, social, and economic development were introduced through social reform measures enacted during the Lyndon Johnson administration (1963–1968). The so-called **Great Society** legislation extended benefits of many existing programs and services designed to help the poor, the disabled, and the aged. The Social Security Act was amended to provide for health care benefits to the aged under the Health Insurance Program (Medicare) and to public assistance recipients through the Health Assistance Program (Medicaid). New legislation also was designed to meet needs not specifically addressed through existing resources. The Older Americans Act (1965) established a legal base for developing senior luncheon programs, health screening, transportation, meals-on-wheels programs, and recreational activities. The Civil Rights Act (1964) sought to put an end to discrimination in employment and in the use of public business facilities. It also was targeted toward nondiscriminatory extension of credit. Education bills were passed that sought to rectify many of the educational disadvantages experienced by children of the poor.

Perhaps the most significant—and controversial—effort to achieve social reform came through the Economic Opportunities Act (1964), dubbed the War on Poverty. The objective of this act was to "eliminate poverty" through institutional change. Poverty was viewed traditionally as an individual matter, and its causes generally were thought to be the result of personal failure, the lack of motivation, or personal choice. Poverty program designers came to a different conclusion. Poverty was considered to be the result of inadequate social institutions that failed to provide opportunities for all citizens. Traditional approaches to solving the problems of poverty were considered unsuccessful. Changing the status of the poor would come not through working with them on an individual basis but rather through the modification of institutions that produced the problems in the first place. Hence, Economic Opportunities Act programs were structured to assure the poor a greater likelihood of success by creating opportunities for decision making and participation. Educational programs such as Head Start, Enable, and Catch-up sought to extend relevant learning experiences to educationally disadvantaged children. Community Action Agencies encouraged the poor to become more vocal in community affairs and to organize efforts for community betterment. Special employment incentives were generated to teach job skills. Youth job corps programs provided public service jobs contingent upon remaining in school, thus assuring greater potential for employment upon graduation. Job Corps centers taught teenage dropouts employment skills. Small-business loans were made to individuals with potential for developing businesses. Rural programs extended health and social services for the poor in rural areas.

In a nation that boasted the highest standard of living in the world, it was believed that the scourge of poverty could be eliminated forever. The euphemism of "War on Poverty" was selected to rally the population to a full-scale commitment to assure that the enemy, poverty, would be overcome. Social action advocates found the climate produced by the Economic Opportunities Act favorable for their efforts. It was a heyday for the expansion of social programs, with spending often outstripping planning. The War on Poverty was short-lived because federal funds were channeled to the war in Vietnam. Social legislation is invariably affected by the political climate. As government resources and attention were diverted to the Vietnam War, the domestic "war" was soon neglected and ultimately terminated.

Conservatism in the Sixties and Seventies

The period from the mid-1960s through the mid-1970s was one of both do-mestic and foreign conflict. While the Vietnam War was raging, the antiesta-blishment movement in the United States was well under way, rioting was occurring in the Watts section of Los Angeles and in Detroit, Martin Luther King was championing the cause of disenfranchised Americans, and inflation was depleting the buying power of those who were working.

In reaction to these disconcerting changes, many middle-class Americans initiated a wave of conservatism that led to an effort to dismantle many of the social programs enacted during the New Deal and expanded through the Great Society programs. The welfare "establishment" was viewed as being costly, ineffective, and counterproductive. The conservatives maintained that the fed-eral government was much too large and cumbersome and that many functions, including social welfare, could be assumed by the states. Although federal involvement in welfare had emerged largely because states had lacked sufficient resources to provide supports, conservatives were convinced that states and localities were better suited to determine policies and administer social pro-grams. One result was the reorganization—and eventual termination—of the federal poverty program. This resulted in its subsequent termination. Several popular programs, such as Head Start and job-training programs, were trans-ferred to other government agencies. Under the Nixon administration, a major welfare reform measure, the Family Assistance Program (FAP), was submitted for congressional approval as House Bill 1. Although never enacted into law, the reform would have eliminated the public assistance program and substituted in its place a proposal that was designed to provide incentives for recipients to work without losing all of their government benefits. The level of defined need, $1,600 per year for a family of four, was far below benefit levels already in existence in the higher-paying states but higher than the benefits in over half the states.

The Family Assistance Act failed, but on a more positive note, public as-sistance programs for the aged, disabled, and blind were combined by the enactment of the Supplemental Security Income (SSI) Act in 1974. SSI increased benefit levels for millions of recipients. Since the AFDC category, which would have been abolished by the Family Assistance Act, failed to pass, AFDC con-tinues to be funded and implemented under the federal-state arrangements already in effect. Thus, AFDC benefits continue to vary appreciably from state to state. Table 2–1 illustrates the differences in the average monthly AFDC payments per person in the various states.

Welfare Reform and the Late Seventies

The policymakers of the mid-1970s inherited a welfare system that had no positive constituency. Recipients, social workers, public officials, and tax-conscious groups agreed only on the inadequacy of the existing system. Each of the four constituencies had in the immediate past initiated a welfare reform effort, and each constituency had failed to achieve its reform, largely because of the op-position of the others. Because of the political costs that had come to be associated with welfare reform efforts, no knights-errant were ready to cham-

Table 2–1 Average Monthly AFDC Payment per Person, for Fiscal Year
1990 by State

Alaska	$269	Delaware	$113
California	$229	Wyoming	$113
Connecticut	$220	Colorado	$109
Hawaii	$186	Illinois	$107
Massachusetts	$185	Nevada	$100
New York	$185	Oklahoma	$100
Vermont	$183	South Dakota	$ 99
Rhode Island	$180	Idaho	$ 98
Minnesota	$173	Virginia	$ 97
Washington	$164	Indiana	$ 93
Michigan	$162	North Carolina	$ 93
New Hampshire	$162	Arizona	$ 92
Wisconsin	$160	Florida	$ 92
Maine	$145	Missouri	$ 92
Oregon	$143	Georgia	$ 88
Iowa	$133	Kentucky	$ 85
North Dakota	$133	West Virginia	$ 85
Maryland	$132	New Mexico	$ 77
Pennsylvania	$130	South Carolina	$ 72
New Jersey	$125	Arkansas	$ 67
Ohio	$121	Tennessee	$ 65
Utah	$117	Texas	$ 57
Kansas	$116	Louisiana	$ 56
Montana	$115	Mississippi	$ 41
Nebraska	$115	Alabama	$ 40

Average = $133.69

Source: "Annual Report on AFDC Expenditures," Texas Department of Human Resources, Austin, Texas, 1991.

pion a new welfare reform effort. The problems that had drawn such attention in earlier decades persisted. The rapidly expanding welfare costs in the Nixon and Ford years, in juxtaposition to the intractability of poverty, made welfare reform an urgent but unpleasant necessity.

Thus, welfare reform again became an issue. The Carter administration proposed that $8.8 billion be appropriated to create up to 1.4 million public service jobs. It was expected that 2 million persons would hold such jobs in a given year, as they were processed through these jobs on their way to regular employment in the public or private sector. According to the proposal, most of these jobs would pay a minimum wage (projected to be $3.30 in 1980) and would be full-time, full-year jobs, thus yielding an annual income of $6,600.

In addition, a family would receive an income supplement. The size of the supplement would be geared to family size. The jobs would not be eligible for the earned income tax credit. A worker would always have an income incentive to move from the public job to regular employment in the public or private sector. Those eligible for such jobs would be adults—one per family—in the "expected to work" category of the second part of the program but could not find employment in the regular economy. Care was to be taken to assure that these jobs would not replace ordinary public jobs, thus removing the objections to the plan from the labor unions. However, Carter's proposal was not adopted, and debate about the most effective way to overhaul the welfare system continued.

Cutbacks in the Eighties

The 1980s were characterized by relentless efforts to reduce and eliminate social entitlement programs. Public expenditures for welfare were viewed as antithetical to economic progress. Mounting inflation was considered to be the result of federal domestic spending. The sad state of our economy was considered the work of social progressives who had engineered welfare expansionism and, as a result, had caused the economy to falter. Many social support programs were reduced dramatically or eliminated. Funds supporting Title XX of the Social Security Act—which provided a wide range of benefits, upgraded the quality of the social service delivery system, and provided services to the aged, children and other populations at risk—were reduced drastically. Many transportation and job-training programs were discontinued.

The administration during the Reagan years promoted a policy of social and income assistance programs to be administered by states through block grants. The effect of this program would have been to decentralize government and return it to the pre–New Deal era, when states assumed responsibility for their own social problems. An unlikely coalition of conservative governors and liberal mayors joined efforts to defeat the Reagan initiative of welfare reform.

As part of his State of the Union message in 1982, President Reagan proposed his version of welfare reform. It went under the title *New Federalism.* The centerpiece was a plan whereby the states would assume financial and administrative responsibility for food stamps and AFDC, while the federal government would assume responsibility for the Medicaid program. Figure 2–1 shows the projected federal expenditures for social programs as compared with real expenditures of the Carter administration. The program was dubbed "The Welfare Swap." The plan went through a number of variations before it was dropped by the administration as politically unfeasible. The problem was that neither conservative governors nor liberal mayors liked the idea. Following his reelection in 1984, President Reagan began again to push for reshaping welfare responsibilities among the various layers of government. A presidential task force was appointed, and it was to issue its report after the congressional elections in 1986. That election resulted in a Democratic landslide, and the responsibility for welfare reform has now shifted from the White House to Capitol Hill.

Lack of Policy in the Nineties

The Bush administration in the 1990s continues to be influenced by conservative views of welfare and welfare reform. With the winding down of the cold war,

Figure 2–1   The Poor Lose, Who Wins?

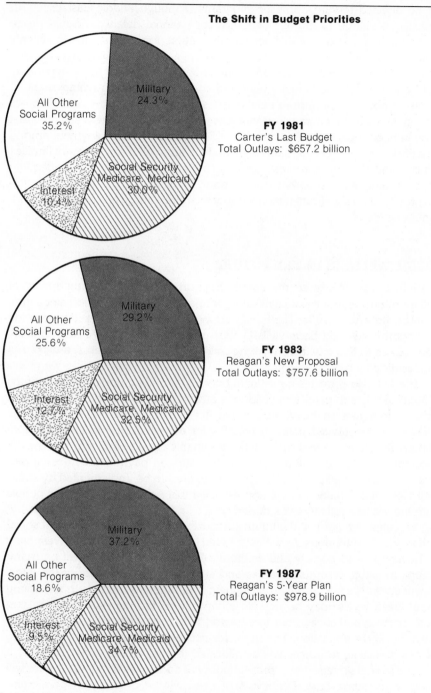

The Shift in Budget Priorities

FY 1981
Carter's Last Budget
Total Outlays: $657.2 billion

FY 1983
Reagan's New Proposal
Total Outlays: $757.6 billion

FY 1987
Reagan's 5-Year Plan
Total Outlays: $978.9 billion

Source: Coalition for a New Foreign and Military Policy, Washington, D.C. Reprinted by permission.

progressives hold hopes that monies appropriated for defense spending can not be directed toward domestic programs, although Middle East crises, in particular, continue to impose demands for national defense. Should peace become achievable during this decade, the nation, for the first time in seventy years, would be confronted with the challenge of establishing a peacetime economy. Such a transition period might be one of turmoil as those dependent on jobs in the defense industry relocated and sought suitable employment.

As of now, many human needs issues remain to be addressed. Debates over national health insurance continue as programs become less able to assist those in need meet the rising cost of medical services. Unemployment among minority group members remains high, and the number of single-parent families is increasing. The need mounts for day-care centers and for more adequate income maintenance programs for the poor. Thus far, the Bush administration has proposed no significant national policy to address these and other important human needs.

SOCIAL WELFARE IN THE FUTURE

In 1988, Congress passed the Family Support Act, hailed by proponents of welfare reform as the most significant piece of domestic legislation since the Social Security Act in 1935. The Family Support Act mandates that states provide job opportunities and basic skills (JOBS) programs for most AFDC recipients (some, such as those with very young children or health problems, are exempt from participation).

The Act also provides transitional benefits, including up to twelve months of Medicaid (health care) and child care after recipients find jobs to give them a chance to transist to the workforce. The Act also mandates that states provide AFDC-UP (unemployed parents) benefits for a limited time to those families with previously employed males who are unable to find employment. The Act also requires stronger enforcement of child support payments by absent parents. Because not all parts of the Act are required to be implemented by states until 1992, it is too soon to tell how effective this Act will be in moving people from the welfare rolls to self-sufficiency.

Speculation regarding the future structure, organization, and focus of social welfare is at best tenuous. As we have noted in this chapter, a society's response to the needs of its socially and economically deprived is contingent on many factors: available resources, values and attitudes, an acceptance of the interdependence of its people, and a willingness to commit resources to those lacking them. Need levels may be defined stringently to include only those lacking food, clothing, and shelter, or more broadly to include supports such as student loans for higher education. The more restrictively the level of need is defined, the fewer societal resources will be allocated to meet needs.

The federal government's present policy of social welfare retrenchment will continue for some time. Definitions of need will become more specific and limited with the consequence that benefits will no longer be available through federal auspices. The result will be that persons with marginal incomes now eligible for limited supports will lose them, many prospective college students will be denied the privilege of attending college, individuals needing health care

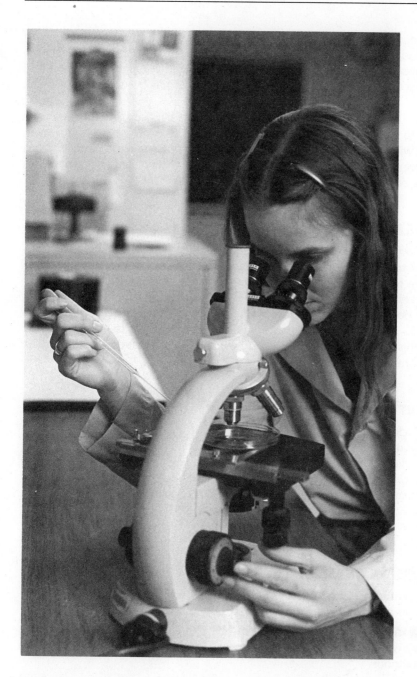

The Family Support Act of 1988 places increased emphasis on helping AFDC recipients obtain training and employment that lead them to become self-sufficient. Here, an AFDC recipient who has just completed a training program and has been hired at a hospital demonstrates her new skills.

will not receive the necessary treatment, and children with special learning problems will be denied access to special educational programs. These are but a few of the implications and realities of major federal welfare reductions.

In all likelihood, there will be a resurgence of initiative by private and philanthropic agencies to provide care for the casualties of federal reductions. Unfortunately, resources will not be adequate to meet present need levels.

Volunteerism, a worthwhile and helpful activity, cannot replace the skills of professional workers. State and local governments will attempt to be responsive. Those with greater resources should be able to compensate for some of the lost federal resources. Poorer states, however, will be unable to bear the burden.

The challenge of finding alternative resources to support the poor will culminate in innovative programs and techniques to meet the need; however, funding will continue to be a problem at all levels. It may take many generations to restore the gains that have been made through the past fifty years. In a humane society, we have no other alternative.

SUMMARY

The history of the development of social welfare reveals the influence of many factors. Periods of economic downturns and upheaval, wars, shifts from conservative to liberal perspectives on governmental versus individual responsibilities, and fluctuations in the resources available are all factors in determining welfare policy. As a result, social welfare development has been fragmentary and lacks a comprehensive conceptual framework for its development. The aim of this chapter has been to reveal how some of the issues in social welfare programming have emerged over the years.

KEY TERMS

Great Society
health and welfare services
indoor relief
institutional programs
laissez faire
outdoor relief
Poor Law

public assistance
residual programs
social insurance
Social Security
Social Security Act
values

DISCUSSION QUESTIONS

1. Of what significance was the Elizabethan Poor Law to the subsequent development of public welfare in the United States?

2. How did the Speenhamland Act of 1795 differ from the Elizabethan Poor Law? What effect did the Speenhamland Act have on resolving the problem of the poor?

3. Argue the case that the Social Security Act has been the most significant social legislation passed in the United States.

4. What were the goals of the Economic Opportunities Act? How successful was this act in reducing poverty? Why was it discontinued?

5. Contrast President Johnson's Great Society programs with President Nixon's position on social welfare.

6. Discuss President Reagan's views on social welfare and his administration's plan to provide assistance for the poor.

7. Compare and contrast the views of social welfare held by the Carter Administration vs. the Bush Administration.

8. Identify at least two social factors that have influenced social legislation in the past twenty years.

REFERENCES

Axinn, June, and Herman Levin. 1975. *Social welfare: A history of the American response to need.* New York: Dodd, Mead.

Federico, Ronald D. 1983. *The social welfare institution.* 4th ed. Lexington, Mass.: Heath.

Fink, Arthur E. 1974. *The field of social work.* 6th ed. New York: Holt Rinehart & Winston.

Friedlander, Walter, and Robert Z. Apte. 1974. *Introduction to social welfare.* 4th ed. Englewood Cliffs, N.J.: Prentice-Hall.

Klein, Phillip. 1968. *From philanthropy to social welfare.* San Francisco: Jossey–Bass.

Leiby, James. 1978. *A history of social welfare and social work in the United States.* New York: Columbia University Press.

National Association of Social Workers. 1977. *Encyclopedia of social work.* New York: Author.

Piven, Francis Fox, and Richard A. Cloward. 1971. *Regulating labor.* New York: Pantheon.

Wilensky, Harold L., and Charles N. Lebeaux. 1965. *Industrial society and social welfare.* rev. ed. New York: Free Press.

SUGGESTED FURTHER READINGS

Compton, Beulah R. 1980. *Introduction to social welfare and social work.* Homewood, Ill.: Dorsey.

Danziger, Sheldon H., and Daniel H. Weisberg, eds. 1986. *Fighting poverty.* Cambridge, Mass.: Harvard University Press.

Fine, Sidney. 1964. *Laissez faire and the general welfare state.* Ann Arbor: University of Michigan Press.

Howell, Joseph T. 1973. *Hard living on Clay Street.* Garden City, N.J.: Anchor Books.

Janson, Bruce S. 1988. *The reluctant welfare state.* Belmont, Calif.: Wadsworth.

Louchheim, Katie, ed. 1983. *The making of the new deal: The insiders speak.* Cambridge, Mass.: Harvard University Press.

Piven, Frances F., and Richard A. Cloward. 1971. *Regulating the poor.* New York: Random House.

Ryan, William. 1971. *Blaming the victim.* New York: Vintage Books.

A Systems/Ecological Perspective to Understanding Social Work and Social Welfare

Juan, a twelve-year-old Hispanic boy, is in the seventh grade in an urban school in Texas. His teachers are concerned about him and are recommending to Christina Herrera, the school social worker, that he be enrolled in the school's dropout prevention program. Recently, Juan has been socializing during school with a group of much older students who are members of a local gang. He has been skipping classes, not completing class assignments, fighting with other students, and arguing with his teachers when they confront him about his behavior. During the past two weeks, he has been caught smoking marijuana and pulling a knife on a classmate. Ms. Herrera has talked with both Juan and his mother. She has suggested that Juan participate in a school support group and has referred Juan and his mother to the local teen/parent outreach center for counseling as soon as there is a counseling slot available. Juan's mother is very concerned about him. However, she also has indicated to Ms. Herrera that she is under a great deal of stress and is angry that Juan is adding to it.

Juan lives in a one-bedroom apartment with his mother and his younger brother, who is five years old. Six months ago, Juan's parents divorced, and his father moved to a neighboring state 300 miles away. Juan always had a fairly close relationship with both his parents. Although he knew that they fought a lot and that his father drank and lost his job, he was surprised when his parents told him that they were getting a divorce.

When Juan's father moved out, his mother had to get an extra job to make ends meet. The family also had to move into a small apartment in another part of the city. Juan's mother's relatives and friends, all devout Catholics, were very much against the divorce and have not been at all supportive. When she is not working, Juan's mother spends much of her time crying or sleeping. At first, Juan tried hard to be supportive of his mother, cooking meals, cleaning the house, and taking care of his little brother. However, at times he doesn't cook or clean exactly the way his mother wants him to. When his brother gets noisy, Juan gets in trouble for not keeping him quiet. Lately, Juan's mother has begun yelling at or hitting Juan when this happens. Because she was abused as a child, Juan's mother feels guilty when she gets so angry at Juan, but she cannot understand why he can't be more supportive when she is trying so hard to keep the family together.

Juan has felt abandoned by everyone since the divorce. His mother is usually angry at him, and his two long-time friends, who come from two-parent families, seem less friendly to him. When they do ask him to do things with them, he usually can't anyway because he has to take care of his younger brother or he doesn't have any money. Transportation is also a problem, since Juan's friends live across town in his former neighborhood. Although he used to do well in school, Juan has lost interest in his classes. He can't get used to the new school, and he doesn't know any of the teachers there. However, he has several new friends who seem to accept him. They are older, and their interest in him makes him feel important. Juan is excited that they want him to be a member of their gang. As long as school is so boring, he can spend time with them during the day and still take care of his brother after school, although he is seriously considering running away from home and moving in with one of the gang members, who lives with his older brother. The friend's older brother recently got out of prison and has promised that Juan can make a lot of money as a drug runner for him.

Juan's case illustrates the many factors that influence how people react to what is going on in their lives. Juan's present situation is affected by his developmental needs as he enters adolescence; his relationships with his mother, father, younger brother, friends, and school personnel; his father's alcoholism and unemployment; his parents' divorce; the fact that his mother was abused as a child; his family's tenuous economic situation; the lack of positive social support available from relatives, friends, the workplace, the school, the church, and the neighborhood to the members of Juan's family; the lack of programs available to divorced parents and teens in Juan's community; Juan's cultural and ethnic background; and community and societal attitudes about divorce, female-headed households, and intervention in family matters. From Juan's perspective, the family system, the economic system, the political system, the religious system, the educational system, and the social welfare system have not been there to meet his needs. Yet he continually interacts with all of these individuals, groups, and social structures and also depends on all of them in some way.

In this chapter we explore the **systems/ecological framework**, which can be used to understand social problems and issues faced by individuals and families in today's world. This framework also provides the broad base for the problem-solving approach, an intervention strategy used by generalist social work practitioners with Bachelor of Social Work (BSW) degrees. The problem-solving approach also is discussed as a way to address both social welfare problems and individual problems.

THE IMPACT OF WORLD VIEWS ON INTERVENTION IN SOCIAL PROBLEMS

All individuals perceive what is going on in their lives and in the world somewhat differently. All college students know that an argument between a parent and a teenager over almost any topic usually is perceived quite differently by the parent and the teenager. People view their environments and the forces that shape them differently depending on many things: biological factors, such as their own heredity and intelligence; personal life experiences, including their childhood; ethnicity and culture; and level and type of education. How people perceive their world determines to a large extent how involved they are in it and how they interact with it. Women who perceive themselves as unimportant and powerless may continue to let their husbands beat them and may not be successful at stopping the abuse or being self-sufficient if they decide to leave the batterer. On the other hand, women who perceive that they have some control over their lives and feel better about themselves may get into a counseling program and get a job at which they can be successful.

As with individuals, professionals from different disciplines also view the world somewhat differently. A physicist, for example, is likely to have a different explanation about how the world began than a philosopher or a minister. A law enforcement officer and a social worker may disagree about how best to handle young teens from poverty areas who join gangs and harass the elderly. A physician may treat a patient who complains of headaches by meeting the patient's physical needs, whereas a psychologist may treat the person's emotional needs through individual counseling to ascertain how the individual can better cope. The way professionals who work with people perceive the world largely determines the type of intervention they use in helping people.

The Difference between Causal Relationships and Association

In the past, many professionals who dealt with human problems had a tendency to look at those problems in terms of a **cause-and-effect**, or **causal relationship.** The causal relationship viewpoint is not usually appropriate when examining social welfare problems. A cause-and-effect relationship suggests that if x causes y, then by eliminating x, we also eliminate y. For example, if we say that smoking is the sole cause of lung cancer, then eliminating smoking would mean eliminating lung cancer. This limited worldview presents problems for many reasons. First, even in relation to smoking, we know that it does not always cause lung cancer, and sometimes people who do not smoke get lung cancer. The relationship between smoking and lung cancer is also not always unidimensional. Other intervening variables or factors, such as living in a city with heavy smog, also increase a person's chances of getting lung cancer. The chances of getting lung cancer are more than twice as great for a person who smokes and lives in a city with heavy smog than for someone who does neither.

Juan's case definitely cannot be discussed in terms of a cause-and-effect relationship. Are the problems Juan is experiencing caused by the abuse his mother suffered as a child, by the divorce, by his father's drinking problem, by his mother's worries about money, by his use of marijuana, by his association with gang members, by the limited social support system available, or by discrimination because he and his family are Hispanic? It is unlikely that one of these factors caused Juan's problems; however, they all probably contributed to them in some way. In looking at factors related to social welfare problems, it is more appropriate to view them in **association** with the problem, meaning that all factors are connected to or relate to the problem, rather than saying that one isolated factor, or even several factors, directly causes a social problem.

The Need: A Conceptual Framework for Understanding Social Welfare Problems

The fact that there are obviously many factors associated with or that contribute to social welfare problems suggests the need for a broad theory to understand them. First, it is useful to define theory and to discuss why theories are important. A **theory** is a way of clearly and logically organizing a set of facts or ideas and defining procedures to analyze these facts.

All of us use theories in our daily lives. We are continually taking in facts, or information, from our environment and trying to order them in some way to make sense about what is going on around us. Although some of our theories may be relatively unimportant to everyone else, they are useful to us in being able to describe, understand, and even predict our environment. For example, a college student has a roommate who always turns up the stereo to full volume whenever the student gets a telephone call. Over the year that they have shared a room, the student has gathered a great deal of information about when this happens. He is now able to articulate a theory he has based on this information to describe the situation, to understand why it happens, and to be able to predict when his roommate will exhibit this behavior. Making sense of the facts in this situation has made it easier for him to deal with this trying behavior. A theory can be relatively insignificant, such as the one just described, or it can have major importance to many people.

A theory can be used to describe something, such as Juan's family situation; to explain or to understand something, such as why a family in crisis would exhibit some of the behaviors of Juan's family; or to predict something, such as what behaviors another family in a similar situation might experience. The same set of facts can be ordered in different ways, depending on who is doing the ordering and the world view of that person or group. If you think of facts as individual bricks, and a theory as a way of ordering the bricks so that they make sense, you can visualize several different theories from the same set of facts, just as you can visualize a number of different structures built from the same set of bricks.

A good theory must have three attributes, if it is to be widely used. First, it must be **inclusive,** or able to explain consistently the same event in the same way. The more inclusive a theory is, the better able it is to explain facts in exactly the same way each time an event occurs. For example, if the person in the roommate situation could describe, explain, or predict the roommate's behavior exactly the same way every single time the telephone rang, he would have a highly inclusive theory.

A good theory must also be **generalizable.** This means that one must be able to generalize what happens in one situation to other similar situations.

Even though the person may be able to explain the facts about his roommate in a highly inclusive way, it is not likely that exactly the same situation would occur with all roommates in the same university, much less in the same city, the United States, or the world. The more a theory can be generalized beyond the single situation it is describing or explaining, the better it is as theory.

Finally, a good theory must be **testable.** This means that we must be able to measure it in some way to ensure that it is accurate and valid. This is the major reason why we have very limited theory in understanding and predicting social welfare problems and human behavior. Only limited measures have been developed relating to what goes on inside people's minds, their attitudes, and their behaviors. How do we measure, for example, behavior change such as child abuse, particularly when it most often happens behind closed doors? Can we give psychological tests to measure attitudes that would lead to abuse, or can we measure community factors such as unemployment to predict child abuse? Any time we try to measure human behavior or environmental influences, we have difficulty doing so. This does not mean that we should stop doing research or trying to develop higher-level theories. In fact, this is an exciting area of social work, and the problems merely point out the need to develop skilled social work practitioners and researchers who can devote more attention to the development of good social work theory.

Because social work draws its knowledge base from many disciplines, many theories are applicable to social work. These include psychological theories such as Freud's theory of psychoanalysis and its derivatives, economic and political theories, sociological theories such as Durkheim's theory relating to suicide, and developmental theories such as Jean Piaget's. All of these theoretical perspectives are relevant to social work and an understanding of social welfare problems, but looking at only one limits one's understanding and, in turn, one's intervention. Thus, it is important to focus on a framework or perspective that allows one to view social problems and appropriate responses that incorporate a multitude of factors and a multitude of possible responses, yet one that does not eliminate or prohibit the rich array of theories available from other disciplines, such as those just delineated.

THE SYSTEMS/ECOLOGICAL FRAMEWORK

Social workers, more than any other group of professionals, have focused both on the individual and beyond the individual to the broader environment. Consider the definitions of social work discussed in Chapter 1. All focus on enhancing social functioning of the individual or in some way addressing the relationships, the interactions, and the interdependence between persons and their environments. This is exemplified by the many roles social workers play within the social welfare system—true generalists, they advocate for changing living conditions of the mentally ill and obtaining welfare reform legislation that enables the poor to succeed in obtaining employment and economic self-sufficiency; lead groups of children who have experienced divorce; educate the community about parenting, AIDS, and child abuse; and provide individual, family, and group counseling to clients. A broad framework is needed that allows for identifying all of the diverse, complex factors associated with a social welfare problem or an individual problem; understanding how all of the factors interact to contribute to the situation; and determining an intervention strategy or strategies, which can range from intervention with a single individual to an entire society and can incorporate a variety of roles. Such a framework must account for individual differences, cultural diversity, and growth and change at the individual, organizational, and societal levels.

The generalist foundation of social work is based on a systems framework, which also incorporates an ecological perspective. The authors choose to use the term *systems/ecological framework* rather than *theory* because the systems/ecological perspective is much broader and more loosely constructed than a theory. It is most useful in understanding social welfare problems and situations and determining specific theories that are appropriate for intervention. Additionally, whereas various systems (see for example, works by Talcott Parsons, Max Siporin, Allen Pincus, and Anne Minahan) and ecological approaches (see for example, works by Urie Bronfenbrenner, James Garbarino, Carel Germain, Alex Gitterman, and Carol Meyer) have been extensively described in the literature, they have not been tested or delineated with enough specificity to be considered theories. A number of advocates of the systems/ecological framework, in fact, refer to it as a metatheory, or an umbrella framework or perspective that can be used as a base from which to incorporate additional theories.

A general systems framework has been discussed in the literature of many disciplines—medicine, psychology, economics, political science, sociology, and education—for many years, and has been used somewhat differently in each discipline. Its principles, as well as similar principles associated with social systems, or systems associated with living things, have been incorporated into the social work literature since the beginning of social work. Mary Richmond,

A systems/ecological perspective focuses on interactions between individuals and their environments. With these Hispanic children, the social worker assesses and builds on their strengths, including their relationships with family, friends, and classmates and the importance of their culture to them and their families.

the social work pioneer discussed in Chapter 1, wrote in 1922, "The worker is no more occupied with abnormalities in the individual than in the environment, is no more able to neglect the one than the other" (p. 989). Since then, many social work proponents, such as Hearn, Pincus and Minahan, Siporin, Perlman, and Bartlett, have developed specific approaches or explored varying aspects of social work from within the boundaries of this framework.

More recently, other social work theorists such as Germain, Gitterman, and Meyer have advocated an ecological perspective, which incorporates many of the same concepts as the systems framework. It should be noted that some social work theorists (Meyer, 1983) clearly separate the systems perspective and the ecological perspective, and consider them two distinct frameworks. These theorists view the systems framework as largely relating to the *structure*, or the systemic properties of cases, which helps us to focus on how variables are related and to order systems within the environment according to complexity. In contrast, they view the ecological perspective as one that focuses more on *relationships* of person and environment, with greater emphasis on interactions and transactions than on structure. Others (Compton & Galaway, 1989) incorporate the very similar concepts of both and refer to one framework, the systems/ecological framework. This is the approach the authors take in this text. Rather than get confused over semantics, readers should focus on the broad definitions and principles of the various frameworks discussed and their commonalities rather than their differences. We emphasize these important points in understanding a systems/ecological perspective and its significant contributions to social work.

The Perspective of Systems Theory

Systems theory was first used to explain the functioning of the human body, which was seen as a major system that incorporated a number of smaller systems: the skeletal system, the muscular system, the endocrine system, the circulatory system, and so on. Medical practitioners, even ones in ancient Greece, realized that when one aspect of the human body failed to function effectively, it also affected the way that other systems within the body functioned and, in turn, affected the way the human body as a whole functioned. This led to further exploration of the relationships between subparts of living organisms. (For example, Lewis Thomas's *The Life of a Cell* clearly articulates the intricate interrelations among the many complex parts of a single cell that enable the cell to maintain itself and to reproduce.)

Synergy The contribution from biology to systems theory is the emphasis on the fact that the whole is greater than the sum of its parts—that is, when all of the smaller systems or subsystems of an organism function in tandem, they produce a larger system that is far more grand and significant than would be the combination of those smaller systems working independently. The larger system, when it functions optimally, is said to achieve **synergy,** or the combined energy from the smaller parts that is greater than the total if those parts functioned separately. Imagine for a moment that your instructor for this course has given you an exam on the chapters you have covered thus far in this text.

Each student takes the exam separately, and scores of each student are listed. The lowest score is 50; the highest is 85. Now, suppose that your instructor decides to let the entire class take the exam together. Each individual in the class now functions as part of the total group, together solving each exam question. As a class, your score on the exam is 100. Your class has demonstrated the concept of the whole being greater than the sum of its parts, or synergy.

Von Bertalanffy (1968, 38) defines a system as "a set of units with relationships among them"; Compton and Galaway describe a system as "a whole, consisting of interdependent and interacting parts" (1984, 112). One of the advantages of the systems/ecological framework is the fact that it is a conceptual framework and can be applied in many different ways to many different situations.

Boundaries An important aspect of a system is the concept of **boundary.** A system can be almost anything, but by its definition, it usually is given some sort of boundary or point when one system ends and another begins. The system's environment encompasses everything beyond this boundary. For example, the human body can be seen as a system, as discussed earlier, with the skin as a boundary and the various body subsystems as smaller components of the larger system. From a different perspective, the human mind can be seen as a system, with Freud's id, ego, and superego as components within that system that interact together to form a whole greater than any of the three components alone: the human mind.

An individual can also be part of a larger system, for example, a family system, which might include one or two parents, a child, and the family dog. One might wish to expand the boundaries of the family system and include the grandparents and the aunts and uncles. We can establish larger systems, such as school systems, communities, cities, states, or nations, and focus on their interactions and interdependence with each other. We can also look at a political system, an economic system, a religious system, and a social welfare system and the ways that those broader systems interact with each other.

The important thing to remember when using a systems perspective is that the systems that we define and the boundaries that we give those systems are conceptual; that is, we can define them in whatever ways make the most sense in looking at the broad social welfare or the more narrow individual problem that we are addressing. For example, if we were to conceptualize Juan's family as a social system, we could include within its boundaries his mother, his younger brother, and Juan. We may also choose to include Juan's father as part of his family system (even though he is out of the home, he is still part of Juan's life, and his absence is a major emotional issue for Juan). We could also include grandparents or other extended family members because although they are not actively involved either physically or emotionally in any supportive way with the family, they are a possible source of support since they have been very involved in the past. (see Figure 3–1). If we were looking at another family system, however, we might well include a larger number of other members. The systems/ecological framework is a useful way to organize data to help understand a situation, and its flexibility allows us to define systems and their boundaries in a number of ways.

Figure 3–1 Using an Eco-Map to Understand Juan's Family Situation

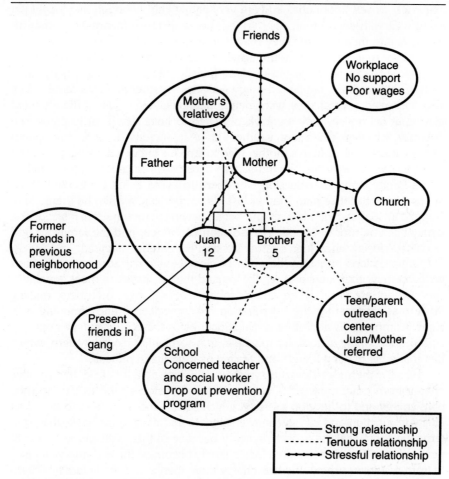

Source: Adapted from Ann Hartman, "Diagrammatic Assessment of Family Relationships," *Social Casework* (October 1978).

Open and Closed Systems While we can draw boundaries wherever it seems appropriate when using a systems/ecological framework, it is also important that we be able to ascertain how permeable those boundaries are. Some systems have easily permeated boundaries between units (e.g., people) in the system and those outside; we call those systems **open systems.** Some families exemplify open systems. Those are the families that readily incorporate others; when someone rings the doorbell at dinnertime, a plate is always added. A cousin or a friend may live with the family for a short or a long time period, and it is often difficult to tell exactly who is a family member and who isn't. For example, in some families, members become overly involved in each others' lives. In other families parents do not set consistent limits for their children and there are no clear boundaries between the parents and the children. Unclear boundaries within systems can lead to family problems, such as incest.

On the other hand, some families represent **closed systems;** they have extremely closed boundaries and are very tightly knit. Although they might get along well with each other, they are isolated and rarely incorporate other individuals into their system. They may have special family nights and traditions where they make it clear that the activities are for family members only.

Before Juan's father began drinking heavily, his family was a fairly open system. Although his family did many activities together just as a family, they also socialized a great deal with friends and relatives. If Juan's friends were playing at his house, they were often invited to have dinner or to participate in family activities. When Juan's father's drinking increased, his family system became more closed. Juan's mother tried to limit his father's drinking by limiting the family social activities. When relatives became more critical of his drinking, Juan's family stopped socializing with them to avoid being confronted about the problem. Because Juan's father lost his temper easily when he drank, Juan stopped inviting his friends over and began playing at their houses instead. The family became more isolated. The isolation continued, and the family system remained closed when Juan's father left and his parents divorced.

Organizations also may be open or closed systems. Some organizations welcome new members and readily expand their activities to meet new interests. Others are very closed and do not encourage new members, making those that try to enter the organization feel unwelcome and shunning new ideas. Communities and other social structures can also be viewed as open or closed. Juan's new school, for example, is a somewhat closed system, which has made his making friends and feeling as if he fits in difficult.

Usually, the more closed a system is, the less able it is to derive positive energy from other systems. Over time, closed systems tend to use up their own energy and to develop **entropy,** which means that they tend to lose their ability to function and can eventually stagnate and die. (In contrast, open systems are more likely to achieve synergy because of their willingness to accept new energy.) The more isolated Juan's family becomes, the less energy it takes in from the environment, the less energy there then is within the family system for family members, and the less able the family is to function. The family system becomes more and more lethargic and will eventually either change or die, with the family separating and members becoming part of other family systems. If, for example, Juan's mother were to become extremely abusive and Juan were to become involved in the gang and serious criminal activities, his brother might be placed in foster care and Juan in a correctional facility for youth.

Interactions and Interrelations Boundaries and open and closed systems are structural aspects of systems. An additional feature of the systems/ecological framework is its emphasis on the interactions and interrelations between units rather than on the systems or subsystems themselves. This lends itself well to the need for focusing on associations among large numbers of factors rather than on cause-and-effect relationships between two factors. The interactions and interrelatedness between systems suggest constant motion and fluidity, as opposed to the stasis of those systems that stand still and do not move or change. The relatedness and interactions also incorporate the concept that a change or movement in one part of the system, or in one system, will have an impact on the larger system, or other systems, as well. Imagine a room full of constantly moving Ping-Pong balls, each representing a system or a sub-system of a larger system. Hitting one Ping-Pong ball across the room will change the movement of the other balls. Similarly, a change in the economic system (for example, inflation) will result in changes in other systems: the educational system could be affected because fewer students could afford to go to college; the social welfare system could be affected because more people would have financial difficulties and need public assistance and social services; the criminal justice system could be affected because more persons might turn to crime; and the political system could be affected because the dissatisfied populace might not reelect the party in office.

The results of interactions and interrelatedness between systems can also be seen when viewing Juan's family. His father's drinking led to his job loss, which then resulted in an increased pattern of drinking. Both of these factors affected his parents' relationships with each other, or the marital system; the parents' relationships with Juan and his younger brother, or the parent–child system; the communication patterns between the family as a system; and relationships between Juan's family system and other systems beyond the family, such as his father's workplace, his family's church, and Juan's school.

Such interactions and interrelatedness occur continually. There are usually constant flows of energy within and across systems. This creates natural tensions, which are viewed as healthy if communication is open, because the energy flow creates growth and change. Feedback among systems is an important part of the systems/ecological perspective, which emphasizes communication. It is important that social workers and others who work within and across various systems understand the goals of those systems and their communication patterns. In unhealthy systems, for example, the various members of the system may be communicating in certain ways and may have certain unspoken goals that maintain the system because its members are afraid to change the system or the system is in some way productive for them. In a family such as Juan's where a parent is an alcoholic, the other parent or an older child may perpetuate the alcoholism and unconsciously try to keep the family system as it is because the nonalcoholic may see his or her role as one of caretaking—keeping the family together and protecting the younger children from the alcoholism. If the family system changes, the nonalcoholic parent or older child will no longer be able to maintain that role and thus may try to force the system back to the way it once was. In a social services agency that began a new program to get women off welfare, the social workers became fearful that they would not get good evaluations if they didn't get large numbers of women into jobs. Thus, the goal of the agency unconsciously became placing women in "dead-end" jobs, which were easy for them to get, rather than getting them into training programs or more challenging, better-paying jobs, which required more time from the workers and gave them fewer job entries to report.

Steady State   Another important concept of the systems/ecological framework is that of **steady state,** in which systems are not static but are steadily moving, as we have already suggested. The concept of steady state means that the system is constantly adjusting to move toward its goal while maintaining a certain amount of order and stability, giving and receiving energy in fairly equal amounts to maintain equilibrium. A healthy system, then, may be viewed as one that is not in upheaval but is always ebbing and flowing to achieve both stability and growth. If Juan and his family receive counseling and other support from the broader environment, his family system should achieve equilibrium. The system will not stop changing but will move toward its goals in a less disruptive manner.

Equifinality   One last concept of the systems/ecological framework is that of **equifinality,** or the concept that the final state of a system can be achieved in many different ways. Because there are many ways to interpret a given situation, there are usually many options available regarding how to deal with it. A number of alternatives can be considered, for example, when working with Juan and his family to help them function better as individuals and as a family unit. Options could include individual and family counseling, support or therapeutic groups for Juan and his mother, a child care program for his younger brother, increasing interactions between Juan and his father, enrollment in a chemical dependency program for Juan's father, enrollment in a job-training program for Juan's mother and/or father, involvement in positive recreational programs for Juan, and membership in a supportive church. Although not all of these options might be realistic for Juan and his family, various combinations of them could lead to the same positive results.

Critiques of the Systems/Ecological Framework

One criticism of the systems/ecological framework in social work is that it encompasses the broad environment yet ignores the psychosocial and the intrapsychic aspects of the individual. Proponents of the systems/ecological framework argue that the individual is perceived as a highly valued system itself, and that intrapsychic aspects and psychosocial aspects, which incorporate the individual's capacity and motivation for change, are parts of any system involving individuals that cannot and should not be ignored.

Another criticism of the systems/ecological framework is that, because it incorporates everything, it is too complicated, making it easy to miss important aspects of a situation. The ecological perspective articulated by social scientists Urie Bronfenbrenner and James Garbarino attempts to address this concern. Bronfenbrenner and Garbarino incorporate individual developmental aspects into the systems perspective of the broader environment, but they break the system into different levels, or layers of the environment. They suggest that, for all individuals, both risks and opportunities exist at each of these environmental levels. Opportunities within the environment encourage an individual to meet needs and to develop as a healthy, well-functioning person. Risks are either direct threats to healthy development or the absence of opportunities that facilitate healthy individual development.

Levels of the Environment   Bronfenbrenner (1979) and Garbarino (1982) suggest that risks and opportunities can be found at all levels of the environment.

They describe these levels as being like a series of Russian eggs, with a large egg cut in half that opens to reveal a smaller egg, that also opens to reveal a still smaller egg, that opens to reveal a still smaller egg (see Figure 3–2 and Table 3–1). They suggest that one consider the tiniest egg to be the **microsystem level,** which includes the individual and all persons and groups that incorporate the individual's day-to-day environment. The focus at this level would incorporate the individual's level of functioning, intellectual and emotional capacities, and motivation; the impact of past life experiences; and the interactions and connections between that individual and others in the immediate environment. Also, the focus would be on whether the relationships are positive or negative,

Figure 3–2   The Levels of the Ecological System

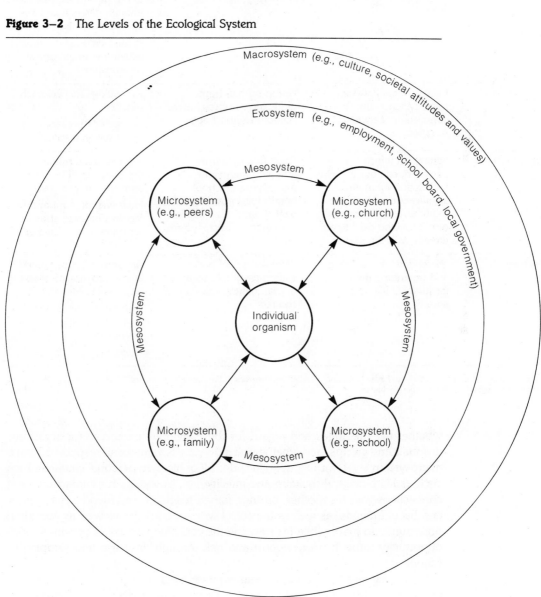

Source: Reprinted with permission from James Garbarino. *Children and Families in the Social Environment* (New York: Aldine de Gruyter). Copyright © 1982 by James Garbarino.

Table 3–1 A Summary of the Ecology of Sociocultural Risk and Opportunity to Individuals as They Interact with Their Environments

Ecological Level	Definition	Examples	Issues Affecting Person
Microsystem	Situations in which the person has face-to-face contact with influential others	Family, school, workplace, peer group, church	Is the person regarded positively? Is the person accepted? Is the person reinforced for competent behavior? Is the person exposed to enough diversity in roles and relationships? Is the person given an active role in reciprocal relationships?
Mesosystem	Relationships between microsystems; the connections between situations	Home-school, home-workplace, home-church, school-neighborhood	Do settings respect each other? Do settings present basic consistency in values?
Exosystem	Settings in which the person does not participate but in which significant decisions are made affecting the person or others who do interact directly with the person	Place of employment of others in the person's microsystem, school board, local government, peer groups of others in the person's microsystem	Are decisions made with the interests of the person and the family in mind? How well do supports for families balance stresses for parents and children?
Macrosystem	"Blueprints" for defining and organizing the institutional life of the society	Ideology, social policy, shared assumptions about human nature, the "social contract"	Are some groups valued at the expense of others (e.g., sexism, racism)? Is there an individualistic or a collectivistic orientation? Is violence a norm?

Source: Reprinted with permission from James Garbarino. *Children and Families in the Social Environment* (New York: Aldine de Gruyter). Copyright © 1982 by James Garbarino.

whether the messages and regard for the individual are consistent across individuals and groups, and whether the individual is valued and respected. Juan's microsystem level, for example, includes all of his own personal characteristics such as his biological makeup and intelligence, as well as his interactions and connections with his mother, brother, father, teachers, and friends. His mother and his old friends, as well as the social worker, could be viewed as providing opportunity to Juan, while his new friends could be viewed as providing both opportunity through peer support and risk through drug use and skipping of school.

The next level is termed the **mesosystem level.** This level incorporates the interactions of the individuals and groups within the individual's microsystem and the ways that those individuals and groups relate to each other but not to the individual upon whose microsystem we are focusing. This would mean, for example, relationships between a child's mother and father, or a child's teacher and her parents, or a child's friends and her family. If they are not getting along, even though the child is not directly involved in the interactions, it has an impact on the child. The marital problems of Juan's parents, for example, even though he was not directly involved in their problems, obviously had a serious impact on Juan and his younger brother and can be seen as environmental risks. The conflicting messages to Juan from his school and family settings versus his peer setting also had an impact on Juan and are additional risks. While his mother and school personnel advocated against skipping school and experimenting with marijuana, his new peers encouraged him to become involved in these activities. His mother's involvement with the school social worker, however, can be viewed as an opportunity for Juan at this level.

The third level is the **exosystem level.** This level includes community-level factors that may not relate directly to the individual but affect the way the individual functions. This includes factors such as the workplace policies of the parents (if they cannot take sick leave when the child is sick, for example, this has an impact on the child), school board and community policies, community attitudes and values, and economic and social factors that exist within the neighborhood and community. For Juan's family, exosystem risk factors include the lack of jobs that pay well for persons with his mother's skill level, lack of affordable child care for Juan's younger brother, and community attitudes toward divorce, Hispanics, and single-parenting. The teen/family outreach center provides an exosystem opportunity for Juan, if it is not too overloaded with other clients.

The final level is the **macrosystem level.** This level includes societal factors such as the cultural attitudes and values of the society (for example, attitudes toward women, minorities, the poor, and violence); the role of the media in addressing or promoting social problems (some suggest, for example, that the media promotes violence and teen pregnancy); and federal legislation and other social policies that affect a given individual. Lack of governmental programs for single parents and potential school dropouts, societal attitudes toward divorce and single parents, discrimination toward Hispanics, and the media's glamorization of gangs and violence all contribute to Juan's current life situation and can be viewed as environmental risks. However, in spite of these risks, there are opportunities for Juan, such as democracy, freedom of religion, and education, that might not be found within other macrosystems.

Many advocates of the ecological framework as conceptualized by Bronfenbrenner and Garbarino agree that it is a derivation of systems theory and another way of defining boundaries of systems. They suggest that it is advantageous to use because it allows one to see the interdependence and interaction across levels from the microsystem level to the macrosystem level and also allows us to target intervention at a variety of levels to address social problems and individual needs. For example, we could provide individual counseling to Juan, counsel his family, and help him develop a new network of friends at the microlevel; work with Juan's mother, teachers, and peers to help them become more consistent in the messages they are conveying to Juan at the mesolevel; advocate for the establishment of a community program to assist teens who experience family problems and of low-cost child care for working parents at the exolevel; and lobby for legislation to develop national media programs that educate the public about gangs, drugs, and the working poor at the macrolevel.

Problems in Living   Social workers Carel Germain and Alex Gitterman (1980) incorporate the ecological perspective somewhat differently in their approach, adding still another important way of viewing individuals within their environments. They suggest that all persons have problems at some point in their

The systems/ecological perspective allows social workers to facilitate change at all levels of the environment. Parents, social workers, and other community representatives attend a Parent Teacher Association (PTA) meeting and advocate for a substance abuse intervention program at their local high school.

lives, or what they term "problems in living." The first problem area they discuss includes those problems associated with life transitions—marriage, the birth of a first child, movement into middle age, movement of children out of the family, and so forth. They suggest that all individuals go through such transitions, and that as one moves from one life stage to another, transitional problems and needs develop that may need social work intervention. Juan's family, for example, is experiencing the transitions of divorce and a child moving into adolescence.

The second area Germain and Gitterman identify includes problems associated with tasks in using and influencing elements of the environment (1980). Juan's mother has had difficulty locating affordable child care for her youngest son, and Juan is having difficulty adjusting to a new school setting. The limited social networks available to Juan and his family suggest the need for intervention in this area.

A final area of focus suggested by Germain and Gitterman is that of maladaptive interpersonal problems and needs in families and groups. Juan's family, for example, has developed some of the unproductive communication patterns typically found in families where alcoholism is a problem. Although these patterns maintained the family as an intact unit for many years, they will continue to stifle individual and family growth unless they change. Germain and Gitterman reinforce the need to incorporate the transactional patterns between persons and their environment when planning any social work intervention.

In summary, a systems/ecological framework emphasizes the fact that our lives are shaped by the choices we make, and that the environment shapes our choices, while our choices shape the way we interact with our environment. This continual interaction and cyclical perspective suggest that we cannot discuss the individual without focusing on the environment, nor the environment without the strong forces that individuals play in its formulation. The individual and the environment are continually adapting to each other. The primary role of the social worker is to ensure that this adaptation is mutually supportive to both the individual and the environment.

THE UTILITY OF THE SYSTEMS/ECOLOGICAL FRAMEWORK

The systems/ecological framework is intended to be used as a mechanism to order facts about social welfare problems or individual problems in such a way that appropriate theories can be identified to further explore the problems or to determine interventions. Box 3–1 examines some ways the framework aids social workers. It is useful to think of this framework as a way to "map the territory" or gather and fit together pieces of a puzzle to understand a situation. When dealing with a problem such as poverty, for example, which is addressed in Chapter 4, many individuals may have unidimensional ways of explaining the problem—it is because people are lazy, for example, or the victims of their own circumstance. A systems/ecological perspective would identify many factors—a large, complex territory and a puzzle with many pieces. Individual factors, family factors, community factors, and societal factors such as the impact of the economic system and of unemployment, racism, sexism, and so forth—all contribute to poverty in some way. Table 3–2 lists just some of the factors that shape the interactions between individuals and their environments.

Box 3–1 Value of Systems/Ecological Perspective to Social Welfare Problems and Social Work Practice

The systems/ecological perspective makes a number of valuable contributions as an organizing framework for social work practice.

1. The systems/ecological perspective allows one to deal with far more data than other models and to bring order to these large amounts of data from a variety of different disciplines.

2. The concepts relating to systems are equally applicable to the wide range of clients served by social workers, including individuals, families, groups, organizations, communities, and society.

3. The systems/ecological framework allows for identifying the wide range of factors that have an impact on social welfare problems and their interrelationships.

4. The systems/ecological framework shifts attention from characteristics of individuals or the environment to the relationships between systems and their communication patterns.

5. The systems/ecological framework views persons as actively involved with their environments, capable of adaptation and change.

6. The systems/ecological framework views systems as goal-oriented, supporting client self-determination and the client's participation in the change process.

7. If systems require constant transactions with each other to survive, the purpose of the social worker is to provide and maintain such opportunities for transactions for all populations and to work to reduce isolation of individuals and systems.

8. Social workers need to work to ensure that change and tension are not resisted in systems and to remove the notions that change and conflict are pathological.

9. Social workers need to be aware of the systems within which they work and how change within those systems affects the whole. This means that social workers must choose points of intervention with care.

10. Social workers are a social system and components of a social systems network.

Adapted from: B. Compton and B. Galaway, *Social Work Processes* (Homewood, Ill.: Dorsey Press, 1984), pp. 124–25.

Once the territory is mapped out or all of the puzzle pieces (or as many as possible) are obtained, then the systems/ecological framework can also allow for further exploration of certain factors, parts of the terrain, or pieces of the puzzle. Once the larger picture is obtained, we can better ascertain where to focus; whether more information is needed and in what areas; and if intervention is required, at what level and within which system or systems within the environment. One or more additional theories or frameworks can then be used to obtain more information or to guide intervention. The advantage of the systems/ecological perspective is that we are less likely to miss a major aspect of a situation or intervene inappropriately. This perspective also allows for individualization and diversity, which also means that cultural and gender differences are readily accounted for. (See Table 3–2.)

The Utility of Other Theories and Frameworks

Although social workers use other theories and frameworks in their professional practice, those are more limiting than the systems/ecological perspective. Two other useful types of frameworks include psychosocial frameworks and cognitive/behavioral frameworks (Whittaker & Tracy, 1989). These and other frameworks commonly used by social workers are discussed in greater depth in Chapter 13.

Psychosocial Frameworks Psychosocial frameworks include psychoanalytic theory, ego psychology, and life-span development frameworks. These frameworks are often used together and are not always viewed as mutually exclusive.

Psychoanalytic Theory Psychoanalytic theory, based largely on the works of Sigmund Freud, is built on the premise that children are born with biologically rooted functions, termed "drives," that dictate individual functioning. These drives are primarily related to sexual expression and aggression. Psychoanalytic

Table 3–2   Factors that Shape Individual Functioning and Relationship with the Environment

Personal Factors:

Level of prenatal care received
Intellectual capacity/ability
Emotional capacity/mental health
Level of social functioning
Physical health
Age
Ethnicity/culture
Motivation
Life stage/transitional period
Crisis level

Family Factors:

Support systems/availability of significant others
Family patterns/structure/values
Economic level/employment
Level of functioning/family crisis

Community Factors:

Social class compared to rest of community
Ethnic/cultural/class diversity/attitudes and values
Social roles available within community
Community support
Economic conditions
Employment opportunities
Educational opportunities
Environmental stress

Societal Factors:

Societal attitudes and values
Racism, sexism, poverty levels
Supportive or lack of supportive legislation/programs/policies
Media role

theory is also a stage or developmental framework, since its premise is that persons cope with different changes in biological, psychological, and social functioning at different stages of their lives. This framework focuses on both conscious and unconscious drives and on internal interactions within an individual between the person's id, ego, and superego. The focus on interaction between the individual and the broader environment is more limited than it is in many other theories, although the psychoanalytic theory includes attention to the impact of past life experiences, primarily during early childhood; on later functioning; and on the development of internal defense mechanisms to cope with the environment, such as denial and rationalization. If Juan's situation were to be viewed from this framework, his sexual drives during preadolescence and the impact of his father leaving during this time would be major focal points. This framework is complex and based largely on individual psychopathology, or emotional illness. If one uses this framework for persons who have problems, the suggested intervention is individual psychoanalysis to work through intrapsychic conflicts.

Ego Psychology and Life-Span Development Frameworks Ego psychology stems from psychoanalytic theory but focuses mainly on the development of a strong ego as opposed to interactions between the id, ego, and superego. The ego psychology perspective also focuses more on the transactions between the person and environment and the impact of the environment in shaping the development of a healthy ego (Erikson, 1959). The impact of Juan's family situation during his childhood would be explored, and ways to help Juan feel better about himself and to increase his self-esteem would be major issues for intervention within this framework.

Both psychoanalytic and ego psychology are life-span development frameworks. These frameworks suggest that individuals interact with their environments in different ways to meet different needs at different points in the life cycle, and that the ways needs are met in previous stages shape individual functioning and later development. Like psychoanalytic theory, there is a strong emphasis on ways that early life experiences shape later behavior. However, the emphasis is much more on the ways that the environment shapes the resolution of these issues. For example, using a life-span development framework developed by Erik Erikson, an individual addresses issues of basic trust versus basic mistrust during the first year of life. If an infant is placed in an environment where his basic needs, such as feeding or nurturing are not met, or are met inconsistently, the child does not develop a sense of trust. If trust is not developed later, the child has difficulty in other stages of life, for example, in developing intimate relationships during young adulthood. Within this framework, Juan's developmental needs involve developing a sense of identity, primarily through peer relationships. Thus, for example, the gang members are filling a major developmental need for Juan that he does not feel can be met in other ways.

Although important and useful to social workers, these frameworks are more limiting than the systems/ecological framework. They place more emphasis on early life experiences than later experiences and less emphasis on interactions and transactions among broader levels of the environment and the impact on the individual. Finally, they suggest intervention primarily at the individual level. However, they are especially useful in helping individuals understand how past experiences have shaped current life situations and how issues are often related to one's developmental stage or age.

Cognitive/Behavioral Frameworks A second set of frameworks can be termed cognitive/behavioral frameworks. These frameworks place little emphasis on past life experiences or biological aspects of an individual. Their premise is that environment, and not heredity, largely determines behavior. These frameworks focus primarily on the present and on shaping individual thinking and behavior within the person's immediate environment. The goal is to shape behavior, not to change personality. For example, Juan may have developed a series of self-messages that suggest he is not competent. These repeated messages have led to his poor schoolwork and his attempts to seek competence in other areas, such as drug use and illegal activities. By helping Juan change his self-messages to positive affirmations about himself, Juan will begin to see himself as competent and begin reengaging in school. The interventions within these frameworks are largely at the individual level, and there is much greater emphasis on the present and the environment. Cognitive/behavioral frameworks, however, are extremely useful to social workers. They can help individuals not only understand ways that unproductive thought patterns shape behaviors but also develop new thought patterns and behaviors that can lead to healthier functioning.

Social workers often use these frameworks, as well as other frameworks, in a variety of ways and often in tandem with each other. Although the systems/ecological perspective can also be used when intervening with an individual or the broader environment, it is almost always used by social workers as the major framework for understanding a given situation/problem. However, once the problem is understood and the broad terrain is mapped out using this framework, other frameworks may be used for further assessment as well as intervention.

The Systems/Ecological Framework and Professional Practice

Because the generalist model of social work incorporates all different levels of the environment and the interactions and interdependence within and between levels, the systems/ecological framework is especially useful as an organizing framework for professional practice. Specifically, the framework:

1. allows the social worker to deal with large amounts of information from many different areas and to bring order to that information;
2. includes concepts that are applicable to the full range of clients served by social workers, including individuals, couples, families, groups, organizations, communities, and broader societal systems;
3. incorporates not only the structures of the social units involved, but the interrelatedness and interactions within and between units;
4. shifts attention away from the characteristics of units to the transactions and interactions between them;
5. views individuals as active participants in their environments, capable of change and adaptation, including shifting to new environments;

6. incorporates the concept of client self-determination and recognizes that multiple approaches in bringing about change;

7. focuses social workers on the need to provide and maintain continual transactions between persons and their environments for all populations and to monitor social systems heading for isolation;

8. provides a constant reminder to social workers that change is healthy and necessary for systems to grow but that systems often resist change;

9. places both the social worker and the agency within the client's environment;

10. reminds social workers that since a change in one level of the system creates changes at other levels, interventions must be thought through and chosen with care (Compton & Galaway 1989, 138–39).

Applying the Systems/Ecological Framework: The Social Welfare System and Poverty

The systems/ecological framework is especially useful in understanding the complexities of large systems within our environment, such as the social welfare system. The social welfare system in place at any given moment is the product of the interactions and interrelatedness of historical, economic, and political forces. As a large system, it is constantly reshaped by changes in societal values and events beyond its boundaries. Changes in societal values, for example, result in increased public acceptance of programs for battered women and child care for children of working mothers. An economic recession results in extensive cutbacks in social welfare services.

The scope of social welfare systems in the United States is not as broad, comprehensive, and integrated as most social workers would like, nor is it as constrained and limited as some others would contend. In a sense, it is not a formal system at all, but rather a collection of ad hoc programs developed in diverse and special political circumstances. Thus, although we have programs for the aged, the disabled, the blind, and dependent children, each program has its own political history and its own political constituency.

As a matter of practice, if not of principle, the target populations of social agencies are those subgroups in our society that do not fare well and that are not adequately served by the primary social systems in our society, which include the economic system, the political system, the family system, the religious system, the health system, and the educational system. Typically, the social welfare system functions as a result of family breakdown, problems in income distribution, and institutional failure in the religious, education, health, and/or business sectors. While each of us would probably give a somewhat different statement of mission for an ideal social welfare system, at a minimum we would likely all agree that such a system should guarantee to each person a socially defined minimum standard of well-being. In meeting this standard, the social welfare system interacts with primary social systems within our society: the family system, the economic system, and the political system. Each of these primary systems, in its turn, has a principal function as illustrated in Table 3–3. The social welfare system is most frequently perceived as a residual

Table 3–3 Social Systems

Systems	Functions
Primary:	
Family	The primary personal care and mutual assistance system between parents and children, between adults and elderly
Political	The authoritative allocation of public social goals and values
Economic	The allocation and distribution of scarce resources to competing entities
Secondary:	
Other goal-specific systems, i.e. education system, health care system, defense system	The list and functions of secondary systems are dependent on individual choice. What would you include?
Social Welfare System:	To respond to failure and/or dysfunction in primary and secondary systems

social system that comes into play when there is a failure in the primary system, or the primary system generates undesirable consequences. (Wilensky & Lebeaux 1975).

As stated earlier, the organized social welfare system, comprised of numerous and varied social services and institutions, is designed to help individuals and groups attain satisfying standards of life and health. This view implies recurrent failure in other social systems. It assumes that individuals sometimes need outside help in coping with a complex social order. Social welfare institutions that comprise the social welfare system assist in time of crisis of the individual, but since recurrent and random crisis is the ordinary condition of social life, a structured set of social agencies needs to stand ready to respond to crises and failures—to overcome the crisis and enhance problem-solving and coping skills of communities, groups, families, and individuals, so that crisis is less frequent.

In this view, the social welfare system is seen as the structured set of responses developed to deal with the dysfunction of other systems. For example, the family system is intended to meet the physical and emotional needs of children. However, at times, the primary family system fails and is unable to serve this function. At that point, the social welfare system provides child welfare services, such as respite child care, foster care, and services to abused and neglected children. When the social welfare system functions to assist or replace the family in its child care roles, this exemplifies a social welfare response to a primary system failure. A second example of a social welfare system response to a primary system dysfunction can be seen in relation to the economic system. We know that the economic system distributes income unevenly, leaving some people poor. Thus, we have generated an income security system to provide various income guarantees to specific classes of persons in need.

Objectively speaking, an overview of the American social welfare institutions and social work practice reveals an incredible range of public and voluntary agencies seeking to respond to social problems. For some problem areas, the response is well conceptualized and generous; for others the response is hasty and scanty; still other social problems invoke no response at all. One of the major problems with our social welfare system is the fact that each problem is usually treated as a separate issue, rather than an interactive and interdependent part of a larger issue. Seldom, for example, is attention given to how a response to problem A is related to its impact on problem B. The passage in 1988 of welfare reform legislation, for example, is intended to help large numbers of individuals receiving public assistance become self-sufficient through gainful employment. However, the staff of employment and training programs established to work with clients as part of the legislation quickly learned that many of them cannot read and write well. This has resulted in a tremendous and often unanticipated overload of the education system, which is being asked to provide remedial education programs for this group of clients. The original legislation unfortunately did not allow for allocation of additional resources to the education system.

A second example of the interrelatedness between systems and social problems can be seen in the area of health care. In a number of states in the past five years, state legislators, concerned about costs being paid for health care for the poor, reduced the funds allocated in this area rather than raise taxes. Unfortunately, they overlooked the fact that most of these state dollars were being used to provide the match for federal dollars allocated to states for health care. For every five dollars that the states contribute, the federal government matched the amount with five dollars of federal money. The reduction in dollars by the states cut the amount of federal money into the states in half, seriously reducing the number of clients that could be served by state public assistance health programs. No longer served by these health programs, the states' poor did not seek health care until they were desperate, and when they did, they came to local hospitals as indigent (unpaying) patients. This meant that local hospitals had to foot these bills, now higher than they might have been if care had been sought earlier. It also meant that all of the higher costs were footed by local taxpayers in these states who all pay local taxes to support the hospitals. Thus, what the legislators ultimately intended as a moneysaving measure for their states' citizens turned out to be far more costly.

Obviously, the systems/ecological framework can be used to help understand issues at every level of the environment and across levels. The framework can also be used to determine types of intervention at all levels of the environment once the complex issues are understood. Although the following discussion focuses primarily on the use of the framework and the problem-solving approach at the microlevel, the framework and the problem-solving approach are just as applicable for planning interventions at broader levels of the environment.

A PROBLEM-SOLVING APPROACH

The generalist model of social work practice taught at the BSW level suggests a problem-solving approach in working with clients at the individual, family, group, organizational, community, or societal level. Two social workers in the early 1970s, Allen Pincus and Anne Minahan, incorporated many aspects of the systems/ecological perspective into a practice framework that could be used in assisting clients. They suggested that individuals with whom the social worker interacts to bring about planned change can be grouped into four different systems (1973, 54–74). The first, the **client system**, includes the person or persons who has either asked for or been mandated to receive services. In Juan's situation, for example, the client system initially included his teachers, since they referred Juan to the school social worker. Since Juan and his mother both asked for help when the social worker met with them, they then became part of the client system.

The second system, the **target system**, includes the person or persons who need to change or be influenced in order to assist the client system. Note that this system and the client system, as in Juan's case, often overlap, although it may be that others, such as Juan's father, could be included in the target system. Sometimes, however, the client and the target systems are different. For example, if Juan and his mother had not asked for help, the teachers would have remained the client system, while Juan and his mother would have been the target system. If a group of migrants comes to a health clinic because their children are sick from drinking polluted water, they would be considered the client system. The target system would be the farmers who own the land where the migrants are working and providing the unhealthy living conditions for the migrants and their families.

The **change agent system** is the social worker, agency, and other persons who will be facilitating the planned intervention. In Juan's situation, this would be the school social worker, social worker at the teen/family outreach program, the school, the teen/family outreach program staff, and any other helping persons involved with the family.

The **action system** includes all of those persons involved with the social worker to bring about the change. When working with Juan's family, this would include Juan and his family, his teachers, other helping professionals, and possibly Juan's peers. This system could also include a church or neighborhood group and other levels of the environment beyond the microsystem.

Pincus and Minahan's model can be useful in helping social workers organize information about who their clients are, who and what are being changed, and how this change will take place. The model is especially advantageous when dealing with complex situations. For example, let's suppose that Juan and his mother had not asked for help, but the school social worker saw them, and not the teachers, as the client system. She probably would have been met with extensive pressure from the teachers to change Juan and resistance from Juan as she attempted to work with him to change. Realizing that the client system and the target system differed would help her focus on the teachers as the client system and change the type of intervention to one that was more realistic and appropriate.

The beginning generalist social work professional is seen as a "problem solver" who can assist client systems in identifying needed change, developing strategies to make the change, implementing those strategies, and monitoring and evaluating throughout the process to ensure that the desired change is taking place. BSW social workers are trained to use the problem-solving approach, which can be used to solve problems that are a part of everyday life as well as to help client systems, which may be individuals, families, groups, organizations, communities, or larger social entities. No matter what level of the environment the social worker selects as an intervention point, the problem-solving approach can be a useful tool in bringing about planned change. The problem-solving process has three major phases (Compton & Galaway 1989, 390–91):

Contact (or engagement) phase

○ The social worker and the client begin to develop a relationship.

○ They begin to identify and define the problem(s) to be addressed.

○ They identify short-term and long-term goals to address the problem.

○ They develop a preliminary contract and commitment regarding work to be done together on the problems to be addressed.

Contract phase

○ The social worker and the client conduct an assessment, gathering as much information as possible about the client and all areas within the client's environment.

○ They determine what problem areas and environmental factors are most critical in addressing the problem and how those are related and they identify factors that can be addressed to bring about change.

○ They identify available resources, including client strengths, that can be used to address problems and bring about planned change.

○ They select the most appropriate resources and determine availability.

○ They formulate a plan of action and determine who will be involved and what their roles will be.

Action Phase

○ The social worker, the client, and others involved carry out the plan.

○ The plan is monitored and revised as necessary.

○ Termination of the social worker–client relationship takes place when goals are met.

○ A final evaluation occurs at the time of termination, and referrals to other resources are made if additional work or follow-up is needed.

After reviewing the phases of the problem-solving process, it is easy to see the "goodness of fit" between this process and the systems/ecological framework and the many ways that the two are related. Ms. Herrera's involvement with Juan and his family can be used to demonstrate how this framework can be applied to understand or to intervene at various levels of the environment.

Applications with Juan and His Family

During the contact phase of the problem-solving process, Ms. Herrera, the school social worker, used all of the concepts of the systems/ecological framework. In developing an initial relationship with Juan and his mother, she used preliminary knowledge about areas such as twelve-year-old boys and their developmental needs during this preadolescence stage, single-parent women and their special needs, the Hispanic culture, and ways that preadolescents and parents might view a professional from an authoritative organization such as a school. She empathized with both Juan and his mother as she realized how they might view life from their day-to-day reality.

As she conducted an assessment, she gathered information about Juan from Juan himself, his mother, his teachers, his friends, and others within his environment who could help her obtain as holistic a picture of him and his needs as possible. Ms. Herrera looked not only at the characteristics of Juan, his mother, his teachers, and his friends, but also at their interactions with Juan and with each other. She focused not only on problem areas but also on strengths. She saw that both Juan and his mother were motivated to change, and that his teachers were very committed to helping him. She incorporated information she learned about Juan's family with her knowledge about the dynamics of a family where substance abuse had been a problem, about long-term effects of child maltreatment on parents, about gangs and peer relationships when adolescents feel lonely and isolated, and about Juan's family's church, Juan's mother's jobs, and the community and its attitudes toward Juan and his family. She was especially concerned about the lack of resources in the community and the lack of support for young adolescent males and single-parent mothers.

As she assessed Juan's situation, Ms. Herrera began to sort out who is part of the client system, the target system, the change agent system, and the action system. She decided that these systems had many strengths and the potential for change. She set up a meeting with Juan and his mother to identify problem areas and to establish preliminary goals based on the information she had gathered. The three of them agreed that three initial problem areas related to Juan's anger about having so much responsibility at home, his sense of loss over his father's leaving and anger because he had left, and his lack of a positive peer support group. They identified goals that focused on reducing the pressure from Juan's mother to take care of his brother and do so much at home, helping Juan deal with his feelings about the divorce, and helping Juan develop a positive peer support group. The three of them agreed that, although the presenting problem related to Juan's school behavior and performance, these underlying problems were more critical and would, in fact, most likely improve his school performance if they were addressed.

After these three goals were identified, Ms. Herrera began meeting, sometimes together and sometimes separately, with Juan and his mother. They considered all possible options regarding how these goals might be met, listing potential resources available that might be helpful. Some resources, such as more financial help from Juan's father and Juan's mother quitting her job and going on public assistance, were rejected for various reasons. Finally, the three of them developed a contractual agreement that specified how these problems would be addressed.

Ms. Herrera referred Juan's mother to the local human services agency, where she was able to qualify for low-income child care for her youngest child. She also was given information about a job-training program to upgrade her skills so that she could get a higher-paying job and be able to work one job instead of two. This would allow her to spend more time with Juan and his brother. Ms. Herrera, Juan, and his mother negotiated specific tasks Juan would do at home and agreed that he would have two hours after school every day to spend time with friends. They also agreed to rules regarding how he could spend his time with them. Juan and his mother also agreed that if Juan followed the rules and completed his chores, he could spend time weekly with his previous friends in his old neighborhood. In addition, Juan agreed to participate in a school support group for seventh-grade boys whose parents have experienced divorce. Ms. Herrera felt that this would not only help Juan work through some of his feelings about the divorce, but also develop a new set of peers with whom he could become socially involved. Juan and his mother also began counseling at the local teen/parent center, and the counselor and Ms. Herrera conferred regularly about his progress there. Ms. Herrera, while maintaining confidentiality about Juan's specific family issues, communicated with Juan's teachers, and they agreed to help Juan feel more accepted in his new school and to provide opportunities for him to get to know other students.

After three months, Juan's teachers reported that he was coming to class, participating in class discussions, handing in his homework, and no longer exhibiting behavior problems. His grades also improved significantly. Juan dropped his friends who were gang members and formed several solid friendships with his classmates at his new school. Two of his friends were from the support group. Although the group was terminated after eight weeks, Ms. Herrera still met with Juan every two weeks or so to be sure that he was doing well. Juan spent a great deal of time in the group talking about the divorce and his feelings about his father. He visited his father twice and was looking forward to seeing him during his spring vacation. Juan and his mother, and sometimes his younger brother, also participated in family counseling sessions at the teen/parent center. Juan's mother developed a new set of friends and a support system through her youngest son's child care center, where there were also many other single parents. She enrolled in a computer-programming training course and was looking forward to the opportunity to upgrade her skills.

As the positive changes in one system occurred, they had a positive impact in other systems as well. The fact that Juan's mother was able to obtain child care, for example, reduced her stress and enabled her to interact more positively with Juan. Ms. Herrera's talking with Juan's teachers and helping them to understand his needs for acceptance also enabled them to view Juan more positively. This, in turn, reduced some of the pressure on him, increased his self-esteem, and gave him the needed confidence to seek out new friendships and find more positive ways to gain acceptance.

Although she felt that she was able to make a difference when helping Juan and his mother, Ms. Herrera was increasingly frustrated about the large number of students she had who were like Juan. She had referrals on her desk for twelve more students in similar situations. She decided that it would be a more productive use of her time to develop additional resources at other levels of the environment than to deal with each student on a case-by-case basis. Ms. Herrera contacted the head of the teen/counseling center and a number of other individuals in the community who were also concerned. A group of fifteen community representatives began developing plans for a comprehensive program that would help teens and their families. The plan called for staff from the teen/parent resource center to come to the school weekly to lead additional support groups, for outreach efforts to be made to local businesses to locate adult mentors to work on a one-to-one basis with teens in need of additional adult support, and for after-school, evening, and weekend recreational programs to be developed for teens. The group also decided to work with a state legislative group to advocate for additional funding for adolescent services and for single-parent families.

Ideally, the social welfare system requires social workers at all organizational levels to be able to deal with the micro, meso, exo, and macro aspects of identified problem areas. Identified needs addressed by social workers range from individual intrapsychic problems to problems of social role performance and role interaction to broad community or total social system problems. Intervention can take place anywhere throughout the social system. The social welfare system, as an ideal, is perceived to encompass the family, political, medical, educational, and economic needs of its clients and to integrate these needs into the solution of the client's current problem.

SUMMARY

Social welfare problems involve many complex and interrelated factors. These factors may be ordered in a number of ways to describe social welfare problems, to understand them, and to predict when they will occur and under what conditions. Because the problems are so complex and involve human behaviors and environmental influences that are difficult to measure, as well as a variety of disciplines, there is no theory that can be used to address all social welfare or human problems. However, the systems/ecological framework, which incorporates the concept that an individual may be seen as part of a larger environment with whom he or she continually interacts and is an independent part of that environment, is useful in organizing information to determine what else is needed and to develop an appropriate intervention strategy. This framework incorporates factors at the individual, family, group, organizational, community, and societal levels and allows for a variety of interventions at one or more levels.

KEY TERMS

action system

association

boundary

cause-and-effect (causal)
   relationship

change agent system

client system

closed system

entropy

equifinality

exosystem level

generalizable

inclusive

macrosystem level

mesosystem level

microsystem level

open system

steady state

synergy

systems/ecological framework

target system

testable

theory

DISCUSSION QUESTIONS

1. Why is it difficult to develop good theory to address social welfare problems?

2. Briefly identify the key components of the systems/ecological perspective. Compare and contrast open and closed systems, and static and steady state systems.

3. Using a systems/ecological perspective, identify the systems that currently affect Juan's life.

4. Using the ecological perspective as delineated by Bronfenbrenner and Garbarino, identify at least one strategy you might use if you were a social worker to help Juan and his family at each of the four levels of the ecological framework: the microsystem, the mesosystem, the exosystem, and the macrosystem.

5. Identify at least four advantages of using the systems/ecological perspective to understand social welfare problems.

6. Briefly describe the problem-solving approach and its advantages to social workers within social welfare institutions. What type of intervention plan would you suggest if you were the school social worker assigned to work with Juan?

REFERENCES

Bronfenbrenner, U. 1979. *The ecology of human development.* Cambridge Mass.: Harvard University Press.

Compton, B., and B. Galaway. 1989. *Social work processes.* Homewood, Ill.: Dorsey.

Erikson, E. 1959. Identity and the life cycle: Psychological issues. Monograph no. 1. New York: International Universities Press.

Garbarino, J. 1982. *Children and families in the social environment.* New York: Aldine.

Germain, C. and A. Gitterman. 1980. *The life model of social work practice.* New York: Columbia University Press.

Hartman, A. Diagrammatic assessment of family relationships. *Social Casework* (October 1978) 59:(8).

Pincus, A., and A. Minahan. 1973. *Social work practice: Model and method.* Itasca, Ill.: Peacock.

Von Bertalanffy, L. 1968. *General system theory.* New York: Braziller.

Whittaker, J., and Tracy. 1988. The search for coherence. In C. Meyer (Ed.), *Clinical social work in the eco-systems perspective.* New York: Columbia University Press, 5–34.

Wilensky, H., and C. Lebeaux. 1965. *Industrial society and social welfare.* New York: Free Press.

SUGGESTED FURTHER READINGS

Anderson, R., and I. Carter. 1984. *Human behavior in the social environment: A social systems approach.* New York: Aldine.

Bronfenbrenner, U. 1979. *The ecology of human development.* Cambridge Mass.: Harvard University Press.

Buckley, W., ed. 1968. *Modern systems research for the behavioral scientist.* Hawthorne, N.Y.: Aldine.

Council on Social Work Education. 1982. *Curriculum policy for the master's degree and baccalaureate degree programs in social work education.* New York: Author.

Garbarino, J. 1982. *Children and families in the social environment.* New York: Aldine Press.

Germain, C. 1979. *Social work practice: People and environments.* New York: Columbia University Press.

Martin, P., and G. O'Connor. 1989. *The social environment: Open systems applications.* New York: Longman.

Zastrow, C., and K. Kirst-Ashman. 1990. *Understanding human behavior in the social environment.* Chicago: Nelson-Hall.

Part
II

**Fields of
Practice and
Populations
Served**

This section explores the settings in which social workers practice and the special populations they serve. Although not all settings and special populations can be presented in the limited space of this text, this section provides an overview of the major social problems and populations that are the domain of the social welfare system and social work practitioners. Each chapter presents a broad systems/ecological perspective to help the reader understand the issues social work practitioners face in addressing the specific social problem or special population. The specific roles and functions that social workers play in dealing with each field of practice and population served also are explored, so that the reader will have an idea of what types of social work jobs are available in that field of practice and what the nature of those jobs entails.

Chapter 4, "Poverty and Income Security," focuses on how poverty is defined, why people are poor, who is poor in the United States, and what types of policies and programs exist to help reduce poverty levels in the United States. The roles social workers play in the fight against poverty also are discussed.

Chapter 5, "Mental Health, Substance Abuse, and Developmental Disabilities," explores definitional issues concerning mental health, mental illness, and developmental disabilities. Critical incidents are addressed that have shaped the way mental health problems are viewed and the types of mental health services available. Several mental health issues, including substance abuse and homelessness, are highlighted. The many functions that social workers, who constitute the majority of mental health professionals in the United States, provide also are explored.

Chapter 6, "Health Care," provides an explanation of the current health care system in the United States, the problems it faces, and the types of health care policies and programs available. Health issues highlighted include increased costs of care, ethical decisions when balancing available technology with costs and needs, and AIDS. Health care is the fastest growing area of employment for social workers today, and career opportunities for social workers in this setting also are highlighted.

Chapter 7, "The Needs of Children, Youth, and Families," provides an overview of the many problems facing families today. Divorce, substance abuse, child abuse and neglect, family violence, and teenage pregnancy are among the problem areas discussed. Factors that place families more at risk to experience these problems also are identified.

Chapter 8, "Services to Children, Youth, and Families," focuses on current policies and programs that prevent or alleviate the problems discussed in Chapter 7. The current service delivery focus on family preservation is highlighted. The activities that social workers provide in serving children, youth, and families are described, including child protective services and school social work.

Chapter 9, "Criminal Justice," discusses the nature of crime and the criminal justice system, including the roles of law enforcement, the courts, and the prison system. A special section focuses on the juvenile justice system and differences in treatment of adult and juvenile offenders. Roles of social workers, including probation and parole officers, also are explored.

Chapter 10, "Business and Industry," explores a field of social work that is resurging and gaining popularity today. Changes in workplace demographics and implications for employers and families are emphasized. Important issues discussed are considering both the impact of the family setting and the work setting in understanding individual functioning and needs. The chapter also examines what social workers in the workplace do to help employees function better both in the workplace and beyond.

Chapter 11, "Social Work in Rural Settings," focuses on an important segment of social work often not addressed. This chapter discusses important differences between rural and urban life and the implications for social workers who choose to practice in rural settings.

Chapter 12, "Old Age: Issues, Problems, and Services," discusses a special population that increas-ingly needs attention from the social welfare system and social work practitioners. This chapter examines issues and problems that an older population creates for society and identifies resources developed to provide physical and social support systems to meet their needs. Social work for the aged is a rapidly growing field, as more people fit this age category. The types of activities undertaken by social workers who assist this population also are explored.

These nine chapters demonstrate the need for social services for individuals from birth through death in a variety of settings. They suggest that some individuals, by the nature of their age, ethnicity, and social class, are more at risk to need social services than others. They also demonstrate that social workers are employed in many settings—government poverty programs, mental health clinics, hospitals, prisons, schools, churches, rural areas, and nursing homes—and that opportunities for social work practitioners in terms of setting and population are almost limitless.

Poverty and Income Security

Robert and Robin Warren, both aged sixty-five, have just retired from very satisfying jobs. Their three children are well established with families and jobs. By any standard the Warrens are well off, emotionally and physically. Financially their retirement was planned around social insurance. Their Social Security Insurance benefits raise their annual retirement income from $45,000 to just under $60,000. This, along with income derived from savings, means their retirement income is actually larger than their income during their working years. Neither Robert nor Robin thinks of their old-age benefits or their Medicare benefits as a form of welfare because, in their view, they paid for these through taxes while working. Robert wrote his congressman to complain about a tax to fund supplemental nursing care insurance, because they are already covered by a private plan. During their working years the social insurance system provided much-needed cash during brief periods of unemployment. Now the social insurance system has provided them with both security and income.

Mary Smith, widowed and aged seventy-two, is a more typical recipient of social insurance. Her $484-a-month Social Security check provides 80 percent of her income. The remaining amount is from the invested income received from the sale of her home six years ago. She lives in a pleasant apartment and with public old-age health insurance, or Medicare, she is covered for major illness and hospitalization. She is not covered for the more immediate threat of a long stay in a nursing home. Her investment income and Social Security payments are not sufficient for the monthly fees, which run to over $2,000.

Maria and Joe Saldana live in an inner-city area in a large northern city. Both in their early thirties, they have five children, ranging in age from two to fourteen. Joe works on construction jobs when he can, and Maria works as a maid at a local hotel when she can find child care for her younger children. Joe and Maria have a combined income of $14,000—well below the poverty level for a family of seven (roughly $19,000). The rent for their two-bedroom house is $350 a month. Money for bus fare, utilities, and other necessities often leaves the Saldanas with no money for food at the end of the month. Last year the children often had to miss school during the winter because they didn't have any warm clothes. Neither of the Saldanas works at a job that provides health insurance, which means that the family usually goes without medical care when someone is sick. Both of the

Saldanas grew up living in poverty, and both quit school in junior high school to earn money to help their parents provide for their brothers and sisters. Although they have a strong value system and are hard workers, they find it difficult to get jobs with adequate pay and benefits, because of their limited education. Maria became sick after the birth of their last child, and shortly after that, Joe lost his job. When his unemployment benefits ran out, he couldn't find another job. Changes in the welfare law in 1988 allowed the family to receive AFDC-UP and Medicaid while Joe looked for a job. There would have been an automatic termination of these benefits after six months in the state where they live, but Joe found a construction job before the termination. Because of income limits they are no longer eligible to receive AFDC. During a transition from AFDC to full-time employment, the family retains eligibility for Medicaid. The family still qualifies for food stamps. However, Joe and Maria have not applied for either program because of a sense of pride and a desire to turn to "welfare" only when desperate.

INTRODUCTION

The Saldanas, Mary Smith, and the Warrens are beneficiaries of the U.S. income security system. The Saldanas, when they receive help, look to a variety of social assistance programs designed to help low-income Americans. Mary Smith's and the Warrens' cash payments and health insurance—considered social insurance—not only are more generous but they carry no stigma of welfare. The two forms of income security are at the core of the American social welfare system. Although the proportion of persons with undergraduate and/or graduate degrees in social work actually employed in income security programs is small, what is accomplished by income security programs shapes all the rest of the social welfare system. The income security system has two essential functions: (1) to respond to the condition of poverty when it occurs, and (2) to maintain the flow of income to households when the normal stream of income is interrupted by employment-related life events.

Since the New Deal era, social welfare in America has been shaped by the duality of the U.S. income security system. The **social insurance** programs, which are central, are designed to replace income lost to factors associated with old age, disability, short-term unemployment, and the death or permanent disability of one parent in the household. By comparison, a far more modest program of **public (social) assistance** exists to funnel cash and in-kind benefits when income shortfall is the result of single parenthood, underemployment, or long-term unemployment. Table 4–1 provides information about the patterns of expenditures for income security programs. It shows that programs for both social insurance and social assistance have grown since 1960 but that the far greater growth has been in programs of social insurance. Social insurance has grown with the economy; public assistance has not.

Table 4–1 The Structure of Income Security and the Economy, 1965–1990.

	1965	**1970**	**1980**	**1990**
Disposable Per Capita (Average) Income, 1982 $s[1]	6,362	7,257	8,783	10,624
OASDI Benefits as Share of Personal Income[2]	2.7	4.2	5.3	5.3
Public Assistance Benefits as Share of Personal Income[2]	.432	.700	.964	.824
Social Insurance Outlays as % GNP[3]	2.5	3.0	4.4	4.5
Public Assistance Benefits Outlays as % GNP[3]	.4	.5	.8	.7

[1]*Economic Report of the President*, 1990, p. 325.
[2]Author's calculation, data from *Overview of Entitlement Programs*, House Ways and Means Committee Print, 1990.
[3]*Overview of Entitlement Programs*, House Ways and Means Committee Print, 1990, p. 1372.

The Concept of Poverty

The concept of "poverty" is elusive. **Poverty** generally means that a household's income is inadequate as judged by a specific standard. The translation of this concept into practical terms produces technical as well as ideological debates. Even defining *household* for a census count is not simple. Is the unit composed only of the nuclear family, or do we count elders, boarders, roommates, and others who share the dwelling? Similarly, at first such concepts as "income" appear easy to define, but should income include goods given or traded outside the regular economy; for example, should it include employer or government benefits given in kind? What should be the time frame—a year or a month? Clearly, as each such question is confronted, the problem of definition becomes more complex.

In defining poverty, we must first consider the distribution of incomes among households in the United States. This distribution is unevenly grouped around the median (i.e., the exact middle of the total income range—50 percent of households have a higher annual income, and 50 percent have a lower one than the median). It is true now, and has been for years, that if we cut the median income in half, we find roughly 20 percent of the population below that income level. If we multiply the median income by 2.5, we find about 5 percent of the households above that line. The 75 percent between these two points are the "great middle class." This rough distribution is how Americans tend to classify themselves—about one-fifth describe themselves as poor, and only about 5 percent think of themselves as rich or well-off.

After-tax income data show how our income is distributed, as reflected in Table 4–2. If there was an even distribution of income each quintile would, of course, have 20 percent of the money income. This information leads to many observations and debates. Basically, we see the poor in America as now having even less of a share than they had in 1960. The largest gainer, particularly in recent years, has been the highest quintile. Nevertheless, although the poor may be less well off in relative terms (i.e., a smaller share of the whole) this does not mean they are necessarily less well off in absolute terms (i.e., dollar amount available).

An alternate measure of poverty is the so-called absolute market basket approach. This is considered the official measure of poverty, or **official poverty,** and provides a set of income thresholds adjusted for household by size, composition, age of the household head, and urban or rural location. The specific thresholds for a working-age household head with a spouse and minor children are given in Table 4–3, reflecting annual adjustments in the figures to account for inflation. This official income-line concept includes calendar-year income from all money sources: wages, salary, bonuses, private and social insurance, money payments for welfare, net child support, and net alimony. It does not include the value of in-kind welfare benefits, such as food stamps, Medicaid, Medicare, and public housing subsidies not given in cash, or of employer-provided noncash benefits. The most serious drawback in the official definition of poverty is that it fails to reflect nearly $40 billion of expenditures on such in-kind benefits. The numbers thus overstate the proportion of the population that is poor.

Three additional important points need to be made: (1) There is no one "right" or correct measure of poverty; (2) the progress against poverty has been unsteady over time; and (3) the progress against poverty has been uneven among the various groups defined as poor. Before examining the types of anti-poverty strategies and the social worker's role in the reduction of poverty rates, it is necessary to look at these three confounding problems.

MEASUREMENT OF POVERTY

The first problem in measuring poverty has to do with a debate over the standard itself. According to some observers, a poverty standard should reflect how well those at the bottom of the income distribution fare relative to all others. Poverty lines thus should reflect the proportion of households that fall below a threshold expressed as a fixed fraction or percentage (such as half or 50 percent) of median income. Such a perspective views poverty as a problem that would disappear only if incomes were equally distributed. In the United States there has been very little shift in the distribution of income throughout this century. As suggested earlier in this chapter, about one-fifth of U.S. households have real incomes below one-half of the median income. Other observers suggest that the poverty threshold should instead be fixed by the total cost of some fixed market basket of goods and services. If in 1988 a person needed an

Table 4–2 Distribution of Money Income of American Households; after Taxes

Quintile	1960	1965	1970	1975	1980	1985	1988
Lowest	4.8	5.2	5.4	5.4	5.3	4.6	3.5
Second	12.2	12.2	12.2	11.8	11.6	10.9	9.2
Third	17.8	17.8	17.6	17.6	17.5	16.9	15.8
Fourth	24.0	23.9	23.8	24.1	24.1	24.2	24.6
Highest	41.3	40.9	40.9	41.1	41.6	43.5	46.9

Source: Data for 1960–1985 from *Statistical Abstracts of the U.S., 1987,* table 733; data for 1988 from *Overview of Entitlement Programs,* 1990, p. 1073.

income of $10,000 to buy a minimal level of food, clothing, and housing but needed $12,000 in 1990 to buy the same things, then the poverty line would need to be raised. For practical purposes, the debate surrounding poverty in America has focused on such an absolute definition of poverty.

Even if there is agreement to use an absolute concept of poverty, the problem of measurement still is not resolved. According to David Stockman, President Reagan's first director of the Office of Management and Budget, the U.S. Census Bureau's estimates of the number of people below the cash-income threshold fail to reflect poverty accurately. Stockman (1984) said,

> In the mid 1960's when we began to measure poverty, such programs as Medicaid, food stamps, housing subsidies, and the like were only an insignificant share of government's direct aid to the poor. By 1973, over half of all

Table 4–3 Weighted Average Poverty Thresholds for Nonfarm Families of Specified Size, Selected Years, 1959–89

	Unrelated Individuals			Families of 2 or More Persons							
				2 Persons							
Calendar Year	All Ages	Under Age 65	Aged 65 or Older	All Ages	Head Under Age 65	Head Aged 65 or Older	3 Persons	4 Persons	5 Persons	6 Persons	7 Persons or More
1959	$1,467	$1,503	$1,397	$1,894	$1,952	$1,761	$2,324	$2,973	$3,506	$3,944	$4,849
1960	1,490	1,526	1,418	1,924	1,982	1,788	2,359	3,022	3,560	4,002	4,921
1965	1,582	1,626	1,512	2,048	2,114	1,906	2,514	3,223	3,797	4,264	5,248
1970	1,954	2,010	1,861	2,525	2,604	2,348	3,099	3,968	4,680	5,260	6,468
1975	2,724	1,797	2,581	3,506	3,617	3,257	4,293	5,500	6,499	7,316	9,022
1976	2,884	2,959	2,730	3,711	3,826	3,445	4,540	5,815	6,876	7,760	9,588
1977	3,075	3,152	2,906	3,951	4,072	3,666	4,833	6,191	7,320	8,261	10,216
1978	3,311	3,392	3,127	4,249	4,383	3,944	5,201	6,662	7,880	8,891	11,002
1979	3,689	3,778	3,479	4,725	4,878	4,390	5,784	7,412	8,775	9,914	12,280
1980	4,190	4,290	3,949	5,363	5,537	4,983	6,565	8,414	9,966	11,269	[1]12,761
1981	4,620	4,729	4,359	5,917	6,111	5,498	7,250	9,287	11,007	12,449	[1]14,110
1982	4,901	5,019	4,626	6,281	6,487	5,836	7,693	9,862	11,684	13,207	[1]15,036
1983	5,061	5,180	4,775	6,483	6,697	6,023	7,938	10,178	12,049	13,630	[1]15,500
1984	5,278	5,450	4,979	6,762	6,983	6,282	8,277	10,609	12,566	14,207	[1]16,096
1985	5,469	5,593	5,156	6,998	7,231	6,503	8,573	10,989	13,007	14,696	[1]16,656
1986	5,572	5,702	5,255	7,138	7,372	6,630	8,737	11,203	13,259	14,986	[1]17,049
1987	5,778	5,909	5,447	7,397	7,641	6,872	9,056	11,611	13,737	15,509	[1]17,649
1988	6,024	6,155	5,674	7,704	7,958	7,158	9,435	12,092	14,305	16,149	[1]18,248
1989[2]	6,314	6,452	5,947	8,075	8,341	7,503	9,890	12,675	14,994	16,927	[1]19,127

[1]Poverty threshold for 7 persons, not 7 persons or more.   [2]Estimated.

Sources: Data from Bureau of the Census, technical papers. Table from House Ways and Means Committee, 1989, *Background Materials,* Committee Paper 101-4, p. 941.

aid was in-kind rather than in cash. Today, roughly 70 out of every 100 dollars of direct aid is given in-kind. Much of this aid goes to people who are lifted out of poverty by virtue of these programs.

Many of the poverty measures are akin to hat tricks. The best measure available of how many really are considered poor has been provided by Sheldon Danziger, of the University of Michigan. Danziger's 1986 data, his most recent available, distinguished among four definitions of income (Danziger and Weinbeg 1989). Table 4–4 summarizes the percentages of the poor in the United States according to these four definitions. First, there is pretransfer income, or market income. This concept includes all income from wages, rent, interest, dividends, pensions, alimony, and child support to the family who receives it and, at the same time, subtracts each amount from the household paying it. This figure reflects a snapshot of poverty if there were no social insurance or

Table 4–4   Percentage of Poor by Various Definitions of Poverty

Year	Pretransfer Poverty (1)	Prewelfare Poverty (2)	Official Measure (3)	Adjusted for In-Kind Transfers Only (4)
1964	—	—	19.0	—
1965	21.3	16.3[2]	17.3	16.8
1966	—	—	14.7	—
1967	19.4	15.0	14.2	—
1968	18.2	13.6	12.8	—
1969	17.7	13.3	12.1	—
1970	18.8	13.9	12.6	—
1971	19.6	13.8	12.5	—
1972	19.2	13.1	11.9	—
1973	19.0	12.4	11.1	—
1974	20.3	13.1	11.2	—
1975	22.0	13.7	12.3	—
1976	21.0	13.1	11.8	—
1977	21.0	13.0	11.6	—
1978	20.2	12.6	11.4	—
1979	20.5	12.9	11.7	9.0
1980	21.9	14.2	13.0	10.4
1981	23.1	15.1	14.0	11.7
1982	24.0	15.9	15.0	12.7
1983	24.2	16.1	15.2	13.1
1984	22.9	15.3	14.4	12.2
1985	22.4	14.9	14.0	11.8
1986[b]	—	—	13.9	—

Source: Data are from S. Danziger and D. Weinberg. *Fighting Poverty*. (Cambridge, Mass.: Harvard Press, 1986), 54.

welfare programs. The second definition includes prewelfare income. In addition to the first figure, this includes any money received from social income benefits, such as Old Age Survivors Disability Insurance (OASDI), Unemployment Insurance (UI), railroad and federal retirements, and military service benefits. The third definition, which is related roughly to the official count presently used, adds payments from Aid to Families with Dependent Children (AFDC), Supplemental Security Income (SSI), and General Assistance (GA). The fourth definition also uses an adjustment for the money equivalent value of the various in-kind payments (housing subsidies, Medicaid, Medicare, etc.) to the poor. Not only is poverty difficult to measure, but the number of poor persons in comparison to all persons in the United States continues to change even with a constant definition. The number of persons falling below the defined line divided by the total population creates the poverty line, by definition. The important thing to look for is how the poverty line is defined. Once a useful definition is devised, one can examine how poverty changes over time and, equally important, how poverty rates differ among various demographic groups.

DEMOGRAPHICS OF THE POOR ARE CHANGING

We can see that the problem of deciding just who is poor is the key to deciding what the government can do to help. Being against poverty is a lot like being against war: it is hard to find anyone on the other side. Yet wars and poverty occur because we cannot agree on how to prevent them. Although many people are frustrated about how many Americans are poor, almost no one is satisfied with current public efforts to respond to poverty. If poverty is defined as the government does so officially, in terms of a fixed market basket of goods, then one perspective emerges. When the federal government began measuring poverty in the early 1960s, the continued existence of poor people in an "affluent society" seemed anomalous. Then, many believed that with sufficient commitment, poverty could be eliminated within a generation. At first the promise seemed to hold: between 1960 and 1973 the rate of poverty was cut in half, but between 1973 and 1983 it rose from 11.1 percent to 15.2 percent. Since the mid1980s the poverty rates have fallen back to 13.1 percent. The data on these trends are presented in Table 4–5 and in Figure 4–1. Figure 4–1 is constructed from figures in the 1990 and earlier versions of the *Economic Report of the President*. It reflects the shift from 1960 to 1990 in the proportion of Americans who were classified as poor.

Many factors interact to produce short-run shifts in who is poor and how many individuals are poor. Basically, however, four factors predominate in causing these shifts: (1) shifts in the overall performance of the economy; (2) shifts in the composition of households within the nation (for example, more single-parent households headed by women); (3) shifts in the level of expenditure on social programs; and (4) shifts in the effectiveness of social programs. The first two factors significantly influence the second two factors.

There is little doubt that the most profound influence in determining how many people are poor and who they are is the performance of the overall economy. Except for the elderly, who largely have left the labor market, shifts in the performance of the economy almost perfectly track the performance of the poverty rate. In John Kennedy's famous metaphor, "the rising tides reach

Table 4-5 Number and Median Income by Race, 1970-1988 (in 1988 dollars) of Families and Persons, and Poverty Status

Year	Families[1] Number (millions)	Families[1] Median Income	Below Poverty Level — Total Number (millions)	Below Poverty Level — Total Rate	Below Poverty Level — Female Householder Number (millions)	Below Poverty Level — Female Householder Rate	Persons Below Poverty level Number (millions)	Persons Below Poverty level Rate	Median income — Males All Persons	Median income — Males Year-round Full-time Workers	Median income — Females All Persons	Median income — Females Year-round Full-time Workers
ALL RACES												
1970	52.2	$30,084	5.3	10.1	2.0	32.5	25.4	12.6	$20,337	$28,002	$6,821	$16,586
1971	53.3	30,042	5.3	10.0	2.1	33.9	25.6	12.5	20,164	28,132	7,034	16,653
1972	54.4	31,460	5.1	9.3	2.2	32.7	24.5	11.9	21,085	29,824	7,356	17,131
1973	55.1	32,109	4.8	8.8	2.2	32.2	23.0	11.1	21,465	30,556	7,450	17,287
1974[3]	55.7	30,960	4.9	8.8	2.3	32.1	23.4	11.2	20,281	29,328	7,396	17,215
1975	56.2	30,166	5.5	9.7	2.4	32.5	25.9	12.3	19,467	28,902	7,443	16,973
1976	56.7	31,099	5.3	9.4	2.5	33.0	25.0	11.8	19,597	28,814	7,435	17,281
1977	57.2	31,252	5.3	9.3	2.6	31.7	24.7	11.6	19,762	29,419	7,693	17,206
1978	57.8	32,006	5.3	9.1	2.7	31.4	24.5	11.4	19,841	29,143	7,381	17,493
1979[4]	59.6	31,917	5.5	9.2	2.6	30.4	26.1	11.7	19,194	28,482	7,091	17,160
1980	60.3	30,182	6.2	10.3	3.0	32.7	29.3	13.0	17,989	27,526	7,064	16,641
1981	61.0	29,136	6.9	11.2	3.3	34.6	31.8	14.0	17,534	26,929	7,103	16,212
1982	61.4	28,727	7.5	12.2	3.4	36.3	34.4	15.0	17,101	26,547	7,217	16,750
1983[3]	62.0	29,307	7.6	12.3	3.6	36.0	35.3	15.2	17,414	26,732	7,608	17,208
1984	62.7	30,096	7.3	11.6	3.5	34.5	33.7	14.4	17,762	27,331	7,820	17,559
1985	63.6	30,493	7.2	11.4	3.5	34.0	33.1	14.0	17,933	27,485	7,935	17,868
1986	64.5	31,796	7.0	10.9	3.6	34.6	32.4	13.6	18,473	27,949	8,214	18,180
1987[3]	65.2	32,251	7.0	10.7	3.7	34.2	32.3	13.4	18,522	27,785	8,638	18,291
1988	65.8	32,191	6.9	10.4	3.6	33.5	31.9	13.1	18,908	27,342	8,884	18,545
WHITE												
1970	46.5	31,209	3.7	8.0	1.1	25.0	17.5	9.9	21,376	28,804	6,909	16,879
1971	47.6	31,173	3.8	7.9	1.2	26.5	17.8	9.9	21,139	28,924	7,151	16,845
1972	48.5	32,685	3.4	7.1	1.1	24.3	16.2	9.0	22,115	30,900	7,404	17,468
1973	48.9	33,558	3.2	6.6	1.2	24.5	15.1	8.4	22,522	31,440	7,522	17,580
1974[3]	49.4	32,174	3.4	6.8	1.3	24.8	15.7	8.6	21,246	30,060	7,480	17,361
1975	49.9	31,374	3.8	7.7	1.4	25.9	17.8	9.7	20,450	29,450	7,520	17,013
1976	50.1	32,303	3.6	7.1	1.4	25.2	16.7	9.1	20,660	29,673	7,497	17,414
1977	50.5	32,679	3.5	7.0	1.4	24.0	16.4	8.9	20,699	30,020	7,811	17,316
1978	50.9	33,327	3.5	6.9	1.3	23.5	16.3	8.7	20,781	29,684	7,470	17,658
1979[4]	52.2	33,305	3.6	6.9	1.4	22.3	17.2	9.0	20,051	29,305	7,158	17,310
1980	52.7	31,447	4.2	8.0	1.6	25.7	19.7	10.2	19,135	28,312	7,102	16,802
1981	53.3	30,606	4.7	8.8	1.8	27.4	21.6	11.1	18,605	27,562	7,183	16,483
1982	53.4	30,161	5.1	9.6	1.8	27.9	23.5	12.0	18,080	27,254	7,315	16,975
1983[3]	53.9	30,688	5.2	9.7	1.9	28.3	24.0	12.1	18,320	27,445	7,741	17,439
1984	54.4	31,523	4.9	9.1	1.9	27.1	23.0	11.5	18,749	28,267	7,912	17,734
1985	55.0	32,051	5.0	9.1	2.0	27.4	22.9	11.4	18,813	28,248	8,089	18,121
1986	55.7	33,255	4.8	8.6	2.0	28.2	22.2	11.0	19,494	28,730	8,376	18,458
1987[3]	56.1	33,725	4.6	8.1	2.0	26.9	21.2	10.4	19,687	28,433	8,859	18,629
1988	56.5	33,915	4.5	7.9	1.9	26.5	20.8	10.1	19,959	28,262	9,103	18,823

Table 4–5 Number and Median Income by Race, 1970–1988 (in 1988 dollars) of Families and Persons, and Poverty Status
(Continued)

Year	Families[1] Number (millions)	Families[1] Median Income	Below Poverty Level – Total Number (millions)	Total Rate	Female Householder Number (millions)	Female Householder Rate	Persons Below Poverty level Number (millions)	Persons Rate	Median income – Males All Persons	Males Year-round Full-time Workers	Females All Persons	Females Year-round Full-time Workers
BLACK												
1970	4.9	19,144	1.5	29.5	.8	54.3	7.5	33.5	12,675	19,620	6,290	13,830
1971	5.2	18,811	1.5	28.8	.9	53.5	7.4	32.5	12,607	19,778	6,266	14,874
1972	5.3	19,426	1.5	29.0	1.0	53.3	7.7	33.3	13,395	20,867	6,917	14,943
1973	5.4	19,368	1.5	28.1	1.0	52.7	7.4	31.4	13,164	21,190	6,789	14,907
1974[3]	5.5	19,211	1.5	26.9	1.0	52.2	7.2	30.3	13,164	21,316	6,752	16,022
1975	5.6	19,304	1.5	27.1	1.0	50.1	7.5	31.3	12,226	21,655	6,832	16,254
1976	5.8	19,215	1.6	27.9	1.1	52.2	7.6	31.1	12,439	21,252	7,065	16,281
1977	5.8	18,668	1.6	28.2	1.2	51.0	7.7	31.3	12,283	20,697	6,745	16,183
1978	5.9	19,739	1.6	27.5	1.2	50.6	7.6	30.6	12,449	22,735	6,726	16,366
1979[4]	6.2	18,860	1.7	27.8	1.2	49.4	8.1	31.0	12,412	21,120	6,515	15,861
1980	6.3	18,196	1.8	28.9	1.3	49.4	8.6	32.5	11,498	19,920	6,575	15,670
1981	6.4	17,265	2.0	30.8	1.4	52.9	9.2	34.2	11,063	19,501	6,381	14,886
1982	6.5	16,670	2.2	33.0	1.5	56.2	9.7	35.6	10,835	19,357	6,452	15,172
1983[3]	6.7	17,295	2.2	32.3	1.5	53.7	9.9	35.7	10,714	19,568	6,615	15,480
1984	6.8	17,570	2.1	30.9	1.5	51.7	9.5	33.8	10,757	19,291	7,018	15,981
1985	6.9	18,455	2.0	28.0	1.5	50.5	8.9	31.3	11,839	19,758	6,901	16,041
1986	7.1	19,001	2.0	28.0	1.5	50.1	9.0	31.1	11,681	20,256	7,087	16,152
1987[3]	7.2	19,168	2.1	29.4	1.6	51.1	9.6	32.6	11,679	20,330	7,237	16,639
1988	7.4	19,329	2.1	28.2	1.6	49.0	9.4	31.6	12,044	20,716	7,349	16,867

1. The term *family* refers to a group of two or more persons related by blood, marriage, or adoption and residing together; all such persons are considered members of the same family. Beginning 1979, based on householder concept and restricted to primary families.
2. Prior to 1979, data are for persons 14 years and over.
3. Based on revised methodology; comparable with succeeding years.
4. Based on 1980 census population controls; comparable with succeeding years.

Note: The poverty level is based on the poverty index adopted by a Federal interagency committee in 1969. That index reflected different consumption requirements for families based on size and composition, sex and age of family householder, and farm-nonfarm residence. Minor revisions implemented in 1981 eliminated variations in the poverty thresholds based on two of these variables, farm-nonfarm residence and sex of householder. The poverty thresholds are updated every year to reflect changes in the consumer price index. For further details, see "Current Population Reports," Series P-60, No. 160.

Source: *Economic Report of the President 1990*. Table C–30; p. 328.

Figure 4–1   Proportion of Individuals Classified as Poor, 1960–1990

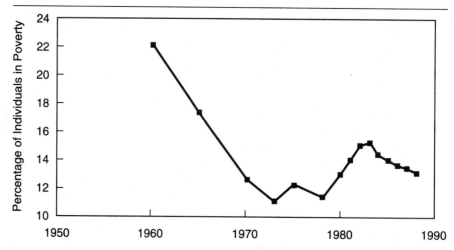

all ships, dinghy and yacht alike." When an economy is strong, the rich get richer and the poor get less poor, with some raised above the poverty line. When the economy performs poorly, the rich get less rich and the poor get more poor, with some sinking below the poverty line.

A second factor to be evaluated in discussing poverty is the shift in the composition of the nation's population. Most dramatic in this regard is what is happening to the black population. Shifts to a much lower marriage rate, a much higher divorce rate, a much higher birthrate among unmarried women, and a larger proportion of single black women neither marrying nor remarrying all have led to revolutionary changes in the composition of black families. The number of black families headed by a single woman increased by 97.5 percent between 1969 and 1982, and the proportion of such families that were poor went from 53 percent to 56 percent. An increase in the number of black single-parent households headed by women and a very high rate of unemployment among black men (six out of ten compared to one out of ten white men) have resulted in higher proportions of blacks than whites living in poverty. A more detailed assessment of demographic shifts and the resulting changes in poverty rates is shown in Table 4–6. The progress against poverty is decidedly uneven by demographic groups. By posttransfer estimates (i.e., the number poor after cash transfers are calculated), the poverty rate among the aged has dropped most dramatically. The poverty rate among female-headed families, however, has increased from its 1969 low but is down from the mid-1980s. No matter how poverty is defined or measured, in a more pragmatic frame the central political questions remain: Who shall have their income maintained, at what level, and for what reasons?

A SYSTEMS/ECOLOGICAL APPROACH TO UNDERSTANDING POVERTY

In understanding the problems associated with poverty, it is also necessary to understand the public and private systems within our society that attempt to ensure that all households have an opportunity to acquire the basic goods and

Table 4-6 Number of Persons in Poverty and Poverty Rate for Individuals in
Selected Demographic Groups, 1959–99

Year	Overall	Aged	Children[1]	Individuals in Female-headed Families[2]	Blacks	Hispanic Origin[3]	Whites
				Number Below Poverty (thousands)			
1959	39,490	5,481	17,552	7,014	9,927	NA	28,484
1960	39,851	NA	17,634	7,247	NA	NA	28,309
1961	39,628	NA	16,909	7,252	NA	NA	27,890
1962	38,625	NA	16,963	7,781	NA	NA	26,672
1963	36,436	NA	16,005	7,646	NA	NA	25,238
1964	36,055	NA	16,051	7,297	NA	NA	24,957
1965	33,185	NA	14,676	7,524	NA	NA	22,496
1966	28,510	5,114	12,389	6,861	8,867	NA	19,290
1967	27,769	5,388	11,656	6,898	8,486	NA	18,983
1968	25,389	4,632	10,954	6,990	7,616	NA	17,395
1969	24,147	4,787	9,691	6,879	7,095	NA	16,659
1970	25,420	4,793	10,440	7,503	7,548	NA	17,484
1971	25,559	4,273	10,551	7,797	7,396	NA	17,780
1972	24,460	3,738	10,284	8,114	7,710	2,414	16,203
1973	22,973	3,354	9,642	8,178	7,388	2,366	15,142
1974	23,370	3,085	10,156	8,462	7,182	2,575	15,736
1975	25,877	3,317	11,104	8,846	7,545	2,991	17,770
1976	24,975	3,313	10,273	9,029	7,595	2,783	16,713
1977	24,720	3,177	10,288	9,205	7,726	2,700	16,416
1978	24,497	3,233	9,931	9,269	7,625	2,607	16,259
1979	26,072	3,682	10,377	9,400	8,050	2,921	17,214
1980	29,272	3,871	11,543	10,120	8,579	3,491	19,699
1981	31,822	3,853	12,505	11,051	9,173	3,713	21,553
1982	34,398	3,751	13,647	11,701	9,697	4,301	23,517
1983	35,303	3,625	13,911	12,072	9,882	4,633	23,984
1984	33,700	3,330	13,420	11,831	9,490	4,806	22,955
1985	33,064	3,456	13,010	11,600	8,926	5,236	22,860
1986	32,370	3,477	12,876	11,944	8,983	5,117	22,183
1987	32,341	3,564	12,963	12,278	9,577	5,442	21,249
1988	31,878	3,482	12,584	12,103	9,426	5,379	20,765

Source: House Ways and Means Committee, 1989, *Background Materials,* Committee Paper 101–4.

services required for a "good life." Depending on how specific one cares to be, it is usually sufficient to focus on three basic interacting systems and a fourth system structured specifically to deal with the failure and/or breakdown of those three basic systems. The three basic systems are the family system, the employment system, and the private and social insurance system. When, for whatever reason, one of these systems malfunctions and the family is left unable to acquire basic necessities of life, the welfare system is expected to anticipate, respond to, and correct that deficiency. As suggested earlier, the income security system is usefully separated into two subsystems: social insurance and social assistance. Alternatively, one can conceive of the insurance system as having a public and private sector. From a systems/ecological perspective, success or failure in one system generates success or failure in other systems. Therefore, it is useful to explain briefly each system's functions and interactions with other systems, then focus on the welfare system.

The Family System

The family is the primary social unit of Western society. Each family member contributes to and receives from the social productivity of the family. It is a social ideal that marriage is a lifetime commitment, and that parents assume the major responsibilities for home care and work so that the children's needs are met as well as their own. The children, in turn, assume responsibility for care of aged parents. The reality is quite different. In the United States half of all marriages are terminated before death of a spouse. At any given time almost one quarter of all children live apart from at least one of their birth parents who is still alive. Only a small proportion of the elderly live with or are directly financially dependent on their adult children. The welfare system needs to respond to these facts.

The Employment System

Our basic social expectation is that those who are physically and mentally able to work will work. We exempt from this responsibility those who are in school or training programs, those who have accepted basic family care responsibilities, the disabled, and the aged. The basic public expectation is that governments will manage the economy and education programs so that there is a fit between job seekers and available jobs. Generally speaking, the number of jobs available ebbs and flows with progress and decline in the overall economy: when the number of jobs decreases, the poverty rate increases. A vigorous economy is the best way to combat poverty. Poverty rates rise faster than the economy in general falls, when the economy is hurting. When the economy improves, poverty rates fall faster than the economy rises. Those who live at the edge of the poverty line are particularly vulnerable to even small shifts in the nation's economic well-being.

The Private and Social Insurance System

Most people now recognize that the family's income cannot always be met from employment-related income and needs to be supplemented by insurance. The function of employment-related insurance is to replace the flow of income from work when that flow is disrupted due to unemployment, disability, retirement, or death. There are two basic categories of employment-related insurance. Private insurance for health care and untimely death is purchased on the open market, often by employers who then make these plans available to their employees. The private insurance subsystem is fundamentally integrated into a subsystem of public or social insurance.

*Many people liv-
ing in poverty are
unable to find af-
fordable housing
and are forced to
live on the streets.
Some, like this
woman, carry all
of their posses-
sions with them
as they move
from place to
place.*

Social insurance is provided by the government. The two major types of
social insurance in the United States are Unemployment Insurance (UI) and
Old Age Survivors and Disability Insurance (OASDI). Not all private and social
insurance programs are discussed in this chapter. For example, **workers' compensation** programs that pay for work-related disability are part of our employment system. Sometimes the payments for disability are so low that the
disabled workers also need to receive social insurance or social/public assistance
to supplement the disability income.

The better the employment system works, the better the private and social
insurance system works. This is true for two reasons. First, full employment
means less strain on social insurance, and second, most of our private and
social insurance plans are designed so that the premiums are paid out of wages.
The larger the share of the population tied directly to the labor force by regular
work or tied indirectly by the labor force participation of a family member, the
larger is the share of the population protected by earning-related insurance.
This means that fewer people have to look to the next line of defense: earnings
replacement programs. Table 4–7 shows how public and private insurance
programs work together to close income gaps generated by the various factors
that cause a disruption or cessation of wage income.

Clearly the mixed results in reducing poverty in the United States over the
last several decades are a reflection of many factors. Chapter 2 reviewed the
political history of American welfare. One important fact from that history is
that we have structured our assistance programs around narrow categories.
The form and amount of the aid have been determined not by the degree of
need but by the immediate cause of the change in family income. Our programs,
principally shaped in the 1930s, have dealt with drastic downward shocks to
income rather than with persistent poverty. The issue has not been the elimi-

Table 4–7 The Social and Private Insurance System

Reason for Earnings Loss	Earnings Replacement Program
Temporary unemployment	Unemployment Insurance (UI)
Disability	
Resulting from work, total and partial	Workmen's Compensation (WC)
	Veteran's Compensation
Not resulting from work	Sick leave (provided by public and private employers)
Short term	Temporary Disability Insurance (TDI) both public and private)
Long term, total	Social Security (OASDI)
	Long-term disability insurance, Early retirement pensions
Retirement	
Low-to-middle-income retirees	Social Security (OASDI)
	Some private provision (pensions, annuities)
Middle-to-upper-income retirees	Social Security (OASDI)
	Considerable private provision
Death	Life Insurance Social Security

Source: Michael C. Barth, George J. Carcagno, and John L. Palm, "Toward an Effective Income Support System: Problems, Prospects, and Choices". (U. of Wisconsin–Madison: Institute for Research on Poverty, 1974).

nation of poverty but the provision of income security. Further, the problems of public responsibility have been dealt with in terms of what was occurring with regard to families finding jobs, deciding how many family members will work, and determining how well their earnings are keeping pace with inflation. We now know the problem of poverty is much more complex. People become poor or lose their income security because of what happens to them socially as well as economically. Changes in marital status, the birth of children, the departure of older children from the home, and other changes in family life cause changes in a family's economic status as much as do finding or losing a job.

Without regular, adequate wage labor and without a stable marital status, the American family is vulnerable to major shifts in economic well-being and perhaps serious material and social deprivation. "Material deprivation" is a relative concept, however. Does it make sense to provide a $12,000 Social Security income to supplement the Warrens' $45,000 postretirement income from private pensions while bringing Mary Smith above the poverty line but leaving her in constant fear of losing her small savings to a relative brief stay in a nursing home, or while giving the Saldanas less than $5,000 in cash and in-kind benefits a year—and then only if neither adult is fully employed and the family is nearly destitute? Such seeming contradictions indicate that we hardly know how to state, let alone evaluate, the goals of American welfare.

No small part of the political and intellectual confusion stems from the simple fact that the goals of social welfare include far more than the reduction of the incidence of poverty. They also include the elimination of dependency on the assistance forms of government welfare and the maintenance of income levels far above the poverty line. With regard to aid to the poor, the twin goals of the reduction of poverty rates and the reduction on dependency on welfare often appear to be on a collision course. This need not be the case, but the politics of welfare makes it so. (Cottingham and Elwood 1989).

INCOME SECURITY PROGRAMS

U.S. income security programs, and programs in most of the Western democracies, represent three broad classes: (1) social insurance, (2) cash public assistance, and (3) in-kind benefits.

Social Insurance

Social insurance is based on "contributory taxes," that is, earmarked taxes that fund special trusts. These special trusts in turn provide funds for the programs. The major social insurance programs are **Old Age Survivors and Disability Insurance (OASDI),** social security payments made to retired elderly persons who have previously been employed; **unemployment insurance (UI),** limited benefits paid to eligible persons who become unemployed; and health insurance for the aged and some disabled persons **(Medicare).** All insurance programs are entitlement programs. The benefits are based on prior contributions and on demonstrated membership in the class of persons being aided—the aged, the unemployed, and so forth. The benefits are not based on need and go to the rich as well as the poor. These programs of social insurance are often called "welfare for the middle class." More specifically, this refers to the fact that much of our social welfare spending does not tax the rich to help the poor but taxes some middle-class citizens to pay benefits to other middle-class citizens, particularly by placing taxes on those now working to provide benefits for those who have retired. (See Table 4–8.) Taxes on the middle class pay for the programs, and the bulk of the benefits go to those, like the Warrens, who are members of the middle class. The earmarked payroll tax that supports the

Table 4–8 Income and Social Security Taxes Paid by Families in the United States

Wage Income (dollars)	Income Tax (dollars)	Social Security Tax (dollars)	Total Tax (dollars)	Income Tax Rate	Federal Tax Rate	Social Security Tax Rate
10,000	−953	765	−188	−0.095	−0.019	0.077
20,000	957	1540	2497	0.048	0.125	0.077
30,000	2760	2295	5055	0.092	0.168	0.077
50,000	6534	3825	10359	0.131	0.207	0.077
100,000	21034	3924	24958	0.210	0.250	0.039

Source: Background Materials and Data on Programs for Programs Within the Jurisdiction of the House Ways and Means Committee, 1990, p. 1148.

social insurance programs has continued to rise while income tax rates have fallen. As a result the combined tax rates have become less progressive.

The bulk of social welfare spending is to secure the income of retired workers. Since the Social Security program is funded from a proportional tax and since the benefits are roughly proportionate to taxes paid, the net result is that American welfare does not shift large sums of money from rich to poor but rather shifts large sums of money from workers in their productive years to workers in their retirement years. The current debate in Congress over the future funding of Social Security reflects the deep divisions that surround America's basic commitment to welfare for the middle class.

Public Assistance

Public assistance programs are both need based and **categorical.** That is, eligibility is established by proof of being a member of the category being helped and proof of need. Currently, the programs are funded out of general revenues from all three levels of government—national, state, and local. The major public assistance programs in the United States are **Aid to Families with Dependent Children (AFDC), Supplemental Security Income (SSI),** and **general assistance (GA).** AFDC aids families with children who are impoverished because there is only one parent in the home. A small subprogram called AFDC-UP (Unemployed Parent) provides time-limited cash benefits to two-parent households where UI has been exhausted. The AFDC-UP benefits have been mandatory in all states only since October of 1990, and the duration of benefits to any family is limited to six months in many states. SSI provides federal assistance to families and individuals impoverished by problems associated with aging, blindness, or disability when the OASDI benefit is absent or too small to provide an income above poverty level. GA is a state/local program to provide cash assistance when there is no income or eligibility to the programs just described. The terms of eligibility and the generosity of the benefits vary widely among the states, as they do for AFDC, as indicated in Table 4-9.

The student who is interested in more numbers will find that detailed descriptive data for the cash programs OASDI, unemployment insurance, SSI, and AFDC are published annually in *Background Materials and Data on Programs for Programs Within the Jurisdiction of the House Ways and Means Committee.* Known as "the Green Book," it comes out each spring.

In-Kind Programs

At the core of American antipoverty strategy lies a dependence on in-kind transfers. The in-kind programs are designed to help poor families obtain the basic necessities of life. Although each of the major in-kind welfare programs has its own unique history, twin notions undergird all of them: (1) some goods are so essential that government will provide them directly if they are not otherwise available; and (2) the poor cannot be trusted to buy these essential goods with cash assistance. The stark contradictions of American welfare become readily apparent in the in-kind programs. On the one hand is the compassionate view that no one should be without these essentials; on the other, the stern belief that those who are without somehow cannot be trusted with the cash to buy them.

Table 4-9 Gross Income Limit, Need Standard, and Maximum Monthly Potential Benefits, AFDC and Food Stamps, One-Parent Family[1] of Three Persons, January 1990

State	Gross income limit (185 percent of need standard)	100 percent of "need"	Maximum AFDC grant[2]	Food stamp benefit[3]	Combined benefits	Combined benefits as a percent of 1989 poverty threshold[4]	AFDC benefits as a percent of 1989 poverty threshold[4]
Alabama	$1,069	$578	$118	$260	$378	46	14
Alaska	1,565	846	846	220	1,066	103	82
Arizona	1,149	621	293	258	551	67	36
Arkansas	1,304	705	204	260	464	56	25
California	1,284	694	694	138	832	101	84
Colorado	779	421	356	239	595	72	43
Connecticut	1,201	649	649	152	801	97	79
Delaware	616	333	333	246	579	70	40
District of Columbia	1,317	712	409	224	633	77	50
Florida	1,550	838	294	258	552	67	36
Georgia	766	414	273	260	533	65	33
Hawaii	1,783	964	602	338	940	99	64
Idaho	1,025	554	317	251	568	69	38
Illinois	1,437	777	[5]367	242	609	74	45
Indiana	592	320	288	260	548	67	35
Iowa	919	497	410	223	633	77	50
Kansas	757	409	[5]409	234	643	78	50
Kentucky	973	526	228	260	488	59	28
Louisiana	1,217	658	190	260	450	55	23
Maine	1,206	652	453	210	663	80	55
Maryland	1,014	548	[5]396	245	641	78	48
Massachusetts	997	539	539	185	724	88	65
Michigan (Washtenaw County)	1,130	611	[5]546	205	751	91	66
Michigan (Wayne County)	1,064	575	[5]516	214	730	89	63
Minnesota	984	532	532	187	719	87	65
Mississippi	681	368	120	260	380	46	15
Missouri	577	312	289	260	549	67	35
Montana	803	434	359	239	598	73	44
Nebraska	673	364	364	237	601	73	44
Nevada	1,018	550	330	247	577	70	40
New Hampshire	936	506	506	194	700	85	61
New Jersey	784	424	[5]424	227	651	85	51
New Mexico	488	264	264	260	524	64	32
New York (Suffolk County)	1,301	703	[5]703	151	854	104	85
New York (New York City)	1,067	577	[5]577	189	766	93	70
North Carolina	1,006	544	272	260	532	65	33
North Dakota	714	386	386	230	616	75	47
Ohio	1,367	739	[5]334	250	584	71	39
Oklahoma	871	471	325	249	574	70	39
Oregon	799	432	[5]432	252	684	83	52
Pennsylvania	1,136	614	421	220	641	78	51
Rhode Island	1,005	543	[5]543	221	765	93	66
South Carolina	775	419	206	260	466	57	25
South Dakota	697	377	377	233	610	74	46
Tennessee	716	387	184	260	444	54	22
Texas	1,062	574	184	260	444	54	22
Utah	955	516	387	230	617	75	47
Vermont	1,800	973	662	148	810	98	80
Virginia	727	393	354	240	594	72	43
Washington	1,678	907	[5]501	213	714	87	61
West Virginia	919	497	249	260	509	62	30
Wisconsin	1,197	647	517	191	708	86	63
Wyoming	666	360	360	238	598	73	44
Guam	490	265	265	384	649	79	32
Puerto Rico	333	180	90	0	90	NA	11
Virgin Islands	387	209	171	335	506	61	21
Median AFDC State[6]	673	364	364	237	607	73	44

1. In most States these benefit amounts apply also to 2-parent families of 3 (where the second parent is incapacitated, or, as permitted in almost half the States, unemployed). Some, however, increase benefits for such families.

2. In States with area differentials, figure shown is for area with highest benefit.

3. Food stamp benefits are based on maximum AFDC benefits shown and assume deductions of $289 monthly ($112 standard household deduction plus $177 maximum allowable deduction for excess shelter cost) in the 48 contiguous States and D.C. In the remaining four jurisdictions these maximum allowable food stamp deductions are assumed: Alaska, $499; Hawaii, $411; Guam, $439; and Virgin Islands, $229. If only the standard deduction were assumed, food stamp benefits would drop by about $53 monthly in most of the 48 contiguous States and D.C. Maximum food stamp benefits from October 1989 through September 1990 are $260 for a family of three except in these 4 jurisdictions, where they are as follows: Alaska, $325; Hawaii, $396; Guam, $384; and Virgin Islands, $335.

4. Except for Alaska and Hawaii, this column is based on the Census Bureau's 1989 poverty threshold for a family of three persons, $9,890, converted to a monthly rate of $824. For Alaska, this threshold was increased by 25 percent; for Hawaii, by 15 percent, following the practice of the Office of Management and Budget.

5. In these States part of the AFDC cash payment has been designated as energy aid and is disregarded by the State in calculating food stamp benefits. Illinois disregards $18. Kansas disregards $36. Maryland disregards $59. Michigan disregards $74. New Jersey disregards $25. Ohio disregards $14. New York disregards $53, the full amount of a benefit boost enacted in 1981 ($30) and in 1985 ($23). Oregon disregards $118. Rhode Island disregards $127.85. Washington disregards $56.

6. With respect to maximum AFDC benefit among 50 States and D.C.

Note—Puerto Rico does not have a food stamp program; instead a cash nutritional assistance payment is given to recipients.

Source: Table prepared by CRS from information provided by a telephone survey of the States. Background Materials and Data for Programs under the Jurisdiction of House Ways and Means Committee, U.S. Congress, Jan. 1990, pp. 540–41.

In the United States children are the largest group experiencing poverty.

In the United States the principal in-kind transfer programs are **food stamps, Medicaid,** and the housing assistance programs. Expenditures for in-kind programs have grown more rapidly than expenditures for cash assistance, as shown in Table 4–5. Various justifications have been given for the substitution of in-kind programs for cash assistance. The first is historical. All three of the major in-kind programs were inaugurated when clear problems existed in the markets for each of these essentials. In the food market there was a food surplus, and the food stamps were originally designated only for foods in surplus supply and for which government subsidies had already been paid. In the housing market, a complex housing shortage existed because of problems in both the supply of affordable housing and the effective demand for low-cost housing. The deficiency in demand was a function of the lack of long-term mortgage availability to low-income workers. In the medical market there was a poor distribution of medical facilities and the absence of employment-related health insurance for low-income workers. Each of the in-kind programs was generated to respond to these unique structural problems. They have continued after the original structural condition was modified. Second, justification for in-kind programs is the continuing belief that poor families cannot be trusted to "spend properly," thus, aid to the poor is made in ways that restrict their options only to socially approved alternatives. Related to both the historical and the individual perspectives is the widespread belief that the total amount of assistance currently available to the poor is more than what would be available through unrestricted cash assistance. Providers of medical care, housing, and food promote in-kind programs that touch their sectors of the economy, but these same groups may not support a similar amount of cash aid.

It is clear that the poor benefit by in-kind transfers. That the poor would be better off if all the current in-kind programs were simply transferred into cash payments is, and will continue to be, a hotly disputed subject (Morris and Williamson 1982). In-kind and cash programs present difficult choices; some people benefit from one, others from another. Cash benefits provide autonomy and flexibility for the recipients. Increased in-kind payments, however, bring not only more transfers but more transfers targeted to minority groups. Table 4–10 shows the increase in in-kind programs during the 1970s and the 1980s. The Family Support Act of 1988 (discussed later) will increase the trend toward more in-kind payments, whereas cash benefits probably will not change. When fully implemented, this act will more than likely accentuate this trend. The shares spent on cash transfers, in-kind benefits, and service programs reflect latent objectives for the social welfare system. (Sandefur and Tienda 1988). The most recent evidence suggests that if the value of food stamps, Medicaid coverage, and housing assistance were actually counted as income, the number of poor persons would drop by about one-third (U.S. Bureau of the Census 1983).

THE POLICY ISSUES OF 1990

A number of policy issues will be faced in the last decade of this century. We cannot discuss all of the issues in this text, but we will focus on income for the aged and programs for families.

Table 4–10   Federal State Expenditures for Five Programs in Millions of 1989 Dollars

Year	Public Housing	Food Stamps	Medicaid	AFDC	SSI
1970	NA	NA	11,506	14,211	9,393
1975	NA	9,625	29,126	20,753	13,548
1980	8,925	13,124	38,796	18,007	11,950
1985	17,340	14,812	47,153	17,439	12,746
1989	17,310	13,837	61,271	17,468	14,791

Note: Table uses 1989 dollars; figures reflect millions of dollars expended, e.g. 9,625 million dollars.
Source: Data derived from various tables in *1990 Overview of Entitlement Programs*

Incomes for the Aged

When the principal wage earner leaves the labor force for retirement, those who have been better off in their working years become even better off, whereas those in the middle fall and those who were worse off during their working years become even more disadvantaged. The principal reason for this is not changes in policy but changes in the economy and changes in private pensions. Manufacturing employment is on the decline, and employment in lower-wage service-sector jobs is on the increase. Such jobs typically provide little or no pension protection. The hope that OASDI would become more of a supplement to retirement income and less a mainstay is fading. The changing picture of retirement income is shown in Table 4–11.

Incomes for Families: The Family Support Act of 1988

The Family Support Act of 1988 is thought by some to reflect a new consensus on what to do with the bottom tier of the welfare system. The liberal image of the lower tier of welfare was an institutional system that provided transitional aid and the necessary services when family units or employment and insurance programs were not working. The conservative image was that the "safety net" was too generous and caused many households to select permanent welfare. In the 1980s a new consensus evolved that both views were right and that there were two populations on welfare: (1) the transitory poor, for whom the welfare system was designed, and (2) the underclass, who were trapped by a system where employment offered less than welfare.

The principal consequence of the new consensus was the passage of the Family Support Act of 1988. The new law, only now being implemented by the states, will place more emphasis on the collection of child support payments from absent fathers, provide transitional assistance such as Medicaid and child care to those who leave welfare for work, establish strong mandates to the states to establish effective service and training programs for those not yet ready to seek work, and require all states to have a temporary program to aid the intact family (AFDC-UP). However, these four measures together are not

Table 4–11 Sources and Shares of Income of American Households with Head Over 65, 1976 and 1986

Source	% Receiving Source		% of Those with This Source for Whom It Is Over 50% of Total Income	
	1976	*1986*	*1976*	*1986*
Public Employment Pensions	9	14	44	36
Wages	25	20	43	41
Private Pensions	20	27	9	7
Asset Income	56	67	13	17
OASDI	89	91	66	62

Source: Employee Benefits Association, Social Security Administration, as reported in *New York Times*, 29 May 1990, p. 1, col. 4.

expected to reduce the rate of poverty; that task falls to a reinvigorated economy. The four together are expected to reduce the number of families permanently dependent on the lower tier of the welfare system. Yet the new consensus may already be crumbling. Between 1960 and 1990 a major policy shift has occurred, but it has occurred gradually. The shift has been from a preoccupation with the reduction of poverty to a preoccupation with the reduction of dependency.

In 1960 the goal was to eliminate poverty, and one way of doing so was to pay benefits to the family to bring it above the poverty line. One consequence of this approach, however, is that the families receiving benefits are viewed by some as being dependent on the government. The goal of eliminating poverty and dependency makes for good rhetoric, but meeting the goal may involve contradictions. That is, for some people in our society poverty is the central problem to be resolved; for others, dependency. When working-poor families receive supplemental benefits to bring them above the poverty line, this fact can be seen as a form of dependency. When the benefits are eliminated and no help designed to enable the family to "earn" a poverty-free income is provided, we reduce dependency but fail to address the poverty problem for that family.

THE ROLES OF SOCIAL WORKERS IN THE FIGHT AGAINST POVERTY

Social work, more than any other profession, maintains a strong commitment to fighting poverty at all levels of the environment. Social workers provide direct services to individuals and families living in poverty; advocate for programs and policies that improve the lives of the poor and reduce poverty at the community, state, and federal levels; and develop and administer policies and programs that serve our nation's poor.

Some BSW graduates become income eligibility or public assistance workers in federal, state, and local human services agencies. They help individuals apply for public assistance programs, such as AFDC, food stamps, Medicaid and general assistance. They also help individuals apply for social insurance programs such as social security and Medicare and oversee the provision of both public assistance and social insurance benefit programs.

The Family Support Act has increased the roles of social workers in the fight against poverty by mandating that all AFDC clients receiving employment services be assigned a case manager to help them obtain self-sufficiency. Case managers use a problem solving approach to assess their clients' strengths and needs; work with their clients to develop appropriate goals to work toward getting off AFDC and achieving adequate employment; develop appropriate service plans with clients to accomplish their goals; assist their clients in accessing needed resources and provide support to them in accomplishing their established goals; and terminate with their clients when the plans have been completed. Case managers also assist clients in developing skills in areas such as interviewing, assertiveness, and handling stress on the job; help them enroll in job training and education programs; and help them locate appropriate resources such as transportation, housing, child care, health care, or family counseling.

Social workers also are employed by churches and other religious organizations, the Salvation Army, local social services agencies, housing programs, Head Start and other child development programs, drop out prevention and teen pregnancy and teen parenting programs, and health clinics and hospitals that provide a variety of services to adults, children, youth and families who live in poverty. Additionally, social workers work with federal, state and local agencies and governments; state legislatures and the U.S. Congress; and advocacy organizations such as the Children's Defense Fund in developing, lobbying for, and administering anti-poverty programs. The values base of the social work profession mandates that social workers treat all clients, including those in poverty, with dignity and respect and work to empower them to be in charge of their own lives.

SUMMARY

The concept of "poverty" is complex, and attempting to define it often results in considerable debate. Because there are a number of different ways to measure poverty, its incidence varies depending on the definition and measurement used. No matter what the definition, the progress against poverty in the United States has been uneven historically. Many people remain poor. Those most at risk to live in poverty are children, women, the elderly, the disabled, and members of ethnic minorities. Because of the economic downturn in the United States in recent years, increased numbers of working citizens, including married couples, are also joining the ranks of the poor.

Public assistance programs for the poor are insufficient to meet individual needs and to help individuals living in poverty become self-sufficient. Social workers are joining other groups in calling for welfare reform that could provide social services, education, employment training, health care, child care, and other resources to enable larger numbers to move out of poverty. However, the U.S. economic structure and availability of jobs are the factors that influence poverty most strongly. Welfare reform alone, no matter how well-planned and implemented, is not sufficient to reduce poverty in the United States significantly.

KEY TERMS

Aid to Families with Dependent
   Children (AFDC)
categorical assistance
food stamps
general assistance (GA)
Medicaid
Medicare
official poverty

Old Age Survivors and Disability
   Insurance (OASDI, or Social
   Security)
poverty
public (social) assistance
social insurance
Supplemental Security Income (SSI)
unemployment insurance (UI)
workers' compensation (WC)

DISCUSSION QUESTIONS

1. Do you believe that a preference for welfare keeps AFDC recipients out of the work force?

2. How does the changing shape of the American economy change the shape of American poverty?

3. To what degree is the number (or percentage) of poor people a good measure of a society's commitment to social welfare?

REFERENCES

Danziger, S., and D. Weinberg. 1989. *Fighting poverty.* Cambridge, MA: Harvard University Press.

Ford Foundation. 1989. *The common good: Social welfare and the American future.*

Morris, Michael, and John Williamson. 1982. *Poverty and public policy: An analysis of federal intervention efforts.* New York: Greenwood.

Sandefur, Gary D., and Martha Tienda. 1988. *Divided opportunities: Minorities, poverty and social policy.* New York: Plenum.

Schorr, Lisbeth B. 1988. *Within our reach: Breaking the cycle of disadvantage.* New York: Anchor/Doubleday.

Stockman, David. 1984. Press release for 13 December. Washington, D.C.: Office of Management and Budget.

U.S. Bureau of the Census. 1983. *Estimates of poverty including non-cash benefits.* Technical paper no. 91. Washington, D.C.: GPO.

U.S. Congress. House. Committee on Ways and Means. 1989. *Background material and data on programs under the jurisdiction of the House Ways and Means Committee.* 101st Cong., 1st session. Committee Print 101–4. (also known as the "Green Book")

U.S. Congress. House. Committee on Ways and Means. 1990. *Overview of entitlement programs.* 101st Cong., 2d session. Committee Print 101–29.

Wilson, William. 1987. *The truly disadvantaged: The inner city underclass and public policy.* Chicago: Univ. of Chicago Press.

SUGGESTED FURTHER READINGS

Ellwood, D. 1987. *Divide and conquer.* New York: Ford Foundation.

Phillips, K. 1990. *The politics of rich and poor.* New York: Random House.

Mental Health, Substance Abuse, and Developmental Disabilities

Twenty-four-year-old Joanna Barclay currently lives in a halfway house in the inner-city area of a large northern city. She has lived there for three months, after being released from her fourteenth stay at a state mental hospital since the age of sixteen. Joanna and her roommates earn money for food and part of the rent by working for an industrial cleaning company. They are supervised by a social worker from the local mental health outreach center, who meets with them as a group twice a week and is available on an on-call basis whenever they need support. Joanna, with her social worker's help, is planning to enroll in a job-training program next month and to move into her own apartment with one of the other residents of the halfway house within the next six months. Joanna is excited about the opportunity to live on her own.

Joanna enjoyed a relatively stable childhood, growing up in a rural area of the South with her middle-class parents and four brothers. During junior high school, she began to experience severe headaches and what she terms "anxiety attacks." Her parents took her to several doctors, but no physical reasons could be found for these problems. At about age fifteen, Joanna's behavior changed from calm and stable to erratic,

ranging from screaming rages to long periods of crying to fun-loving, carefree behavior. She began experimenting with drugs, ran away from home a number of times, and got into several physical altercations with other girls at school. Her family had difficulty coping with her behavior. After one serious incident when Joanna threatened her mother and her younger brother with a knife, she was hospitalized in a local private psychiatric hospital for thirty days. She was placed on medication to help stabilize her erratic behavior, and she and her family received therapy. After her release from the hospital, Joanna functioned better for several months. However, she soon reported feeling overwhelmed and pressured and told her family she "could not stop the frightening thoughts that kept running through her head." Her psychiatrist wanted to rehospitalize her, but her family's insurance benefits had been exhausted during her first hospitalization, and Joanna did not want to admit herself to the state mental hospital nearby.

After continual arguments with her family and school personnel and several minor altercations with the law, Joanna quit school and moved with a boyfriend to California, where she held a series of temporary jobs. When the boyfriend left her because he could not handle her mood swings, her behavior became even more erratic. Finally, after she was found asleep in a dumpster and unable to remember who or where she was, the police picked her up and took her to the state hospital. During the next six years, Joanna repeated a pattern of briefly holding a menial job, losing the job, living on the streets, entering the state hospital, and being released in a more stable condition. When Joanna was released from her last hospital stay, the local mental health center in Joanna's area finally had space available at the halfway house where she currently is living.

The mental health needs of Americans are receiving increased attention. The 1980 National Commission on Mental Health concluded that 15 percent of the U.S. population at any given time is in need of mental health services and that 25 percent of the population suffers from some type of emotional problem. However, services are available to only one out of every eight individuals who need them. Because of increases in individual stress, financial pressures, divorce and marital problems, and work-related pressures, most individuals will experience emotional problems at some point in their lives.

How does one determine who needs mental health services and who should receive them? The stigma placed on individuals with mental health problems and the stereotypes about the services provided them cause many individuals with mental health problems to avoid seeking services. People think of mental health services and those who receive them as portrayed in popular movies and books, such as *One Flew Over the Cuckoo's Nest* (Kesey 1962). For this reason, many communities and neighborhoods are developing zoning ordinances and other means to squelch attempts to move into the community people who have mental health problems but do not need institutionalization.

INCREASED FOCUS ON MENTAL HEALTH

The rights of those with mental health problems also are receiving increased attention. Should persons be forced to be hospitalized, receive electric shock treatments, or receive drug therapy against their wishes? Or, like Joanna, when they so desperately need treatment that is not available due to scarce resources, do they have a right to demand services, especially if it means they will be less likely to need more intensive services, such as institutionalization, in the future? Does someone in an institution who could function in a less restrictive environment have the right to demand such a placement? What about the rights of those in our society who may encounter persons with serious mental health problems? Concern is being expressed about the accountability of those with serious mental health problems and what should happen when such individuals become dangerous to themselves and others. This was exemplified by several recent court cases. The young adult who shot President Reagan in 1981 was not sentenced for the act due to "reasons of insanity." At the same time, a young adult who killed a number of women over a period of several years, diagnosed by a number of psychiatrists as having severe psychological prob-lems, was sentenced to death in a Florida court and executed in 1989. And a retarded young adult who aided in a murder at the age of seventeen, when his mental age was about six, recently was put to death in that same state.

Current studies also show a strong relationship between mental health problems and physical health problems. When persons do not get help in addressing their mental health problems, they are much more likely to become physically ill. For example, IBM researchers found that 50 percent of persons going to company physicians with health-related problems were experiencing mental health problems (Comprehensive Care Corporation 1981). A recent study of over 40,000 persons in Hawaii (Hiratsuka 1990) found that persons who received short-term mental health services for a specific psychological problem experienced a 35 percent to 38 percent drop in subsequent medical costs. The high costs of health care could be reduced if more attention were given to the mental health needs of individuals.

Mental health problems, if left untreated, also disrupt families and increase the financial costs to taxpayers, as well as decrease productivity at the work-place. Researchers recently found that mental health problems cost the United States $64.2 billion in 1980 (U.S. Department of Health, Education, and Welfare 1980). Direct costs for publicly and privately provided mental health care in the United States were estimated to be $20 billion in 1980 (Rochefort 1989), with costs for mental illness the third largest expenditure for all categories of health care. Other researchers (Mechanic, 1987) estimated that the public cost of providing services to persons with serious mental illness in 1983 was $11.1 billion, with 59.5 percent of those dollars coming from the federal government, 37.8 percent coming from state governments, and 2.7 percent coming from local governments.

Over half of the individuals providing mental health services today are social workers employed in state mental hospitals, private psychiatric treatment fa-cilities, community outreach facilities, schools for the developmentally disabled, child guidance clinics and family service agencies, alcohol and drug treatment facilities, emergency hotlines, crisis centers, and private offices. Thus, services for mental health and developmental disabilities are rapidly growing and offer many critical roles for social workers. Substance abuse, although considered a mental health issue, has received such extensive attention in recent years that it can almost be considered a separate area.

In this chapter we discuss definitions of mental health, mental illness, substance abuse, and developmental disabilities. Critical incidents that have shaped the ways individuals with mental health problems, including substance abuse, and developmental disabilities are viewed and the types of services provided are also addressed. Current service needs and issues are considered, and the roles that social workers play in meeting service needs and addressing these issues are discussed.

MENTAL HEALTH OR MENTAL ILLNESS? DEFINITIONAL ISSUES

Societies have always developed their own systems for labeling acceptable and unacceptable behavior. What is tolerated in one society may not be in another.

For each society there is a continuum, with certain definitely unacceptable and inappropriate behaviors at one end and definitely acceptable and appropriate ones at the other. Typically, although the behaviors at either end of the continuum are almost uniformly agreed upon by most members of that society, the behaviors in the middle of the continuum tend to cause much debate and disagreement. For example, although murder would be considered a definitely unacceptable behavior by most, where on the continuum would continually talking to oneself fall, or being convinced that you were King Tut? Some societies tolerate little deviance from acceptable behavior. For example, for a brief period in colonial times in Salem, Massachusetts, some persons whose behavior was considered "deviant" were labeled as witches possessed by the devil, and they were tortured and burned at the stake. Later research (Mechanic 1980) suggested that many of these individuals had severe psychological problems. In other societies, those whose behavior deviates from the norm are given special roles and, in some instances, elevated to high-status positions within the society. For example, in many American Indian tribes, nonconforming individuals often became shamans, or medicine men—high-status positions within the tribes.

Historically, those labeled as mentally ill or retarded often have been isolated or punished. In colonial times, individuals frequently were locked in attics or cellars or warehoused in lunatic asylums. Today, our society is still ambivalent about how such individuals should be regarded. Attempts at deinstitutionalization or mainstreaming emotionally disturbed and disabled individuals into classrooms and communities have met with much resistance. Various people (e.g., Goffman 1961, Mechanic 1980) have suggested that for many individuals who have emotional or developmental problems, the stigma attached to the labels they are given is far more damaging to them than the extent of their problems. David Mechanic, a prominent social policy analyst in the mental health field, argues that definitions of mental illness are made at varying levels in the social structure. Early informal definitions are made in groups within which the person operates, usually among family members or co-workers. Such definitions depend on the norms of the particular group and what is tolerated, as well as the position the person occupies within the group. A boss's behavior, for example, may be defined as outside of the group norms much less quickly than a file clerk's. Definitions of this type also depend on whether or not the other members of the group can empathize, that is, whether they can fit that behavior into their own frames of reference. For example, a person who continually carries on an imaginary conversation with his mother while on the job is more likely to be tolerated if the group is aware that the mother recently died and the son had a very close relationship with her. However, if there is no apparent context for the behavior or if the behavior persists, such individuals are likely to be labeled as strange or odd (Mechanic 1980).

Definitions of so-called abnormal behaviors typically are based on visible symptoms, such as talking to people who are not present, rather than the severity of the actual problems. Anytime one is attempting to define a condition based on nonvisible factors, such as what is going on inside an individual's mind, specific definitions are difficult to achieve. Only those who in some way enter the mental health system are likely to be specifically defined as having some type of emotional problem. The mental health system, in spite of its problems, is likely to accept, at least for short periods of time, almost all individuals who seek its services, including the unwanted, the aged, the indigent, the lonely, and those with nowhere else to go. At times, this results in over-estimates of the number of individuals defined as having emotional problems and underestimates of those who should enter the system.

Mental Illness

Formal definitions of mental illness traditionally have followed a **medical model,** which considers those with emotional problems as sick and thus not responsible for their behavior. This model also assumes that sick people are entitled to be helped and that help or treatment should be guided by the medical profession in medical settings or settings such as psychiatric facilities directed by medical professionals. The medical model conceptualizes mental illness as severe emotional problems caused by brain dysfunction or intrapsychic causes, with little attention to systems or environmental influences. Traditionally, mental illness also has been viewed from a genetic or physiological perspective as a disease of the mind or a disturbance in the functioning of the individual.

The American Psychiatric Association has monitored the categorization and definition of various types of emotional disorders through a classification system termed the **Diagnostic and Statistical Manual of Mental Disorders,** or the *DSM.* This classification system, revised significantly in 1980 as the *DSM-II* and again in 1987 as the **DSM-III-R** (third edition, revised), uses a multiaxial system for evaluation, which focuses on the psychological, biological, and social aspects of an individual's functioning. The system incorporates information from five axes in diagnosing an individual. Axes I and II incorporate all of the mental disorders, such as schizophrenic and psychotic disorders. Axis III incorporates physical disorders and conditions. Axes IV and V rate the severity of the psychosocial stressors that have contributed to the development or the mainte-nance of the disorder and the highest level of adaptive functioning that the individual has maintained during the previous year (Williams 1987, 389).

The *DSM* classification system is an important one for social work profes-sionals, as it incorporates a systems/ecological perspective in assessing an individual, allowing a focus on either organic factors or environmental factors, or both, that affect an individual's condition. It also allows for the incorporation of the individual's strengths, as well as problems, when completing an as-sessment. This classification system has been used increasingly in recent years for third-party insurance reimbursement when mental health services are pro-vided. Although many social workers find the *DSM-III-R* helpful, its use by social workers and other professionals to label conditions of clients in order to obtain third-party insurance reimbursements has raised questions about whether such labels really are beneficial in improving services. Critics suggest that such a diagnostic process may actually be more detrimental to clients, because labels such as "schizophrenia" or "conduct disorder" can negatively affect clients and the way others treat them, particularly if such labels included in clients' records are obtained and misused.

Mental Health

Many individuals view mental health and mental illness at opposite ends of a continuum. Others, like psychiatrist Thomas Szasz (1970), suggest that mental

A Retired Senior Volunteer Program volunteer helps build the self-esteem of a participant in a neighborhood summer youth olympics festival sponsored by a local mental health agency.

health and emotional problems are issues that defy specific boundaries. Szasz objects to labeling the mentally ill and argues that there is no such thing as mental illness. He agrees that there are illnesses due to neurological impairment, but he believes that such illnesses are brain diseases rather than mental illnesses. Although he acknowledges the existence of emotional problems, Szasz contends that labeling nonorganic emotional problems implies a deviation from some clearly specified norm. He feels that the label not only stigmatizes individuals, but may cause them to actually assume those behaviors.

Szasz argues that instead of talking about definitions of mental illness, we should talk about problems of living; that is, an individual's struggle with the problem of how to live in our world requires attention. He and others suggest that positive mental health is promoted by one's competence in dealing with the environment and one's confidence of being able, when necessary, to cause desired effects. Szasz advocates a systems/ecological perspective for viewing mental health. Within his framework, problems in living can be viewed as being due to biological/physiological, economic, political, psychological, or sociological constraints. Promoting positive interactions between individuals and their environments is viewed as congruent with the promotion of optimal mental health and social functioning for individuals. Szasz (1960) proposes a classification system with the following categories of mental health problems:

1. Personal disabilities, such as depression, fears, inadequacy, and excessive anxiety
2. Antisocial acts, such as violent and criminal behaviors
3. Deterioration of the brain, such as Alzheimer's disease, alcoholism, and brain damage

Many mental health experts prefer this system and its emphasis on healthy functioning to a system that emphasizes mental illness. This system assumes that all individuals have difficulties at some point negotiating their complex environments. Mental health services are viewed as available to and needed by all individuals at some time during their lives rather than as something to be avoided.

THE DEVELOPMENT OF MENTAL HEALTH PROBLEMS

There is considerable debate on how mental health problems are created. In many instances, it is difficult, if not impossible, to say that any one specific factor caused a mental health problem. More than likely, mental health problems are the result of a variety of factors. Research suggests a number of possible explanations:

○ Hereditary and Biological Factors—Researchers have identified genetic traits that suggest that individuals with the same gene pools may be prone to certain mental health disorders. For example, among identical twins, if one has schizophrenia, the other is also highly likely to have the disorder, even if the twins were separated at birth and raised in different environments. Some researchers suggest that genetic factors alone do not cause mental health disorders, but that some individuals are predisposed to certain problems through heredity, and that under certain environmental conditions, this predisposition is triggered, resulting in the emotional problem. A variation of this position is that, due to genetic traits or physiological characteristics, some individuals are biologically less capable of coping with environmental stress.

○ Psychosocial Developmental Factors—This perspective, based on the work of developmental theorist Erik Erikson and others, suggests that mental health problems result from environmental experiences during childhood. Research shows that individuals who experience severe trauma during childhood—such as physical or sexual abuse, separation from a close family member, or alcoholism or other drug abuse among family members—are much more likely to experience mental health problems later in life.

○ Social Learning—The social learning perspective suggests that mental health problems are the result of learned behaviors. Such behaviors may be learned by observing parents or other role models or be developed as survival mechanisms to cope with difficult life experiences.

○ Social Stress—This perspective, based on the work of Thomas Szasz, focuses on the relationship between environmental stress and mental health, suggesting that individuals who are under greater stress—including the poor, ethnic minorities, and women—are more likely to experience mental health problems.

○ Societal Reactions and Labeling—This perspective suggests that society creates individuals with mental health problems through a societal reaction process. By establishing social norms and treating as deviant those who do not subscribe to the norms, a society identifies individuals with mental health problems. Additionally, individuals identified or labeled as somehow different will assume the role prescribed to them; that is, individuals labeled as having mental health problems will behave as they would be expected to if they had the problem.

○ Systems/Ecological Perspective—This perspective suggests that mental health problems are the result of a variety of factors that interact in a complex fashion and vary according to the uniqueness of the individual and the environment within which he or she interacts. Within the systems/ecological framework, for example, many factors that shape a person's self-concept, competence, and behaviors can be addressed, such as the person's biological characteristics; ethnicity; gender; place within the broader environment, including family, peer groups, and the neighborhood and community in which the person functions; and cultural and societal expectations.

Application of the Systems/Ecological Perspective

The systems/ecological perspective can include a combination of the other perspectives identified earlier as well. For example, a person may be predisposed biologically to experience mental health problems, may have suffered as a child from sexual abuse, may have had a parent who also experienced mental health problems, and currently may be in an extremely stressful living situation (e.g., experiencing an unhappy marriage, a stressful job, or financial problems). If such an individual experienced mental health problems, it would be impossible to state which of those factors directly caused the problems.

A systems/ecological perspective allows us to focus on all of the factors within an individual's past and present environment, as well as the individual's physiological characteristics, in addressing mental health problems. If we know which factors are most important, we are much more likely to be able to intervene successfully in alleviating the problems. This focus on both the individual and the individual's environment allows the social worker and the client to "map out" the critical factors most likely to account for the problems, and then to develop an intervention plan that specifically addresses those factors.

Whether one takes a mental illness perspective or a broader perspective, how and when an individual's emotional problems are identified and defined depend on a number of factors:

1. The visibility, recognizability, or perpetual occurrence of inappropriate/deviant behaviors and symptoms;
2. The extent to which the person perceives the symptoms as serious;
3. The extent to which the symptoms disrupt family, work, and other activities;
4. The frequency of the appearance of the signs and symptoms, or their persistence;
5. The tolerance threshold of those who are exposed to and evaluate the signs and symptoms;
6. The information available to, the knowledge of, and the cultural assumptions and understandings of the evaluator;

7. The degree to which processes that distort reality are present;

8. The presence of needs within the family/environment that conflict with the recognition of problems or the assumption of the "sick" role;

9. The possibility that competing interpretations can be assigned to the behaviors/signs once they are recognized;

10. The availability of treatment/intervention resources, their physical proximity and costs of money, time, and effort as well as costs of stigmatization and humiliation. (Mechanic 1980, 68–69)

The identification of individuals with mental health problems and the ways those problems are defined are hotly debated issues among mental health professionals. A number of years ago, psychologist David Rosenhan and his associates conducted a study that exemplifies this concern. Rosenhan (1973) and his seven associates went separately to the admissions offices of twelve psychiatric hospitals in five different states, all claiming that they were hearing voices. In every instance, they were admitted to the hospitals as patients. Immediately upon admission, they all assumed normal behavior. At least one of the researchers did not try to hide his role as a researcher—he sat on the ward and took copious notes on legal pads about all of the events going on around him.

In spite of the fact that the researchers all behaved completely normally while hospitalized, hospital professionals were unable to distinguish them from other patients. In a number of instances, however, the other patients were able to determine that they were not mentally ill! Rosenhan and his associates remained at the hospitals as patients from time periods ranging from seven to fifty-two days, with an average stay of nineteen days, before they were discharged. The diagnosis at discharge for each of them was "schizophrenia in remission" (Rosenhan 1973).

ALCOHOLISM AND CHEMICAL DEPENDENCY

Problems of alcoholism and chemical dependency can be related not only to the area of mental health, but also to developmental disabilities, child and family issues, poverty, criminal justice, and the workplace. Special populations, including women, the elderly, minorities, and gays and lesbians, are also at greater risk for experiencing serious problems with alcoholism and chemical dependency than are other groups.

What constitutes alcoholism and drug abuse, the ways that these problems are conceptualized, and their causes are undergoing increased debate among professionals from a variety of disciplines. Historically, most attention has been directed toward alcohol abuse and alcoholism, which were until recently considered to be moral issues. The general societal perception was that persons drank too much because they were weak, and that they could stop drinking if they wanted to.

Although many people still hold this view, during the 1940s and 1950s attention began to focus instead on the concept that alcoholism is a disease and that it must be treated as one might treat a person with diabetes or another chronic illness. In 1957 the American Medical Association recognized alcoholism as a disease, and this concept is well established today. One definition of alcoholism, for example, views it as a chronic condition, meaning it is treatable but incurable; progressive, meaning it becomes worse if the drinking does not stop; and fatal, since if untreated, death can result. Although debate continues on whether alcoholism should be viewed as an individual disease, a family or societal disease, or an individual, family, or societal problem rather than a disease, there are advantages to the disease model. First, individuals and their families may be more likely to accept the alcoholism and become involved in an intervention program if they view the alcoholism as a disease rather than as a moral weakness or a social problem. Second, conceptualizing alcoholism as a disease also allows for coverage of treatment and hospitalization by insurance companies and public health care programs. Because of recent legislation in many states, the serious abuse of other drugs also must be treated as a disease. However, because use of drugs other than alcohol more often involves illegal and/or counterculture activities, there has been much more reluctance to consider the abuse of drugs other than alcohol as a disease.

Alcoholism and drug abuse are denied by many substance abusers and their families, who define a substance abuser in various ways—as someone who takes one more drink or drug than they or their family member takes; as someone who only drinks excessive amounts of hard liquor and not beer or wine, as they do; as someone who uses more dangerous drugs and not marijuana, which they use; or as someone who drinks and uses alcohol or other drugs every morning or every day and not only evenings or weekends, as they do. More recent definitions of alcoholism and chemical dependency focus on the personal implications of the drinking or drug use rather than the amount or frequency. **Alcoholism,** for example, has been defined as any use of alcohol that interferes with personal life, including school, jobs, family, friends, health, spiritual life, or the law (Royce 1989, 10). Definitions of drug abuse are similar.

Although the abuse of alcohol is considered more socially acceptable than the abuse of other drugs, it is increasingly difficult to separate abuse of alcohol and alcoholism from the abuse of other drugs and chemical dependency. Some experts in the field prefer to keep the two separate to call attention to the fact that alcohol is still the most widely misused drug and that it, too, has serious individual and societal costs. However, others point out that 80 percent of persons under twenty and 60 percent of persons under forty abuse more than one substance. Current research on addiction also shows that many individuals treated for one type of **substance abuse** stop using that substance and "cross-addict" to another drug. Thus, persons in the field of chemical dependency often refer to the substance a person has abused as his or her "drug of choice" and to those who abuse more than one drug as "polyaddicts."

Other experts in the field of chemical dependency and alcoholism conceptualize the problem as one of dependency or the broader concept of **addiction,** which can be defined as a "physical and/or psychological dependence upon mood changing substances, including, but not limited to, alcohol, drugs, pills, foods, sex, or money" (Parkside Medical Services Corporation, 1988). Some experts believe that treatment should focus on addiction and eliminating addictive behaviors in all areas of a person's life, including food, work, and relationships, as well as drugs.

Types of Commonly Abused Substances

Alcohol, the most commonly abused drug, is most often viewed as a depressant, although it can also be a stimulant, and, for some individuals, a hallucinogen. Other depressants include sedatives, such as sleeping pills, tranquilizers, and pain killers. Women and persons who have experienced or are experiencing chronic pain are two groups more at risk to abuse depressants than other groups.

Narcotics such as opium and its derivatives, morphine and heroin, are also highly addictive. Although, legally, cocaine is considered a narcotic, it often acts more like a stimulant, creating a high in its users. Crack, a relatively inexpensive cocaine-based drug, has a similar, but much more euphoric and highly addictive, effect. Because of its easy availability and highly addictive nature, crack has resulted in sharp increases in crime, overdoses, prostitution, AIDS, and homelessness. Recent publicity has also focused on "crack" babies, who are born addicted and at risk to die during the first year of their lives or to survive with serious physical and emotional problems. Stimulants that are often abused include caffeine—legal, but not as safe as was once thought— and amphetamines such as speed.

Illicit drugs also include the hallucinogens, such as LSD, and marijuana, the most commonly used. One group of substances that is abused and often overlooked is inhalants. Use of inhalants is especially prevalent among Hispanic youth and often results in retardation or death. A wide variety of inhalants are used, including petroleum products such as gasoline, freon, aerosol products, and typewriter correction fluid. Amyl nitrate and butyl nitrate, commonly called "poppers," are also inhalants.

Incidence and Social and Economic Costs of Drug Abuse and Alcoholism

Although it is difficult to estimate the number of individuals who are dependent on alcohol or other drugs, current estimates suggest that thirty-six to forty-three million persons in the United States, or 15 percent to 18 percent of the population, will become dependent on at least one drug during their lifetime (Royce 1990). The majority of media attention is devoted to the abuse of drugs other than alcohol, primarily cocaine, crack, and heroin. Although it is difficult to obtain accurate numbers, recent national studies suggest that there are ten million regular users of cocaine and that 25 million Americans have tried cocaine at least once.

However, alcohol remains the most common drug of choice for most drug abusers in the United States. It is estimated that there are fifteen million alcoholics in the United States and that fifty million Americans are affected directly by alcohol abuse by a family member. Most people's image of an alcoholic is the skidrow bum—old, male, unkempt, unemployed, living on the streets, and derelict. In reality, only 3 percent of alcoholics can be characterized this way. About 45 percent of alcoholics are in professional or managerial positions, 25 percent are white-collar workers, and 30 percent are manual laborers. Physicians, air traffic controllers, airline pilots, law enforcement officers, attorneys, and clergy all have high rates of alcoholism (Royce, 1989).

Similar patterns are also found among the family members of both alcoholics and abusers of other drugs. Studies have found that 25 percent of males and 10 percent of females who grow up in families where their parents abused either alcohol or other drugs become substance abusers themselves. Even those who do not develop substance abuse problems themselves often develop other addictive behaviors or experience emotional problems. Although fewer women repeat the pattern of drug abuse, they are much more likely to select a mate who is a drug abuser. Royce (1989) surveyed alcohol-related literature and journals, which reported that alcohol was involved in 67 percent of child abuse cases, 40 percent of forcible rapes, 80 percent of spouse abuse cases, 83 percent of homicides, and 90 percent of incest situations.

Although alcohol abuse and chemical dependency are widespread among all age groups, their increased use among adolescents has caused increasing concern. Recent reports have shown that use of drugs other than alcohol is decreasing among teens, but alcohol use continues to increase. Researchers who conducted a study in 1990 found that 40 percent of high school seniors had gotten drunk at least once within the previous two weeks prior to being surveyed. The study also found that 3.5 million 12–17 year olds had tried marijuana at least once and that one-third of the teens surveyed said they were regular users (Lipman 1990). Whereas the death rate for other age groups has decreased, the death rate for adolescents has increased significantly in recent years, with most deaths due to traffic accidents and suicides and related to abuse of alcohol or other drugs.

Drug abuse, particularly alcoholism, among the elderly is also a problem. This age group, like adolescents and young adults, also has a high death rate due to alcoholism, due primarily to chronic alcohol-related diseases such as cirrhosis of the liver, digestive diseases, and hepatitis.

Members of minority groups are also more at risk to abuse alcohol and drugs. Blacks, for example, are three times as likely to die as a result of alcoholism than whites, and American Indians have the highest incidence of alcoholism of any ethnic group in the United States. It is unclear whether this is due to factors associated with unemployment and poverty, different cultural patterns in the use of drugs and alcohol, or genetic differences. Some researchers, for example, suggest that more American Indians metabolize alcohol in ways that predispose alcoholism than members of other groups. The heightened risk of minority groups for suffering the personal, emotional and economic consequences of substance abuse raises a number of issues about our society, since nonminorities are most often the ones who oversee large-scale production and sale of drugs and reap the economic profits.

Abuse of alcohol and other drugs has also increased among women. Female substance abusers experience greater stigma than males. Researchers in one study found that 23 percent of women encountered opposition from friends and family when entering substance abuse treatment programs, compared to 2 percent of men (Royce 1989). Other studies show that in families where alcoholism is a problem for male spouses, women remain in the relationship in 90 percent of such situations. In families where alcoholism is a problem for female spouses, men, however, remain in the relationship only 10 percent of the time (Ackerman 1983). It is estimated that six million women are addicted to drugs other than alcohol, with the largest increases among younger women.

This drug use has also resulted in increases in AIDS, prostitution, and homelessness among women.

Alcoholism and chemical dependency also affect children seriously. Increased attention has been given recently to the large numbers of infants born addicted or impaired because of their mothers' addiction or misuse of either alcohol or drugs. Five thousand infants born each year to addicted mothers in the United States have fetal alcohol syndrome, now the third leading cause of birth defects associated with mental retardation. Thousands more babies born to mothers who abused alcohol or other drugs during their pregnancies have less serious disabilities.

Child welfare advocates are suggesting that the United States has not yet begun to experience the long-term effects of having such a large number of children born to women who are drug addicts. A recent study by the Alcohol and Drug and Mental Health Administration, for example, found that 11 percent of all babies born in twenty-eight cities in the United States were exposed to some type of illicit drug. One urban Michigan hospital identified 43 percent of infants delivered there as being prenatally exposed to drugs (Select Committee on Children and Youth 1990). Estimates are that it will cost the United States $15 billion each year to care for addicts' offspring during the first five years of their lives, to prepare them to enter the public schools (Associated Press, December 1, 1989).

As abuse of drugs becomes more widespread, the implications are becoming more obvious, more costly, and of greater concern. Costs not only include intervention for alcoholics and substance abusers, but also lost productivity, motor vehicle losses from accidents, and property losses from violent crimes. However, cost estimates typically do not include personal costs such as physical and emotional injury and loss of life. The economic costs of alcoholism and alcohol abuse in the United States have been estimated at $120 billion in 1986 by the University of California at Berkeley School of Health. In 1987 the National Institute of Drug Abuse estimated that $80 billion was lost from the abuse of other drugs. Furthermore, Americans spent an estimated $71.9 billion on alcohol, $60 billion on cocaine, and $80 billion on other drugs in 1987 (Royce 1989). General Motors estimates that consumers pay an additional $242 for each automobile that they purchase due to workers who have problems with substance abuse. Other studies have shown that productivity also declines for family members of the abuser: absenteeism rates have been found to be five times greater than for persons from families without substance abuse problems (Royce 1989).

Why Substance Abuse Occurs

Reasons why substance abuse occurs parallel reasons why emotional problems occur among individuals. New research suggests that there are genetic factors associated with substance abuse. Some researchers believe, for example, that substances are metabolized or broken down differently for some individuals, resulting in an inability of the body to eliminate some chemicals that then not only build up in the body but also serve as stimulants for even greater use when the addictive substance is used again.

Other researchers suggest that for some individuals, substance abuse is a form of self-medication, or a way for them to attempt to regulate their emotions or the pain that they are experiencing. People who have been sexually abused, have experienced a significant personal loss or series of losses, or are depressed may use alcohol or other drugs to moderate their moods or try to deaden the pain they are experiencing (See Box 5–1). Other substance abuse experts suggest that people use drugs to experience excitement, fit in with peers, alleviate pressure, or try to function better; others see it as behavior learned from family members.

There probably are multiple reasons why persons use drugs, just as there are multiple reasons for other mental health problems. For example, research suggests that a person with a biological or chemical predisposition to abuse drugs who is also experiencing personal or family stress is more at risk to become an alcoholic or an addict than others. Further research is needed to learn more about the factors associated with substance abuse so that prevention and treatment programs can be more effective.

DEVELOPMENTAL DISABILITIES

Generally, the term **developmental disability** refers to developmental problems, such as mental retardation or cerebral palsy, that developed before adulthood. Although, in the past, these persons were often referred to as "mentally re-tarded" or "mentally handicapped," the terms *developmentally disabled* or *physically challenged* are now preferred because they are viewed as less neg-ative. In 1984 the U.S. Congress passed the Developmental Disabilities Assis-tance and Bill of Rights Act (P.L. 98-527), which defined developmental disability as follows:

> A severe, chronic disability of a person which (a) is attributable to a mental or physical impairment or combination of mental and physical impairments; (b) is manifested before the person attains age twenty-two; (c) is likely to continue indefinitely; (d) results in substantial functional limitations in three or more of the following areas of major life activity: (i) self-care, (ii) receptive and ex-pressive language, (iii) learning, (iv) mobility, (v) self-direction, (vi) capacity for independent living, and (vii) economic self-sufficiency; and (e) reflects the per-son's need for a combination and sequence of special, interdisciplinary, or generic care, treatment, or other services which are of lifelong or extended duration and are individually planned and coordinated. (P.L. 98-527, Title V, 1984)

Although over 75 percent of those classified as having developmental dis-abilities are **mentally retarded,** other individuals also may be so classified due to cerebral palsy; epilepsy; autism; spina bifida; or speech, hearing, vision or orthopedic handicaps. Other individuals may have learning disabilities, such as dyslexia, a reading disability where symbols are perceived differently than they are, or attention deficit disorder, a disability that results in hyperactivity and an inability to pay attention to an activity for a reasonable amount of time. Of those individuals classified as mentally retarded, 75 percent are only mildly retarded and can be educated to function fairly independently or with some supervision; 20 percent are moderately retarded; and only 5 percent are pro-

Box 5-1   A Young Adult's Story

Three years of drinking pushed a seemingly outgoing, good student to the depths of depression and despair. This is her story:

I began ninth grade excited about starting high school. I was like most other teenagers—I wanted to make good grades and be accepted by my teachers and peers. The peers I sought out were popular, cheerleaders and on the student council, and they seemed to know everyone. I liked being included in their parties and other activities.

My mom asked me questions about my friends and the rules their parents had for them, but she usually let me go with them if I was waiting for her when she picked me up. At games and the other teen hangouts there was lots of drinking and it looked like people drinking were having a good time. One night I stayed over at a friend's house and we went to a party. When I was offered a beer I drank it. When the alcohol hit my body, I found I wanted more. That night I drank 7 beers. I was 14 years old.

After that, I drank almost every weekend. I drank to be accepted, escape day-to-day pressures of my home and school life, and forget the pain from some experiences I had while growing up. When I drank, I usually laughed and clowned around a lot. People told me how much fun I was and what a great sense of humor I had. I felt relaxed and accepted when I drank.

I continued to drink on weekends, and my activities with my friends usually centered around sneaking beer or other alcohol from our parents' pantries or having older friends buy it for us. We drank it at games, parties, or at each other's houses after the parents were asleep. Soon we went to the mall to meet older guys. We had no sense of risk. Our parents dropped us at the mall, we hopped in some guy's car to go to a party where everyone was drunk. Then we were dropped back at the mall in time for our parents to pick us up. We sprayed ourselves with perfume, chewed gum, and somehow managed to hide our drinking from our parents most of the time. I often felt guilty about my drinking and worried about what my parents would do if they found out, but I also enjoyed it. I felt grown up, and my friends enjoyed telling me how hilarious I had been with all of my antics. Boys paid a lot of attention to me and I discovered that it was much easier to relate to them when I had been drinking.

I became more popular and was elected to the student council. I rationalized that drinking even helped my grades, since the few times I decided that I was drinking too much and stopped for a week or two, I became depressed and my grades went down. I became more involved in school activities, got a part-time job at the mall, and partied even more. When my parents confronted me with their suspicions about my drinking, I either managed to convince them that everyone else was drinking except me or to tell them that I had a little bit now and then, but didn't every teenager?

During my junior year I made the dance team. I thought all my feelings of insecurity and my drive to fit in would be over, and that I could slow down my drinking. To my surprise, being on the dance team meant even more pressure. I had to maintain my popularity, be more involved in school activities, and work even harder to be sure that I wasn't surpassed by the many girls who I thought were almost all smarter, prettier, and had more personality than I did. Soon I was drinking in the locker room in the morning before dance practice "just to wake me up and help me stretch better," in the parking lot or the bathroom after lunch "just to make it through the afternoon," or at my job "just to make it until closing," and always on the weekends.

I still could hide my drinking from teachers and my parents. I sat in the back of the classroom, answered questions, and did my homework and handed it in on time. I always gave my parents a plausible explanation what I would be doing when I went out and I was lucky enough to be where I said I would be when they checked up on me. When I didn't drink a lot, I came home at or before my curfew.When I did drink a lot, I stayed overnight at friends' homes. I began blacking out

continued on next page

at parties and waking up at a friends' house and not remembering how I got there. I rode with drivers who were drunk and I would drive when I was drunk too. I also began to get involved with a lot of guys who I never would have gotten involved with if I had been sober. I got really scared about getting pregnant, since I knew someone could take advantage of me during my blackouts.

At that point my drinking wasn't fun anymore, but I couldn't stop. In fact, I began drinking more and more. It was nothing for me to drink 16 or 17 cans of beer all by myself in one night. All of my friends could still drink and enjoy it but it started getting me in trouble. My grades went down and I started skipping school. I became edgy and worried about everything. I started having fights with my friends and my family over little things. The drinking was controlling me. The more I drank, the worse I felt, and the worse I felt, the more I needed to drink to ease my pain. What had started out to be fun was now completely out of my control.

During the summer my parents suspected something was really wrong. I started seeing a psychologist, and both she and my parents tried to convince me that my drinking was a problem and that I was using it to escape the pain I had about some of the things that had happened in my life. I got angry at them and refused to see the psychologist. I began to rebel more and more. One night a party I was at turned into a brawl. I got knocked out when I tried to break up a fight. I left with a friend and a guy I barely knew. I woke up the next morning in the guy's apartment, and couldn't remember what had happened. Driving home I was still so drunk that I had to stop and get out of the car to read the street signs and I was only a half mile from home. I told my parents we'd stayed up all night talking at my girlfriend's house and I slept the whole next day.

Gradually I stopped caring what everyone thought of me and trying to hide my drinking from my parents. Finally one weekend I stayed out all night when I had a midnight curfew. When I came home and got grounded, I ran away and stayed with a friend for 3 days, mostly drinking. When my friend went to work, I got a six-pack of beer and drank it alone. When I came home my parents grounded me for a month and took away my car. They told me I had to see the psychologist. I was going to leave home for good, but I knew that I had reached a dead end and that my life was out of control. I didn't care about myself, my parents, or anything any more. Life had no purpose.

When I was confronted with my drinking again, I decided to enter a treatment program. I was tired of fighting, and at that time I thought that anything, even treatment, would be better than living at home and being nagged about my behavior. I now realize that entering treatment was the most important risk I have ever taken. The 6 weeks that I spent there were some of the hardest days of my life, but they were also some of the best. I was able to get rid of some of the pain, hurt, and anger that I had stored up for so many years. I learned new ways to communicate, share my feelings, and how to have fun while I was sober instead of drunk. I realized not only had I hurt myself, but also my family and other people who cared about me. My whole family took part in my treatment and we all grew together. They began going to Alanon while I went to Alcoholics Anonymous.

After I got out of treatment, I continued to attend AA regularly. I had found a place where I fit in. AA members understood how I felt and where I was coming from. Each day got better for me. I became more content and gained self-confidence. I also found the peace I had never had before. I got in touch with myself and met many wonderful people in the process. Today, I am a recovering alcoholic and have now been sober for two years. Finding sobriety at 17 has meant a whole new world for me. I have fallen in love with a wonderful person who understands my need for sobriety, and we are building our life together. My family and I enjoy being together. I am a college sophomore and plan to attend graduate school and work with children. I have goals and a sense of purpose I didn't have before. Although life is still difficult, I have learned to take things as they come, one day at a time. I am grateful that I had the courage to change myself.

Source: *Journal.* Anonymous student, University of Texas at Austin, 1991.

foundly retarded and need constant care and supervision. A number of factors are associated with developmental disabilities:

○ Hereditary and Fetal Developmental Factors—Factors such as metabolic disorders, brain malfunctions, or chromosomal abnormalities can result in disabilities such as Tay-Sachs disease and Down's syndrome.

○ Prenatal Factors—Chemical and alcohol addiction, radiation, and infections such as rubella (a form of measles) can result in disabilities, as can fetal malnutrition if mothers do not receive adequate prenatal care.

○ Perinatal Factors—Premature birth, trauma at birth, and infections transmitted during birth, such as herpes, can cause disabilities.

○ Postnatal Factors—Postnatal infections such as meningitis, trauma as a result of automobile accidents or child abuse, lack of oxygen during illness or an accident, and nutritional deficiencies can result in developmental disabilities. Environmental factors, such as lead poisoning, parents with severe emotional problems, or parental deprivation, also are important factors that often lead to developmental disabilities. Children who do not receive appropriate nurturance, especially during their early years, are often developmentally delayed; and if intervention does not occur soon enough, mental retardation, learning disabilities, or other types of problems can result and may be permanent.

Specific causes of developmental disabilities often cannot be identified. Many parents who give birth to children with such problems often spend a great deal of time—sometimes their entire lives—blaming themselves because their children have disabilities. Research has enabled the early identification of many types of disabilities, such as phenylketonuria (PKU), which results in retardation. A simple test at birth can allow for immediate treatment, which has virtually eliminated this problem in most western countries. More attention needs to be given to understanding how and why such disabilities occur.

CHANGING VIEWS TOWARD EMOTIONAL AND DEVELOPMENTAL PROBLEMS

The early treatment of individuals with mental health and substance abuse problems and developmental disabilities depended primarily on the reactions of the individuals' families. In most cases, individuals remained at home and were at the mercy of family members. Although, in some instances, individuals were treated humanely, many mentally ill and retarded persons were chained in attics and cellars, and sometimes they were killed. When there were no family members to provide for them, they were often transported to the next town and abandoned. Later, almshouses were established (see Chapter 2). Some mentally ill or developmentally disabled individuals were placed in jails if they were deemed too dangerous for the almshouse. Most alcoholics also were jailed, with their family members sent to almshouses.

The Pennsylvania colony's hospital, established in 1751 for the sick poor and "the reception and care of lunatics," was the first hospital in the United

States that provided care for the mentally ill, although treatment of mentally ill patients was little better than it had been in jails and almshouses. Individuals deemed mentally ill were assigned to hospital cellars and placed in bolted cells, where they were watched over by attendants carrying whips, which were used freely. Sightseers paid admission fees on Sundays to watch the cellar activities.

From Inhumane to Moral Treatment

During the late 1700s, people throughout the world began to seek better approaches to address the needs of the mentally ill. What mental health historians describe as the first of four revolutions in caring for the mentally ill actually began in France rather than the United States, with a shift from inhumane to moral treatment. Philippe Pinel, director of two hospitals in Paris, ordered "striking off the chains" of the patients in 1793, first at the Bicêtre Hospital for the Insane in Paris. Pinel advocated the establishment of a philosophy of **moral treatment,** which included offering patients hope, guidance, and support, and treatment with respect in small family-like institutions.

The moral treatment movement soon spread to America. Benjamin Rush, a signer of the Declaration of Independence, wrote the first American text on psychiatry, advocating that the mentally ill had a moral right to humane treatment. However, not until the 1840s, through the efforts of Dorothea Dix, a schoolteacher, did the mentally ill in the United States actually begin to receive more humane treatment (see Chapter 2). Dix became aware of the plight of the mentally ill through teaching Sunday School for a group of patients in a Massachusetts hospital. Appalled by what she saw, she gave speeches, wrote newspaper articles, and met with government officials to bring attention to the inhumane and abusive treatment she observed in the many facilities she visited. As a result of her efforts, a bill was introduced in Congress to use the proceeds from the sale of western land to purchase land for use in caring for the mentally ill. This bill was vetoed by President Franklin Pierce, which set a precedent for the federal government's refusal to be involved in state social services programs that remained unchanged until the New Deal era.

Refusing to give up, Dix turned her efforts to the individual states. By 1900, thirty-two states had established state mental hospitals. However, Dix and other advocates for the humane treatment of the mentally ill soon had additional cause for concern. What began in many hospitals as humane treatment changed as hospitals became overused and overcrowded, admitting all who couldn't be cared for elsewhere. State insane asylums became warehouses, commonly described as snake pits.

Dorothea Dix and her group of reformers demanded that strict guidelines be established for the treatment of mental hospital patients. Again, states responded, and expanding facilities soon were heavily bound by detailed procedures. Although abuse and neglect of patients decreased dramatically, the guidelines left little room for innovation, and until the 1960s, patients in state mental hospitals received little more than custodial care. In the years immediately following the Dix reform, nearly half of patients who had been admitted were released, often only to make room for new admissions and to alleviate overcrowding. Once the population stabilized somewhat, however, long stays in mental hospitals became the norm, with discharge rates falling to as low as 5 percent. Although these state institutions had been intended to house a transitory patient population, the absence of a treatment technology forced the retention of many patients until their deaths. The desire for single state facilities to house large populations of mentally ill patients resulted in their location in rural areas, where land was less expensive and expansion of facilities possible. Thus, the state mental hospital became—and, in many instances, still is—the "principal industry" in the area where it is located.

Although much less attention was given to the developmentally disabled, institutionalization became prevalent for this group as well. During the 1850s, many states established state training schools for the retarded, which housed persons who ranged from profoundly to mildly retarded.

More Reforms Needed   In spite of the efforts of Dorothea Dix and others, overcrowded conditions and neglect of the mentally ill and developmentally disabled still existed in many state facilities. Facilities continued to be overcrowded, with large numbers of immigrant residents. Although the staff could provide moral treatment, love, and respect to some residents, it was difficult for many to transfer this philosophy to foreigners. Also it was increasingly hard to get medical staff willing to work in state mental institutions. Graduates from medical school were repelled by the foreigners, alcoholics, and severely disturbed individuals who populated the institutions.

A second effort to reform conditions in state mental hospitals was undertaken in the early 1900s by Clifford Beers, a Yale graduate from a wealthy family who had been hospitalized in a Connecticut mental hospital for three years. After his release, Beers almost immediately suffered a relapse and was hospitalized for a second time. During this stay, he began to formulate plans for more effective treatment of the mentally ill. He kept careful notes of the maltreatment he received from physicians and the well-intended but ineffective care he received from caretakers. After his release in 1908, Beers wrote a book, *A Mind that Found Itself,* which was intended to be a parallel to *Uncle Tom's Cabin* but focused on conditions in mental hospitals. This book led to the formation of state mental health advocacy organizations, such as the Connecticut Society for Mental Health. Later, state organizations formed the National Association for Mental Hygiene, which became a lobbying force for the continual reform of state hospitals and the development of alternative systems of care.

The Introduction of Psychoanalysis

What is described as the second revolution in the mental health field occurred in the early 1900s with the introduction of Sigmund Freud's writings and the use of **psychoanalysis** in the United States. Professional mental health workers trained in Freud's techniques attempted to gain cooperation and insight through verbal or nonverbal communication with patients, seeing them at regular intervals over long periods of time.

The first social workers hired to work in state mental hospitals actually were hired before Freud's teachings were introduced into the United States. Their primary role was to provide therapy to clients, but it was based on a limited knowledge about what the therapy should entail. As psychoanalysis gained popularity in the United States, psychiatric social workers, like others working with the mentally ill, were quick to adopt a system of therapy that was reportedly much more effective than the often haphazard treatment they were using. In 1905, Massachusetts General Hospital in Boston and Bellevue Hospital in New York City hired psychiatric social workers to provide therapy to patients. However, because of staff shortages and the large number of patients, few patients actually received psychotherapy, which requires highly trained therapists, fairly verbal patients who speak the same language as the therapist, and long hours of treatment to be effective. In most instances, psychotherapy as a treatment approach for dealing with mental health problems was used more in outpatient facilities, either private practices established by psychiatrists or child guidance centers, which were established in the United States in the 1920s and focused primarily on promoting healthy relationships among middle-class children and their parents.

The Shift to Community Mental Health Programs

The third revolution in mental health, a shift in the care of individuals with mental health problems and developmental disabilities from institutions to local communities, began in the 1940s and still continues. Public interest in mental health issues and treatment of the mentally ill remained at a fairly constant level until the 1940s and the onset of World War II. The military draft brought mental health problems to the attention of Congress. Military statistics showed that 12 percent of all men drafted into the Armed Forces were rejected for psychiatric reasons. Of the total number rejected for any reason, 40 percent were rejected for psychiatric reasons (Felix 1967). Serious questions began to be raised about the magnitude of mental health problems within the entire U.S. population.

Initial Postwar Developments   After the war ended, state hospitals, which had been neglected during the war, again began to receive attention. Albert Deutsch wrote a series of exposés on state mental hospitals, later published as *Shame of the States* (1949). This stimulated a series of similar books, one of which was made into a film, *The Snake Pit*. The attention resulted in a widespread public outcry and created a climate for reform. In 1946, Congress passed the National Mental Health Act, which enabled states to establish community mental health programs aimed at preventing and treating mental health problems. The act also provided for the establishment of research and educational programs and mandated that each state establish a single state entity to receive and allocate federal funds provided for by the act.

In 1949 the U.S. Governors' Conference sponsored a study of mental health programs in the United States. That same year, Congress created the **National Institute of Mental Health (NIMH)**, the first federal entity to address mental health concerns. In 1955, with impetus from a working coalition of leadership from the National Institute of Mental Health and the **National Association of Mental Health (NAMH)**, university medical schools and schools of social work, and organizations of former mental patients and their families, the National

Mental Health Study Act was passed. This act signified the belief among both mental health experts and government officials that large custodial institutions could not deal effectively with mental illness. The act authorized an appropriation to the Joint Commission on Mental Illness and Health to study and make recommendations in the area of mental health policy. The commission published a series of documents in the late 1950s and early 1960s calling for reform. Commission reports called for a doubling of expenditures within five years and tripling within ten years in mental health expenditures to be used for comprehensive community mental health facilities, increased recruitment and training programs for staff, and long-term mental health research. The commission suggested expanding treatment programs for the acutely mentally ill in all facilities while limiting the number of patients at each hospital to no more than a thousand inpatients.

The commission also recommended that the majority of emphasis be placed on community programs, including preventive, outpatient treatment, and aftercare services that could reduce the number of institutionalized patients and allow for their successful treatment within their local communities. The group also recommended that less burden be placed on states to provide services and that the federal role be increased in addressing mental health needs. President John F. Kennedy also made mental health issues a high priority and strongly supported the efforts of the commission, becoming the first U.S. president to publicly address mental health concerns. Furthermore, the public was beginning to see the effectiveness of **psychotropic drugs** in the treatment of the mentally ill and consequently was becoming more receptive to the idea of community care.

Community Mental Health Initiatives Congress passed the Mentally Retarded Facilities and Community Mental Health Center Construction Act in 1963. This act provided major funding to build community mental health centers and community facilities for the developmentally disabled. This and subsequent legislation mandated that centers built with federal funds must be located in areas accessible to the populations they serve and must provide the following basic service components: inpatient services, outpatient services, partial hospitalization (day, night, or weekend care), emergency services, consultation, and educational services. By 1980 there were over 700 community mental health centers in the United States partially funded with federal funds. The intent of the community mental health care legislation was to replace the custodial care within a large-scale institution with therapeutic care within a community through the provision of a comprehensive array of services available locally. Emphasis was to be placed on **deinstitutionalization,** or keeping individuals from placement in hospitals whenever possible, and on least restrictive alternatives, or providing the **least restrictive environment** appropriate. The 1978 President's Commission on Mental Health defined the purpose of providing a least restrictive environment as "maintaining the greatest degree of freedom, self-determination, autonomy, dignity, and integrity of body, mind, and spirit for the individual while he or she participates in treatment or receives services" (44). Such programs were not only deemed cost effective, as many individuals could work at paid jobs and live in situations requiring less expense than an institution, but also were seen as increasing individual self-esteem and feelings of contributing to society.

The community mental health center legislation, coupled with the use of psychotropic drugs, significantly reduced the number of individuals in mental institutions. In 1955, 77.4 percent of all patients received inpatient services; 22.6 percent received outpatient services. By 1980 only 28 percent received inpatient services and 72 percent, outpatient services (Mechanic, 1980). Emphasis on treatment had shifted from custodial care, shock treatment, or long-term psychotherapy to short-term treatment, group therapy, help to individuals in coping with their environments, and drug treatment.

Programs for Developmental Disabilities and Alcohol and Substance Abuse Efforts to improve conditions for the developmentally disabled continued to focus on institutionalization through the 1950s. Greater attention shifted to this population when parent advocates in 1950 formed the Association for Retarded Children, which later became the Association for Retarded Citizens. This group has been instrumental in advocating for national and state legislation and improved conditions for the developmentally disabled. Additional attention to the needs of the disabled came during President Kennedy's administration. Kennedy's retarded sister, Rosemary, received extensive publicity, and he established a Presidential Panel on Mental Retardation during his term, which called for additional research and the development of a system that provided continuity in caring for the disabled. The Mentally Retarded Facilities and Community Mental Health Center Construction Act, passed in 1963, included funding for research and facilities for this population.

Initial efforts to address problems of alcoholism and substance abuse were aimed at moral rehabilitation, prohibition, and temperance. The most significant breakthrough in the alcohol field came in 1935 with the establishment of **Alcoholics Anonymous (AA),** a self-help group for alcoholics. AA began in Akron, Ohio, when a New York stockbroker named Bill W. and an Akron physician named Dr. Bob met and discovered they could maintain sobriety by supporting one another and following a program philosophy, which has since been incorporated into the twelve steps of AA. During the next several decades, as AA continued to grow in numbers and in popularity, various physicians also developed research and intervention efforts that shifted attention from the moral concept of alcoholism to the disease concept. The formation of education and advocacy groups such as the National Council on Alcoholism in 1944 also aided in increased attention to alcoholics' problems.

However, much-needed federal attention to the problem of alcoholism did not occur until 1970 when Senator Harold Hughes of Iowa, a recovering alcoholic at the time of his election, advocated for the passage of the Comprehensive Alcohol Abuse and Alcoholism Prevention, Treatment and Rehabilitation Act. This act provided financial assistance to states and communities to establish treatment, education, research, and training programs and established the National Institute on Alcohol Abuse and Alcoholism. The act also provided for the withdrawal of federal funding from any hospital that refused to treat alcoholics.

AVAILABILITY OF RESOURCES AND RESPONSIBILITY FOR CARE

Perhaps the overriding issue in the mental health, substance abuse, and developmental disabilities arena is how to manage limited resources to best address the needs of those who require services. The mentally ill and developmentally disabled, unable to advocate well for themselves, often fail to receive their just share of funding. Public attitudes about alcoholism and substance abuse as moral issues also have continued to limit funding for substance abuse programs.

Many of the gains in mental health and developmental disabilities programs established in the 1960s have been lost as governments battle over who should have the responsibility for the care of the mentally ill and the disabled and what the level of services should be. Although attitudes have changed significantly since colonial times, much change must yet be made.

Deinstitutionalization

Many states and local communities have successfully moved large numbers of mentally ill and developmentally disabled individuals from institutions to community programs and facilities, but some are reluctant to do so. Some states are under court order, as a result of suits brought by citizen advocate groups, to move more quickly to deinstitutionalize. Reasons for resistance to deinstitutionalization include inadequate funds and other resources, economic disruption caused by shutting down institutions in areas where they are the major source of employment, and lack of appropriate facilities at the community level to house individuals who could be deinstitutionalized.

In some instances, deinstitutionalization has resulted in individuals, like Joanna in the opening vignette, falling through the cracks. Many individuals who could function well within an institutional setting do not do as well in a community setting, particularly with little day-to-day supervision. Deinstitutionalization also means decentralization and the potential for both shoddy standards of maintenance and the failure to provide follow-up services to clients. This decentralization points to the necessity for a case-management system, where social workers or other mental health professionals are responsible for a specific number of clients, ensuring that their living conditions are appropriate, that they are maintaining health care and taking medication, and that their other needs are being met.

Some deinstitutionalization programs, however, have been extremely successful. For example, George Fairweather, a noted mental health expert, has established a series of community programs for individuals who previously have been institutionalized. Called Fairweather lodges, these facilities provide supervised living for individuals in small groups, with residents sharing housekeeping chores. Residents also work in the community, with a lodge coordinator who ensures that residents are successful in the workplace. The coordinator also facilitates support group meetings for residents' families as well as for lodge members. The recidivism rate for this program has been extremely low. Although some communities that have established lodge programs were reluctant to do so at first, they now view the lodges and their residents as important parts of the community. Cottages for disabled persons and recovering substance abusers have also met with success.

Wide-ranging Program Alternatives   Other beneficial community programs that have been established include partial hospitalization, where persons attend hospital day programs and receive treatment, returning to their homes at night or to work in the community and return to the hospital for treatment and monitoring in the evenings. Day programs for the developmentally disabled that provide education, supervision, and, in some instances, limited employment opportunities have also been successful. Halfway houses and refurbished apartment complexes for the mentally ill, developmentally disabled, and recovering substance abusers, with resident supervisors who oversee and lend support to residents, have been especially successful. Many persons have been able to return to their own homes. Some go to adult or special children's daycare centers during the day while parents work, returning home at night. Respite-care programs established in some communities, using trained volunteers, make it possible for family members to find substitute caretakers so they can occasionally have some time away from the person to regain their energies.

Community-based alternatives for the elderly have also received greater attention. Many residents of both state mental hospitals and state schools for the developmentally disabled once were, in fact, elderly persons who could function in a less restrictive environment if they had someone to care for them. A number of elderly individuals have been successfully placed in nursing homes, often in integrated facilities that take people without mental health or disability problems. Other alternatives such as those mentioned in the preceding paragraph have also been developed for older people.

The passage of Public Law 94-142, the Education for All Handicapped Children Act (1975), also has made deinstitutionalization more feasible for children. This law mandates that public school systems provide educational and social services for children with a range of disabilities, including emotional disturbances, mental retardation, and speech, vision, hearing, or learning disabilities. Parents and educators are required to develop jointly an individualized educational plan (IEP) for each child. The law also requires each child to be placed in the least restrictive setting possible, with the intent that children with disabilities and emotional problems be placed in the regular classroom to the extent possible and in special education classes as a last alternative.

Many deinstitutionalized individuals have difficulty adjusting to community living, particularly when adequate programs are not available. As one former state hospital resident commented, "At the hospital, I had hot coffee every morning, three meals a day and a warm bed every night, and people to talk to if I wanted to talk. Here, I have the street and that's about it. No food on a regular basis, no bed, and no one to talk to. I didn't have a bad life at the hospital." (Iscoe, 1982) The biggest problem with deinstitutionalization is the fact that large numbers of individuals have been released from institutions to communities that have been unable to respond quickly enough to develop programs at the community level to meet their needs adequately.

Homelessness

Increased attention has been given to the rising number of homeless persons in the United States. Advocates of more effective services for the mentally ill, the developmentally disabled, and the chemically dependent suggest that dein-stitutionalization and the lack of community services have resulted in a significant increase in homelessness among these three groups. Recent estimates show that approximately 30 percent of the homeless are mentally ill and about 15 percent of homeless women and 45 percent of homeless men have serious problems with alcoholism or drug abuse (Cohen, 1989; Koroloff & Anderson 1989). In one study researchers tracked individuals released from a state hospital in a large Ohio metropolitan area for a six-month period after their release, and they found that 36 percent became homeless during this period. Of that group, approximately 75 percent were chronically mentally ill and 15 percent were both mentally ill and substance abusers (Cohen, 1989). Many homeless mentally ill people have serious cognitive disturbances, like Joanna, and are out of touch with reality, unaware of where they are going or where they have been. Their most frequent contacts with community resources are with the police and emergency psychiatric facilities. They most often remain on the streets, extremely vulnerable, until they are unable to function and then are rehospitalized. For many, their lives become a pattern of homelessness and hospitalization. The major response to date to homelessness has been the McKinney Act of 1988, which established limited funding for services and shelter for homeless people who are mentally ill and/or chemically dependent. The act also established the National Resource Center on Homeless and the Mentally Ill, which is compiling information and research about the problem and providing assistance to states and communities in strengthening or developing programs for these populations.

Suicide

Suicide is a serious mental health problem in the United States, which has a higher suicide rate than many western countries. In 1990, suicide was the ninth leading cause of death among all age groups and the second leading cause of death among teens 15–19. The teenage suicide rate has tripled in the last 30 years (Lipman 1990). Suicide is increasing at a faster rate among the elderly than any age group, with a 60 percent increase in suicides among persons over 65 in the past decade. In 1985, 25 percent of all suicides in the U.S. were among persons over 65 (Zastrow and Kirst-Ashman 1990). Females are more likely than males to make suicide attempts. However, once males attempt suicide, they are more likely to succeed because their methods are usually more lethal.

While the majority of persons contemplate suicide at some point in their lives, persons who make suicide attempts are likely to have experienced one or more significant losses in their lives—the loss of a parent, sibling, spouse, close friend, good health, or a job. They also feel helpless and hopeless and are experiencing so much pain that they do not see any options other than ending their pain. Loneliness and isolation and lack of a stable support system and environment are other significant factors associated with persons who attempt suicide.

Persons at risk to attempt suicide also often abuse alcohol and drugs, since they may turn to these as ways to ease their pain. Because alcohol and some other types of drugs are depressants, these substances tend to make a depressed person more depressed, as well as impairing the person's ability to think rationally. Poor health, particularly among the elderly, who may not see any hope of getting better and may not want to be an emotional or financial burden to anyone, is another important factor. Other factors that suggest a person is serious about suicide include previous attempts, a change from a depressed, hopeless perspective to suddenly seeming to get better, and giving possessions away. Suicide threats by any person should be taken seriously. Persons dealing with someone who is suicidal should locate appropriate resources that can assess the mental health of the person and intervene appropriately.

Legal Rights of Clients

Mental health and developmental disabilities experts have identified clients' rights as the next revolution in the mental health/disabilities arena. With the increased number of options available to individuals with mental health and development disabilities problems—including placement in less restrictive facilities, new counseling techniques, and drug treatment—a number of legal issues also have surfaced. On one hand, do individuals have the right to refuse treatment? On the other hand, if treatment technology or knowledge about more appropriate types of treatment exists but such treatment is not available, do individuals have the right to demand treatment? In some states, class-action suits have been brought on behalf of patients in institutions demanding that they be placed in less restrictive settings and receive treatment unavailable to them in the institutions.

The NAMH and other advocacy organizations have forced the U.S. court system to establish a series of patients'/clients' rights, which include the right to treatment, the right to privacy and dignity, and the right to the least restrictive condition necessary to achieve the purpose of commitment. The courts also have determined that persons cannot be deemed incompetent to manage their affairs; to hold professional, occupational, or vehicular licenses; to marry and obtain divorces; to register to vote; or to make wills solely because of admission or commitment to a hospital.

Patients in mental institutions have the same rights to visitation and telephone communication as patients in other hospitals, as well as the right to send sealed mail. They also have the right to freedom from excessive medication or physical restraint and experiments and the right to wear their own clothes and worship within the dictates of their own religion. Finally, patients also have the right to receive needed treatment outside of a hospital environment (Mechanic 1980).

Most states make it difficult to commit a person to an institution involuntarily. In many states, however, a law enforcement agency can order that a person be detained in a state institution for a limited period without a court hearing. At that time, a court hearing must be held, and a nonvoluntary commitment can be ordered only if the person is found to be dangerous to himself or herself or to others. Individuals who are not really capable of functioning on their own but who are not found to be dangerous often are released to be on their own. Because of this system, many individuals receive what some mental health experts have termed "the revolving-door approach" to treatment, getting picked up on the streets because they are too incapacitated to function on their own, admitted to the hospital, given medication and food and rest, and then released quickly because they legally cannot be held any longer against their wishes.

Children's right to refuse or to demand treatment is an issue that has received even less attention. In some instances, parents commit children to institutions because they do not want to or are unable to care for them. In other instances, the child's problems are the result of family problems that the parents do not want to accept. Currently, both the rights of individuals to avoid treatment and the rights of individuals to receive treatment are unclear and need to be clarified further by the U.S. Supreme Court.

Deinstitutionalization and Access to Care   The mental health field has been subjected to considerable shock within the last decade. Some individuals have argued that deinstitutionalization has resulted in the "ghettoization" of the mentally ill and disabled, meaning that communities in many instances have neither the funding nor the commitment to accept recently released patients, forcing them to subsist in subhuman conditions in poverty areas.

For example, two social workers from the Mental Health Law Project in Washington, D.C. visited Mr. Dixon, an individual who won his right to freedom in a class-action suit several months after he was transferred from the hospital to a boarding-care facility. They gave the following description of their observations in testimony before a Senate subcommittee:

> The conditions in which we found Mr. Dixon were unconscionable. Mr. Dixon's sleeping room was about halfway below ground level. The only windows in the room were closed and a plate in front of them made it impossible for Mr. Dixon to open them. There was no fan or air conditioner in the room. The room had no phone or buzzer. There would be no capacity for Mr. Dixon to contact someone in case of fire or emergency and this is significant in the face of the fact that Mr. Dixon is physically incapacitated. Mr. Dixon had not been served breakfast by 10 A.M.. He stated that meals were highly irregular and he would sometimes get so hungry waiting for lunch that he would ask a roomer to buy him sandwiches. He can remember having only one glass of milk during his entire stay at his new home. (U.S. Senate Subcommittee on Long-Term Care 1976, 715)

Shortly after this testimony, Dixon returned to St. Elizabeth Hospital in Washington, D.C. and was placed in a more suitable home. However, there are numerous cases similar to or worse than Mr. Dixon's.

A major problem for many persons who experience mental illness and/or developmental disability has been the denial of basic rights that others take for granted. The most significant piece of federal legislation for disabled persons, the Americans with Disabilities Act, was passed in July 1990. This act bans discrimination based on disabilities among private employers with a work force of more than fifteen persons or in public accommodations, public services, transportation, and telecommunications. The act also extends protections included in the 1964 Civil Rights Act to an estimated forty-three million people with physical and mental disabilities, including protections for persons with AIDS.

The quality of life for those who are mentally or developmentally impaired rests on the fate of federal and state legislation and funding, which decreased markedly during the 1980s. It is clear that we have both the technology and the capacity to maintain those with mental health problems and developmental disabilities in community settings. However, it also is clear that to meet the needs of these individuals adequately, substantial and continuing resources will be required.

Prevention versus Treatment

The issue of prevention versus treatment, especially within the confines of scarce resources, is a final consideration. Mental health experts address prevention issues at three levels: **primary prevention,** or prevention targeted at an entire population (e.g., prenatal care for all women to avoid developmental disabilities in their infants, parenting classes for all individuals to decrease mental health problems among children); **secondary prevention,** or prevention targeted at "at-risk" populations, those groups more likely to develop mental health problems than others (e.g., individual and group counseling for family members of schizophrenics or alcoholics); and **tertiary prevention,** or prevention targeted at individuals who have already experienced problems to prevent the problems from recurring (e.g., alcohol treatment groups or mental health programs for individuals who have attempted suicide).

Although numerous studies have shown that prevention programs are cost-effective ways to reduce developmental disabilities and mental health problems, it is difficult to create such programs when resources are scarce and so many individuals need treatment. Still, policymakers often focus on short-term solutions to problems, ignoring long-term and more favorable solutions. For example, although drug abuse prevention programs cost money in the short-term, the costs are far less than those to house individuals in institutions or to provide other extensive treatment programs.

Other mental health problems also are currently in the limelight. These include child physical and sexual abuse, suicide, and spouse abuse. These problems, while not new, are being recognized as having significant negative impacts on not only the individuals experiencing these problems but the entire family. This emphasis on intergenerational, cyclical problems has focused attention on the need to provide resources not only to children and their families experiencing these problems but to adults who grew up in such families (see Chapters 7 and 8).

Cultural and gender differences must also be considered when discussing mental health, mental illness, substance abuse, and developmental disabilities. The importance of gender and culture differences and societal and institutional racism and sexism and their impact on individuals must be considered in relation to several things: theories used to understand human behavior and to identify "normal" and "pathological" behavior; the use of diagnostic classification systems such as the *DSM-III-R*; the ways that practitioners view and relate to individuals with whom they interact; and the ways that mental health and developmental disabilities services are organized and delivered (Goldstein, 1987).

SOCIAL WORKERS: MENTAL HEALTH AND DEVELOPMENTAL DISABILITIES SERVICES

The first social workers credited with providing mental health services were the psychiatric social workers hired in New York and Boston mental hospitals in the early 1900s. They were responsible primarily for providing individual therapy to hospitalized mental patients and overseeing the care of discharged patients in foster homes. The mental health field expanded during the 1920s with the establishment of child guidance centers. At these centers, professionally trained social workers provided services to children and their families, most often psychotherapy with children on an individual basis.

Social workers today are involved in the total continuum of mental health and developmental disabilities services. They provide these services in a variety of settings, including traditional social services agencies—such as community mental health centers, child guidance centers, and public social services departments—as well as nontraditional settings—such as the courts, public schools and colleges and universities, hospitals and health clinics, child care centers, workplaces, and the military. While they fulfill a variety of roles, social workers currently form the largest group of psychotherapists in the United States.

Many social workers in mental health settings still provide individual counseling, including psychotherapy, to clients. However, instead of being referred to as psychiatric social workers, most are called **clinical social workers.** The majority of agencies that hire clinical social workers require that they meet the qualifications of the National Association of Social Workers Academy of Certified Social Workers (ACSW) certification or obtain appropriate state certification or licensing. In order to receive ACSW certification, an individual must have a master's degree in social work (MSW) from an accredited graduate school of social work, two years of social work experience under the direct supervision of an ACSW social worker, and a satisfactory score on a competency examination administered by the National Association of Social Workers. State licensing and certification programs have similar requirements but vary by state.

Many social work jobs also are available in the field of mental health and developmental disabilities for social workers with a bachelor's degree in social work (BSW). BSW social workers provide such services as crisis intervention for women and their children at battered-women's centers and operate suicide, runaway youth, child abuse, and other types of crisis hotlines (see Chapter 1). They also provide counseling to adolescents and their families at youth-serving agencies and work as social workers in state hospitals for the mentally ill and state schools for the developmentally disabled. In these settings they provide counseling to residents and serve as the primary professional involved with the individual's family.

Social workers also work in schools with troubled students and their families, not only providing individual counseling, family counseling, and family outreach, but also leading groups for children and their families in areas such as divorce, child maltreatment, ways of dealing with anger, techniques for getting along with adults, and alcohol and drug abuse. The reauthorization of P.L. 94-124 in 1990 included the use of social workers in the act's definition of social services. Many social workers are employed as counselors in alcohol and drug treatment programs. In fact, wherever mental health services are provided, social workers are likely to be employed. In the 1980s social workers comprised the largest professional group in public mental health services. Over half of the labor force employed in mental health–related jobs are social workers, and over one-third of the federally funded community mental health centers have social workers as their executive directors.

Social workers in the field of mental health fulfill a variety of functions. Many work in direct practice and clinical settings, providing therapy to individuals, groups, and families. Many mental health programs use a **multidisciplinary team approach**, hiring social workers, psychiatrists, physicians, psychologists, psychiatric nurses, child development specialists, and community aides, who work together to provide a multitude of services. Although social workers on multidisciplinary teams are involved in all aspects of treatment, most often they are given the responsibility of working with the client's family and the community in which the client resides. Because of their training from a systems/ ecological perspective, social workers usually are responsible for obtaining any resources needed from another agency and then ensuring that they are provided.

Many social workers in mental health settings provide case-management services, even if they are not employed in agencies that use multidisciplinary teams. Case managers are responsible for monitoring cases to ensure that clients receive needed services. A case manager does not necessarily provide all services directly but manages the case, coordinating others who provide the services. Many states are employing case managers at community mental health centers to oversee clients who are living in the local community, including those previously in institutions, who can function fairly independently with supervision and support. The case manager regularly meets with the client and contacts his or her family members, employers, and other appropriate individuals to ensure that the client is functioning adequately.

Still other social workers involved in the mental health field function as advocates. Organizations such as the Association for Retarded Citizens advocate for disabled persons on an individual basis, ensuring that they receive needed services. For example, a fourteen-year-old mentally retarded girl in a junior high school in an urban area was not receiving special education services and had been suspended several times for behavior problems. An advocate assigned to her arranged for the school district to provide the needed testing, saw that she was placed in a special education program that reduced her anxiety level and allowed her to function in a setting where she felt better about herself, and arranged for her to receive counseling. Advocates also work to ensure that groups of citizens are provided for, such as working within a community to ensure that housing is available to individuals with mental health problems and developmental disabilities. Social workers also function in the mental health arena as administrators and policymakers. Many direct mental health programs, and others work for government bodies at the local, state, and federal levels. They develop and advocate for legislation, develop policies and procedures to ensure that the needs of individuals with mental health and disability problems are met, and oversee governing bodies that monitor programs to ensure that services are provided.

New Trends in Services and Social Work Roles

Although the intent of the Community Mental Health Act was to provide services to individuals within specific geographic areas with the greatest need, particularly in poverty areas with diverse populations, studies have shown that in many instances persons receiving services largely have been middle class and white. The Commission on Mental Health established by President Jimmy Carter in the 1970s found that minorities, children, adolescents, and the elderly were underserved, as were residents of rural and poor urban areas. The commission also found that many services provided were inappropriate, particularly for those persons with differing cultural backgrounds and life styles. In many instances, when mental health centers were first established, they were directed by psychiatrists trained in psychotherapy or influenced by educational psychologists accustomed to providing testing and working with students. As a result, the staff members often were inexperienced at dealing with nonvoluntary clients, who did not want to be seen, failed to keep appointments, and were unfamiliar with the concept of one-hour therapy sessions. They often were also unequipped to deal with problems such as family violence, physical child abuse, and sexual abuse.

As programs developed, many centers became skilled at reaching special populations and developing more effective ways of addressing client needs. In the 1970s, centers were required to establish special children's mental health programs. Currently, many centers provide programs that address the needs of special populations such as abused or developmentally disabled children, individuals with alcohol and drug abuse problems, and Vietnam veterans. Mental health professionals also assist in the establishment of self-help groups, such as Alcoholics Anonymous, Adult Children of Alcoholics, Alateen, Parents Without Partners, and Parents Anonymous (a child abuse self-help program).

Today, social workers in mental health settings provide crisis intervention, operate telephone hotlines, conduct suicide prevention programs, and provide alcoholism and drug abuse services. Mental health services increasingly are provided in settings other than mental health centers, including churches, nursing homes, police departments, schools, child-care centers, the workplace, and health and medical settings. Problems addressed by mental health professionals have expanded to include loneliness and isolation, finances, spouse and child abuse, male–female relationships, housing, drugs, and alcohol. Mental health staff members have become more multidisciplinary, using teams of professionals, as well as volunteers. Increasingly, the focus of services has been on case management and short-term counseling.

SUMMARY

Services for individuals with mental health needs and developmental disabilities have changed significantly since colonial times. Four major revolutions have occurred in the area of mental health, including (1) the shift from inhumane to moral treatment; (2) the introduction of psychoanalytic therapy; (3) the move from institutions to community programs; and (4) the development of psychotropic drugs that effectively treat many types of mental health problems.

Current issues in the mental health field include scarce resources and conflict over the roles of federal, state, and local governments in providing services; the legal rights of clients and whether they should be able to refuse or demand treatment; attention to substance abuse and the expansion of private alcohol and drug abuse treatment facilities; increased services and advocacy for the developmentally disabled; the need for more effective services for women, minority groups, and individuals in rural settings; and additional services that address problems such as child maltreatment, alcohol and drug abuse, particularly for low-income groups, posttrauma stress for Vietnam veterans, and the special needs of rural and ethnic populations. Social workers currently play a critical role in the provision of mental health services, serving as therapists, advocates, case managers, administrators, and policymakers. These roles are expected to continue and expand in the future. With increased social change and the resulting stress to all individuals in our society, it is anticipated that the mental health needs of all individuals will become an even more important area of focus.

KEY TERMS

addiction
Alcoholics Anonymous
alcoholism
clinical social worker
deinstitutionalization
Diagnostic and Statistical Manual (DSM)
developmental disability
least restrictive environment
medical model
mental retardation

moral treatment
multidisciplinary team approach
National Association of Mental Health
National Institute of Mental Health
primary prevention
psychoanalysis
psychotropic drugs
secondary prevention
substance abuse
tertiary prevention

DISCUSSION QUESTIONS

1. Discuss the problems in defining *mental illness.*
2. Identify and briefly describe at least four frameworks that can be used in understanding mental health problems.
3. Identify the four major revolutions in the field of mental health.
4. Identify at least three different ways that substance abuse may be conceptualized.

5. Identify at least four ways that substance abuse is costly to society.

6. Discuss the meaning of the term *developmental disabilities*. How does this term contrast with previously used terminology to identify persons within this category?

7. Discuss the advantages and disadvantages of current efforts at deinstitutionalization.

8. Identify at least five areas in which social workers employed in mental health settings might work. What are some of the roles in which they might function?

9. Do you agree with Szasz's concept of mental health? Discuss your rationale for either agreeing or disagreeing.

REFERENCES

Ackerman, R. 1983. *Children of alcoholics.* 2nd edition. Oshtemo, MI: Learning Publications.

Alcoholics Anonymous World Services. 1976. *Alcoholics Anonymous.* N.Y.: Author.

American Psychiatric Association. *Diagnostic and statistical manual of mental disorders* 3d ed., rev. 1987. Washington, D.C.: Author.

Associated Press. 1989. "Epidemic" of drug babies will drain economy, Bentsen says. *Austin American Statesman* (Dec. 1, 1989), A4.

Cohen, M. 1989. Social work practice with homeless mentally ill people: Engaging the client. *Social Work* (Nov. 1989) 34: 6, 505–9.

Comprehensive Care Corporation. 1981. *Employee assistance programs: A dollar and sense issue.* Newport Beach, Calif.: Author.

Deutsch, A. 1949. *Shame of the states.* New York: Columbia University Press.

Felix, R. 1967. *Mental illness: Progress and prospects.* New York: Columbia University Press.

Goffman, E. 1961. *Asylums: Essays on the social situation of mental patients and other inmates.* Garden City, N.Y.: Doubleday.

Goldstein, E. 1987. Mental health and illness. In *Encyclopedia of social work,* 18th ed. vol. 2, 102–9. Silver Springs, Md.: National Association of Social Workers.

Iscoe, I. 1982. Summary of interviews with previous mental hospital patients. Austin, Tex: University of Texas at Austin Center for the Study of Human Development.

Kesey, K. 1962. *One flew over the cuckoo's nest.* New York: Basic Books.

Kirk, S. and Therrien, M. 1975. Community mental health myths and the fate of former hospitalized patients. *Psychiatry,* 38(8); 209–17.

Koroloff, N. and S. Anderson, 1989. Alcohol-free living centers: Hope for homeless addicts. *Social Work.* (Nov. 1989) 4:6, 497–504.

Lipman, L. 1990. Study finds U.S. youth on dangerous track. *Austin American Statesman,* (Jun. 8, 1990), A1.

Mechanic, D. 1987. Improving mental health services: What the social sciences can tell us. In R. Lamb (ed.) *New Directions for Mental Health Services 36,*(Winter, 1987), San Francisco: Jossey.

Mechanic, D. 1980. *Mental health and social policy.* Englewood Cliffs, N.J.: Prentice Hall.

Parkside Medical Services Corporation. 1988. Participant Handbook. Parkridge, Ill: Author.

Public Law 98-257. 1984. Developmental Disabilities Assistance and Bill of Rights Act. Washington, D.C.: 98th Congress.

Rochefort, D. 1989. Handbook on mental health policy in the United States. New York: Greenwood Press.

Rosennan, D. 1973. On being sane in insane places. *Science* (January) 179: 250–57.

Royce, J. 1990. *Alcohol problems and alcoholism: A comprehensive survey.* New York: Free Press.

Szasz, T. 1970. *The manufacture of madness.* New York: Harper & Row.

Szasz, T. 1960. The myth of mental illness. *American Psychologist.* (February 15: 113–18.

U.S. Department of Health, Education, and Welfare. 1980. *Health: United States, 1980.* Washington, D.C.: DHEW.

U.S. House of Representatives. Select Committee on Children, Youth, and Families. Women, Addiction, and Perinatal Substance Abuse Fact Sheet. 1990. Washington, D.C.

U.S. Senate Subcommittee on Long-Term Care. 1976. *Hearings on long-term care.* Washington, D.C.: DHEW.

Williams, J. B. 1987. Diagnostic and statistical manual (DSM). In *Encyclopedia of social work,* 18th ed. vol. 1, 389–93. Silver Springs, Md.: National Association of Social Workers.

Zastrow, C. and K. Kirst-Ashman. 1990. Understanding human behavior and the social environment. Chicago: Nelson-Hall.

SUGGESTED FURTHER READINGS

Black, C. 1987. *It will never happen to me.* New York: Ballantine.

Green, Hannah. 1964. *I never promised you a rose garden.* New York: Holt, Rinehart & Winston.

Report of the President's Commission on Mental Health. 1978. Washington, D.C.: GPO.

Scheff, Thomas, 1966. *Being mentally ill.* Chicago: Aldine.

Szasz, T. 1970. *The manufacture of madness.* New York: Harper & Row.

Chapter

6

*to individuals to prevent or
...ca is in a crisis state. On
Alice Mendoza, are faced
...sult of life-threatening
...percent, do not have
...provides only limited
...have increased at
...illion in 1980 to
...rise almost 12
...ensus 1990).
...ceded only
...oncerns:
...th care?
...ge and
...area
...re-
...rs*

*...ed as a
...g town.
...e became
...e she and Ruben
...health insurance, Alice
...ted until she was five months
pregnant to see a doctor. Two
months later, she gave birth
prematurely to a daughter. Shortly
after the birth, the baby began
experiencing severe respiratory and
cardiac problems, and the doctors
decided to fly her to the regional
neonatal center 300 miles away.
The baby remained at the neonatal
center for three months, requiring
intensive care and heart and lung
surgery.*

*When Carmen finally was
allowed to return home, she
required extensive care, and Alice
was unable to return to work.
Already financially strapped, the*

*...v faced with a
...or the
...n's care. A visit
...an services
...o seek Medicaid was
...sful. Although Alice and
...n's income was less than
...10,000 per year, they earned too
much to qualify for the medical
assistance. Alice's boss and other
friends held a dance to raise
money for the family, which
netted $4,000.*

*At this point, Alice and Ruben
are overwhelmed with medical bills
and are unsure whether they will
ever be able to pay them all.
Doctors say that Carmen is
developmentally delayed and will
likely need extensive physical
therapy and possibly more surgery
later on. Although Ruben and Alice
had hoped to have a larger family,
they have decided they cannot
afford to have any more children.
Over the last six months, Ruben
has developed kidney problems
and has already missed five days
of work. However, he feels that he
can't afford to see a doctor with
the already-extensive medical bills
and so is hoping that whatever is
wrong will clear up by itself.*

141

At the present time, **health care,** care provided
promote recovery from illness or disease, in Amer
one hand, many of America's citizens, like Ruben and
with the payment of mammoth medical bills as a r
situations. Thirty-seven million Americans, or about 15
any health insurance at all; most have health insurance that
coverage (Children's Defense Fund 1990).

On the other hand, national expenses for health care
incredibly high rates—from $12.7 billion in 1950 to $247.2 b
$757.9 billion in 1990. Health care expenses currently comp
percent of the U.S. gross national product (U.S. Bureau of the C
The health care industry is the third largest in the United States, p
by agriculture and construction.

Debates over national health care issues focus on two primary
First, how much of our country's resources should be allocated to hea
And second, how should those resources be allocated? As our knowled
technology in the health care arena continue to expand, decisions in the
of health care increasingly will become moral and ethical. Given scarce
sources, for example, should an infant who requires tens of thousands of doll
to be kept alive be given maximum treatment to save its life, particularly whe
the child may live a life continually fraught with health problems and possibly
retardation? And what about organ transplants and kidney dialysis—should
these be made available to everyone? And if not, who should get them? Given
the growing number of persons with AIDS, how many dollars should be allocated to research, education, and treatment, and who should pay what costs?
Does the government have the right to mandate good health practices for
women drug users who are pregnant or to impose penalties on persons with
AIDS who do not practice safe sex? With more U.S. citizens living longer, to
what extent should resources be allocated toward health care for older persons?
And to what extent should attention be given to environmental concerns, such
as nuclear power, sanitation, and pollution, and their impact on personal health?
Finally, given the high costs of health care, who should pay for health care for
the indigent—the federal government, states, local communities, or individuals
and their families themselves? And if individuals cannot afford health care,
should it be denied to them?

Increasingly, social workers are playing a central role in helping policymakers, medical practitioners, and family members make these critical decisions. Social workers provide services in a variety of health-related settings,
ranging from traditional hospitals to family planning clinics, rape crisis centers,
home health care programs, and hospice programs for dying individuals and
their families. Studies project that the area of health care, particularly as it relates
to the elderly, is the fastest-growing area of employment for social workers
today.

This chapter provides an overview of our country's current health care
system, the problems it faces, and the types of health care policies and programs
currently available. The roles social workers play in making those policies and
programs possible are also discussed.

A SYSTEMS/ECOLOGICAL APPROACH TO HEALTH CARE

Because the systems/ecological perspective was first introduced as a mechanism to explain the functioning of the human body, this perspective has a longer history within the health care arena than other arenas in which social workers function. As early as the Greek and Roman eras of civilization, it was observed that many health problems were precipitated by changes in the environment. An ancient Greek medical text entitled *Airs, Waters, and Places,* said to have been authored by Hippocrates, explained health problems in terms of person–environment relationships. This work attributed human functioning to four body fluids: blood, phlegm, and black and yellow bile. As long as these body fluids were in equilibrium, an individual was healthy. However, Hippocrates attributed changes in the balance of these fluids to ecological variations in temperature, ventilation, and an individual's live-style in relation to eating, drinking, and work. Negative influences in the environment caused these fluids to become unbalanced, which in turn resulted in illness to the individual.

Other early works subscribed to germ theory, which is based on the premise that illness is a function of the interactions among an organism's adaptive capacities in an environment full of infectious agents, toxins, and safety hazards. The Greeks and Romans also were cognizant of the relationship between sanitation and illness. Early Roman writings suggested that one could predict and control health through the environment and prevent epidemic diseases by avoiding marshes, standing water, winds, and high temperatures. Public baths, sewers, and free medical care were all ways that early civilizations used to promote health and reduce disease (Catalano 1979).

The focus on the relationship between individual health and the environment continued during later centuries. J. Frank's medical treatise, *System of a Complete Medical Policy,* written between 1774 and 1821, advocated education of midwives and new mothers, a healthy school environment, personal hygiene, nutrition, sewers and sanitation, accident prevention, collection of vital statistics such as birth and death rates, and efficient administration of hospitals to care for the sick.

Numerous studies throughout the years have attributed the incidence of infant mortality, heart disease, and cancer to environmental influences. A number of studies, such as Dohrenwend and Dohrenwend's well-known research on individual financial status and mental health (1974), show strong relationships between stressful life events and the subsequent development of physical disorders, supporting Hippocrates' earlier theories of the ways that a negative life-style can affect one's health. Brenner (1973) demonstrated the relationships between health problems such as heart disease, infant and adult mortality rates, and other health indicators and national employment rates between 1915 and 1967. He found that when employment rates were high, health problems were low, and that low employment rates were associated with higher incidences of health problems. Lazarus (1970) takes a somewhat different systems perspective, presenting research findings that show that persons who perceive their environments as stressful, such as those living in highly urban or highly rural areas, place their psychological systems in jeopardy and develop ways to cope that are tied to the perception of the situation. An elderly man, for example, living in a rural area, who perceives himself as being extremely isolated and without the resources to get to a hospital quickly if he becomes ill is more likely to experience health problems than an elderly man who perceives that he is living in an area where health care is more readily available to him. As can be seen in Table 6–1, the greatest contributions to premature death are not individual hereditary factors, but environmental and life-style factors. Studies show that a number of specific factors affect health status significantly.

Income

The higher one's income, the more likely one is to be in good health. The poor are much more likely to have health problems. This can be attributed to the fact that individuals with higher incomes are more likely to have health insurance, seek medical care earlier and more often, buy and eat more nutritious foods (which may be more expensive), and experience less mental stress. The poor also are more likely to live in areas that are environmentally negative, such as areas with poor sanitation or close to hazardous wastes.

In one 1987 study, for example, researchers found that although most Americans reported themselves to be in good health, the numbers were much lower for persons with low incomes (Schoenborn and Marano 1988). Although 22 percent of individuals with incomes below $10,000 reported that they were in fair to poor health, only 6.7 percent of persons with incomes of $20,000 to $34,999 and 4 percent of persons with incomes above $35,000 did so. Persons living in poverty experience much higher rates of diabetes and tuberculosis and report that they spend more days each year with illnesses serious enough to confine them to bed than do the nonpoor.

Studies show that the impact of low income on health is especially damaging to infants and children. Newborns' chances of death or serious illness at birth can be linked directly to whether or not their mothers have health insurance. Uninsured babies are 30 percent more likely to die or to experience serious medical problems at birth than insured babies. Half of all poor children in the United States are not covered by either Medicaid, the federal medical care plan for the poor, or by private health insurance (Braveman 1989).

Ethnicity

Primarily because of incomes, whites as a group enjoy better health than nonwhites. Whereas 69 percent of whites report themselves to be in good health, only 55 percent of blacks do so. **Infant mortality rates,** the number of infant deaths compared to total infants' births during a given time period, are twice as high for nonwhites as for whites. Infants born to uninsured black mothers are twice as likely to die or to experience serious medical problems than babies born to insured white mothers. Nonwhites are less likely to seek health care for themselves and their children. Half of all black preschoolers, for example, are not fully immunized, and 40 percent of all black women, compared to 20 percent of white women, do not receive any prenatal care during their first trimester of pregnancy (Edwards 1990).

Table 6–1   Major Factors Contributing to Premature Death: Estimated Percent Contribution to Cause of Death

Leading Causes Death	Age-adjusted Death Rate*	Life Style	Environment	Inadequacy of Health Care Services	Genetic/ Hereditary Factors
Cardiovascular Disease	216.8	54%	9%	12%	25%
Cancer	133.2	37%	24%	10%	29%
Non-motor Vehicle Accidents	35.2	51%	31%	14%	4%
Motor Vehicle Accidents	19.4	69%	18%	12%	1%
Pulmonary Diseases	18.8	50%	22%	7%	21%
Influenza/ Pneumonia	13.5	23%	20%	18%	39%
Suicide	12.7	60%	35%	3%	2%
Diabetes	9.6	34%	0%	6%	60%
Cirrhosis	9.2	70%	9%	3%	18%
Homicide	8.5	63%	35%	0%	2%
TOTAL: All 10 Causes Together	541.7	51%	19%	10%	20%

*Per 100,000 population

Source: Centers for Disease Control. 1988. Ten Leading Causes of Death in the U.S., 1985. U.S. DHHS.

Nonwhites are also more at risk to develop heart disease, diabetes, and cancer. Black males are 85 percent more likely to experience strokes than white males, and black females are 80 percent more likely to experience strokes than white females. Health problems that should not be major problems in a wealthy industrialized country such as the United States are increasing among all groups, but particularly among minorities. Studies of health care along the U.S.–Mexico border, for example, show high rates of tuberculosis, hepatitis, and malaria. Life expectancies for nonwhites are also much shorter than for whites: Average lifespan is 72 years for white men compared to 66 years for nonwhite men, and 79 years for white women compared to 74 years for nonwhite women (Zastrow and Kirst-Ashman 1990).

Gender

The average life expectancy for both men and women has increased in recent years—six years for men and seven years for women since 1950. Although the fact that the average life expectancy for women is greater than for men can be viewed as an advantage for women, it is also a disadvantage for them. Because of the difference in life expectancy and the fact that women have less built up in Social Security due to staying at home and raising children, increasing numbers of elderly women who become widowed have little or no health insurance coverage and limited Social Security benefits. Thus, they are more likely to spend their last years living in poverty, which in turn places them at even more risk to experience poor health.

Age

Our country's oldest and youngest citizens are at the highest risk to experience poor health. The elderly are at risk as a result of both the aging process and the fact that one-third of today's elderly are poor and do not seek health care as needed due to the high costs. Eighty percent to 90 percent of the more than a million and a half persons in the United States afflicted with Alzheimer's disease, for example, are sixty-five and older. The aging factor will be of greater significance as the U.S. population continues to age: by the year 2000, 13 percent of the population will be over sixty-five. Current estimates indicate that the nursing home population will grow four times faster than the population of all other Americans during the next fifty years (Ford Foundation 1989).

Although the United States is one of the wealthiest countries in the world, it continues to have the highest infant mortality rate, which is the rate of children who die at birth, of any Western country. As the number of children growing up in poverty continues to increase, U.S. children will be at a greater risk to experience serious health problems.

Disability

Individuals with both permanent and temporary disability are much more at risk to have serious health problems than nondisabled persons. The fact that they may be less resilient due to their disability is often compounded by the lack of affordable, accessible, appropriate health care that allows them to practice good preventive health practices.

Rural/Urban

Individuals living in extremely rural or highly populated urban areas are more at risk to have health problems. This can be attributed to the increasing environmental hazards such as pollution and increased stress from living in a highly populated urban area and the lack of medical facilities for prevention and early medical care found in extremely rural areas. Over half of all the people at the poverty level live in rural areas, and individuals in rural areas are more likely to suffer from emotional disorders than people in urban areas (see Chapter 11). People living in urban areas also are more likely to be poor than those living in suburban areas, and are also more at risk of experiencing stress and injury as a result of violence than people in non-urban areas.

Application of a Systems/Ecological Perspective

It is vital that a systems/ecological perspective that focuses on the interaction and interdependence between person and environment be used in understanding **health risk factors,** or those factors which affect individuals' health and place them at risk for serious health problems and health conditions (see Table 6–1). A 1979 national health report, *Healthy People,* emphasized the important link between physical and mental health, noting the "importance of strong family ties, the assistance and support of friends, and the use of common support systems" in promoting healthy individuals (U.S. Surgeon General 1979).

The current emphasis on holistic health care stems from a systems/ecological approach to health care. This perspective views all aspects of an individual's health in relation not only to how that individual interacts with family members, the workplace, and the community but also to how the environment, including community quality of life as well as legislation and funding available to support quality of life, has an impact on a person's health. This perspective slowly is replacing the more traditional medical model used by health practitioners, which often only focuses on symptoms and malfunctions of one part of the body without focusing on other body systems or the environment within which the individual interacts. The World Health Organization defines **health** as "a state of complete physical, mental, and social well-being and not merely the absence of disease or infirmity" (Schlesinger 1985). This definition reflects the systems/ecological perspective in viewing health as clearly dependent on a combination of environmental, physiological, sociological, and psychological factors.

THE EVOLUTION OF HEALTH CARE IN AMERICA

Early emphasis of health care in the United States focused on keeping people alive. Persons born in the United States 200 years ago only had a 50 percent chance of surviving long enough to celebrate their twenty-first birthday. One-third of all deaths were of children less than five years old. Even then, nonwhites had higher death rates. In the late eighteenth century, the death rate was 30 per 1,000 for whites and 70 per 1,000 for slaves (U.S. Public Health Service 1977). Health practitioners at that time were limited in number and in training and faced great difficulties in keeping their patients alive due to environmental constraints, such as poor sanitation and extreme poverty. Many illnesses resulted in catastrophic epidemics, which claimed the lives of entire families. In 1793 during a yellow fever epidemic in Philadelphia, three physicians were available to care for 6,000 patients stricken with the disease. Thus, early attempts to improve health care in the United States included national and state legislation relating to control of communicable diseases, sanitation measures such as pasteurization of milk, and education for midwives, physicians, and young mothers (U.S. Public Health Service 1977).

Although more recent legislation and programs have focused on control of chronic, degenerative diseases such as heart disease and cancer, as well as those illnesses that are self-inflicted, such as cirrhosis of the liver, and other health problems such as accidents and violence, most efforts are still directed to restoring health after illness has occurred. The health care system in the United States still allows large numbers of U.S. citizens to remain unserved or underserved, and mortality rates remain higher than in many developed countries (Ford Foundation 1990).

CRITICAL ISSUES IN CURRENT HEALTH CARE DELIVERY

Presently many domestic policy experts believe that the United States is experiencing a crisis in health care. While health care costs are increasing significantly, greater numbers of Americans are finding health care inaccessible to them. Health care statistics show that more infants are dying at birth and other people are experiencing serious health problems that often are treatable.

Funding and Costs of Health Care

The rapidly increasing costs of health care at all levels of our country—for consumers, local health care practitioners, community hospitals and local governments, and state and federal programs—is considered to be one of the most, if not the most, critical issues facing the United States today (see Figure 6–1). The United States currently spends over $1 billion a day on health care alone, and predictions are that this amount will increase to $5 billion a day by the year 2000, or $2 trillion per year (Mechanic 1986). Individuals like the Mendozas are not the only ones experiencing financial bankruptcy because of health care costs; physicians are leaving independently owned practices, particularly in rural and poverty areas; hospitals are closing; insurance companies are going out of business; communities and states are in the red due to increased costs of indigent health care; and the federal government's Medicaid and Medicare systems are not supporting themselves and are facing the possibility of significant projected cuts in the coming years. In spite of the costs, services are increasingly fragmented, inaccessible and unattainable for many U.S. residents and not well matched with the needs of those receiving them when they are provided. In fact, the health care system in the United States unfortunately is an excellent example of how lack of planning and funding has created an

Figure 6–1 Health and Medical Expenditures under Public Programs

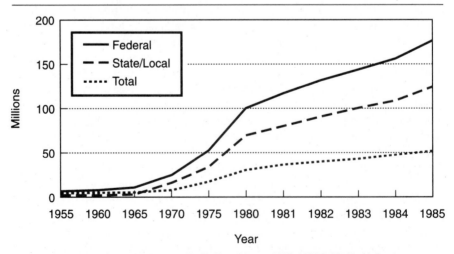

Source: National Center for Health Statistics, Health, United States, 1987. 1988 Public Health Service. Washington, D.C.: U.S. GPO.

Figure 6-2   Cost Comparison: Preventive Measures versus Costly Health Care Problems

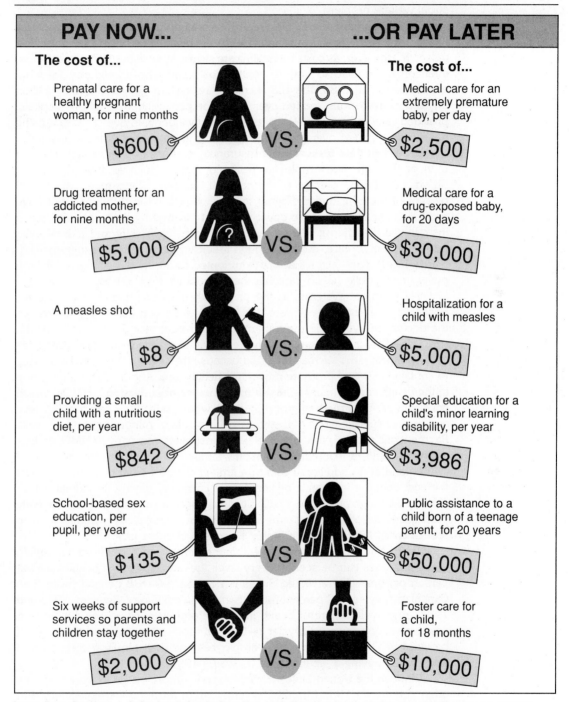

Source: From "Pay Now . . . Or Pay Later" chart by Steve Hart. 1990. *Time* (October 8): 45. Copyright 1990 The Time Inc. Magazine Company. Reprinted by permission.

ineffective, narrowly focused, fragmented, and expensive approach to a major social welfare problem.

Emphasis during the 1950s and 1960s was on providing the best possible health care to all Americans and improving health personnel, services, and research. However, as costs for health care skyrocketed in the 1970s and 1980s, attention has shifted to how to control costs and who should pay for what expenditures. In 1980, the U.S. health care system provided over 1 billion physical examinations, treated over 33 million persons in over 8,000 hospitals, provided care to over 1 million persons, mostly elderly, in over 19,000 nursing homes, and treated over 181 million persons in outpatient visits to hospitals.

In 1987 **private insurance,** or insurance purchased by individuals on their own or through their employers from companies such as Blue Cross/Blue Shield, paid for 31 percent of the costs of this care. Consumers paid for 26 percent of the care directly, either to cover health costs if they did not have health insurance at all, or to cover costs not covered by their personal health insurance if they had it. **Public insurance** funds, both state and federal, paid for 41 percent of care, mostly through Medicaid and Medicare programs (Edwards 1990). One factor that has contributed to the increased costs for both private and public health care has been the shift from retrospective to prospective payment systems. In the past, with the exception of insurance for hospitalization, most health care was paid for after you used it—you went to the doctor, and you paid the full amount after your visit. Today, most health care is paid for in advance through premiums to private insurance companies or federal programs such as Medicaid because the health care industry is trying to contain costs and promote preventive health care. Another important group in the health care industry is **health maintenance organizations** (HMOs) which consist of pre-paid medical group practices where individuals pay monthly fees and receive specific types of health care at no cost or minimum costs per visit. Payment of a monthly amount, to a health insurance company or HMO, entitles a person—and, if insured, the person's family—to either needed health care on demand at no additional cost or a limited cost, for example, 15 percent of the cost with the insurance or health care company paying the additional 85 percent. Although prospective health care has been an attempt to promote early preventive use of care to create a nation that is physically healthier and to reduce costs, it has not been highly successful at either task.

Health care costs continue to escalate rapidly in spite of efforts to contain costs. Increases can be seen at every level: the average cost of health care per person per year in the United States is now $2,200—38 percent more than Canadians pay and 49 percent more than the Swedish pay. Between 1980 and 1987, employees' share of health insurance premiums increased 50 percent. When someone buys a Chrysler or General Motors car, $700 of the amount provides health care coverage for employees and their families, compared to $200 when buying a Japanese car (Edwards 1990).

Although the United States currently spends more on health care than any other country, in 1988 it ranked seventeenth in terms of life expectancy and twentieth in terms of infant mortality among countries of the Western world (see Table 6–2).

Almost one-fourth of all U.S. women who deliver babies at public hospitals have received no prenatal care. Although studies show that as much as fourteen

Table 6–2   Comparison of Amount of GNP Allocated to Health Care with Infant
Mortality Rates, 1987

Country	Percent of GNP Allocated to Health Care	Infant Mortality Rate*
United States	11.4	10
Sweden	9.1	6
Canada	8.5	8
France	8.5	8
Germany	8.1	9
Switzerland	8	7
Japan	6.7	6
United Kingdom	6.2	9

*Deaths per 1,000 live births

Source: National Center for Health Statistics. 1988. Health, United States, 1987. DHHS. Washington, D.C.: GPO.

dollars a day can be saved for every dollar invested in immunizations, large
numbers of children in the United States remain unimmunized: in 1985, 20
percent of two-year-olds had not been immunized against polio; 18.3 percent
had not received measles immunizations, 22.7 percent had not received rubella
immunizations; and 21.1 percent had not received immunization for mumps.
In 1990 a number of children died because of a large measles outbreak in the
United States and increasing numbers of children are getting whooping cough

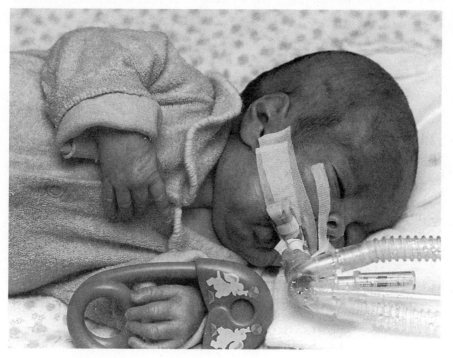

*This infant was
born prematurely.
Prenatal care can
prevent early de-
livery that often
results in ex-
tremely high costs
for health care.*

and other illnesses that had declined significantly in recent years (Ford Foundation 1990).

Although costs of health care, like costs in other areas, have increased due to inflation, other reasons for rising health expenditures also must be considered. Some attribute increased costs to more extensive use of medical resources by a more educated population interested in preventive health care. They argue that accessibility to group insurance plans through the workplace and the increase in health maintenance organizations and other health programs aimed at reducing health costs actually increase costs because of more extensive use. Statistics show, however, that many Americans, particularly poor persons—minorities, single-parent females, and the elderly—work for employers who do not offer health insurance or are paid such low wages that they cannot afford the health insurance offered. Thus, they are less apt to use health care resources, but when they do, they are more likely to need more costly services because they have not sought preventive care.

However, even with today's emphasis on wellness and public awareness about the damages smoking, alcohol and drug consumption, and lack of exercise can do to one's health, few dollars are spent on prevention by private citizens and by all levels of U.S. government, even though studies show that dollars spent for preventive care pay for themselves as much as eight times over in the long run (Comprehensive Care Corporation 1981).

There are other, more reliable explanations for the extreme costs of health care in the United States. First, because of the increased access to health care, improved knowledge and technology, and a better quality of life, people are living longer, resulting in increased need for medical care for those sixty-five and older. Comprising approximately 11 percent of the population and more likely to be poor and unable to pay for health care than other groups, persons over sixty-five have three times more health problems and needs than persons in other age groups. As this population continues to increase, costs will also increase. Few insurance premiums cover the costs of nursing home care, and those that do are rapidly increasing their premium charges. The insurance system, particularly in care for the elderly, is also fragmented, with separate systems paying for home health care, medical equipment, nursing homes, and transportation to and from health care facilities (Ford Foundation 1989).

A second factor is the greater availability and technology for saving lives: neonatal procedures for infants born prematurely; heart, lung, and other organ transplants; and heart surgery to restore circulation and reduce incidence of heart attacks and other cardiac problems. Currently, the extent of and knowledge about technology exceed the dollars necessary to support such sophisticated systems and make them available to everyone in need (see Box 6–1). In many instances, heroic procedures are covered by health care policies, whereas preventive care, such as long-term care, rehabilitative services, and health education, are not (Ford Foundation 1989). Although values issues are inherent when discussing health care, our current health technologies have become very costly. Current studies suggest, for example, that persons who receive heart transplants live an average of four years longer than persons who do not receive transplants, at a cost of $100,000 per transplant or $25,000 for every additional year of life.

Box 6-1   Ethical Dilemmas which Balance Health Care Costs and Human Life .

Brackenridge to Pay $15,300 for Equipment to Move Girl

Patty Carnes' special wish to have a family of her own is closer to coming true.

Brackenridge Hospital officials Tuesday decided to buy the $15,300 worth of medical equipment the 6½-year-old girl needs to stay alive in the home of a Portland, Ore., family who plan to adopt her.

"We don't want Patty to wait any longer," said Sandra Bockelman, an assistant city attorney. Brackenridge is a city-owned hospital.

Patty, who was left paralyzed and unable to breathe on her own by a spinal cord inflammation when she was an infant, has been in the hospital for six years—longer than any other Brackenridge patient. A ventilator breathes for Patty, but it does not prevent her from talking, laughing, or making wishes like any other child.

Patty's move from Children's Hospital of Austin at Brackenridge to the home of Diane and Ken Stacy in Oregon will cost nearly $45,000—$15,300 for a ventilator and other equipment, $20,000 for a van with a wheelchair lift, and $9,600 for an air ambulance.

Brackenridge's decision to buy the equipment came one day after Travis County commissioners voted to pay for the air ambulance, which doctors say is the safest way to transport Patty.

The van, which the Stacys need to take Patty to school and to the doctor, "is the only thing that stands in her way" of moving, said Stephanie Crowell, a pediatric social worker at Brackenridge. "That's the glitch."

"If we can get this money for the van, I think this little girl is going to go home," said Crowell, who has spent years trying to locate a family to adopt Patty.

Patty is a ward of the state because her mother gave up her parental rights when she realized she could never properly care for her daughter. Last week, a state judge ordered the Texas Department of Human Services to have Patty moved to the Stacy's home by Feb. 15. During a hearing before State District Judge Jeanne Meurer, representatives of the state, county and city argued that the other governmental entities should pay for Patty's move.

City officials decided to buy the medical equipment because it appeared that DHS and the county have not found any money for equipment, Bockelman said.

"We'll buy the equipment and put it on (Patty's) bill," she said, but "we're all hoping somebody will drop out of the sky with the money" to reimburse Brackenridge.

Patty's unpaid hospital bill totals more than $2 million, and charges of more than $1,500 are added each day, officials said.

Source: Denise Gamino, "Brackenridge to Pay $15,300 for Equipment to Move Girl," *Austin American Statesman*, 24 January 1990, sec. B.

Additionally, with increased numbers of private hospitals and the difficulties public hospitals face in remaining solvent, health care has become increasingly competitive. Many private hospitals are now owned by large corporations with real estate subsidiaries and their own insurance divisions. The increased competition has resulted in duplicative purchases of expensive equipment by hospitals in close proximity in many instances. While hospitals struggle to compete with each other for paying clients, the number of persons who are unable to pay hospital bills continues to increase. The limits on public insurance (i.e., Medicare and Medicaid) reimbursements to hospitals also have created serious financial problems for many hospitals that are unable to provide services at reimbursement levels. In Texas, for example, 105 hospitals have closed since 1980, 73 percent in rural areas. Eighty percent of rural hospitals in Florida were leased or sold between 1982 and 1987. During the third quarter of 1989, Texas hospitals lost $1.6 billion in uncompensated care, or an average of $619 for each Medicare patient and $601 for each Medicaid patient. One in ten patients was indigent and could not pay for medical costs at all.

A third health care cost factor that has been suggested is the use of third-party billing by many medical practitioners (billing an insurance company directly rather than billing the patient). Many physicians and hospitals charge the maximum amount allowable under an insurance system, whereas they might be reluctant to charge individual clients the same amount if they knew the clients would be paying for the services directly. Faced with rapidly increasing costs, the 1,500 private insurance companies in the United States that cover about half of the population are now minimizing their risks by reducing benefits covered, requiring second opinions in many instances, and excluding the chronically ill. At the same time, insurance premiums continue to increase, with high costs to both employers who pay portions of employees' premiums and employees themselves. In 1965, 9 percent of corporate profits was spent on employee health care, whereas in 1989 it was 46 percent. As a result, many employers, particularly smaller ones, are now either no longer covering employees or their families or are covering a smaller percentage of premiums, with employers paying much larger shares. Increasing numbers of individuals who carry health insurance on an individual, rather than an employee, policy are being forced to cancel their policies because they cannot afford them, requiring local communities to pick up the rising costs of their health care when they become ill and cannot pay their bills.

Federal and state governments are also struggling with the high costs of health care as the number of poor individuals who need health care and cannot afford to pay for it continues to increase. However, efforts to reduce Medicaid and Medicare expenditures by setting ceilings for reimbursable costs have led some physicians and nursing homes to refuse to accept clients under these health care assistance plans, claiming they lose too much money because the actual costs are much higher then the ceilings allowed.

Even though there are problems with the Medicaid system of health care for the poor and with group insurance programs, of greater concern are the many persons who have no health coverage at all. Over half of the poor in the United States are either not covered by Medicaid or do not use the system. Those persons who have neither Medicaid nor other health insurance coverage often become destitute immediately when they or members of their family suffer health problems. Few families can afford even several thousand dollars in health care costs, and many health problems can easily cost a family over $10,000. Unfortunately, when individuals and other available health care programs cannot pay for health care, local communities and taxpayers must bear the costs. One study (Kingston et al. 1988) of poor persons aged fifty to sixty-four who received services at a New York City shelter for the homeless and did not qualify for federal health care programs found that 75 percent had had some type of medical treatment during the past year, 30 percent had been hospitalized, and 76 percent received emergency room services. The city had to pay for the health care.

Many local public hospitals that must accept all patients are operating in the red; one local hospital spent over $2 million on a young child with serious health problems, as the child was not covered by any type of private or public health care plan. Thus, the hospital—and the local taxpayers—absorbed the costs of her care. The story had a happy ending—the child was adopted and moved to a home with parents equipped to provide for her special needs at a cost much less than the $1,500 per day cost for her hospital care (see Box 6–1). However, the costs of indigent health care to local communities are increasing. Many state legislators and citizens do not understand the complicated reimbursement system for the government programs such as Medicare and Medicaid. For every dollar of Medicaid money spent, for example, the state contribution is forty cents and the federal contribution is sixty cents. However, conservative legislatures limit dollars allocated for health care, not always understanding that limiting state costs reduces the number of federal dollars available to the state and ultimately results in more money, not less, paid by that state's citizens. One large southwestern state, for example, consistently limits its legislative authorization of state dollars for health care coverage for the poor, particularly dollars to draw down federal Medicaid and Medicare funds. As a result, fewer federal money comes into the state and more goes to other states. In 1989, for example, for every $3.00 that a citizen of the state paid in federal income taxes, only $1.89 was returned to the state. The other $1.11 went to other states for their programs. Yet because the state only authorized a limited Medicaid program, large numbers of women and children were not eligible to receive Medicaid benefits. When they became ill, they went to local public hospitals, funded by local tax dollars, with the hospitals having to absorb the costs of their unpaid care. Thus, from a cost standpoint, the health care the women and children received that could have cost state citizens forty cents per dollar if they had been covered by Medicaid ultimately cost the citizens the entire dollar—and this does not include the extra tax money the state citizens are paying in federal taxes that is going to other states.

Our society's encouragement of lawsuits is another cost-raising factor. Many medical practitioners fear the increasing number of malpractice suits being filed. One study found that all practitioners face at least one suit during their careers, no matter how competent they are. This has resulted in extremely high costs for malpractice insurance, and practitioners who feel compelled to order numerous tests, exploratory surgery, and other medical procedures when they are not sure what is wrong with an individual, to eliminate the risk of a lawsuit for a wrong decision.

CURRENT MAJOR HEALTH PROBLEMS

Current major health problems are facing the United States and its citizens including heart disease, strokes, cancer, AIDS, and catastrophic illnesses.

Heart Disease, Strokes, and Cancer

Although many health problems that faced Americans in the past have all but been eliminated, new ones arise upon which attention must be focused. Heart disease, strokes, and cancer remain the three leading causes of death in the United States. Although heart disease and strokes are declining because of increased attention to personal health including fitness and diet, it is estimated that almost 50 percent of U.S. citizens will die from heart disease. Cancer rates continue to rise and are increasingly associated with environmental factors. Eventually cancer will strike one out of every three persons. Breast cancer is the leading cause of death for women and rates of breast cancer are increasing in the United States. While new technology and medications have made treatment of these diseases more effective, they remain major causes of death.

AIDS

Acquired immune deficiency syndrome (AIDS) is the greatest health-related tragedy to strike the world in decades. AIDS has affected all of our social institutions and most communities in the United States. People who are diagnosed with clinical AIDS usually live an average of two years after the diagnosis, and the disease continues to spread to all segments of the population.

AIDS first came to the attention of health authorities in the early 1980s, and after ten years there have been an estimated 270,000 cases identified and approximately 180,000 deaths. Currently, an estimated one to two million people in the United States and five to ten million people throughout the world are infected with the human immune deficiency virus (HIV) associated with AIDS. Most will likely die of AIDS-related causes.

There are three conditions associated with the AIDS virus: the **HIV-positive,** or seropositive, state; **AIDS-related complex (ARC);** and clinical, or "full-blown," AIDS (Rothstein 1989). The seropositive state refers to a person who has tested positively for AIDS, meaning that the person has HIV (human immunodeficiency virus) antibodies present in his or her blood and has been infected with the virus. Most individuals become infected two to three months after exposure to the virus. Although persons who test positive for AIDS may not show symptoms of either ARC or AIDS for many years, they are carriers of the virus and can infect others with it.

The second condition, AIDS-related complex, is diagnosable using a series of criteria developed by the National Centers for Disease Control. At least two of the following signs must be present for at least three months for a person to be diagnosed as having ARC: fever, weight loss, swollen lymph nodes, diarrhea, fatigue, or night sweats. In addition, at least one of the following must be present: low white blood cell count, low red blood cell count, low platelet count, or elevated levels of serum globulins. The person must also have a low number of T-helper cells and a low ratio of T-helper to T-suppressor cells. This condition moderately damages the body's immune system.

The third condition, clinical AIDS, is diagnosed when the disease moves from ARC to a major collapse of the body's immune system. This results in the recurrent development of otherwise treatable infections that continue to break down the body's resistance and stress the entire system. Kaposi's sarcoma, a rare skin cancer, is a common disease associated with AIDS. About half of persons with AIDS die from a rare form of pneumonia caused by the organism *Pneumocystis carinii* (Rothstein 1989).

Recent studies suggest that the incubation period between the time of infection and the onset of clinical AIDS is up to seven years, with the time increasing as physicians become more knowledgeable about ways to promote positive health among HIV-infected persons and to keep the immune system from breaking down. Unfortunately, AIDS is fatal an average of two years after diagnosis as clinical AIDS. Little is known about how the disease can be treated effectively, and current research efforts have yet to find a cure or vaccine to prevent its spread.

AIDS is transmitted by exchange of body fluids, primarily blood and semen. To date, there is no evidence that AIDS is transmitted by casual contact such as shaking hands, sharing drinks from the same glass, getting an insect bite, sneezing, or living or working with a person infected with the virus. Persons at the highest risk to be exposed to AIDS are homosexual and bisexual men, intravenous drug users who share needles, persons who are exposed to the virus through blood transfusions, and babies born to mothers who are infected with the AIDS virus. In 1990, 73 percent of persons with AIDS were sexually active gay and bisexual men (90 percent were twenty to forty-nine years of age); 19 percent were intravenous drug users; 4 percent were heterosexuals;

This social worker from an AIDS services program has just completed a home visit to one of her clients. Many social workers assist persons with AIDS and their families in a variety of ways, including helping them access services as well as counseling them and providing emotional support.

1 percent were hemophiliacs; 2 percent were infected through blood transfusions; and 1 percent were newborn infants.

AIDS experts have suggested that because it takes several years for AIDS symptoms to show up, instead of looking at data relating to the numbers of persons with full-blown AIDS, we should focus on the number of persons who have the HIV virus in their blood. Recent projections of blood testing of persons in the military and from other studies suggest that whereas rates among homosexual and bisexual men have stabilized, rates among the heterosexual population, particularly intravenous drug users, and children are increasing. One recent study of two inner-city hospitals in the East found that 6 percent of persons tested carried the AIDS antibody. In one of the hospitals, in an area with a high number of drug users, 30 percent of black males aged twenty-five to forty-four carried the antibody. Heterosexuals, drug users and their partners, and children born to persons with AIDS now make up over twenty-five percent of new cases. Pediatric AIDS cases make up 2 percent of all cases, with the average age of diagnosis six months and the average life span two years. Many of these children never leave the hospital after birth, which becomes expensive both in dollars and emotional costs to hospital employees who work with the children and their families.

Because of the long incubation period for AIDS, most of those who will die of the disease do not know that they have it. Most AIDS victims lose their jobs and most often their health insurance before the disease takes their lives. Currently, only limited funding has been made available for research, treatment, or public education. The disease remains a controversial one, but it is gaining much-deserved attention throughout the United States. Estimates are that it costs $80,000 to cover all health care costs of a person with AIDS once the AIDS antibody is discovered. Persons with AIDS and their families face not only serious financial problems but also discrimination both in communities and the workplace and problems in obtaining health care, housing, employment, social services, and emotional support (see Box 6–2 for NASW policy statement on AIDS).

Other Illnesses and Health Problems

Other illnesses receiving increased attention are diabetes, musculoskeletal diseases such as arthritis and osteoporosis, and respiratory diseases. These problems are much more likely to be experienced by the poor, minorities, and the elderly, who are less likely to be able to afford both preventive and rehabilitative health care.

Recent research is finding that some life-threatening diseases, such as Huntington's disease and cystic fibrosis, are genetically linked. Researchers indicate that within the next several decades, prenatal genetic screening will likely be able to indicate the presence of hypertension, dyslexia, cancer, sickle-cell anemia, manic-depression, schizophrenia, Type 1 diabetes, familial Alzheimer's disease, multiple sclerosis, and myotonic muscular dystrophy (Rothstein 1989). Others predict that genetic screening will also show a predisposition for addictions to alcohol and other drugs.

These discoveries will increase the level of debate regarding moral and ethical choices in relation to birth, fetal and parental rights, abortion, and emo-

Box 6–2 Humane Treatment for Persons with AIDS: the National Association of Social Workers Policy Statement on AIDS

Because of the complex biopsychosocial issues presented by AIDS, ARC, and HIV infection, social workers, with their special knowledge, skills, and sensitivity, can make a unique contribution to the management of this crisis by pursuing action in eight areas:

1. **Research.** Basic research, including epidemiological, clinical, and psychosocial studies, is imperative. Social workers, particularly in the area of psychosocial research, have a special contribution to make. They have been at the forefront of issues relating to AIDS and have demonstrated significant leadership in identifying critical issues and needs and have a responsibility to continue in these research efforts.

2. **Public Education and Dissemination of Information.** Accurate information about AIDS; HIV infection control measures; prevention; treatment; and medical, financial, and psychosocial resources available should be widely distributed. The fears of caregivers and the general public must be addressed with appropriate education and interventions. Adequate public funds must be authorized for educational efforts among the general public to reduce the fear of AIDS, ARC, and HIV infection and the stigmatization of persons assumed to be at risk for infection. Adequately funded public education programs should encourage prevention, early treatment, and formulation of new behaviors to reduce the risks of HIV infection. Professional health care organizations, training programs, and continuing education programs should incorporate the latest information and address especially the needs of minority groups, adolescents, women, infants and children, the developmentally and physically disabled, and the chronically mentally ill. Education and training programs must accommodate differences in culture and ethnicity among people. Program materials must be clear and explicit and targeted to individuals of all sexual orientations. Social workers should work cooperatively with existing AIDS-related educational, treatment, and research organizations. Especially important, social workers should be educated and updated on all AIDS-related issues, including prevention strategies, and should play major roles in reducing public hysteria and prejudice.

3. **Psychological and Social Support.** Comprehensive psychological and social support is necessary to help persons with AIDS, ARC, and HIV infection and all individuals close to them. Extended families, including domestic partners and significant others, represent rich resources of emotional and social support, just as they represent a network of persons likely to be affected by the disease-related changes, including death, of persons with AIDS and HIV infections. All care providers should respect the individuality of people with AIDS, ARC, and HIV infection and the importance of the individual's relationships with family, domestic partners, and close friends.

    The diversity of interpersonal relationships and support systems should be recognized, nurtured, and strengthened. Supplemental services, including support groups, counseling, and therapy, should be made available to

continued on next page

people with AIDS and AIDS-related conditions and their loved ones as well as to others who feel vulnerable. In addition, all providers of care should have access to support groups and related services to alleviate the stress inherent in assisting persons with AIDS-related conditions. All AIDS-related service organizations should provide for support, supervision, respite, and recognition of social workers engaged in the emotionally demanding work of serving people with AIDS.

4. **Service Delivery and Resource Development.** A comprehensive service delivery system to respond to AIDS based on a case management model must include suitable housing, adult-child foster care, home health and hospice care, appropriate, affordable health care, access to legal services, and transportation services. Children needing foster care should be provided care at the least restrictive level in nonsegregated settings. Traditional health and social welfare agencies including income maintenance programs must become responsive; eligibility requirements and coverage by health insurance and income maintenance should be adapted to meet the rapid onset and catastrophic effects of AIDS. The health status of people with AIDS-related disorders may vary daily. Currently, service delivery systems do not take health care needs and work requirements into consideration. Systems should be more flexible in providing services for individuals with AIDS-related disorders.

    Adequate funding both from public and private sources should be provided to assist alternative health and social services that deal with AIDS and AIDS-related conditions in various communities. Such services, many of which are complementary to and cooperative with mainstream services, help broaden and strengthen the range of traditional supports available to persons with AIDS and AIDS-related conditions. Social workers should be encouraged to be involved in the initiation of—and serve as membership on—local, statewide, regional, and national AIDS task forces.

5. **Civil Rights.** No person should be deprived of civil rights or rights to confidentiality because he or she has been diagnosed as having contracted AIDS, is infected with HIV, or is assumed to be at risk for infection. Nondiscrimination laws should be extended and existing legal protection should be vigorously enforced to protect individuals with AIDS, ARC, and HIV infections from being presumptively deprived of health care, employment, housing, and immigration rights.

6. **HIV Testing.** Social workers should be concerned particularly with the violation of human rights and the psychosocial consequences to people taking HIV antibody tests. Given the potential for serious discrimination, all testing should be voluntary, anonymous, and conducted with informed consent. Social workers should make certain that the limits of the predictive value of such testing are known in advance by clients. Appropriate pre- and post-test counseling must be offered by social workers or other skilled professionals. Social workers are mandated to protect client confidentiality.

7. **Professional Accountability.** The helping professions and appropriate licensing authorities should use their full range of persuasive and regulatory powers to assure that people with AIDS, ARC, and HIV infection and their significant others are not discriminated against in their eligibility for or receipt of services because of their illness or lack of financial or social resources.

continued on next page

8. **Political Action.** Social workers, individually and organizationally, should participate with other groups to lobby actively at local, state, and federal levels on behalf of people with AIDS in order to improve their quality of life; protect their civil liberties; and to advocate for increased funding for appropriate education, prevention, interventions, treatment, services, and research.

The National Association of Social Workers (NASW), as the organizational arm of the profession, must help coordinate a response to AIDS, ARC, and HIV infection by pursuing the multifaceted strategy outlined in this policy statement.

tional and financial costs to individuals and society. If it is certain that a child will be born with multiple sclerosis, AIDS antibodies, or cancer, who should decide whether to continue the pregnancy? If the child is born, who should pay the costs for care? Current termination rates for women who decide to have genetic screening are nearly 100 percent for muscular dystrophy and cystic fibrosis, 60 percent for hemophilia, and 50 percent for sickle-cell anemia. But what if the disease is one that occurs much later in life, such as Huntington's disease; is not fatal, such as Down's syndrome; or reveals a "predisposition" to a disease, such as cancer, heart disease, or schizophrenia? The field of **bioethics,** which deals with the moral and ethical decisions associated with advanced technology in the health care field, is a fast-growing one in which social workers can play a major role.

Another health concern is the increased number of persons with serious head or spinal injuries who are brain injured and/or multiply disabled. Many require years of rehabilitation, and some require institutional care for the remainder of their lives. As technology enables many more persons who experience such injuries to remain alive more often than in the past, costs for their care also increase. Because large numbers of persons have received head and/or spinal injuries in motorcycle accidents when they were not wearing helmets, or in alcohol- or drug-related accidents or car accidents when they were not wearing seat belts, additional concerns are raised about who should pay for health costs and how much should be paid.

Catastrophic Illness

Increased national attention is also being given to the problems encountered by families when a **catastrophic illness** occurs. A catastrophic illness is a chronic and severely debilitating condition that results in high medical costs and long-term dependence on the health care system. Although many families can provide health care for themselves during typical, less serious bouts of illness, a catastrophic illness most often can wipe out the savings of even a fairly wealthy family. To date, proposals have failed for legislation to provide national health insurance for individuals and families who experience a catastrophic illness when their available health insurance is exhausted and the costs for the care have reached a certain limit. The Catastrophic Health Care bill passed by both the U.S. House and Senate in 1988, which provided coverage for families and elderly persons who experienced catastrophic illness or disability, was repealed in 1989 after a strong lobby by middle- and upper-middle-class elderly persons who protested increased Medicare premiums included in the legislation. The bill provided Medicare benefits at full coverage after one year of hospitalization but increased the deductible for benefits as well as the costs for premiums. The bill also did not cover long-term nursing home care. Although many national groups and health care lobbyists will continue to advocate for a national health insurance program that provides some type of health care coverage for all individuals in the United States, coverage limited only to catastrophic health care is a compromise measure more likely to be approved. Thus, it is likely that some sort of catastrophic health care bill will pass in the near future.

Teenage Pregnancy

Attention has been directed toward at-risk groups that generate additional health problems. Recently, the group most publicized has been teenage parents. Studies show that pregnant teens receive little or no prenatal care, poor nutrition during pregnancy, and limited services (USDA 1990). As a result, they are at more risk of having miscarriages, and of giving birth to premature and low-birth-weight infants and ones with congenital problems.

Although availability of family planning and other preventive services, as well as prenatal health care, is viewed by many as a moral issue because such services supposedly promote teen pregnancy, such services are cost-effective and more likely to result in healthy infants better able to grow up to become healthy adults. A one-year study by the U.S. Department of Agriculture found, for example, that low-income pregnant women who participated in the food and nutrition education program saved an estimated $573 for every newborn. Birth weights increased and the number of premature births declined among program participants.

Environmental Factors

Increased attention also is being paid to environmental factors and their impact on the health of individuals. These include hazardous household substances and other poisons, as well as the quality of household building materials, such as lead-based paints and formaldehyde in insulation. Workplaces also present risks to health, and increased attention is being given to environmental protections for employees from dangerous chemicals, pollutants in the air, and hazardous jobs. An estimated one-fifth of all cancer deaths are associated with occupational hazards. A recently publicized environmental hazard has been the harmful asbestos discovered in many older buildings and associated with increased incidence of cancer and respiratory diseases. Yet in spite of the known health risk, workers hired to remove asbestos in many instances have not been provided with needed precautions to limit exposure to the disease. Fifty percent of persons who have long-term exposure to asbestos die. Other environmental risks associated with some occupations also receive little attention. For example, 30 percent of uranium miners develop lung cancer (Employee Assistance Quarterly 1989).

For all persons living in the United States, regardless of occupation, the environment is an increasing health hazard. The rising amount of ozone in the air and of other pollutants in the air, the soil, and food products has resulted in significant increases in heart disease, cancer, and respiratory diseases in the United States in comparison to other countries. States and communities are paying increased attention to road and traffic safety; unsafe housing; contaminated food, meat, and dairy products; pest and animal control; biomedical and consumer product safety; and other public health risks, such as inappropriate disposal of chemical and human wastes, storage and treatment of water, and control of nuclear energy plants.

Smoking is being seen increasingly as an environmental hazard. New studies suggest that smoking not only poses a health threat to smokers but to others who inhale their smoke. Recent federal and state legislation, local community ordinances, and workplace policies limit smoking to specially designed areas or prohibit it completely. For example, smoking is not allowed on airline flights within the continental United States.

Prevention and Wellness Programs

Increased attention is also being given to preventive aspects of health care, although prevention is still secondary to intervention after a health problem has occurred. The 1979 surgeon general's report, *Healthy People,* found that the United States spends only about 5 percent of all health care dollars on promotion of preventive measures. However, some businesses have established wellness programs, with exercise and fitness programs, nutrition and weight control programs, smoking cessation workshops, and other prevention efforts. A number of employers are working with insurance companies to offer incentives to employees who are low health risks, such as salary bonuses or reduced insurance rates. Problems in the workplace and the broader society due to substance abuse have also led employers and insurance companies to establish substance abuse prevention programs in the workplace.

ETHICAL ISSUES

As health care costs continue to increase, more people need health care, and new technology and knowledge make it possible to keep people alive who previously could not have been helped. For these reasons, ethical dilemmas in the area of health care continue to increase. Many of these issues are already before our courts. When infants born three and four months premature can be saved, at what point, if at all, should abortion be prohibited? When infants require extensive neonatal care in order to survive, should such care be made available (see Box 6–1), even if the parents cannot afford the costs? Should the circumstances change to provide such care if the infant can survive but with serious mental and/or physical disabilities? If technology for heart and lung transplants is available, should everyone of all ages and income groups have equal access to these procedures? If genetics testing reveals that a fetus has a serious illness or disability, what choices should be considered, and who should be involved in the considerations? If persons can survive with medical care or special procedures, should they have a right to decide whether to receive the care or to be allowed to die? Do persons have the right to choose unsafe behaviors, such as riding motorcycles without helmets, not using seat belts, or using drugs or alcohol heavily, when injuries or other health problems may result in high costs to others—taxpayers, state and local governments, and others in the same insurance group? Does a pregnant woman have the right to drink, smoke, or use drugs if such actions can compromise the survival of her child? Who makes such decisions? What are the rights of the individual? Of the parents if the person is a child? Of the state or local governments if they are to pay for the care (see Box 6–3).

Several recent court cases have attempted to address some of these issues. In the early 1980s, the so-called Baby Doe case received national attention. This case involved an infant born with serious health problems who would have been seriously disabled, physically and mentally, with surgery and would have died immediately without surgery. The parents did not want the child to have surgery or to suffer, but instead to die a peaceful death. Some members of the hospital staff wanted the child to have the surgery, and others wanted the child to die. Concern has been raised in similar situations throughout the country. In some instances, it was reported that infants had been starved to death or had experienced great pain when life supports were removed from them before they died. Special federal legislation was introduced that would have required local child welfare agencies to handle all such situations as child protective services cases and conduct investigations before medical decisions were made to ensure that children were being protected. The legislation was changed before it passed, so that this did not happen, but the final legislation did mandate that hospitals establish special review boards to deal with such cases.

Some states have also made legislative decisions that have addressed serious ethical issues. In 1987 the state of Oregon voted to stop using its Medicaid funds to pay for liver, heart, bone-marrow, and pancreas transplants and to use the $2.3 million saved to provide prenatal care for women in poverty. Other states, including Alabama, Arizona, Texas, and Virginia, have set limits on what they will pay for organ transplants. Illinois passed transplant legislation allowing funding for transplants but only appropriated a limited amount to pay for them. The California legislature decided to pay for transplants but then reduced its Medicaid funding shortly thereafter, cutting health care benefits to 270,000 Californians. Citizens' groups throughout the United States are forming to address such ethical decisions. One of the first, Oregon Health Decisions, formed in 1983 and has held meetings throughout the state to determine and then advocate for priorities for health funding.

Another major ethical issue relates to decisions surrounding the right to die. The Karen Quinlan case and other similar cases involving persons who are kept alive only because of life-support systems but are in a coma have generated increased debate over the issue. Other situations involving persons who have serious health problems and decide that they wish to die are also receiving attention. For example, recent cases of women who wanted to die involved a

Box 6–3 Bioethics: The Challenges of Genetic Discoveries

The medical system is the core around which other institutions build their use of new diagnostic techniques. Their acceptance in medical settings is encouraging their use outside the clinical context: in insurance companies, in schools, in the workplace, in the courts. The accumulation of diagnostic information about individuals can indicate preventive actions or therapeutic procedures. On the other hand, nonclinical institutions may use the tests in ways that the medical profession did not intend, with devastating results.

Imagine, for example, a small electronics firm planning to manufacture an intricate navigational system. Part of the system must be assembled manually, and the company must carefully select an individual for the arduous training this new job requires. One of the company's employees seems ideal. Dependable, bright, and particularly quick with her hands, she is thirty-five years old and has worked for the company for eight years. This company routinely uses the latest diagnostic tests to screen its employees, and has her biological profile on record. The company physician does a computer scan of it, searching for disabilities that could affect her motor coordination in the future. He discovers an unexpected problem: the woman's DNA markers show, with a high degree of certainty, that she will develop Huntington's disease, an inherited degenerative neurological disorder that results in loss of motor control, depression, personality changes, and death. Symptoms may begin to develop when she is about forty, and soon after she may be unable to work. Her condition would eventually become debilitating and require costly medical care. Thus she would be an economic drain on worker's compensation and the corporation's health insurance and long-term disability policies. From the employer's perspective it would hardly be rational to promote and to train this person. But for the individual, the consequences of this information are disastrous. Her employer might begin to question her ability to function in her current job. If she is terminated, who else would employ her? And who would pay her costly medical bills?

Sophisticated diagnostic tests serve many useful and humane purposes: in clinical settings they may point the way to particular therapeutic measures. They can provide families the opportunity to avoid the anxiety and cost of bearing a child with an untreatable disease; they can identify potential health or behavioral problems for remedial or preventive action. In nonclinical contexts, they can help in the early recognition of learning-disabled children, protect vulnerable workers from exposure to harmful toxic substances, and provide solid evidence for legal decisions about a person's criminal responsibility or competence to stand trial. The language used to describe diagnostic techniques speaks mostly of such benefits. The tests emerging from research in the neurosciences will "generate clinical successes" and provide "answers to disabling mental illness," claims the National Institute of Mental Health. "New genetic clues to heart disease, cancer, AIDS, and other killers could save your life," reports a journalist. "We'll achieve the ideal in medical care, the prevention of disease," predicts the director of a biotechnology firm.

Yet information from tests is not always beneficial or even benign, for in many cases nothing can be done to prevent the predicted disease. What will

continued on next page

happen to a twenty-year-old who discovers that he is likely to develop a fatal disease in middle age? The genetic flaws detected by tests will not necessarily translate into functional impairment; yet knowing about the potential problem without being able to prevent it will be a source of extreme anxiety for him. Moreover, it could subject him to considerable discrimination. He may be denied a job, and his insurance costs will surely increase. Even if something can be done to prevent the manifestation of a predicted condition, awareness of the predisposition can be used in ways that harm the individual. A diagnosed genetic vulnerability to heart disease may encourage a preventive life-style, but the prediction itself could affect a person's career. After all, tests have often been abused, serving, for example, as a means to justify racial or gender bias, to legitimate arbitrary exclusionary practices, and to enhance institutional power with little regard for the rights or personal fate of individuals.

Source: D. Nelkin and L. Tancredi. 1989. The new diagnostics. *National Forum* 69:4, 2–4. Reprinted with permission.

women seriously disabled and in constant pain from cerebral palsy and a woman who was still fairly healthy but had been diagnosed with Alzheimer's disease. The first woman was denied the right to die by a state court and the second committed suicide with the assistance of a physician, who was later acquitted of related charges. Although those situations obviously involve some degree of choice, the American Medical Association estimates that 70 percent of the 6,000 deaths that occur each day involve some sort of negotiation regarding life or death. A recent U.S. survey found that 80 percent of persons interviewed approved of laws allowing medical procedures withheld if the patient wishes (Malcolm 1990).

In many instances, such ethical dilemmas can be avoided, and dollars saved, by providing accessible and affordable health care before the problem occurs. For example, pregnant women who don't receive care during the first three months of pregnancy are 30 percent more likely to deliver infants with low birth weights. Costs for providing such infants neonatal intensive care average $20,000 per child. Not only is $772 saved for each day that an infant remains in its mother's uterus between the twenty-ninth and thirty-fourth week of pregnancy, but the ethical dilemmas that often occur with such cases also are avoided (Metropolitan Council 1985).

HEALTH PLANNING

To eliminate problems in costs of health care, duplication of care in some areas and gaps in others, and interface of public and private sector health care delivery, several important pieces of legislation have been passed. These include the following.

Hill-Burton Act

Passed in 1946, the Hill-Burton Act funded construction of a number of rural hospitals. Amendments in 1964 authorized the development of areawide hospital planning councils and the concept of areawide hospital planning. The act also specifies that hospitals who receive funding through this legislation cannot refuse to serve clients if they are unable to pay for services.

Medicare and Medicaid

These programs provide the majority of federal financing for health care. Medicare is a special health care program for the elderly to be used as a supplement to their other insurance programs (see Chapter 12), whereas Medicaid is available only to low-income individuals and families (see Chapter 4). The growth of both programs has been extensive, with the annual cost for each now being $50 billion.

Medicare is currently experiencing a serious financial crisis, and predictions are that the Medicare trust fund will not be able to pay for services shortly after the year 2000. Although Medicare pays many costs, it does not provide long-term care for chronic needs, particularly nursing home care, or for other costs such as special wheelchairs that might enable more elderly to be cared for in their own homes. Because of increases in premiums for Medicare, in 1990 it paid for less than 50 percent of the total costs of health care for senior citizens.

Although costs for Medicaid have also increased, many of the poor do not qualify for coverage; in 1990, for example, only 37 percent of our nation's poor were covered by Medicaid. The Omnibus Budget Reconciliation Act of 1989 mandated states to increase the number of pregnant women and children covered under Medicaid from those at or below 130 percent of the poverty level to those at or below 133 percent. This 3 percent increase cost the state of Texas alone $26 million in state dollars, with the federal government paying the remainder of costs. By 1992, proposed federal legislation could extend Medicaid coverage to families who are at or below 185 percent.

The 1988 Family Support Act also extends Medicaid coverage to AFDC (Aid to Families with Dependent Children) recipients for up to one year after they become employed. Although more expensive initially, it is hoped that this will actually reduce government health care costs, since large numbers of recipients who leave the AFDC rolls have been forced to return when they or their children experience health problems and they have not been able to become financially stable enough to afford health insurance. It is hoped that the employment programs for public assistance recipients in states required by the Family Support Act will result in human services agency staff helping more recipients find long-term jobs that offer health insurance, and that the extension of Medicaid as a transitional benefit also will help recipients to remain off AFDC once they obtain employment.

Although Medicare was intended to provide the bulk of health care for the elderly, with Medicaid intended to serve children and families, increasing amounts of Medicaid dollars are being used to pay for nursing home care that is not provided under Medicare. In 1987, for example, 41 percent of all nursing home costs were paid for by Medicaid. State and federal budget crises in Medicaid are not because of increased costs to serve families, but to cover nursing home and other extensive health care costs for the increased number of elderly persons who cannot afford to pay for health care not provided by Medicare.

Maternal and Child Health Act

Title V of the Maternal and Child Health Act, through the Women and Infant Care (WIC) program, provides screening, counseling, and food supplements for pregnant women and for children up to five years old who are at nutritional risk due to low income. Studies show that WIC reduces infant deaths, low birth weight, and premature births and increases good health and cognitive development among preschoolers. Since the Reagan administration significantly reduced funding for the program, some states have been able to document that infant deaths, low birth rate, and premature births are on the increase and can be tied to the reduction in WIC programs. Additionally, because states have the option of offering the program, only half of eligible women and children in the United States were receiving WIC services in 1990.

Comprehensive Health Planning Act

Passed in 1966, the Comprehensive Health Planning Act expands on the concept of local health planning districts to coordinate services and also requires review of other factors affecting the health of area residents, such as life-style and environmental conditions. The National Health Planning and Resources Development Act of 1974 further mandates the establishment of health systems agencies and statewide health coordinating councils to monitor hospital bed supply and occupancy rates, obstetric and neonatal special care units, pediatric beds, open heart surgery, and availability of expensive technological equipment such as megavoltage radiation equipment. The focus of this legislation is to increase availability of services in rural or other underserved areas and eliminate duplication in other areas, as well as to provide high-quality care at reduced costs by requiring rate review panels and professional standards of care.

Health Maintenance Organization Act

Passed in 1972, this act allows the development of health maintenance organizations (HMOs) to reduce health care costs for individuals. Most HMOs require a monthly fee, which allows free or low-cost visits to a special facility or group of facilities for health care. HMOs are intended to reduce health costs and encourage preventive health care.

Ryan White Comprehensive AIDS Resources Emergency Act of 1989

This act, named in honor of eighteen-year-old Ryan White, who died of AIDS in 1989, authorizes emergency funds to metropolitan areas hardest hit by AIDS, grants to states for comprehensive planning and service delivery, early intervention with HIV-infected infants, and the development of individual pilot projects to serve children with AIDS and to provide AIDS services in rural areas.

Proposed Legislation

Efforts continue to be made through legislation and other policy arenas to balance health care costs with quality of care. It appears likely that some sort of mandated universal health care program will be established. Currently, the United States and South Africa are the only two industrialized countries that do not have some type of government-funded universal health care system.

Many advocates for a universal health care system in the United States are calling for a national health insurance program for all types of health care, not just catastrophic illness. Those in favor of such a program argue that costs for health insurance are too high for large numbers of individuals to afford, that many local hospitals are going in debt because they are having to pay health care costs for the increasing numbers of indigent persons, and that health care costs are higher because persons are not seeking preventive health care, which would be more likely were there a national health insurance program with such an emphasis. Those against such a program argue that it means going to a system of socialized medicine, that the costs would be too high, and that people would clog the health care delivery system with trivial health problems that do not require medical attention.

Proponents of government-funded health care programs have proposed a variety of alternatives, including having the federal government collect funds for the program from various taxes, with the program administered by private insurance companies; having the government collect and administer the program, developing an expanded Medicare program available to everyone; having persons claim a tax credit on their income tax form if they use health care; and providing health coverage only for catastrophic illnesses.

Local states also are passing health care legislation; limiting the amounts that can be collected in malpractice suits, in an attempt to keep medical costs down; mandating availability of health care for indigent persons and reducing the burden on local hospitals in poor areas of states; and establishing procedures for decision making about organ transplants and life-threatening situations. More states will follow the path set by Oregon and California, passing legislation limiting the types of health care allowed with state dollars.

Legislation, planning, and service delivery at all levels will need to focus on reducing the costs of health care while increasing the accessibility. Other critical issues in the next decades include reducing the fragmentation of care, developing private and/or government insurance plans for long-term health care for the elderly, and increasing the availability of funding for home health and respite care.

SOCIAL WORK ROLES IN THE DELIVERY OF HEALTH SERVICES

Today, social workers play many roles in a variety of health care settings. In fact, social work in health care, particularly in working with the elderly, is one of the fastest-growing occupational areas today. Health care is the third largest field of social work practice, with 14 percent of social workers employed in health care settings. Three recent developments have expanded the social work profession's involvement in health care. In 1989, federal legislation relating to nursing homes mandated that by October 1990 all nursing homes in the United States with 120 or more beds must have a social worker with a BSW or MSSW degree. Changes in legislation relating to Medicare also now require that social workers with an MSW degree who also have professional social work certification should be reimbursed for providing outpatient mental health services to the elderly. Previously, only psychiatrists or psychologists could be reimbursed under Medicare for these services. Also, for the first time, federal legislation providing training monies for persons interested in health care includes social workers as well as nurses and physicians.

Both social work roles and practice settings have increased significantly since the first social worker was employed at Massachusetts General Hospital in Boston in 1905. At that time, hospitals and general physicians were the major sources of health care. The social worker worked with the physician, other hospital staff, and the patient's family to ensure that high quality care and attention continued after the patient returned home.

Although the responsibility for care after a patient leaves the hospital is still a major one for many social workers in health care settings, social workers in these settings now provide a variety of other tasks as well. Social workers often serve as a liaison between the patient's family and the health care staff. They help the staff understand family concerns and how family constraints and other environmental factors may affect a patient's ability to recover. They also help patients and their families understand the implications of illness and issues relating to recovery and care. In many instances, the social worker provides support to the family when a death occurs or a patient's condition worsens.

Social workers in health care settings provide a number of functions, including

○ conducting screening and assessments to determine health risk factors, particularly those involving the family and the broader environment;

○ offering social services to patients and their families, such as individual counseling to help a patient deal with a major illness or loss of previous capabilities due to accident or illness, helping family members grieve over a dying individual, or helping a teenage mother accept her decision to place the child for adoption;

○ providing case management services, including working with other social and health services agencies regarding patient needs, such as helping arrange for financial assistance to pay hospital bills, nursing home or home health care for patients when they leave the hospital, or emergency child care for a single parent who is hospitalized;

○ serving as a member of a health care team and helping others understand a patient's emotional needs and home/family situation;

○ advocating for the patient's needs at all levels of the environment, including the patient's family, hospital and other health care settings, school, workplace, and community;

○ representing the hospital and providing consultation to other community agencies, such as child protective services agencies in child abuse cases;

○ providing preventive education and counseling to individuals relating to family planning, nutrition, prenatal care, and human growth and development;

○ providing health planning and policy recommendations to local communities, states, and the federal government in areas such as hospital care, community health care, environmental protection, and control of contagious diseases.

Increasingly, social workers in health care settings serve as case managers, working with patients and their families to identify needs, locating appropriate resources to meet those needs, developing an intervention plan delineating how resources will meet specific needs, and then overseeing the implementation of the plan to ensure that the resources are effectively meeting the patient's and the family's needs.

Whereas many social workers function in agencies administered by and hiring primarily social workers, called **primary settings,** health care settings are considered **secondary settings** because they are administered and staffed largely by nonsocial work professionals. Social workers in health care settings must be comfortable with their roles and be able to articulate their roles and functions clearly to non–social workers. A strong professional identity is important for health care social workers. Additionally, social workers in health care settings must be able to work comfortably within a medical setting. Knowledge and understanding of the medical profession and health care are important for social workers, as is the ability to function as a team member with representatives from a variety of disciplines. Social workers in health care settings, particularly hospital settings, must be able to handle crisis intervention, and they most often prefer short-term social work services rather than long-term client relationships. They must also be able to work well under pressure and high stress and be comfortable with death and dying.

Hospital Settings

The American Hospital Association requires that a hospital maintain a social services department as a condition of accreditation. Social workers in hospitals may provide services to all patients who need them or may provide specialized services. Larger hospitals employ emergency room social workers, pediatric social workers, intensive care social workers, and social workers who work primarily on cardiac, cancer, or other specialized wards. M. D. Anderson Hospital in Houston, Texas, for example, has over twenty social workers. It is a large hospital that specializes in treating cancer patients. A number of large hospitals have added social workers who provide social services primarily to AIDS patients. Other hospitals use social workers in preventive efforts, providing outreach services, including home visits to mothers identified during their hospital stay as potentially at risk to abuse or neglect their children. Still others use social workers to coordinate rehabilitative services, acting as a case manager to ensure that occupational, physical, recreational, speech, and vocational therapy services are provided. Social workers work in both public and private hospitals, providing both inpatient and outpatient care. Many are employed by Veterans Administration (VA) hospitals, which have a long-time tradition of using social workers to work with persons who have served in the armed forces. Many VA social workers provide specialized counseling relating to physical disabilities and alcohol and drug abuse. A number of VA social workers now specialize in post-Vietnam stress syndrome and provide services to Vietnam veterans and their families.

Because of accreditation standards, most hospital social workers must have a master's degree in social work. Many graduate schools of social work offer specializations in medical or health care.

Long-Term Care Facilities and Nursing Homes

Many persons who suffer from illness or disability do not need the intensive services of a hospital but cannot care for themselves in their own homes without assistance. For some individuals, particularly the frail elderly, **long-term care facilities,** programs that provide medical care and other services to individuals including the elderly and the disabled, such as nursing homes, are most appropriate. There are various levels of care facilities, with licensing and accreditation requirements for each. From 1965 to 1972, social work services were mandated for all nursing homes that cared for residents covered by Medicare. Beginning in 1990, all nursing homes with 120 or more beds must employ a social worker. Social workers in these settings help residents adjust to the nursing home environment, help families deal with their guilt and feelings of loss after such placements, serve as liaisons to other social services and health care agencies, and provide individual and group counseling and other social services for nursing home residents and their families.

Provision of social work services to the elderly in health care settings is probably the fastest-growing area in the field of social work, and many schools of social work are offering specializations at the master's degree level in health and gerontology and special courses at the BSW level in these areas to meet the demand.

Community-Based Health Care Programs

Many social workers, both at the BSW and MSW levels, are employed in local community-based health care programs. Most state health departments operate local health clinics, which provide a variety of health services available to low-income residents as well as community education programs for all residents. Such programs include immunizations, family planning services, prenatal care, well-baby and pediatric services, nutrition and other types of education programs, and basic health care. Many health clinics employ social workers to work with patients and their families as other health care services are provided. For example, some clinics operate high-risk infant clinics, which include social services for parents of infants at risk for abuse, neglect, or other serious health problems or those who already have serious health problems and whose parents need monitoring and support. Social workers also work with local community groups and schools, providing outreach programs to publicize such concerns as sexually transmitted diseases and teen pregnancy.

Social workers are also employed in family planning clinics, such as those offered through Planned Parenthood, providing counseling and help in decision making regarding pregnancy prevention or intervention, such as planning for adoptive services when an unwanted pregnancy has occurred. With new technology that can diagnose problems in embryos in the uterus, many health providers also are employing social workers to provide genetic counseling, helping patients to understand possibilities of giving birth to infants with potential problems, and to make appropriate decisions regarding whether to become pregnant or to terminate a pregnancy.

Many social workers are employed in community health care settings that provide services to persons with AIDS and their families. Social workers provide individual, family, and group counseling; serve as case managers assisting clients and their families in accessing community resources; provide advocacy for clients and their families; and offer community education programs.

Increasingly, other health care settings are recognizing the impact of environmental factors, such as unemployment, on mental and physical health. To help address the relationship, previously traditional health care settings increasingly are employing social workers. In many areas, for example, local physicians' clinics, usually operated by a small group of physicians who share a practice, are hiring social workers to provide counseling to patients in an effort to improve mental health and reduce stress. HMOs are also hiring social workers to perform similar functions.

Home Health Care

Many states and communities are recognizing the need for **home health care,** or services that enable persons with health problems to remain in their own homes. Home health care services most often preserve self-esteem and longevity for the individual and are far less costly than hospital or nursing home care. Trained nurses and home health aides, as well as social workers, provide health care in a person's home. Social workers provide counseling to both the client and the family, help clients cope emotionally, and serve as case managers, ensuring that appropriate resources are provided to deal with client needs. Home health care allows the elderly, persons with AIDS, and other persons who do not need to be hospitalized the right to have greater control over their lives. Such care also offers them dignity and emotional support they might not receive in a hospital or other institutional setting. Because home health care programs are more cost-effective than hospitalization or other institutional care, these programs will be expanded during the next several decades, and more social workers will be needed to work in them.

State Departments of Health and Health Planning Agencies

Many social workers at both the BSW and MSW levels are employed in health care policy and planning jobs. They help make critical decisions regarding funding, policies, and programs for state legislatures, federal officials, and state and local health departments and planning agencies. A social worker might determine how many more elderly could be served by Medicaid if the income eligibility requirements were changed from 130 percent to 150 percent above the poverty line, develop plans to implement a community wide AIDS education program, or suggest ways that a local hospital can be more responsive to the needs of the primarily black and Mexican-American population it serves. In one state, for example, planners in the state health department recommended that the agency solicit bids for infant formula for infants served by the WIC program instead of contracting with the same company the agency had always used. The bids received were much lower than the amount the department was paying for the formula, enabling the department to serve many more clients while still saving money.

The impact of environmental changes on individuals, disease prevention and control, monitoring of solid waste and water facilities, and emergency and disaster planning are other areas in which social workers in these programs become involved. State health departments provide services relating to dental health, family planning, nutrition, and teenage pregnancy; nutrition programs for pregnant women and young children; periodic health screening programs for infants and young children; drug and alcohol programs; and teenage parent services. Health departments and other federal, state, and local agencies also develop policies and implement plans for the provision of emergency and disaster services. Social workers from a number of federal, state, and local public and private agencies, for example, were involved in planning and overseeing emergency services after hurricane Hugo hit the Carolinas and a major earthquake occurred in California in 1989.

The National Public Health Service provides health and health-related services to indigent populations in areas with few medical practitioners, such as American Indian reservations and migrant areas. The service also monitors communicable diseases and provides research in a variety of health areas. Many individuals who receive federal funds to attend college or professional schools in health-related areas, including social work, are required in return to provide a set number of years of service through the Public Health Service after graduation. Other federal programs such as the National Institutes of Health (NIH) also provide research and policy alternatives. Both the Public Health Service and the National Institutes of Health employ social workers at the BSW and MSW levels. The National Institutes of Health, for example, employs social workers in direct care settings established to develop new techniques in health care, such as its pediatric AIDS program in Washington, D.C.

Other Health Care Settings

Social workers are involved in numerous other health-related programs. Many work for the American Red Cross, for example, providing emergency services to families when disaster strikes. Recently developed health programs that often employ social workers include women's health clinics, which currently number over 1,000 and provide gynecological and primary care using a holistic health approach; genetic counseling centers; and rape crisis centers. Many EMS (emergency medical service) programs in large cities are employing social workers to assist in crisis intervention during family violence, child maltreatment, rape and homicide.

Hospices are multiplying throughout the country and employing social workers. Originally begun in England, hospice programs allow terminally ill persons to die at home or in a homelike setting surrounded by family members rather than in an often alien hospital environment. Using the stages of grief described by Elizabeth Kübler-Ross as a framework, many hospices employ social workers to work with families and the dying person or to supervise a cadre of volunteers who provide similar services. As more elderly persons and persons with AIDS continue to live longer, the need for hospice programs will increase. As critical issues in health care continue to be identified, the functions of social workers in all types of health care settings will continue to expand.

SUMMARY

The state of health care in the United States has been declared a national crisis by many policymakers and health care experts. Issues relating to health care continue to be controversial and complex. As health care costs continue to rise, new technology and medical discoveries continue to be made. Ethical issues in health care—such as who should receive services at what cost, who should be allowed to make decisions about the right to refuse medical care, and who should be held accountable when a person's health is jeopardized by that person or another individual—are becoming increasingly complex and arising more often than in the past.

The AIDS epidemic has focused additional attention on the health care system. With more persons living longer, concerns about health care will become increasingly evident. The relationships between environmental factors and health need additional exploration. Finally the large number of Americans, particularly children and members of minority groups, who receive inadequate health care, if any, and the long-term implications for these individuals in all areas of their lives and for our country as a whole must be addressed.

Finding a balance of health care that is available, accessible, acceptable, and affordable, yet accountable to funding sources, is the highest priority for the United States in the next decade. Whatever the balance established, social workers will play an ever-increasing role in both the planning and the delivery of health care services. Social work in health care settings is one of the fastest-growing areas of social work today.

KEY TERMS

acquired immune deficiency
  syndrome (AIDS)
AIDS-related complex (ARC)
bioethics
catastrophic illnesses
health
health care
health maintenance organizations
  (HMOs)
health risk factors

HIV-positive
home health care
hospices
infant mortality rates
long-term care facilities
primary setting
private insurance
public insurance
secondary setting

DISCUSSION QUESTIONS

1. Discuss some of the changes in the focus of health care that have taken place in the United States since colonial times.

2. Identify at least three reasons why health care costs have increased over the last decade.

3. Which groups of persons in the United States are most at risk to experience problems with their health? Why?

4. What are some of the ethical issues faced by health care providers and policymakers? Who do you think should receive priority in access to basic health care services if costs prevent it being available to everyone?

5. What are some preventive programs social workers can implement to reduce the need for health care in the United States?

6. Identify at least three roles social workers might play at various levels of the environment in dealing with the AIDS epidemic. Why is AIDS such an important issue for the world today?

7. Identify at least five roles social workers can play in the delivery of health care services. How do careers for social workers in health care compare to careers in other areas in terms of availability and opportunity? Why?

REFERENCES

Braveman, P. 1989. *New England Journal of Medicine.*

Brenner, M. H. 1973. Fetal, infant and maternal mortality during periods of economic stress. *International Journal of Health Sciences* 3:145–59

Catalano, R. 1979. *Health behavior and the community: An ecological perspective.* New York: Pergamon.

Children's Defense Fund. 1988. *Children's Defense Fund budget: An analysis of the FY 1989 federal budget and children.* Washington, D.C.: Author.

Comprehensive Care Corporation. 1981. *Employee assistance programs: A dollars and sense issue.* Newport Beach, Calif.: Author.

Dohrenwend, B. S., and B. P. Dohrenwend, eds. 1974. *Stressful life events: Their nature and effects.* New York: Wiley.

Edwards, R. 1990. Health system's crisis calls for a cure. *NASW News,* 35:6. 2 and 4.

Employee Assistance Quarterly. 1989.

Ford Foundation. 1989. *The common good: Social welfare and the American future.* New York: Author.

Gibbs, N. 1990. Shameful bequests to the next generation. *Time* (October 8) 42–46.

Kingston, E., C. S. Petersen, J. Magaziner, E. D. Lopez, C. Joyce, E. Kassner, and S. Sowers. 1988. Health, employment and welfare histories of Maryland's older General Assistance recipients. *Social Work.* 33:2 105–109.

Malcolm, A. 1990. Whose right to die? *Austin American Statesman,* (June 10) D1, D4.

Mechanic, D. 1986. *From advocacy to allocation: The evolving American health care system.* New York: Free Press.

Nacman, M. 1977. Social work in health settings: A historical review. *Social Work in Health Care* 2 (Summer): 407–17.

Nelkin, D., and Tancredi, L. 1989. The new diagnostics. *National Forum: Phi Kappa Phi Journal* (Fall):2–6.

Rothstein, M. 1989. AIDS, rights and health care costs. *National Forum: Phi Kappa Phi Journal.* (Fall):7–10

Schlesinger, E. 1985. *Health care social work practice: Concepts and strategies.* St. Louis, Mo.: Times Mirror-Mosby.

Schoenborn, C. and M. Marano, Current estimates from the national health review survey: United States, 1987. *Vital and Health Statistics,* Series 10, No. 166. Washington, D.C.: Public Health Service, 115.

Scott, J. Insurance vital to babies, study says. 1989. *Austin American Statesman,* 24 August, p. A3.

U.S. Bureau of the Census. 1987. *Statistical abstract of the United States.* Washington, D.C.: GPO.

U.S. Congress. Office of Technology Assessment. 1981. *The implications of cost-effectiveness analysis of medical technology: Case Study No. 10: The costs and effectiveness of neonatal intensive care.*

U.S. Department of Agriculture. 1990. *Five state study of women, infants and children program.* Washington, D.C.: GPO.

U.S. Public Health Service. 1977. 200 years of child health. In *200 years of children,* ed., F. Grotberg. Washington, D.C.: GPO.

U.S. Surgeon General. 1979. *Healthy people: The surgeon general's report on health promotion and disease prevention.* Washington, D.C.: GPO.

Zastrow, C. and K. Kirst-Ashman. 1990. *Understanding human behavior and the social environment.* Chicago: Nelson Hall.

SUGGESTED FURTHER READINGS

Biomedical ethics and the Bill of Rights. 1989. Special issue. *National Forum: Phi Kappa Phi Journal.* Baton Rouge, La.: Louisiana State University.

Bracht, N. 1978. *Social work in health care.* New York: Haworth.

Dougherty, C. 1988. *American health care: Realities, rights and reforms.* New York: Oxford University Press.

Estes, R. 1984. *Social work in health care.* St. Louis, Mo.: Green.

Germain, C. 1984. *Social work practice in health care: An ecological perspective.* New York: Free Press.

Marmor, T., and Christianson, J. 1982. *Health care policy: A political economy approach.* Beverly Hills, Calif.: Sage.

Schlesinger, E. 1985. *Health care social work practice: Concepts and strategies.* St. Louis, Mo.: Times Mirror-Mosby.

Shilts, R. 1987. *And the band played on: Politics, people and the AIDS Epidemic.* New York: St. Martin's.

The Needs of Children, Youth, and Families

Divorced for two years, Ernestine Moore is struggling to survive. Her five children are in a foster home while she tries to stabilize her life. Mrs. Moore is looking forward to the day when she and her children can live together as a family again.

Mrs. Moore came from a large family. Her father drank often and beat her mother, her siblings, and Ernestine. Pregnant at age sixteen and afraid of what her father would do, she eloped with the father of her child, a nineteen-year-old high school graduate who worked at a fast-food restaurant. The first year was fairly peaceful for the Moore family, although money was a continual problem. Lacking health insurance, it took them several years to pay the bills for the birth of the baby. However, both of the Moores were excited about the baby, and Mrs. Moore worked hard to provide a good home for her husband and her baby. She wanted desperately to have the kind of home and family she had not had as a child.

The Moores had three more children during the next six years. Because one of the children had a number of health problems, financial pressures continued to mount, and life became increasingly stressful. Mr. Moore began to drink heavily and beat

Mrs. Moore often. He also physically and verbally abused the middle child, a boy who was diagnosed as mildly developmentally disabled. When Mrs. Moore became pregnant again, her husband left her. Since that time, he has only paid child support for six months.

After her husband left, Mrs. Moore moved in with a sister, who had three children. To support her children and help contribute to the rent her sister was paying, she got two jobs, one in a fast-food restaurant and one at night cleaning a bank. Shortly after her new baby was born, this arrangement ended because of the continual arguments between the two sisters over money, space, and child rearing.

At that point, Mrs. Moore applied for food stamps and medical assistance and moved into a two-room apartment. She applied for low-income housing, and although she was eligible, she was told there was a two-year waiting list. Mrs. Moore hired a young teenage girl to babysit for her children while she worked. Tired and overwhelmed, Mrs. Moore had little time to spend taking care of the children or the apartment. She became increasingly abusive toward the children. The older children did poorly in school and *were continually fighting, stealing, and vandalizing. Neighbors in the apartment complex saw the younger children outside at all hours, unsupervised, often wearing only diapers. They often heard Mrs. Moore screaming and the baby crying throughout the night.*

Mrs. Moore's babysitter quit because Mrs. Moore was behind in paying her. When Mrs. Moore missed two days of work while trying desperately to find another sitter, she was fired from her fast-food job. Afraid that she would also lose her cleaning job, she began putting the younger children to bed at six o'clock and leaving the oldest child, eight, in charge until she returned home. Finally, the Moores were evicted from the apartment because Mrs. Moore was unable to pay the rent. For two weeks the whole family slept in a friend's car. Finally, when the oldest child came to school with multiple bruises and complaining of a sore arm and revealed the family's living situation to her teacher, the local child protective services agency was called. The social worker discovered all of the children badly bruised and malnourished, and the

oldest girl had a broken arm. Mrs. Moore was overwhelmed and angry, and she felt extremely guilty about what had happened to her children.

The children were placed in foster care with an older, nurturing couple. With more structure and a stable living situation, the children began doing better in school and were able to develop some positive relationships with others. Mrs. Moore visited the children often and began to see the foster parents as caring individuals who seemed almost like parents to her.

She enrolled in a job-training program and was hired as a health care aide for a local nursing home. She enjoys her job and is talking about getting her high school equivalency certificate and going to nursing school. Mrs. Moore's social worker encouraged her to join Parents Anonymous, a support group for abusive parents. For the first time, Mrs. Moore has developed positive, trusting relationships with others. She has located an affordable duplex, and she and her social worker are making plans to have the children return home permanently.

For all individuals, the family is probably the most significant social system within which they function. Within the family we first develop trusting relationships, a special identity, and a sense of self-worth. Traditionally, despite difficulties in society, the family has been viewed as a safe, protective haven where individuals can receive nurturing, love, and support. It is increasingly difficult for children and their families to grow up in today's complex and rapidly changing world. Daily, children are confronted with family financial pressures, the need for one or both parents to work long hours, or the physical or mental illness or loss of a family member.

Unable to cope with these pressures, family members often turn to substance abuse, resort to violence, or withdraw from other family members and do not respond to their needs. Sometimes, because they did not receive love and nurturing when they were children, the parents cannot provide this for their own children. Other parents do not know how to provide for their own children because they never learned what children need at certain ages or what to expect from them. Other families, although generally functioning well, may be unable to meet the needs of family members adequately during some type of crisis, such as death or a serious illness.

How well a family is able to meet the needs of its members also depends on other systems within the family's environment. The workplace, the neighborhood, the community, and the society with which that family interacts have a tremendous impact on its well-being. Urie Bronfenbrenner (1979) and James Garbarino (1982), two researchers interested in the development of children and families, suggest that more attention should be given to intervention in these broader systems, rather than just providing services to individual family members. A family that functions within an unsupportive environment is much more susceptible to family problems than a family functioning within a supportive environment. If the family lives in a community that has no programs available to family members, that also may threaten the family's well-being.

Consider Mrs. Moore's situation. Her children were at risk for many reasons. Abused as a child, she learned to distrust others and failed to have her emotional needs met during her childhood. This left Mrs. Moore feeling worthless and inadequate. Individuals with low self-esteem are more likely to get pregnant during their teenage years. They also are more likely to abuse their children than are other parents. Parents like Mrs. Moore also have learned from their own parents that anger is dealt with by hitting. Like Mrs. Moore, they may be used to living with an alcoholic and may have learned many behavior patterns that they carry into their own lives.

In this chapter we discuss general issues and trends that must be considered when focusing on the needs of children, youth, and families; the types and extent of problems that can have an impact on children and their families; and factors that place families more at risk to experience those problems. Chapter 8 focuses on services and policies that prevent or alleviate problems experienced by children, youth, and families. The roles that social workers play in providing these services and developing and implementing policies are also discussed in Chapter 8.

ISSUES TO CONSIDER WHEN ADDRESSING CHILD AND FAMILY NEEDS

What Is a Family?

The typical American family in the 1950s through 1970s included a husband, a wife, and 2.6 children. Today, only about 11 percent of American families are of this type. Twenty percent of all families are headed by only one parent, usually a woman, although an increasing number of men are assuming responsibility for raising children following a divorce or separation. Many families have extended-family members, such as grandparents, aunts, uncles, or cousins living with them. Others have children adopted through the court system or taken in informally; still others have foster children. It is also becoming more common for individuals to live together who are not related by blood or marriage.

During the 1970s, the federal government funded a program to develop a national policy that supported families. The program's first task was to define *family*. The program staff determined that this task was impossible! Others, however, provide a broad definition of a **family**, exemplified by the following: Any group of individuals who are bonded together through marriage, kinship, adoption, or mutual agreement (Goode 1964). When referring to needs of children and families, a family is referred to within the context of a parent figure or figures, and at least one child. Perhaps the most important issue in relation to what constitutes a family is that whereas all children and families have similar needs—to be loved, wanted, accepted, fed, clothed, given shelter, and protected—no two families are alike. Each family may be viewed as its own system, and each family system must be viewed as unique.

How Are Families of Today Viewed?

There are many frameworks used when studying the family. Two of the most relevant when considering the family within the context of the social welfare system are the systems/ecological framework and the life-span-development framework. The systems/ecological framework allows one to explore interactions and relationships between family members as well as between the family and other levels of the environment, such as extended family members, other families, the neighborhood, the school, the church or snynagogue, the workplace, the community, the state, and other larger systems such as the economic system and the political system. Mrs. Moore's family was discussed briefly using the systems/ecological framework.

A second framework that can be used is the life-span development framework, previously discussed in Chapter 3. The family as a social system has more impact on the individual throughout the life cycle than any other system. Even before birth, the physical and emotional health of the family in which the child will be born and the environment in which the family functions significantly affect the child's future. How well individuals learn to trust others, to develop autonomy, to take initiative, to be industrious, to have a positive identity, to be intimate with others, to give something of themselves back to others, and to face death with integrity are all shaped extensively by relationships within the family.

Families also go through stages of development. Carter and McGoldrick (1980) identify six stages of family life, each with emotional transitions and changes in status: the unattached young adult, early marriage, the birth and care of young children, raising adolescents, launching children, and aging. The family's needs and interactions with the social welfare system differ according to its stage of development.

What Is a Healthy Family?

Unfortunately, much of the literature about families focuses on family problems without considering what constitutes a healthy family. The perfect family portrayed in television situation comedies does not exist, and all families experience some type of problem at some point during the family life cycle. However, some families are better able to cope with family problems because of the availability of financial resources and social support systems, and the physical and mental health of family members. A major crisis—no matter how healthy the family is—will have a serious impact on the family and will likely result in at least a temporary need for assistance from the social welfare system in some way.

Studies show that there are a number of factors associated with healthy families. These include the opportunity to express all ideas and feelings, no family secrets, a valuing of everyone's opinions and feelings, rules that are flexible yet enforced with consistency, positive energy, and opportunities for growth and change. Children are more likely to grow up to be successful adults able to develop intimate relationships, maintain employment that allows self-sufficiency, and experience relatively good health and mental health if they experience nurturing, consistent parenting, particularly during their first month of life; are two years or more apart in age from any siblings; and have access to others who can provide emotional support if their immediate families cannot do so (Werner and Smith 1977).

How Are Family Problems Defined?

What constitutes a family problem depends a great deal on the perspective of the individual defining the problem. How a problem is defined depends on a variety of factors, including the social and historical context within which the problem takes place; the attitudes and values of the culture or society of the family; the attitudes and values of the community in which the family resides and the norms of the community; the attitudes, values, culture, previous life experiences, and professional background of the person defining the problem; legal definitions of the problem; and the availability of resources to address the problem.

Cultural attitudes, values and practices shape how family problems are defined. In cultures where women become sexually active as soon as they reach menses, teenage pregnancy is not likely to be considered a problem. Some cultures think it abusive that we make young children sit in a dental chair and force them to open their mouths and have their teeth pulled out. Some family policy experts suggest that the United States as a society is less supportive of children and families than other countries, when legislation and programs supportive of families are considered. In many Scandinavian countries, for example, the government provides free health care to children, subsidies for working parents to stay home when their children are young, and free child care. Other policy experts suggest that our country's fascination with violence as exemplified through the media and sports events has a strong impact on the high incidence of violence within the family, and that the emphasis placed on sex in the media contributes to the high incidence of teenage pregnancy.

The *norms and values of the community* also shape the way family problems are defined. If everyone within a community is unemployed and lives in housing without plumbing and with dirt floors and all children are poorly fed and clothed, the families within that community living under those circumstances are not likely to be seen as neglecting their children. However, a family living like that in a wealthy community with high employment and stability most likely would be considered neglectful. Whipping a child with a belt is not as likely to be considered child maltreatment in some communities or parts of the country as in others.

The *attitudes, values, personal life experiences, and professional background of the person* defining the problem also influence how a problem is defined. A person raised in a conservative family, where drinking of any alcoholic beverages was considered taboo, might define alcoholism differently than a person raised in a family where drinking alcoholic beverages was commonplace. A physician may be more likely to define child abuse only in terms of bruises or broken bones, whereas a social worker may be more likely to argue that emotional neglect or harassment also constitutes an important form of child abuse.

Legal statutes also provide definitions of some types of family problems. These definitions vary by country and state and often leave a great deal of room for interpretation at the personal, professional, and community levels. For example, child maltreatment has been defined at the national level as "the physical or mental injury, or threatened physical or mental injury, of a child by the acts or omissions of the child's parent or other person responsible for the child's welfare" (National Center on Child Abuse and Neglect 1980c). Terms such as *mental injury, threatened,* and *acts or omissions* often are difficult to interpret. At the same time, they allow leeway for additional protection of children who may be subject to just as much risk as a child in a more easily defined situation. For example, a child who is constantly threatened with a knife or gun, even though never actually hurt, is at risk of suffering emotional problems.

The *availability of resources* to address the problem may be the most important factor of all in how a problem is defined. The broader the definition, the more children and families will be identified as having the problem and needing assistance; the narrower the definition, the fewer identified as having the problem and needing assistance. The legal definition just given, for example, allows for the inclusion of neglected and emotionally maltreated children. In fact, when a similar state definition was first implemented, three times as many cases of child neglect were reported as cases of child abuse. Almost ten years later, due to scarce resources and significantly more cases reported, physical abuse and neglect cases are investigated and substantiated about equally, and only the most serious cases are defined as such. Resources are so stretched to their limits in many states that more narrow definitions of child maltreatment are being used. During the Kennedy and Johnson administrations, when resources to address domestic social problems were abundant, the emphasis was on developing programs to "achieve the maximum potential of all children." The emphasis shifted under the Nixon administration to "meeting minimum levels of care for children and their families," thus significantly narrowing the numbers of families and children who fit within the definition of needed services (Steiner 1976). The latter emphasis has continued under subsequent presidential administrations.

What Causes Families to Have Problems?

Families have problems for many reasons—and some families experience similar problems but for different reasons. There is no single cause for a given problem, which is why it is important to use a systems/ecological perspective in addressing family problems. It also is more appropriate to say that there are certain factors *associated* with specific family problems, rather than factors that *cause* those problems. This means that a family experiencing a problem may have other problems as well, but it is often difficult to determine which problem caused the other.

We know that problems often go together. One is likely to find child abuse, spouse abuse, alcoholism, teenage pregnancy, and divorce within the same family. Individuals with these problems are more likely to be under stress; worried about financial pressures, whether rich or poor; have low self-esteem; and come from families where similar problems existed when they were children than individuals in families without these problems.

Services for children and families often are provided by problem area—for example, specialized services for alcoholism, child abuse and neglect, and spouse abuse—rather than services that focus on the family as a system. This is due largely to the categorical basis on which state and federal funding generally is allocated. This categorical funding system has resulted in fragmented and duplicated services, as well as gaps in services in which client groups "fall through the cracks."

How Do Cultural and Gender Differences Affect Family Problems?

Statistics show that more children and families who experience family problems in the United States are white and headed by two parents, but that is only because there are more white, two-parent families than other types of families (Children's Defense Fund 1988). Thus, it is important to consider not only raw counts but rates; that is, numbers of individuals of a certain group experiencing problems compared to the total population of that group. Such comparisons show that some groups are more vulnerable, or at risk, to experience certain problems than other groups.

In the United States single women with children are more at risk for experiencing family problems than are men; similarly, members of ethnic minority groups are more at risk than whites. The reader should not infer from this statement that women and members of ethnic minority groups are in any way less competent, genetically impaired, more prone toward violence, or self-absorbed than others. Instead, there are a number of very critical reasons why women and minority groups are more at risk than other groups. Whereas one out of four children in the United States grows up in poverty, nearly half of all black children and nearly 40 percent of Hispanic children are poor (Children's Defense Fund 1988). The unemployment rate in this country in 1988 was 12 percent for white youth aged eighteen to twenty-four not enrolled in school and 30 percent for minority youth. Twenty-five percent of all households in 1990 were single-parent families, most headed by women. More than 50 percent of all households headed by women and 80 percent of all households headed by women under twenty-five years of age fall below the poverty level. Only 13 percent of all two-parent families are below this level (Children's Defense Fund 1988). In 1990, 80 percent of all white children, 67 percent of all Hispanic children, and 38 percent of all black children lived in two-parent families. It is estimated that by the year 2000, 70 percent of black families will be headed by single-parent women, and 30 percent of black men will be unemployed (Moyers 1986).

Because individuals who experience poverty are far more likely to experience stress, they are far more at risk of experiencing other family problems. Thus, women and minority groups, by the very nature of their positions within the socioeconomic hierarchy, are more likely to experience family problems. Additionally, these groups traditionally have had less power than other groups and not only are more vulnerable to being ignored or blamed for causing problems but also are unable to advocate for solutions and resources to address the problems they face. Women, for example, are often paid less and hired into lower level jobs than men. Those who reenter the workplace after or while in more traditional marriages where they have not been employed outside the home ("displaced homemakers") are at a disadvantage in getting jobs that allow them to adequately support their families. They also most often must bear the brunt of child care and other child-related needs. Traditional attitudes about women and ethnic minorities are changing, but because of a scarcity of resources available to address their needs, they continue to be at the bottom of the social structure in our country.

Children growing up in families where social support is not available are more likely to experience problems in development, have low self-esteem, drop out of school, become pregnant at an early age, and have difficulty in finding adequate employment. Because they often lack appropriate role models and have been raised in an environment of hopelessness and despair, having children is often the only way they feel competent as people. With few skills and even fewer resources, the cycle of the at-risk family is repeated with their own children.

Although some attention is being given to the special needs of women and minorities and their families, this attention does not always address the problems from a broad context. For example, with the increased divorce rate and the growing number of people having children out of marriage, women have been targeted as "America's new poor," and much attention has been given to the **feminization of poverty** (DiNitto and McNeese 1990). However, in addition to providing more social supports to women and their families, the problem needs to be addressed from a systems/ecological perspective—women alone are not responsible for pregnancy or divorce, and men's responsibility in such situations also must be addressed.

Additional factors also must be taken into account when considering the relationship between family problems and minorities and women. While such families also are more likely to experience poverty and stress and, thus, more likely to experience alcoholism or spouse or child abuse or be too overwhelmed by these pressures to parent their children adequately, they are also more likely to be labeled as having such problems. A black parent who abuses a child, for example, is much more likely to take the child to a public hospital or clinic for treatment, where the case is likely to be reported to authorities. A white parent, however, is much more likely to take the child to a private physician, and perhaps to a different private physician if the child is reabused. Minority families and single-parenting women also are more likely to seek help for family problems at public services agencies, such as local mental health centers, than at private psychological counseling programs. White parents having problems with children are far more likely to be able to afford to send them to residential treatment facilities for therapy, whereas minority children are much more likely to be sent to juvenile detention centers, where such treatment usually is not available.

Not all minority or female-headed families have problems, and one must be careful not to stereotype such families. However, individuals studying social problems need to be aware that children who grow up in families headed by minorities and women are more vulnerable than children growing up in other families. Family problems must be considered within the context of the broader environment, and these considerations are important as we work to shape the environment to make it more supportive for children and their families.

TYPES OF FAMILY PROBLEMS

Divorce and Separation

The divorce rate in the United States has increased dramatically during the past several decades. In 1980, it was projected that over one-third of married persons of child-rearing age would divorce, with each marriage involving an estimated two children. Current projections suggest that over half of today's children will spend at least some time in a single-parent household (Children's Defense Fund 1988). Divorce and separation result in crises for family members. For adults, the separation or divorce signifies the loss of an intimate relationship that also brought security and support. Separation or divorce also signifies a loss of hopes and dreams as well as feelings of failure. Although there may be relief over the divorce, being alone also brings fear, anxiety, loneliness, and guilt, especially if there are children involved. Initially, parents are so caught up in dealing with their own emotions that they have little energy left to help their children cope. Thus, at a time when their children need them most, many adults find themselves unable to function adequately as parents.

For children, the initial impact of the divorce almost always is traumatic. If a great deal of fighting existed in the family, children may feel a sense of relief. However, they, too, experience anger, guilt, fear, and sadness. Often, children blame themselves for their parents' divorce. Many times, they try to change their behavior, either acting overly good or overly bad in the hope that this will bring their parents back together. Parents often fail to say anything to their children about an impending divorce, because of their own grieving and the belief that their children will cope better if they are not burdened with adult problems.

Studies suggest that the most important factor that helps children get through a divorce is having someone to listen and provide support to them. Parents need to explain that they are divorcing each other and not the child, and that both of them will continue to love and spend time with the child. Some children may not react visibly when they are informed that their parents are separating or divorcing. However, if children do not react immediately after the divorce, they are likely to hold their feelings inside and express them at a later age (Wallerstein & Kelly 1979).

Talking about the divorce and giving them a chance to express their feelings are important aspects in helping children cope with divorce. Children experiencing a divorce in their family usually regress at the time of the divorce. Children may exhibit such behaviors as nightmares and bed-wetting, thumb sucking, behavioral problems at school and at home, drop in academic performance at school, listlessness and daydreaming, changes in eating habits, increases in illness, and, if preadolescents or adolescents, experimentation with alcohol, drugs, sexual activity, and other risk-taking behaviors. Particularly if one parent has much less contact than in the past, children may develop extreme fears that they will be abandoned by the other parent or worry about what will happen to them if the parent they are living with dies (Wallerstein & Kelly 1980).

Although children are likely to cope better with divorce if the adults cope well, it usually takes them longer to recover, primarily because they have no control over the situation. Various studies (Wallerstein & Kelly 1980, Wallerstein & Blakeslee 1989) show that it takes children an average of three and a half years to work through the divorce and be on equal footing again. Children fare better after a divorce if they maintain a positive relationship with both parents and if the parents do not speak negatively about each other through the children or use the children to fight their battles with each other.

Custody and visitation problems often have a negative impact on a child following a divorce. Although the situation is changing, mothers are much more likely to obtain custody in a divorce, with fathers, as the noncustodial parents, having children visit them on holidays and during summer vacations. Courts have emphasized a long-held doctrine that, in a child's "tender years," the mother is more important in the child's life, and unless totally unfit, she should receive custody of children in a divorce. Although in many instances today fathers want custody and are equally and often more capable of caring for children, less than 10 percent of divorces result in children living with their fathers. Because the average woman's income decreases significantly following a divorce, whereas the average man's income increases, children of divorce often view their fathers as "Santa Clauses" who buy them presents and take them special places, let them stay up later, and let them have fewer rules than their mothers, who are buying the necessities and maintaining the daily routine, which usually requires more discipline. Mothers resent that they cannot give their children the same fun aspects of life, whereas fathers often find visitation time with their children artifical and awkward and don't know what else to do with them.

Parents also often expect the child to decide where to live and where to spend holidays, creating undue pressure on the child, who knows he or she will be forced to hurt one parent no matter what the decision. Experts recommend that children be allowed to give input in such decisions, but that final decisions be made by either the parents or, if they cannot agree, by a trained mediator skilled in divorce conflicts or by the court (Gardner 1970).

Increasingly, parents are opting for joint custody, where both parents equally share custody and, often, time spent living with the child. Some parents alternate the child's living with them every three or four days, whereas others have the child with them for six months and then switch the living arrangements. In some instances, to maintain stability for the child, the parents move in with the child, who remains in the same home, one at a time for a specified period of time. Studies conflict as to the benefits of different types of custody. Many experts suggest shared custody if the parents have a positive relationship with each other, as this provides the child with two strong role models who love and pay attention to the child and communicates that the child is wanted and loved by both parents equally. Other experts suggest that shared custody, particularly if it involves a great deal of moving back and forth on the child's part, creates instability and a lack of permanence, and that the child has no place to truly call his or her own.

The need for support to families experiencing divorce, particularly for children, is receiving increased attention. Many cities have established family **mediation** centers, where a team of social workers and attorneys work together with families in the divorce process. This helps parents maintain positive relationships with each other in an adult way, resolving conflicts together rather than forcing them to take adversarial roles, as is often the case when individuals have separate attorneys and a court action. Public schools and family service agencies also have established special programs and support groups for children experiencing divorce and their parents.

Single Parenting

Currently, 25 percent of families in the United States are headed by a **single parent,** either because of divorce or separation or, increasingly, because of unmarried women giving birth to children. Currently, 62 percent of all black children are being raised in single-parent homes. As indicated earlier, projections suggest that, by 2000, the number of children of all ethnic groups being raised in single-parent homes will increase significantly. There is no evidence that suggests that growing up in a single-parent family is inherently positive or negative. However, single-parent families are more likely to be associated with factors that place the children in these families more at risk of other types of family problems, such as alcoholism, child maltreatment, teenage pregnancy, and juvenile delinquency.

These families, with a single income most often earned by a woman, are more likely to be poor and, if not within the poverty definition of poor, experiencing financial stress. In addition to financial pressure, single parents must maintain sole responsibility for overseeing the household and child rearing. As a result, children growing up in single-parent families often are used to different life-styles than others. It is a paradox of children growing up in single-parent families that, on one hand, they are likely to have more freedom than other children, and on the other hand, they must take on much more responsibility. Children of single parents often have increased freedom because they must spend more time by themselves while their parents are working. Because child care is so expensive, many children of single parents, especially school-age children, become "latch-key" children, responsible for themselves until their parents get home from work. Others must be responsible for younger siblings. It is not unusual for a child of a single parent to come home from school alone, do homework and household chores, and prepare the evening meal. Single-parent children also must assume more responsibility for themselves because of the unavailability of supervision.

Single-parent children who are the same gender as the parent who has left the home also may assume many of the roles of the absent parent, for example, mowing the lawn and doing household repairs. They also may serve as companions to their parents, who may be lonely or too busy or hurt to establish adult relationships. Parents may confide in children about money, relationships with their ex-spouse, and other adult matters, and expect children to accompany them on activities such as shopping trips, meetings, or parties. They also may place children in a situation of role reversal, expecting children to comfort them and meet their needs. Other parents become overly protective, worrying that since they have lost a significant relationship with an ex-spouse, they also may lose the relationship with the child.

Children in single-parent families may experience inconsistent discipline. A parent may be too tired to discipline at some times or stressed and likely to overdiscipline at others. Parents' dating and development of opposite-sex relationships also can be stressful to children in single-parent families. Many children, particularly if they feel abandoned by the absent parent or do not have a positive relationship with that parent, may be anxious for the parent with whom they reside to remarry. Other children, particularly older children who have been in a single-parent family for a longer period of time, may see any dating by their parent as a threat to their own relationship and may do everything possible to destroy such relationships. Such issues as how much to tell children about dating, how involved they should be in decision making about serious relationships or remarriage, how to handle "overnight" guests and live-in partners, and how to help children handle a relationship that has ended are of concern to single parents and their families.

Children growing up in single-parent families also may have fewer options regarding long-range plans for their future. Income and time limitations of such families may preclude college or other post–high school education.

Other issues children growing up in single-parent families may face include kidnapping or fear of being kidnapped by the noncustodial parent, sexual abuse or other types of child maltreatment by the parent or parent's friends, alcoholism or drug abuse by one or both parents, and concerns about the child's own sexuality and ability to establish long-term opposite-sex relationships.

Increasingly, schools, child guidance centers, and community mental health centers are offering special programs for children growing up in single-parent families. Programs include individual and group counseling, family counseling, and the development of self-help groups for children. Big Brother and Big Sister programs, which match adult role models in one-to-one relationships with children, also help children in single-parent families develop healthy relationships with adults of the opposite sex of the custodial parent figure to ensure that children experience positive relationships with both male and female adults. A number of books and other materials are also available to help both children with single parents and their families. Longitudinal studies of children growing up in single-parent families are also helping to identify strengths of such families, as well as problem areas, to be better able to help children growing up in this type of family constellation.

Homosexual Parenting

Many homosexuals have children; studies show that many homosexuals have been married prior to declaring their homosexuality. In addition, many gay people who never marry are also likely to have children. Difficulties often arise, however, when gay parents seek custody of children in court battles; both men and women often have difficulty gaining custody if they are gay.

Studies show that there are few differences between gay families and nongay families. Children born and/or raised in families where one or both parents are gay are no more or less likely to be gay themselves than children born and/or raised in families where both parents are heterosexual. Studies also have found that gay parents do not influence their children to become gay and that children raised by homosexual parents are not emotionally impaired. Although a number of individuals suggest that children are at risk to be molested by gay parents, researchers have found that a child is more at risk to be molested in a heterosexual household than in a homosexual one. There is supportive evidence that gay parents are just as effective at parenting as nongay parents (Moses and Hawkins 1982).

There are some specific issues families with gay parents must address, however. For example, gay parents may not want their employers to know that they are gay because they fear being fired. Thus, children may have to keep the homosexuality a secret from others. Many gay parents also worry about how their children's friends and their parents will react to their being gay, and as their children grow older and more aware, they may fear this as well. Gay parents may also fear that their children will be ridiculed or discriminated against. As in any family, children who are dealt with honestly and have open communication with their gay parents usually have less difficulty dealing with a gay parent than children who find out about the homosexuality from others or sense the homosexuality but are not allowed to discuss it with their parents.

Stepparenting and Blended Families

With increased numbers of single-parent families, second marriages also are on the increase. Eighty percent of divorced adults remarry, and 60 percent of remarriages involve at least one child. In 1980, 13 percent of children in the United States were living in a stepparent family (U.S. Department of Health and Human Services 1980). A number of these families involve marriages between partners who each have children from previous marriages. Such families are often referred to as **blended families.**

Remarriage typically generates a number of strong feelings among both children and adults involved. Whereas adults may feel a sense of joyousness and security, children are likely to feel a sense of loss in relation to the parent, who must now be shared with the spouse, as well as anxiety over what the addition of another adult will mean to their own well-being. They also may experience concern about balancing the stepparent relationship with that of the absent birth parent. If the new marriage brings other children, relationships between stepsiblings may bring forth feelings of competition and jealousy.

The development of stepfamily relationships can be a difficult process, and time and effort are required on the part of all family members to make the new family constellation work. Children frequently feel distant from their new stepparent and may see that parent as a replacement for their absent parent. Even if they like the stepparent, conflicts over loyalty to their birth parent may prevent them from establishing a positive relationship. If the child functioned as more of a "partner" in the family than a child prior to the new marriage, feelings of displacement and jealousy toward the stepparent can occur. Additionally, many children, no matter how old, still have fantasies of their birth parents reuniting, and the remarriage represents a threat to these fantasies. Stepsiblings also may mean less attention for birth children, as well as possible competition outside of the family boundaries regarding friends, sports, and school.

In addition to the development of emotional bonds among family members, adjustments to changing family roles, responsibilities, and family identity must be made in a blended family. Rules often are readjusted, and many times are more strict than they were in the single-parent household. If children are still in contact regularly with their other birth parent, they are now essentially members of two households, each with its own distinct culture and rules. Problems regarding multiple role models and parental figures can create confusion for children. Some experts in stepparent family relationships suggest that the stepparent should not in any way undermine the absent birth parent relationship but should establish himself or herself as a parental figure in the family and take an active role in immediate family issues such as rules and discipline. Other experts argue that the parenting should be left completely to the child's parents, with the stepparent working to establish a positive bond with the child, but as an adult friend rather than a parental figure, staying out of decisions regarding rules and discipline.

Although remarriage can increase the stability, security, and financial resources for children, working through the implications of such changes takes a great deal of time before there is acceptance. Special parent education classes for stepparents; support groups for stepparents, spouses, and children in stepparent families; and family counseling programs are available in many communities to help focus on strengths of such families and provide support in working through problem areas.

Substance Abuse

Current evidence indicates that over 10 percent of individuals in the United States are being raised or were raised in alcoholic homes. An increasing number of children are being raised in homes where abuse of other substances is common. There are 30 to 50 million children of alcohol and drug abusers in the United States (Ackerman 1983). Until recently, substance abuse has been viewed as an individual disease rather than a family problem. However, recent studies have found that individuals raised in such families are five times as likely to become substance abusers themselves. Twenty percent of juvenile delinquents and children seen in child guidance and mental health clinics come from families where alcohol abuse is a problem. Other studies show high correlations between substance abuse and family violence. The U.S. Advisory Board on Child Abuse and Neglect (1990) cited increased use of substance abuse as the most important factor in the rise in incidence and severity of child maltreatment. Researchers in one study found that two-thirds of reported cases involve substance abuse. Seventy percent of infants abandoned in hospitals have parents who are addicts; many of the children they abandon are born addicted to drugs as well. Children who manage to "survive" in substance abusive families seldom escape unscathed. Experts in substance abuse suggest that adult children of alcoholics manifest coping characteristics they developed as children within their own families, including a compulsion to control, a need to overachieve, and a need to please others continually (Black 1979).

In looking at a substance abusive family from a systems/ecological perspective, the family develops a way of functioning with the abuser as the central family member that, although dysfunctional to outsiders, is functional to the family in that it facilitates survival. Family members or others who facilitate continuation of substance abuse are called **enablers.** For example, a spouse may assume the major responsibility for maintaining the family, protecting the children from the substance abuser, and making excuses for his or her behavior. An older child may take on a "hero" role, believing that by being a perfect child and pleasing the parents, the substance abuse will stop or be less likely to disrupt the family. This child is likely to get excellent grades in school, take care of younger children, nurture both parents, and work toward keeping family members happy no matter what the costs to the child. Another child in the family may take on a "scapegoat" role, subconsciously believing that negative attention directed at him or her will take the attention away from the parent who is the substance abuser. Conflict between the parents over the substance abuse may instead be directed at the child, who is always getting in trouble at home, at school, and in the neighborhood. Yet another child may assume the role of the "lost child," believing that the family is better able to cope if he or she is out of sight. These children are always in their rooms, under the table or in the corner, or at friends' homes. They seek little attention and, in fact, go out of their way not to call any attention to themselves at all. A final role a child in such families may assume is the "mascot" role. These children, often the youngest, become the pets or clowns of the family, always available to be cuddled when cuddling is demanded or to entertain when entertainment can alleviate some of the family's pain (Ackerman 1983).

Ackerman and others who have identified such roles in substance abusive families, however, point out the enormous costs of these roles on the individual family members throughout their whole lives, as well as the total family. Such roles actually promote the substance abuse, and family members are seen as unknowingly encouraging the substance abuse. This is why current substance abuse intervention strategies view the abuse as a family systems problem; if communication patterns and roles within families are not changed concurrently with treatment for the substance abuser, the substance abusive behavior is likely to return quickly, reinforced by the behaviors of other family members.

The ways that families typically cope with substance abuse can be divided into four phases. The first phase is the reactive phase, in which family members deny that the substance abuse exists and develop their own coping strategies around the substance abusive parent, usually—sometimes intentionally—enabling the abuse to continue. These strategies range from nagging to making excuses or covering up abuse (often without directly confronting the fact that there is a substance abuse problem) to staying at home and trying to prevent the substance abuse to denying emotional feelings. Children in such families may be victims of birth defects as a result of the substance abuse, may be torn between parents wondering why one is angry or feeling sorry for or angry at the abuser, may avoid activities with peers because of fear and shame, may not trust others, and may learn destructive and negative ways to get attention (Ackerman 1983).

The second is the active phase, where family members become aware that there is a substance abuse problem, that this is not a normally functioning family, and that help is available. Family members begin to realize that the abuser does not control the family and that they have the power to make changes in their own behaviors and cannot assume responsibility for the substance abuser. At this point, members may join self-help groups such as Al-anon or Alateen, where others going through similar experiences within their own families can lend support.

The third phase in a substance abusive family is the disequilibrium phase. This phase is difficult for all family members but must be experienced if the problem is to be alleviated. This phase occurs after family members are aware that a problem exists, but all efforts to change the abuser or the family dynamics have been unsuccessful. During this phase, family members consider openly whether disruption is the only alternative. This often leads to polarization among family members. This phase often ends in divorce, with subsequent separation of family members. It is doubly traumatic for children, who then have to experience the problems of both alcoholism and divorce. It is estimated that divorce occurs in approximately 40 percent of family situations that reach this phase (Ackerman 1983). For those families who do not choose separation, the traditional family communication patterns may be shaken enough that the family begins to change actively. Whether disruption occurs or the family member who is the substance abuser agrees to make a concerted effort to change, the family is forced to reorganize. This requires new and different roles for family members (Ackerman 1983).

The final phase that families involved in substance abuse experience is the family unity phase. Many families with substance abuse problems either disrupt or maintain the substance abuse problem and never reach this phase. Being free of substance abuse is central to this phase; however, it is not enough. Acceptance of the family member as a non–substance abuser and lasting changes in family communication patterns must take place if the family is to remain free of recurring substance abuse problems.

Spouse Abuse

Although definitions of **family violence** differ across state lines, a general definition often used is "an act carried out by one family member against another family member that causes or is intended to cause physical pain or injury to that person." Family violence typically has been separated into two major categories: spouse abuse and child abuse. Recent attention also has focused on elder abuse and children battering their parents. Child abuse first received attention as a major national issue in the 1960s, with impetus from the medical profession and other professionals and concerned child advocates; however, spouse abuse did not gain attention until a number of years later. Attempts to combine forces by women's advocates were met with resistance from child abuse advocates. Early attempts to develop programs and secure legislation for spouse abuse were spin-offs from rape crisis centers, which often were run by feminists at the grassroots level.

Professionals, particularly those from the medical profession, were concerned that joining forces with feminists might jeopardize child abuse programming. Thus, in 1990 only limited legislation and few centralized programs existed to deal with spouse abuse, although significant efforts in both legislation and federal programs existed for child abuse. More important, very limited federal dollars have been appropriated for spouse abuse programs. Some states have allocated funding for spouse abuse programs; however, these programs usually are either small adjuncts to child welfare/child abuse departments or under the auspices of special women's commissions, implying that spouse abuse is a woman- or child-related problem rather than a family problem of concern to everyone. Some child abuse programs have funded spouse abuse programs only by suggesting that children raised in a home where spouse abuse is present are emotionally abused.

An additional reason why attention to spouse abuse was late in developing relates to ways men and women are viewed in our society: Men are regarded as more powerful both within and outside of the home. Although men are seen as having power over children as well, it is much easier for the general public to become concerned about abused children than abused women. Many individuals will subscribe to the myth that women who are beaten somehow deserve it, or that they must enjoy it or they would not put up with it.

Violence between couples extends beyond the marital relationship. In one recent study researchers found that between 22 percent and 67 percent of dating relationships involve violence of some sort (Straus, Steinmetz, and Gelles 1980). Milder forms of violence, such as slapping, pushing, and shoving, are more common; but more severe types of violence, including kicking (commonly done in the stomach to pregnant women), biting, punching, and threatening with a knife or gun also are surprisingly common. A sad commentary on the implications of family violence is the fact that more than 25 percent of the victims of the violence and more than 30 percent of the abusers interpreted the violence as a sign of love.

Although it is difficult to determine the exact incidence of family violence because it happens behind closed doors, it is estimated that half of all women will be hit at least once during their marriage. Violence among couples is thought to occur in about one in every four marital relationships. A recent study determined that slightly under 7 percent of all women in heterosexual relationships experience serious, repeated violence (Dutton 1988).

A number of factors commonly are associated with spouse abuse. Men who assault their wives generally have low self-esteem and feel inferior. Feeling powerless outside of the family, they exert their power within the domain of their homes. It is more difficult to interpret factors associated with women who are abused. Lenore Walker (1983) has identified "learned helplessness" as a common trait among abused women. She suggests that women have learned to act passive and helpless as a way of coping with their violent spouses and have been conditioned to believe that they are powerless to get out of the violent situation. Others (Frieze & Browne 1989) suggest that battered women exhibit symptoms consistent with post–traumatic stress syndrome, a diagnosis commonly given to persons who have suffered severe trauma. Earthquake victims, persons involved in accidents where they have witnessed deaths or serious injuries, and Vietnam veterans are often given this diagnosis. Frieze and Browne suggest that women in violent domestic situations react emotionally to their experiences. They are often paralyzed and unable to act to defend themselves or their children, they exhibit the characteristics of learned helplessness identified by Walker, they blame themselves for their abuse because they did such things as not getting dinner ready on time, or they redefine the event, rationalizing that it wasn't that serious or that it was a rare occurence.

Many times, abused women are reluctant to leave violent situations. They often have no employable skills and are concerned abut being able to survive, particularly if they have children. Other studies show that battered women are not always passive and often seek help in dealing with the abuse although they love their husbands in spite of the violence and believe they will reform. In many violent situations among spouses, the period following the violence is almost like a honeymoon period, with the abusive spouse often crying, being extremely sorry for the violence, threatening suicide if he is deserted, promising never to be violent again, and being extremely loving and supportive. It is difficult for a woman who loves her husband not to be taken in by this Jekyll and Hyde personality, at least initially.

Other studies show that women with low self-esteem, particularly those who were physically or sexually abused as children, feel so worthless that they believe they deserve the violent treatment. Such women are more at risk to be abused than other women. Whereas in some situations the woman is passive and the man abusive, in other situations both spouses are violent; however, because of size differences, it is most often the woman who is hurt. Other factors that place couples more at risk for spouse abuse include substance abuse, financial stress and poverty, and the male's unemployment or underemployment.

Although programs that address spouse abuse are extremely limited, many communities are establishing safe houses and battered women's shelters, where battered spouses and their children can seek refuge. These programs also provide counseling for both women and children, and assist them in settling legal issues, locating housing and unemployment if they decide not to return to the batterer, and developing support networks. Sadly, in 1985, three out of every four women seeking shelter at such a program were turned away because of lack of space. Additionally, although some programs have been developed that focus on helping the batterer learn to control anger and on improving communication patterns in couple relationships, most programs usually begin to treat the violence after it has reached an intolerable point and change is difficult.

Child Maltreatment

Child maltreatment has received far more attention, and far more resources, than spouse abuse. However, reported cases of child abuse continue to increase at epidemic rates, and current resources are unable to serve the many abused and neglected children and their families who come to the attention of available programs. In 1989 there were 2.4 million reported cases of child abuse and neglect in the United States, a 71 percent increase since 1981 (National Advisory Committee on Child Abuse and Neglect 1990). A recently conducted national study (U.S. Department of Health and Human Services 1981) suggests that reported cases of child maltreatment represent less than one-third of children who actually are maltreated (see Figure 7–1). Exact figures on numbers of abused and neglected children do not exist because most maltreatment happens within the confines of family privacy, and when cases are known to others, they are often not reported.

There are four categories of child maltreatment: **physical abuse, sexual abuse, neglect,** and emotional maltreatment, which includes **emotional abuse and neglect.** Neglect is the most frequently reported type of maltreatment, with almost half of all reports of this type. Reports of sexual abuse, however, have increased most in recent years, probably because of increased awareness about sexual abuse and less secrecy about the problem. Children of all ages are maltreated. Although infants are at the greatest risk of being abused or neglected severely, most abused and neglected children are school age. Large numbers of adolescents are also maltreated; however, because of scarce resources, these cases are least likely to gain the attention of authorities.

Physical Abuse. The National Center on Child Abuse and Neglect's national child abuse reporting system indicates that 2.2 of every 1,000 children in the United States received severe physical injuries as a result of abuse in 1989 (National Advisory Committee on Child Abuse and Neglect). In addition, 15.4 per thousand children received less serious physical injuries, and 4.1 per thousand received unspecified physical injuries. Physical abuse is a result of someone beating, kicking, spanking too severely, slapping, biting, punching, throwing, burning, or shaking a child. Most children who are physically abused receive bruises, welts, or abrasions. These injuries are caused by parents whipping or spanking children with objects such as belts, extension cords, hair brushes, or coat hangers. Often imprints of the objects can be seen on the child's body. Child abuse is suspected when these types of injuries occur on the face or head of an infant—unlikely places for infants to bruise themselves—or on more than one plane of child's body, such as the back and arms, and are in various stages of healing, as with bruises in varying colors.

Children also receive broken bones and burns, as well as internal injuries, as a result of physical child abuse. Physicians can use X-rays, for example, to determine what types of breaks occurred and when. Children with spiral fractures, for example, may have experienced the break when a caretaker became angry and twisted one of their limbs. Children who are physically abused and brought to the hospital with one suspected broken bone will often have fractures in various stages of healing in several areas of the body. This condition, termed "battered child syndrome" by physician C. Henry Kempe, is a diagnosis now recognized by medical professionals (Kempe and Helfer 1968). One of the most serious types of child maltreatment is an internal injury to the head, which results in internal bleeding and often brain damage or death. Shaking a child severely can also result in serious injury, including blindness due to detached

Figure 7–1 Conceptual Presentation of the Recognition of Maltreated Children: An Iceberg

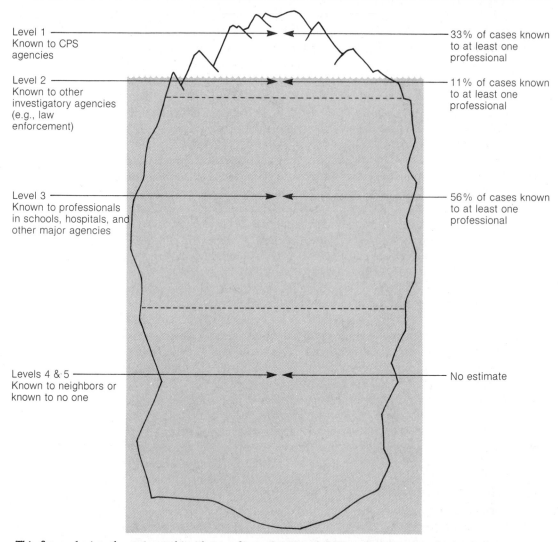

Level 1
Known to CPS
agencies — 33% of cases known to at least one professional

Level 2
Known to other
investigatory agencies
(e.g., law
enforcement) — 11% of cases known to at least one professional

Level 3
Known to professionals
in schools, hospitals, and
other major agencies — 56% of cases known to at least one professional

Levels 4 & 5
Known to neighbors or
known to no one — No estimate

This figure depicts the estimated incidence of actual cases of child maltreatment and who in the community knows about these cases. As the figure shows, the child protective services agencies that are mandated to provide services in such cases actually know about only 33% of cases that other professionals know about. This percentage does not even include those cases which only neighbors or immediate family members know about, suggesting that known cases of maltreatment are only the "tip of the iceberg" when it comes to how much child maltreatment actually exists.

Source: Figure adapted from *National Study of the Incidence and Severity of Child Abuse and Neglect* (1981), Washington, D.C.: U.S. Department of Health and Human Services.

retinas, brain injury, and death. Many children are also burned on their hands, feet, and other parts of their bodies with cigarettes or lighters. Parents with unrealistic expectations about toilet training often burn children by placing them in extremely hot water when they have soiled themselves.

Many children who grow up in dysfunctional families experience the repercussions of substance abuse, sexual abuse, violence, or neglect.

Many times, abusive parents lose their tempers and do not intend to harm the child severely. Many factors are associated with families who physically abuse children, including economic problems (with unemployment and poverty), isolation, unrealistic expectations about children's developmental milestones and about children's abilities to meet parental needs for love and attention, alcoholism and drug abuse, maltreatment or abuse of the parent during childhood, lack of education about nonphysical alternatives to discipline, low impulse control and inability to cope well with stress, and marital problems. Studies show that only about 10 percent of parents who maltreat their children are seriously psychologically disturbed (Gelles 1973).

Studies also show that some children are more at risk to be physically abused than others. Children who were born prematurely or with congenital problems, children who somehow do not meet parental expectations or are perceived as different by their parents, and children who are the result of unwanted pregnancies are more at risk to be abused physically than other children. Many parents who abuse children begin with role reversal within the family system, expecting the child, even as an infant or toddler, to meet their emotional needs. When the child resists or is unable to do so because he or she is too young, the parent may feel rejected, become angry and frustrated, and abuse the child.

Using a systems/ecological perspective, one can also see that children who grow up in communities with few economic resources and few support systems available to families also are more at risk to be abused. Cultural conditions also have an impact on physical abuse. Studies show that cultures where children are valued and where parenting is shared by extended family members or others beyond the nuclear family have less child abuse than other cultures (Korbin 1982).

Sexual Abuse Sexual abuse, more than any other type of child maltreatment, has received increased attention in recent years. Reported cases of sexual abuse have increased by as much as 65 percent in some states for two main reasons. First, with increased public awareness, many more individuals, including the children themselves, are reporting cases. Second, with children today exposed to more adults than in the past, including child care providers, stepparents, and other adults, the likelihood of being abused is increased.

Child sexual abuse can be defined as "contacts or interactions between a child and an adult when the child is being used as an object of gratification for adult needs or desires" (National Center on Child Abuse and Neglect 1980b). Thus, child sexual abuse can include acts such as fondling in addition to sexual intercourse. Recent legislation also mandates that state child abuse laws include child pornography and sexual exploitation in definitions of sexual abuse. This expands the definition to include acts such as taking pictures of children in sexual poses or for purposes of sexual gratification. Although the true incidence of sexual abuse is not known, the National Center on Child Abuse and Neglect reports that 11.7 of every 1,000 children in the United States were found to be sexually abused in 1989 (National Center on Child Abuse and Neglect 1980b). Many individuals are unaware until later in life that they have been sexually abused, either because they have repressed the experience, since it was so horrifying to them, or because they have no idea what healthy interactions are like and have assumed that all children experience such treatment. Others—males more than females—are reluctant to report the abuse because they are ashamed, embarrassed, have been threatened, or are worried about possible repercussions for themselves and their families. Thus, the incidence reported by the National Center is much lower than that found in other studies, namely, that one out of every four women and one out of every seven men experience some type of sexual abuse before the age of eighteen (Finkelhor 1984).

Although most individuals think of sexual abusers as strangers who accost children in the park, the majority are known and trusted by the children they abuse. The first category of abusers consists of parents. Sexual abuse by birth parents, commonly referred to as **incest,** is considered by many to have the most serious personal and social consequences. Abusers also may be other parent figures, such as stepparents. The second category of abusers consists of family members other than parent figures, such as siblings, grandparents, and uncles or aunts. Sexual relationships between siblings are reported to be the most common. The broadest definition of incest includes sexual relationships between any family members. The third category of sexual abusers includes trusted adults. These may be teachers, babysitters, neighbors, coaches, leaders of children's groups, or other adults. The last, and least frequent, types of sexual abusers are strangers or remote acquaintances.

The reasons why adults sexually abuse children are complex and vary according to the individual abuser. Some experts involved in the treatment of sexual abusers classify them as falling somewhere on a continuum, with two opposite types of abusers. At one end of the continuum is an abuser who is primarily interested in having intimate adult relationships but is emotionally unable to feel good enough about himself or herself (although the majority of reported sexual abusers are men) to have a positive emotional relationship with another adult. This type of adult is insecure and usually is experiencing some type of personal crisis. They are likely to be married but in relationships that have deteriorated significantly. Feeling too inadequate to seek emotional fulfillment from their spouses, they often turn to their children to meet their needs. Although time spent together at first may be nonsexual and regarded by both parent and child as special, over time such fulfillment becomes sexual as well for the adult. In this situation, the adults involved see themselves in an adult relationship and are more than likely also to view the child as a pseudoadult. Individuals involving children in such relationships are far more likely to go from fondling to full intercourse in an attempt to have an adult–adult relationship, but they feel more comfortable with a child replacing the adult partner because of their own feelings of inadequacy.

At the opposite end of the continuum are adults who view the experience with the child as feeling like a child themselves and seeing the child in a child role. These abusers are more likely to be labeled **pedophiles** (meaning "lovers of children"). Individuals at this end of the continuum have a sexual fascination with children, but from a child's perspective rather than from an adult one. Some experts view pedophiles as having arrested stages of sexual development; others suggest that pedophilia may be due to a hormonal imbalance or genetic inclination.

Most abusers engage in a seductive power role with children with whom they become involved. Children, wanting affection and not knowing how to draw boundaries themselves between positive affection and sexual abuse, initially may become involved and then feel too afraid to tell anyone what is going on. Although the sexual abuse acts themselves may not involve physical force on the part of the adult, the child is trapped in the situation because adults are in power positions with children. Some abusers tell children that the relationship is the only thing keeping the family together, or the abuser is the only one who really loves and understands the child. Other abusers threaten physical harm to the child or to other family members if the child refuses to cooperate or tells anyone what is going on. For example, the abuser may say that the child's mother will "go crazy," the child will be taken out of the home, or the adult will sexually abuse a younger sibling.

Studies on the effects of sexual abuse show that it is extremely harmful to children emotionally and that many individuals who have been sexually abused suffer long-term effects. The impact of sexual abuse on children depends on factors such as the age of the child when the abuse occurred, the type of sexual abuse that took place, the relationship of the abuser to the child, how long the abuse continued, how long it was between the time the abuse occurred and someone found out that it was going on, other characteristics of the child's family and available positive support to the child, and the reactions from family members and professionals when the sexual abuse finally was discovered (Sgroi 1982). Many persons who have been sexually abused see themselves as victims due to the trauma of the abuse and have extremely low self-esteem; difficulty in establishing intimate, trusting relationships with others; and problems with their own families and marriages when they become adults. Without intervention for the sexually abused child and the family, persons who have been sexually abused are more at risk than others to turn to alcohol, other drugs, or suicide to ease their pain. Many communities have established programs that promote public awareness of sexual abuse and early intervention with families once cases are reported to attempt to address such long-term effects.

Child Neglect   Child neglect can be defined as "a condition in which a caretaker responsible for the child either deliberately or by extraordinary inattentiveness permits the child to experience available present suffering and/or fails to provide one or more of the ingredients generally deemed essential for developing a person's physical, intellectual and emotional capacities" (National Center on Child Abuse and Neglect 1980a). As opposed to child physical abuse, in which damage to a child is inflicted, neglect is characterized by acts of omission; this usually means that something that should have been done to or for a child was not done.

Many states include specific categories in their definitions of child neglect, including failure to provide adequate food, clothing, or shelter for a child, often termed physical neglect; failure to provide adequate supervision for a child, for example, leaving young children alone for inappropriate periods of time, often termed lack of supervision; leaving a child alone or not returning when expected to care for a child, often termed abandonment; failure to provide medical care for a child, often termed medical neglect; failure to provide an education for a child, often termed educational neglect; and failure to provide for a child's emotional needs, often termed emotional neglect. The National Center on Child Abuse and Neglect's national reporting system determined that 55.7 per 1,000 children were deprived of necessities for survival in 1989, and 5.7 per 1,000 were abandoned (National Advisory Committee on Child Abuse and Neglect 1990).

Although some individuals view neglect as less dangerous to a child than abuse, this is not the case. Studies have shown that just as many children die each year from neglect as from abuse. Many are burned in fires while left alone or with inadequate supervision, some drown in bathtubs while left unsupervised, and others die because their parents did not obtain medical care for them soon enough when they became ill. Other studies show that neglected children, in fact, may suffer from more long-term consequences of their maltreatment than abused children. Adults who did not have their physical or emotional needs met as children are much more likely to have problems in finding and maintaining jobs, developing positive relationships with other individuals and remaining in marriages, and parenting their own children adequately.

One type of neglect that is receiving increased attention is **nonorganic failure to thrive,** a form of parental deprivation. Failure to thrive has been medically defined as the condition of any child who is three percentiles or more below the normal weight for his or her age, who apparently is fed regularly, and who has nothing organically wrong yet does not gain weight and literally "fails to thrive." When such a child is placed in a hospital and given nothing more than regular feedings of a normal diet, coupled with love and attention (e.g., holding and cuddling), however, he or she begins to gain weight immediately. Bowlby (1951) studied maternal deprivation and children raised in European orphanages without love and attention and found a high death rate and significant differences in intelligence quotient (IQ) and physical and emotional development when compared to children raised in environments where they received love and attention. Similar findings are evident among children diagnosed with failure-to-thrive syndrome.

Parents who neglect their children differ from other parents at the same socioeconomic level. Although a strong relationship exists between poverty and neglect, not all parents who are poor neglect their children. Research studies have shown that the typical neglectful parent, as compared with nonneglectful parents also living in poverty, is more isolated, has fewer relationships with others, is less able to plan and less able to control impulses, is less confident about the future, and is more plagued with physical and psychological problems (Polansky et. al. 1985). They also are more likely to say that they have never received love and were unwanted by their parents. Many have been raised by relatives or in foster care. Neglectful parents often began life lonely, and they continue to live in isolation. Polansky, Ammons, and Gaudin (1985) found that neglecting parents had difficulty identifying neighbors or friends with whom they could leave their children if they needed emergency child care or from whom they could borrow five dollars in an emergency. They are extremely isolated from both formal and informal support networks; many neglecting parents describe their social workers as being their best or only friends.

Polansky and associates (1975) classified two types of neglecting parents. The first type suffers from what they term **apathy-futility syndrome.** These neglecting parents have all but given up on life. They see little hope for the future and view all efforts to try to relate to either their children or others as futile. They convey an attitude of hopelessness and despair. Usually neglected themselves as children and, in many instances in the past, beaten down whenever they tried to make a go of life, they lack the physical or emotional energy to relate to their children. A neglectful parent with apathy-futility syndrome is likely to be found lying on the couch in a chaotic household that hasn't been cleaned or cared for, with children unkempt and uncared for, left largely to fend for themselves. Children raised by this type of neglectful parent may suffer from physical, medical, educational, and/or emotional neglect, as well as lack of supervision.

The second type of neglecting parent characterized by Polansky and colleagues (1975) is one with **impulse-ridden behavior.** This type of parent may be loving and caring and may provide adequate food, clothing, and medical care most of the time. However, this parent has trouble making appropriate decisions and often behaves impulsively. Such parents suddenly may decide to go to a party and leave their children alone or may answer the telephone and become so engrossed in the telephone conversation that they forget that their child is unattended. They often get in trouble with employers over impulsive behavior at work, with creditors because of impulsive spending habits, and with friends because they make commitments and then impulsively change their minds and go off with others instead. Neglectful parents with impulse-ridden behavior are restless, intolerant of stress, and inconsistent. Their children never know exactly what to expect and, in fact, may be abandoned for long periods by an impulsive parent who suddenly decides to go off somewhere on a trip. Sometimes, when such parents seem to be making great progress in being more consistent in their child care, they ask their social worker to babysit for their children so they can go off to the beach (or elsewhere), or they go to the beach and seem to forget completely that their children are left unsupervised. Children of neglecting parents of this type are likely to suffer from abandonment, lack of supervision, and emotional neglect. Additionally, because of the inconsistency they experience, they are likely to have difficulty trusting others, developing positive relationships, and being consistent themselves.

Neglecting parents often are more difficult to help than abusive parents, particularly those who are apathetic and feel hopeless. Unlike abusive parents, who still have enough spirit to be angry, many neglecting parents experience feelings of despair and futility. These feelings are much more difficult to change. By helping neglecting parents develop trust in other individuals and increase their self-esteem, particularly through links with supportive individuals, social workers can help them begin to care adequately for their own children. Most of the attention and resources in the area of child maltreatment has gone to child physical and sexual abuse rather than to neglect. Because studies show that neglect is just as detrimental to children as abuse—and in some instances, more so—increased concern needs to be given to this type of child maltreatment.

Emotional Maltreatment.   Emotional maltreatment is the most elusive form of child maltreatment and the most difficult to define, to substantiate, and to obtain resources for. It probably, however, also is the most common type of child maltreatment, and like other types of child maltreatment, it can result in serious long-term consequences for the child. Experts suggest that there are two types of emotional maltreatment: emotional abuse and emotional neglect (Whiting 1978). Definitions parallel those of abuse and neglect. Emotional abuse is viewed as acts of commission, or emotional acts against a child. Emotional abuse is often verbal; it includes a child being told continually how bad he or she is, being told that he or she was (and is) unwanted, and being blamed for all the parents' and family's problems.

Almost all parents emotionally abuse their children at some times; one child development expert notes that children receive six negative messages about what they do for every one positive message (Ginott 1965). However, continual emotional abuse can lower self-esteem and undermine a child's feelings of competence. Parents also emotionally abuse children in other ways; some parents, for example, give away children's prize possessions to "another child who will appreciate it," telling children that they don't deserve special things because "they are bad." Less often, parents emotionally abuse children by shaving their heads or cutting their hair or doing other humiliating things as forms of punishment. Children who are forced to watch parents or others in the family being beaten or otherwise abused also experience emotional abuse.

Emotional maltreatment is probably the most common type of child maltreatment. The National Committee for the Prevention of Child Abuse and other programs have developed media campaigns to focus attention on this problem.

Sexually abused children are also emotionally abused; in fact, some experts suggest that the emotional abuse has just as severe, if not more severe, consequences for the sexually abused child than the sexual abuse (National Center on Child Abuse and Neglect 1980c).

Emotional neglect, like neglect itself, relates to acts of omission involving a child and includes the failure to meet the child's emotional needs. Parents who emotionally neglect children may provide for their physical needs, but they usually interact very little with their children in an emotional sense. Common parent-child activities such as cuddling and holding or reading, singing, going places, or just talking together are nonexistent for children who are emotionally neglected. Not having their emotional needs met when they are children is likely to result in adults who cannot give emotionally to their own children. Such adults may not only neglect their own children emotionally but mistreat them in other ways as well.

James Garbarino (1987) provides a broader conceptualization, using the term "psychological maltreatment," which he defines as "a concerted attack by an adult on a child's development and social competence, a pattern of psychically destructive behavior" (p. 8). He suggests that psychological maltreatment takes five forms: (1) rejecting, where the adult refuses to acknowledge the child's worth and the legitimacy of the child's needs; (2) isolating, where the adult cuts the child off from normal social experiences; (3) terrorizing, where the adult verbally assaults the child, creating an environment of fear and terror; (4) ignoring, where the adult deprives the child of essential stimulation and responsiveness; and (5) corrupting, where the adult stimulates the child to engage in destructive antisocial behavior and reinforces deviance (p. 8). Garbarino's conceptualization is based on a systems/ecological perspective, which suggests that emotional deprivation or emotional trauma in one domain of children's lives increases their vulnerability to similar experiences in other domains.

Problems Associated with Adolescents

Little attention has been given to the special needs of adolescents in literature about children and family problems. Many family development experts are quick to point out that prevention and early intervention efforts aimed at young children and families would eliminate many adolescent problems. They note that adolescents who come through the juvenile justice system as delinquents, runaways, or pregnant teens most often come from families who have experienced many of the problems discussed in this chapter but have not received appropriate services and support. Although delinquent adolescents are required by law to be treated differently than adults, the current juvenile justice system does not have the resources to address the numerous family problems and provide the extensive treatment that many juveniles need. Many who are released from the juvenile system quickly enter the adult criminal justice system. However, as juveniles commit more severe crimes at younger ages, how to address their needs effectively and how to protect others from them are becoming more pressing issues.

Currently in the United States, because of the scarcity of resources available to address family problems, most resources are targeted toward younger children, who are more vulnerable than adolescents. In one state with few resources, school personnel find themselves agreeing with teenagers when they determine that their only recourse to escape a serious family situation is to run away from home. Because youth shelters and services are limited, a youth advocate in one state suggested that her only alternative to ensure that teens had safe shelter was to suggest that they get arrested so they could be booked into the juvenile detention center!

Adolescents labeled as delinquent often should more appropriately be considered "throwaways" or "push-outs," as more and more families fail to provide for the needs of their children and find themselves with emotionally damaged adolescents. Estimates suggest that 1.2 million to 1.5 million children and adolescents run away each year; most of these are teenagers who are gone only a night or two, but many never return to their homes (Children's Defense Fund 1988). Most runaways are running in an attempt to cope with serious problems, including physical and sexual abuse, family alcoholism or drug abuse, divorce or spouse abuse, other family problems, or failure in school. A study

Rates of teenage pregnancy, particularly among young girls 12–14, are growing rapidly in the U.S. Few comprehensive programs are available in the U.S. that meet the needs of both the infant and the parenting teen.

of New York runaway-youth shelters found that between one-third and two-thirds of teens who came to them for help did not feel that they had a home to return to (CDF 1986).

Many adolescents experiencing problems also suffer academically. Family problems often result in learning disabilities and other learning problems, and young persons who do not feel good about themselves and who face daily problems at home are not likely to do well in school. Increased concern is being expressed about dropout rates of youth and the high illiteracy rate among youth and adults. In 1990, 31 percent of Hispanic youths dropped out of school before reaching age eighteen, whereas 18 percent of blacks and 14.3 percent of whites did so. In New York City and Los Angeles, the dropout rate for

Hispanics that year was 80 percent. Even with a high school education, increasing numbers of persons in the United States are illiterate. A recent study found that 56 percent of Hispanic adults, 44 percent of black adults, and 16 percent of white adults in the United States are illiterate (National Council of La Rasa 1990).

Youths who do not complete high school suffer in their ability to locate suitable employment. There is a serious lack of employment available for young adults, particularly those who are black or Hispanic, even when they do graduate from high school. In 1983, more than half of all black high school graduates not enrolled in college were unemployed, whereas only approximately 25 percent of white high school dropouts were unemployed (Children's Defense Fund 1988). The increasing dropout and illiteracy rates, especially for Hispanic and black populations, have raised serious questions about the ability of the United States to maintain qualified workers in light of the demand for employees with a minimum of a high school education and technological skills. The limited availability of job skills training and adequate employment suggests that poverty rates, particularly for blacks and Hispanics, will continue to increase.

Another major problem facing our country today is teen pregnancy. In 1988, 1.1 million teenagers became pregnant, resulting in 500,000 births. In 1990, demographic studies showed that 20 percent of white and 45 percent of black women become pregnant at least once by age twenty. Over 20 percent of these births were to mothers fifteen years old and younger. For teenagers who are not developmentally prepared, parenthood interrupts, sometimes permanently, their successful transition into adulthood (Ford Foundation 1989).

Teens today face a great deal of pressure from many sources—peers, the media, advertising—to see their primary self-worth in terms of their sexuality. With limited opportunities to be successful in other arenas, such as the family, school, and the workplace, many male and female teens feel that their sexuality, and producing a baby, are the only ways they can feel good about themselves and have someone to love them. The United States has one of the highest teen pregnancy rates in the Western world, and the number of younger teens, age twelve to fourteen, becoming pregnant is increasing each year. Many factors are associated with teen pregnancy, including poverty, low self-esteem, lack of information about reproduction, school failure, lack of appropriate health care and other services, and poor family relationships.

Additionally, emphasis on pregnancy prevention and intervention has focused on teenage girls, and little has been done in regard to prevention and intervention with teenage boys. Even more important, attention to pregnancy prevention often only begins when teens (girls) reach age thirteen. Developing positive self-esteem, effective decision-making skills, a strong value system, and a sense of responsibility for one's self and others—all major deterrents to teen pregnancy—are factors shaped from birth on.

Whereas, in the past, most teens who became pregnant relinquished their babies for adoption, either formally through agencies or informally through relatives, today the majority of teens are choosing to keep their babies. This places tremendous pressure on both the teen mothers and their children. Infants born to teenagers are much more likely to have low birth weight, be premature babies, or have congenital and other health problems. Their mothers also are more likely to drop out of school, remain un- or underemployed, and raise their children in poverty than are nonteenage parents.

The cycle often repeats itself: teen pregnancy is both a cause and a result of poverty. In 1986, minority teens, more likely to grow up poor, constituted 27 percent of the teenage population, about 50 percent of poor adolescents, and about 40 percent of teenage mothers (Children's Defense Fund 1986). Nearly 90 percent of babies born to black teens fifteen to nineteen years old are born to single mothers. Teen pregnancy is viewed by many concerned about family problems as the hub of the cycle of poverty in the United States ("Children Having Children" 1985).

Suicide and Children's Mental Health

Changes in society, communities, and the family have resulted in increased instability of many children and adolescents in the United States. Children are too often the victims in divorce, family and community violence, substance abuse, and other types of family, community, and societal dysfunction. In one recent study researchers found that 12 percent of all U.S. children suffer some type of emotional illness. Many children and adolescents become involved in substance use, becoming alcoholics or addicts themselves, often at young ages, or suffering serious physical and emotional injuries as a result. In 1990, drinking and driving was the number-one cause of death among adolescents. Suicide was the second leading cause of death. Suicide rates among children and adolescents of all ages are higher in the United States than in most other countries. Ten percent of all boys and 18 percent of all girls attempt suicide at least once before they reach age eighteen (House Select Committee on Children, Youth, and Families 1990). These individuals often try other ways to stop their pain first, frequently with drugs and alcohol, before turning to suicide. Children and adolescents who attempt suicide feel helpless, hopeless, and powerless, and they are often experiencing or have experienced a series of losses in their lives. When they are in an environment over which they feel they have no control, sexual experimentation, use of alcohol and drugs, suicide attempts, eating disorders, and other risk-taking behaviors become ways either to gain control over what they perceive as an uncontrollable environment or to escape from it.

Homelessness

There is a strong relationship between other problems discussed in this chapter and homelessness. As rents and purchase prices of homes throughout the United States continue to escalate and federal funds to build low-income housing continue to be reduced, more and more families and their children are becoming homeless. Although it is impossible to determine the exact number of homeless people in the United States because they cannot be readily located, in 1988 it was estimated that as many as 500,000 children were homeless (Children's Defense Fund 1989). Families are the fastest-growing group of homeless persons. Many families are forced to live in welfare hotels in unsafe neighborhoods, tents, or automobiles. Without a permanent address, it is difficult for parents to locate employment and for children to attend school. The psychological consequences of being homeless can be developmentally devastating to children, who may then repeat the same patterns with their families.

SUMMARY

There are many reasons why children, youth, and families in the United States experience problems. Many families experience a number of problems, and families who are at risk to experience one type of problem are likely to be at risk to experience others as well. From a systems/ecological perspective, factors associated with family problems are complex and interactive.

Societal and cultural factors, as well as the level of support available to families from the communities in which they reside, have an impact on the nature and extent of problems that families experience. Finally, all families have strengths that can be used to draw from when they do experience problems. Effective intervention and prevention programs can capitalize on these strengths when working with children, youth, and families. However, effective intervention and prevention efforts must be undertaken within the broader context of understanding the complexities of the family problems just discussed.

KEY TERMS

apathy-futility syndrome	feminization of poverty
blended families	impulse-ridden behavior
child neglect	incest
custody	mediation
emotional abuse	nonorganic failure to thrive
emotional neglect	pedophile
enabler	physical child abuse
family	sexual abuse
family violence	single-parent-family

DISCUSSION QUESTIONS

1. Identify and discuss at least three of the issues that must be considered when defining a family problem.

2. Discuss briefly at least three issues that often surface in families who experience divorce.

3. Describe at least four roles family members might play where substance abuse is a problem.

4. Identify and briefly describe the four types of child maltreatment.

5. Identify at least five factors likely to be associated with families who abuse or neglect their children.

6. Briefly discuss at least four reasons why teenagers today are likely to become parents.

7. Why are minority children, youth, and families more likely to be at risk of serious problems than white children, youth, and families?

REFERENCES

Ackerman, R. 1983. *Children of alcoholics*. Holmes Beach, Calif.: Learning Publications. American Humane Association. 1986. *National analysis of child neglect and abuse reporting*. Denver: Author.

Black, C. 1979. Children of alcoholics. *Alcohol Health and Research World* 4(1): 23–27.

Bowlby, J. 1951. Maternal care and mental health. *Bulletin of the World Health Organization* 3: 355–534.

Bronfenbrenner, U. 1979. *The ecology of human development.* Cambridge, Mass.: Harvard University Press.

Carter, E. and M. McGoldrick. 1980. *The family life cycle: A framework for family therapy.* New York: Gardner Press.

Children having children. 1985. *Time,* Dec. 9, 78–90.

Children's Defense Fund. 1988. *Children's defense budget: An analysis of the FY 1988 federal budget and children.* Washington, D.C.: Author.

DiNitto, D. and C. A. McNeece. 1990. Social Work: *Issues and opportunities in a challenging profession.* Englewood Cliffs, N.J.: Prentice Hall.

Finkelhor, D. 1984. *Sexual abuse: New theory and research.* New York: Free Press.

Frieze, I. and A. Browne. 1989. Violence in marriage. In L. Ohlin and M. Tonry (eds.): *Family Violence.* Chicago: University of Chicago Press, pp. 163–218.

Ford Foundation. 1989. *The common good: Social welfare and the American future.* New York: Author.

Garbarino, J. 1982. *Children and families in the social environment.* New York: Aldine Press.

Garbarino, J., E. Guttmann, and J. Seelely. 1987. *The psychologically battered child.* San Francisco: Jossey Bass.

Gardner, R. 1970. *The boys and girls book about divorce.* New York: Bantam Books

Gelles, R. 1973. Child abuse as psychopathology: A sociological critique and reformulation. *American Journal of Orthopsychiatry* 48: 408–424.

Gelles, R. 1979. Violence toward children in the United States. In *Critical Perspectives on Child Abuse,* ed. R. Bourne and E. Newberger. Lexington, Mass.: Lexington.

Ginott, H. 1965. *Between parent and child.* New York: Avon Books.

Goode, W. J. 1964. *The family.* Englewood Cliffs, N.J.: Prentice-Hall.

House Select Committee on Children, Youth and Families. 1990. *Opportunities for success: Cost effective programs for children.* Washington, D.C.: GPO.

Kempe, C. H. and R. Helfer. 1968. *The battered child.* Chicago: University of Chicago Press.

Korbin, J. 1982. *Cross-cultural perspectives on child abuse.* Berkeley: University of California Press.

Moses, A. and R. Hawkins. 1982. *Counseling lesbian women and gay men: A life-issues approach.* St. Louis: C. V. Mosby.

Moyers, W. 1986. *The vanishing black family.* New York: ABC Television.

National Center on Child Abuse and Neglect. 1980. *Neglect: Mobilizing community resources.* Washington, D.C.: Department of Health and Human Services.

_____. 1980b. *Selected readings in sexual abuse.* Washington, D.C.: Department of Health and Human Services.

_____. 1980c. *The role of the child protective services worker.* Washington, D.C.: Department of Health and Human Services.

National Council of la Raza. 1990. *Report on the status of Hispanic youth.* Washington, D.C.: Author.

Polansky, N. A., G. Hally, and N. F. Polansky. 1975. *Profile of neglect: A survey of the state of knowledge of child neglect.* Washington, D.C.: Department of Health, Education, and Welfare.

Polansky, N., P. Ammons, and J. Gaudin. 1985. Loneliness and isolation in child neglect. *Social Casework* (Jan.): 38–47.

Sgroi, S. 1982. *Handbook of clinical intervention in child sexual abuse.* Lexington, Mass.: Lexington.

Steiner, G. 1976. *The children's cause.* Washington, D.C.: Brookings Institute.

Steinmetz, S., and M. Straus. 1974. *Violence in the family.* New York: Harper & Row.

Straus, M. A., R. J. Gelles, and S. K. Steinmetz. 1980. *Behind closed doors. Violence in the American family.* Garden City, N.J.: Doubleday.

U.S. Advisory Board on Child Abuse and Neglect. 1990. *Child abuse and neglect: Critical first steps in response to a national emergency.* Washington, D.C.: GPO.

U.S. Department of Health and Human Services. 1981. *National study of the incidence and severity of child abuse and neglect.* Washington, D.C.: Author.

————. 1980. *Helping youth and families of separation, divorce, and remarriage.* Washington, D.C.: Author.

Walker, L. 1983. The battered women's syndrome study. In *The dark side of families,* ed. D. Finkelhor, R. Gelles, G. Hotaling, and M. Straus, 31–48. Beverly Hills, Calif.: Sage Publications.

Wallerstein, J. and S. Blakeslee. 1989. *Second chances: Men, women and children after a decade of divorce.* New York: Ticknor and Fields.

Wallerstein, J., and J. Kelly. 1980. *Surviving the breakup: How children and parents cope with divorce.* New York: Basic Books.

————. 1979. Children and divorce: A review. *Social Work* (Nov.) 24: 468–75.

Werner, E. and Smith, R. 1977. *Kauai's children come of age.* Honolulu: University Press of Hawaii.

Whiting, L. 1978. Emotional neglect of children. In *Proceedings of the second annual National Conference on Child Abuse and Neglect, Vol. 1 209–13.* Washington, D.C.: Department of Health, Education and Welfare.

SUGGESTED FURTHER READINGS

Billingsley, A., and J. Giovannoni. 1972. *Children of the storm: Black children and American child welfare.* New York: Harcourt, Brace, Jovanovich.

Child welfare: A sourcebook of knowledge and practice. 1984. Frank Maidman (ed.) New York: Child Welfare League of America.

Children and families (special volume). 1990. *Social Work* 35:6.

Garbarino, J., and H. Stocking. 1980. *Child abuse and neglect.* New York: Aldine Press.

Kadushin, A. and J. Martin. 1988. *Child welfare services* (4th edition). New York: Macmillan.

Kozol, J. 1988. *Rachel and her children: Homeless families in America.* New York: Fawcett Columbine.

McGowan, B., and W. Meezan. 1983. Child welfare: *Current dilemmas, Future directions.* Itasca, Ill.: Peacock.

Schorr, L. and D. Schorr. *Within our reach: Breaking the cycle of disadvantage.* 1989. New York: Anchor.

Services to Children, Youth, and Families

*J*uanita Kingbird, a social worker with the local family services agency, is involved in a number of activities that prevent families from becoming dysfunctional, as well as activities that help families when problems occur. Her agency provides a variety of programs: Parenting programs teach child care to teenage parents; an outreach program and parent groups seek out and help parents who are under stress or having problems with their children; and the agency provides individual, family, and group counseling for children and family members of all ages. Recently, the agency developed a shelter for adolescents who cannot remain in their own homes and a respite care program for families of developmentally disabled children. The agency also provides homemaker services, child care, and employment services to help families remain economically self-sufficient and able to stay together.

On a typical day, Juanita begins by returning a crisis call from a mother whose son ran away from home the night before after a family argument. She calls the school social worker and arranges for her to try to locate the boy if he is in school and talk with him. After two counseling sessions with adolescents who are staying in the shelter, focusing on their feelings about becoming independent and separating from their families, Juanita leaves for the local high school, where she leads a support group for teenage parents. After the group, she meets individually with several of the girls and helps one of them obtain an appointment with a specialist for her developmentally delayed infant. She has a quick lunch with the school social worker to coordinate services both are providing to some of her clients, and then she meets with the runaway boy, who did come to school, getting him to agree to meet with her and his mother later on in the day. On the way back to her office, Juanita stops off to make a home visit to one of her clients who has been emotionally abusing her two young children. Juanita interacts with the mother and her children, role modeling good communication patterns and ways to give feedback and set limits positively. She returns to the office in time to attend a staffing on another family with social workers from the five other agencies involved. Although the family has many serious problems, the coordinated intervention plan developed by the agencies seems to be effective, as everyone reports that the family is making progress. Juanita then meets with the runaway boy and his parents.

They negotiate family rules and boundaries and agree to try to live together without major conflicts, returning in a week for another family counseling session. Juanita leaves the agency to go home, glad that she has a supportive family waiting for her who will help her so that she does not burn out from getting too emotionally involved with her clients.

Juanita enjoys her job a great deal. Although she finds it difficult

to deal with the many problems faced by the families with whom she is assigned to work, especially when children are suffering, she has learned to share small successes with family members. "If I can make things better in some small way each day for one child or one parent, my job is more than worthwhile," she stated in a recent newspaper interview.

Programs and policies that address the needs of children, youth, and families are as diverse as the types of needs experienced. Traditionally, the system that has provided programs and policies that address child and family concerns has been called the **child welfare delivery system.** This system includes the "network of agencies, public and private, denominational and non-denominational, offering direct social services to children and families" (Kadushin 1980, 3).

This chapter focuses on services provided that address the family-related problems discussed in Chapter 7. The roles that social workers play in providing services to children, youth, and families are also discussed.

CURRENT PHILOSOPHICAL ISSUES

All policies and programs that address the needs of children, youth, and their families must consider not only the social and cultural framework of the child's family, the community, and the broader environment but also a number of current philosophical issues.

The Right to a Permanent, Nurturing Family

The first assumption is that every child has a right to grow up in a permanent, nurturing home and that every attempt must be made to provide such a home whenever possible. This assumes that the child's own home should be seen as the best option for that child whenever possible. Such a philosophical position dictates that services should be provided first to the child's family and that every attempt should be made to keep the child and the family together. This position has led to the development of family preservation programs, or services provided to a child and family while they remain together, as opposed to placing a child in a foster home or other type of substitute care. Increasingly, special attention is being given to those services that will keep families together rather than quickly removing the child from his or her family setting.

In the past, many children receiving services in an overloaded service delivery system became lost in the system, with no chance either to return

With appropriate intervention, children and adolescents growing up in troubled families can become well-functioning, healthy adults.

home, be adopted, or become emancipated. There was no way of determining exactly how many children were in substitute care, and in some instances, children were sent to other states because care was less expensive and responsibility for their care could be shifted elsewhere. Although foster care was, and still is, supposed to be temporary, many children placed in foster care at young ages needed extended care and left only because they had reached age eighteen and the system did not provide care for adults. Children often lived in five or more foster homes and had five or more social workers. Some children moved around so much they never went to the same school for an entire school year.

Concern among many individuals and advocacy organizations has led to legislation at both the state and federal levels that mandates **permanency planning.** This concept ensures that when a child and family first receive services, a specific plan is developed that states what is planned to help that family remain together if possible and, if not, what will be done to provide a permanent, nurturing home for the child. Specific plans are developed to take place within time limits and are monitored by the court and/or a citizens' review panel. This way, if a family receives services without making enough progress to provide for a child's most basic needs, the parents' rights can be terminated and the child placed in an adoptive home, rather than the child remaining in limbo in the foster care system. Such planning assists agencies in making more realistic decisions about helping children and their families and ensures that families know specifically what they need to do in order to be allowed to continue to parent their children.

The Best Interests of the Child

Decisions about needs of children and families should be based on what is in the **best interests of the child.** Sometimes, even with the most appropriate intervention, it is questionable whether it is best for children to remain with their own families. In such circumstances, should decisions regarding where a child is placed (i.e., remain with his or her own family or be placed elsewhere) focus on the child's best interests, the parents' best interests, or the family's best interests? Although experts agree that the rights of both the parents and their children need to be considered carefully, current trends give attention first to the best interests of the child. This means that before any decision is made, careful attention must be given to what the most beneficial outcome will be for that particular child. In *Before the Best Interests of the Child* (1979) and *Beyond the Best Interests of the Child* (1973), Goldstein, Freud, and Solnit give careful consideration to this issue. They argue that in considering what is best for a child, the **least detrimental alternative** for that child must be considered. In other words, if it is detrimental for a child to remain with his or her family, one must then ask what the least harmful alternative would be.

Legislation now requires that courts appoint a guardian *ad litem* (one who acts for the minor on a limited and specific basis) in certain child welfare situations, such as hearings when a parent's rights are being terminated. The guardian *ad litem's* sole purpose is to represent the best interests of the child and to make a recommendation to the court with this in mind. This is especially important in situations where the parents have an attorney advocating one decision to a judge, such as returning a child to the parents, and the state child welfare agency has an attorney advocating another decision, such as placement in substitute care or termination of parental rights.

Goldstein, Freud, and Solnit (1973) also focus on considerations of who is most significant and should be involved in planning changes in a child's life. Until recently, decisions regarding where a child should be raised usually involved the child's biological mother, and then father. However, the early rearing of many children is by a relative or a foster parent rather than their biological parents. Goldstein, Freud, Solnit, and others stress the importance of considering the child's **psychological parent** rather than biological parent, who might not always be the same individual.

Considerations before State Intervention

Another important philosophical issue is under what circumstances the community or state should intervene in family matters. As indicated previously, in the past, families were considered sacred, and intervention in family matters seldom took place. Such intervention, when allowed, has been based on the doctrine of *parens patriae.* This doctrine is based on the concept that the state is a parent to all of its children and has the obligation, through regulatory and legislative powers, to protect them and, when necessary, provide them with resources needed to keep them safe.

Now, with increased attention to such family problems as child abuse, child neglect, spouse abuse, and alcoholism, many children are growing up in unsafe and unnurturing environments. Many family advocates argue that early intervention is necessary to keep a family together, as well as protect the child from growing up with severe emotional damage. Recently, other advocates have suggested that intervention in families should take place less often, because there are too many instances when the intervention—especially when limited resources do not often allow for the family to be rehabilitated—is more harmful than no intervention at all. These advocates suggest that intervention in families should take place only when requested by a parent, such as in child custody disputes; when a parent chooses to relinquish the rights of a child and place that child for adoption; or when a parent is seriously abusing a child and the effect of the abuse on the child can be visibly observed.

The issue of when a government entity has the right or the obligation to intervene is increasingly before the courts. Many state child advocacy groups have filed class action suits against state agencies mandated to provide child protective services, charging failure to provide needed services to protect children from serious maltreatment. However, in 1990, the Wisconsin State Supreme Court ruled that the state cannot be expected to protect all children in the state who are at risk from serious injury or death. This case will likely end up in the United States Supreme Court.

Prevention of Family Disruption and Dysfunction

Another major issue is whether scarce resources should be targeted toward prevention or treatment of family problems. And, if toward prevention, should it be primary, secondary, or tertiary? All three are important in strengthening families.

Most intervention with families today is treatment oriented rather than prevention oriented, and even those programs are not available to many parents and families in need of such services. Because resources are scarce, little attention is given to any type of prevention at all. Of the few prevention programs available, the focus is tertiary in nature. For example, the current focus is on family preservation; however, children often must be severely abused or families must experience a serious crisis before services are available, and by that time family preservation is not likely to be a realistic option.

How Accountable Are Parents?

A final issue receiving increased attention is the extent to which parents should be held accountable in regard to caring for their children, and what should be done to parents who do not care for them adequately. A number of specialists in family problems suggest that punishment is more likely to make parents angry and less likely to teach them how to be better parents. These specialists hold that effective treatment programs and the availability of resources are much more optimal for children than punishment of their parents and likely separation from them. Other experts suggest that a compromise is most effective: that parents whose family problems pose severe consequences for their children be brought before the court and ordered to receive treatment, with punishment ordered if they refuse treatment.

The relationships between parents' problems and consequences for a child are also being debated increasingly and coming before the courts for decisions. Should a woman who fears for her own life if she intervenes to protect her child be held accountable for the injury of the child, for example? In two recent child abuse fatality cases, one in New York and one in Texas, a battered woman was charged with failing to protect her child from her violent husband. In the New York case, the mother was found not guilty; in the Texas case the mother pled guilty in a plea bargain and was sentenced to six years in prison. The court also terminated the mother's parental rights.

DEFINING SERVICES TO CHILDREN, YOUTH, AND FAMILIES

Traditionally, services to children, youth, and families have been defined as **child welfare services.** Kadushin (1980,5) suggests that "child welfare involves providing social services to children and young people whose parents are unable to fulfill their child parenting responsibilities, or whose communities fail to provide the resources and protection that children and families require," and that the goals of child welfare services are "to reinforce, supplement or substitute the functions that parents have difficulty in performing; and to improve conditions for children and their families by modifying existing social institutions or organizing new ones."

The Social Security Act, the most significant piece of national legislation ever passed in relation to providing support to children and families, has a specific section (Title IV-B) that mandates states to provide a full range of child welfare services, defined as:

> *public social services which supplement, or substitute for parental care and supervision for the purpose of:*
>
> *1. preventing or remedying, or assisting in the solution of problems which may result in the neglect, abuse, exploitation or delinquency of children,*
> *2. protecting and caring for homeless, dependent, or neglected children,*
> *3. protecting and promoting the welfare of children of working mothers and*
> *4. otherwise protecting and promoting the welfare of children, including the strengthening of their own homes where possible or, where needed, the provision of adequate care of children away from their homes in foster family homes or day care or other child care facilities. (Section 425)*

Because of negative connotations associated with the term *welfare* and the current emphasis on the importance of strengthening the family in order to support the child, child welfare services today more often are referred to as services to children, youth, and families or child and family services. Both Kadushin's definition and the definition in the Social Security Act are broad enough, however, to be congruent with either of the more currently preferred terms.

THE HISTORY OF SERVICES TO CHILDREN, YOUTH, AND FAMILIES

In colonial times, children were considered to be the responsibility of their families, and little attention was given to children whose families were available to provide for them, no matter whether the family actually met the child's needs. Children usually came to the attention of authorities only if they were orphaned and relatives were not available to provide for them. Churches and a few private orphanages cared for some dependent children; however, prior to 1800, most orphans were placed in almshouses or indentured, that is, given to families to function as servants. Focus during this time period was on survival, as death often occurred at early ages; fewer than half of all children born in the United States prior to the 1800s lived to reach the age of eighteen.

During the 1800s, increased attention began to be given to the negative effects of placing young children in almshouses along with insane, retarded, delinquent, and disabled persons. In 1853, Charles Loring Brace founded the Children's Aid Society of New York, which established orphanages and other programs for children. Brace and others felt that such programs were the most appropriate way to "save" many children from the negative influences of their parents and urban life (Bremner 1974). Brace viewed rural Protestant families as ideal parents for such children, and he recruited many foster families from the rural Midwest to serve as foster parents. During the mid-1800s, "orphan trains" carrying hundreds of children stopped at depots throughout the Midwest, leaving behind those children selected by families at each stop.

By 1880, the Children's Aid Society of New York had sent 40,000 children to live with rural farm families (Bremner 1974). A number of individuals and organizations strongly criticized this move. Although some called attention to the negative effects of separating children from their parents, the greatest criticism targeted religious conflicts. The majority of children placed in foster homes were from Irish immigrant families who were predominantly Catholic, whereas their foster families were primarily German and Scandinavian Protestants. The outcry led to more emphasis placed on the development of Catholic orphanages and foster homes.

Still, little attention was focused on children living with their own families or with other families as a result of informal placement by their families, and no standards or system of intervention existed to address the needs of abused and neglected children and their families. This changed in the 1870s as the result of a now-famous case involving a young girl in New York named Mary Ellen. Abandoned by her parents at birth, Mary Ellen was living with relatives who beat her severely, tied her to her bed, and fed her very small amounts of food from a bowl like a dog. A visitor to Mary Ellen's neighborhood was appalled at the abusive treatment she was receiving from her caretakers and reported the situation to a number of agencies in New York City. When none would intervene, the visitor, reasoning that Mary Ellen fell under the broad rubric of "animal," finally got the New York Society for the Prevention of Cruelty to

Animals to take the case to court and request that the child be moved from the family immediately.

As a result of the Mary Ellen case, New York and other cities established a Society for the Prevention of Cruelty to Children. These organizations, however, focused primarily on prosecution of parents rather than on services to either children or their families. The establishment of Charity Organization Societies (COS) and settlement houses in the late 1800s gave increased attention to children and families, as well as to the environments in which they functioned.

The majority of other efforts in the 1800s and early 1900s focused on the health needs of children. This was because illness was frequent and the death of children was commonplace during this time period and also because middle- and upper-middle-class families saw prevention of disease as a way to keep the diseases of immigrants from spreading to their own children (Bremner 1974). Immunization laws, pasteurized milk legislation, and other sanitation laws passed easily during this time period. Other relevant legislation focused on child labor laws and compulsory school attendance legislation. Increased attention began to be given at both state and national levels to the responsibilities of government to provide for children and families, and many states passed legislation establishing monitoring systems for foster care and separating facilities for dependent, neglected, and delinquent children from those for adults.

The most significant effort toward the establishment of a true service delivery system for children, youth, and families during the early 1900s was the creation of the **U.S. Children's Bureau** in 1912. This was a result of the first White House Conference on Children, held in 1910, and a coalition of child advocates from the settlement houses, COS groups, and state boards of charities and corrections. The legislation establishing the U.S. Children's Bureau was significant because it was the first national legislation recognizing that the federal government had a responsibility for the welfare of its children. Julia Lathrop was appointed the first chief of the bureau, and the agency's first efforts were aimed at birth registration and maternal and child health programs, in an attempt to reduce the high infancy mortality rate and improve the health of children. One of the bureau's first publications, *Infant Care,* a booklet for parents, has undergone over twenty revisions and remains the most popular document available from the Government Printing Office. Today, the Children's Bureau is responsible for a number of federal programs for children, youth, and families and is a part of the U.S. Department of Health and Human Services.

During the first thirty years of the 1900s, states continued to become more involved in services to children, youth, and families, particularly in the South West, where strong private agencies did not exist. Many states established public departments of welfare that also were responsible for child and family services, including protecting children from abuse and neglect, providing foster homes, and overseeing orphanages and other institutions for children. The establishment of the American Association for Organizing Family Social Work (which later became the Family Service Association of America) in 1919 and the **Child Welfare League of America** in 1920 gave further impetus to the provision of child and family services. Both of these organizations stressed the role of the social work profession and established recommended standards for the provision of services. During the 1920s, attention turned to parenting and facilitating the development of healthy parent–child relationships. Child guidance centers were established and the emphasis on psychoanalysis led to increased attention to child therapy. Establishment of adoption as a formal child welfare service and subsequent passage of adoption legislation also occurred during this period.

Services to children, youth, and families became more formalized with the passage of the Social Security Act in 1935. This act established mothers' pensions, which later became the AFDC program, and also mandated states to establish, expand, and strengthen statewide child welfare services, especially in rural areas. The definition of child welfare stated earlier in this chapter incorporated the following trends currently seen in state and federal child welfare services:

1. Recognition that poverty is a major factor associated with other child and family problems;
2. A shift from rescuing children from poor families and placing them in substitute care to keeping children in their own homes and providing supportive services to prevent family breakup;
3. State intervention in family life to protect children;
4. Increased professionalization and bureaucratization of child welfare services;
5. An emphasis at the federal level that it is the responsibility of the federal government to oversee the delivery of child welfare services within states to ensure that all children and families in the United States have access to needed services.

In spite of the Social Security Act, there continued to be problems with the delivery of services to children, youth, and families. Access to services remained unequal, and many children continued to grow up in poverty. Some child welfare services, such as adoption, were provided primarily to white middle-class families, and few child welfare services adequately addressed the needs of black, Native American, and Hispanic children and their families. Many children, particularly minority children, spent their entire childhood in foster care. What initially was meant to be temporary care until families stabilized enough for their children to return became a permanent way of life for many children.

In the 1960s the Kennedy and Johnson administrations took a strong interest in children, youth, and families. Services during these administrations were broader and were targeted at the prevention and elimination of poverty. Many of these programs were based on then-new studies that suggested that children could be shaped by their environment and that heredity played only a minimal role in individual outcomes. The focus became to "maximize the potential of all individuals" and to help them become productive adults. As a result, programs were implemented such as infant care centers and **Head Start** (a preschool program focusing on social, emotional, and cognitive development), and increased emphasis was placed on education, as well as job training and employment programs for youth and their parents. With this broad-based focus, traditional child welfare services received less attention in favor of strengthening families and preventive services.

When President Nixon took office, resources were perceived as being more scarce. The focus shifted from providing maximum resources to meeting minimum standards in regard to child and family services. With only a few exceptions that Congress actively advocated, services to children, youth, and families narrowed. In addition, funding, programs, and policies shifted back to more traditional child welfare services, including protective services to abused and neglected children and their families, foster care, and adoption.

In 1974, attention to the **battered child syndrome**—a medical diagnosis given to a child who comes to a medical setting with a broken bone and whose X-rays reveal previously broken bones throughout the body in various stages of healing—resulted in strong advocacy from the medical profession and key congressional leaders, such as Walter Mondale. As a result, Congress passed the Child Abuse and Neglect Prevention and Treatment Act. This act mandated establishment of the National Center on Child Abuse and Neglect as part of the Department of Health, Education and Welfare (now the Department of Health and Human Services). It required states receiving federal dollars to strengthen child maltreatment programs to meet a number of mandates, including state definitions and reporting laws regarding child maltreatment; established research and technical assistance programs to assist states in developing child maltreatment prevention and treatment programs; and established special demonstration programs that could later be adopted by other states. When the act was renewed three years later, a new section was added to strengthen adoption services for children with special needs, or those children who were waiting to be adopted and were considered difficult to place because of ethnicity, age, or developmental disabilities.

During the Nixon administration, because of increased concern about the high costs of child care and the number of children left alone because their parents could not afford child care, Congress attempted to pass legislation that would give states funding for child care subsidies for low-income working parents. It was reasoned that this would not only keep more children safe but also reduce the number of women on AFDC and the number of families living in poverty. In 1990 the A Better Child Care (ABC) Act was introduced in Congress with a wide base of support. That legislation, which was not supported by the Bush administration, also failed, as has most other child and family services legislation since the Carter administration.

Significant legislation that has passed in recent years includes the 1974 Juvenile Justice and Delinquency Prevention Act, which establishes limited funding for runaway youth programs; the Indian Child Welfare Act (1978), which attempts to prevent disruption of American Indian families; and the Education for All Handicapped Children Act (1975), which mandates the provision of educational and social services to handicapped children through public school systems.

In 1980, Congress passed the Adoption Assistance and Child Welfare Act. For many years advocates had been urging that legislation of this type be passed because they had become increasingly concerned about the large number of children "drifting" in the foster care system and those who were legally free for adoption but for whom homes were not being found. A number of studies (Maas & Engler 1959; Vasaly 1976) indicated that the child welfare services delivery system perhaps was doing more harm to children than they would experience if they had remained in their own homes. Researchers in one study (Shyne & Schroeder 1978) found that, although foster care philosophically was (and is) intended to be short-term (six months or less) while parents prepare for family reunification through counseling and other types of assistance, this was not the experience of many children. The average age of children studied in foster care was approximately thirteen; the average number of years a child had been in foster care was approximately five; the average number of social workers managing the child's case while in foster care was approximately five; and the average number of different foster homes in which the child had lived was approximately five.

The Adoption Assistance and Child Welfare Act has changed the thrust of services to children, youth, and families. Through ceilings on funding allowances, it encourages the establishment of own-home services and reductions in the number of children in foster care; it requires case plans and six-month reviews for all children receiving child welfare services so that they do not languish in foster care; and it provides federal funding to subsidize the adoption of special-needs children.

Unfortunately, however, the act has not received the funding appropriations needed to implement successfully what it was designed to do. Because the act offered financial incentives to states if they reduced the number of children in substitute care and strengthened services to children while they remained in their own homes, foster care rates dropped nationwide during the early 1980s, from an estimated 500,000 to an estimated 270,000. However, as child abuse and neglect reports have increased and funding for services has decreased, more children have been seriously injured or have died when they have remained in their own homes. Although the act put no ceiling on federal payments for foster care of children who qualify for AFDC benefits, it severely restricted funding for in-home services such as family counseling. The more frequently required court hearings have also overloaded an already overextended court system, making it difficult for legal proceedings to take place that can free children for adoption. Thus, substitute care rates are again on the increase, with an estimated 360,000 children in foster care nationwide in 1990 and rates showing no signs of decreasing; furthermore, funding for in-home services and other programs that keep families together is seriously lacking. For example, in 1990, funding under the authorization of the act was $1.5 billion for foster care and $252 million for preventive programs. Still, child and family advocates point to important gains in philosophy, practice, and management of cases since the passage of the act. There is now increased recognition given to children's right to remain in their own home or to return to their home as soon as possible, more special needs children have been adopted, and innovative in-home services have been developed in many parts of the country (Kamerman & Kahn 1990).

During the Reagan administration, federal legislation for children and youth services was limited, and the same has held true during the Bush administration. However, several significant pieces of legislation have been enacted which have had an impact on services to children, youth, and families. The Developmentally Disabled Assistance and Bill of Rights Act (1990) requires states to establish services in the least restrictive settings possible. The Special Education for Infants and Toddlers Act (1989) provides special identification and intervention for developmentally delayed infants and toddlers. The Public Health Act (1987) authorizes establishment of adolescent family life demonstration programs to prevent teenage pregnancy and to service pregnant and parenting teens and their families. Another drawback to these legislative acts, in addition to the limited funding authorized to implement the requirements of each act, is the continued categorization of legislation. Such categorical legislation, targeted toward areas such as child abuse, alcoholism and drug abuse, runaway youth, school dropouts and adolescent pregnancy, leads to the establishment of programs limited to narrow populations and reinforces the fragmentation of services rather than a holistic approach.

Recent sessions of Congress have placed additional ceilings on amounts available for child and family services. During the 1980s increased focus due to publicity has been given to substance abuse, sexual abuse, teenage pregnancy, pediatric AIDS, and increased gang activities and more serious crimes among juveniles. However, due to budgetary constraints and attention to other priorities, increased attention has not meant increased funding.

The federal legislation that has the potential to be the most significant for children and families since the Social Security Act of 1935 is the Family Support Act of 1988, commonly referred to as the "welfare reform act." Proponents of the legislation believe that the provision of transitional benefits for AFDC recipients—such as health care, child care, and transportation; the emphasis on education, job training, and placement in a job that leads toward self-sufficiency; and the case management approach, which views the client and family from a holistic perspective—may reduce some of the problems with previously fragmented services created by categorical legislation. However, funding to provide such massive changes is limited, and implementation of the act at the state and local levels requires extensive coordination and services provided by human services agencies, school districts, community colleges and universities, employment and job training programs, child care programs, health care providers, transportation programs, and private and public sector employers. Initial efforts to initiate or strengthen welfare reform programs will be more expensive than previous efforts. If increased numbers of families achieve self-sufficiency, however, the long-term benefits to future generations of public assistance recipients, as well as to the national economy and the well-being of our society, will be far more substantial than the initial costs.

PREVENTIVE SERVICES TO CHILDREN IN THEIR OWN HOMES

Although preventive services receive less attention than other types of services, there are many programs that strengthen families and reduce chances for family dysfunction.

Natural Support Systems

Given the scarcity of resources, increased attention is being given to the strengthening of **natural support systems** to assist families. Many families develop social networks of friends, relatives, neighbors, or co-workers who provide emotional support; share child care, transportation, clothing, toys, and other resources; offer the opportunity to observe other children, parents, and family constellations and how they interact; and provide education about child rearing and other family life situations. However, studies show that many families who experience problems are isolated and lack such support systems. Many social services agencies, churches, and other community organizations are assisting communities in the establishment of support systems for new families and other families who lack natural support systems to help them meet their needs. Some communities have established telephone support programs for various groups, such as a Parents' Warmline or Teen Help Line, where individuals can receive support and information about appropriate resources.

Recently in the United States there has been increased attention given to the provision of **home-based family-centered services,** or services delivered to children and families in their own homes, with a focus on preserving the family system and strengthening the family to bring about needed change. Comprehensive services, which are usually overseen by a single case manager assigned to the family, include homemaker services, respite care, child care, crisis intervention, financial assistance, substance abuse treatment, vocational counseling, and help with various concrete services, such as locating housing or transportation. Most home-based service programs include the following features (Lloyd & Bryce 1980):

o A primary worker or case manager who establishes and maintains a supportive, nurturing relationship with the family;

o Small caseloads of 2–6 families with a variety of service options used for each family;

o A team approach with team members providing some services and serving as a backup to the primary worker/case manager;

o A support system available 24 hours a day for crisis calls or emergencies;

o The home as the natural setting, with maximum use of natural support systems, including the family, extended family, neighborhood, and community;

o Parents remaining in charge of and responsible for their families as educators, nurturers, and primary caregivers;

o A willingness to invest at least as much in providing home-based services to a family as society is willing to pay for out-of-home care for their children.

Most families receiving home-based family-centered services are multi-problem families who have received fragmented services for long periods of time from a number of agencies. Many children from these families have also previously spent time in substitute care. However, due to the chronic and severe problems and the repeated crises such families often experience, past efforts have been largely ineffective.

Home-based family-centered services are based on a systems/ecological approach to family intervention, viewing the entire family as the focus of treatment. Intervention is short-term and goal-oriented, focused on behavioral change. Intensive services are usually provided to families for sixty to ninety days, which averages out to the same number of families a worker providing traditional child welfare services carries during a one-year period. However, the ability to focus on a limited number of families intensively has important benefits. First, it gives workers a chance to stabilize more families so that they can function either independently or with fewer services while allowing children to remain in their own homes. Second, it allows workers to make a better determination more quickly and with more documentation that the family cannot be stabilized, allowing children to be placed more quickly in adoptive homes rather than remaining in limbo in either a dysfunctional life-threatening family situation or the instability of foster care.

Studies comparing home-based family-centered service programs to more traditional child welfare services show that when 18 percent to 20 percent of children who would otherwise enter substitute care can be maintained safely in their own homes, the home-based services pay for themselves. Evaluations of home-based family-centered programs show that 75 percent to 90 percent of children are able to remain in their own homes when such services are provided (Bryce & Lloyd 1980).

Parent Education

Whereas most people are required to learn math and English in school, little attention is given to one of the most important roles they are likely to play as adults—that of being a parent. Many communities offer parenting classes aimed at a wide range of parents: prenatal classes for parents prior to the birth or adoption of their first infant, classes for parents of toddlers and preschoolers, classes for parents of school-age children, and classes for parents of adolescents. Such programs not only offer education about basic developmental stages of children and adolescents and alternative methods of child rearing and discipline, but they also encourage the development of mutual support systems among participants, who often relax about their roles as parents when they realize that other parents have similar concerns and struggles.

Child Development and Child Care Programs

Accessible, high-quality child care programs that are affordable for working parents, particularly single parents, also can be seen as preventing family breakdown. Such programs help parents ensure that during working hours their children are happy and safe in a comfortable, nurturing environment, thus reducing parental stress. Many child care programs offer additional opportunities for parents, including parenting education classes, babysitting cooperatives, social programs, and the opportunity to develop support systems with other parents and children. However, affordable, high-quality child care programs often are available to working parents, particularly in rural areas. Child care for infants, for school-age children during vacations and holidays, and when children are sick also is not widely available in the United States. An additional gap in services is the availability of evening and night child care for parents who must work late shifts.

Special programs are available for low-income parents. However, these are often limited in the hours and in the number of children they can serve. Head Start, perhaps the most successful program established under the Office of Economic Opportunity in the 1960s, provides not only a developmental learning program for preschool children but also health care, social services, and parent education. Infant–parent centers, which allow parents the opportunity to learn how to interact and play with their children in order to stimulate their development, also are available to some parents on a limited basis.

Recreational, Religious, and Social Programs

When discussing services for children, youth, and families, attention is seldom given to the major roles that community resources other than social services agencies play in meeting family needs. From a systems/ecological perspective, the broader social, recreational, and religious programs must be seen as primary services available to all persons and families; and social services agencies are to be viewed as residual services to address the needs of those families not served by these primary services. The church meets the spiritual, emotional, social, and recreational needs of many children, youth, and families and often plays a major role in establishing special preventive services, such as child care programs, outreach centers, and parent education programs. Increasingly, the business community is providing preventive services through the workplace, including bag-lunch programs for working parents, recreational facilities and programs for employees and their families, and the facilitation of co-worker support systems. Many communities offer extensive free recreational programs that provide family entertainment. Serious gaps exist in most communities, however, in providing appropriate recreational programs for adolescents. Some experts attribute increases in adolescent problems, including teenage pregnancy and delinquency, to the lack of available programs for this age group.

Health and Family Planning Programs

Early screening of health problems also reduces child and family problems. Health problems place increased stress on families, and access to affordable health care from prenatal care to adulthood is an important aspect of preventing family breakdown. Additionally, access to programs that provide help in responsible decision making about becoming a parent, through family planning clinics, churches, and other community resources, reduces the risk of unwanted children and provides assistance in exploring options when pregnancy occurs.

Education about Family Problems

Finally, education about the various types of family problems—and, should they occur, about resources available—is a significant form of prevention. Many communities provide programs for children that focus on prevention of sexual abuse by teaching them about types of touch and what to do when they find themselves in an uncomfortable situation with an adult or older child. Other communities provide alcohol and drug awareness programs.

Appropriate Educational Opportunities

Most studies identify strong relationships between difficulties in school and individual and family problems. Programs that provide an opportunity for children to learn in ways that help them feel good about themselves and develop a sense of competence prevent family- and child-related problems in the long run. Children who have such encouragement are less likely to become pregnant, drop out of school, and live their lives in poverty. School-based social services allow for close cooperation between children and adolescents, teachers and school administrators, parents, and the community.

SCHOOL SOCIAL WORK

Another specialized field that focuses on services to children, youth, and families is **school social work**, or social work services provided in a school-based setting. Such services provide an opportunity to identify needs of children and their families early and to facilitate early intervention before problems become more serious. Social workers in school settings provide preventive services such as parent education and facilitate the development of positive mental health for children through special outreach programs in the school. School social work includes individual, family, and group counseling, as well as crisis intervention services. School social workers deal with suicidal students; students and their families and friends after a serious injury or death has occurred; and students in conflict with family members, peers, or school authorities. School social workers serve as members of intervention teams who work with developmentally disabled and other children with special needs, often serving as the liaison to parents and the community when special services are needed. The recent renewal of the Education for All-Handicapped Children Act specifies that schools may hire social workers to provide social services to special-needs children, and dropout prevention legislation in some states also suggests the hiring of social workers.

School-based social work services are advantageous for many reasons. First, the social worker gets to see the child or adolescent in a natural setting, interacting with peers, teachers, and school administrators, which provides a different perspective than seeing a client in an office or an agency. Second, they allow the social worker access to large numbers of children and families in need of services; most children aged five to eighteen attend school. Third, they allow the social worker to help parents and school personnel use a systems/ecological approach to better address the child's needs, focusing on the relationships between the child, the home, the school, and the broader community. Often, in school, the staff focus on academic performance and school behavior. A social worker with a systems/ecological perspective can help school personnel understand the importance of family and community variables in relation to the child's capacity to function in the school setting.

SERVICES TO CHILDREN AND FAMILIES AT RISK

Although, because of a scarcity of resources, it is sometimes easier to locate community resources for children and families already at risk than preventive services, such services are also limited and fragmented. Many studies of child and family services find that coordination among service providers is a problem identified by both service providers and recipients. Some communities have made special efforts to increase coordination, avoid duplication, and reduce gaps in services available to at-risk children and families. Efforts include development of computerized data bases and information and referral systems that can provide instant information about the types, location, eligibility requirements, and costs of available services.

Other efforts involve "first-stop" resource centers where families at risk can receive thorough assessments identifying needs so that they can be referred to appropriate agencies rather than going from agency to agency only to learn that services are not available to them or do not meet their needs. In some communities, multiservice agencies have been established where a number of agencies are located in the same facility with a single assessment point and agency staffings to share information about families and determine which agencies can best meet a family's needs. At-risk families, often reluctant to trust service providers and without transportation to access services, can receive individual and family counseling, complete forms to receive public assistance, get help in finding employment and housing, and attend parenting classes and parent support groups all at the same location. A variety of programs are available, particularly in urban areas, to help meet the needs of at-risk children and families.

Health and Hospital Outreach Programs

Many health clinics and hospitals have established special programs to address the needs of children and families who are at risk of family disruption or dysfunction. (These and other services to families at risk are shown in Figure 8–1.) Some clinics have high-risk infant programs, for example, that provide intensive services to teenage parents; parents of low-birth-weight, premature, or handicapped infants; parents with alcohol or drug abuse problems; and parents who never seem to have established appropriate relationships with their children. Clinics offer a variety of services, such as weekly outreach programs conducted by a public health nurse, individual counseling, play groups for children and support groups for parents, role modeling of appropriate child care, and assistance in obtaining other resources as needed.

Hospitals offer similar programs. In some hospitals, specially trained nurses identify at-risk mothers in the delivery room and provide intensive care and support to those mothers during their hospitalization in addition to outreach services to both parents after the hospital stay. In a number of instances, such programs help parents realize they do not wish to be parents and help them relinquish children for adoption or place them in foster care while they receive additional help. More often, such programs prevent child abuse or neglect and help parents establish positive relationships with their children. Pediatric-AIDS programs have also been established in many major-metropolitan-area hospitals. Such programs attempt to stabilize the health of infants and older children infected with the AIDS virus. Because many parents do not want to or cannot care for children with AIDS and it is difficult to locate foster families willing to do so, many children with AIDS remain in the hospital for extensive periods of time, sometimes longer than a year.

In some areas, special health clinics have been established to provide services for adolescents. Clinics provide basic health care; information on adolescent development, puberty, and sexually transmitted diseases; and in some instances, pregnancy tests, contraceptive information, and prenatal care. Some clinics are located in public high schools. Although this has caused some controversy, studies show that physical and emotional problems, sexually transmitted diseases, and pregnancies have decreased significantly in these schools.

Figure 8–1 Support Service Options for Families at Risk

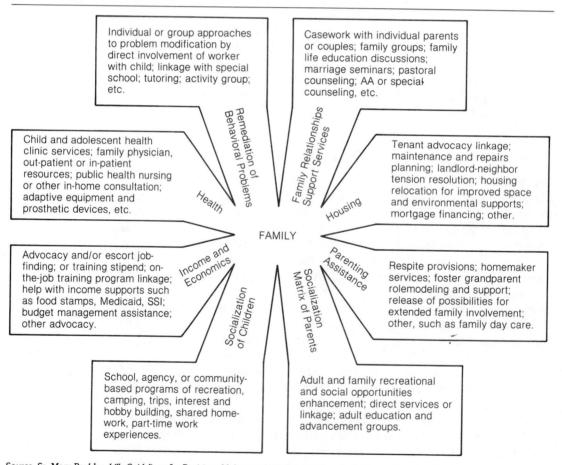

Source: Sr. Mary Paul Janchill, *Guidelines for Decision–Making in Child Welfare*. New York: Human Services Workshops, 1981, p. 13.

Child Care

Although attention usually is given to child care for working parents, child care also is used as a service for at-risk parents that enables children to remain in their own homes. Many parents need respite from their children and cannot provide for their needs twenty-four hours a day. Child care provides parents time to meet their own needs and provides children the emotional support they may not be getting at home. It allows families to stay together and is less costly than foster care and less traumatic for the child. In many states, some child care providers receive special training to enable them to work more effectively with at-risk parents and children. In some instances, child care providers develop surrogate-parent or positive role relationships with parents, giving them and their children much-needed emotional support.

Many times parents under stress reach a point where they need a break from their child or they will abuse or neglect the child. Other times, emergencies occur and parents lack natural support systems to help them in times of crisis. In other situations, families with severely developmentally disabled children need time for themselves but must cope with their needs twenty-four hours a day. Many communities have established various forms of crisis or respite care programs for such families. Some agencies have respite care programs for developmentally disabled children, where specially trained adults care for children evenings or weekends so parents can have time to themselves. Other communities have established crisis nurseries or shelters, where parents under severe stress or in a serious emergency can leave their children for a limited amount of time. Some programs even provide emergency transportation for the children; most require counseling for parents under extreme stress while their children are in crisis care.

Some communities provide respite care for adolescents who need time away from their parents. Emergency shelter facilities for teens also most often provide crisis and family counseling to help stabilize the situation so the teens can return home. However, special services for teens are lacking in many areas. In some communities, the only resource available for teens as young as twelve or thirteen is the Salvation Army's general shelter.

Increased attention is also being given to child care for working parents, particularly under the provisions of the Family Support Act of 1988. The inability to access affordable child care can often be the last straw that creates an additional crisis for families who are already at risk and under severe stress. Many at-risk working parents lose or are forced to quit their jobs because of a lack of child care.

Homemaker Services

Many agencies provide homemaker services to families who are at risk or who have abused or neglected their children. Homemakers are specially trained individuals, often indigent persons from the community who have been parents themselves and can serve as a nurturing, supportive role model for the parents and children in the home. Homemakers offer practical suggestions and education about housekeeping, child care, nutrition and cooking, health and safety, shopping, budgeting, and access to community resources. Additionally, they may serve as surrogate parents to both parents and children in a family and often develop positive, trusting relationships with family members who may have been previously isolated. Homemaker services are far more cost-effective than foster care and often prevent the necessity to separate children from their parents.

Crisis Intervention Programs

Various community agencies provide **crisis intervention** services to families in crisis, which deescalate the crisis and often result in a subsequent referral for additional help, such as counseling. Law enforcement agencies in many communities have crisis intervention teams that handle domestic disputes, including situations of spouse and child abuse. Some runaway youth shelters provide crisis intervention for adolescents and their parents. Hospitals also provide crisis intervention services in emergency rooms, dealing with child maltreatment, family violence, and other serious family problems. From a systems/ecological perspective, intervention often can be more effective in a crisis situation than in a noncrisis situation, because the family system is thrown into disequilibrium. Studies show that families are more receptive to change and to agreement to services such as counseling during disequilibrium, because regular defenses and the family balance are no longer intact.

Counseling

Individual, marital, and family counseling services are available in many communities for families experiencing problems. Mental health centers, social services agencies, child and family services agencies, child guidance clinics, employee assistance programs, churches, schools, youth services programs, and hospital outreach programs often provide various types of counseling services. Unfortunately, services often are available on a limited basis, due to scarce resources and the large number of persons needing services, and services may not always be available free or on a sliding scale. Additionally, specialized counseling to address family problems such as family violence or sexual abuse often is unavailable in many communities. For example, only five dollars per child was available for counseling services for the large number of sexually abused children in one large city, when one hour of counseling cost $40–$80 and children needed long-term counseling in most instances.

Studies show that for many problems, group counseling is more effective than individual counseling, or a combination of both is more effective than individual counseling alone. For example, when dealing with sexual abuse, children who have been sexually abused need to hear from other children that they are not the only ones who have had such an experience. Sexual and physical abusers, as well as others with family problems, often deny that there is a problem, and group therapy sessions with others in similar situations typically break down their defenses more quickly than individual counseling.

Increased attention by helping professionals is being given to family counseling as an effective way to strengthen individual functioning and address problems. Family counseling is effective in helping families understand behavior and coping patterns, establish more productive communication patterns, resolve problems, and support each other as family members. In almost all situations where a family member is experiencing a problem or undergoing a stressful change—for example, substance abuse, family violence, rape, a serious illness or disability, death of a family member, divorce, or remarriage—family counseling can help the entire family reinforce positive changes and address negative patterns appropriately, and also serve as a source of support to each other.

Some agencies have initiated multifamily groups, or groups of families that receive therapy jointly. Many times individuals can see their own issues and family dynamics more clearly while watching other families interact, because they are too involved when such interactions occur within their own families. Teenagers, for example, may be more likely to listen to another parent who provides feedback rather than their own parents, and parents are often more likely to listen to other teens or parents rather than family members.

Social workers, because of their emphasis on a systems/ecological perspective, have played an important role in this shift in focus from individual to family counseling. Social workers in particular focus on the strengths of family members and of the family as a total system, building on those strengths to make the system more supportive of its individual members.

Support and Self-Help Groups

Support groups and **self-help groups** also are effective ways of helping children, youth, and families cope with family problems. Such groups help individuals

School-based programs for parenting teens help reduce drop-out rates and also provide supportive services to teen parents. Here, teen parents interact with their babies during a lunch-time support group meeting with the school social worker.

realize that they are not the only ones coping with a given problem. Support and self-help groups also help members develop new ways to cope as they learn from each other. Perhaps most important, persons who may see themselves as being inadequate have a chance to reach out and give something to someone else. Examples of self-help groups include twelve-step programs such as Alcoholics Anonymous for alcoholics, Al-anon for family members of alcoholics, Alateen for teen family members of alcoholics, Narcotics Anonymous, and Adult Children of Alcoholics; Parents Anonymous for abusive or potentially abusive parents; Parents United for sexually abusive parents; Tough Love for parents of out-of-control adolescents; and Parents Without Partners for single parents.

Many communities have established support groups for adults, children, or teens dealing with divorce, stepparenting, death of a loved one or other type of loss, or stress associated with having a developmentally disabled or emotionally disturbed family member. Schools have established support groups for students experiencing difficulty functioning within the school setting, coping with family problems such as divorce or abuse, recovering from substance abuse, and teen parents. As resources become more scarce, social service agencies are realizing that in many instances more individuals and families can be served effectively through support and self-help groups.

Volunteer and Outreach Programs

Many traditional social services agencies are overloaded with cases and can provide only limited services—and those only to families with the most severe problems. A number of agencies have established volunteer components, whereas other agencies have been established that use only volunteers. In many instances, because they can spend more extensive time with families, volunteers can be highly successful in intervention and prevent family disruption. Most volunteer programs have established effective screening mechanisms that recruit volunteers with good nurturing skills who can relate well to clients. Many have been parents themselves, some are grandparents, and others are students or already involved in human services. Volunteers usually receive extensive training and are supervised by a social work case manager.

Many communities and states have successful volunteer programs. SCAN (Suspected Child Abuse and Neglect) of Arkansas and Family Outreach Centers established by the National Council of Jewish Women both use highly trained volunteers to work on a one-to-one basis with abusive and neglecting families. The SCAN model is based on a reparenting framework, which focuses on developing trust and then helps the parent work through all the stages of psychosocial development that they missed during childhood. Volunteers in such programs visit often and converse with parents and children, assist in problem solving and accessing community resources, and serve as a surrogate parent/role model/friend to the parent and family members. Similar programs have been developed that pair volunteers with teenage parents and abused and neglected children. The national Big Brothers and Big Sisters program uses volunteers as friends and role models to children from single-parent families. Studies show that volunteer programs can keep families together. Given the continuing increase in the number of families needing services and the lack of resources, volunteer programs are likely to increase.

Programs for at-risk families are funded by federal, state, and local governments as well as the private sector. The United Way funds numerous programs for families at risk in many communities. Churches, foundations, and private contributions fund other programs. Increasingly, public–private partnerships are being developed with funding from a variety of sources. In many instances, state and local governments contract with private agencies to provide services, and many private agencies receive funding from multiple sources, both public and private. Which entity should pay for what type of services is an increasingly complex issue at all levels in the United States. As the number of at-risk families continues to increase and as federal and state funding continues to be limited, more emphasis is being placed on local communities to fund such programs. However, local governments, employers, and private contributors are also becoming financially strapped as inflation continues and recessions are predicted. New ways of providing services and more effective cost-sharing are issues that will have to be explored in more depth during the 1990s.

CHILD PROTECTIVE SERVICES

The federal Child Abuse and Neglect Prevention and Treatment Act mandates that all states must designate a single agency to oversee services to abused and neglected children and their families. Such services are usually termed **child protective services.** Families reported to state human services agencies with child protective services divisions as being abusive or neglecting must be investigated by the agency to ascertain whether the maltreatment report can be substantiated. Legislation in all states, although often vague, establishes a minimum standard of care that caretakers are expected to provide to their children. If the social worker (commonly referred to as a child protective services worker) finds that abuse or neglect is a problem, and the minimum standard of care is not being met by the parent, the family receives protective services. This is a nonvoluntary program—that is, parents did not request or volunteer to receive the services.

Investigations of Child Maltreatment

In implementing the mandated services, child protective services workers cooperate closely with other professionals, including law enforcement officers, attorneys, health care providers, and educators. Child protective services workers provide a variety of roles in providing protective services in cooperation or jointly with other agencies. They may provide intake services, where they screen reports of child maltreatment, interviewing persons reporting cases over the telephone to obtain appropriate information needed to make a preliminary determination about how serious the report is and whether it needs to be investigated immediately. Most states require life-threatening situations to be investigated immediately or within twenty-four hours and less serious cases to be investigated within ten days.

Child protective services workers, by themselves or jointly with law enforcement officers, also conduct investigations of child maltreatment, interviewing children, parents, other family members, and collateral contacts such as teachers and neighbors, to determine the nature and extent of the reported maltreatment. Investigations involve examining and interviewing the child, attending to the child's immediate emotional needs during the investigation and making a preliminary assessment about whether maltreatment is occuring. If it is, investigators determine whether the maltreatment is causing or could cause permanent damage to the child's body or mind, how severe the maltreatment has been, and whether the situation is life-threatening and warrants immediate removal to a safer environment. In some instances, other resources, such as physicians, may be used to assist in gathering needed information. Investigations of child maltreatment require knowledge and skill in the identification of various types of maltreatment, interviewing techniques appropriate with children and adults who may be apprehensive and reluctant to cooperate, and a balance of compassion and firmness. Striking a balance between the use of authority and the use of compassion, or between the ability to confront and the ability to be empathic, is one of the challenges of being a child protective services worker (Maidman 1984).

Determination of Intervention Approach

The outcome of an investigation of child maltreatment is an assessment of the situation and the most appropriate actions to take. Child protective services workers are not expected to prove that maltreatment has actually taken place or to determine who perpetrated the maltreatment—those actions are within the domain of the courts. Their role is to determine whether the child needs to be protected and what is needed to provide the protection. Workers must assess a number of risk factors to determine whether the child is at risk and how severe the risk is. They have four options when assessing a possible situation of child maltreatment: to determine that the child is not being maltreated and withdraw from the case; to offer help to the family; to determine that the child is at serious risk and/or the parents are uncooperative and make arrangements to take the family to court; and with the court's permission to remove the child from the home immediately and place the child in emergency care, and later, usually foster care.

Child protective services workers most often determine that, although services are required, it is safe to leave the child in the home while the services are being provided. When children are removed, it is most often because the child or a sibling has been seriously injured or abandoned, the parent or caretaker states that he or she is going to kill or injure the child, evidence suggests that the child has experienced sexual abuse and the perpetrator is still in the home or has easy access to the child, there is a current crisis such as a psychotic parent or a parent in jail because of substance abuse, or there is little or no cooperation from parents and the child is at serious risk for substantial harm.

If, after trying to provide mandated services to families, the protective services workers feel that the families are resistant to the services, or the state in which they work mandates court involvement, they may take cases to court and request that the court order services, such as counseling. This way, if the family does not comply, the worker can bring the case back into court and request more serious options, such as placing the child in foster care.

Child protective services workers provide a variety of services to the families with whom they work. Their primary goal is to keep the child safe, and they make every effort to ensure that the child can be safe in his or her own home. They often serve as case managers, arranging for community resources such as housing, employment, transportation, counseling, health services, child care, homemaker services, or financial assistance. They provide counseling, parent education, and support. They may assist a client in getting involved in a church or other support group, or they may suggest (or require) that the client attend Parents Anonymous or be assigned a volunteer. Often, they develop a specific contract with a parent delineating specific goals the family must accomplish in order to be removed from the child protective services caseload.

Child protective services is challenging work because of the emotional aspects of working with abused and neglected children and the multiple roles that child protective services workers must play. Increased attention is being given to the importance of child protective services staff, and a number of national organizations, including the Child Welfare League of America, the American Association for Protecting Children, and the American Public Welfare Association, have established specialized training programs for staff and worked with states to explore new ways to provide protective services.

As reports of child maltreatment continue to increase and often involve children more severely injured than in the past, the role of child protective services as part of the child and family service delivery system is undergoing extensive debate. Due to the scarcity of resources, child protective services are the dominating child welfare service in many communities. However, whereas child protective services agencies in the past publicized their role as providing services to children and families to prevent child maltreatment from occurring or recurring, their current message is that they protect children. Because of staff shortages, many agencies can barely respond to all reports received and are unable to investigate all but the most serious reports. With increases in child maltreatment due to more extensive crack and cocaine use, poverty, and homelessness, the emphasis of child protective services is more often one of "damage control" rather than intensive services. This shift in philosophy leaves other community organizations to prevent child maltreatment and often to provide the extensive services needed to keep it from recurring, while child protective services must monitor to ensure that children are protected and refer cases to the courts for action when they are not. (Kamerman and Kahn, 1990)

SUBSTITUTE CARE

Although every attempt is made to keep children in their own homes, sometimes this is not possible. Parents may have too many unmet needs of their own, have serious health or emotional problems, or be too little interested in parenting to be able to care for their children adequately. In such situations, substitute care is located for the children involved. Unless the situation is an emergency—which many state laws define as a life-threatening situation—a child protective services worker cannot remove a child from a family without a court order. Even with emergency removals, court orders must be obtained, usually within twenty-four hours, and hearings must be held with parents present.

Types of Substitute Care

There are a number of different types of **substitute care.** Many communities have established crisis shelters, available to take children twenty-four hours a day until a family situation can be stabilized or other care that best meets a child's needs can be located. Although attempts are made to place children with relatives or neighbors so that they can remain in their immediate environment, this is not always possible. Other types of substitute care include foster homes, group homes, residential treatment facilities, and psychiatric treatment facilities.

Once a child is placed in substitute care, the child must have a plan developed that focuses on either returning the child home or, less often, terminating the parental rights and placing the child in an adoptive family. Each case must be reviewed by the court every six months to ensure that the child is not in limbo in the child welfare system.

If a child does need to be placed in substitute care, every effort should be made to ensure that the placement is the least restrictive option, although this is not always done. Thus, relatives, neighbors, and others with whom the child is familiar should be considered first if they meet criteria to be positive substitute parents for the child. Consideration also should be given to finding care for the child consistent with his or her cultural background, preferably in the same neighborhood or school area. Since it is important that the birth parents visit the child, if this is in the best interests of the child, attention also needs to be given to accessibility of the parents as well.

Foster Care If appropriate placements with relatives or other suitable arrangements cannot be made, the child most often is placed in foster care with a foster family. **Foster care** means the child will live in a home with a family that is not related by blood and nurtured until the child can return to his or her birth parents or be adopted. Foster parents are recruited and trained to relate to children and their birth parents. They often have children of their own and may take in more than one foster child. Many foster parents keep in touch with their foster children after they leave, and some adopt the children if they become available for adoption.

All states have strict standards regarding training that individuals must complete prior to becoming foster parents and to be able to continue as foster parents, the number of children foster parents can take, appropriate discipline and treatment of children, and supervision of foster parents. A number of states train foster parents to parent certain types of children, for example, adolescents, children with AIDS, or children who have been sexually abused. Foster parents also develop support systems, and many belong to local and national foster parent organizations. Although foster parents are paid a limited amount each month to care for each child, they often spend more than they receive and in almost all instances give large amounts of love and attention to the children they parent, who are often needy and may take out their frustrations on the foster family.

Currently, almost all children who require foster care have been abused or neglected. Because more children whose safety is threatened are being removed from their homes, additional foster parents are needed nationwide. Many localities are having difficulty finding foster parents willing to parent adolescents and younger children with serious emotional problems that often have resulted from child maltreatment.

Some children have difficulty handling the intimacy of a foster family, particularly if they have been seriously abused or neglected. In other instances, a foster family may not be found for a particular child—it is difficult to find foster homes for adolescents, for example. Group homes, which usually have a set of house parents to care for five to ten children or adolescents, are an alternative to foster care. Such homes attempt to maintain a homelike atmosphere and provide rules and structure to children and adolescents. They also may include regular group counseling sessions for residents.

Residential Treatment   Children and adolescents who need more structure than foster care or group homes can provide may be placed in **residential treatment** programs. Such programs, more expensive to maintain than foster care and group homes, provide consistent structure for children and adolescents, as well as intensive individual and, usually, group counseling. Most residential treatment programs help the child establish the boundaries that may be missing from home, build self-esteem and competence, and resolve anger and other issues from his or her family experience.

The goal of residential treatment is to develop enough coping skills that the child can return home better able to deal with the family situation. Ideally, the family also has undergone counseling, so they do not enter into old roles that may force the child back into previous behaviors in order to survive. Family counseling does not always occur, however, and it is often up to the child to cope on returning to the family and community.

Children and adolescents with more serious problems may be hospitalized. In hospital settings, more intensive therapy is provided and it is more likely that medication will be used. In other instances, children or adolescents, primarily delinquent adolescents, are placed in juvenile detention facilities. Studies suggest that white, middle-class children and teens are more likely to be placed in residential treatment or hospital programs, whereas poor and minority children and teens are more likely to be placed in juvenile detention facilities.

Although recent attempts have been made to strengthen the substitute care system, problems remain. Perhaps the greatest problem is the lack of resources available to birth parents that enable them to reunite with their children. Overloaded service delivery systems often thwart social workers from providing needed services to parents. As a result, social workers are reluctant to terminate parental rights and free children for adoption. On the other hand, because they cannot provide needed services, they are also reluctant to return children to unsafe homes. Thus, children languish in the foster care system. Emlen (1977) shows, however, that when intensive services are provided to parents, even those who have multiple problems and have been separated from their children for long periods of time can be reunited successfully with them.

ADOPTION

When parents choose not to or cannot provide for their children, parental rights are terminated by the court and the child becomes legally free for **adoption.** However, many children in the United States, particularly black children, are adopted informally by relatives without a formal court hearing ever taking place. The focus of adoption has changed significantly in recent years. In the past, the emphasis was on finding a perfect child for a couple who biologically could not have children, with an attempt to match the child to the parents according to physical features such as hair and eye color. Today, the emphasis is on finding an appropriate parent for a child—that is, one who can best meet the child's needs.

The types of adoptions that are taking place in the United States have also changed. Until the 1970s, most formal adoptions in the United States were couples who adopted healthy infants. However, most adoptions that take place today are adoptions by step-parents, which is a result of the increasing rates of divorce and remarriage. Today, there are also fewer infant adoptions. This is because many young women of all ethnic groups are choosing to keep their babies rather than place them for adoption. However, there are still traditional maternity homes/adoption agencies that provide residential and health care and counseling services before birth and, in some instances, postadoption counseling as well.

Adoption of Special-Needs Children

Many adoption agencies, however, have changed their focus to the more than 120,000 **special-needs children** available for adoption in the United States. Such children, while traditionally considered by many to be unadoptable, have been placed successfully in a variety of family settings. Special-needs children are those who are members of a minority group, older, physically or emotionally disabled, or members of sibling groups. Agencies also have focused on parents they had not previously considered. Whereas in the 1960s and 1970s emphasis was on transracial adoption, currently most agencies focus on finding parents who are of the same ethnic or cultural background as the child, if possible. Advocacy by groups such as the Association of Black Social Workers and passage of the Indian Child Welfare Act (1978)—which mandates that when placing Indian children, efforts must first be made to place a child with a family of the child's same tribe, then with another Indian family, and only then with a non-Indian family—have provided impetus to the emphasis on ethnicity when placing children for adoption. A number of agencies have established special outreach programs to black and Hispanic communities to recruit adoptive parents. In the 1980s Father George Clements, a black priest in Chicago, worked to establish the "One Church, One Child" campaign, based on the premise that if each church in the United States, particularly churches with primarily minority congregations, could work to have one child adopted by a member of its congregation, the adoption of special-needs children would no longer be so critical. This campaign has spread throughout the United States and has been one of many successful efforts; however, many special-needs children still need adoptive families.

Adoption agencies also are recruiting single parents, working parents, foster parents, and parents with large families already. Experience is showing that all of these families can successfully parent. An additional emphasis is on placing siblings together in the same adoptive family. Previously, many siblings were separated, often forever.

The Adoption Assistance Act, previously discussed, allows monthly living allowances and medical expenses for families who could not otherwise afford to adopt special-needs children. More assertive outreach efforts, such as Father Clements's One Church, One Child program, television's "Wednesday's Child" programs that portray children available for adoption, and national comput-erized services listing waiting children and waiting parents, have resulted in children being adopted who were previously considered unadoptable, including many who in the past would have been relegated to a life in a state institution.

Other current adoption trends include foreign-born adoptions and open adoptions, which allow the birth parent(s) to be involved in the selection of the adoptive parents, and, in some instances, to be able to maintain contact with the child as the child grows up. While adoption services have been strengthened, there are still barriers to successful placements, particularly of special-needs children. Agencies and individuals still consider some children unadoptable, and some agencies are reluctant to work on placing children across state lines, even when parents in other states can be located, or vice versa.

As the number of special-needs adoptions has increased, agencies and adoptive parents have also recognized the need for postadoption services for children and their adoptive families. Children who have experienced not only the loss of their birth parents but also extensive child maltreatment have special needs that often continue or do not surface until long after the adoption has been finalized. Adoptive parent groups have been instrumental in advocating for legislation, in establishing adoption programs, and in providing support to other adoptive parents. Currently, they provide the primary support after place-ment in many communities.

Additional issues relating to adoption will continue to be raised in the next decade, including the extent to which adopted children should have contact with birth parents and siblings, the ethics of paying young pregnant girls large amounts of money for their unborn children without going through an agency, and what rights surrogate parents should have.

SOCIAL WORKERS AS PROVIDERS OF SERVICES TO CHILDREN, YOUTH, AND FAMILIES

Social workers play many roles in the provision of services to children, youth, and families. In fact, this is the most traditional area of social work practice. The "child welfare worker"—first a volunteer during the 1800s and then a trained social worker in the 1900s—is most often the stereotype of social workers. However, the roles of social workers in this area have expanded significantly, and social workers at the BSW, MSW, and PhD levels are actively involved in the provision of services to children, youth, and families. At the

BSW level, social workers are involved as child care workers in group homes and residential treatment centers, as women's and children's counselors at battered women's shelters, as counselors at runaway youth shelters, as crisis counselors in law enforcement agencies, and as child protective services and foster care workers in public social services agencies.

An entry-level position in the area of child and family services usually provides a broad-based experience that allows a great deal of flexibility to move to other jobs, either into supervisory positions or other areas of social work. Some states require a minimum of a BSW for certain child and family positions, such as child protective services and foster care staff. A growing number of social workers specialize in child protective services, investigating reported cases of abuse and neglect and intervening when necessary. They work closely with the courts, law enforcement agencies, and community-based family intervention, self-help, and volunteer programs. Foster care staff recruit foster families and oversee their training, and they often work with the child and foster family while the child is in foster care, helping the child to adjust.

Many BSW graduates work as child care workers in residential treatment and psychiatric care facilities, serving as members of treatment teams and working directly with children and adolescents to implement the team's plan. Such experience is valuable in learning skills in working with emotionally disturbed children and their families. Other social workers are employed in agencies such as Big Brothers and Big Sisters of America, assessing children and potential volunteers and monitoring the matches after they are made. Increasingly, BSW graduates are being hired as case managers in home-based, family-centered programs, family support programs that assist families in getting off public assistance, and programs that provide services to developmentally disabled children and their families. Social workers at the BSW level are also hired to work as substance abuse counselors in inpatient and community-based adult and adolescent treatment programs. Special certification in the area of alcohol and drug abuse is often required for such jobs.

School social workers also often require special state certification, which varies from state to state. In some states, BSW graduates can be hired as school social workers, whereas in other states you must have teaching experience and graduate-level courses or an MSW degree. With increased attention to school dropouts and increases in such problems as teenage pregnancy, school social work is a rapidly growing area. School social workers work closely with teachers, school administrators, and other school support staff, including school counselors, nurses, and psychologists. They provide individual, parent, and family counseling; lead groups of students who are teen parents, on probation, recovering from substance abuse, experiencing family problems such as divorce or abuse, or having problems relating to teachers and peers; provide crisis intervention services such as suicide intervention; organize parent education and parent support groups; advocate for the needs of children and families within the school system and the community; and network with other social services agencies in the community to assist parents and their children in accessing appropriate services. The National Association of Social Workers has a school social work division, and two school social work journals are published nationally.

A number of social work jobs in the child and family services area require an MSW degree. This is partly due to the standards established by the Child

Welfare League of America, which many agencies follow, as well as the fact that some child and family services are highly specialized. In almost all instances, an MSW is required of an adoption worker. Most child guidance centers and child and family service agencies also require MSW degrees. Many social work or therapist positions in residential treatment centers require an MSW, as do clinical social work positions in adolescent and child psychiatric treatment programs. Most schools of social work have child and family or child welfare specializations at the graduate level, which provide special coursework in this area, as well as field placements in child and family services settings.

With the implementation of the PhD degree in social work, some child guidance or child and family services agencies are attempting to hire agency directors at this level. Additionally, persons who want more highly specialized clinical experience are earning PhD degrees, enabling them to do more intensive therapy with children, youth, and families.

If students are interested in a social work career in the area of child and family services, there are a number of child welfare and child and family journals, as well as numerous books on all areas discussed in this chapter, readily available. In addition, because many child and family services programs have volunteer programs, volunteer experience will not only help students determine whether they are interested in this area but also provide sound social work experience.

SUMMARY

Policies and programs that focus on the needs of children, youth, and families are developed and implemented within the context of society and community attitudes and values, awareness about needs, and the availability of resources. The currently preferred focus is prevention and early intervention, keeping families together, and making decisions based on the best interests of the children. However, lack of resources places large numbers of children, youth, and families in jeopardy of disruption and serious dysfunction. Because individual and family needs are diverse, as are available programs to address them, there are many opportunities for social workers interested in children, youth, and family services.

KEY TERMS

adoption
battered child syndrome
best interests of the child
child protective services
child welfare delivery system
Child Welfare League of America
child welfare services
crisis intervention
foster care
Head Start
home-based family-centered
    services

least detrimental alternative
natural support systems
permanency planning
psychological parent
residential treatment
school social work
self-help group
special-needs children
substitute care
U.S. Children's Bureau

DISCUSSION QUESTIONS

1. What is meant by the concepts "in the best interests of the child," "least detrimental alternative," and "psychological parent"?

2. Describe briefly at least three prevention programs used with children and their families.

3. Compare home-based family-centered services with substitute care and adoption. What are the advantages and disadvantages of each?

4. Identify at least two areas in which social workers at the BSW and MSW levels might be employed in a child and family services position.

5. What is meant by "special-needs adoption"?

6. Select one of the "family problem areas" discussed in Chapter 7. Identify at least one prevention and one intervention program you would suggest to address that problem area.

7. Identify at least three problems with the current children, youth, and families service delivery system.

REFERENCES

Bremner, R. 1974. *Children and youth in America.* Cambridge, Mass.: Harvard University Press.

Children's Defense Fund. 1989. *Children's defense budget: Analysis of the FY 1988 federal budget and children.* Washington, D.C.: Author.

Emlen, A. 1977. *Overcoming barriers to planning for children in foster care.* Portland, Oreg.: Portland State University.

Goldstein, J., A. Freud, and A. Solnit. 1979. *Before the best interests of the child.* New York: Free Press.

————. 1973. *Beyond the best interests of the child.* New York: Free Press.

Kadushin, A. and J. Martin. 1988. *Child welfare services.* 4th ed. New York: Macmillan.

Kamerman, S., and A. Kahn. 1990. Social services for children, youth and families in the United States. *Children and Youth Services Review* 12 (1–2), New York: Pergamon.

Lloyd, J., and Bryce, M. 1980. *Placement prevention and family unification: Planning and supervising the home-based family-centered programs.* Oakdale, Iowa: National Clearinghouse for Home-based Services, School of Social Work, University of Iowa.

Maas, H., and R. Engler. 1959. *Children in need of parents.* New York: Columbia University Press.

McGowen, B., and W. Meezen. 1983. *Child welfare: Current trends and future directions.* Ithaca, Ill.: Peacock.

Maidman, F. 1984. *Child welfare: A source book of knowledge and practice.* New York: Child Welfare League of America.

Shyne, A., and A. Schroeder. 1978. *National study of services to children and their families.* Washington, D.C.: U.S. Children's Bureau, DHEW.

Social Security Act. 1935. Title IV-B, Section 425. Washington, D.C.: U.S. Congressional Record.

Vasaly, S. 1976. *Foster care in five states.* Washington, D.C.: U.S. Department of Health, Education and Welfare.

SUGGESTED FURTHER READINGS

Child Welfare. A bimonthly journal published by the Child Welfare League of America, New York.

Children's Defense Fund. *Children's defense budget: analysis of the federal budget and children* (published annually). Washington, D.C.: Author.

Kamerman, S., and A. Kahn. 1990. Social services for children, youth and families in the United States. *Children and Youth Services Review* 12 (1–2), New York: Pergamon.

Janchill, M. 1981. *Guidelines for decision-making in child welfare.* New York: Human Services Workshops.

U.S. Department of Health, Education, and Welfare. 1978. *Child welfare strategy in the coming years.* Washington, D.C.: GPO.

Criminal Justice

Joe is a thirty-two-year-old man whose current address is Huntsville State Prison. He is serving a twenty-year sentence for armed robbery. This is not Joe's first term in prison, but he hopes that it will be his last.

Joe first came to the attention of the criminal justice system when he was fourteen years old. He was arrested for stealing a car. The third child in a family of six children, Joe grew up with his mother and siblings in a poverty-stricken area in a large eastern city. He was abused physically during his childhood and received little positive attention from his mother. From first grade on, Joe had difficulty in school. He had a short attention span, disrupted the classroom, and rarely completed his schoolwork.

At the time of his first arrest, Joe was in the seventh grade for the second time. He was placed on probation, and his family was referred for counseling. However, because his mother worked long hours, she was never able to arrange the sessions. Joe became more of a problem in school and the neighborhood. He began skipping school, experimenting with drugs, and committing a series of burglaries. His mother could not handle his frequent bursts of anger nor get Joe to respond to her limits.

When Joe was sixteen, he spent three months in a juvenile detention facility, where he did well with the structure provided by the program. When he left the program, he was assigned a probation officer and returned to his family. His conditions of probation stipulated that he attend school on a regular basis, maintain a specified curfew, and report to his probation officer monthly. Joe followed these conditions for several months; however, he continued to have difficulty in school and dropped out four months after he returned home. He held a series of jobs at fast-food restaurants but had difficulty coming to work regularly and became frustrated because he was not earning very much money. Increasingly, he gravitated toward older young adults who hung out on the street and seemed to have the freedom and the money he yearned for. They liked Joe, and he felt accepted by them and enjoyed being with them. Joe soon became involved with them in selling drugs and committing burglaries.

Joe then began a series of arrests for drug dealing, burglary, and assault, which resulted in several stays in various detention facilities. Just before his last arrest, Joe married a nineteen-year-old, who recently had their baby. He is anxious to get out of prison and begin to get to know his son and support his family. He is frustrated by the limited work programs and the lack of counseling available at the prison. He has enrolled in a prison education program to try to earn his high school equivalency certificate and hopes to be released to a community halfway house and enroll in a job-training program. He knows that he will need job skills and help in dealing with his anger and frustration if he is to maintain a successful marriage and job and to stay out of prison.

Public social problems are specific conditions in the society that are perceived as sufficiently bothersome to merit intervention by government. Crime is clearly such a condition. Citizens have a right to expect government protection from crime. Society has a need to apprehend suspended offenders, to convict the guilty and free the innocent, and to appropriately punish and rehabilitate the convicted. These steps constitute the ordered processes of the criminal justice system.

The criminal justice system is expected to act as both a specific and a general deterrent to crime. A **specific deterrent** is structured to prevent crimes very directly. In capital cases, for example, the execution itself is obviously a specific deterrent; the fear of capital punishment serves as a further **general deterrent.** This does not mean a society can impose capital punishment without cost.

In our society the criminal justice system is evaluated not only by its capacity to contain crime but also by the justice meted out by the system. That is why we refer to the *criminal justice system* rather than the *criminal containment system.* The system's dual responsibility to protect the citizenship rights of criminals as well as their victims constitutes the core of the criminal justice system. The constitutional safeguards of our society are expected to follow criminals from their first apprehensions by police, through their arraignments, trials, imprisonments, and reentries into society. That these constitutional safeguards increase the costs and, perhaps, lower the effectiveness of police, courts, and prisons in containing crime is seen as one of the costs of democracy.

All systems of public policy face policy dilemmas, but the dilemma of the criminal justice system is particularly acute. This is reflected by the rise of vigilantism, a public expression of discontent with the balance that has been struck within the criminal justice system. This system is charged with the deterrence of crime and the maintenance of justice. Its desired goals include (1) efficient, but not intrusive police work; (2) fair and impartial trials for the accused, and an awareness of the rights of the victims; (3) safe, yet secure and humane, prisons; and (4) parole programs that provide reentry into the free society for ex-offenders but protect the community at large.

Law-abiding citizens want to be protected from criminal behavior but also want protection from unwarranted intrusion of the criminal justice system into their private lives. The duality of these demands imposes costs and constraints on police, court officers, and prison and parole officials. Since in the final analysis "law and order" exponents and "civil libertarians" want the same things, where does the policy problem lie? It lies in the question of emphasis and balance, and the latter seldom seems to exist.

VIEWS OF CRIMINAL BEHAVIOR

A number of views of criminal behavior compete to explain why people commit crimes. Crime can be viewed as psychologically aberrant behavior, as socially induced behavior, as a consequence of rational thought where criminals simply see crime as just another way to make a living, or as a complex interactive process of an individual's personal characteristics and the many factors that constitute his or her environment. The explanation accepted by various citizens constitutes the structure upon which they wish the criminal justice system to be built.

Psychological Views of the Criminal Personality

One school of thought suggests that criminals differ from noncriminals in some fundamental way, other than the obvious one of having been convicted. The distinguishing trait has been found over the years to be reflected in body or head shape, skull size, chromosome structure, specific patterns of response to projective tests, or in the complex labeling process of psychiatric diagnosis. Of course, there is a circular reasoning process in all of the psychological-physiological attempts to establish a criminal type. There also is a kind of satisfaction in the notion of a criminal type, because crime policy then becomes, simply, segregation of the criminals from the rest of society.

A second psychological interpretation of the **etiology of crime** is only slightly more sophisticated. Crime is seen simply as a manifestation of a compulsion derived from unresolved conflicts between the superego and the id. Someone with a criminal personality—by definition a defective ego—is unable to overcome the desire to defy social taboos, yet the conflict reflects itself in an unconscious desire to be caught.

Anecdotal evidence suggests that criminals do operate this way—they may deliberately, albeit unconsciously, leave the clues that lead to their arrests. Were it not for the seriousness of the incidents, this behavior often would be truly comic. One young criminal brought a pair of slacks to the cleaners and, after being presented with the claim check, he pulled a gun and robbed the attendant. He returned three days later with the stub of the claim check to pick up his slacks and was patient enough to wait when the same attendant said the slacks were on the way. The young man waited calmly for the police to come and arrest him. Another pair of criminals left the motor running in the getaway car, but because they had failed to check the fuel gauge before the robbery, their car ran out of gas while they were holding up the bank. Anecdotal, but not systematic, evidence suggests such a pattern in all crime (Silberman 1980). If there is any basis for such a theory of crime, it leads to the conclusion that punishment is not a deterrent to crime but, in fact, is a stimulant.

A more sophisticated psychological theory of the etiology also contains in its assumptions the prescription for a proper anticrime policy. The following is a summation of what can be classed as a psychosocial theory of crime:

1. Criminal behavior is learned.
2. There is a relationship between the type of criminal behavior learned by individuals and their socioeconomic status in society. Certain classes of persons will learn different ways of crime.
3. The processes involved in learning criminal behavior are the same as those in learning other behavior that involves learning a technique as well as values.

This view of criminality is less encompassing than the more simple etiological-psychological views of crime. It does not attempt to explain which people will commit crimes—an impossible task—but rather, why and how those who have committed crimes are systematically different from those who do not.

Social Views of Criminal Behavior

Another perspective suggests that crime is not caused by individual physical or mental deficiencies but rather by societal breakdown. Proponents of this perspective focus on industrialization, racism, poverty, and family breakdown as major factors that create social disorganization, and, in turn, increase in crime. Discussions of crime and society too often are presented as a conflict between straw men. As an illustration, the journalist Charles Silberman and the political scientist James Q. Wilson, both popular writers on crime policy, are portrayed as prototypical advocates of extreme positions. In fact, both see the relationship between crime and social conditions as inordinately complex. Whereas Wilson believes that criminal sanctions would deter crime, Silberman places more faith in indirect social reforms. Both would argue that we need more carrots (job opportunities, antipoverty programs, etc.) and more sticks (swift and certain prison terms as a deterrent), but they would disagree on mix and emphasis.

Sociological inquiries into crime frequently are based on statistical correlates, such as the increasing breakdown of the traditional family or variations in unemployment and crime rates. The more sophisticated inquiries fall short of establishing a direct path of causation. Crime is seen as a result of many factors within the context of the offender's society. Street crime and white-collar crime are seen as very different expressions of social maladjustment. Regardless of specifics, the essence of the sociological perspective is that general deterrence, rehabilitation, and reeducation of offenders constitute the best safeguards against repeated crimes.

The social view of crime advocates a criminal justice system that offers a variety of social intervention strategies (Cullen 1982). One such strategy of importance to social work practitioners is collaboration between social worker and police officer at the earliest intervention point. When the suspected offender is first in police custody, social workers and police officers are expected to concur on the case disposition. The argument is made that, despite their disparate professional orientations, both social workers and police officers are experienced in dealing with troubled people at crisis points in their lives. Individualization of response is seen as critical (Treger 1975).

No one sociological perspective is seen as dominant. Rather, a number of theories are offered, depending on the type of crime committed. Marshall Clinard (1967) suggests the following classification of crimes:

1. Violent personal crimes: i.e., murder
2. Sexual offenses
3. Occupational/white collar crimes
4. Political crimes
5. Organized crimes
6. Professional crimes
7. Crimes without victims

Each of these types of crime has its own sociological pattern, and each crime type places a unique set of demands on the criminal justice system.

Economic Rationale of Crime

A final perspective is that crime is simply another form of entrepreneurship, which happens to be illegal. This view sees the criminal as an amoral person who calculates the costs and benefits of a particular crime, much as a businessperson calculates the costs and benefits of opening a new store. In the economic formulation, potential criminals assess the costs of getting caught and sentenced against the probable benefits of successful completion of the crime. They decide to be criminal or not, depending on the outcomes of their calculations. People who are not poor commit fewer crimes because the costs of going to prison (in lost wages, deprivation of status, amenities of life, etc.) are higher for them than for others. If we subscribe to this theoretical perspective, to contain crime, all we need to do is increase the probable chances of being caught, sentenced, and sent to jail. There is little or no empirical evidence to suggest a valid basis for this theory (Hillman 1980).

Each of these views of crime—and we have listed only three—provides a policy paradigm for the criminal justice system, from the role of the arresting officer to the responsibilities of the parole and probation workers. One's beliefs about why some people commit crimes are the obvious source of ideas about how to contain crime.

PROGRAM ALTERNATIVES

For every thirty-six crimes committed, one person is sentenced to prison. Only one crime in every four reported results in an arrest of a suspected offender. There is roughly one arraignment for every three arrests, and although nearly 95 percent of all criminal arraignments result in criminal conviction or guilty pleas, only one in three results in a prison term. These numbers mislead as much as they reveal, for tracking a particular crime (acknowledging that crimes are greatly underreported) to a particular sentence is a Herculean statistical task. One thing that is unambiguous in these numbers is the enormous amount of discretion that operates within the criminal justice system. Figure 9–1 portrays the complex pathways in the criminal justice system. At each new stage (represented by the rectangles) an opportunity exists for diversion out of the criminal justice system. Only a small percentage of all crimes result in criminal convictions.

The American criminal justice system largely is an English invention, but it includes some important innovations that are the peculiar products of the United States. These innovations are the elements of the system in which social work is most explicitly and importantly involved; these are the programs of probation, parole, and juvenile procedures. The American system is perhaps more fragmented than the criminal justice system in most countries. The criminal justice system can be seen first as composed of three parts: police, courts, and correctional arrangements. With federal, state, and local involvement at each level and a separation into adult and juvenile divisions, a multipartite system emerges. More dramatic is the fact that no subsystem views the criminal problem from

Figure 9–1   The Path through the Criminal Justice System

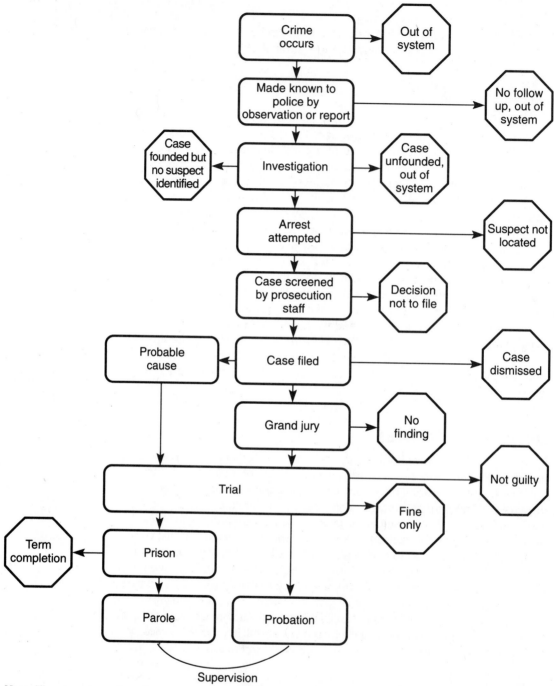

Note: The stop signs show how a crime drops out of the system. Rectangles represent stages in the system.

a total perspective. Each entity is busily resolving its own problems. The result is a highly fractured system that is difficult to describe, evaluate, or control.

Despite the lack of cohesion and the internal tensions, actions within one subsystem clearly have reverberations throughout the entire system. "Success" or "failure" in one part may generate significant problems for another part. Should state and local police, by virtue of more personnel or better investigation, apprehend 25 percent more offenders, both the courts and the correctional system would have to absorb more defendants and prisoners. If the prison system released a higher proportion of recidivists, police and the courts would have to deal with a larger population of criminals. On the other hand, over-crowded prisons generate backups in local jails. All of the elements of the criminal justice system must respond to the factors in the larger society that accelerate criminal behavior. Because the criminal justice system is not examined or funded as an entity, each component accepts and adopts its own strategies. The fundamental adaptation for one part often produces particular problems for another entity within the system.

The Police

A suspect formally becomes involved in the criminal justice system at the point when he or she is questioned in connection with a crime. Arrest does not always occur. If arrest is followed by a formal charge, the path may lead to *indictment* and trial. Often the questioning does not even lead to arrest; the questioning of a suspect could lead to the conclusion that "successful" prosecution is unlikely.

The Courts

After the indictment, the suspect moves into the court stage of the process. An **arraignment** is held, where the suspect, now a defendant, is able to enter a plea of guilty or not guilty. If the defendant enters a guilty plea, a date is set for sentencing. The defendant who enters a not guilty plea may request to have a jury trial or to be tried by the court without a jury. At the time of that plea, the court has the opportunity to dismiss the charges for lack of sufficient evidence and remove the defendant from the criminal justice system.

The **prosecutor** is the public official in the criminal justice system charged with presenting the evidence that the state has against a defendant. Prosecutors are officers of the court (attorneys) but in fact have responsibilities that go beyond this. A conceptualization of the role of the prosecutor has some limitations and caveats. Prosecutors are in a critical position in the criminal justice system. Because they work in close cooperation with the police, the courts, and the correctional arrangement, they are the persons most likely to provide leadership in any efforts to coordinate the activities of the various agencies within the system. The criteria utilized by the prosecutor in deciding whether to proceed within the criminal justice system or to divert the case in a particular direction are of central importance. The prosecutor has the opportunity to drop the charge or to engage in various forms of plea bargaining to facilitate the operations with regard to a particular defendant.

In a criminal trial a human being's freedom is at stake. The **defense attorney** is the person whose performance in large measure will determine whether the individual receives a fair shake from the state. Prosecutors and judicial officials have competing loyalties. By the ethics of our judicial system, the defense attorney's loyalty primarily is to his or her client, whereas the prosecutor's loyalty is to the society as represented by the state. The rights of defendants were established in the famous case of *Gideon v. Wainwright* (Lewis, 1964). Indigent defendants are represented through the public defender system.

The judge is the principal officer of the court, who presides over the court and has the final responsibility for organizing the process at the trial stage to ensure that justice is administered. The nature of the judge's office is unique in the system of criminal justice. Because of the nature of their duties and their power, the staffs of judges are critical to the conduct of their offices and thus of the entire criminal justice system. No other individual within the criminal justice system has as much largely unsupervised discretion as the judge. In 1984 the President's Commission on Law Enforcement and Administration of Justice recommended that state criminal justice systems be strengthened by improving the quality of judicial officials. An important ancillary to improving the quality of the judicial system is to provide judges with adequate staffs.

A major problem with the criminal justice system is that it is so overloaded, particularly the court system. Public defenders' offices, public prosecuting attorneys' offices, and judges often are unable to devote the appropriate time to their cases needed to ensure that judicial decisions are fair to both society and the individuals who come before the courts.

Corrections

The corrections component of the criminal justice system includes those programs that deal with a criminal after sentencing by the court. Corrections programs include various types of incarceration or detention facilities (such as prisons and jails), parole, and probation.

The state penitentiary is one of America's most unchanged social institutions. The striped suit and the ball and chain have disappeared, but the social climate of the prison remains. The type of prison constructed in 1819 remains as a prototype. Enforced degradation and hopelessness have proven imprisonment to be a costly failure in the war against crime.

Confusion about the purposes of imprisonment remains a hallmark of the American system. What is the mission of the prison? Is it reform—to alter the perception of inmates so that crime is no longer seen as acceptable behavior? Is it isolation—the mere sequestering of the criminal from society so that the only opportunity for crime is against one another? Is it retribution—a mechanism for society to "get even," to extract its revenge on those who lawlessly punish others? Is it general deterrence—for the prisons to serve as a reminder to those contemplating crime how costly to the perpetrator the crime could be? Each mission requires a differently structured prison operation. There is considerable evidence to suggest that in trying to perform all four missions, the American prison fulfills no mission whatsoever (Silberman 1980).

The quality of U.S. prisons varies greatly and in many dimensions: security, therapeutic mode, rehabilitation potential, even basic human amenities. As a

Social workers participate in the criminal justice system and are often called to testify in court cases.

general rule, federal prisons are more tolerable than state prisons, which, in turn, are better than jails. The one common denominator is that all prisons are horrible places. With rising costs and lower societal expectations of prisons, several states have turned to contracting with private enterprise, not only to build but to operate the prisons.

Some states are turning to types of detention facilities other than large-scale prisons. A number of states and communities have established minimum security centers for nonviolent offenders and those guilty of less serious crimes. These centers allow them to work in the community but otherwise be incarcerated. Other states and communities have set up halfway houses for persons who have served time in prison but are not yet ready to be released into the community without some sort of structure and supervision. A new type of incarceration made possible by modern technology allows persons to be incarcerated in their own homes. A person wears an unremovable band with a radio transmitter that trips a signal in a correction-monitoring center when the person goes beyond the front yard. This system is cost effective and may reduce significantly the number of persons in prison facilities. Studies show that prisons may actually teach more about crime than reform, creating persons likely to return to prison for more serious offenses than their first ones. Thus, this system also may serve to encourage repeat offenses, as well as allow already scarce rehabilitation programs within prisons to focus more intensively on fewer individuals.

Probation is an official correctional option in which the offender is given an opportunity to remain free from detention or have a fine held in abeyance in return for accepting supervised living. The supervisional constraints could not legally be placed on a free citizen but are accepted by the convicted person as a contract in lieu of detention or fine. Rather than going to prison, the offender is supervised by a probation officer who monitors his or her activities and ensures that the conditions of probation are met. These conditions can include abstaining from use of drugs and/or alcohol, observing a curfew, not leaving the county of residence, holding a job, and obtaining counseling. If the conditions are violated, the offender can be ordered back before the court, the probation can be revoked, and a prison sentence can be given instead.

Parole is the opportunity given to a person who has been imprisoned to serve the remainder of the sentence outside of prison in a supervised situation. Again, the constraints could not be placed on the free citizen, but a prisoner may choose to accept parole as a means for an earlier reentry into society. Originally conceived of as a policy available to individualize the rehabilitation of the offender, both probation and parole now principally are mechanisms for managing the size of the prison population.

Judges grant probation, often as part of a prearranged plea bargain, where a defendant agrees to plead guilty to or to accept a guilty finding for a lesser crime rather than risk a guilty finding for a more serious offense and a possible prison term. It should be noted that suspension of sentence is unconditional, whereas probation is conditional. If the individual fails to live up to the conditions of probation, there are civil and criminal procedures to revoke probation and impose the sentence. In unconditional suspension, the individual is found guilty but the judge feels that conviction alone is sufficient, and thus suspension has the effect of satisfying the offender's criminal liability.

If suspension or probation is not appropriate, a sentence is imposed. After serving some portion of the sentence in detention, the prisoner is considered for parole, either automatically or by petition. Probation and parole decisions essentially are similar. The judge in probation, or a citizen board in the case of a parolee, considers a report that includes information about the crime, the social history of the individual, social support available to the person, current conditions, and so on. These reports are now highly uniform in accordance with a court decision on procedural rights. The philosophy of individualized decision making remains, but in reality the procedure for parole and/or bargained probation is fairly automatic. Myth and reality stand far apart in probation and parole practice.

Diversion

Clearly, there is a need to divert persons from the criminal justice system, because the size and complexity of running all those guilty of criminal behavior through the system would overload and break down the system. **Diversion** is the formalization of the old process by which police officers did not make arrests in certain crimes and/or crime areas, or prosecutors dismissed charges, diverting individuals to other programs, such as counseling or DWI (driving while intoxicated) classes. Much criminal behavior is better dealt with outside the criminal justice system and inside the social services network. Police and prosecutors often view crimes likely to be diverted as either not serious or beyond their purview but too important as social problems to be either condoned or ignored (Nimmer 1974).

Traditional or old-style diversion procedures have been criticized for the ad hoc nature of their operation. One police officer may think that a crime was committed in a family dispute and enter one or more members into the criminal justice system, whereas a second officer may respond to the identical circumstance with counseling on the scene. A third may extract a promise from the family to contact a social services agency as the price of nonarrest. These ad hoc judgments violate equality. A number of communities have elected to formalize the diversion procedure. Descriptions of two such procedures follow.

Court employment programs (CEPs) originally were funded in part by the federal government. Local communities, using their own unique but jurisdictionwide criteria, established alternative paths to prosecution or disposition. Social work counselors contacted the clients prior to disposition and referred them to employment and/or vocational training programs from a list of participating private employers. The counselors would seek 12-day adjournments and, if the case appeared to be headed toward resolution, the traditional path of prosecution, trial, prison, and parole was cut short. A second and far more common practice was to establish local "dispute settlement services," such as New York's Family Crisis Intervention Unit. This process is the same as just described: the social services unit contacted the client and established a treatment strategy that included individual or family counseling, or substance abuse treatment, and prosecution was postponed. If this intervention was successful, the case did not proceed through the criminal justice system.

The Juvenile Court

The juvenile courts in this country were first established in Cook County, Illinois, in 1899. The philosophy of the juvenile courts then as now is that the courts should be structured to act in the best interest of the child. In essence, juvenile courts thus have a treatment and rehabilitation orientation that sometimes dominates their adjudicative function. In adult criminal proceedings, the focus is on a specific crime. In contrast, the focus of juvenile courts is often on the psychological, physical, emotional, and educational needs of the defendant, as opposed to the child's specific guilt in a unique case. Of course, not all juvenile court judges live up to these principles, and there is the ever-present danger that the juvenile court process can be subverted.

In the 1960s, Gerald Gault (a fifteen-year-old youth) was tried in the Arizona juvenile court for allegedly making an obscene phone call to a neighbor. Neither the accused nor his parents was given advance notice of the charges against him. He was not informed of his legal rights and, if found guilty, could have been held within the criminal justice system until he reached the age of majority. The procedures used by the Arizona officials in the Gault proceeding were not unreasonable. They were in accord with the thinking of the times, namely, that advance notice and formal trial are likely to stigmatize a child and violate many confidentialities. The focus of concern was on the state as a parent rather than the state as the embodiment of a social conscience. Thus, Gault was brought before the juvenile court and tried without proper safeguards.

In 1967 the case went to the Supreme Court. The majority opinion, written by Justice Abe Fortas, vehemently criticized the juvenile correctional establishment and made it clear that regardless of intent, juveniles should not be deprived of their liberty without the full set of due process rights available to an adult. This case restored to juvenile procedures safeguards that often had been ignored, including notification of charges, protection from self-incrimination, confrontation, cross-examination, and the like (Niger 1967).

The wisdom of the Gault decision is still disputed. There is no doubt that it gives minors the same basic constitutional rights enjoyed by adults. They should never have lost them. However, the return to a focus on whether or not a young person has committed a crime often masks the need for help exhibited by young persons caught up in the court processes. This case has brought about a critical reassessment of juvenile procedures and has suggested that the treatment and rehabilitative role of the juvenile correctional system must be secondary to the process of protecting the rights of the juvenile before the criminal justice system. Youth crime is a particularly troublesome problem to society. The way in which we have addressed this in the past has been either to treat juveniles as though they were adults or to treat juveniles in such a fashion that their basic rights were not protected. The necessity to reassess this responsibility is one of the most challenging problems that social work will face in the 1990s.

The Criminal Justice System

American patterns of dealing with crime and its consequences have survived largely because the criminal justice system is a patchwork. When one patch fades or is weakened or burned out, a new one can usually be cut and put in its place. Although the solution to a problem might not fit exactly, nor blend well with the surrounding pattern, no one notices for long because the complexity of the overall design conceals this fact well. The unevenness of solutions in the criminal justice system has not worked well enough to deter people from committing crimes. People commit crimes because they assume the crime will benefit them in some way.

Criminals do not think about the monetary and moral costs to society. Try viewing the would-be crime in terms of the benefits minus the costs to the person considering the crime. Clearly, we want to decrease the would-be criminal's benefits from crime and increase his or her costs. The goal is to make the expected value of compliance with the law greater than the expected value of crime. This produces three non-mutually exclusive alternatives: (1) Increase the probability of arrest, conviction, and a punishment that is seen as costly to the criminal; (2) decrease the benefit of crime by providing less opportunity for crime and greater opportunity for similar benefits by noncriminal activity; and/ or (3) increase the cost of crime by ensuring a harsher life and more suffering in prisons and probation programs. The goal is not to select one strategy that accomplishes the end of making crime less attractive. By increasing the probability of conviction, making the crime less attractive, and/or making the consequence of conviction more costly, the net benefit of crime to the criminal is decreased or eliminated. Crime would not disappear, but it would become less likely.

Crime is not easily contained or eliminated, and the incidence of crime throughout this nation is very high, as indicated in Table 9–1. This variation in the crime picture clearly indicates a need for careful development of crime policy uniquely in each state. As can also be seen in Table 9–1, in most instances, states with high rates of violent crimes also spent less on public

Table 9–1 Violent Crime Rate among the Contiguous States in Relation to Public Welfare Spending

State	Violent Crime Rate (crimes/100,000 population)	Per Capital Welfare Cost ÷ Per Capita Corrections Cost, 1988*
Florida	1118	0.699
New York	1097	1.868
California	930	1.300
Illinois	810	1.747
Maryland	807	1.210
Nevada	781	0.504
Michigan	742	2.392
S. Carolina	741	1.216
Louisiana	717	1.312
Georgia	665	1.246
Texas	653	0.986
New Mexico	638	1.070
Massachusetts	620	2.395
Arizona	610	0.758
New Jersey	583	1.402
Alabama	559	1.164
Missouri	553	1.401
Oregon	546	1.113
Tennessee	533	1.788
N. Carolina	502	1.231
Colorado	473	1.262
Washington	466	1.629
Connecticut	455	1.857
Delaware	452	0.927
Ohio	452	2.081
Oklahoma	435	1.932
Arkansas	423	2.298
Rhode Island	397	2.741
Indiana	380	2.125
Kansas	365	1.445
Pennsylvania	362	2.302
Kentucky	330	2.077
Mississippi	325	2.098
Wyoming	314	1.009
Virginia	299	0.996
Minnesota	290	2.804
Nebraska	273	1.972
Iowa	257	2.160
Utah	243	1.351

continued on next page

Table 9–1 Violent Crime Rate among the Contiguous States in Relation to Public Welfare Spending *(Continued)*

State	Violent Crime Rate (crimes/100,000 population)	Per Capital Welfare Cost ÷ Per Capita Corrections Cost, 1988*
Idaho	235	1.290
Wisconsin	214	2.633
Maine	157	3.312
New Hampshire	148	1.984
Vermont	143	2.685
W. Virginia	131	2.993
Montana	123	2.123
S. Dakota	114	1.772
N. Dakota	59	3.195

*Calculations by author
Note: Violent crimes involve threatening a person or causing bodily harm to that person.
Source: Data from *U.S. Statistical Abstract, 1990,* pp. 171, 181.

welfare compared to the costs of maintaining their correction systems, while states with low rates of violent crimes also spent more on public welfare compared to the costs of maintaining their correction systems. In Figure 9–2 each state's expected crime rate as a function of its spending on welfare and correction is plotted against its actual crime rate. The relation is very close.

Figure 9–2 Estimated and Actual U.S. Crime Rates, 1988

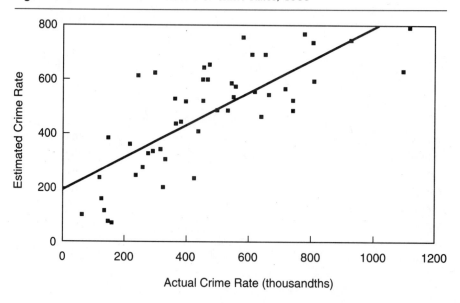

THE ROLE OF SOCIAL WORK IN THE CRIMINAL JUSTICE SYSTEM

The role played by the social work community in the criminal justice system has been relegated almost exclusively to the correctional components of the system. Police agencies only recently have begun to use social workers; these social work functions have low priority in the police budgets and fall quickly to budget cuts. Adult courts have made relatively little use of professional social workers. Social workers most frequently work in the criminal justice system in the juvenile courts, rehabilitation centers, prisons, and parole programs. Such uses of social workers, however, need to be assessed within a systemwide context.

Some law enforcement experts suggest that the majority of police calls are family or crisis oriented rather than crime related. When crimes occur, they often are the result of family problems—many homicides, for example, occur among family members rather than outside of the family. Increasingly, crime is associated with other social problems, such as alcohol or drug abuse.

Social workers play various roles in police departments. Many departments have crisis intervention teams, consisting of both police officers and social workers, that respond to domestic violence calls or calls to assist victims of rape or other violent crimes. Some police departments have established special victim assistance programs. Often staffed by social workers, these programs provide follow-up services to victims of crime, helping them work through their

Many courts operate diversion programs for young people when they first come into the juvenile justice system to prevent kids from becoming repeat and more serious offenders. Here, a social worker leads a group of juveniles in a discussion on career choices, helping them to focus on positive options and a sense of future.

feelings. They also help victims locate emergency funding, shelter, employment, counseling, and other needed services.

Many police departments also have special child abuse or sex crimes units, which include social workers on their staffs. The social workers assist in investigating suspected cases, interviewing children and other individuals involved, contacting other agencies such as child welfare departments and hospitals, and arranging for emergency services when needed. A number of police departments also hire social workers to work in youth programs. In Pittsburgh, for example, social workers operate inner-city recreation programs. In Austin, Texas, the police department has had a social worker managing a dropout prevention program in the public schools. Such social workers provide counseling and drug and alcohol education, and serve as positive law enforcement role models to youth at risk of becoming involved in crime.

The role of the social worker in prison and prison life is very much peripheral. The social worker most likely is involved only when convicts enter or leave prison. The classification and assignment process at entry point is heavily influenced by social work practice. The pardon and parole recommendation also is influenced by social workers. The provision of service within the walls themselves, while influenced by social work knowledge, typically is done by others.

SUMMARY

In the sad history of crime and punishment, reform is always just beyond the horizon. As the chapter shows, a dreary picture is drawn from practice and current procedures. Police practices do not deter crime, the courts do not dispense justice, the corrections system does not correct, and the parole system does not facilitate ex-prisoners' reentry into society as law-abiding citizens. Clearly, part of the problem is that insufficient funds are spent on the criminal justice system. Too much is expected for too little expended.

Funds alone are not the problem. Despite a considerable and growing body of knowledge of what works and what does not work in police, court, and correctional settings, there is insufficient attention to integration within the system. Each unit of the system seeks to improve its operation and to clarify its mission, but at the expense of other components within the system. A more effective integration of police, court, and prison practices is required.

The failure of the criminal justice system also is due to uncertainty about what it is expected to deliver: Is it safe streets, a just system, effective rehabilitation, or simple containment? Effective policies require clarity, choice, commitment, and closure. The segmented structure of the criminal justice system precludes all of these. As a consequence, during some periods society throws money at certain aspects of the overall problem; during other periods, other aspects are funded. Clearly, careful diagnosis and prescription are needed.

KEY TERMS

arraignment
defense attorney
diversion
etiology of crime
general deterrent

parole
probation
prosecutor
specific deterrent

DISCUSSION QUESTIONS

1. To what extent is the policy dilemma of the criminal justice system reflected in the juvenile justice system? To what extent does the juvenile justice system have its own unique policy dilemma?

2. Which of the three views of crime, if any, is most consistent with social work practice theory?

3. If systems integration is the central problem of the criminal justice system, how can the contemporary social worker enhance the probability of that integration?

REFERENCES

Clinard, Marshall. 1967. *Criminal behavior systems.* New York: Holt, Reinhart & Winston.

Cullen, F. T. 1982. *Rethinking crime and deviance.* Totowa, N.J.: Rowman & Allanheld.

Hillman, Darrell. 1980. *The economics of crime.* New York: Routine Press.

Lewis, Anthony. 1964. *Gideon's trumpet.* New York: Random House.

Niger, Allen. 1967. The Gault decision, due process and the juvenile court. *Federal Register* 31 (4): 8–18.

Nimmer, Raymond. 1974. *Diversion: The search for alternatives.* Chicago: American Bar Foundation.

Silberman, Charles. 1980. *Criminal violence and criminal justice.* New York: Random House.

Treger, H. T. 1975. *Police and social work teams.* Springfield, Ill.: Thomas.

Wilson, James Q. 1983. *Thinking about crime.* New York: Basic Books.

SUGGESTED FURTHER READINGS

Byrne, J. M., and R. J. Sampson. 1986. *The social ecology of crime.* New York: Springer-Verlag.

Curtis, Lynn A. 1985. *American violence and public policy.* New Haven, Conn.: Yale University Press.

Feinman, Clarice. 1986. *Women in the criminal justice system.* New York: Praeger.

Felkenes, G. T. 1978. *The criminal justice system: Its functions.* Englewood Cliffs, N.J.: Prentice-Hall.

Gordon, Diana. 1990. *The justice juggernaut.* New Brunswick, N.J.: Rutgers.

LaFree, Gary D. 1989. *Rape and criminal justice.* Belmont, Calif.: Wadsworth.

Nagel, Stuart S. 1986. *Law policy and optimizing analysis.* London: Quorum Books.

Scheingold, Stuart A. 1984. *The politics of law and order: Street crime and public policy.* New York: Longman.

Wilson, Colin. 1984. *A criminal history of mankind.* New York: Putnams.

Chapter 10

Occupational Social Work

Bill and Meredith Hunt, both thirty-two years old, live in a small house in a rapidly deteriorating part of the city with their three children, ages two, four, and eight. Bill works at a large manufacturing plant, as one of several workers who monitors a largely automated assembly line. Meredith works as a word processor for a large company. The Hunt's two youngest children attend a child care center, and their oldest child attends school. Until recently, Bill's job has been the most important aspect of his life. He is well liked as an employee, and his neighbors view his job as desirable. However, Bill is finding that his job is a lot less meaningful to him than it has been in the past. His raises are less frequent and are not enough to pay even for necessities. Last year, Bill and the other assembly-line workers were laid off for two months due to a production slowdown. Most manufacturing companies in the area are buying their parts from abroad, and Bill's company increasingly is automating its operations, reducing the need for employees. There is even talk of shutting down the plant and moving it to Mexico. Bill is frustrated about the recent layoff and the lack of pay and is concerned about how long his job will last. Although he knows that

his wife has to work in order to make ends meet, Bill resents the fact that she has less time for him and feels bad because he can't provide for his family on his own.

Within the last two years, Bill has begun drinking heavily. He has beaten Meredith several times, and he yells at the children and spanks them more often. Bill's supervisor has noticed a change in his job performance and is ready to give him formal notification that he needs to improve or risks being fired. Bill feels tired, financially pressured, and emotionally defeated. Meredith also finds herself strained emotionally. In addition to her job, Meredith maintains primary responsibility for care of the house and the children. She gets up at 5:30 A.M., and it is always after midnight before she has everything done and can collapse into bed. Because the child care for the Hunt's two children costs over half of Meredith's take-home pay, they can't afford child care for their oldest son before and after school. Meredith worries about him being at home alone and makes several telephone calls to him each afternoon. Additionally, neither of the companies the Hunts work for allows employees to take sick leave when their children are sick, and all three children have been sick a lot lately. Meredith has missed six days of work in the last two months to care for her sick children. On three other occasions, Meredith has kept her oldest son home from school to take care of the younger children.

Meredith's mother, who lives in a neighboring city, recently was diagnosed with cancer and is scheduled to have surgery. Meredith would like to spend several days with her mother during and after the surgery since her other siblings live out of state. However, she has used all of her vacation days for her children's illnesses, and her company has no policies that provide for leave in such situations.

Recently, Meredith has been having difficulty sleeping and has had stomach problems. Her doctor prescribed tranquilizers, which she takes more often than the

prescription calls for. Meredith's co-workers are worried about her but resent having to do extra work when she is absent or not able to work as quickly as she usually does. Her boss has commented on her slip in job performance. Meredith likes her job very much but also is very worried about her husband, her children, and her mother. She feels guilty because her working places extra pressures on her family. Her oldest son is not doing well in school, and Meredith is too tired to help him. All of the children vie constantly for her attention. Both Meredith and Bill feel caught between the pressures of work and their family, and they are becoming increasingly overwhelmed by the demands of both.

Most individuals over the age of eighteen have two major domains in which they interact: the family and the workplace. While attention to social problems and individual needs usually includes an emphasis on the family, rarely is there any focus on the relationship between the individual and the workplace. This omission has caused us to help individuals and their families less often and not as effectively as we could.

Consider again the systems/ecological perspective to understanding problems discussed in Chapter 3—the way systems overlap and interact with each other and the individuals who function within those systems. Think about this perspective in relation to the Hunt family. Although until recently the Hunts have been a close-knit family, work is a primary focus in their lives. It produces the economic resources needed to provide food, clothing, shelter, and the recreational activities affordable to them. When someone meets Bill or Meredith, the first question asked usually is not "to what family do you belong?" but rather "where do you work?" In our society, a person's status in life is defined largely by occupation. Much of our self-respect, self-fulfillment, identity, and status is defined by the type of work that we do. Until recently, both Bill and Meredith received fulfillment from their workplaces. They got along well with co-workers and received raises, recognition for jobs well done.

At first, their two jobs allowed the Hunts to support their family adequately. The positive aspects of work spilled over into the family, and they also maintained positive support within the family. However, the overlap between the two domains began to create additional pressures for both Bill and Meredith. Conflicts began about which came first—home or work—when there didn't seem to be enough energy for both; what to do when children or relatives were sick; how much money to spend on child care, eating out when tired or cooking meals at home, and other items; and what types of jobs and career paths to pursue when the type of work available seemed to be changing. All these had an impact on Bill and Meredith's relationships and ability to function, both at home and at work.

For both Bill and Meredith work currently has many negative implications. Ideally, they will seek help from some type of social service program before either their family or their jobs become jeopardized further. A social worker or other helping professional who becomes involved with the Hunt's problems cannot help them effectively if work issues are not taken into consideration.

In this chapter we explore current and projected demographics regarding the work force; the changing nature and meaning of work; problems within the family and at the workplace created by work and family tensions; and the roles the workplace and social workers can play in attempting to prevent such problems from occurring or recurring.

A HISTORICAL PERSPECTIVE ON WORK AND FAMILY RELATIONSHIPS

In most Western countries, particularly in the United States, much of the basis of society can be traced to the Protestant work ethic, which stems from the Protestant Reformation of the seventeenth century. The work ethic suggests that work is an expectation of God and that laziness is sinful. Attitudes toward paupers during the early colonization of the United States and toward welfare recipients today stem from the impact of the work ethic on our society.

For women, however, the emphasis was different: the primary role of women was to maintain the family and to support the ability of men in the family to work outside the home. Until the 1970s this pattern changed only during wartime, when women were needed in the factories because men were away at war. However, as soon as peace came, women returned home and men to the workplace. Those women who did work outside of the home, because of either necessity or interest or both, often were considered to be outside of their appropriate role. It is interesting to note, for example, that until the 1970s most studies regarding work focused on the negative impact of the unemployed man on his family, or on the negative impact of the employed woman on her family (Bronfenbrenner & Crouter 1982).

Within recent years much has changed in regard to the relationship between the individual and the workplace. Probably the biggest change has been due to the large number of women who are working, including those with children. Other changes have taken place as well. Individuals today expect more from the workplace than just a paycheck: recognition, a say in decision making, benefits, and flexible working hours. Numerous studies have focused on the alienation of some workers and the fact that many workers today put other priorities ahead of their jobs. Additional problems receiving increased attention from the workplace include alcoholism and drug abuse; increased costs of health care and other benefits; maternity, paternity, and sick leave; and the overall increase in employees' stress (Kanter 1977).

A growing number of experts view the relationship between work and family life as one of the most critical policy issues to be addressed during the next decade. In many instances, special social services and other programs have been established within the workplace to assist employees and their families in order to maintain or increase productivity.

Occupational social work (sometimes called "industrial social work") has emerged as a growing field for social workers. By applying a systems/ecological perspective, social workers have the potential to play a major role in strengthening relationships between the individual, the family, and the workplace.

THE CHANGING NATURE OF THE WORK FORCE

Today's workforce is very different from the workforce of past decades. While in past years the workforce has consisted largely of middle-aged white males, the workforce of the 90's includes more women, single parents, older persons, and minorities.

More Women in the Work Force

The majority of today's work-related programs and policies are based on work and family demographics as they existed during the 1950s: an almost totally male work force and a male breadwinner supporting his stay-at-home wife and 2.6 children (an average figure). However, in 1987 only about 10 percent of American families could be classified this way. Over 50 percent of two-parent families had both parents employed full-time. Over 60 percent of all working women had children under eighteen, and 57 percent had children under six years of age. Almost half of all women with children under one year of age were employed outside the home (U.S. Department of Labor 1988).

It is estimated that by the year 2000, approximately 47 percent of the work force will be women, and 61 percent of all women will be working outside the home. As Figure 10-1 indicates, women will comprise approximately 60 percent of the new entrants into the work force between 1985 and 2000 (Johnston & Packer 1987). The increase in the number of women employed outside of the family has been fairly sudden, leaving both employers and families unprepared to deal adequately with the resulting implications.

Many individuals argue that the reason for this phenomenon has been primarily economic—that the majority of women work as an economic necessity rather than by choice. Others argue that the women's movement and the realization that women have choices open to them other than remaining at home have created this shift. Still others counter that the women's movement occurred because women were forced by economics to enter the work force, and once there, they faced unfair conditions and began lobbying for changes and more options. Still others argue that more women are working because of the increased emphasis on self-fulfillment (the "me" generation) and consumption among both genders. Although studies indicate that some women work because of choice, most women who are mothers want to work fewer hours than they do now. A recent Gallup poll found that although 52 percent of respondents held full-time jobs, only 13 percent preferred working full-time

Figure 10–1 Most New Entrants to the Labor Force Will be Non-white, Female or
Immigrants

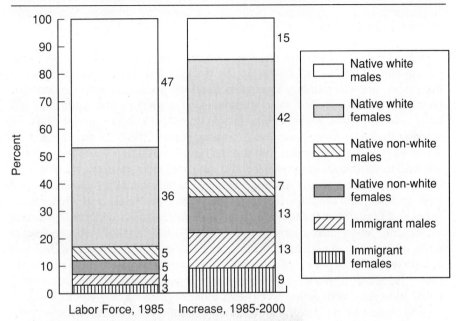

Source: Hudson Institute. Workforce 2000: *Work and workers for the 21st century.* 1987. Indianapolis:
Author. p. 95.

work hours (8 A.M. – 5 P.M.). Sixty percent preferred part-time employment,
flexible hours, or stay-at-home jobs, whereas 16 percent preferred not working
at all (Johnston & Packer 1987).

Whatever the reason or reasons for the increased number of women in
the labor force, this factor more than any other has focused attention on the
relationship between work and family. As sociologist Rosabeth Kanter (1977)
explains, when only one family member left the home each day and operated
within the work system, there was less necessity for overlap or interaction
between the work and family systems, and it was fairly easy to keep them
separate. However, when two family members become involved in the work
system, it is impossible to keep the two systems separate.

Single-Parent Families Other demographic shifts require special attention as
well. In 1990, 25 percent of all families in the United States were one-parent
families, most headed by women (Associated Press 1990). Nationally, women
in general earn less than their male counterparts in the work force. For every
dollar that a man earned in 1987, a women earned seventy cents. One study
projects that this figure will increase to seventy-four cents by the year 2000
(Johnston & Packer 1987). In 1987, the median income for all couples with
both spouses employed was $40,000, while for married couples whose wives
were not in the labor force it was $25,500. Financially, single-parent families
headed by women fare much worse than other families. The median income
for a single-parent household headed by a female in 1987 was close to $15,000,

which is approximately 55 percent of the median income for a two-parent family where only one spouse was employed. Over half of the single-parent households headed by females in the United States are below the poverty level (Mishel and Simon 1988).

Emerging Issues   For women and their families, issues such as patterns of child rearing and affordable child care, flexible working hours, transportation to and from work, and job training, in addition to salary, benefits, compensation, and pensions, are crucial. For their employers, absenteeism and tardiness, sick leave, and employee stress become factors no matter how competent and hard working their employees are. Johnston and Parker (1987) of the Hudson Institute in Indianapolis predict that the increased numbers of working women will lead to more heavily subsidized and regulated child care; readjustments to tax systems such as the "marriage penalty," which penalizes families where both spouses are employed outside the home, and child care deductions; decreased flexibility of the work force as two-career families become less willing to relocate; fewer distinctions between males' and females' jobs and wage rates; an increase in part-time, flexible, and stay-at-home jobs and a decrease in total work hours per employee; a restructuring of private benefit policies to reflect the needs of two-income families and single workers; and more stringent public programs, with access to benefits more segregated between those available to wage earners and those available through government to low-income earners and the unemployed (Johnston and Packer 1987).

A Smaller, Aging Work Force

As a result of the decrease in the number of babies being born, the work force will become smaller and older. Between 1985 and 2000 the labor force is projected to grow by about 22 percent, the slowest gain since the 1930s. This in turn will decrease the national rate of economic growth. Economic growth also will depend more heavily on the increased demand for products such as travel and tourism, restaurant meals, luxury goods, and health care.

Whereas the overall population between 1985 and 2000 is projected to grow by only 15 percent, the number of persons age 35 to 47 will increase by 38 percent and the number of persons age 48 to 53, by 67 percent. The average age of the work force, which was 35 years in 1984, will reach 39 by the year 2000. The increased aging of the work force and of society will likely have the following impacts:

○ A more experienced, stable, and reliable work force should increase U.S. productivity.

○ A continuing decrease in the number of workers available to assume responsibility for those not in the work force will have long-term implications for areas such as Social Security.

○ Although initially, jobs in areas such as fast-food service may be plentiful due to the decreasing number of younger workers, the labor market for younger workers may actually tighten as companies forced to raise wages to attract young workers develop other strategies such as increased automation.

○ If workplaces continue the trend to reduce middle-management positions and develop hierarchical work organizations, there will be more competition among workers to move up within organizations, and those workers who leave or lose jobs will have a difficult time seeking new jobs at their previous levels.

Greater Ethnic Diversity in the Work Force

During the next decade, blacks, Hispanics, and other minorities will continue to enter the work force in greater numbers. Nonwhites will comprise 29 percent of new work entrants and more than 15 percent of the work force in the year 2000. Black women will account for the largest share of this increase, outnumbering black male workers. This is in contrast to the pattern among whites, where men will outnumber women by almost three to two (Johnston & Packer 1987).

The number of immigrants within the work force will also continue to increase. Estimates suggest that if immigration patterns continue, even under the most conservative estimates Hispanic and Asian populations in the United States will double by the year 2000. This population shift will be most significant in the South and the West, particularly in California.

The increase in ethnic diversity within the work force is likely to have a number of implications (see Figure 10-2).

○ Members of minority groups will continue to be discriminated against, to be in lower-paying jobs, and to be promoted to management positions less often than whites. A recent study, for example, found that although women of color comprised 10 percent of the workforce, they were in only 2 percent of managerial positions. Black males comprise 3 percent of management positions, whereas white females are in 23 percent of such positions (Alexander 1990).

○ Members of minority groups will continue to earn less than whites, and unemployment rates and earnings may actually worsen for these groups (Johnston and Packer 1987). Whereas black family income compared to white family income increased from 54 percent of white family income in 1950 to 61 percent in 1970, it decreased to 56 percent in 1983. Hispanic family income dropped from 71 percent to 66 percent of white family income from 1978 to 1983 (Johnston and Packer 1987).

○ Unemployment rates will continue to be higher for members of minority groups. Black unemployment rates were 2.4 times higher than rates for whites from 1978 to 1983, whereas the rate for Hispanics was 1.6 higher than for whites during that same time period (Johnston and Packer 1987).

○ Blacks and Hispanics will continue to be overrepresented in dead-end jobs and in declining occupations. An Equal Employment Opportunity Commission study found that both blacks and Hispanics were 35 percent more likely to be employed in occupations projected to lose the most employees (Johnston and Packer 1987).

○ Over fifty percent of blacks and Hispanics, compared to 25 percent of whites, will continue to live in inner-city areas with severe problems that

Figure 10–2 Black Men and Hispanics Face the Greatest Difficulties in the Emerging Job Market

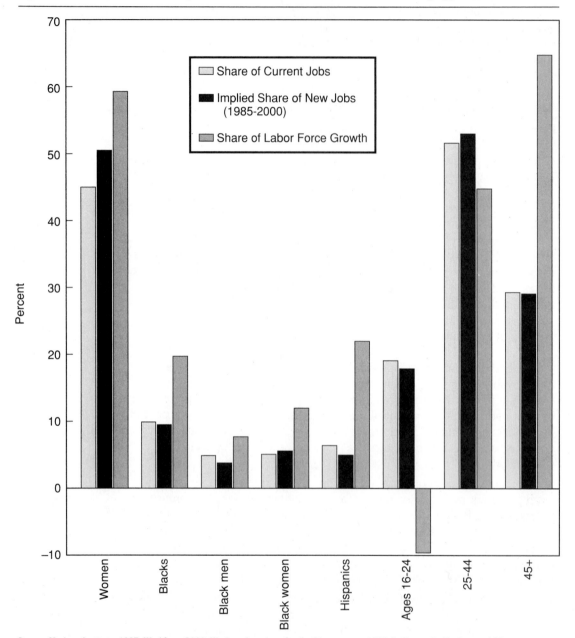

Source: Hudson Institute. 1987. Workforce 2000: Work and workers for the 21st century. 1987. Indianapolis: Author, p. 102.

place their residents more at risk for unemployment. (Johnston and Packer 1987).

○ Immigrants will represent the largest share of the increase in both the population and the work force since World War I and will also often experience barriers to employment due to language and lack of education (Johnston and Packer 1987).

Employment experts are concerned that unemployment and low earnings rates will worsen for minority groups because they also have disproportionately high dropout rates and more problems with literacy than whites.

The changing nature of the work force will have significant implications for employers and employees alike, particularly for companies that have hired primarily young white males. By the year 2000 only 15 percent of new entrants to the work force will be young U.S.-born white males, compared to 47 percent in 1987. Sixty percent of all women over sixteen will be in the work force, and 29 percent of the work force will be nonwhite, or over twice as many nonwhite workers as there were in 1987 (Johnston and Packer 1987).

Types of Jobs Available

The types of jobs in which workers are employed also have changed. Through the 1960's, the majority of workers were employed in blue-collar jobs. However, as the United States has shifted from a manufacturing-based society to a services-based society, more and more workers have been employed in white-collar jobs. In 1988, over 50 percent of the work force was in white-collar jobs (Mishel and Simon 1988). Jobs in the least-skilled job classifications will continue to be eliminated, while the number of white-collar and skilled professional jobs will continue to grow. Most new jobs will require higher levels of education and greater skills in mathematics and language. As high school dropout rates increase, the number of jobs requiring less than a high school education continues to decrease. It is estimated that by the year 2000 only 10 percent of jobs will require less than a high school degree. Whereas in 1987 only 22 percent of all occupations required a college degree, it is estimated that more than half of all new jobs created by the year 2000 will require college degrees (Johnston and Packer 1987).

Shifts in the types of jobs available are likely to lead to a dual work force— more jobs available in the white-collar and skilled areas, primarily in services, requiring high levels of education, and a limited number of jobs available in manufacturing and low-level service jobs that require less education and skill. Such changes are likely to make the work force even more segregated, with more minorities, immigrants, and women in the less-skilled, lower-paying jobs and more white males in the higher-paying jobs requiring greater education and skill.

The shift in jobs away from major industrial centers in the North and East to the Sunbelt and West Coast states, as well as the move away from small agricultural production, also has had a significant impact on workers and their families. Many individuals and families who have remained in industrial centers or farm areas have been forced to take lower-paying jobs or to seek financial assistance for the first time in their lives. Having depleted their savings, they often have lost their homes, farms, and businesses and face an unpredictable future.

THE CHANGING NATURE OF WORK

Futurists disagree when discussing projections regarding the workplace of the future. Some speculate that the marked decline in manufacturing jobs will be counterbalanced by increases in service jobs, including the provision of care for children and the elderly, since working individuals will be unable to provide these supports to either their children or their parents. Others project fewer jobs due to automation and the general decline of labor-intensive industries (Etzioni 1984; Friedman 1983; Galambos 1984; Katzell 1979). Such issues have important implications when addressing employee concerns and the roles social workers and others can play in dealing with them. These contradictory projections make it difficult to predict accurately the future needs of employees and their families, how those needs will surface at the workplace, and which strategies are most likely to meet them.

Unemployment and Underemployment

Although employed individuals often bring numerous problems to their families, and vice versa, the ramifications of unemployment are far more serious. Layoffs and unemployment are expected to increase as the nature of work continues to change. From 1981 to 1985, 20 million jobs disappeared due to plants either closing or moving overseas (Foster and Schore 1989). An increasing number of jobs are being lost due to **outsourcing,** or the contracting out of production of parts or complete products by U.S. companies to plants in countries other than the United States. For example, many major companies operate twin plants (maquiladores) in U.S. and Mexican border cities. The major production takes place in the Mexican plants, where labor is relatively inexpensive compared to the costs to hire workers to complete the same tasks in the United States.

Because work not only provides economic support to families but defines, in one sense, an individual's self-worth, increased unemployment is an issue of national concern. Studies show that unemployment and low economic status are associated with poor family cohesion and family deterioration (Bronfenbrenner & Crouter 1982).

Although official unemployment rates have remained at 6 percent to 6.5 percent during the past few years, some employment experts suggest that they actually have increased as much as 25 percent, because the rates do not reflect those individuals who have become discouraged and are not actively seeking employment. Unemployment rates for blacks are double those for whites. Underemployment, or persons placed in jobs that are at a lower level than they are qualified for, is also an increasing problem. In one recent study researchers found that one-third of Americans reported that they were underemployed in their current jobs (Foster and Schore 1989).

When faced with unemployment or underemployment, many individuals and their families relocate to a supposedly more opportune area. Such areas, however, usually are largely unprepared to address the many needs created by a rapidly expanding population. Housing and other necessities are unavailable or more expensive than anticipated; the availability of work for certain types of workers is inflated or exaggerated; and transportation, utilities, and education are often lacking or underdeveloped. The absence of support from family and friends also plagues those relocating; and social services agencies, overwhelmed by the population influx, are unable to provide resources to meet many employee and family needs.

For employees and their families who remain in unproductive areas, as well as for those who relocate to new areas, stress increases significantly. Social services agencies in these areas report significant increases in suicides, family violence, alcoholism and drug abuse, marital problems, juvenile delinquency, and other mental health problems. They also report significant increases in family financial problems and pressures. For example, as a result of increased economic stress to farm families in the Midwest, spouse abuse rates have increased 300 percent from 1985 to 1988 in Iowa, suicide rates have increased significantly, and depression is the most common mental health problem in the rural Midwest (Select Committee on Children, Youth, and Families 1989).

THE CHANGING WORK FORCE: ATTITUDES AND VALUES

Demographic changes in the work force have had a considerable impact on changing attitudes and values toward work. Although most employees continue to be fairly satisfied with their jobs, there is a growing discontent among certain segments of the labor force over the nature and meaning of work. Employers today are experiencing a new type of worker, described by one policy analyst, Daniel Yankelovich (1979), as the "new breed worker." Yankelovich contrasts today's worker with the "organization man" described by Theodore Whyte in the 1950s (1956). (This term would be considered sexist today, but was appropriate at that time, since the work force was primarily male.) Whyte's organization man was one who put the needs of the organization for which he worked above all else. He came to the company intending to remain there for his entire career, worked long hours, willingly traveled and relocated for the company, and viewed his paycheck as his primary reward for his loyalty and hard work.

Today's worker is much different from Whyte's organization man. Concerns about quality of life and a willingness to express such concerns to employers have forced an emphasis on additional incentives beyond the paycheck. An insistence on individual accomplishment and self-fulfillment, priorities given to interests outside of the workplace, and personal recognition on the job suggest that employees expect work to have meaning beyond the extrinsic rewards of a paycheck. Not only is the meaning of work changing, but it must be viewed differently for different individuals. In a study conducted for *Working Woman* magazine, Yankelovich found that men viewed the meaning of work and satisfaction with their jobs along two dimensions, salary and a say in decisions. Women, however, viewed job satisfaction among six different dimensions, primarily related to relationships with and recognition from co-workers and supervisors (Kagan 1983).

Bureaucratization of the workplace has resulted in a lack of clarity regarding the self-identity of individuals and what should be valued most in a person's life: job, as was true for individuals in the past; family; or one's self and one's own needs. Less support from family members and lack of time to develop supportive relationships with others have resulted in a growing number of individuals who maintain a strong identity with the workplace and expect the majority of their needs to be met by their work. One investigator recently found that employees were more likely to seek help when dealing with problems, including marital and other family problems, from co-workers than from neighbors or family members (Anderson 1985).

In addition to the increased expectations that the workplace should meet personal needs, a growing number of younger, more educated workers expect high salaries, rapid promotions, and challenging jobs (Katzell 1979). Because of increased acceptance of alternate life-styles, the fact that the cost of refusing a job is reduced due to an extensive social welfare system, and the large number of families where more than one individual is employed, Yankelovich and others suggest that for many workers, the traditional work ethic has diminished significantly.

The changes in the types of workers in today's work force and their attitudes toward work have occurred so rapidly that the workplace, for the most part, has been unable to adjust at a comparable pace. Many workplaces still expect not only the loyalty of the organization man, to which they were accustomed, but also the willingness of the employee's wife and children to remain at home and out of the realm of the workplace.

IMPLICATIONS FOR EMPLOYEES AND THEIR FAMILIES

Most of the attention relating to changes in the types of individuals now in the workplace has been directed toward the impact on the family rather than on the workplace. The majority of this attention has been focused on two-parent families. As we suggested earlier, it is when multiple members of the family work that the work and family domains begin to overlap and, in many instances, create conflict. Such conflicts result in lack of time for individuals for themselves and family members; stress caused by balancing work and family schedules and priorities; problems in obtaining adequate child care and other parenting issues; feelings of isolation due to lack of time and energy to develop friends and support systems; and financial difficulties (Kamerman & Hayes 1982; Kanter 1977; Piotrkowski 1978).

Several studies focusing on the impact of work on family life have stemmed from Wilensky's (1960) suggestion that people experience a **spillover effect**, where feelings, attitudes, and behaviors from the workplace spill over into leisure life and vice versa. Evans and Bartolome (1980) suggest five possible work–family relationships:

1. Spillover effect, where one domain affects the other in either a positive or negative way—for example, if you really like your job, this will add satisfaction to your family life.

2. Independent, where work and family life exist side by side but are independent from each other, making it possible to be satisfied and successful with your job but not your family, for example.

3. Conflict, where work and family are in conflict with each other and cannot be reconciled. In a conflict relationship, sacrifices are required in one area in order to be satisfied and successful in the other—for example, spending less time at home with family members in order to be successful at your job.

4. Instrumental, where one domain is primarily a means to obtain something for the other—for example, a job is seen only as a way to earn money to maintain a satisfying family life.

5. Compensation, where one domain is a way of making up for what is missing in another—for example, a recently divorced man puts all of his energies into his job, works long hours, and socializes only with co-workers.

In helping both employees and their family members understand how they can better balance work and family life, it is useful for social workers and other helping professionals to help them look at how they view their work–family relationships.

When examining the impact of work on the individual and family, one additional perspective that deserves attention is the importance of life events. Rapoport and Rapoport (1980) advocate the use of a **life-span model,** in which the meaning of work and family changes as individuals move through childhood, adolescence, youth, adulthood, midlife, and old age. Individuals often are pressured to give full attention to both work and family life at the same period of life—for example, beginning a successful career at the same time that they have recently married and are beginning to have children. Some policy analysts suggest that companies should consider not focusing on promotions and moves up the career ladder for their employees until they are middle-aged and have already dealt with the child-rearing years. The importance of looking at life span can also be seen when focusing on the large number of individuals who make midlife career changes, not because they are necessarily unhappy with their jobs, but because they are dealing with personal developmental issues that are age related.

The majority of attention given to the impact of work on the family has been devoted to working wives and mothers. For all families where mothers work, the impact on the family, particularly the children, is an issue that has been well researched. Current findings indicate that, taken by itself, a mother's employment outside the home has no negative effects on the child. Factors that may affect children of working mothers include the quality of child care that the child receives while the mother is working; the overall stability of the family itself; the type of employment; the socioeconomic status of the family; and the quality and quantity of time that either parent spends with the child (Bronfenbrenner & Crouter 1982).

Increased Stress

Not surprisingly, the majority of studies focusing on work and family issues find that increased stress on the employed family member and the family itself is the issue most often identified by those individuals studied. Some mental health experts suggest that the tremendous increase in the number of individuals seeking mental health services can be attributed to increased pressures faced by more and more individuals trying to balance the demands of job and family.

Recent studies have also focused on **dual-career families,** which are families that have both spouses pursuing their own careers, particularly in relation

Employee problems in the workplace are costly in monetary and human terms. This male employee shares his problems with his coworkers, explaining to them why he has been unable to complete his share of the workload.

to the changes in family roles and responsibilities when both parents work. Although most studies find that both parents in dual-career families experience stress and less time for themselves and family members, it is the wives and mothers who feel these pressures the most. Although in many dual-career families, husbands share more in child-rearing responsibilities, the majority of child-rearing responsibility still falls on the wife. Studies also show that although husbands take on more of the parenting tasks, housekeeping responsibilities fall almost totally on the wives, even among families where both husbands and wives view themselves as being less traditional in the division of household tasks than other couples (Klein 1983). Both men and women from dual-career families list strengths as being additional income, greater opportunities for meaningful communication and growth because both individuals are stimulated by jobs, and more sharing in parenting roles. However, women in such families face numerous role conflicts, citing lack of time to accomplish tasks both at home and at work, lack of time for self, lack of time for spouse, and lack of time for children as major concerns. Furthermore, some studies find that career-oriented couples are not having as many children as in the past. When such couples do have children, childbearing occurs within a shorter span of years so that parents can continue working (Portner 1978).

Relocation

Increases in the number of dual-career families have also resulted in problems when one spouse has a job opportunity in another geographic location. Which spouse's job should prevail and under what conditions present conflicts in many marriages when such opportunities arise. These dilemmas have resulted in more employers providing relocation services that include help in finding employment for spouses, as well as an increase in the number of commuter families, or families where spouses are employed in different locations, often in different parts of the country. Many more workers are also refusing promotions that require relocation.

Financial Problems

Individual and family finances is another area of work–family problems. In many families, both parents are employed outside of the home, but their incomes are below or barely above the poverty level. Financial pressures are especially great for women, minorities, and other workers less likely to be well educated or trained and, as a result, more likely to be employed in low-paying jobs. Those individuals who are single parents (also most likely to be women and minorities) are especially vulnerable to financial pressures. Increasingly, the majority of poor in the United States are working. In a 1987 study, staff of the Center on Budget and Policy Priorities found that the number of working poor in 1987 was 43 percent higher than in 1978, with 28 percent of poor people working full-time. In 1987, 1.9 million people in the United States worked full-time year-round and remained poor. Half of all people living in poverty that year lived in households where at least one member worked during the year, and two of every three children in poverty came from families with one or more workers (Shapiro and Greenstein 1987). Because of the low minimum wage, even those persons who work fulltime at that rate find it difficult to support themselves and their families. A full-time worker earning the minimum wage in 1989 supporting a household of three persons earned $2,900 below the poverty level (National Center for Children in Poverty 1990). Advocates for the working poor suggest that continuing to ignore the working poor will result in substantial costs to both families and the U.S. economy. Suggested options to aid them include a dual approach of restoring the minimum wage to an adequate level that would lift a family of three out of poverty and expanding allowable income tax credits for working parents (Shapiro & Greenstein 1987).

Additionally, 25 percent of the U.S. work force is not covered by employee health insurance. These employees, more likely to be women and minorities, have eight times as many dependents as individuals who are covered by insurance. When these families do have health crises, they are likely to face severe financial problems. Many employers continue to hire workers as temporary or part-time workers so that they will not have to pay part of their health insurance and other benefits. For women employees who become pregnant, maternity leave (without pay) is only available 29 percent of the time. Paid vacations, taken for granted by most individuals, are unavailable to 20 percent of the work force (Kamerman & Kingston 1982). In 1990, both houses of Congress passed the Family and Medical Leave Act, which would have provided workers in workplaces with fifty or more employees the right to twelve weeks of unpaid, job-protected leave to care for new babies or seriously ill children, spouses, or parents. Advocates for the act stated that it would have helped businesses as well as families by improving worker morale and productivity, and 71 percent of Americans favored its passage. However, President Bush vetoed the bill, and Congress did not muster enough votes to override the veto.

Accidents and Other Occupational Hazards

Accidents and other on-the-job health hazards create additional stresses for employees and their families. Coal miners whose daily contact with coal dust results in black lung disease, workers in chemical plants who contract cancer and miscarry or produce children with congenital deformities, and construction workers who may be hurt by heavy equipment place themselves and their families in jeopardy. A number of individuals have successfully sued employers for mental anguish that they and their families experienced as a result of such situations.

The United States continues to have a much higher rate of industrial health and safety accidents than other countries. In 1970 the federal Occupational Safety and Health Act was passed to address this problem. The act sets health and safety standards in industrial workplaces through on-site inspections and citations for violations. The regulatory function is through the Department of Labor, while research and technology are addressed through the National Institute of Occupational Safety and Health (NIOSH), housed within the Department of Health and Human Services. NIOSH also sets standards that relate to hazardous materials. However, cutbacks in staff and the fact that anonymous reports from workers are less likely to be investigated than those that are from companies and relate to immediate danger have jeopardized the effect of the act. Approximately 25 deaths each day, or 6,000 each year, result from industrial accidents. Blacks and Hispanics are most likely to be employed in the most dangerous jobs and the most dangerous occupations and are most at risk to suffer accidental injury or death while on the job. Although increased publicity has been given to occupational hazards such as exposure to asbestos and other dangerous chemicals, efforts to deal effectively with such concerns have been limited at both state and federal levels (Lewis 1989).

Lack of Dependent Care for Working Parents

Nationally, an estimated 5.2 million children under the age of fourteen are without adequate child care while their parents work. Often, infants and toddlers are left sleeping alone at night by working parents. It is not unusual for children ages four and five to be left at home alone for long periods of time, and children as young as eight are often left in charge of much younger children. Increased numbers of children are being injured, often fatally, as a result of fire or other accidents while left unsupervised by working parents. In New York City recently, five children five years old and younger died in a fire; they had been left alone in a locked apartment while their mother worked as a waitress. The same day in Texas, a twelve-year-old girl, left in charge of her ten-year-old brother while her parents worked, heard a noise in the front yard and, becoming scared, got out her father's gun. The gun went off accidentally, killing her younger brother. (The noise had been made by the family dog.) Increases in vandalism and other youth-related delinquent acts, as well as increases in teenage pregnancy, are being attributed partly to the lack of supervision provided to adolescents while their parents work.

New attention has also been given to the increased number of elderly and the need for members of the work force to care for them. In one recent study researchers found that 20 percent of workers thirty years of age and older provide some type of care for older persons, usually parents, who are not in institutions. Many middle-aged women are projected to have dual responsibilities for dependent children and elderly parents, a situation described as the "sandwich phenomena" (Anastas, Gibeau, & Larson 1990). The stress to these caregivers is considerable.

Changing Expectations about Balancing Work and Family Life

Changing expectations regarding what is important in life have also had implications for both families and the workplace. Researchers in one recent study found that increasing numbers of individuals are reassessing tradeoffs between work and family life. The investigators found that 50 percent of persons surveyed would reduce their salaries by 25 percent to have more personal or family time. Forty-five percent of persons surveyed indicated that they would turn down a promotion if it seriously jeopardized the amount of time they could spend with their families (Stanush 1990). The term **downshifting** has been used to refer to the voluntary limiting of job demands so one can devote increased time to one's family or to oneself.

Implications for Mental Health of Employees and Families

Escalating divorce rates and numbers of individuals living alone have left the affiliational needs of many individuals largely unmet. Increasingly, employees and their families, lacking a support system and unable to cope with life's pressures, succumb to divorce, family violence, alcoholism or drug abuse, suicide, or other health or emotional problems. Researchers who conducted a study for the IBM Corporation found that 50 percent of individuals seen by the company's medical department had problems that were emotional or psychological in nature (Compucare Corporation 1981). For workers and their families facing such pressures, however, options often are limited. Many individuals work because they have to in order to support their families, often as the sole source of support for those families. For those who earn low wages and cannot rely on other family members to offer emotional support or to meet family needs such as child care, the toll on them and their families can be extensive. Consider again the situation of the Hunts, the family described at the beginning of the chapter. Even for those who have more options, such as being able to afford child care or rely on relatives, or who work different hours than other family members, balancing work and family pressures is still difficult.

IMPLICATIONS FOR THE WORKPLACE

The problems that have an impact on the individual employee and his or her family also have a significant effect on the workplace. The United States is currently ranked eighth in productivity among Western countries. Job turnover, absenteeism, and other costs created by employee and family problems are expensive to both the workplace and the consumer, who ultimately is forced to absorb these costs.

Researchers in a 1975 study determined that a typical manufacturing company invested an average of over $1,000 per worker during the first year of employment for training. The turnover rate was as high as 31 percent, resulting in a substantial loss of dollars for those companies each time an employee left. Of those individuals who left the companies, 76 percent listed child care problems as the major reason for leaving, and 95 percent listed it as either the first or second reason (Texas Industrial Commission 1977). Absenteeism and lost work time to deal with parenting issues are also costly to employers; a number of Houston, Texas, companies have indicated that their telephone lines are completely tied up between three and four o'clock in the afternoon when children arrive home from school (Center for Social Work Research 1983).

Costs of Alcohol and Drug Abuse

Although child care problems have received much attention in relation to the workplace in recent years with the increased numbers of mothers in the work force, other employee problems are even more costly. In 1980, lost productivity due to alcoholism in the United States totaled $30.1 billion. Drug abuse cost $8.3 billion in lost productivity, and other mental health problems cost $25.8 billion (U.S. Department of Health, Education, and Welfare 1980). Forty percent of industrial fatalities and 47 percent of industrial accidents are related to alcohol use, and the average cost of one employee grievance relating to poor job performance due to alcoholism is over $1,500. At General Motors Corporation absenteeism costs $1 billion each year, and costs related to alcohol, drug abuse, and other mental health problems add hundreds of dollars to the cost of each automobile. In one recent study investigators found that consumers pay an additional $237 per automobile due to alcohol-related costs alone (Compucare Corporation 1981). Such costs are not only attributed to the individual with the problem; one study found that individuals from families where one person was an alcoholic were absent from work ten times more often than persons from families where alcohol was not known to be a problem (Hopson 1977).

Increasing Demands on Employers

Many studies suggest that increased individual and family problems that are emotionally based exact a heavy toll on both the individual and the workplace in relation to health care costs. In 1983, fringe benefits accounted for almost 37 percent of salaries and wages paid by employers in the United States. The average hourly worker received benefits worth $7,582 in that year (U.S. Chamber of Commerce 1984). Wages increased 20 percent between 1969 and 1984, and benefits increased 171 percent (U.S. Bureau of Labor Statistics 1984). The high cost of health care is a major issue for employers. Many are not only increasing employee-paid costs of health care but also are reducing the extent of benefits available.

The fact that more and more workers are looking to the workplace to meet affiliational needs has created additional problems in the job. Co-workers and supervisors find themselves spending increased amounts of work time listening to employees' problems, ranging from marital disputes to more serious problems such as alcoholism, drug abuse, and spouse abuse. A supervisor for a large company who oversees fifteen employees recently noted that in one day she had helped find temporary shelter for a woman employee who had been beaten the previous night by her husband, listened to another employee whose son was in jail for cocaine abuse and theft and referred him to a counseling center, confronted an employee regarding a job error and learned that he was in the midst of a divorce from a twenty-five-year marriage, and covered for another worker who had to leave early because she had a sick child.

ADDRESSING WORK AND FAMILY PROBLEMS: WHOSE RESPONSIBILITY?

Given the serious costs to workers of employee- and family-related problems, their families, and the workplace, many groups have become involved in developing strategies to address these problems. Social services counselors are much more likely to address factors related to the job when working with individuals and family members than they have been in the past. Many communities have developed task forces and programs to provide affordable child care and transportation for employees. A number of public schools have established before- and after-school child care programs, and some schools schedule parent—teacher conferences and other events during evening hours so that most working parents can attend. Social services agencies in some communities have come into the workplace to provide noontime seminars and other programs relating to topics such as coping with divorce, alcoholism and drug abuse, and parenting.

A growing number of employers have also realized that they have a social responsibility to address such problems. Today, many employers are replacing their personnel departments with human resources departments that have expanded roles which include a more holistic approach to employee needs. Human resources departments oversee personnel, social services, health and wellness, along with other employee-related programs. Some employers have used social workers as consultants to assist managers in determining how they can better meet the needs of their employees. Using a systems/ecological approach, appropriate interventions can be directed at all levels of the workplace, from the total corporate environment to the individual employee. Some companies have established **employee assistance programs (EAPs)**, which provide counseling and other social services to employees, and often their families, through the company. Others have expanded health coverage to include alcoholism, drug abuse and mental health counseling, and dental care. A number of both public and private employers have established flexible working hours for their employees, also called **flextime**, which allows employees to work hours that vary from a typical 8 A.M. to 5 P.M. workday. For example, a worker could work four ten-hour days each week or work a different set of hours from other employees, perhaps 6 A.M. to 3 P.M. Other employers allow **job sharing**, a system that allows two people to share the same job which means each person usually works half-time. Another alternative for employers is to create permanent part-time positions. Some employers also allow employees to work in their homes. For example, disabled workers and women workers with children can access employers' computer networks to complete word-processing and other tasks without leaving their homes. This practice is sometimes referred to as **flexiplace**. Still other employers have stress reduction and health promotion programs, including on-site fitness centers where employees and their families can exercise. Some employers also provide on-site child care for employees or arrange for other programs that provide child care; several companies have even established special programs that provide care for school-age children during the summer or when the children are sick.

EMPLOYEE ASSISTANCE PROGRAMS

Nationally, over 5,500 organizations have established formal employee assistance programs (EAPs) to provide counseling to their employees. An additional 1,000 EAP specialists contract with companies to provide services to employees. Originally, EAP programs were established to provide counseling and treatment for employees with alcohol problems; and a recovered alcoholic, often one of the company's own employees, usually worked as the program coordinator. Today, a wide variety of EAPs are available. Although many are still primarily alcohol related, others are broad-based programs that address a wide range of employee problems, including divorce, child rearing, spouse abuse, and financial problems (Shain & Groeneveld 1979). Many innovative programs have been developed for employees and their families through EAPs. Kennecott Copper Company's Insight Program operates a twenty-four hour hotline. Other EAPs provide computerized networks that locate services such as child care. An increasing number of EAPs are offering services relating to the care of elderly parents. One EAP, for example, was able to locate a nursing home in a distant state for an employee's elderly father. EAPs are also called on when workers are relocated or laid off or when companies close. Social workers employed in EAP programs become involved in a wide range of situations involving employees—discrimination, including unfair treatment of minorities, women, new immigrants, and persons with AIDS; the needs of disabled workers; the effects of toxic chemicals and pollutants on employees; and effects of the physical and emotional demands of the workplace.

There are two major types of EAP programs—those provided in house and those provided through referral to an outside organization that actually provides the services. Most workplaces that use external service providers have a full-time coordinator employed by the company who trains supervisors in how to recognize troubled employees and make referrals and who publicizes the program within the company. This coordinator provides the initial screening of employees to ensure that the EAP services are appropriate; however, a referral is then made to a contracting social services agency or trained professional outside of the company who provides the services. In other instances, the coordinator oversees an in-house EAP, where the majority of services, including counseling, are provided directly by company employees, often social workers. Studies have found such programs to reduce employee absenteeism as well as health care costs and increase employee productivity. General Motors Corporation found that it saved $3,700 per year for each employee successfully enrolled in its EAP, or a total of $37 million in a single year (Compucare Corporation 1981). One company spent $65,000 to establish an EAP and saved

$750,000 in sick leave alone. ITT estimates that it has saved $30 million over a ten-year period since establishing its EAP (Royce 1989).

Increasingly, with the rise in health and mental health care costs, EAPs also oversee managed health and mental health care for employees, attempting to reduce inadequate and ineffective services. EAP staff in this role assess employee needs and then make a determination about the most appropriate type of care needed and refer the employee or family member to the most appropriate resource. EAP personnel also often serve as case managers in such situations, ensuring that the services are provided and monitoring regularly until the case is terminated. Employees receive an incentive in reduced co-payments for using these services. This role has raised ethical issues for social workers in some instances if the emphasis is on saving costs for the employer at the expense of providing the most appropriate services for the client.

Another critical issue that EAP workers find themselves confronted with is confidentiality, with increasing numbers of EAPs adopting clear guidelines about the circumstances under which information should be given to management about employees. Most programs advocate total confidentiality between the EAP and the employee unless a crime has been committed or the client is dangerous to himself or others. An employee must sign a written consent form before information will be shared.

CHILD CARE PROGRAMS

Companies are responding to employees' needs in other ways. Many organizations have helped to establish a variety of child care programs. In some instances, companies have established on-site child care programs, allowing parents to bring children to the program on their way to work, to see them during their lunch periods, and to be close by if a child should become sick. Other companies have worked with communities in establishing child care referral systems, helping employees to locate appropriate child care that best meets individual needs. Some companies provide vouchers for child care, or they offer flexible spending packages in which employee benefits can be designed for care of elderly or child dependents. Others provide a variety of after-school and summer child care programs and programs for sick children. Some companies, realizing the amount of money lost every time a child is sick, provide nurses to go to parents' homes and care for children, paying a portion of the cost of their service.

Although not yet well documented, child care programs appear to be cost-effective for employers. The turnover rate for one company was 1.8 percent for those employees with children in its child care program, compared to 6.4 percent for employees who did not enroll their children in the program. One company in Houston, Texas, reported saving 3,700 hours in absenteeism in one year after its child care program was established. The company had a waiting list of potential job applicants, whereas a similar company without child care was having difficulty recruiting workers (Center for Social Work Research 1983). Still, nationally, only about 1,800 organizations provide or assist in the provision of child care for their employees; about half of these are hospitals (Friedman 1985). Although a limited number of work sites have special provisions for sick children, most organizations do not allow employees to take

Increasing numbers of workplaces are developing child care programs for their employees. Parents at this employer-supported center enjoy visiting their children on their lunch breaks and hearing about their day.

personal leave time when children are sick. In 1980 the Conference Board, a national organization that focuses on workplace issues and programs, found that only 13 percent of U.S. companies provide personal leave time when children are sick (Friedman 1985).

Some firms have implemented other programs to increase productivity, including flexible work schedules, health and wellness programs, transportation systems, recreation teams, and employee work groups that work together to improve the workplace and its environment. Co-workers also play an important role in lending support to other employees and their families. Many co-workers are turning to their fellow employees for support during times of crisis. Help with child care, transportation, and advice about coping with teenagers or divorce are all types of assistance provided increasingly by co-workers rather than neighbors, friends, or relatives.

In spite of this assistance, the need for affordable, accessible child care for working parents was recently identified as the most critical need for families in the United States. Twenty-nine million children currently need child care. However, many parents cannot afford the costs of good care, particularly those at or near the poverty level. In 1987 the average weekly cost of child care was forty-nine dollars per child, a 17 percent increase since 1984, in comparison to a 10 percent cost-of-living increase during the same time period. Child care costs are 7 percent of total expenditures for the average family, but over 20 percent of total expenditures for the working poor (*EAP Quarterly* 1989).

SOCIAL WORK IN THE WORKPLACE

One of the areas in which the profession of social work is expanding is in the provision of social services in the workplace. Termed industrial or **occupational social work**, many view this specialization in social work as relatively new; however, this is not the case. In fact, it is interesting to note that the profession of social work owes its name to industry. The term *social work,* introduced in the United States in the early 1890s, apparently as a direct translation of the German phrase *arbeiten sozial,* was used to refer to housing, canteens, health care, and other resources provided to employees by Krupp munitions plants to support the industrial work force (Carter 1977). Although in many other countries industry is the largest field in which social workers practice, in the United States industrial social work was developed and practiced between 1890 and 1920, but then was largely dormant until the 1970s.

Historical Development

The development of welfare and social work programs in industry began with mutual aid societies and volunteer programs established as a result of many of the progressive reform movements during the late 1800s and early 1900s. Positions of "social secretary," "welfare manager," or "welfare secretary" existed in many American industries, including textile mills in the South, Kimberly-Clark, and International Harvester. Welfare secretaries had backgrounds primarily in religious or humanitarian work, with little previous experience in either social work or industry. In general, they were responsible for overseeing the physical welfare (safety, health, sanitation, and housing), cultural welfare (recreation, libraries, and education programs), economic welfare (loans, pensions, rehabilitation, hiring, and firing), and personal welfare, which included social work (then called "case work") with employees and their families (Carter 1977).

According to a Bureau of Labor Statistics survey, by 1926, 80 percent of the 1,500 largest companies in the United States had at least one type of welfare program and about half had comprehensive programs. Sociologist Tamara Hareven recently reviewed old records and conducted a historical study of work and family relationships at the Amoskeag textile mill in New Hampshire in the late 1800s and early 1900s. The company, like many other industries during that time period, provided corporate housing close to the mill for working parents; boarding houses for young single employees; English, sewing, cooking, and gardening classes; nurses who provided instruction in housekeeping, health care, and medical aid and visited the sick and elderly regularly to provide food and assistance; a charity department to provide needy families with clothing, food, and coal and assistance to widows with large families if their husbands died or were injured on the job or were former employees; a hospital ward for employees injured on the job; a dentist for employees' families; a child care program and kindergarten; a children's playground with attendants to supervise the children; a swimming pool and ice-skating rink; an Americanization program; an athletic field and showers; lectures, concerts, and fairs; and a Boy Scouts program (Hareven 1982). Although many companies were generous with assistance, services were denied if an individual refused to work. Thus, the system was designed to encourage loyalty to the organization. Since many industries employed entire families, often in the same work unit, it can also be argued that this system made it less difficult for workers to make the transition from family to factory, with many family members seeing little difference between work life and family life.

During the late 1920s, opposition to these programs came from a number of fronts, including employees themselves. Many employees were immigrants, including women. As they became more acculturated within the Untied States, they saw such welfare programs as paternalistic. The rise of the labor movement also increased negativism toward corporate welfare programs. Labor leaders considered such programs antiunion, believing that the welfare secretary diffused employee unrest without bringing about changes that would improve working conditions for employees. The emergence of scientific management of the workplace turned the focus to improving efficiency of workers. Later, scientific management and welfare work merged into a new field, personnel management. At the same time, public and private social services agencies became more prevalent, decreasing the need for business to provide the many services they had previously provided. Thus, corporate welfare programs declined.

During World War II, the National Maritime Union and United Seaman's Service provided an extensive industrial social work program, providing assistance to the families of the more than 5,000 union members who had been killed during the war. Because unions feared social workers hired by companies would not be sympathetic to unions, other unions initiated industrial social work programs. Until the mid 1970s, unions were responsible for the majority of industrial social work programs in the United States (Carter 1977).

Social Workers' Roles

With the decline in manufacturing and other industries and the shift to a service economy, the term *industrial social work* has been replaced by the term *occupational social work*. Historically, occupational social work has served a variety of functions in business and industry. Profit often has been a major motivation of employers who provide social work services in hopes that these services would increase productivity and morale much as fringe benefits have. However, social workers have affected the workplace in addition to providing social services to employees and their families. Social workers also have played a role in integrating new groups of inexperienced workers such as women, minorities, and immigrants into the work world; providing affirmative action consultation; designing policies to protect workers with AIDS; strengthening relationships between the corporate world and the community; and promoting organizational development through redesign of work to make the workplace more humane for employees. In addition to expertise in working with troubled individuals and families, social workers also are trained in the art of effective communication and negotiation, skills that lend themselves well to advocating for employee needs or working to improve conditions within a workplace, and increasing the understanding between employees and employers.

It seems logical that social workers should become more actively involved in the workplace. Occupational social work lends itself to the provision of services within a natural setting—the majority of adults, after all, are employed. The opportunity for a universal service delivery system that goes beyond services to the poor, the elderly, and the sick also is ideal for the provision of preventive services, an area that is almost negligible from the broader perspective of total services provided.

Although individuals with specializations in fields other than social work, such as personnel or human resources management and industrial psychology, also are employed in human relations capacities in business, such as in personnel or employee counseling positions, social work as a profession is strengthening its interests and capabilities in the area of occupational social work (see Box 10–1). The two major professional bodies that guide the profession, the National Association of Social Workers and the Council on Social Work Education, have established task forces, developed publications, and held conferences that focus on occupational social work. In some instances, these programs are interdisciplinary in nature and operate jointly with other departments such as business administration. All programs provide future occupational social workers with knowledge and skill in dealing with alcoholism and drug abuse, marriage and family problems, and other individual and family problems. They also offer courses relevant to working in organizations and the corporate world. To be successful in the workplace, social workers need special

---

Box 10–1 The Occupational Social Worker

A job description for an occupational social worker might include the following:

o Counseling and carrying out activities with troubled employees and their families to assist them with their personal problems and to achieve maintenance of their productive performance;

o Advising on the use of community services to meet client needs and establishing linkages with such programs;

o Training front line personnel to enable them to (1) identify when changes in job performance warrant referral to a social service unit and (2) carry out an appropriate approach to the employee that will result in such referral;

o Developing and overseeing the operation of a management information system, which will record service information and provide data for analysis of the unit's program;

o Developing a plan for future programmatic direction and staffing of the industrial social work program;

o Offering consultation to management decision makers concerning human resource policy;

o Helping to initiate health, welfare, recreational, or educational programs for employees;

o Advising on corporate giving and on organizational positions in relation to pending social welfare legislation.

Source: From S. Akabas and P. Kurzman, "The industrial social welfare specialist: What's so special?" In *Work, workers and work organizations: A view from social work*, S. Akabas and P. Kurzman, eds. © 1982, pp. 201–202. Reprinted by permission of Prentice-Hall, Englewood Cliffs, N.J.

knowledge and skill in business principles, planning and management, marketing, financial management, personnel adminstration, family counseling, and organizational behavior. Students in occupational social work programs also are placed in field internships in corporations and with unions, where they work directly with troubled employees and their families or are involved in adminstration and planning activities within the corporation.

Much of the focus of occupational social work to date has been on the client as a worker. Although it is important that social work as a profession recognize the importance of work within the individual's life, the emphasis of occupational social work has been primarily at the individual casework level through employee assistance programs and other forms of one-to-one counseling or information and referral services. The central focus appears to be on the relationship of work to emotional problems. Social workers have also played a role in addressing work-related social policy issues such as the appropriate division between corporate and social welfare sectors in the provision of social services; the relationships between work and family roles for men and women; the impact of affirmative action programs on women, minorities, and disabled individuals; and unemployment. However, future directions suggest a broadened role social work could play from an organizational change perspective.

Applying a Systems/Ecological Perspective

Because social workers operate from a systems/ecological perspective, focusing on the interaction between the individual and his or her environment, they are well equipped to develop strategies of intervention at a variety of levels of systems within which the individual functions (see Box 10–2). Consider again, for example, the Hunt family discussed at the beginning of this chapter. Social work intervention could include individual counseling for Bill and Meredith Hunt relating to their respective jobs. However, because the problems that the Hunts face are associated with their relationship to each other, a social worker might propose marital counseling for the couple, seeing both of them together. Remember, though, that the Hunt children also were having difficulties within the family. It also might be appropriate for a social worker to provide counseling for the entire Hunt family.

Other individuals within the systems in which the Hunts operate may need to be involved, too. Co-workers and supervisors with whom the Hunts interact may be exacerbating their problems. The oldest son's teacher also might be helpful in providing insight into the boy's problems. A social worker might wish to work with these individuals in addition to the Hunts, to help others with whom they interact be more supportive of their needs. There may also be other resources within the community that the social worker might refer the Hunts to, such as a low-cost after-school child care or recreational program for the son, parenting classes, Alcoholics Anonymous, or a battered women's program.

The role of a social worker can go beyond the individual and family intervention level. The social worker might realize that there are numerous individuals at the workplace experiencing the same kinds of problems as the Hunts, so he or she might establish support groups for employees with similar concerns and needs. An additional role of the social worker could be to advocate with management for company policies that better support the needs of employees

Box 10–2 Assessment of Problem(s)

A comprehensive social worker's problem(s) should
include the following:

I. Worker

    A. Work History

    B. Current Position—Occupation, Hours, Salary, Fringe Benefits

    C. Job Duties and Responsibilities

    D. Adequacy of Job Performance

    E. Degree and Type of Autonomy and Control in Work Role

    F. Relationships with Colleagues, Supervisors, Subordinates

    G. Specific Work Strains and Satisfactions

    H. Career Goals

    I. Self-Concept as a Worker

II. Work Organization

    A. Size, Location, Function, Physical Setting

    B. General Ambiance

    C. Organizational Structure

    D. Opportunities Provided to Worker for Advancement

    E. Expectations regarding Loyalty, Performance, etc.

III. Interface Between Work and Family

    A. Mesh between Worker's Time and Family Time

    B. Adequacy of Income to Meet Personal and Family Needs

    C. Degree to which Work Role and Responsibilities Intrude on Family
       Life

    D. Degree to which Family Roles and Responsibilities Intrude on
       Work Life

    E. Degree to which Work Role Meets Expectations of Significant
       Others, e.g., Spouse, Children, Family of Origin, Friends

    F. Overlap between Work and Leisure Activities

Source: From J. Cohen and B. McGowan, "What do you do?" An inquiry into the potential of work-
related research. In *Work, workers and work organizations: A view from social work*, S. Akabas and
P. Kurzman, eds. © 1982, pp. 126–27. Reprinted by permission of Prentice-Hall, Englewood Cliffs,
N.J.

like the Hunts. The social worker might work with others within the workplace
to implement child care programs, flexible work hours, and adequate sick leave
policies. Also, the social worker might work with others beyond the workplace
to develop state and federal legislation to mandate policies that are more supportive of employees and their families, such as parental leave, and sick-leave
policies that allow for time off when illness among family members occurs.

Service Models

The University of Pittsburgh school of social work has developed three models of service for occupational social workers that incorporate a variety of roles inherent to the profession of social work. The first model, the employee service model, focuses primarily on the microlevel of the systems within which employees and their families function. In this model, social work functions include counseling employees and their families; providing educational programs to employees; referring employees to other agencies; implementing recreational programs; consulting with management regarding individual employee problems; and training supervisors in recognizing and dealing appropriately with employee problems.

The second model, the consumer service model, focuses on intervention at a broader level within the same systems. This model views employees as consumers and assists them in identifying needs and advocating to get those needs met. Social workers work with consumers-employees in assessing their needs and developing strategies to best meet those needs; identifying and providing community resources to meet the needs; serving as liaison between consumer-employee groups and social services agencies; and developing outreach programs to meet employee needs.

The third model, the corporate social responsibility model, focuses on intervention at the exo and macrolevels within the various systems in which employees and their families function. Social workers operating within the realm of this model work with the workplace, community, and society in general in developing and strengthening programs that support individual employees and their families. They provide consultation about human resources, policy, and donations to tax-exempt activities within the workplace and to community organizations such as the United Way; analyze relevant legislation and make recommendations for additional legislation; administer health and welfare benefits; conduct research to document needs and evaluate programs and policies; and serve as community developers, providing a link between social service, social policy, and corporate interests (Akabas & Kurzman 1982).

These models often overlap in actuality, with social workers in workplace settings providing tasks that fall within more than one model. The majority of social work activity in the workplace to date has been with the employee service model. It is anticipated that as a growing number of social workers practice within an occupational setting, more of their activity will fall within the other two models.

SUMMARY

A systems/ecological approach to social problems focuses on the interactions between the individuals and their environment. Until recently, little attention has been given to the interactions between the individual, the individual's place of employment, and the individual's family. However, as more women, both with and without children, enter the workplace, and as rapid social change continues to negatively affect many individuals, the relationship between the workplace and the family can be ignored no longer. Individuals experiencing stresses at the workplace invariably bring their stresses home. Conversely, individuals experiencing stresses at home bring those to the workplace. The costs of employee and family alcoholism, drug abuse, marital problems, parenting problems, and other mental health problems are extensive to both the family and the workplace.

A number of communities and workplaces have developed programs that help individual employees and their families better balance work and family pressures. These include employee assistance programs, as well as child care, transportation, and health and wellness programs. Studies show that these programs are effective in preventing family and workplace dysfunction. The field of occupational social work is emerging as an area where some impact can be made through intervention in the workplace to improve family functioning, and prevent negative consequences of change, as well as increasing profitability and productivity for the work organization. It is anticipated that social work as a profession will begin to play a more major role in developing programs within the workplace, as well as advocating for appropriate policies and legislation, that provide increased support to employees and their families.

KEY TERMS

downshifting

dual-career family

employee assistance programs
  (EAPs)

flexiplace

flextime

job sharing

life-span model

occupational social work

outsourcing

spillover effect

DISCUSSION QUESTIONS

1. List four ways that the composition of the workplace has changed over the past thirty years. How have these changes had an impact on the workplace?

2. Using a systems/ecological perspective, discuss the relationships between an individual, his or her workplace, and his or her family.

3. Name three types of employee- and family-related problems and describe how these problems affect the workplace.

4. Name three types of work-related problems that an employee might experience. In what ways might these problems affect the employee's family?

5. Describe five types of programs employers have established to address employee and family needs.

6. Describe the three models on which an occupational social work program might be based. List at least three of the roles an occupational social worker employed in a workplace setting might play.

REFERENCES

Akabas, S., and P. Kurzman. 1982. The industrial welfare specialist: What's so special? In *Work, workers, and work organizations: A view from social work*, ed. S. Akabas and P. Kurzman. Englewood Cliffs, N.J.: Prentice-Hall, 197–235.

Alexander, K. 1990. Minority women feel race, sexism are blocking the path to management. *Wall Street Journal,* 25 July, B1.

Anastas, J., J. Gibeau, and P. Larson. 1990. Working families and eldercare: A national perspective in an aging America. *Social Work* 35(5): 405–411.

Anderson, R. 1985. *Employer-based support to employees and their families.* Austin: University of Texas.

Bronfenbrenner, U., and A. Crouter. 1982. Work and family through time and space. In *Families that work: Children in a changing world,* ed. S. Kamerman and C. Hayes. Washington, D.C.: National Academy Press, 39–83.

Bureau of Business Research. 1984. *Private sector employee benefits in Texas: The relevance to working families.* Austin: University of Texas.

Bureau of Labor Statistics, 1988. *Current Population Survey.* Washington, D.C.: U.S. GPO.

Carter, L. 1977. Social work in industry: A history and a viewpoint. *Social Thought* 3:7–17.

Center for Social Work Research. 1983. *Achieving organizational excellence: Issues of personal and family life—A report of the Texas Corporate Leadership Forums.* Austin: University of Texas, School of Social Work.

————. 1983. *Work and family life issues: A report of a series of corporate forums held with selected work-related organizations in Texas.* Austin: University of Texas, Center for Social Work Research.

Children's Defense Fund. 1989. *America's children and their families: Key facts.* Washington, D.C.: Author.

Cohen, J., and B. McGowan. 1982. "What do you do?" An inquiry into the potential of work-related research. In *Work, workers, and work organizations: A view from social work,* ed. S. Akabas and P. Kurzman. Englewood Cliffs, N.J.: Prentice-Hall, 117–146.

Compucare Corporation. 1981. Employee assistance programs: A dollar and sense issue. Newport Beach, Calif.: Author.

Etzioni, A. 1984. The two-track society. *National Forum: The Phi Kappa Phi Journal* 64(3):3–5.

Evans, P., and F. Bartolome. 1980. The relationship between professional life and personal life. In *Work, family, and the career: New frontiers in theory and research,* ed. C. Derr. New York: Praeger.

Foster, B., and L. Schore. 1989. "Job loss and the occupational social worker." *Employee Assistance Quarterly* Vol. 5, No. 1, 77–98.

Freeman, R. 1979. The workforce of the future: An overview. In *Work in America: The decade ahead,* ed. C. Kerr and J. Rosow. New York: Van Nostrand Rienhold, 58–79.

Friedman, D. 1983. *Encouraging employer support to working parents: Community strategies for change.* New York: Carnegie Corporation.

————. 1985. *Report on corporate child care assistance.* New York: Conference Board.

Galambos, E. 1984. A "high-tech" or a service economy future? *National Forum: The Phi Kappa Phi Journal* 64(3):38–39.

Hareven, T. 1982. *Family time and industrial time.* Cambridge, England: Cambridge University Press.

Hopson, A. 1977. Where are the other victims of alcoholism? *Labor–Management Alcoholism Journal* 7(2):22–23.

Johnston, W., and A. Packer. 1987. *Workforce 2000: Work and workers for the twenty-first century.* Indianapolis, Ind.: Hudson Institute.

Kagan, J. 1983. Survey: Work in the 1980's and 1990's. *Working Woman* (April 1983):26–28.

Kamerman, S., and C. Hayes. 1982. *Families that work: Children in a changing world.* Washington, D.C.: National Academy Press.

Kamerman, S., and P. Kingston. 1982. Employer responses to the family responsibilities of employees. In *Families that work: Children in a changing world,* ed. S. Kamerman and C. Hayes. Washington, D.C.: National Academy Press, 144–208.

Kanter, R. M. 1977. *Work and family in the United States: A critical review and agenda for research and policy.* New York: Russell Sage Foundation.

Katzell, R. 1979. Changing attitudes toward work. In *Work in America: The decade ahead,* ed. C. Kerr and J. Rosow. New York: Van Nostrand Reinhold, 35–57.

Kerr, C., and J. Rosow. 1979. *Work in America: The decade ahead.* New York: Van Nostrand Reinhold.

Klein, D. 1983. Trends in employment and unemployment in families. *Monthly Labor Review.* 106(12):21–25.

Lewis, B. 1989. Social workers' role in promoting occupational health and safety. *Employee Assistance Quarterly* 5(1):99–118.

Masnick, G., and M. J. Bane. 1980. *The nation's families: 1960–1990.* Cambridge, Mass.: MIT and Harvard University, Joint Center for Urban Studies.

Mishel, L., and J. Simon. 1988. *The state of working America.* Washington, D.C.: Economic Policy Institute.

National Center for Children in Poverty. 1990. *Five million children: A statistical profile of our poorest young citizens.* New York: Columbia University School of Public Health.

Piotrkowski, C. 1978. *Work and the family system: A naturalistic study of working class and lower middle class families.* New York: Free Press.

Portner, J. 1978. *A literature search: Topics relevant to a consideration of impacts of work on the family.* Minneapolis: Minnesota Council on Family Relations.

Rapoport, R., and R. Rapoport. 1980. Balancing work, family and leisure: A triple helix model. In *Work, family and career: New frontiers in theory and research,* ed. C. Derr. New York: Praeger.

Royce, J. 1989. *Alcohol problems and alcoholism.* New York: Free Press.

Shain, M., and J. Groeneveld. 1979. *Employee-assistance programs: Philosophy, theory, and practice.* Lexington, Mass.: Lexington Books.

Stanush, M. 1990. An executive decision: Family life taking top priority. *Austin American Statesman* (September 16, 1990): E-1, E-13.

Shapiro, S. and R. Greenstein. 1987. *Making work pay: A new agenda for poverty policies.* Washington, D.C.: Center on Budget and Policy Priorities.

Stapleton, D., and D. Young. 1984. The effects of demographic change on the distribution of wages, 1967–1990. *Journal of Human Resources* 19(2):175–201.

Texas Industrial Commission. 1977. *Industry-sponsored child care: A question of productivity.* Austin: Author.

U.S. Bureau of the Census. 1988. *Current population survey.* Washington, D.C.: GPO.

U.S. Bureau of Labor Statistics. 1984. *Employment and Earnings* 31(12). Washington, D.C.: GPO.

————. 1984. *Report of U.S. growth in productivity, June 1984.* Washington, D.C.: GPO.

U.S. Bureau of Labor Statistics. 1988. Mothers participating in labor force. March 1988. Washington, D.C.: GPO.

U.S. Chamber of Commerce. 1980. *Employee benefits, 1979.* Washington, D.C.: Author.

U.S. Chamber of Commerce. 1984. *Employee benefits, 1983.* Washington, D.C.: Author.

U.S. Department of Health, Education, and Welfare. 1980. *Health: United States, 1980.* Washington, D.C.: GPO.

U.S. House Select Committee on Children, Youth, and Families. 1989. Hearing summary. *Working families at the margins: The uncertain future of America's small towns.* April 11, 1989. Washington, D.C.: Author.

Whyte, W. 1956. *The organization man.* New York: Doubleday.

Wilensky, H. 1960. Work, careers and social integration. *International Social Science Journal* 7(4):543–60.

Yankelovich, D. 1979. Work, values, and the new breed. In *Work in America: The decade ahead,* ed. C. Kerr and J. Rosow. New York: Van Nostrand Reinhold, 3–26.

SUGGESTED FURTHER READINGS

Akabas, S., and P. Kurzman. 1982. *Work, workers, and work organizations: A view from social work.* Englewood Cliffs, N.J.: Prentice-Hall.

Googins, B., and J. Godgrey. 1987. *Occupational social work.* Englewood Cliffs, N.J.: Prentice-Hall.

Occupational social work today. 1989. (special issue). *Employee Assistance Quarterly.* 5(1).

Social Work in Rural Settings

*E*lizabeth Jones is a children's protective services worker assigned to a western county in Iowa. The largest city in the county is the county seat, a community of 5,500 persons. Elizabeth is employed by the Department of Human Services and, along with one co-worker, Norman Johnson, is responsible for covering the entire 2,300-square-mile county area. Her task is to investigate reports of child abuse and neglect, report her findings to the court, and make recommendations related to disposition of the case. As a social worker, she finds that locating and supervising foster homes for children, providing support to abusive parents, and networking with other support resources often require far more time than the forty-hour work week allows.

Elizabeth enjoys her work, but she occasionally has to travel great distances. Also, she sometimes feels frustrated because other formal agencies' supports are limited. On the other hand, she enjoys the rural environment and its informal systems and the opportunity to work with the local community leaders in seeking the best plan for abused children and their families. She has learned that informal relationships in the rural environment and the personal concern of rural residents are real strengths that can be effectively utilized in problem solving.

Today, millions of Americans live in rural communities that are characterized by limited resources and isolation. Although the majority of our citizens reside and work in urban areas, the population of small towns and outlying areas has increased over the past several decades. As more individuals and families become disenchanted with the fast pace and overcrowded conditions of cities, it is likely that the rural population will continue to expand.

Rural areas, with their small towns, farms, and ranches of varying sizes, offer an appreciably different environment and life-style than those in cities. Although automobiles and airplanes have provided many rural inhabitants access to the resources of major cities, isolation and long distances continue to pose problems for others. On the average, people living in rural areas have more limited resources than do urban residents. Farley et al. (1982) have illuminated many of the urban–rural differences, pointing out that over half of America's substandard houses, half of our poor, the majority of our untreated ill, and substantial numbers of unemployed individuals live in rural areas. In this chapter, we review some of the more salient characteristics of rural America and identify social welfare and social work resources available in rural areas.

RURAL: AN OPERATIONAL DEFINITION

Arriving at a universally agreed upon definition of **rural** is more difficult than the reader might think. Generally, such definitions are based on population counts (the census) of a specified area rather than upon the behavioral traits and customs of people. For example, the "hillbillies" from Tennessee, Arkansas, and West Virginia who migrated into many northern cities brought along with them their customs, values, and traits. Disadvantaged and unsophisticated in the ways of urban life, they had a great deal of difficulty adapting to the demands of urban life. Uneducated and unskilled, they were relegated to poverty and a continual struggle for survival. Although their customs and habits positioned them clearly as rural transplants, once in the urban environment, they were no longer considered rural. Urban dwellers moving into rural areas have experienced similar "culture shock." The point is that definitions of *urban* or *rural* are not subject to the behavioral attributes of population groups but rather to population size. Seemingly, such definitions should constitute a rather simple task, yet it is complex.

The U.S. Census Bureau classifies as rural communities those that are composed of 2,500 or fewer people. This classification has limited utility in that it only enables us to separate out those communities statistically identified as rural from those that are not. For example, is a small, isolated rural community of 2,500 in Utah the equivalent of a similarly sized, incorporated, "bedroom" community twenty-five miles from Houston, in terms of access to resources? Probably not.

In addition, millions of Americans live on farms or ranches that are some distance from villages, towns, or cities. In many of these areas, small farms are close together, whereas in others, miles may separate families from each other. Rural inhabitants often are identified as *rural-farm* or *rural-nonfarm* to further clarify and differentiate the nature of rural residency. Clearly, there are differences and distinctions in the daily living requirements and patterns of the small-town resident and those of the farm dweller.

Farley et al. (1982) have suggested that rural life might be conceptualized as ecological, occupational, and sociocultural. Each conceptual aspect provides a basis for differentiating among rural towns and outlying areas. Many of these characteristics are reflected in the discussions that follow. The reader should be aware that the life of a small farmer in Georgia may be appreciably different from that of a goat rancher in West Texas.

CHARACTERISTICS OF RURAL POPULATIONS

Data are available that enable us to gain an overview of rural life. Approximately 70 million Americans are living in rural areas, and that number is increasing. Table 11–1 illustrates the age and sex distribution of the rural population in 1988. Many of the areas in which they live are predominantly agricultural, with crops, poultry, cattle, sheep, or goats as the main sources of livelihood. Inhabitants may live on small acreages and be self-sufficient or work for large commercial farms. Many attempt to do both. Increasingly, major industrial developments are seeking out rural areas to establish plants or factories, thus sponsoring various social get-togethers and recreational opportunities. Religion typically plays a vital role in setting the moral tone and in meeting the spiritual needs of rural residents. Ministers are viewed not only as spiritual advisors but also as community leaders.

In agricultural areas, the county extension office, funded by the **U.S. Department of Agriculture,** provides many services valued by the farm community to assist rural areas, and the county liaison office provides a variety of community and family services. Technical assistance is made available for crop planting and harvesting, ranch management, disease control, care of livestock, food preparation, home canning, and other activities related to farm, ranch, and home management. Informally, the county agent often becomes aware of personal problems and serves as counselor, case manager, and resource finder. The county agent also often functions as an advocate or broker (with the local banker or other lending agencies) for farmers experiencing financial disaster.

Recreational activities are often limited in rural areas. The absence of a local movie house, skating rink, park, library, and other outlets for children and teenagers severely restricts opportunities for leisure-time activities. Many small communities literally "roll up the sidewalks" at dark. As a consequence, the local school often is a prominent source for recreational get-togethers and sponsors dances and holiday programs. Athletic events are usually well attended and serve as the central focus for young people and adults to meet and socialize. The school, along with the church, is among the primary institutions for social organization in the rural community.

SOCIAL PROBLEMS IN RURAL AREAS

Rural areas are often thought of as being peaceful, serene, and devoid of the types of problems that are found in large cities and metropolitan areas. Unfortunately, that typification is not borne out by life experiences of our rural citizens. Rural areas are not devoid of social problems, and the impact of those problems is often far greater on rural residents than those living in cities because of the distance to or absence of support services. A few of the more prominent problems are identified in the following paragraphs.

The Farm Crisis

During the latter part of the 1970s and throughout the 1980s the charac' nature of rural America changed dramatically. Inflation, low farm pri' production costs, imports, and economic recession converged to cre **crisis** for the small landowner-farmer. Within the past decade, th' farm and ranch foreclosures increased dramatically, resulting in' ment of large numbers of farmers and ranchers who depende' production for their livelihood. It is not uncommon for inter' to be lost through foreclosure. Displaced farmers, particular' ranchers, often lack the skills to become readily absorb' of the labor market. Major commercial farm operations demise of small farm operations through volume pr' prices for farm products. The small operator, even ' has great difficulty in competing with the large cc'

Table 11–1   Age and Sex of the Rural Population, 1988, (in thousands)

Age	Both Sexes	Male	Female
All Ages	64,798	32,152	32,646
Under 15	14,935	7,641	7,295
15 to 19	5,131	2,622	2,508
20 to 24	4,097	2,091	2,006
25 to 29	4,869	2,358	2,511
30 to 34	5,431	2,659	2,772
35 to 39	5,196	2,610	2,586
40 to 44	4,525	2,270	2,255
45 to 49	3,802	1,922	1,881
50 to 54	3,145	1,595	1,550
55 to 59	3,047	1,490	1,557
60 to 64	2,976	1,438	1,538
65 to 69	2,693	1,308	1,385
70 to 74	2,087	967	1,120
75 and Over	2,864	1,181	1,683
Median Age:	33.1	32.6	33.6

Source: U.S. Department of Agriculture and U.S. Census Bureau, Rural and rural farm population: 1988. *Current Population Reports*, ser. P-20, no. 439 (Washington, D.C.: GPO, 1988).

providing opportunities for employment. Jennings (1990) has further described rural communities as characterized by the following:

1. Basic trust
2. Basic friendliness
3. Isolation
4. Resistance to change
5. Suspicion toward newcomers or outsiders
6. Tendency for children to take on the identity of their parents
7. Independence of spirit yet vulnerable
8. Similarity to a family system, especially regarding roles
9. Financial and experiential poverty
10. Reliance on informal and/or natural helping systems first for assistance
11. Concrete thinking and more reserved behaviors
12. Traditional values and conservatism
13. More holistic, less compartmentalized lives
14. Multilevel relationships

The strength and intensity of any (or all) of these characteristics may vary, depending on the organization and density of the population of the rural area as well.

SOCIAL ORGANIZATIONS OF RURAL COMMUNITIES

Unlike in major metropolitan areas, social networks in rural communities are more personalized and informal. Many of the prominent and powerful community leaders are descendants of early settlers, are often large landowners, and are leaders in community affairs. Residents, both affluent and poor, tend to be known by many people in the community. Privacy and anonymity are seldom achieved. Good, as well as bad, news travels through the informal community network with amazing speed. Reputations are routinely established for residents and are changed only with great effort. Newcomers often find themselves in an "out-group" category and, regardless of their interest or endeavor, find it difficult to be accepted fully into the inner circles of community life. Judgments concerning the character, ability, and competency of individuals tend to be based on subjective assessments. The success or failure of community residents usually is considered to be the result of personal effort and motivation. Hence, the poor, unemployed, or downtrodden are viewed as individuals who lack the determination to achieve. Divorce and poverty typically are classified as personal failures, and strong negative sanctions serve as constant reminders that deviation from the norm is accompanied by increasing social distance and exclusion from free and full participation in community life.

On the other hand, responses to people in need are often quick and personal. A death in the family or a farm failure stimulates neighbors to respond with goods and services designed to assist the needy through the crisis situation. Droughts, floods, tornadoes, and other natural disasters create a bond among farmers and ranchers and a unity of purpose with shared concern. People often

Because resources are sparse in rural areas, social workers most often provide general services. Here, an elderly couple welcomes the social worker from the area mental health center as she makes a home visit.

show reciprocity by sharing labor for the harvesting of crop. in times of need, and organizing to counteract threats to comm politically conservative, rural communities are characterized by innovation and skepticism concerning modern technological inne slickers are viewed with disdain and are not to be trusted until pro of trust. They are considered to be uninformed as to the needs of rural. Honesty and strong character are valued as desirable traits.

The action hub of rural communities centers around the church, the bank, the county extension office, small businesses, the feed store, and local school system. As a consequence, the local banker, ministers, the coun agent, store owners, and school administrators usually hold powerful influenc over community life. County government is typically relegated to the county judge and county commissioners. The sheriff's office handles law enforcement, although many small towns also have a police force. Violations of the law are considered to be a personal offense against the community, and mitigating circumstances are usually downplayed or viewed as irrelevant. Ginsberg (1976, 7) suggests that rural communities have a style of living that is scaled down from urban areas and states that

> a smaller scale of life does not imply simplicity. Rural communities are often as socially complicated as cities. Many of the things that happen may be based upon little-remembered but enduringly important family conflicts, church schisms, and crimes. It may require months of investigation before a newcomer in a rural area fully understands the power relationships of the community's institutions. Things are often not as they are supposed to be . . . a single civic club may have a disproportionate influence over governmental matters, while the government may be weak.

The social organization of rural communities is as varied as the locations in which they occur. Although there are common threads of roles and relationships that knit the community together in any setting, each locale has its own character.

SUPPORT SERVICES IN THE RURAL COMMUNITY

Many of the support services that urban residents take for granted are often scarce or nonexistent in rural communities. It is not uncommon to find an absence of doctors, nurses, social workers, dentists, or attorneys in small rural towns. Adequately staffed hospitals with up-to-date equipment are expensive to develop and maintain, and small communities lack the resources to finance them. As a consequence, many health-related problems go unattended, or people rely on traditional cures or folk medicine. Resources for the treatment of mental illness are particularly lacking. However, individuals exhibiting "peculiar" behavior often find acceptance in rural areas, and their families may experience considerable understanding and social support from neighbors. Social work and social services are distributed sparsely in rural areas, often because the community's mores or limited financial support capabilities.

As noted earlier, the church is a significant institution in rural life. Congregations are quick to respond to those in need and set the pace for community in time of crisis. The church also is the center for community activities,

Currently, in the United States, few resources are available to assist the small farmer in maintaining property and purchasing the equipment essential for a successful operation. The federal government's preoccupation with the reduction of deficit spending has taken its toll on farm supports. Urbanites must be reminded continually that their survival also depends on a healthy agricultural industry. Along with these problems, the stress and tension associated with the loss (or impending loss) of one's farm create havoc for the families of small farmers and serve as a disincentive for prospective farmers. Many of the victims, once productive and self-sustaining, must turn to welfare as a means of survival.

Mental Health in Rural Areas

The farm crisis has changed the quality of life in the rural environment. Stresses and tensions associated with the instability and unpredictability of maintaining one's farm and productivity have affected the psychosocial environment of the rural resident. Although mental health problems have always existed in rural environments, considerable concern has been expressed over what appears to be an increase in dysfunctional mental health problems since the 1980s. J. Dennis Murray (1990), president of the National Association of Rural Mental Health (NARMH), has pointed out that (1) the prevalence of mental illness in rural America at least equals, if not exceeds, that in cities; and (2) rural areas have higher rates of emotional disorder (especially depression). Murray has expressed concern over the limited resources that are available to address these problem areas. It is also commonly known that the suicide rate in rural areas is similar to that found in cities.

In addition to these more severe and traumatic problems of social dysfunctioning, the psychological and emotional anguish associated with marital discord and parent–child conflicts has intensified as a result of the frustration and insecurity related to the unsettled farm economy. Child abuse, for example, once thought to be a primarily urban problem, is also found in rural areas in ever-increasing numbers. Many view such problems as a reflection of the ecological instability of rural life as it exists today. The abuse of alcohol and other drugs, often viewed as a symptom of economic and social unrest, has also become a more significant problem in rural areas.

The availability of mental health resources to meet the needs of the rural constituency varies with population density, but it is generally considered woefully inadequate. Some of the reasons for the lack of service availability and the limited use of available resources are described in the *Rural Health Reporter* ("Mental Health Services" 1989) as follows:

1. Artificially configured service areas
2. Very large service areas
3. Stigma and the lack of privacy
4. Staff shortages
5. Inadequate facilities
6. Absence of support services
7. Few treatment alternatives

In addition to these problems, inadequate financial resources and community resistance present barriers that must be overcome if individuals and families in need of mental health services are to receive them. As discussed later in this chapter, resources necessary to assist rural families are very limited.

Health Care Problems

Problems associated with health care are also of concern to rural Americans. Health indicators, for example, reflect that infant mortality and chronic disease rates are higher in rural areas than in urban ones. Some estimates suggest that over "50 percent of the rural aged suffer from continuing poor health, with 87 percent of these suffering from some form of chronic illness" (Hyde 1978, 21). Resources such as rural hospitals are being curtailed with increasing frequency, leaving the rural resident with little access to health care treatment centers that are nearby. This results in either postponing necessary care or traveling great distances in order to secure it—often beyond the means of the patients or their families to manage.

Although most rural areas have emergency medical services (EMS), these services are not prepared to handle life-threatening diseases or severe traumatic injuries. In addition, the recruitment of doctors, nurses, and other health care professionals for practice in rural areas has been relatively unsuccessful. For instance, as of 1988 one Texas county consisting of over 960 square miles with a rural population of over 6,000 had only one medical doctor, with the closest hospital forty miles away. Solutions to rural health problems are difficult to achieve, but the health needs of rural residents must become a priority for policymakers. The 1989 Omnibus Health Care Rescue Act (H.B. 18) was designed to provide some relief in the form of additional health care resources, although even with its implementation, major gaps in service continue to exist. Some of the more recent health care concerns such as AIDS create even more demand on rural health resources. A recent California study reported "409 cases of AIDS in the rural areas, and 588 cases in eleven cities," thus dispelling any myths that AIDS is a manifestly urban phenomenon (Wooten 1989). The demands on rural health providers will continue to escalate while resources to meet the needs are limited.

Poverty

Lower incomes and erratic employment opportunities contribute to higher rates of poverty and disease in rural areas. Among the rural population, which comprises slightly more than 26 percent of the total U.S. population, the poverty level is slightly higher than 38 percent—a percentage that has increased over the past decade (Watkins and Watkins 1984). Numerically, whites "constitute a majority of the rural poor, but persons of minority status are overrepresented: about 41% of all rural Blacks and 26% of all rural Hispanics live in poverty" (Uhr and Evanson 1984, 5). The rural poor tend to work primarily at menial jobs; however, their ability to achieve higher-paying jobs is affected by the fact that they are less well educated. The income-earning capacity of the rural poor is also affected by seasonal employment, illness, and injury (Morrissey 1985).

The majority of the rural poor are engaged in crop harvesting, which is often unpredictable, pays poor wages, and often requires that families move from place to place to secure employment. Although many of these families no longer travel great distances to harvest crops, they are generally referred to as migrant workers.

As mentioned earlier, the children of these workers, like their parents, receive less education than their counterparts who live in urban areas. Disease rates and higher infant mortality rates reflect the substandard conditions under which the majority live. Small-town school systems, already strained for financial resources, are not diligent in enforcing mandatory school attendance laws. As a result, many children are not encouraged to pursue an education and, instead, work alongside their parents to help the family make enough income to survive. Consequently, a vicious cycle is set in motion, perpetuating intergenerational patterns of farm laborers who are poor and lack the necessary resources to break out of poverty.

Rural communities are also more segregated than urban areas. Morrison (1976) reports that racial segregation, limited political participation, and impoverishment continue to characterize the plight of minorities in rural communities. Attempts to organize farm labor and implement civil rights legislation have met with only limited success due, primarily, to the resistance of large landowners and commercial farmers who seek to maintain the status quo and exert sufficient power to assure that reform does not occur. In states that border Mexico, such as Texas, New Mexico, Arizona, and California, the many undocumented aliens are often viewed negatively, because they are seen as compounding problems in the farm labor market through their willingness to work for lower wages. However, experience has shown that they do jobs that otherwise go unfilled or that otherwise would not be filled. Since most undocumented aliens are concerned with being detected by federal immigration officials (and returned to Mexico), they are vulnerable to exploitation by landowners who seek cheap labor. The recent decline in the value of the peso has further exacerbated the problem and prompted large numbers of undocumented aliens to cross the border to seek work and better living conditions.

Poor white farm workers experience many of the same problems. Typically less educated than urban whites, they are viewed stereotypically as people with less incentive and motivation to succeed. Limited resources and skill levels keep them on the farm. Illiteracy rates are higher and poverty more pervasive among rural whites than urban whites. When rural whites do migrate to cities, they are relegated to low-paying jobs and often experience considerable difficulty in becoming assimilated into the urban environment.

Perhaps the conditions of the poor are best described in an article by Colby (1987), who cites an anonymous poor rural resident:

> *Poverty is dirt. You say in your clean clothes coming from a clean house, "Anybody can be clean." Let me explain housekeeping with no money. For breakfast I give my children grits with oleo, or cornbread with no eggs or oleo. . . . What dishes there are, I wash in cold water with no soap. . . . Look at my hands, so cracked and red. . . . Why not hot water? Hot water is a luxury. Fuel costs money. . . . Poverty is . . . remembering quitting school in junior high because "nice" children had been so cruel about my clothes and my smell. . . . Poverty is a chisel that chips on honor until honor is worn away.*[9,10]

The problems of the rural poor are compounded by the lack of community support services—public water and sewage, fire and police protection, transportation, employment opportunities, and related services (Bedics 1987).

SOCIAL WELFARE IN RURAL COMMUNITIES

There are many more small communities and towns in the United States than cities or major metropolitan areas. These communities vary in size and in their proximity to major metropolitan areas. For example, Tilden, Texas, a county-seat town of approximately 350 residents, is situated in a county that covers approximately 1,400 square miles. It is the largest town in the county. What type of organized social welfare programs would one find in this community? What is needed? To what extent could the community support social welfare services?

The reader should be wary about generalizations concerning the nature and extent of organized social welfare programs in small towns and rural areas, because they vary greatly in size, nature, and ability to finance needed services. Many rural areas have very few services, and those available tend to be basic ones. Typically, public welfare services, mental health and mental retardation outreach centers, and public health services are found in rural areas, although they usually are minimally staffed, offer only limited assistance, and often may be reached only by a drive of several hundred miles. It is not unusual for counties to offer a limited welfare assistance program and for county administrative officials (usually the county judge) to administer benefits, along with their other duties. A few rural communities have Community Action Agencies (a residual of the War on Poverty programs), although attempts to organize rural areas, in general, have been unsuccessful (Morrison 1976). Senior citizens' luncheon programs may be provided by a branch of an areawide agency on aging. Employment agencies, family planning services, and family counseling agencies and related services are not typically found in rural areas. Ginsberg (1976, pp. 7–8) suggests some innovative changes that would increase the service capacity to meet the needs of rural populations:

1. *The public, basic services must often expand their activities to include functions that they might not carry in cities. For example, a public welfare office might be charged with much more responsibility for family counseling, community development, and social welfare planning simply because it exists, is staffed with knowledgeable people, and needs to help meet problems that occur, despite the absence of agencies. Similarly, a community mental health program may be required to carry some youth services activities that its urban counterparts would leave to other agencies.*

2. *Many activities are voluntary and depend, therefore, on the good will and interest of their supporters rather than upon full-time professional staff. This is particularly true of social welfare planning efforts, which are often the result of social welfare professionals working together without additional compensation to create and sustain a structure for coordination and planning. Some direct service and community development activities are conducted in a similar manner.*

3. *Although formal structures may not exist, many informal services are offered in rural communities. In fact, it is the nature of communities, both*

rural and metropolitan, to develop services for overcoming human problems. For example, the functions carried by Travelers' Aid agencies in large cities may be performed in rural communities by the police or the sheriff's office. A single individual may carry out a program serving children. Churches may assume responsibility for everything from food baskets to family counseling. It is important for social workers in all communities to understand the nature of the service delivery system. In rural America that structure may be hard to identify because of its informal nature.

4. *Some formal agencies in rural areas may carry expanded functions. Youth-serving programs such as 4-H, the Boy Scouts, Girl Scouts, and Campfire Girls may be the only resource for activities that in a larger area would be handled by the YMCA, YWCA, and other programs.*

5. *The importance of individuals and families in serving social welfare needs should not be overlooked. As has already been suggested, one public spirited woman may function almost as effectively as an agency or office. Knowing about such people and gaining their assistance is crucial for the rural worker.*

6. *Perhaps most important is the fact that some formal organizations exist in rural areas that are important but different from those one finds in urban settings. The best example is probably the cooperative extension services, which are sponsored by each state (along with Department of Agriculture standards and funds), usually under the supervision of state land-grant universities. The traditional function of such programs is to provide consultation on agricultural activities to farmers and ranchers as well as home-making information to rural women. However, they have expanded their functions dramatically, with many cooperative extension programs now heavily committed to community improvement and development programs in areas as diverse as housing, drug abuse treatment, and social welfare planning. Working with such organizations, which are most prominent in rural areas, is essential for the rural worker.*

As suggested earlier, public social services are generally extended to rural areas through the auspices of state agencies. For example, state mental health/mental retardation programs generally have satellite offices in rural areas that are implemented through regional offices, as do state departments of human services which offer public assistance programs. Regional Education Service Centers provide resource assistance for rural schools.

In general, however, organized social welfare services in rural areas are not as well developed, well organized, or efficiently staffed as those that serve urban populations. Additional resources must be developed in rural areas if services equivalent to those in urban areas are to exist. In the past decade, efforts have been made to update and improve rural social services. Projects such as the Great Plains Staff Training and Development for Rural Mental Health in Nebraska, the information and advocacy efforts of the NARMH, and the caucus of national rural social workers and rural human service workers are all active in promoting higher levels and quality of service in rural areas.

SOCIAL WORK IN RURAL SETTINGS

The practice of social work in rural communities is both similar and different from that practiced in urban areas. The core of knowledge, methods, and skills of social work practice undergirds practice in both environments. The nature of rural settings, the problems experienced, discussed earlier, and the lack of resources converge to confront the social worker with a unique set of challenges. Creativity and the ability to innovate and influence community members to mobilize in meeting needs are crucial skills for successful practice in rural settings. Bruxton states:

> No other environment compares with rural practice in carrying out the dictum of the "total individual" in the "total environment." The rural social worker by her- or himself must often provide the rural dweller with services, support, and hope while simultaneously helping to change the environment in order to provide better transportation, increased medical care, and a more responsive community (1976, 32).

Unlike urban social workers, the worker in a rural area may feel frustrated by the absence of fellow professionals and a social service network. Opportunities for consultation and feedback are limited, so decision making is often difficult and problematic.

Social workers who both live and practice in rural areas find that they are seen as neighbors as well as professional practitioners. Almost everyone in the community knows who they are, and they may be called on at home as well as the office to provide a wide range of services. Their service constituency may consist of children, adults, the mentally ill, the incarcerated, the bedridden, the distressed, and the abandoned (Bruxton 1976). At any one time, the worker may be assisting a family in securing a nursing home placement for an older parent, securing resources for a disabled child, counseling with a pregnant teenager and her family, collaborating with local ministers in developing leisure-time activities for youth, assisting school personnel in developing management techniques for a hyperactive child, or working with the court in securing re-habilitation resources for a delinquent child. These varied demands require that the worker be flexible, have good communication skills, engage both private and public resources, and have a basic understanding of community values and practices.

As Fenby (1978) suggests, practicing social work in a rural setting subjects the worker to a life in a "gold-fish bowl." Everyone tends to know the worker both professionally and personally. The private life of the worker is closely scrutinized. Since workers, like other community people, have problems, the way they are managed becomes a matter of community concern. Like ministers, the worker is expected to meet high personal and moral standards, and any deviation may lower community esteem. In rural communities, the ability to separate personal life from professional competence is difficult. Often, the credibility of the worker is at stake should personal problems go unresolved.

Maintaining client confidentiality is difficult. Neighbors may become clients. Community residents typically know when problems are being experienced and when professional assistance has been sought. A casual encounter at the grocery store may prompt a resident to inquire as to how a client is progressing. As Fenby has indicated:

> At times a client will be open about his or her knowledge. "I hear you had oil burner problems this morning and Art sent his truck out." At times there is a

subtle change in the therapy hour, and the therapist cannot discount the fact that information from the "outside" is affecting the interaction "inside." For example, a client who had been working well in therapy became evasive and distant, although nothing discernible had caused the change. Probing uncovered that the woman had discovered that my husband was on a yearly contract at the college, and had surmised that therefore I would not be staying in the area. She thought that therapy would end in failure, uncompleted. In a small world it is essential to be aware of contamination from outside information in the process of the therapy (1978, 162).

Social workers who have periodic assignments in the rural area but do not reside there encounter other problems. Typically, they are viewed as outsiders. In some instances, they have not had the opportunity to become aware of community priorities and values. Often, they are viewed as having little vested interest in the community and, as a result, respond to special client problems out of context. Community resistance may become an additional barrier to problem solving. Sensitivity to the importance of interpersonal relationships with community leaders is essential in gaining support for change efforts.

An old social work axiom suggests that "change comes slow." While this premise is open to debate, it is valid in rural social work practice. Timetables and the pace of life tend to be slower. Urgency is offset by practicality and patience. Waiting matters out may be given more credence than intervention. Workers must learn to stifle their frustration and impatience, yet retain their persistent efforts in the helping process. As the credibility and competence of the worker become more established, community resistance will turn into support, and the contribution made to the community as a problem solver will become enhanced.

RURAL SOCIAL WORK AS GENERALIST PRACTICE

By now it should be apparent to the reader that the variety and diversity of the tasks inherent in rural social work practice can best be accomplished by the generalist practitioner. Workers in rural communities are called on to work with individuals, families, and groups, and in community organization. Administrative and management skills are essential in rendering needed services (see Box 11-1). The abilities to define problems operationally, collect and analyze data, and translate findings into practical solutions are requisites for enriched practice. The rural practitioner is a multimethod worker who appropriately facilitates in the problem-solving process. Knowledge of resources, resource development, methods of linking clients with resources, and case management is required of the rural social worker. Other essential requirements for generalist social work practice are discussed in Chapter 1.

THE BACCALAUREATE SOCIAL WORKER
AND RURAL SOCIAL WORK PRACTICE

Social work in rural communities is both challenging and rewarding. Self-reliance and the ability to work apart from social work support systems are attributes that rural social workers must have in order to function effectively. Many un-

Box 11–1   Some Characteristics of Effective Rural Social Workers

1. They are especially skillful in working with a variety of helping persons who are not social workers or who may not be related to the profession of social work, as well as with peers and colleagues.

2. They are able to carry out careful study, analysis, and other methods of inquiry in order to understand the community in which they find themselves.

3. They utilize their knowledge of the customs, traditions, heritage and contemporary culture of the rural people with whom they are working to provide services to the people with special awareness and sensitivity.

4. They are able to identify and mobilize a broad range of resources which are applicable to problem resolution in rural areas. These include existing and potential resources on the local, state, regional and federal levels.

5. They are able to assist communities in developing new resources or ways in which already existing resources may be better or more fully utilized to benefit the rural community.

6. They are able to identify with and practice in accordance with the values of the profession and grow in their ability and effectiveness as professional social workers in situations and settings where they may be the only professional social worker.

7. They are able to identify and analyze the strengths and/or gaps and shortcomings in governmental and nongovernmental social policies as they affect the needs of people in rural areas.

8. They accept their professional responsibility to develop appropriate measures to promote more responsiveness to the needs of people in rural areas from governmental and nongovernmental organizations.

9. They are able to help identify and create new and different helping roles in order to respond to the needs and problems of rural communities.

10. They initiate and provide technical assistance to rural governing bodies and other organized groups in rural communities.

11. They are able to practice as generalists, carrying out a wide range of roles, to solve a wide range of problems of individuals and groups as well as of the larger community.

12. They are able to communicate and interact appropriately with people in the rural community, and adapt their personal life-style to the professional tasks to be done.

13. They are able to evaluate their own professional performance.

14. They are able to work within an agency or organization and plan for and initiate change in agency policy and practice when such change is indicated.

15. On the basis of continuous careful observation, they contribute knowledge about effective practice in rural areas.

Source: Statement on "Educational Assumptions for Rural Social Work" by Southern Regional Education Board, Manpower Education and Training Project Rural Task Force, Atlanta, Georgia.

dergraduate social work programs are located in small cities or large towns adjacent to rural areas and specialize in rural social work practice. Field placements typically utilize rural agencies to familiarize students with skills essential for practice in those settings.

The baccalaureate social worker's generalist practice perspective will prove invaluable in working with rural populations. The opportunity to engage existing formal and informal organizations in extending or developing resources to meet community needs is a continuing challenge the BSW worker can address competently. The worker also will find that individuals and families in rural areas often have problems and need assistance in problem solving. The knowledge and expertise of the worker in problem identification, outreach, linking of target systems with resources, resource development, education, and problem solving help enrich the lives of rural inhabitants as well as strengthen community support systems. The abilities to understand community value systems and to experiment with innovative techniques in working with community residents are essential assets for productive practice.

Until recently, social workers have not been inclined to engage in rural social work practice. Fortunately, this attitude is changing. Job opportunities in rural communities are increasing, and the potential for a satisfying and rewarding career in rural social work practice is greater now than ever before.

SUMMARY

In this chapter we reviewed some of the characteristics that typify rural community life in America, identified the more salient problems that rural residents experience, examined the social organization of rural communities, and presented an overview of the more typical social support networks in rural areas. The methods and functions of social work practice in rural areas have been presented, and the role of the generalist practitioner outlined. Rural social work is a setting ideally suited for the baccalaureate social worker. Job opportunities are increasing, and the challenges for a successful career in providing needed services for rural communities are attracting social workers in greater numbers into rural areas.

KEY TERMS

farm crisis   U.S. Department of Agriculture
rural

DISCUSSION QUESTIONS

1. What problems are involved in defining rural populations?
2. Identify the major "activity" centers in rural communities. Who appears to be among the more significant power brokers in rural areas?
3. Describe the types of problems that are more likely to be found in rural areas. What type of informal network exists to assist with these problems?

4. What types of formal welfare services generally are found in rural areas? How do these services interact with other community resources?

5. What types of services will the social worker more likely be offering in rural areas? What problems will be encountered? Indicate the skills essential in rural social work practice.

6. What roles would the BSW social worker play in rural areas?

REFERENCES

Bedics, Bonnie. 1987. The history and context of rural poverty. *Human Services in the Rural Environment* 11(1): 12–14.

Bruxton, Edward B. 1976. Delivering social services in rural areas. *Social work in rural communities: A book of readings,* ed., Leon H. Ginsberg. 29–38. New York: Council on Social Work Education.

Colby, Ira. 1987. The bottom line: a personal account of poverty. (Anonymous author). *Human Services in the Rural Environment.* 11:1, 9–11.

Farley, O. William, Kenneth A. Griffiths, Rex Skidmore, and Milton G. Thackery. 1982. *Rural social work practice.* New York: Free Press.

Fenby, Barbara L. 1978. Social work in a rural setting. *Social Work* 23(2): 162–63.

Ginsberg, Leon H. 1976. An overview of social work education for rural areas. In *Social work in rural communities: A book of readings,* ed. Leon H. Ginsberg. 6–8. New York: Council on Social Work Education.

Hyde, Henry. 1978. Rural development: What's coming—What's needed. *Human Services in the Rural Environment.* Madison: Center for Social Service, Univ. of Wisconsin.

Jennings, Mary. 1990. Community mobilization. Presentation made to the National Association of Rural Mental Health Workers, Lubbock, Texas.

Mental health services not meeting needs of rural residents. *Rural Health Reporter,* (Fall): Austin, Tex.: Texas Rural Communities, Inc.

Morrissey, E. S. 1985. Characteristics of poverty in nonmetro counties. Department of Agriculture Rural Development Research Report 52. Washington, D.C.: GPO.

Morrison, Jim. 1976. Community organization in rural areas. In *Social work in rural communities: A book of readings,* ed. Leon H. Ginsberg. 57–61. New York: Council on Social Work Education.

Murray, J. Dennis. 1990. Written testimony submitted to the Regional Field Hearing on Mental Illness in Rural America, 12 April.

Watkins, J. M. and Watkins, D. A. 1984. *Social policy and rural settings.* New York: Springer.

Wooten, Donald B. 1989. AIDS in rural California. *Human Services in the Rural Environment* 13(1): 30–33.

Uhr, E. and E. Evanson. 1984. Poverty in the United States: Where do we stand now? *Focus* 7(1): 13.

U.S. Department of Agriculture and U.S. Census Bureau. 1988. Rural and rural farm population: 1988. *Current population reports,* ser. P-20, no. 439. Washington, D.C.: GPO.

SUGGESTED FURTHER READINGS

Clark, Frank, Jon Bertsch, and Edward V. Bates. 1980. Informal helping in a rural boom town. *Human Service in the Rural Environment* 5 (May–June): 19–24.

Martinez-Brawley, Emilia E. 1981. *Seven decades of rural social work.* New York: Praeger.

Martinez-Brawley, Emilia E. 1982. *Rural social and community work in the U.S. and Britain.* New York: Praeger.

Munson, Carlton E. 1980. Urban–rural differences: Implications for education and training. *Journal of Education for Social Work* 16 (Winter): 95–103.

Summers, Anne, Joe M. Schriver, Paul Sundet, and Roland Meinert, eds. 1987. *Social work in rural areas.* Batesville: Arkansas College.

Weber, Gwen K. 1976. Preparing social workers for practice in rural social systems. *Journal of Education for Social Work* 12 (Fall): 110–11.

Whitaker, William H., ed. 1985. *Social work in rural areas.* Proceedings of the Ninth National/Second International Institute on Social Work in Rural Areas. Orono: University of Maine.

Old Age: Issues, Problems, and Services

James Johnson is a seventy-eight-year-old widower who lives alone in the suburbs of a large northeastern city. He has an unmarried daughter who lives near him and a married son who lives in Seattle, Washington. Neighbors have recently been complaining that James's yard has become unkempt and that they do not see him for long periods of time. Recently, a complaint was made against James that resulted in a visit from an adult protective services worker. The worker noted that James's house was filthy, dishes were strewn around the kitchen, garbage had accumulated, and James's personal appearance reflected a lack of personal care. The worker also noted that James

had sores on his hands and face that were not being treated.

The worker contacted James's daughter, who stated that she had attempted to convince her father that he needed to secure placement in a protective environment, such as a nursing home. James refused, indicating that he was doing fine and strongly emphasized that he wished to remain in his own home. Neighbors also were pressuring the protective services worker to have James committed to a long-term-care facility. A final decision has not been made; however, James has secured an attorney to fight attempts to have him placed in a protective setting.

Fortunately, most older adults do not have problems like those experienced by James Johnson; however, far too many must contend with similar experiences. The majority of older adults experience a general sense of satisfaction, accomplishment, and contentment. Others must struggle to survive, which limits their ability to enjoy life. Although older adults are often thought to be very much alike, there is as much variation among the old as there is between the young and the old.

Today the number of people reaching old age is much greater. Life expectancy has increased dramatically since the early 1900s, when only 3 out of every 100 Americans were 65 years of age or over. By 1980, 10 out of every 100 were 65 or over. By the year 2030, 16 out of every 100 will have reached the age of 65 years. On the average, each day of every year results in another 1,700 persons who reach their sixty-fifth birthdays! At no time in recorded history have as many older adults populated a society as is the case in America today. Not only are more individuals reaching age 65; they are also living longer (see Table 12–1). In 1987 the average life expectancy was 75 years, with more and more individuals living into their eighties and nineties. Some experts suggest that we should talk about two groups of elderly, the "old" and the "old-old." Increasingly, older individuals in their sixties are caring for their own parents in their eighties and nineties.

While living a long life is a goal to which most of us aspire, the consequences to society have the potential of being catastrophic. Assuring that essential resources are available to meet the needs of the older population places a heavy burden on government and private resources, including families. More and more, middle-aged Americans are becoming the "sandwich generation," having to provide for their children while they also are providing for their elderly parents. However, many families cannot provide such support, especially when major health problems occur, and many elderly people do not have families available to provide even emotional support. Thus, there is an increasing reliance on federal and state government to provide for such needs. For example, it is estimated that one-fourth of the federal government's expenditures is allocated to meeting the needs of the older population. With continually increasing numbers of older adults in our society, even larger government allocations will be necessary in the future (see Figure 12–1).

In this chapter, we examine the more salient issues and problems an older population creates for society, review their problems of adaptation, and identify resources that have been developed to provide physical and social support systems designed to meet their needs.

PHYSIOLOGICAL AGING

Readers of this book are very much aware of physical changes they have experienced in their lives. The process of change through growth and physical maturation is not fixed but continues throughout the life cycle. During midlife

Table 12–1   Population by Age: 1960–2080 (in thousands)

Year	65 & Over	85 & Over	100 & Over
1990	31,559	3,254	56
1995	33,764	3,912	76
2000	34,882	4,622	100
2010	37,162	5,321	144
2020	48,212	5,397	186
2040	58,835	9,165	228
2080	49,532	9,796	438

Age ranges in the table represent overlapping categories; the figure for those aged 65 and over includes those 85 and over and 100 and over. The figure for those aged 85 and over includes those aged 100 and over.

Source: U.S. census of population, 1988–2080; and Projections of the population of the United States, by age, sex and race, 1989. *Current Population Reports,* ser. P-25, no. 1018, (Washington, D.C.: GPO, 1990).

Figure 12–1 Population 55 Years and Over by Age: 1900–2050

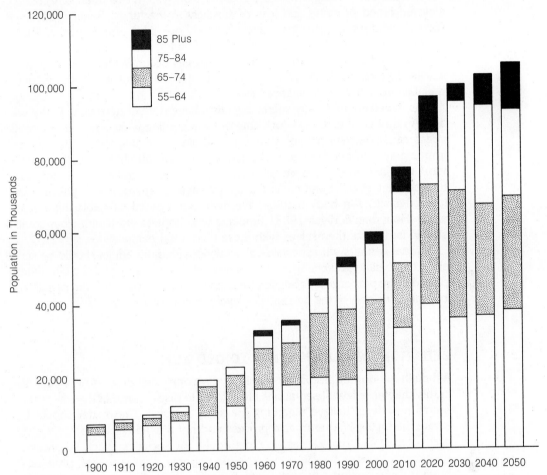

Source: U.S. census of population, 1890–1980, and Projections of the population of the United States: 1983–2080. GPO, 1985. *Current Population Reports,* ser. P-25, middle series (Washington, D.C.: GPO, 1985).

(around the age of forty-five) we go through a stage of physical change that is called senescence. Senescence is generally defined as the onset of the degenerative process. It is at this stage that adults develop an awareness of significant bodily changes—the graying or loss of hair, wrinkling of the skin, a slowing down of the pace, and an awareness that old age will soon be a reality.

Old age may be accompanied by sensory losses. Visual acuity may decrease, and bifocals may became necessary. Hearing problems may increase, and many older adults need hearing aids. In very late life, tactile (touch) and olfactory (taste) senses may lose their fine-tuning. These changes do not, of course, happen at any particular age, nor do they affect the aged to the same degree. Losses may be minor and hardly detectable in some but be major dysfunctions in others. Unless sensory losses are profound, they seldom limit the older adult's ability for social interaction and maintenance of a normal and fulfilling life style. Even when more serious sensory debilities exist, proper prosthetic supports often allow the older person to maintain a normal life.

Although sensory losses are noticeable, even more significant changes occur internally. Changes in the cardiovascular system are often reflected in elevated blood pressure and loss of elasticity in the lungs. Renal capacity is reduced, and the bladder loses approximately one-third of its capacity. There is a loss of brain weight as well as muscular strength. Estrogen and testosterone levels are reduced, and other hormonal changes occur. With the exception of disease factors, however, none of these changes reduce older adults' ability to maintain an active, well-balanced life.

As incredible as it may seem, scientists have not yet determined why we age. A number of theories—including those regarding wear and tear (external stress causes organisms to wear out), autoimmune responses (organism's immune system becomes less effective in throwing off challenges to the system), cellular (cells are reduced in number as well as the ability of the organism to replicate lost cells) and cross-linkage (changes in collagen with subsequent loss of elasticity in body tissue)—have been put forward as viable theories of aging (Hooyman & Kiyak 1988). Students who hope to work with older adults should familiarize themselves with these theoretical perspectives.

Social workers who specialize in working with older adults should be sensitive to physiological changes that are normal processes of growing old. When placed in the proper perspective, these changes should not be viewed negatively but rather as part of the normal life-development continuum.

BEHAVIOR AND ADAPTATION TO OLD AGE

Although we do not discuss in detail the developmental processes of later life in this chapter, a few observations are offered to dispel some of the myths that many individuals believe regarding the aging process. The reader should be aware that **aging** is a normative process and not a fixed dimension of the life cycle. Young children age, as do older adults. All societies attach significance to various stages of the life cycle. Aging is not only a chronological process; it has symbolic meaning as well (Karp & Yoels 1982). Cultures determine, for example, the age at which their members should enter school, marry, begin careers, enter the military, have children, become grandparents, and retire. Norms for behavior are prescribed at various developmental stages of the life cycle. Old age has been viewed too often as a period of dramatic decline. Thus, older adults are expected to be less active, need fewer resources, contribute less to society, and become more content and serene.

Scientific data buttress many of the symbolic definitions assigned to old age. Physiological changes, including the loss of muscular strength, sensory losses, and reduced lung elasticity, are but a few of the measurable differences between older adults and the young. On the other hand, many of the presumed losses associated with cognitive functioning have been demonstrated to have little substance in fact. Intelligence and intellectual functioning, once thought to decline appreciably in old age, are not measurably affected by the process. Behavior in old age is an individual matter and not attributable to the aging process alone. Any accurate assessment of adaptation in late life must take into consideration the effects of the environment on behavior, as well as the physiological and cognitive characteristics present within the behavioral context.

In recent years, several theories of aging have emerged that seek to explain or describe adaptation in late life. Among the more prominent ones are disengagement theory (Cumming & Henry 1961), activity theory (Havighurst 1968), exchange theory (Dowd 1975), and developmental theory (Kimmel 1974). *Disengagement theory* assumes that biological degeneration and social withdrawal are coterminous and functional for the individual and society. This theory contends that as older adults decline physically, they have less need and desire for social interaction and progressively become "disengaged" from social roles. However, more penetrating analysis reveals that it is societal discrimination against older adults that limits the social contexts (and thus opportunities) for social interaction. Social barriers, such as mandatory retirement, constrain the opportunities for participation in society. For some this means limited income resources and fewer friendship networks.

Exchange theory attributes social withdrawal of the aged to a loss of power. Having once exchanged their expertise for wages, the aged must comply with mandatory retirement in exchange for pensions, Social Security payments, and Medicare. Thus, the power advantage has shifted from them as individuals to society (Dowd 1975). The effect of this power loss results in withdrawal from meaningful social interaction and greater dependence on those holding power over them.

Developmental theory emphasizes positive adaptation and life satisfactions based on mastering new tasks as the individual moves through the life cycle, including old age. Life-span development is viewed as a normal process that encompasses new challenges, new tasks, and flexibility in incorporating changes into the repertoire of behaviors. Older adults must accept the physiological changes they experience, reconstruct their physical and psychological life accordingly, and integrate values that validate their worth as older adults (Clark & Anderson 1967).

Developmental theory postulates that the psychosocial crises of late life are "integrity versus despair" and "immortality versus extinction" (Newman & Newman 1987). Integrity, according to Newman and Newman, is "not so much a quality of honesty and trustworthiness . . . as it is an ability to integrate one's sense of past history with one's present circumstances and to feel content with the outcome" (551). Despair suggests that the opposite of integrity will occur, that is, the inability to integrate past history with the present or to achieve contentment with the outcome. Confrontation with the psychosocial crisis of immortality versus extinction occurs in very late life. Immortality refers to the extension of one's life through one's children, contributions to social institutions, spirituality, and positive influences one has had on others. Extinction suggests the lack of connectedness and attachment and the "fear that death brings nothingness" (Newman & Newman 1987, 588–89).

Activity theory "implies that social activity is the essence of life for all people of all ages," who must maintain adequate levels of activity if they are to age successfully (Barrow 1986, 72). Presumably, more active older adults will achieve greater satisfactions and thus age more adaptively. Activity theory has provided the basis for a number of programs developed for older adults, such as the Retired Seniors Volunteer program (RSVP), Senior Luncheon programs, the Foster Grandparents program, the Green Thumb program, and activity programs in nursing homes.

Society's role in creating the behavioral and value context for older adults must be examined in order to gain insights into the problems and issues implicit in understanding adaptation in later life. As the French writer Simone de Beauvoir has indicated in *The Coming of Age*:

> Society cares for the individual insofar as he is productive. The young know this. Their anxiety as they enter in upon social life matches the anguish of the old as they are excluded from it. Between the two ages, the problems lie hidden by routine. . . . Once we have understood what the state of the aged really is, we cannot satisfy ourselves with calling for a more generous "old-age policy," higher pensions, decent housing and organized leisure. It is the whole system and our claim cannot be otherwise than radical—change life itself. (1971, 807)

Our society stresses productivity and distributes varying degrees of rewards and power in relation to it. Retirement serves to disengage older adults from socially recognized productive efforts. Instead of being consumers of products from their own current productive efforts, older adults are forced to be consumers of the products from the efforts of others. As we now turn our attention to the problems and issues confronting older adults, the reader should keep in mind that there are no simple solutions to problems. Casework with older adults who have problems may bring some relief to those individuals helped, but it does not address the causes of those problems. Changing the social systems that produce the problems is a more tenable solution, albeit more difficult.

ATTITUDES TOWARD GROWING OLD

Negative attitudes toward the aged are among many of the harsh realities one faces in old age. Although there has been a pronounced positive shift in attitudes toward aging in recent years, negative attitudes persist (Butler & Lewis 1977). Our society often has been characterized by its emphasis on youth and productivity. Independence is stressed and is enabled by financial supports gained through employment. Retirement often drastically reduces available income and may contribute to dependency. As a result, older adults are often viewed as being of less value to society.

Negative attitudes also are expressed through the process of exclusion. Media, for example, have avoided the use of older adults in television commercials, while advertisements in newspapers and magazines use younger persons to convey messages. Until recently, older adults, when used in film or advertising, were portrayed as dependent, irascible, or sickly. Fortunately, there is evidence that the media are beginning to present a more accurate portrayal of older adults.

Collectively, many societal practices have reinforced negativism toward old age. Many of these practices, such as mandatory retirement, have supported the idea that older adults are less capable of making contributions through work and to society. Various rules and regulations governing employment limit the opportunity for them to make such contributions. The discrimination or differential treatment based on age alone is called **ageism.** Like other forms of discrimination, ageism is institutionalized and, as a result, is often subtle. Individuals are often unaware that they reinforce it through their attitudes and practices. Unfortunately, negative attitudes toward older adults may be expressed by professional practitioners as well as the general public. Riley (1968) identifies nurses, medical doctors, attorneys, the clergy, and social workers, among others, as giving preference to younger individuals as clientele.

Negative attitudes toward older adults often result in the loss of social status, with the accompanying diminished self-concept. Also, real-life issues further compound the problem. For example, as adults grow older, they invariably lose significant others through death, and they must deal with their own physical decline, which may limit activities and opportunities for mobility. Although the majority of older adults are independent and experience high levels of life satisfaction, these changes (or losses) invariably affect their quality of life.

As we review other problem areas experienced by older adults, the reader should keep in mind that attitudes, although not always directly linked with behavior, tend to shape our priorities and practices. Viewing the older population as "excess baggage" is not the bedrock upon which positive responses to the needs of older adults will be achieved.

RETIREMENT

The impact of retirement on human behavior continues to be a topic of major interest. Although retirement often has been viewed as synonymous with old age, that scarcely is the case in our society today. Data indicate that more and more Americans are electing to retire at earlier ages while, on the other hand, many older citizens continue to work either full- or part-time in the labor force. This mixture of age and work (either full- or part-time) clouds our ability to arrive at a precise definition, or line of demarcation, that clearly separates those among us who are retired from those who are not. When, for example, is an individual considered to be retired? Is the military "retiree" receiving a full retirement pension from the military, yet working full-time in a civil service position, considered retired? Or the seventy-two-year-old person receiving full Social Security benefits from the federal government who works full-time as a court bailiff? And what about the sixty-nine-year-old housewife receiving Supplemental Security Income (public assistance for the aged)? Certainly, many other examples would further muddy the already murky waters of the definitional dilemma.

As a result, researchers use operational definitions that seldom are accepted universally. Some view individuals as retired if they receive a pension from their employer for past work performed, regardless of their present work status. Others identify retirees as those individuals who receive retirement pension benefits that exceed any monies earned through present work, and many identify a person in retired status who receives a pension and works half-time or less. Obviously, the retiree living on a pension and not working presents us with far fewer definitional problems. There is agreement that the retired status is achieved only in relation to benefits earned through employment of one type or another (Atchley 1985).

Although it is difficult, primarily due to the definitional problems just described, to ascertain how many individuals are added to the retirement pool each year, it must be large, although 45 percent of those age sixty-five and over continue to participate in the labor force (U.S. Department of Labor 1985). For many retirees, income resources often are reduced drastically upon retirement. Few would disagree that the quality of life is related to available spendable income, and that for many retired individuals meeting basic survival needs is often difficult. Luxurious life-styles and world cruises often portrayed in magazines targeted for the retired "over-fifty" population and sponsored by associations such as the American Association of Retired Persons are options available only to a relatively small percentage of retirees. Understandably, many retirees remain concerned about the stability of the Social Security system, which, incidentally, has been the catalyst for retirement on a grand scale. As Riley and Foner (1968) indicate, finances are important in the relationship between age and attitudes toward retirement.

Income, of course, is not the only factor affecting positive adjustment to retirement. Health is a matter of great importance and concern. As the retired population grows older, good health becomes more problematic. Few survive beyond their seventies without some debilitating health problem, such as arthritis, high blood pressure, poor digestion, or related problems. For most, such problems do not severely restrict mobility or daily activities. For others with more severe conditions, the role of patient tends to eclipse preferred retirement activities. Concerns over meeting medical expenses, or anticipated expenses, may lead to conservative spending patterns that, in turn, reduce options and activities. Most older adults rely primarily on Medicare, a federal health insurance program available to individuals sixty-five and older. For the retiree in poor health, health-related problems may diminish satisfactions in the world away from work.

Future-oriented retirees who have developed interests and activities also seem to achieve greater gratification. It is accepted, generally, that preretirement programs have been successful in promoting greater satisfaction and adjustment in retirement. Unfortunately, such programs are still rather novel, although they seem to be growing in popularity.

The need for research on retirement continues to be crucial. Although social scientists have made great strides in the last several decades, the potential value of retirement-related research becomes more manifest as the number of retirees in this country grows. From past efforts, we have developed an emerging body of knowledge and understanding of the effects of retirement on individuals. Obviously, there is much more to learn. Appropriate and valid social policies must be undergirded with a sound knowledge base.

In the past decade considerable emphasis has been given to preparation for retirement. So-called preretirement planning is based on the notion that people who prepare adequately for retirement adjust better to the life-style changes that accompany it. Many major corporations as well as public agencies have developed preretirement training programs for their employees. These programs usually emphasize estate planning; forecasting of income; identification of federal, state, and private resources for older adults; and strategies for dealing with such issues as relocating, living alone, and planning for leisure-time activities. Although there is no compelling evidence that participation in preretirement planning positively affects adaptation to retirement, there is a mounting consensus that it does. Logic alone would suggest that life changes can best be successfully managed when adequate preparation has been made.

Retirement is emerging as a desirable goal for more Americans as it becomes more commonplace and publicly accepted. Our attention will now be directed in more detail toward the social and adaptive issues related to growing old in our society.

OLDER ADULTS AND THEIR FAMILIES

Facts refute the myth that older adults are abandoned by their families, because family members continue to be the primary source of emotional support and, in times of illness, care for their elderly members (Shanas 1979). Less than 5 percent of the older population is without family members. As Table 12–2 illustrates, the majority of older men are married, but the majority of older women are widowed. As women grow older (seventy-five and up), the likelihood increases that they will become widows and must rely more on family members other than their spouse. Most older married couples express general satisfaction with their marriage and the mutual emotional support that it brings. The majority have adult children with whom they maintain contact. Few older adults live with their children—and most do not want to, preferring instead to remain as independent as possible. Grandchildren also play important roles such as companionship, emotionally gratifying interaction, visitations, reducing loneliness and often caretaking responsibilities.

If older adults become debilitated with health problems, they often turn to their adult children for support. As a consequence, adult children may find the situation stressful, particularly because of the increased time demands. Middle-aged children of older adults have the responsibility of providing physical and emotional support to their own children while also providing support for their parents. Because of this dilemma middle-aged people have been called the "sandwich generation." This strain may push these middle-aged children to their emotional and physical limits. With older adults living longer, they may need familial support for a number of years. Although most families manage the demands adequately, the potential for intergenerational conflict is ever present.

Table 12–2 Marital Status of Older Adults

Marital Status	Percentages for Ages 65–74		Percentages for Age 75+	
	Male	Female	Male	Female
Single	5	5	4	6
Married, spouse present	80	49	67	23
Married, spouse absent	2	2	3	1
Widowed	9	39	24	67
Divorced	4	5	2	3

Source: U.S. Bureau of the Census, Current Population Survey, March 1984.

Families continue to be a viable resource for older adults, providing both comfort and identity. Although research continues to provide inconclusive findings about the overall quality of intergenerational relationships, it does suggest that most older people maintain regular contact with their family members, who are the primary source of assistance when needed.

DYING AND DEATH

Obviously, death can occur at any point in the life cycle; however, death rates increase significantly among those aged fifty or older. (See Table 12–5.) Death in late life generally results from disease rather than accidents.

Every culture shapes attitudes toward death as well as life. Our society tends to overemphasize a rational view of death as a natural, but highly individualized, event. Most of us are not engaged with the dying and consequently have little experience that prepares us for our own death or the death of significant others. Therefore, most people are uncomfortable with the dying and are apprehensive about their own death. In the 1970s Elizabeth Kübler-Ross (1975) laid the groundwork for helping dying persons come to grips with the remaining part of their lives. In recent years, social workers and other professionals have provided assistance for the dying and their families through the **hospice** movement. Hospices are "dedicated to helping individuals who are beyond the curative power of medicine to remain in familiar environments that minimize pain, and to maintain personal dignity and control over the dying process (Hooyman & Kiyak 1988, 451). The hospice movement originated in England, and the first U.S. hospice was established in Connecticut in the 1970s. The movement has grown rapidly since that time, and now hospices are located in major cities as well some rural areas. Social workers who work with older adults will invariably work with the dying. Through the application of their skills, social workers can help individuals and families handle interpersonal losses and protect the dignity and integrity of the dying person.

AGING AND MENTAL HEALTH

The state of mental health among older adults is not appreciably different from that of the population in general. Unfortunately, adaptive problems such as disorientation, memory loss, excessive dependency, and senility are assumed to be inherent to the aging process. The pervasiveness of these myths results in the view that older adults, in general, experience mental health problems. Just as individuals in other stages of the life cycle, older adults may experience problems of a mental nature that result in dysfunction. And, as with younger people, these problems generally are responsive to treatment. In some instances, these adaptive problems have been present throughout the life cycle. Other individuals have managed to function adequately and do not develop mental health problems until late in life, often as a result of interpersonal loss, organic deterioration, or some traumatic event. On the other hand, activity and future orientation appear to be associated with good mental health. Maintaining enthusiasm and working toward goals are antithetical to the development of dysfunctional behavior.

Problems experienced in old age also may be analyzed using a systems/ecological perspective. The way that an individual interacts within the environment strongly influences that individual's mental health. Many of the symptoms of dysfunctional behavior that appear in old age may be attributable to environmental factors. Social isolation and loneliness often appear to produce maladaptive behaviors. Overmedication often results in memory loss, disorientation, loss of vigor, or loss of appetite. Depression, one of the more common mental health problems in late life, may be caused by bereavement, anxiety related to income security, a limited social friendship network, health concerns, relocation, and related factors. Ageism and lack of attention to problems of the elderly have led to increased concern about this group's high suicide rate (Figure 12–2). In 1985, 25 percent of all suicides within the United States were among the over 65 population.

Alzheimer's disease has emerged as one of the more publicized types of organic brain syndromes in later life. Given the nature of the disease, it is difficult to ascertain precisely the extent to which it occurs in the older population; however, it is estimated that 2 percent to 4 percent of adults over sixty-

Figure 12–2 Suicide Rates in the United States by Age, Gender, and Race, 1974

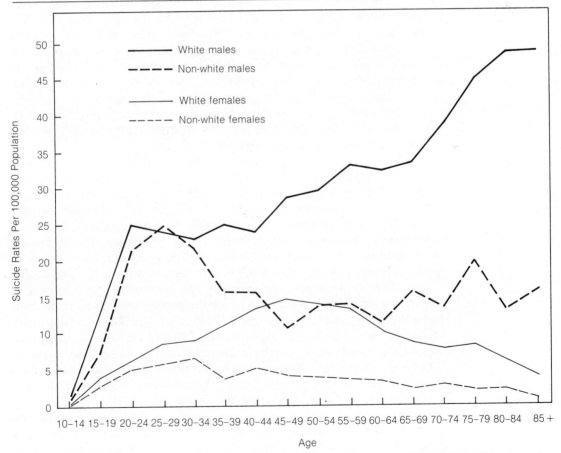

Original Source: National Center for Health Statistics. As it appears in Marv Miller, *Suicide after Sixty: The Final Original Alternative*, p. 4. Copyright 1979 by Marv Miller.

five may have this disease (American Psychiatric Association 1987). Alzheimer's is typically an insidious progressive disease that results in increasing maladaptation. Disorientation, memory loss, wandering, and inappropriate (and often bizarre) behavior are among the symptoms. In the later stages the person requires total care, including feeding, bathing, and all routine maintenance activities. Alzheimer's disease imposes heavy demands on family members, who are the primary caretakers in the initial stages. Both physical and emotional demands related to caring for a disabled loved one increase as the disease progresses. Alzheimer's support groups have been formed in many communities to provide emotional support for caregivers as well as an opportunity to share ideas related to effective techniques in caring for the person.

Dramatic changes in the mental health of individuals are seldom caused by the aging process alone. Individuals possessing well-integrated personalities who prepare themselves for changes related to retirement, develop leisure-time interests, and plan for the future are less vulnerable to age-related stress factors.

INCOME SECURITY

Justifiably, one of the more persistent anxieties experienced by older adults relates to income security. Inflation, with its effect on the price of commodities, has increasingly limited buying power. With few exceptions, income available to individuals after retirement is well below that they received when employed. For many, retirement income is only half of what they received while on the job (Schulz 1980). Few of our present-day older people earned sufficient incomes to have been able to put away money for retirement. Retirement incentive plans such as IRAs, tax-deferred annuities, and Keogh plans were nonexistent during the time of their employment. As a result, the majority of retirees are forced to live on Social Security payments.

Social Security was never intended to be a complete retirement income plan. It was designed to supplement pension plans provided by the individual's employer. Yet today, 75 percent of retired elderly persons have only Social Security to meet their financial needs (Barrow & Smith 1983). A smaller number receive Supplemental Security Income (public financial assistance for the elderly) benefits that average only $300 per month. Slightly less than 50 percent of the aged have an income of less than $10,000 per year. Many live at or below the governmentally established poverty level (see Table 12–3 and Table 12–4). Older single women, for example, had an average yearly income of $5,905 in 1986—only a few dollars above the poverty level. Older single men had a slightly higher average income—$7,580. Older families with heads over 65 had an annual income of approximately $10,140 per year. As these data suggest, older single women are by far the most jeopardized by limited incomes. With the passing of time, inflation will further reduce the buying power of the nation's aged even though Social Security benefits are periodically adjusted to correspond with increases in the consumer price index (CPI).

While money does not always produce happiness, it is related to satisfaction in later life. The common myth that older adults need less income to meet their living needs is hardly buttressed by fact. The need for food, clothing, shelter,

Table 12–3 Percentage of the Aged below the Poverty Line and below 125 Percent of the Poverty Line, 1986

Income	White Married	White Nonmarried Men	White Nonmarried Women	Black Married	Black Nonmarried Men	Black Nonmarried Women
Below Poverty Line	5	13	19	18	35	43
Below 125% of Poverty Line	9	23	32	29	55	57

Note: Categories in the table are divided into race, marital status, and gender. In 1986, the poverty line was $6,630 for a two-person unit aged 65 or older and $5,255 for one person aged 65 or older.

Source: Adapted from Susan Grad, "Income of the Population 55 and Older, 1986," SSA publication no. 13–11871, Table 54 (Washington, D.C.: U.S. Department of Health and Human Services, 1988).

recreation, transportation, and the ability to buy gifts for grandchildren and family members does not decline with age. Lowered standards of living, unmet needs, and the inability to adequately meet these needs may result in feelings of inadequacy and loss of self-esteem.

Income is an enabling resource and affects the options available in life. As income declines so do those options, including the loss of independence.

Recent debates concerning the future of Social Security payments have raised the concern of many citizens. In responding to the increasing federal deficits, the Bush administration favors taxing Social Security benefits along with other income-producing resources such as private pension payments, investments, and earnings. Should Congress pass the measure, it is conceivable that, with higher levels of non-Social Security income benefits, a potential beneficiary would receive little or no Social Security benefits at all! Should these taxing measures become law, it is possible that a worker would (because of a higher aggregate income) in effect receive no Social Security benefits even though contributions to that system were made throughout the work cycle.

Table 12–4 Total Median Income by Age, Gender, Race, and Marital Status, 1986

	White Married	White Nonmarried Men	White Nonmarried Women	Black Married	Black Nonmarried Men	Black Nonmarried Women
Median Income	$19,600	9,270	7,290	11,310	5,890	4,520

Source: Adapted from Susan Grad, "Income of the Population 55 and Older, 1986," SSA publication no. 13–11871, Table 15 (Washington, D.C.: U.S. Department of Health and Human Services, 1988).

Various health and social service resources that have emerged to assist older adults with their needs might not be necessary if retirement income benefits were sufficient to enable the nonworking aged to meet their needs at the marketplace. The United States lags behind other industrialized nations in replacement (retirement) income for its aged, ranking fourth in payments to couples and eighth in income benefits for the single older adult (Wilson 1984).

HEALTH AND HEALTH CARE SERVICES

In later life the probability of developing health problems becomes more pronounced. Unfortunately, this condition has led many observers to conclude that aging and poor health are synonymous. Such is not the case, if one considers that health problems in old age are treatable and correctable, just as they are at earlier stages in the life cycle. Older adults are more prone to develop illnesses such as pneumonia, influenza, and gastrointestinal complaints than the population in general (see Table 12–5). Also, chronic disease, including heart disease, hypertension, cancer, arthritis, diabetes, emphysema, osteoporosis, and visual impairments are more common in old age (Whitney 1976).

Only 5 percent of the older adult population is affected by health problems so severe that their mobility is limited. The majority are able to move about the community even though they may have one or more disease symptoms.

Health care resources are provided primarily through Medicare and Medicaid. **Medicare** is a government health insurance program designed to pay for hospital care and related medical expenses for persons over sixty-five. Because of the costs of medical care, the amount of benefits paid by Medicare has decreased to approximately 50 percent of the total cost of the care. The inability of older adults to pay the portion of medical fees not covered by Medicare has resulted in large numbers not seeking necessary medical attention.

Both Medicare and **Medicaid** (health insurance for the poor) have made it possible for many older adults to obtain needed medical treatment. Due to personal cost-related factors, however, many older adults often are forced to delay seeking treatment until health conditions become severe or life-threatening. Neither of these

Table 12–5 Death Rates for the Leading Causes of Death for Ages 65 and over by Age, 1986 (deaths per 100,000 population)

Cause of Death by Rank	65–74 years	75–84 years	85 years
1. Diseases of the heart	1,043	2,637.5	7,178.7
2. Malignant neoplasms	847	1,287.3	1,612
3. Cerebrovascular diseases	164.1	573.8	1,762.8
4. Arteriosclerosis	149.2	294.8	362.9
5. Influenza and pneumonia	58.6	242.8	1,032.1
6. Diabetes mellitus	59.2	121.9	213.9
7. Accidents	49.0	106.3	252.2

Source: National Center for Health Statistics, "Vital Statistics of the United States," annual. 1987.

Many communities have established home health care programs where social workers and other professionals provide companionship, medical care, and positive support.

health insurance programs is designed to provide funding for preventive health care. Doubtless, many serious health problems could be averted or become less problematic if attention were given to preventive health measures.

As with other government-funded benefit programs, Medicare and Medicaid funds rapidly are approaching deficit spending levels. Various solutions to the financing of health care have been proposed. These include a reduction of benefits, more stringent eligibility requirements, and an expansion of government coverage for catastrophic cases. Solutions to financing must be found if the health needs of our older population are to be met.

ABUSE AND NEGLECT

Because of limited research, little is known about the form and pervasiveness of abuse and neglect of the elderly. Neglect is the failure to perform the needed activities or tasks essential for meeting one's daily needs. Abuse is a physical or psychological act intended to inflict harm. As is the case with battered children or spouses, the knowledge that old persons are the victims of abuse and neglect is antithetical to our social morality.

Self-neglect is perhaps the most common. Many older adults lack the necessary resources or skills to provide adequate nutrition or to maintain daily household living tasks, such as washing dishes, cleaning the house, and securing proper health services. Self-neglect is more frequent when older persons are socially isolated and have little involvement with family or friends. Caretakers, usually family members, also may be involved in the neglect of elderly people's physical and emotional needs. Neglect often occurs when an older adult lives with a son or daughter and is dependent. Ignoring daily and special needs, denying transportation, failing to include aged persons as members of family households, ignoring their desires to contribute, and providing improper clothing and diet are among the more common forms of neglect of the aged.

Like neglect, abuse usually occurs when the older adult is living with a relative. Abusers often are overtaxed mentally and emotionally and lash out when demands are made on them by older family members. Physical abuse takes the form of slapping, shoving, punching, or placing the older adults in restraints. Psychological or emotional abuse results from threats (of sending the older adults to nursing homes, etc.), ignoring, ridiculing, taking their Social Security or other income and giving them no spending money, cursing, and reminding them that they are a burden.

It is estimated that 10 percent of the older population experiences abuse or neglect. The rates may actually be higher, since many victims are reluctant to report experiences for fear of retaliation or placement in a nursing home. Many states have enacted legislation to protect older adults from abuse and neglect. Family violence is an unfortunate and dehumanizing product of our society that generally is directed toward those dependent on others for some aspect of their care. Protective services are designed to shield victims from further harm. Unfortunately, such services do little to alleviate the causes of the problem.

NURSING HOME CARE

Most older Americans enjoy reasonably good health, with only 5 percent experiencing health problems so debilitating that they require nursing home care. The contemporary nursing home industry has emerged primarily as a result of Medicare and Medicaid legislation, which allows third-party payments to the providers of health care services. Nursing homes typically are licensed by state health departments, which have the responsibility of periodically reviewing the homes to ensure that minimal standards of care are maintained. In addition, all states require that administrators of homes be licensed, although there is considerable variation in administrator-licensing requirements among the states.

Nursing homes often are portrayed as dehumanizing warehouses, where little concern and attention are directed toward the needs of residents. In recent years, more stringent state standards and skillful investigation and evaluation techniques by regulatory agencies have resulted in the provision of high-quality services. Many nursing homes provide excellent patient care and extend special efforts to meet the psychosocial needs of their residents. Other homes are skilled in the delivery of medically related services but lack the foresight, knowledge, and skill to address the psychological and emotional needs of their patients.

The majority of nursing homes in this country are proprietary, that is, they are private profit-making businesses. Some homes are nonprofit and are usually operated through the auspices of religious organizations or units of state or local governments. There appears to be little difference in the quality of care between the private profit-making homes and nonprofit ones. Privately owned facilities are more vulnerable to "shaving" services in order to maximize profit. Strict enforcement of standards, however, minimizes any significant differences in the services provided for residents.

Nursing homes will continue to be the most viable resource for the debilitated elderly. Alternatives such as home health care, visiting nurses, and personal care homes enable the older adult to reside in the community for a longer period of time but tend to defer, not replace, the need for nursing home care (see Figure 12–3). As the need for additional nursing home beds increases (400,000 more by the year 2000), financing the needed care will become more critical. Government financing plans are strained already; and should forecasted budget reductions become a reality, alternative financing or other more cost-effective plans must be developed to assure that the debilitated elderly receive essential health care services. In a number of communities, churches, unions, and private profit organizations are developing residential facilities for the elderly.

Figure 12–3 Who Pays Nursing Home Bills?

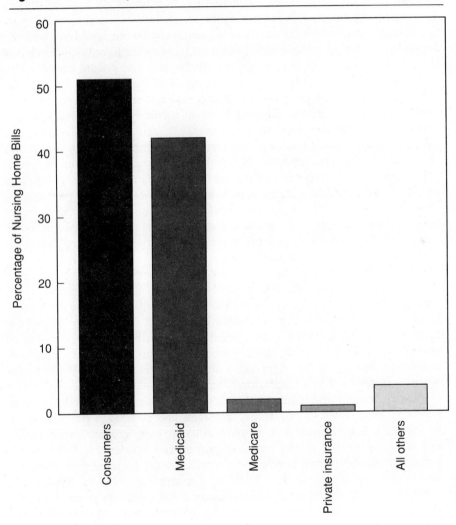

Source: Health Care Financing Administration records

HOUSING AND TRANSPORTATION

Although the majority of older adults are homeowners, housing often is a major concern for them. The rate of substandard homes among the elderly exceeds those for other age groups. Many of their houses become dilapidated over the years, and in later life the ability of older adults to maintain or repair them is often limited by low incomes. In addition, older adults find it very difficult to secure home repair loans. They must be content with progressively deteriorating housing, which often results in inadequate protection from the heat, cold, and other threatening climatic conditions.

Government housing for the aged typically is difficult to secure because of the high demand for low-cost housing units. Even when available, low-cost housing often appears unattractive, impersonal, lacking in privacy, and too noisy. The advantages include low rent, security, and adequate protection from weather extremes. More units are needed for older adults but are not likely to be forthcoming due to government budgetary limits.

Housing alternatives for the more economically secure aged have recently expanded. High-rise, self-contained apartment complexes have been developed through the auspices of both religious organizations and private sponsorship. These facilities are typically attractive, provide all of the amenities for comfortable living, and assure peer interaction and essential social supports. Many of these facilities also provide differing levels of medical care, nursing services, and meals, should individuals become unable to care for themselves in their own apartments. Such facilities, however, are much more costly, and many require substantial down payments before an individual is accepted as a resident. Although housing communes are not abundant, they are growing in popularity and provide a family-type living experience for older participants. This type of housing arrangement develops when several older adults pool their resources to rent or purchase a dwelling and share in its upkeep. Basic living costs for such things as food and utilities are shared, thus enabling each participant to spend less on basic living needs.

Transportation is essential for grocery shopping, attending church services, keeping appointments with doctors and dentists, visiting friends, and maintaining contact with the family. Most older adults must travel some distance in order to procure the necessities for daily living, but it often is very difficult for them to do so. Many who once owned an automobile find the hazards of driving and the cost of vehicle maintenance and insurance beyond their capacity to manage. As a result, they depend on alternate sources of travel. Public transit systems usually are not satisfactory. Bus routes typically are developed for employed workers who regularly use this type of conveyance. Scheduling often results in long walks to bus stops, transfers, and prolonged riding time. In addition, it is extremely difficult for older adults to carry grocery bags onto the bus and walk several blocks from the stop to their residences. A few transit systems have developed specialized services for the handicapped and aged and operate on a door-to-door basis by appointment. Few are available to serve the elderly on an on-call basis. Users must anticipate needs (often as long as two weeks in advance), make the appointment, and hope that they are not forgotten.

Volunteers have been engaged in providing transportation services for the elderly in some communities. Although only a small minority who need such services are able to get them, this option has enabled many older adults to gain mobility for securing needed goods and services. Nutrition programs also have provided transportation to luncheon programs, and some have been able to extend their transportation services to include shopping and social visits. This type of transportation alternative is available only to a comparatively few older adults in need.

The absence of transportation has resulted in many older adults becoming home-bound. Often the result is social isolation, which leads to the loss of incentive, decreased activity, self-deprecation, and eventually psychological and physical deterioration, thus confirming the stereotype that older adults elect not to participate in the mainstream of life.

Unfortunately, little has been accomplished in addressing transportation needs of the aged. Indeed, government budget cuts have significantly reduced transportation programs designed for the elderly in many communities. The reader might ask this question: How do we expect older adults to be independent, shop for themselves, attend meetings, and remain engaged with societal institutions if they lack the transportation resources to do so? Such is the case for many of our aged today.

MINORITY GROUP MEMBERS AS OLDER ADULTS

The problems of adaptation discussed earlier in this chapter are also experienced by older minority group members, but to a much greater extent. Life expectancy for both blacks and Hispanics is appreciably less than for whites (see Table 12–6). Approximately 7 percent of the blacks and 4 percent of the Hispanics are sixty-five or over, compared with 11 percent of the total U.S. population (Watson 1982). Since neither genetics nor heredity has been a factor contributing to a shorter life expectancy for these groups, social and cultural factors are more likely to account for this differential in longevity. As a result of social discrimination, larger proportions of minority populations experience lower incomes, more physically menial and demanding work, and fewer opportunities to achieve essential life-support services. This has resulted in more severe and unattended health problems, inadequate nutrition, fewer opportunities for social advancement, near-poverty wages, and an oppressive cultural environment. Growing old under these adverse conditions has to be difficult. Fortunately, there is some evidence that the social climate is changing and that the opportunity structure in which minorities may compete is becoming more equitable. If such is the case, we can expect to see the life expectancy rates for blacks and Hispanics become more like those of whites.

While retirement income benefits for all older adults are relatively low, they are even less for the minority aged (see Table 12–7). For example, in 1983 the percentage of aged white families living below the poverty level was 6.6 percent, compared to 24.3 percent for aged blacks and 15.5 percent for aged Hispanics. The percentage of white women family heads living below the poverty level was 7.0 percent, compared with 26.4 percent for black women family

Table 12–6 Population 55 Years and Over by Race, 1984 (in thousands)

	Total		White		Black and Other	
	Number	Percent	Number	Percent	Number	Percent
Percent Distribution of Racial Groups by Age:						
All ages	236,416	100	201,555	100	34,861	100
0 to 54	186,220	79	156,420	78	29,809	85
55 to 64	22,210	9	19,805	10	2,400	7
65 to 74	16,596	7	14,959	7	1,637	5
75 to 84	8,793	4	7,981	4	812	2
55 plus	50,195	21	45,136	22	5,509	16
65 plus	27,985	12	25,331	13	2,654	8
85 plus	2,596	1	2,391	2	205	0.1
Percent Distribution of Age Groups by Race:						
All ages	236,416	100	201,555	85	34,861	15
0 to 54	186,220	100	156,420	84	29,809	16
55 to 64	22,210	100	19,805	89	2,400	11
65 to 74	16,596	100	14,959	90	1,637	10
75 to 84	8,793	100	7,981	91	812	9
55 plus	50,195	100	45,136	90	5,059	10
65 plus	27,985	100	25,331	91	2,654	9
85 plus	2,596	100	2,391	92	205	8

Note: Percentages may not add to 100 due to rounding.
Source: U.S. Bureau of the Census. Projections of the population of the United States, by age, sex and race, 1983–2080, ser. P-25, no. 925 (Washington, D.C.: GPO, 1985).

heads. The data are even more revealing when comparing white and black men living alone (18.5 percent and 45.0 percent, respectively). For aged white women living alone, the percentage was 24.5 percent, compared with 63.4 percent for their black counterparts (Grad 1988). Accurate income data for aged Hispanics are more difficult to ascertain, but all estimates are that the percentage living below the poverty line is somewhat less than that for blacks.

Many of the necessary support services often are not available to aged minority members because of discrimination, language differences, lack of information concerning eligibility requirements, limited entitlement, pride, and less-than-vigorous outreach services. Unfortunately, for many elderly minority group members poverty, limited options, and discrimination mean that they cannot attain the security, contentment, and life satisfaction that most other older Americans do.

SERVICES FOR OLDER ADULTS

In recent years a wide array of social, health, and related support services have either been developed or extended to provide for the needs of the aged. On

Table 12–7 Number and Percent of Elderly Living in Poverty by Race, Gender, and
Living Arrangement, 1983

Race and Gender	Living Arrangement					
	Number (thousands)			Percent		
	In Families	*Unrelated Individuals*	*Total Number*	*In Families*	*Unrelated Individuals*	*Total Percent*
White:						
Male	496	298	794	6.1	18.5	8.2
Female	552	1,507	2,059	7.0	24.5	14.7
Total	1,048	1,805	2,853	6.6	23.3	12.0
Black:						
Male	142	105	247	21.9	45.0	28.3
Female	204	340	544	26.4	63.4	41.7
Total	346	445	791	24.3	58.4	36.3
Hispanic Origin:						
Male	38	22	60	17.7	(1)	22.4
Female	35	53	88	13.7	45.7	23.7
Total	73	75	148	15.5	43.7	23.1
All Races:						
Male	656	412	1,072	7.4	22.1	10.0
Female	771	1,861	2.640	8.8	27.7	17.0
Total	1,427	2,273	3,711	8.1	26.5	14.1

Source: Bureau of the Census. Characteristics of the population below the poverty level: 1983. *Current Population Reports*, ser. P–60, no. 147, Table 3 (Washington, D.C.: GPO, 1984).

the federal level, the majority of these programs have their legislative base in either the Social Security Act or the Older Americans Act. Social Security Act programs cover both income maintenance through social insurance and Supplemental Security Income and health services through either Medicare or Medicaid. The Older Americans Act of 1965 provides supplementary services through funding of nutrition programs, transportation, social services, and the coordination of services for the aged.

Through both governmentally and privately sponsored sources, such older-citizen participation programs as Foster Grandparents, Green Thumb, and the Retired Seniors Volunteer program, as well as a variety of self-help programs, have been developed within the past decade. Older adults in the Foster Grandparents program, for example, are employed part-time to work with children in state schools, hospitals, and child-care centers, as well as with pregnant teenagers and with abusive and neglectful parents. Senior centers provide a site in many communities where older adults can interact, partake of nutritious meals, participate in recreational activities, and pursue hobbies or crafts. Through the auspices of the Older Americans Act, areawide agencies on aging (AAAs) have been established throughout the country that coordinate services to the aged. Among their many functions are such activities as assessing the needs of the older population, providing or contracting for congregate-meals programs, developing transportation services, serving as information and referral resources, and acting as advocates for the aged in assuring that communities will be attentive to their needs.

Meals-on-wheels programs provide hot meals for the home-bound aged and attempt to provide essential social contact with older adults who find it difficult to leave their homes because of limited mobility related to a variety of physical debilities. Adult day-care centers enable older adults to remain in the community. Often participants live with a working son or daughter who cannot provide the required daily monitoring for the older person. Day-care centers assume caretaking responsibilities during the periods when their children are away at work. These centers usually have a variety of activities and provide health checkups and supervision for participants. Mental health services are provided through mental health–mental retardation outreach centers, and counseling services usually are available to the aged and their families through many local social services agencies. Older adults living in rural areas often are disadvantaged in that many of these services are not readily available to them, although nutritional and transportation resources usually are offered.

Although community services are helpful in meeting the needs of many older adults, they are not widely available in proportion to the numbers in the community that could potentially benefit from them. Outreach efforts have been reasonably successful in securing participation; however, resources are limited and funding levels limit the number that can be served. Often, agencies are not located strategically, and therefore the participation of many older adults is limited. Also, outreach efforts would be more effective if older adults could be employed as care providers (Stewart et al. 1972).

The need for support services for the aged will continue to grow with the expansion of our older population. New funding sources must be developed to accommodate this growing need. Social, health, and related services are essential in promoting the well-being of the older population.

SOCIAL WORK WITH OLDER ADULTS

In recent years, social work practice with the aged has intensified. In 1982 the Bureau of Labor Statistics estimated that 700,000 new jobs would be available in services to the elderly by the year 2000 ("Growth Industries of the Future" 1982). Gerontologists expect most of these jobs to require skills at the BSW social work level or below (McCaslin 1985). Many schools of social work have developed specializations in **gerontology** (the scientific study of aging, the aging process, and the aged), and social work research has focused on problems of adaptation and life satisfactions in old age. As a result, research and literature on this topic have developed rapidly, and a beginning knowledge base for intervention is being established. It is now recognized that older adults experience many of the same problems evident at other stages of the life cycle: personal adjustment problems, marital problems, relocation, family conflict, adjustment to separation and loneliness, anxiety over limited income, mental illness, and interpersonal loss, among others. Growing along with this recognition is the acknowledgement that the aged are responsive to social work change efforts.

Direct practice is the most common form of social work intervention with the aged. This type of practice includes working with older adults and their families on specific problems, such as enhancing personal adjustment, securing resources to meet their needs, providing emotional support in decision making, dealing with death and dying, and managing family conflict. Direct practice employs a counseling and guidance approach, stresses problem clarification and the development of options and priorities, and provides an opportunity for the client to express anxiety and emotion.

Community-based practice focuses on exo-level community systems as targets for creating a more responsive opportunity structure for the aged. Using an advocacy approach, the social work function is to "identify issues such as poor housing, lack of transportation, health needs, economic needs, and . . . to mobilize community resources to help bring about change through the development of resources to meet these needs" (Johnson 1983, 234).

Social workers with an older-adult clientele must be aware of the special problems they encounter. Many of the aged have been self-sustaining members of society and have developed problems of adaptation only after reaching old age. Accumulated interpersonal losses (e.g., loss of spouse, friends, familiar environment, job, income, physical health) often produce social and behavioral dysfunctioning that inhibits the achievement of life satisfactions and the fulfillment of daily living needs.

Social workers are employed currently in a variety of agencies that serve the elderly, including mental health centers, family service agencies, nursing homes, nutrition programs, recreational centers, hospitals, health and nutrition centers, volunteer programs, transportation and housing programs, protective services programs, and community planning agencies. Social work activity with older adults will continue to be intensified and interventive techniques refined as the theoretical knowledge base expands, resulting in more effective services to the ever-increasing older population in need of them.

SUMMARY

In this chapter we have examined the problems and issues related to growing old in America. As the older population continues to expand, more creative approaches to meeting their needs must be developed. Problems that must be addressed include inadequate income, ever-increasing costs of health care, housing and income inadequacies, abuse and neglect, transportation, and the growing need for services, with special attention to the needs of minority groups.

The majority of our older adults experience few problems of sufficient magnitude to deprive them of their satisfactions in later life. Far too many, however, suffer from deprivation related to limited resources and unattended health concerns. Social workers can attempt to meet this challenge through the development of more understanding, knowledge, and skill in working with older adults.

KEY TERMS

aging
ageism
gerontology

hospice
Medicaid
Medicare

DISCUSSION QUESTIONS

1. Identify at least three consequences to society because the U.S. population is growing older.
2. Contrast disengagement theory, exchange theory, developmental theory, and activity theory in describing aging.
3. What are the implications of retirement for an elderly person?
4. Why is the suicide rate for persons over sixty-five population increasing?
5. Describe at least four programs available to the elderly to help address their needs.
6. What are some jobs in the field of gerontology available for a social worker?

REFERENCES

American Psychiatric Association. 1987. *Diagnostic and statistical manual of mental disorders (DSM-III)*. Washington, D.C.: Author.

Atchley, Robert C. 1985. *Social forces and aging*. 4th ed. Belmont, Calif.: Wadsworth.

Barrow, Georgia M. 1986. *Aging, the individual, and society*. 3d ed. St. Paul, Minn.: West.

Butler, Robert N., and Myrna I. Lewis. 1977. *Aging and mental health*. 2d ed. St. Louis, MO.: Mosby.

Clark, Margaret, and Barbara Anderson. 1967. *Culture and aging*. Springfield, Ill.: Thomas.

Cumming, Elaine, and W. E. Henry. 1961. *Growing old: The process of disengagement*. New York: Basic Books.

de Beauvoir, Simone. 1971. *The coming of age*. New York: Putnam.

Dowd, James J. 1975. Engaging as exchange: A preface to theory. *Journal of Gerontology* 30 (September): 589–94.

Garvin, R. M., and Robert C. Burger. 1964. *Where they go to die: The tragedy of America's aged*. New York: Delacorte.

Grad, Susan. 1988. Income of the population 55 and over, 1986. 55A Publication no. 13-11871, Washington, D.C.: U.S. Department of Health and Human Services.

Growth industries of the future. 1982. *Newsweek* (October 18): 83.

Havighurst, R. J. 1968. A social-psychological perspective on aging. *The Gerontologist* 8 (2): 67–71.

Hooyman, Nancy R., and H. Ausman Kiyak. 1988. *Social gerontology: A multidisciplinary perspective*. Boston: Allyn & Bacon.

Johnson, H. Wayne. 1983. *The social services: An introduction*. Itasca, Ill.: Peacock.

Karp, David A., and William C. Yoels. 1982. *Experiencing the life cycle*. Springfield, Ill.: Thomas.

Kimmel, Douglas. 1974. *Adulthood and aging: An interdisciplinary developmental view*. New York: Wiley.

Kübler-Ross, Elisabeth. 1975. *Death: The final stage of growth*. Englewood Cliffs, N.J.: Prentice-Hall.

Lauderdale, M., J. Stewart, and G. Shuttlesworth. 1972. The poor and the motivation fallacy. *Social Work* (November): 38–42.

McCaslin, Rosemary. 1985. Substantive specializations in master's level social work curricula.

Newman, Barbara M., and Philip R. Newman. 1987. *Development through life: A psychosocial approach*. 4th ed. Chicago: Dorsey.

Riley, Mathilda White. 1968. *Aging and society*. New York: Russell Sage.

Riley, Mathilda White, and Anne Foner, eds. 1968. *Aging and society. Volume 1: An inventory of research findings*. New York: Russell Sage.

Schulz, J. 1980. *The Economics of aging*, 2d ed. Belmont, Calif.: Wadsworth.

Shanas, E. 1979. The family as a social support in old age. *The Gerontologist*. (April) 19:2 169–74.

Stewart, James C., Mitchell Lauderdale, and Guy E. Shuttlesworth. 1972. The poor and the motivation fallacy. *Social Work* 17 (November): 34–37.

U.S. Department of Labor. 1985. *Manpower report to the president, 1983*. Washington, D.C.

Watson, Wilbur H. 1982. *Aging and social behavior*. Monterey, Calif.: Wadsworth.

Whitney, Kevin N. 1976. Health aspects of aging. San Antonio: Trinity University.

Wilson, Albert J. E. III. 1984. *Social services for older persons*. Boston: Little, Brown.

SUGGESTED FURTHER READINGS

Beaver, Marion L., and Don Miller. 1985. *Clinical social work practice with the elderly*. Homewood, Ill.: Dorsey.

Bould, Sally, Beverly Sanborn, and Laura Reif. 1989. *Eighty-five plus: The oldest old*. Belmont, Calif.: Wadsworth.

Burnside, Irene. 1984. *Working with the elderly: Group process and technique*. Monterey, Calif.: Wadsworth.

Foner, Anne. 1986. *Aging and old age*. Englewood Cliffs, N.J.: Prentice-Hall.

Harbert, Anita, and Leon H. Ginsberg. 1979. *Human services for older adults*. Belmont, Calif.: Wadsworth.

Huttman, Elizabeth. 1985. *Social services for the elderly*. New York: Free Press.

Lowy, Louis. 1979. *Social work with the aging*. New York: Harper & Row.

Margolis, Richard J. 1990. *Risking old age in America*. Boulder, Colo.: Westview.

Roff, Lucinda L., and Charles R. Atherton. 1989. *Promoting successful aging*. Chicago: Nelson-Hall.

Social Work:
Its Practice
and
Methodology

Social work practice and methodology are presented in this section. Chapter 13, "Direct Practice: Social Work with Individuals and Families," examines the most prevalent method in professional social work practice—intervention by the social worker with individuals and families who experience problems with social functioning. Both theories and techniques in working with individuals and families are discussed as they relate to problem-solving strategies, with the roles of both social workers and clients identified.

Chapter 14, "Direct Practice: Social Work with Groups and the Community," reviews the professional activities of social workers who use the group method in assisting client populations with a variety of problems and who work at the community level. Group theory is reviewed briefly, and a variety of groups are identified. Issues in group formulation and group process and different methods of working with groups are presented. The importance of the community in working with clients is also discussed, as well as various methods of community organization and community intervention commonly used by social workers.

Chapter 15, "Social Agency Administration," addresses the myriad of tasks essential in bringing together the resources, opportunities, roles, and objectives of the social welfare agency in its problem-solving mission. Various strategies of leadership, administration, and management are reviewed as requisites for increasing the efficiency and effectiveness of the agency's activities.

Finally, Chapter 16, "Research and Practice," emphasizes the interdependence of social work practice and research and the use of social research as an integral part of the problem-solving process. The role of research in policy and practice is explicated to inform the reader of the need to buttress practice continually with data gained from research findings.

The chapters in this section provide the reader with an in-depth awareness of basic social work methodology and its rationale and potential effectiveness in assisting individuals, groups, organizations, and communities with problems.

Chapter 13

Direct Practice: Social Work with Individuals and Families

After twelve years of marriage, Marilyn's husband, Jeff, left her, filed for divorce, and married a younger woman, leaving two children, Timmy, age seven, and Rachel, age four, to the care and custody of Marilyn. To complicate matters, Marilyn recently lost her job at the local savings and loan association, which closed. Without a job and with only minimal child support payments, Marilyn was finding it difficult to make home mortgage payments, meet household expenses, and purchase necessary food items. Marilyn was also very lonely and depressed. Her concerns over being the sole caretaker for the children, securing a well-paying job, and maintaining the home had created new demands, which made it more and more difficult to cope. As a consequence, Marilyn was having suicidal thoughts, sleepless nights, and increased irritability with the children.

While watching television one evening, Marilyn saw the commercial sponsored by the local Family Service Association, a United Way agency. The following morning she called the agency and was given an appointment with Arlene Rankins, a direct practice social worker. Since their initial contact, Arlene has been seeing Marilyn each week, and periodically meets with Marilyn and her children in a group session. Marilyn has been able to talk about her situation and her feelings, and, with Arlene's assistance, she has established some goals regarding employment and single-parenting. With Arlene's encouragement, Marilyn has also joined a group that is composed of members who, just like Marilyn, are learning to cope with the task of restructuring their lives as single parents.

The society and world in which we live are characterized by rapid transition, change, and uncertainty. The technological revolution has contributed to sweeping modifications of life-styles, increased mobility, and shifting values. As the capacity to create new products has increased, the shifting job market has required new skills and more adaptable employees. Relationships among individuals have become tenuous and short-lived. As a result, a sense of roots in the community is becoming increasingly more difficult to achieve. Family life has been affected by social and job-related pressures and upward mobility. The pursuit of success has conflicted with long-cherished values regarding the sanctity of family-first goals. These changes, which began in the 1960s, have given rise to an emphasis on individuation and happiness as contrasted with strong family commitments. Broken families have become commonplace as marriages are being terminated with ever-increasing frequency.

Emotionally disturbed children, the illicit use of drugs by both adults and children, an increasing burden of caring for older adults, and two-career marriages have created demands on individuals and families that often leave them disrupted, confused, tense, and frustrated.

These and many other social pressures generated by our rapidly changing society are experienced by virtually all of us at one time or another. It is neither an unusual response nor a sign of weakness for individuals and families in stressful situations to seek professional help with the hope of alleviating stress and its **dysfunctional** consequences. All of us have needed the steady guidance of a respected friend or professional at some time. When problems become increasingly stressful and self-help efforts fail to produce solutions, professional assistance may be needed. *Direct practice social work*, as defined in Chapter 1, is a method of providing that assistance.

Direct practice with individuals, families, and groups is the oldest social work practice method (traditionally referred to as casework, as noted in Chapter 1). As we indicated in Chapter 2, it had its formal developmental roots in the Charity Organization Society Movement, when "scientific charity" was emphasized and the need for trained professional workers became a fundamental prerequisite to a more studied approach in working with client populations. The distinguishing characteristic of **direct practice** (as contrasted with other social work methods) is its face-to-face involvement with individuals, families, and small groups in helping them seek solutions to perplexing problems. In this chapter we examine the components and characteristics of the direct practice methods used with individuals and families. Direct practice with groups is explored in the next chapter.

DIRECT PRACTICE: A DEFINITION

A social work direct practitioner assists clients in a change process that focuses on producing a higher level of social functioning. Direct practice is both a process and a method. As a process, it involves a more or less orderly sequence of progressive stages in engaging the client in activities and actions that promote the achievement of agreed-upon therapeutic goals. As a method, it entails the creative use of techniques and knowledge that guide intervention activities designed by the direct practitioner. Direct practice also is an art that utilizes scientific knowledge about human behavior and the skillful use of relationships to enable the client to activate or develop interpersonal and, if necessary, community resources to achieve a more positive balance with his or her environment (Bowers 1949). Direct practice seeks to improve, restore, maintain, or enhance the client's social functioning (Boehm 1959). The key converging elements in direct practice are that it

1. is an art—that is, it involves a skill that results from experience or training;

2. involves the application of knowledge about human behavior;

3. is based on client involvement in developing options designed to resolve problems;

4. emphasizes the use of the client's resources (psychological and physical) as well as those extant in the community in the problem-solving process;

5. is based on an orderly helping process;

6. is based on planned change efforts; and

7. focuses on problem solutions.

Although the basis for direct practice was grounded in the philosophy and wisdom of early social work pioneers such as Mary Richmond, Gordon Hamilton, Helen Harris Perlman, Florence Hollis, and others, many changes in practice have occurred over the years. As greater knowledge of human development, ecology, economics, organizational behavior, stress management, social change, and more effective intervention techniques have emerged, direct practice has been enriched and offers a more scientifically buttressed model for intervention. The face-to-face relationship between the social worker and the client has maintained its integrity as a fundamental prerequisite for intervention, as has the emphasis on process (study, assessment, intervention objectives, intervention, evaluation, and follow-up). Democratic decision making and the belief in the dignity, worth, and value of the client system continue to undergird direct practice philosophy. The client's right to self-determination and confidentiality are fundamental practice values in the helping process. These values and practice principles form the fundamental concepts and interventive practice techniques that are identified with direct practice.

PREPARATION FOR DIRECT PRACTICE

Earlier in this chapter, we indicated that a requisite for direct practice is an understanding of factors that affect human behavior. The practitioner must not only be armed with an understanding of personality theory and a knowledge of the life cycle but must also be able to assess the effects of the environmental context within which behavior occurs. Factors such as race, gender, ethnicity, religion, social class, physical condition, occupation, family structure, health, age, income, and educational achievement are among many of the contributing variables that converge to account for behavior within different social contexts. Practitioners obviously cannot master all knowledge related to behavior, but theories allow us to make guided assumptions about behavior from which we can make logical estimates of factors associated with the client's problems. The direct practitioner is able to arrive at probable causes of dysfunction and to establish theoretically plausible interventive activities that will assist client systems in solving problems.

THE DIRECT PRACTICE PROCESS

The orderly process of direct practice consists of social study, assessment, intervention, and evaluation. Each step in this process is guided by the application of theory and knowledge of human behavior.

Many social workers function in direct practice settings. Here, family members participate in a counseling session with a social worker while a social work student observes behind a one-way mirror.

Social Study

The social study consists of obtaining relevant information about the client system and the problem (or problems) being experienced. The client's perception of the problem, its antecedents, ways the problem is affecting life satisfaction and performance, attempts at problem management, and outcome goals are important parts of the social study. The practitioner also obtains information regarding the client's ability to function in a variety of roles and collects data that enhance the practitioner's ability to initiate the process of making initial judgments about probable causes and potential actions that might lead to problem resolution. The social study responds to such questions as: Who is the client? What is the nature of the problems as the client sees and experiences them? What has the client done to alleviate the problems? How effective were the efforts? What other individuals or groups are affected by the problems, and how is the client related or associated with them? What are the client's strengths and weaknesses? How motivated is the client to work toward solutions to the problems?

Assessment

Assessment consists of making tentative judgments about the meaning of the information derived in the social study. It provides the basis for initiating and establishing intervention objectives and formally engaging the client in the intervention process. At this stage of the direct practice process, the perceived reality of the client's behaviors is filtered through the matrix of theory and understanding of human behavior to arrive at probable causes of the problems. Assessment seeks to answer such questions as: What factors are contributing to the client's problems? What is the potential for initiating a successful change?

Goal Setting

Goal setting is the process in which the client and practitioner ascertain intervention options that have the potential to relieve or solve the problem based on the client's abilities and capacities. Short-term and long-term goals are developed after reviewing all options and determining which are most appropriate for the particular client, problem, and situation.

Contracting

In contracting, the practitioner and the client agree to work toward the identified intervention goals. To facilitate and clarify the commitment implied by the contract, the role of the practitioner is identified explicitly, and the client agrees to perform tasks related to the solution of the problem. The contract makes visible the agreement both parties have reached and serves as a framework from which they may periodically assess intervention progress. Contracts may be renegotiated or altered during the course of intervention, as more viable goals become apparent. Contracts also help to maintain the focus of intervention.

Intervention

The focus of direct practice intervention is derived from the social study and assessment and sanctioned by the contract between the practitioner and client. The implementation phase of intervention focuses on the problem and may involve such activities as counseling, role playing, engaging other community resources, establishing support groups, developing resources, finding alternative-care resources, encouraging family involvement, offering play therapy, or employing related strategies. The goal of **intervention** is to assist the client toward an acceptable resolution of problems. The practitioner must skillfully involve the client throughout the intervention process by providing not only regular feedback and support but also an honest appraisal of the problem-solving efforts.

Evaluation

Clients are not likely to remain in the intervention process unless they feel some positive movement has been made toward resolving their problems. Evaluation is an ongoing process in which the practitioner and client review intervention activities and assess the impact on the client's problem situation. Both must intensively examine their behavior, with the goal of understanding the impact on intervention goals. What has changed? What has not changed? Why? How does the client view the problem at this time? Has social functioning improved? Become more dysfunctional? What is the overall level of progress? Are different interventions needed? Evaluation within this context becomes a self-, as well as a joint, assessment process. Based on the evaluation, intervention may continue along the same lines or be modified as implied by the evaluative process.

THE DIRECT PRACTICE RELATIONSHIP

Although it has been many years since Biestek (1957) outlined the components of the casework relationship, they continue to be intrinsic to the direct practice relationship. Briefly outlined, these components are as follows:

○ *Self-determinism:* Social work practitioners respect their clients' rights to make choices that affect their lives. On occasion, those choices may not appear to be in the best interests of the client; however, the role of the practitioner in such an instance would be to point out the potentially dysfunctional aspects of the choices. Of course, this does not preclude or limit the practitioner's effort to assist the client in making more appropriate choices. However, it does indicate that exerting undue influence or belittling the client is unacceptable behavior in "bringing the client around" to more appropriate choices. Social work is based on a democratic process, in which self-determinism is a fundamental part.

○ *Confidentiality:* The client's right to privacy is guarded by the principle of confidentiality. It is based on the notion that information shared between the client and practitioner is privileged. The client must not be compromised by making public the content of information disclosed in the intervention process. Confidentiality assures the client that feelings, attitudes, and statements made during intervention sessions will not be misused. This principle also commits the practitioner to using client information only for professional purposes in working with the client.

○ *Individualization and Acceptance:* Regardless of the nature of the client's problems, each client has the right to be treated as an individual with needs, desires, strengths, and weaknesses different from those of anyone else. Acceptance is the ability to recognize the dignity and value inherent in all clients, in spite of the complex array of problems that characterize their behavior.

○ *Nonjudgmental Attitude:* Recognizing that all human beings have strengths and weaknesses, experience difficult problems, make improper choices, become angry and frustrated, and often act inappropriately, the practitioner maintains a neutral attitude toward the client's behavior. To judge clients and their behaviors is to erect implicitly a barrier that may block communication with them. From the clients' perspective, judgmentalism places the caseworker in the same category as others who may be making negative judgments about them. Nonjudgmentalism does not limit the right of the caseworker to confront the client with inappropriate behaviors. It does suggest that the client should not be condemned because of them.

○ *Freedom of Expression:* The client's need to express feelings and emotions is encouraged. Often, pent-up emotions become disabling to the client and result in more problematic behaviors. The client should be encouraged to engage in free and unfettered self-expression within the safety of the direct practice relationship.

The direct practice relationship is the conduit through which assistance is extended by the worker and is received and acted upon by the client. The principles of the relationship just outlined must represent more than a catechism to be learned by the worker, if an effective helping process is to be achieved. These principles must be "experienced" by the client in interaction with the worker. As the client "tests the water" by investing energy in the problem-solving process, trust will be established only if the relationship principles are a distinctive aspect of client–worker interaction.

THE DEVELOPMENT OF PRACTICE SKILLS

The development of competency in using the direct practice method is acquired through study, role playing, and supervised practice. Since direct practice involves the application of knowledge, it is an effective method of problem solving only if employed skillfully. As in other applied professions, skill is an "art" that is enriched and refined continually through the controlled and thoughtful interaction with clients. Just as one would assume that the skill of a surgeon increases with time and experience, those same principles apply to the development of direct practice skills. We now examine some of the more significant skill areas that are essential for effective direct practice.

Conceptual Skills

The ability to understand the interrelationships of various dimensions of the client's life experiences and problem behaviors and to place them within an appropriate perspective provides a framework from which intervention goals may be established. Conceptual skills enable the worker to view the many incidents and interactions of the client not as discrete entities within themselves but as interacting parts of the client's behavioral repertoire. Without conceptual skills, social study data have little meaning, and assessment may become less accurate. Conceptual skills also involve an ability to place the client's problem within a theoretical framework and to arrive at appropriate intervention strategies directed toward problem solving.

Interviewing Skills

The interview is more than just a conversation with the client. It is a focused, goal-directed activity used to assist clients with their problems. Communication skills are essential in assuring that the interview will be productive. The practitioner must assume the responsibility for maintaining the professional purposes of the interview. Sensitivity to both the client's statements and feelings is necessary. Putting the client at ease, asking questions that enable the client to share observations and experiences, and being a sensitive listener enhance the productivity of the interview. The worker's sensitivity to the client's feelings and the ability to communicate an awareness of those feelings strengthen the helping relationship and provide encouragement and support to the client. Empathy, or the ability to "put oneself in the client's shoes," is a benchmark quality of the helping relationship. Clients who feel that the worker really understands their problems are able to feel more relaxed and hopeful that solutions will be found for them. Not all interviews are conducted for the same purpose. Zastrow (1981) identifies three types of interviews that are used to facilitate the helping process in social work. *Informational interviews* are used primarily to obtain a client history that relates to the problems currently experienced. The history-collecting process should not be concerned with all of the life experiences of the client but with only selected information that may have an impact on current social functioning. The *diagnostic* (assessment) *interview* has a more clinical focus, in that it elicits responses that clarify the client's reactions to problems and establishes some sequential ordering of events that enables the practitioner to make initial judgments about events that affect client behaviors. *Therapeutic interviews* are designed to help clients make changes in their life situations that will help alleviate their problem. Not only are the client's feelings and emotions shared in these interviews, but problem-solving options are developed and efforts at change reviewed.

Recording

Maintaining case records that provide insightful information into the client's background (social study data), judgments about the nature of the problem (assessment), and worker–client activity are essential in maintaining the focus of ongoing activities with the client. Practitioners typically carry a large caseload, with many clients over a long period of time. Properly maintained records enable the worker to review the nature of the problem, objectives, and progress in each individual case prior to appointments. In many instances, cases are transferred both within and outside of the agency, and the case record provides an up-to-date accounting of the client's problems and activities directed toward their resolution. Case records also are useful for research purposes. Properly maintained records strengthen the direct practice process. If viewed within this context, record keeping becomes less of an irrelevant chore and more of a vital tool for effective service delivery.

PRACTICE THEORY

Over the years, a number of theoretical approaches to direct practice have emerged. Practitioners have adopted various models, and many use an eclectic approach; that is, they integrate different aspects of several theories as a framework for practice. Some often find that one particular theoretical model is viable for one type of problem situation, whereas another may have greater utility in other situations. For example, a caseworker may use behavior therapy with children and ego psychology with adults. The point is that there are many different approaches to practice, each offering the practitioner a theoretical framework for intervention. A few of the more widely accepted social work treatment theories are as follows.

Systems/Ecological Framework

This framework for practice, discussed extensively in Chapter 3, is based on the observation that individuals and their environment are in continual state of interaction and that problematic behavior is the result of disequilibrium between these entities (i.e., the individual and the environment). Since people live in a constantly changing environment, adaptive skills are required in order to maintain coping abilities consonant with environmental demands. Adequate coping skills are predicated upon the abilities of individuals, families, and groups to both integrate the consequences of environmental forces into their adaptive response repertoires and to influence (and change) those environmental factors involved in creating dysfunctional stress. As Brieland, Costin, and Atherton (1985, 145) state:

> The human being and the environment shape each other. Styles of coping with stress emerge from their perceptions of environmental demands and their capabilities for response. The "ecological" model seeks a match between personal and adaptive needs and the qualities of the environment.

The systems/ecological framework focuses the social worker's attention on the interacting systems within which the client system lives, as well as providing a theoretical framework for understanding the rationale related to the system's adaptive responses. As an assessment tool, this framework enables the social worker to identify both functional and dysfunctional responses to environmental demands and stresses. Once these have been identified, the social worker can focus on the processes of social work intervention and goal setting with the client system.

Ego Psychology

Often referred to as psychosocial treatment theory, **ego psychology** stresses the interplay between the individual's internal state and the external environment. The individual's developmental experiences, fears, hostilities, failures, successes, and feelings of love and acceptance all converge to form an estimate of self through which life experiences are filtered and responded to. A main feature of this theory deals with the individual's ability to cope with external pressures and to respond in such a way as to produce satisfaction and feelings of security and self-worth. Often, internal stress results from the inability to solve problems of a mental or physical nature. Inappropriate or underdeveloped coping skills aggravate and intensify the problems, thus causing the person to become apprehensive, insecure, unwilling to risk, anxious, or in extreme cases, mentally ill.

Ego psychology also is concerned with environmental factors that affect the individual's adaptive abilities. Job loss, immobility, death, divorce, poverty, discrimination, and child-management difficulties are among many potentially stressful conditions that may overextend coping capacities. Because stress is experienced individually, practitioners must give individualized consideration to the client in the problem situation. Knowledge of stress management, personality organization, and effective coping mechanisms is essential in the assessment process. Ego psychology is an "insight" therapy. Help comes to clients through developing an awareness of their problem and their reactions to it and then learning to develop more adaptive coping skills.

Perhaps the key principle associated with using ego psychology as a treatment therapy is that of enabling the individual to develop more adaptive coping skills. The result should be the reduction of internal stress, more satisfactory role performance, and greater life satisfaction.

Problem-Solving Approach

One of the more widely used approaches in social work practice is identified as the **problem-solving approach.** This approach, developed by Perlman (1957), emphasizes that successful intervention is based on the motivation, capacity, and opportunity of the client systems for change. Recognizing that problems often immobilize the client, that the abilities of the client then are neutralized or applied inappropriately, and that opportunities for problem solutions are not engaged, this approach stresses the need to "free up" the client system so that the client can work toward solving the problem. The problem-solving approach requires that the client do more than just identify and talk about problems—although both are necessary. The client must begin to move toward taking action (within his or her capacity to do so) to resolve or alleviate the discomfort produced by those problems. Often this requires that resources (the opportunity structure) be tapped to achieve these goals. Generally, the opportunity resources include those of the agency involved in the helping process, although it may extend to other community resources.

Conceptually, the problem-solving approach is based on the premise that without motivation (or the will or desire to change), only limited progress can be made with the client. Motivation is often stymied as a result of stress experienced through dysfunctional or unresolved problems. Social workers often experience the client's doubts through statements such as "I know it will not do any good to try," "it has not worked out in the past," or "Nothing ever turns out right for me." In such instances the social worker must provide inducements that will enable the client to risk taking steps toward problem resolution, with the social worker's assistance. As successful problem solving occurs, motivation will likely increase.

In the problem-solving process the social worker must be aware of other issues, too. *Capacity* addresses the limits (or ability) of the client to change and includes physical as well as psychological characteristics. For example, a client with a sixth-grade education probably could not become an electrical engineer, but he or she could possibly attend a vocational training program and thereby develop skills that would enhance job opportunities.

Opportunity relates to possibilities within the environmental milieu in which the client interacts on a daily basis. As indicated in the preceding paragraph, a client might attend a vocational school if one is available within the client's locale. If the client had to travel fifty miles, however, transportation and finances might serve as deterrents, and the client thus might not have opportunity to participate. Optimal problem solving can only be achieved if the three components—motivation, capacity, and opportunity—are engaged in the process.

Behavior Modification

Social learning theory undergirds behavior modification therapy. Based on the assumption that all behavior (adaptive as well as maladaptive) is learned, **behavior modification** is an "action" therapy (see Box 13–1). Developmental processes that contribute to the acquisition of positive human responses also are responsible for the development of inappropriate or dysfunctional ones. Since behavior is learned, it is possible to assist the client in discarding faulty

Box 13-1 Behavior Modification

One case involved a little boy who was unwilling to go to bed alone because he claimed he was afraid of the dark. Many therapists would view such a problem as stemming from underlying dynamic causes, but a careful analysis of the situation indicated that the boy was only afraid of the dark at home. He had no fear when he stayed with his relatives. His parents' attention to the fear seemed to be maintaining it. The clinicians prescribed a simple program in which the parents agreed to play with the child, which they did not ordinarily do, each time the boy went to sleep without crying or fussing. The darkness phobia disappeared within a week.

A more complex case involved a nine-year-old boy who had been very ill in his early years. He was quite demanding and threatened to hold his breath—at times he did so until he actually passed out—if his parents did not give in. Because the parents were so frightened of causing physical damage to the boy, they always gave in to his requests. We were concerned about this physical problem and his parents' apprehension if we advised them to ignore his demands. Hence, we decided to focus on reward for changing behavior rather than extinction. Although we had no control to rule out the effects of novelty or a change in the parents' attitudes, once a point system was set up so that the boy could earn through good behavior the same sorts of things for which he had disrupted the household, the family returned to normal.

Source: Excerpted from Virginia Binder, "Behavior Modification: Operant Approaches to Therapy," in *Modern Therapies*, ed. Virginia Binder, Arnold Binder, and Bernard Rimland, © 1976, pp. 159–160. Reprinted with permission of Prentice-Hall, Englewood Cliffs, N.J.

behaviors and acquiring new and more appropriate response patterns. Recognizing that external events and internal processing result in specific behaviors, change is effected by modifying one's actions, which will result in changing thought patterns. Any attempt to change the internal process (i.e., helping the client develop insight into the problem apart from directly addressing behavior changes) is considered largely ineffective.

Based on these general principles, the practitioner using behavior modification approaches intervention with the following organizing framework:

1. In a social study, only information that is directly related to the current problem is essential for intervention. Antecedent factors are pertinent, such as when the problem began, the circumstances that contribute to the problem behavior, and the client's efforts at problem resolution.

2. Intervention must focus on specific problems, not the entire range of problems, that the client experiences. The practitioner assists clients in resolving each problem in an independent manner rather than treating them in total.

3. Although the client's "feelings" are considered an important factor, the behavioral act is the target, not intrapsychic dynamics. The practitioner assists the client in developing specific techniques and learning more

appropriate behavioral responses, as opposed to altering thought processes related to the problem and its effect. Thought processes are considered to be the results, not causes, of behaviors.

Behavior modification treats the objective, definable dimensions of human response patterns. To facilitate engaging the intervention process, the practitioner and client must agree on the problem to be addressed, contract to work on that problem, agree on the responsibility each will assume in the change effort, specify goals and objectives, discuss the techniques to be employed, and commit themselves to the treatment effort. As with other therapies, monitoring and evaluation are important dimensions of the process. As more functional and acceptable behavior evolves, it is reinforced by more adaptive functioning. Dysfunctional responses are discarded as they become less functional and rewarding for the client.

Reality Therapy

Reality therapy is based upon the assumption that individuals are responsible for their behavior. Maladaptive behavior is viewed as the product of an identity deficiency. Identity, a basic psychological need of all human beings, is successfully achieved through experiencing love and a sense of self-worth. Individuals who have been deprived of love fail to experience a sense of worth and, as a consequence, develop a poor self-concept. Change is effected by confronting clients with irresponsible behaviors and encouraging them to accept responsibility for their behavior. It is assumed that clients cannot develop a sense of self-worth while engaging in irresponsible behaviors.

Since **self-concept** is a person's internal reaction to the perception of how others see him or her, the practitioner's role in establishing a warm, friendly, accepting relationship becomes an important factor in the intervention process. As with the case of behavior modification, the focus of intervention is on the client's actions, as opposed to feelings. Confrontation with inappropriate behaviors is emphasized, as is the rejection of rationalizations (excuses). Many practitioners elect reality therapy as an intervention framework because of its straightforward application and the more informal, relaxed role of the therapist.

Family Practice

Social workers have long recognized that the family unit provides physical and emotional support for its members and shapes their identity. As mentioned in Chapter 1, socialization of the young is one of the basic tasks of the family. When problems occur, all of the family members are affected. For example, when a father loses his job, the income available for food, clothing, shelter, and family recreation becomes limited, thus altering the family's daily patterns. The father may become depressed, which affects relationships with his wife and children. Or, a teenager may experience emotional problems, have difficulty with schoolwork, and, in turn, become slovenly with home-maintenance responsibilities. Again, all family members are affected by this problem. These (and, of course, a myriad of related problems) are problems with which we can all identify. We have experienced times in our family when disruption occurred, and we have witnessed the stress and tension that resulted.

Social workers often focus on the family as a unit of intervention. Recognizing that all members of a family are affected by the problems of any one member, intervention is keyed to treating the family system. This approach recognizes that the attitudes and emotions of each family member are significant components in moving the family toward more healthy functioning. Family therapy (or intervention) does not preclude any individual member from specialized treatment. It does, however, require that all members be included in the treatment process, since everyone in a family unit both contributes to and is affected by ongoing problems within the unit.

Task-Centered Casework

The **task-centered casework** method exemplifies a short-term therapeutic approach to problem solving (Reid & Epstein 1972). This approach stresses the selection and establishment of specific tasks to be worked on in within a limited time period. Although different models of intervention may be used (such as the ones previously discussed), the emphasis on setting brief time limits for problem solutions is an integral therapeutic ingredient. By "compacting" the agreed-upon time limits to work on problems, the client must focus his or her attention and energy on the problem, and tasks for achieving resolution must be adopted quickly. The task-centered approach is an action model that is designed to engage the client quickly and meaningfully in identifying, confronting, and acting on problems.

Other Approaches

Practitioners use a number of other treatment theories and approaches. Rational emotive therapy focuses on "self-talk" as a target for change, and role therapy examines both prescriptive and descriptive roles played by clients and identifies incongruities in role expectations as well as dysfunctional role behavior. Its purpose is to guide the client toward more functional and appropriate role performance.

Throughout their careers, social workers develop a more complete awareness not only of the intervention theories discussed thus far but of others as well.

As new knowledge and understanding of human behavior evolve, social workers must remain vigilant and open to incorporating new theoretical concepts into practice modalities.

Practice Effectiveness

Both students who are just beginning to explore social work as a helping profession and experienced social workers may well be interested in the extent to which direct practice is successful in helping clients with their problems. Research over the past two decades has, to a large extent, produced mixed results. One researcher, however, recently reported that practice using problem-solving models and task-centered methods has resulted in positive outcomes (Rubin 1985, 474). In general, researchers have established that accurate assessment of problems is related to the effectiveness of outcomes where strategic application of interventive techniques was employed. On the whole, recent research has been encouraging with respect to the effectiveness of direct practice with clients. As techniques are refined through practice and as knowledge accrues through research, the direct practice social worker should continue to be more effective as a problem solver.

Direct Practice Supervision

Typically, one thinks of supervision as a management function—that of overseeing and assuring that employees are fulfilling the purpose and goals of an agency or organization. Although this function may be one of the responsibilities of the social work supervisor, he or she must do much more through supervision. The social work supervisor provides enrichment to practitioners by assisting them in the development of practice skills through periodic feedback and discussion of cases. The supervisor regulates the flow of cases assigned to workers and utilizes the unique skills of workers through selective case assignment. The supervisor is at times an educator, a listener, an enabler, and a resource for identifying alternative techniques for addressing problems. In their management functions, supervisors present the need for resources to agency executives and maintain standards for excellence in worker performance. Supervisors play a vital role in helping an agency achieve its purposes.

DIRECT PRACTICE AND THE MSW SOCIAL WORKER

Direct practice is the primary method used by social workers, although contemporary practice generally requires that the worker become involved in group work and community organization methods as well. Competence in the use of all social work methods enhances the effectiveness of the worker in seeking solutions to individual as well as community-related problems. At times, the worker becomes a generalist in the problem-solving effort. Many practitioners are employed in highly therapeutic environments, such as psychiatric or family service settings, whereas others work at agencies, such as a department of human resources, serving people with less specialized problems. Private practice also has increased in recent years, and this typically calls for competence in psychotherapeutic and intensive counseling skills. Practitioners continue to develop resources that enable clients to achieve a more satisfactory level of adaptation regardless of the setting in which social work is practiced.

THE BACCALAUREATE SOCIAL WORKER IN DIRECT PRACTICE

As generalist social workers, practitioners at the baccalaureate level typically find employment in social agencies specializing in direct practice. An appreciation of the nature of client problems in such settings is enhanced by a generalist background and focus. Direct practice with individuals does not always demand in-depth psychotherapeutic treatment. Although interviewing and assessment skills always are essential in establishing intervention goals, the BSW worker need not be concerned with those skills required for intensive psychotherapy. It is important to remember that direct practice with individuals extends far beyond psychotherapeutic involvement. The case of Marilyn, presented at the opening of this chapter, is a good example. The BSW worker could be involved as a case manager in helping Marilyn identify needed resources for reducing stress and then in linking her up with other appropriate resources to insure that her needs were being addressed. The interviewing and counseling skills of the BSW worker would be useful in providing Marilyn with an opportunity to air her problems and explore the resources necessary for resolving them.

The skill of the BSW practitioner in articulating community resources in the problem-solving process must not be underestimated. The knowledge of resources and the preparation of clients to use those resources are paramount in problem resolution. BSW practitioners are employed in a variety of direct practice settings. Among the many opportunities are agencies such as state departments of human resources (or public welfare), mental health and mental retardation programs, children's service agencies (child welfare and child care institutions), halfway houses, nursing homes, areawide agencies on aging, agencies serving battered women, rape crisis centers, and child-care centers.

SUMMARY

In this chapter we defined direct practice with individuals and examined the components of the direct practice process, skills essential for effective practice, and theoretical models that serve to structure intervention. Direct practice has been identified as a direct services process that assists individuals and families through a therapeutic problem-solving process.

KEY TERMS

behavior modification
direct practice
dysfunctional
ego psychology
intervention

problem-solving approach
reality therapy
self-concept
task-centered casework

DISCUSSION QUESTIONS

1. Define direct practice as a social work method. Identify the converging elements of direct practice.
2. Describe the elements of the direct practice process. How is this process enhanced by the direct practice relationship?
3. What types of skills are essential for direct practice? Why?
4. Review and identify the key elements of the various practice theories identified in this chapter. How are they alike? Different?
5. Discuss the role of the BSW social worker in direct practice.

REFERENCES

Biestek, Felix. 1957. *The casework relationship.* Chicago: Loyola University Press.

Binder, Virginia, Arnold Binder, and Bernard Rimland, eds. 1976. *Modern therapies.* Englewood Cliffs, N.J.: Prentice–Hall.

Boehm, Werner. 1959. *The social casework method in social work education,* Curriculum Study, vol. 10, pp. 44–45. New York: Council on Social Work Education.

Bowers, Swithun. 1949. The nature and definition of social casework. *Social Casework* 30 (December): 417.

Brieland, Donald, Lela B. Costin, and Charles R. Atherton. 1985. *Contemporary social work.* New York: McGraw–Hill.

Perlman, Helen Harris. 1959. *Social casework: The problem solving process.* Chicago: University of Chicago Press.

Reid, William J., and Laura Epstein. 1972. *Task-centered casework.* New York: Columbia University Press.

Rubin, Allen. 1985. Practice effectiveness: More grounds for optimism. *Social work* Nov.–Dec. 30:6 469–75.

Zastrow, Charles. 1981. *The practice of social work.* Homewood, Ill.: Dorsey.

SUGGESTED FURTHER READINGS

Compton, Beulah R., and Burt Galaway. 1989. *Social work processes.* Homewood, Ill.: Dorsey.

Hepworth, Dean H., and Jo Ann Larsen. 1986. *Direct social work practice.* Belmont, Calif.: Wadsworth.

Hollis, Florence. 1964. *Casework: A psychosocial therapy.* New York: Random House.

Pincus, Allen, and Anne Minihan. 1973. *Social work practice: Model and method.* Itasca, Ill.: Peacock.

Reid, William J., and Anne W. Shyne. 1975. *Brief and extended casework.* New York: Columbia University Press.

Simons, Ronald L., and Stephen M. Aigner. 1985. *Practice principles: A problem-solving approach to social work.* New York: Macmillan.

Direct Practice: Social Work with Groups and the Community

Chapter 14

By all standards, Charles was a typical thirteen-year-old boy. His parents, Dora and Richard, were well adjusted, had a satisfying marriage, and were both professional career people. It came as a shock to them when they learned that Charles had been picked up, along with a group of older teenagers, in a substance-abuse raid. Seeking help, Dora and Richard turned to the local Family Service Agency, where social worker Heather McMillian listened to their concerns and discussed options for appropriate intervention. Dora, Richard, and Charles agreed that they would commit themselves

to the helping process. Charles joined a teenage substance abusers' group (a therapeutic group) under the direction of social worker Karl Hensen, while Dora and Charles joined a self-help group that consisted of parents of teenage substance abusers. This group was monitored by social worker Clara Perkins. Once each week, Heather, Karl, and Clara would meet with the social work supervisor, Grace Shore, to discuss the status and progress made by Charles, Dora, and Richard and to determine whether other alternative intervention was indicated.

After a period of supervised experience with groups, BSW social workers might find themselves working as a co–group facilitator with Charles and the substance abusers' group or as the monitor of the self-help group that Dora and Richard were participating in. As a generalist practitioner, the BSW recognizes, first, the importance of groups in achieving treatment goals for clients and, second, the usefulness of group methods in helping one identify the most effective methodology for assisting clients with their problems.

SOCIAL GROUPS: A DEFINITION

Social groups are formed for many purposes. The most common type is the **natural group,** in which members participate as a result of common interests, shared experiences, similar backgrounds and values, and personal satisfactions derived from interaction with other group members. A street gang or neigh-

359

borhood group of individuals who "hang out" together is a natural group. Such groups are further characterized by face-to-face interactions and an emotional investment in the role of the group member. Natural groups are seldom formed purposefully to meet specific objectives. All of us are members of natural groups, and seldom is our membership in those groups the result of a planned effort to become involved. In natural groups, a leader often emerges without premeditation or election by group members but rather because one member possesses behavioral attributes or resources that are highly valued by the other group members. Like all groups, natural groups tend to be transitory, with old members exiting and new ones entering throughout the group's life cycle.

Other groups are formed purposefully for a specific reason. For example, apartment house residents may organize to seek building repairs and better living conditions, or a church or synagogue may organize a softball team. Established agencies, such as the YMCA or YWCA, might organize recreational groups within the city. A common characteristic of each of these groups is that they are developed to fulfill a specific purpose.

Regardless of the reasons for which a group is formed, the social group work method may be employed to assist group members in achieving personal growth through the democratic process. Sherif and Sherif (1956, 144) suggest a definition of a **group**, derived from empirical observations:

> *A group is a social unit which consists of a number of individuals who stand in (more or less) definite status and role relationships to one another and which possesses a set of values or norms of its own, regulating the behavior of individual members, at least in matters of consequence to the group.*

GOALS OF SOCIAL GROUP WORK

Group work is a process and an activity that seeks to stimulate and support more adaptive personal functioning and social skills of individuals through structured group interaction. Euster (1975) and Konopka (1954) emphasize the development of communication competency, adaptive coping skills, and effective problem-solving techniques as goals of the group work experience. Group work techniques can be used more effectively when goals and objectives are related to the needs of group members. Effective group work capitalizes on the dynamics of interaction among members of the group. Members are encouraged to participate in making decisions, questioning, sharing, and contributing their efforts toward the achievement of agreed-upon goals and objectives.

GROUP FOCUS

Social workers engage in practice with groups to accomplish a variety of tasks. Generally, however, groups may be classified in terms of a specific purpose. Several of the more common types of groups are identified and discussed in Box 14–1.

Recreation Groups

The primary objective of **recreation groups** is to provide for the entertainment, enjoyment, and experience of participants. Activities such as athletic games or

Box 14–1 Illustrations of Different Types of Groups, Their Focus and Membership

○ *Recreation Group:* A YWCA organizes and promotes dominos, cards (bridge, etc.), basketball, and volleyball groups for interested community residents of all ages.

○ *Recreation-Skill Groups:* The extension division of a local community college offers courses in the manual arts, golf, swimming, volleyball, sewing, and macrame for community residents who wish to develop skill in those areas. Task development is emphasized, and mutual interaction is encouraged in the learning process.

○ *Educational Groups:* A local family service agency offers a group of middle-aged adults opportunities to learn more about the aging process and how to cope with problems of their aged parents. At the same time, the agency sponsors a group on parenting skills for pregnant women and their husbands. In both groups, discussion is emphasized and group members are encouraged to identify their specific concerns for group reaction and discussion.

○ *Socialization Groups:* A halfway house serving delinquent adolescents develops a weekly group meeting for its residents. Discussion focuses on specific problems experienced by group members. Activities are introduced that require cooperative interaction among group members for successful completion (e.g., yard maintenance, household chores). Emphasis is given to democratic participation and personal decision making.

○ *Self-Help Groups:* An Alcoholics Anonymous group is formed by individuals wanting to overcome an alcohol addiction. The purpose of the group is to provide support and reassurance to group members in dealing with alcohol-related problems, with the goal of helping members stay sober.

○ *Therapeutic Groups:* These groups may consist of individuals who have difficulty in dealing with emotional problems associated with divorce, interpersonal loss, alcohol- and drug-related problems, mental health problems, difficulties in parent–child relationships, or other areas in which dysfunctional behavior results. Typically, emotional problems are related significantly to the problems being experienced by group members.

○ *Encounter Groups:* A group is organized by a local service agency to help young men and women who lack assertiveness, are self-deprecating, and feel inadequate. Members are encouraged to be self-expressive, learn to risk, gain insight into their own and others' feelings, provide mutual support, and establish meaningful relationships. A safe, nonjudgmental environment is essential for the successful participation of members.

table games are typical recreational outlets. Community centers, YMCAs and YWCAs, and settlement houses routinely provide this type of group activity, as do senior centers for older adults. Participation provides opportunities for shared interaction, interdependence, and social exchange. Group recreational activities also provide constructive outlets for individuals in a monitored environment. Group workers must be sensitive to scheduling arrangements and willing to develop activities that are of interest to prospective participants.

Recreation-Skill Groups

As differentiated from recreation groups, the purpose of the **recreation-skill group** is to promote development of a skill within a recreational or enjoyment context. Ordinarily, a resource person with appropriate expertise teaches participants the essential skills necessary to develop greater competency in a craft, game, or sport. Tasks are emphasized, and instruction is provided by the resource person (e.g., a coach).

Educational Groups

Educational groups are formed for the purpose of transmitting knowledge and enabling participants to acquire more complex skills. Although educational groups may take on a classroom appearance, emphasis is given to group task assignments, and opportunities for interaction and idea exchange buttress didactic presentations. Educational groups vary in purpose, from learning to repair an automobile to learning the most effective techniques in managing an Alzheimer's disease patient. Group leaders usually are persons with professional expertise in the area of interest for which the group was formed.

Socialization Groups

From a more traditional perspective, **socialization groups** typify the purposes and goals of social group work in that they seek to stimulate behavior change, increase social skills and self-confidence, and encourage motivation (Euster 1975, 220). The group focuses on helping participants develop socially acceptable behavior and behavioral competency. Personal decision making and self-determinism are emphasized as integral aspects of the group process. Typically, socialization groups may consist of runaway youth, predelinquents, or older adults seeking remotivation groups (Zastrow 1986, 588). Leadership is typically provided by a social worker familiar with group dynamics and knowledgeable about the problem area experienced by the participants.

Self-help Groups

Self-help groups are composed of individuals with specific personal or social problems. Membership in the group is usually based on voluntary participation, and members often have "given up" on resolving their problem through community agencies or institutions. Members are expected to make a strong personal commitment to the group, its members, and its goals. Mutual aid and interdependence are given high priority. Personal involvement, face-to-face interaction, and a willingness to respond to other members' needs are expected.

Self-help groups (often identified as support groups) are formed for many different purposes: for recovery and growth, as in the case of Alcoholics Anonymous, Al-Anon, or Synanon; advocacy, such as prolife groups, women's liberation groups, or MADD (Mothers Against Drunk Driving); or a combination of personal growth and advocacy, such as Parents Without Partners or Parents Anonymous (Zastrow 1986, 348).

Most social service agencies provide group experiences for clients in order to serve them more effectively.

GROUP WORK SETTINGS

Traditionally, social group work was practiced in recreational settings, such as the YWCA or YMCA, settlement houses, and community centers. With the growing popularity of group work, along with the redefinition of the scope of social work practice, group work has become a valuable practice method within most direct-service agencies. For example, a family service agency might form a group of prospective adoptive parents to orient them to the adoptive process. A treatment center might compose a group of adolescent substance abusers to assist them in learning to identify and manage stress and interpersonal problems. A recreational center might sponsor athletic teams for middle school youth. Older adults living in a nursing home could constitute a "remotivation" group.

Working with groups not only promotes growth and change through the interaction of the members but also enables the agency and workers to serve a greater number of clients. Although some group members may need the resources of a caseworker in addition to the group experience, in most instances, the group activity is sufficient for personal growth. When direct practice with individuals is not provided by the agency offering the group, referrals are made to an appropriate agency, and a cooperative relationship between the service providers assures the client of maximum assistance with problems.

EVALUATION

Professional practice with individuals and groups must include an evaluative process. Evaluation always is focused on the extent to which the group is able to achieve its objectives. Evaluation may be both an ongoing process as well as an assessment of the total group process, which comes at the termination

Self-help groups do not always seek professional leadership. Effective efforts to resolve problems are based on personal involvement and a willingness to assist fellow members in learning to cope and develop adaptive skills. Since members have experienced the same problem, they may be more empathetic, insightful, and able to provide a more understanding response.

Therapeutic Groups

Therapeutic groups require skilled professional leadership. Group members typically have intensive personal or emotional problems requiring the expertise of a well-trained professional, such as a master's degree–level social worker, a clinical psychologist, or other professional counselor. Monitoring group interaction and its effects on members is an essential requirement of the group leader. Various therapy approaches may be used to promote therapeutic interaction directed toward behavioral change. Therapeutic groups also may be supplemented by individual treatment in some instances.

Encounter Groups

Encounter groups are oriented toward assisting individuals in developing more self-awareness and interpersonal skills. Such groups are characterized by a secure environment in which members can be openly expressive, develop a sense of trust, receive candid feedback, and develop sensitivity to their own and others' feelings and emotions. Assertiveness and confidence resulting from heightened self-acceptance and self-awareness promote more genuine relationships and enhance the quality of interpersonal communication. Encounter groups are identified by many different titles: T (training) groups, sensitivity groups, and personal growth groups.

EFFECTIVE GROUP DEVELOPMENT

The achievement of desired outcomes of the group process is dependent on several key considerations. *Purposefulness* is an essential characteristic for maximum effectiveness of the group work process. Purposefulness involves the establishment of specific goals and objectives and access to their achievement by the group. Purposefulness provides the direction or intent for each group session and provides a framework for monitoring and evaluating the group's progress.

Leadership is essential in helping the group maintain its focus and encouraging maximum participation of members. The group worker may play an active or passive role in the group, depending on the needs of the group as it moves toward the established goals and objectives. The leader must be skilled in group processes and able to perform a variety of roles in supporting the accomplishment of tasks necessary to maintain group integrity and continuing progress. Zastrow (1986, 585) has identified a wide range of role responses that may be required of a group leader, such as "executive, policy maker, planner, expert, external group representative, controller of internal relations, purveyor of rewards and punishments, arbitrator and mediator, exemplar, ideologist, and scapegoat."

Effective leadership is essential to the successful achievement of the group's purposes. The methods that a leader may use to accomplish group goals should be consistent with the values and purposes of social work practice. Wilson and Ryland (1949, 60–99) have identified five leadership styles, four of which are not compatible with social work goals:

1. The *dictatorial* or *authoritarian* method in which the leader orders and the members obey;

2. The *personification* method, where members seek to imitate the group worker and attempt to be like him or her, but they do not explore and find their own abilities;

3. The *perceptive* method, wherein the worker gives instructions, and the group members carry them out and learn skills, although they are not detecting their own resources and capacities;

4. The *manipulative* method, where the group worker goes with the group through a phase of planning and decision making, but the group is only accepting a prearranged program of the leader and is deceived into believing that the group itself came to the decision;

5. The *enabling* method, where the group worker helps the members participate with full responsibility in the life of the group, in its planning and program; in developing their own ideas, skills, and personal attitudes; and in making their own decisions regarding the purposes and actions of the group.

Only the enabling method fully embraces the principles of democratic process and encourages individual responsibility and risk sharing as products of group interaction and decision making. The success of group process and goal attainment is related to a large extent to effective group leadership. Needless to say, the group leader largely is accountable for group maintenance and the success (or failure) of the group in achieving its purposes.

The selection of group members is an important factor in achieving group cohesion. In composing groups, the group worker must accurately assess each individual's needs, capacity for social functioning, interests, and willingness to assume an active role as a group member. Although diversity of background and experience may enhance alternatives for achieving the group's purposes, homogeneous (similar) motives are essential to the formation of the group and identification as a group member. Members with few common interests often have more difficulty in becoming involved in group activities. Age and/or gender may be critical factors, depending on the purposes of the group and the activities designed to achieve those purposes. Individuals with severe emotional problems or behavior disorders may be disruptive to the group process; thus, careful consideration should be given to including them as group members. Members should have the ability to focus on group tasks. Systematic disruptive behavior is not only disconcerting but may lead to group disintegration. The type of group being formed (e.g., recreational, educational) will determine the criteria

for the selection of members. In all instances, selection should be based on the "principle of maximum profit" (individuals with specific needs that would be most likely to achieve the greatest benefit from the group). The assessment of individuals for group membership is enhanced by a personal interview prior to inclusion in the group (Klein 1972, 66).

The size of a group is to a large extent determined by its purposes. To determine in advance that four, six, or fifteen members is the "ideal" size of a group has little validity. It is more effective to examine the goals and purposes of the proposed group when determining group size. If, for example, anonymity (or the ability to "lose" oneself) is a desirable end, a larger number of members may be indicated, thus assuring more limited interaction and group fragmentation (i.e., the emergence of subgroups). Smaller groups, by definition, demand more intimate interaction, and group pressures typically are intensified. Absenteeism affects group process and task accomplishment more in small groups than large ones. Small groups may function more informally than larger ones, which usually require a structured format. The role of the group leader also varies with the size of the group. The democratic process can be achieved in both large and small groups, although it is more difficult in the former. The principles and techniques of social group work are effective with large and small groups alike (Klein 1972).

The number of members selected for the group depends on the desired effect on its individual members, the needs of the members, and their capacity to participate and support group purposes. Generally, a small group may be composed of four to nine members, whereas a large group may consist of ten to twenty members.

THEORY FOR GROUP WORK PRACTICE

Social group work is a direct social work practice method requiring the social worker to be familiar with theories related to group behavior. Group theory provides a framework for promoting guided change through group interaction. The discipline of social psychology has contributed much to our understanding of group formation, roles, norms, values, group dynamics, and cohesion. Sherif and Sherif's (1956) contribution to the understanding of group formation, maintenance, and conflict resolution; Lewin's (1951) conceptualization of field theory; and Moreno's (1953) insights into group configurations have been helpful in gaining greater awareness of how groups function. Early social group work pioneers also contributed valuable experiential and theoretical insights that added to the knowledge base from which an informed approach to working with groups can be employed.

Social group work can be distinguished as a professional social work method by the informed application of theory in helping groups achieve their objectives and goals. Since groups vary extensively in their composition, types, and purposes, the worker also must have a broad-base understanding of the life cycle, emotional reactions to stress, and maladaptive behavior. Group workers must have skill in working with the group and sensitivity in helping the group move toward the achievement of its goals.

of the group. In the former instance, the worker continually "monitors" group behavior, in order to enable the group to focus on its goals. Monitoring also may help the group redefine its purpose and goals, should it become evident that the original ones are unachievable. Monitoring consists of a critical assessment of the group's output.

Evaluation includes an assessment of all activities and behaviors related to the group's performance. Factors such as group leadership, resources, attendance at sessions, changes in group structure, dysfunctional behaviors, characteristics of group members, group norms, and agency support, among others, all are reviewed in relation to the achievement of personal and group goals and objectives. Evaluation has the potential of providing a basis for answering such questions as: What could have increased group productivity? What were the positive achievements of the group? What implications for change are suggested? Efficiency and better quality of service are likely when rigorous evaluative standards are maintained.

GROUP TERMINATION

Groups are terminated when the purposes for which they were established are achieved. Although many groups are initiated with a predetermined expiration period, termination usually is related to meeting group goals and personal goals of the members. Occasionally, a group is aborted when it becomes obvious that its goals are unattainable or when dysfunctional behavior of one or more group members continually disrupts the group's activities.

The worker must be sensitive to the needs of group members at the time of termination and assist them in phasing out their attachment to the group. Often resistance to termination becomes highly emotional and vocal. Frustration, anger, withdrawal, and grief are among the more common reactions to the loss of the close ties that have developed among members throughout the life of the group. By helping the group assess its accomplishments and plan alternatives, the worker can help members develop a more adaptive transition.

SOCIAL GROUP WORK AS A PRACTICE

As we indicated previously, group work is directed toward the enrichment of an individual's life through a group existence. Coyle (1959, 88–105) observes that the group experience may provide assistance to individuals as

1. a maturing process;
2. a supplement to other relationships;
3. preparation for active citizenship;
4. a corrective for social disorganization;
5. treatment of intrapsychic maladjustment.

Although it is unlikely that group members derive equal benefit from the group experience, all can be expected to experience growth in one or more of these areas. Positive group work is a planned-change effort. Change is predicated on benefits derived from group process and interaction. The worker is responsible for assuring that the principles governing social work practice are included in the process. Euster (1975, 232) identifies those principles as follows:

1. *Assuring the dignity, worth, uniqueness, and autonomy of all members;*
2. *A clear working agreement between the worker and the group and an articulated understanding of the group's purpose;*
3. *An assessment of the problems and needs of individual group members and special support by the social worker when the need is indicated;*
4. *Individualization of the group, which reflects its unique character, set of relationships, and needs;*
5. *Strong communications networks, which permit the expression of feelings and emotions of members;*
6. *Relevant program activities, around which constructive interaction, assessment of group process, and the advancement of the group's purpose can be made;*
7. *Preparation for termination.*

Each group also has its own life cycle characterized by developmental stages. Stanford and Roark (1974) identify the stages of a group's development as follows:

1. Beginning—basic orientation and getting acquainted;
2. Norm development—establishing ground rules for operation;
3. Conflict phase—members asserting individual ideas;
4. Transition—replacing initial conflicts with acceptance of others;
5. Production—sharing of leadership, tasks, and trust;
6. Affection—appreciation for the group;
7. Actualization—flexibility, consensus, and decision making.

An awareness of these stages is helpful in monitoring the progress of the group as it moves toward greater cohesion and effectiveness. Dysfunctional "blocking" at any stage (the conflict phase), once identified, can be addressed and resolved by the group, and the developmental progress can continue. Allowed to continue unchecked, the unresolved blockage may result in group dissolution.

Skill in working with groups is an important aspect of social work practice. The efficiency and effectiveness of the group work process have resulted in personal enhancement, skill development, and problem reduction.

SOCIAL WORK WITH COMMUNITIES

Norma Carlson, a BSW social worker, has been working with Brenda Bostwick for several months. Brenda, age sixteen, is a single parent who aspired to complete her high school education in hopes that she could find a good job and better provide for her child. It was difficult for her to concentrate on her schoolwork because she often had to miss school to care for her baby. School officials had suspended her for absences on several occasions, and she was becoming more discouraged day by day. With Brenda's consent, Norma visited with the school officials in order to engage them in working out a special educational program for Brenda so that she would not fall behind in her studies. Norma also contacted a local day-care center and arranged for Brenda's child to be cared for while Brenda was in class. She was also successful in securing reduced-rate transportation with the local bus company, who agreed that Brenda should be supported in her determination to work toward her educational goals.

Successful social work intervention, as in the case of Brenda, often requires the social worker to engage community agencies and organizations in the process. It is doubtful whether Brenda, without Norma's knowledge and skill, could have made the arrangements that resulted in a positive solution to her problem. Clients are often unaware of available resources or the process through which successful solutions can be achieved. Also, in some instances, they may not have the self-confidence to pursue alternatives that result in goal achievement. Social workers in direct practice find that work with the community often becomes an essential ingredient in the problem-solving process. In this section of the chapter, we discuss the concepts and principles of social work with the community.

What Is a Community?

Community is a descriptive term that has many meanings. Communities may be defined as groups of people who live within certain incorporated limits, such as Philadelphia, Pennsylvania; Boise, Idaho; or Mena, Arkansas. Or, others may speak of a "religious community," which refers to a group of people who share common religious values. A community may also be a subunit of a larger metropolitan area, such as Watts in Los Angeles, or Shadyside in Pittsburgh. Members of an ethnic group who live close together are often referred to as a community. Illustrations are endless, and our purpose here is to identify the ambiguity of the concept. How, then, do we arrive at a usable definition that enables us to understand the focus of social work with communities? It is obvious from the preceding illustrations that "communities" vary considerably in terms of organization, resources, values, and purpose. It is also obvious that a client may well be a member of several communities—for example, an incorporated city or town, a religious group, an ethnic minority, and a well-defined neighborhood. Social workers need to be familiar with the community systems that serve as behavioral contexts for their clients. Keeping these definitional variations in mind, we will, for our purposes, consider **community** as a *group of individuals who live in close proximity to one another, who share a common environment, including public and private resources, and who identify themselves with that community.*

Social workers often feel overwhelmed with the concept of working with the community. Perhaps a better perspective could allay some of these fears: If one considers that the community consists of interacting individuals, then work with the community would consist of working with the individuals and groups who interact. As Zastrow (1986, 582) has indicated, "the most basic skill needed in community practice is to be able to work effectively with people [and such practice] . . . primarily involves working with individuals and groups."

As indicated earlier, generalist social work practitioners constantly engage in community practice.

Social work with the community may focus on a wide range of problems and issues. The case illustration with which we initiated this discussion is only one example. Social workers may, as in the case of Brenda, serve as a **broker** with several agencies in order to obtain sources necessary for the achievement of treatment goals. In the broker role, the social worker helps clients plow through the maze of different agencies in locating resources that are most appropriate to problem resolution. In addition to the active role of negotiation with agencies, the worker also gathers and transmits information between client systems and action systems.

At other times the social worker in community practice may serve as an **enabler** in seeking to help people identify and clarify their problems (assessment) and in providing support and stimulation for the group to unite in their efforts to secure change. For example, a group of tenants in a rat-infested tenament might be encouraged to unite and confront the owners or landlords with the problem and seek redress for those conditions. At other times, the social worker in community practice may function in the role of *advocate* for a client system in confronting unresponsive representatives of community institutions. In the advocate role the social worker is clearly aligned with the client system in seeking to nudge unresponsive institutions to take action. A worker may, for example, represent the client system in increasing police protection in high-risk neighborhoods. Finally, a social work community practitioner might serve as an *activist* who seeks change in institutional response patterns. For example, a worker may serve as an activist in seeking modification of discriminatory hiring practices or in trying to secure the rights of disenfranchised groups.

COMMUNITY PRACTICE APPROACHES

Social work with the community, like other methods of social work practice, is based on planned change and assumes familiarity, skill, and expertise on part of the worker, including the basic social work skills of problem identification, data collection, assessment, analysis (or interpretation), and the development of planned intervention. Social workers who routinely practice with communities generally use a "social action, social planning or community development" approach. The **social action** strategy was popularized by Saul Alinsky (1969) and was used extensively by oppressed groups in the 1960s "War on Poverty" programs. This approach stresses organization and group cohesion in confrontational approaches geared to modify or eliminate institutional power bases that negatively impact the group. **Social planning** emphasizes modification of institutional practices through the application of knowledge, values, and theory—a practical, rational approach to problem solving that assumes well-intentioned people will be responsive to sound arguments. The **community development** approach considers and respects the diversity of the population and uses those differences as strengths in achieving community betterment for all citizens. Often citizens become polarized as an action group when "superordinate goals" (Sherif & Sherif 1956) are identified, requiring concerted community efforts for a satisfactory resolution.

Social work with the community is an integral practice role of the generalist social work practitioner at the BSW level. It is a rewarding, challenging activity that requires an awareness of theory, knowledge, and practice for effective intervention.

SOCIAL WORK WITH GROUPS AND THE COMMUNITY

The baccalaureate social worker, or BSW, has developed familiarity with and a beginning competency in working with groups and the community as part of the generic educational program. Both theory and practice in working with groups are required by accredited BSW programs. Many opportunities exist for work with groups and the community at the BSW level. Most agencies use the group and community methods as part of their practice modalities. Agencies such as family service agencies, state departments of human services, hospitals, correctional centers, mental health and mental retardation agencies, school social services, youth organizations, and a variety of related service delivery organizations use group and community practice methodologies. It should also be noted that social workers with advanced degrees (the MSW) are also often employed as community organization workers, often specializing in that area as a field of practice. At this level, they may serve as administrators of state or federal programs, as department heads in a city's human services division, or directors of agencies.

SUMMARY

Social work with groups and social work with the community are social work methods that promote the personal growth of individual members (group work) and enhance the capacity of the community to better serve the needs of its diverse members (community practice). Groups may be identified by their purpose: recreational, recreational-skill, educational, socialization, encounter, self-help, and therapy. Community change efforts are facilitated through social action, social planning, and community development approaches. In all of these, members of the group or community establish goals and objectives, and the group leader helps the members achieve their goals. Democratic decision making is important to the process. Monitoring and evaluation are major activities used to help the group and community achieve their goals and to enrich practice methods.

KEY TERMS

broker	natural group
community	recreation group
community development	recreation-skill group
educational group	self-help group
enabler	social action
encounter group	social planning
group	socialization group
group work	therapeutic group

DISCUSSION QUESTIONS

1. What is a group? Differentiate between a natural group and groups organized for specific purposes.

2. Identify the role of the social worker in helping groups achieve their goals.

3. Explain how the following groups differ and how they are alike: Socialization groups, encounter groups, self-help groups, recreational groups, and therapy groups.

4. Describe the goals of social group work. How are these goals achieved?

5. Discuss the principles of group work practice. How important are these principles in securing group goals?

6. What considerations should be made in terminating the group? Why are these considerations important to members of the group?

7. What are some of the problems in arriving at a definition of *community*?

8. Identify the roles that social workers play in social work with the community.

9. Differentiate among the social action, social planning, and community development approaches to social work with communities.

10. Why are most generalist social workers involved in community practice?

REFERENCES

Alinsky, Saul. 1969. *Reveille for radicals.* New York: Basic Books.

Coyle, Grace. 1959. Some basic assumptions about social group work, in Marjorie Murphy, ed., *The social group work method in social work education* (88–105). New York: Council on Social Work Education.

Euster, Gerald L. 1975. Services to groups, in Donald Brieland, Lela B. Costin, and Charles R. Atherton, eds., *Contemporary social work* (Chap. 13). New York: McGraw–Hill.

Klein, Alan F. 1972. *Effective groupwork.* New York: Association Press.

Konopka, Gisela. 1954. *Group work in the institution.* New York: Whiteside.

Lewin, Kurt. 1951. *Field theory in social science: Selected theoretical papers.* D. Cartwright, ed. New York: Harper & Row.

Moreno, J. L. 1953. *Who shall survive?* rev. ed. New York: Beacon.

Sherif, Muzafer, and Carolyn Sherif. 1956. *An outline of social psychology.* New York: Harper & Row.

Stanford, Gene, and Albert E. Roark. 1974. *Human interaction in education.* Boston: Allyn & Bacon.

Wilson, Gertrude, and Gladys Ryland. 1949. *Social group work practice.* Cambridge: Houghton Mifflin.

Zastrow, Charles. 1986. *Introduction to social welfare institutions.* 3rd ed. Chicago: Dorsey.

SUGGESTED FURTHER READINGS

Boulette, Teresa R. 1985. Group therapy with low income Mexican Americans. *Social Work* (September): 403–4.

Dunham, Arthur. 1970. *The new community organization.* New York: Crowell.

Harford, Margaret. 1971. *Groups in social work.* New York: Columbia Univ. Press.

Henry, S. 1981. *Group skills in social work: A four dimensional approach.* Itasca, Ill.: Peacock.

Papell, C., and B. Rothman. 1966. Social group work models—Profession and heritage. *Journal of Social Work Education* 66–77.

Roberts, Robert W., and Helen Northen. 1976. *Theories of social work with groups.* New York: Columbia Univ. Press.

Shulman, L. 1979. *The skills of helping individuals and groups.* Itasca, Ill.: Peacock.

Simons, Ronald, and Stephen M. Aigner. 1985. *Practice principles: A problem-solving approach to social work.* New York: Macmillan.

Social Agency Administration

*R*achill Johnson was recently promoted to the position of director of a city's Family Service Agency in an area with a large Hispanic and black population. When Rachill interviewed for the job, the agency's board of directors and representatives from the state mental health agency, which partially funds the program, informed her that the center needed to make a number of changes and that she would be responsible for determining how to make them.

The agency that Rachill now directs has been in the community for seventy-five years, established when the area was populated largely by poor white immigrants. As the community changed from poor immigrant to stable working class, the agency also changed. Now these families have moved to the suburbs and become middle class, and the agency still serves many of them, as well as other white middle-class families. It has few minority clients and almost none from the immediate neighborhood. None of the staff, except Rachill, is black or Hispanic.

Many staff members see no need to serve the immediate community, since they say the residents would not be receptive to the traditional psychotherapy services they provide. Other staffers, along with some individuals living in the local community, believe the agency needs to change its central purpose.

Rachill realizes that she faces a myriad of problems in administering the agency. She thinks she is especially skilled at getting individuals with different backgrounds and viewpoints to work together to meet common goals. She plans to establish working groups of board members, staff members, and community members to develop ideas about ways to change the agency and to involve them throughout the planning and implementation process. She understands that she will need to use her existing skills as a line-level social worker and develop some new ones. Directing the staff, finding the funds, and responding to the community will be a tough challenge.

The social work agency is many things to many people. It is a place where people go for help when problems occur and a place society holds responsible for addressing specific problems. It also is a place of employment for some and a setting for voluntary action by others. With the multiple motives of multiple actors, there is no single purpose of the social agency but rather a myriad of purposes. Above all else, the major task of the administrator of a social agency is to bring resources, opportunities, and goals together in such a way that a variety of social missions are accomplished. The focus of this chapter is on the management activities and the administrative processes of the local agency. Management activities are not the sole responsibility of agency executive directors and their assistants. All workers in the agency, the members of the board of directors, and the clients play vital roles in the administrative process.

The dominant view of agency administration used to be "organizational rationality." The notion was that the agency director, responsive to the board of directors, identified cost-efficient means of attaining the board's ends, indicated the costs and benefits of the various alternatives, and then implemented their choice. This view met with criticism from proponents of two positions. First, theories of politics demonstrated that organizations do not have single rational goals but multiple goals emanating from many sources. Second, social workers and other professionals viewed organizational decisions as the product of many forces, of which goal-directed rationality is but one (Grummer 1990).

ADMINISTRATIVE STRATEGY

The administrative processes of an agency can be thought of first as a strategic task. **Strategy** is ongoing, dynamic thinking formulated to analyze problems and to establish specific objectives. This process may best be described in terms of a cycle of administrative activity, as depicted in Figure 15–1. The parts of the cycle are as follows:

1. Strategic Formulation—analysis of problems and of objectives with input from staff, community leaders, those with funding authority, clients served, and the media.
2. Planning and Budgeting Implementation—development of specific budgets, resource budgets, fiscal budgets, and time budgets, and deployment of these resources.
3. Control and Management—direction of activities, which are constantly evaluated, establishing a feedback loop back to strategic formulation.

To be effective, the cycle must be completed, so that analysis of the data generated by those working directly with clients and community groups leads back to a more precise problem formulation at the highest level of the organization. It is typical to think of strategic formulation as the first phase of the administrative process. However, at any point in time, strategic formulation also is the product of many previous administrative cycles.

As an example, since the late 1980s, the Episcopal Community Service Agency of North Fork, Nebraska, has been expected to devise a strategy to deal with AIDS, child and substance abuse, suicides, crime, and other social problems linked to the many farm foreclosures in River Fork County. The agency was created in the 1940s to provide social and chaplain services to the residents of the county poor farm. It was established by wealthy farmers, whose des-

Figure 15–1 The Administrative Cycle

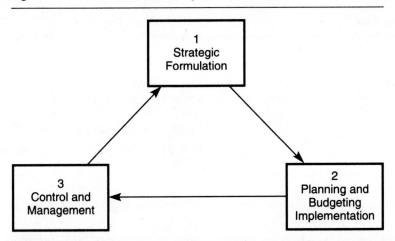

cendants now face the loss of their family farms. How the agency functions today is related to many earlier decisions. For example, the agency provides a food pantry and thrift shop, as well as traditional marriage counseling by a parish priest. However, in developing the strategic plan to meet current social problems, the staff must review the agency's traditional role within the community as well as factors in the current environment, such as the following:

1. Economic forces—What are the most likely sources of funds to address current problems?
2. Government policies—What are state, local, and national governments going to do that will reduce or exacerbate the problem?
3. The current social structure of the agency—Specifically, what are the talents and dispositions of the current staff? This is most often the strongest force in strategic planning.

APPLYING A SYSTEMS/ECOLOGICAL PERSPECTIVE

A key aspect of strategic planning is the recognition that the problems addressed lie far beyond the control of any given agency. As the board members, with the assistance of the executive director, contemplate these problems and the appropriate responses, they find that opportunities, risks, resources, and responsibilities interact and reverberate along the way. A systems/ecological perspective suggests that an agency's resources and its goals overlap and interact. Clearly, the goals specified influence the capacity to generate resources, just as the manner in which resources are obtained and the nature of those resources affect and change the goals of the agency (Anthony & Herzlinger 1975).

Perlman and Gurin (1972) suggest that there are five types of resources to which the local social agency manager needs to respond (see Table 15–1):

1. A supply of clients, who expect to receive from the agency some valued product or service. These clients may seek the service/product on their

Table 15–1 Organizing Principles of Social Agencies

Resource Base	Some Examples
Clients	Children, delinquents, disabled workers, retired persons
Fiscal Base	Public, private, voluntary funds
Social work method	Direct practice, case management, advocacy
Human Resources	Paid staff, volunteer staff, mixed staff
Mandate	Legislative mandate, United Way charter, license to practice

own accord, or the service/product may be imposed upon the client, as in the criminal justice system.

2. Financial resources, which are made available to the agency by a system of grants, taxation, fees for service, and/or voluntary contributions.

3. A social work method, by which the financial resources are transformed into the service/product sought by its clients. The technology of the social work agency typically is one or more of the social work processes: direct practice, client advocacy, and so on.

4. The people, or human resources, who comprise the agency staff. These paid or volunteer workers are the ones on the front line, who interact directly with the clients to provide the service/product.

5. A continuing mandate to operate. The mandate may be in the form of a license, a legislative directive, or a charter of some sort.

In administering any social agency, there are five essential elements that must be considered: the agency, its clients, its product, its goals, and its staff. A specific agency has a set of social programs related to its service or product and its goals. The fit between the agency's product and its goals is one way the agency is judged. An essential administrative task is to achieve an optimal fit between the product and the goal. Similarly, the product and the staff must have some degree of congruence, if the agency is to operate efficiently. The staff members clearly need the training and competency to deliver the service effectively or to produce the product. Since social agencies tend to be labor-intensive organizations, assuring such staff readiness is one of the most crucial aspects of the administration of an agency.

Pairing these five essential elements in various combinations, as indicated in Figure 15–2, dictates the specific administrative tasks that must be performed successfully. There are ten essential pairs or choices to be made. Each choice affects the other choices, so the agency can be understood as a system. Three of the most important pairs are discussed in the following paragraphs.

Goal and Product

An organization provides a product, and although that product is the end stage in the organization's directly visible activities, the product is provided in pursuit

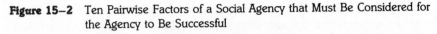

Figure 15–2 Ten Pairwise Factors of a Social Agency that Must Be Considered for the Agency to Be Successful

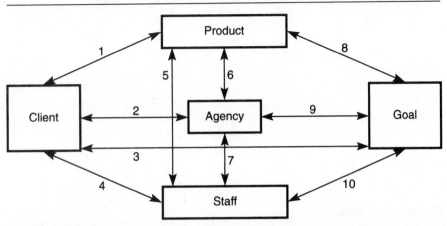

of stated, manifest, or latent organizational goals. A retail store sells a particular product presumably in order to make a profit for the store owners. It is not the purpose of the bookstore at the local mall to provide employment to its workers or to make first-class literature easily available to potential readers, even though it may serve those ends. For the retail store, the ultimate purpose is profits, and failure to produce profits will cause the enterprise to cease.

In the absence of a profit motive to guide choices, the administrator of a social agency faces several questions: If profit, defined as total revenues minus total costs, is not to be maximized, what should be—the number of people served, the quality of service to those who are served, or some appropriate combination of these? Attempts to answer such questions will force the administrator to think about some of the other pairwise considerations.

Staff and Product

The agency director has to identify staff or position needs, recruit and retain qualified persons to fill those positions, and promote an effective, task-centered work environment. An agency requires human resources: professional and technical staff members, as well as volunteers. Board members, who help to ensure that the links between the community and the agency are sustained and current, also need to be recruited and retained. The nurturing and development of staff, volunteers, and board members are sufficiently complex to be the subject of specialized graduate-level courses. However, some general principles are of interest to other students.

Staff management must begin with clear specification of staffing requirements. The specific objectives of developing staffing standards are

1. to determine the requirements of the specific task essential to organizational maintenance and goal attainment;

2. to determine the qualities, abilities, knowledge, and skills required to perform these tasks successfully;

3. to develop a pattern of task assignments so that staff members are neither underutilized nor expected to accomplish tasks beyond their skill levels.

With a chart of staff needs and staff availability, the agency administrator can specify position requirements and expectations. This task-oriented staff structure needs to address a number of elements. For example, a pattern of supervisory controls must be specified; that is, the nature, extent, and procedure for reviews of task performance and the means available to correct and respond to substandard performance must be addressed. Also needed are ways to measure accountability, review, coordination, and perhaps most important, the ways in which the agency's services help the clients meet the problems that led them to seek help.

Product and Client

The identification and specification of the problem call for organized intervention, which involves a political process rather than a rational, technical one. With some problems, such as crime, little conflict exists regarding goals. However, various groups strongly disagree about what legitimate social interventions to employ in controlling crime. In another area, such as child care for children of working parents, conflict exists over the desirability of intervention itself. Some see quality child care as both benefiting children and allowing parents— especially single parents—to become self-supporting; others see child care simply as a way to watch the "kids" while both parents work. Still other groups oppose child care and view it as a significant factor in the decline of the American family. Clearly, political ideologies constitute the core by which individuals judge the nature of social problems and the propriety of social intervention. A social work credo suggests that the agency needs to be responsive to the clients served. However, the clientele directly served are not the only interest group that affects the resource base of the agency. For example, who is served by a public housing project? Is it the people who live there, the real estate interests, or the building trade unions and construction companies who completed the facility? Clearly, depending on the degree of one's cynicism, one can specify a myriad of legitimate interests involved in implementation of public housing policy, or any other policy.

Weighing the Clients' Best Interests

Pluralistic politics do not provide the administrator with any set of substantive rules for specifying the appropriate product of the agency. Social service agencies that represent clients with little or no political power have very special problems. Too much concern with the wants and desires of the clients directly served clearly can erode the economic and political support necessary for the very existence of the agency. However, too little concern will result in exploitation of the clients the agency purports to serve. The very fact that the social agency typically is accused of both errors reflects the delicate balance that an agency administrator faces, and this is only one of many critical administrative choices.

One very specific concern is who makes what choices? Children, the mentally ill, the mentally retarded, and others may not know what is in their own best interest. The phrase caveat emptor, "let the buyer beware," implies that the customer in a store knows and can best judge his or her own self-interest. For example, a bookstore clerk is not expected to help a customer decide between the hardback or the paperback edition of a book. Presumably, the ethical responsibilities of the firm are satisfied when the client knows of the availability of both books. However, problems become more complicated as choices become more complicated. A surgeon, for instance, is expected to guide a patient through a decision about having an operation or getting chemotherapy when each has different costs and different benefits and, most particularly, different probabilities of being effective. The problem becomes most acute when the client being served directly cannot choose his or her own best interest.

The professional social worker in the service agency needs to steer between two dangers. On the one hand, rigid adherence to the rules that benefit the agency or the taxpayers who fund the service agency can quickly result in a subtle but debilitating form of tyranny. On the other hand, the agency has a responsibility not to become captives of its clientele or to surrender to its clients the power to determine the structure and nature of the services being offered. When interests are in conflict, there is no one correct way to resolve that conflict. The problem becomes particularly acute in the social agency in which the social worker has to represent the interests of clients incapable of knowing just what their own best interests may be.

IMPLEMENTATION

Failure in strategic thought or process can render a social program, however well intended, useless—or worse. Even brilliant strategy has to be put into effective operation. **Implementation** involves deciding on the actions and coordinating them. It is a process of turning general thoughts into specific actions, where real people are charged with things they must do within established time frames. Implementation involves selecting the tactics required to carry out the strategy. Further, patterns of communication need to be designed, systems of monitoring and accountability instituted to ensure that activities have been put into place, and the necessary staff recruited and trained.

The key to success in the implementation phase is getting staff and volunteers to understand and support the selected objectives and pattern of attainment. The process is sure to fail if the human aspects of the implementation process are not addressed adequately. The implementation process flows imperceptibly into the specific management activities.

MANAGEMENT ACTIVITIES

The management function, often simply called administration, has to do with getting things done on a day-to-day basis. The essence of administrative tasks has been stated in many ways.

In 1937, Luther Gulick popularized the abbreviation POSDCORB to describe the activities of the agency executive (Sharkansky 1982, 124). POSDCORB

Social services administrators must be skilled in many areas and able to work with civic leaders as well as clients. Here, an agency administrator works with clients as they try out new forms the agency has developed to help staff determine their needs more effectively.

stands for planning, organizing, staffing, directing, coordinating, reporting, and budgeting. Although this acronym has been subjected to three generations of academic criticism—some of it quite savage—it stands up well as a reasonably structured and easily remembered set of tasks to describe the multifaceted activities of agency administration. To place the problem of management of an agency in perspective, one needs to examine these tasks.

○ *Planning*—working out in broad outline the things that need to be done and the methods for doing them to accomplish the purpose set for the enterprise.

○ *Organizing*—the establishment of the formal structure of authority through which work subdivisions are arranged, defined, and coordinated for the defined objective;

○ *Staffing*—the whole personnel function, bringing in and training the staff and maintaining favorable conditions of work;

○ *Directing*—the continuous task of making decisions and embodying them in specific and general orders and instructions and serving as the leader of the enterprise;

○ *Coordinating*—the all-important duty of interrelating the various parts of the work;

○ *Reporting*—keeping those to whom the executive is responsible informed as to what is going on, which includes keeping the entire staff informed through records, research, and inspection;

○ *Budgeting*—fiscal planning, accounting, and control.

Planning

Planning is sensing what needs to be done in order to accomplish the purposes of the agency. Agency planning functions can be subdivided into strategy (broad, overall plans) and **tactics** (day-to-day, specific plans), as well as into short-term and long-term planning. Planning activities should be structured to anticipate future resource needs and delineate specific tasks in an ordered and sequenced pattern in order to accomplish the goals of the agency. Planning receives its most visible form in the development of the agency budget.

Effective planning incorporates the following steps:

1. Identification of the precise goals of the agency
2. Ranking of those goals in their order of importance
3. Identification of the resources currently available to accomplish the goals
4. Identification of the resources available to meet next week's, next month's, and next year's goals
5. Measurement of resources used and goals accomplished in order to have a guide for future actions

Organizing

Organizing is the establishment of the formal structure of authority through which resources are allocated and transmitted to the goals or targets of the agency. There are alternative ways of organizing an agency, but typically an agency is structured by place, process, or purpose, as shown in Figure 15–2.

The range of organizing patterns is nearly infinite, and most agencies are in the process of either reorganizing, planning a reorganization, or adjusting to having just been reorganized. In the most typical structure, the ongoing director will work out for some particular agency a unique plan for ongoing authority. Social workers in an agency do not just wake up in the morning and go out to "do good" but are required to report on their time use, their accomplishments, and the ways they achieved these accomplishments.

Staffing

Staffing encompasses the entire personnel function: recruiting, training, and retraining the necessary personnel to carry out the tasks of the agency. In a small agency these functions may be but one of the tasks of the single agency executive, whereas in a very large agency, they may be done by an entire subunit of the agency devoted entirely to personnel, including staff training.

Directing

Directing is the continuing task of making decisions about client needs and the resources to which clients are entitled. These decisions are allocated to the organized process in a structured way to ensure that all clients are served as nearly identically as possible without regard to the particular social worker that they see. On first blush, this may appear to be a highly impersonal approach, but on reflection, it means that an agency's resources—in dollars, goods, or staff time—are not dispensed haphazardly but in accordance with an established set of criteria to ensure that all clients receive their due share of the agency's resources. The agency director needs to set forth guidelines for discretion by being clear but not rigid—social problems are much too complex for that. Nonetheless, the public has the right to be assured that the social worker is not free to act capriciously, tyranically, or in ways that contravene the socially sanctioned goals of the agency. There are specific problems to be addressed. All clients should be treated alike on the basis of clear rules known to both social worker and client, yet there is a need for responsiveness. The agency director must ensure that in those cases where following the letter of the rule defeats the clear intent of the rule, workers are trained to use their intelligence and are free to do that but not to substitute their own personal standards. This is a tricky problem for administrators and directors to solve.

Coordination

Coordination involves timely and effective use of an agency's various activities to achieve the maximum social benefit. This means not only that each unit of the agency knows what the others are doing, but that agency activities are structured and sequenced to serve the client most fully. For example, the educational and the therapy units of a family service agency need to have their activities structured and attuned to each other, if they are to achieve their best results, because they utilize a common staff and serve the same clientele for a shared purpose.

Reporting

The agency director has an ethical, and often a legal, responsibility to inform board members and fiscal supporters about the activities, problems, and accomplishments of the agency. Information about the administration of the agency should flow both from director to the staff and vice versa. The agency director monitors the agency activities through regulations, records, statistical reports, on-the-spot inspections, research, memos, newsletters, and other appropriate reporting devices. Workers, in turn, inform their supervisors through regular reports of their day-to-day use of time, special reports of unusual activity, and informal talks.

Budgeting

Budgeting is the process of allocating dollars to specified purposes. In the standard budget, dollars are allocated for specific categories, such as staff salaries, utilities, and mortgage payments. A second budget also needs to be prepared, which has been called the process budget. In a process budget, dollars from the agency are allocated not to specific entities but to the function for which they are intended. For example, the proportions of staff salaries, supplies, and fixed costs needed to operate the agency's community education program are calculated and assigned to that function.

SUMMARY

Finding the best pattern of rules and behavior to follow in the administration of a social work agency is difficult—if not impossible. Ways of doing things change constantly because circumstances vary so much. Regulations can appear to be arbitrary and frustrating, yet they reflect judicial and legislative decisions and beliefs about the relative merits of particular goals and actions. Who gets what and why are the key questions in evaluating administrative rules. Ideally, regulations of practice are the result not of good or bad luck but of careful decision making. There is no magic formula that social workers can use or that administrators can apply. The best they can hope for is that clients, social workers, directors, and board members will respect one another and assess each situation with sensitivity and care.

KEY TERMS

implementation   strategy
planning   tactics

DISCUSSION QUESTIONS

1. What are some of the factors that need to be considered when developing a strategy for an agency?

2. How might existing personnel and agency policies shape the direction an agency takes in developing and implementing new programs?

3. Distinguish between strategy and tactics.

4. If an agency was reorganized and services were provided by place instead of process, how might that change the services offered?

REFERENCES

Anthony, Robert, and Regina Herzlinger. 1975. *Management control in nonprofit organizations.* Homewood, Ill.: Irwin.

Etzioni, Amitai. 1975. Alternative conceptions of accountability: The example of health administration. *Public Administration Review* 35(3).

Grummer, Burton. 1990. *The politics of social administration.* Englewood Cliffs, N.J.: Prentice Hall.

Perlman, Robert, and Arnold Gurin. 1972. *Community organization and social planning.* New York: Wiley.

Sharkansky, Ira. 1982. *Public administration: Agencies, policies, and politics.* San Francisco: Freeman.

SUGGESTED FURTHER READINGS

Flynn, John P. 1987. *Social agency policy: Analysis and presentation for community practice.* Chicago: Nelson-Hall.

Mayer, Robert R. 1985. *Policy and program planning: A developmental perspective.* Englewood Cliffs, N.J.: Prentice Hall.

Schulman, Kary, and Fred Setterberg. 1985. *Beyond profit.* New York: Harper & Row.

Williams, Walter. 1980. *The implementation perspective: A guide for managing social service delivery programs.* Berkeley: University of California Press.

Research and Practice

B *ecause of a budget crisis, the directors of the human resources agency in a northwestern state were considering a policy change that would reduce AFDC payments. They asked a policy analyst from the agency to determine the probable impact of such reductions. The analyst concluded that the state, rather than saving money, would actually spend more because of having to pick up emergency relief and* *indigent health care costs for families who could not survive without AFDC and Medicaid, both of which are largely federally subsidized. Based on this information and other data the analyst provided, the agency directors increased funding for low-income child care and employment training to reduce the number of AFDC recipients, but they did not reduce the actual payments.*

Research, in its most general sense, refers to any disciplined strategy of inquiry. The term sometimes elicits an image of a white-coated individual in a sterile laboratory, but this conception is unduly restrictive for our purposes. On the other hand, research is sometimes equated with the mere gathering of facts. For our purposes, this concept is too broad. Research within a profession such as social work has many manifestations, but in this chapter we focus on three reasonably specific modes, or forms, of research: (1) **disciplinary research,** (2) **policy research,** and (3) **evaluative research.**

All three modes are scientific in that all depend on the scientific method. All three are objective in that the investigator is required to conform to established canons of logical reasoning and formal rules of evidence. Further, all three are ethically neutral in that the investigator does not take sides on issues of moral or ethical significance. Each mode seeks to generate a proposition, or set of propositions, capable of falsification. Although similar in their demand for objectivity, each of the modes has its own specific intents.

DISCIPLINARY RESEARCH

Disciplinary research is the term used to distinguish investigations designed to expand the body of knowledge of a particular discipline. In the social sciences that means to expand or modify the understanding of social and psychological processes so that social behavior can be explained. The intent is explanation for its own sake. This is sometimes called pure, as opposed to applied, research. Disciplinary research begins with a paradigm. The paradigm is a perspective, perhaps a school of thought, that structures the research, the research goals, and hence the research methods that are seen as appropriate in the analysis of a particular topic. The paradigm directs the investigator as to where and how to seek evidence. Complex social behavior cannot be explained except in terms of a paradigm. The political scientist, the economist, and the sociologist each would describe, analyze, and explain identical phenomena in different ways. No single one is right and the others wrong; rather, each paradigm generalizes its own special insight into the problem at hand. The social worker uses all of these paradigms in his/her effort to identify a pragmatic method of intervention.

The desire to understand the intergenerational transmission of poverty and dependency can be used as an illustration. Investigators do not disagree about whether psychological immaturity, social isolation, or the lack of economic alternatives produces multigenerational welfare. Investigators know that they all do and that when all three are present, the likelihood of multigenerational poverty becomes very large. In science, for the most part, explanations are seen as additive. The economist might think of intergenerational poverty in terms of the job structure or the lack of job opportunities. The social psychologist may explore the problem in terms of role models or the lack of them. The nutritionist will explore food consumption patterns and cognitive development, school failure, and dependency. There is no one route to poverty and dependency.

The social investigator is interested in providing an explanation of why something happened. The first requirement then is to identify a dependent variable (that which we wish to explain) and show how it is related to one or more independent variables (those factors that produce changes in the dependent variable.) In the physical sciences we know that as the temperature falls, or rises, changes occur in the way we see H_2O—as ice, water or as steam. Complex molecular theories are used to explain that simple observable phenomenon. Similarly, as changes in economic circumstances occur, observable changes in employment opportunities occur. Just establishing the direction of causality can be a profound problem. Careful selection of variables, careful use of both inductive and deductive reasoning, and precise application of the established rules of evidence are required to produce correct inferences about relationships. This is what is meant by an explanation.

The glue that holds together a disciplinary investigation is theory. A **theory** is a set of logically related, empirically verifiable generalizations that intend to explain relationships clearly. Since the process of theory building and research is cyclical and constitutes a single feedback loop, we can break into the process at any point.

In science, theory and research interact; in practice, observation and generalization interact. Together they form the whole of an investigation process. The normal presentation is that of a circle, as depicted in Figure 16–1. A theory is derived from a set of generalizations. The theory, in turn, sparks a **hypothesis,** which focuses attention on certain observations, which then yield more carefully phrased empirical generalizations.

The economist, the sociologist, and the psychologist would provide widely different explanations for the shifts in family structure associated with shifts in general economic conditions. No one theory is right or wrong; some are more useful to practice patterns than others.

Sometimes the research process begins with observation. For example, the renowned nineteenth-century French sociologist Émile Durkheim looked at

Figure 16-1 The Investigation Process

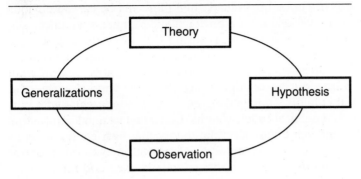

crude data on suicides and found that suicide rates were lower for Catholics, married persons, and people in rural areas. The common feature of these correlates was a sense of social involvement. This led him to articulate the theory of linking a lack of social integration—which he called "anomie," or the sense of being without norms and standards—and suicide. Legions of scholars have deduced various hypotheses from Durkheim's groundbreaking work, which led to a number of empirical generalizations about the social consequences of anomie. These have been adopted into practice modes to reduce the sense of anomie via specific practice methods. These, in turn, ultimately are utilized to expand, modify, and sharpen Durkheim's original theory.

POLICY RESEARCH

Policy planners and policy advocates frequently use specific research methods as they ply their craft. A political decision maker who needs to resolve uncertainties before making a policy choice often will seek the aid of policy research. In deciding whether to expand maximum-security cells or dormitory-type rooms, the individual prison official will want to know more about the effectiveness of various ways of housing prisoners and the reliability of these predictions regarding their postconfinement behavior. Using scientific methods to reduce, or at least minimize, uncertainty is part of the social worker's task.

Policy research is a specialized form of inquiry whose purpose is the provision of reliable, valid, and relevant knowledge for public officials, agency managers, and others in the decision-making processes of government. It is used (or misused) at all levels of government and at all bureaucratic strata. Research studies employ techniques that vary from the simple collection and collation of available data to the design of sophisticated econometric models and social experiments.

Scientific research does not guide or control policy choices. History is replete with examples of public officials rejecting the advice of the research community. The rejection of research findings does not inevitably lead to negative results, nor does the acceptance of the recommendations of the research community always yield the intended beneficial results. Deciding on the contribution to and limits of the research to public decision making is a complex topic that has been treated extensively in other books (e.g.,

Haveman 1987). For example, if welfare benefits are to be raised and if eligibility standards are to be broadened, then there will be certain obvious consequences. There will also be less obvious, and perhaps even uncertain, consequences. Identifying or at least reducing the policy uncertainty is a central task of policy research. How a society uses this knowledge once it is generated is a political issue. The answer clearly depends not on what we know but on how our knowledge is related to the various social conditions and how that information is congruent—or incongruent—with particular ideologies and political belief systems. Conservative and liberal actors on the political scene will often select the theory that best fits the ends or goals they seek. Just as prosecution and defense attorneys both produce expert medical testimony, so also, social science is used and misused for larger political gain.

Today, almost all graduate schools of social work have created policy tracks or concentrations designed to prepare the professional social worker to assist in the formulation and analysis of policy alternatives in specialized areas, such as social work, public health, city management, or education. The use of research methods to discover and delineate means available to government to respond to problems is a practice as old as government. However, specialized education in research procedures, especially structured to policy choice, is a recent development.

Problems arise in the design, execution, and interpretation of research for specific policy choices that are not encountered in disciplinary research. Policy analysis frequently is expected to produce specific kinds of information in a short time on a limited budget. Policy and disciplinary research differ in other ways as well. Both policy research and disciplinary research are governed by the canons of scientific methodology. Disciplinary research is structured to provide theoretically relevant explanations of social phenomena. However, policy research is structured to provide an identification, assessment, and evaluation of public strategies used to produce public ends. As described by Majchrzak (1984), policy research is both an artistic and a scientific process, where the solution specifies a desirable relationship between manipulable means and obtainable ends. That is, the investigator directs the social worker to identify the best use of limited but available means to analyze those ends or goals that are realistic in light of what we know about the problem at hand.

Adequately executed social science research often is an inadequate guide to policy choice, because it often fails to be timely or is structured in a way that is unusable to the public official or agency manager. On the other hand, practitioners in the field often have failed to use the most elementary forms of inquiry before instituting a policy action. The connection between scientific demand on inquiry and political demands on action needs to be appraised.

EVALUATIVE RESEARCH

Policy evaluation is a specific kind of policy research. The ordinary method used to develop a policy perspective on an anticipated change in a program is to review the literature generally available. When this is done, the social worker typically has a mass of written documents, all of which are generally relevant

Professionals at all levels in the social welfare system rely on many types of research to help them develop new programs and policies. Here, staff at a substance abuse treatment program review the results of a study they conducted to evaluate their program.

but none of which is precisely related. One useful way to begin is with a particularly influential report, such as a study by the federal government or perhaps a study done in a state similar to one's own. Then the social worker can examine all of the principal bibliographies for relevant references for the new topic. Few social problems are brand new, and even a cursory examination of how other governments deal with similar problems is a valuable way to use existing knowledge to choose among policy options. Sometimes the investigation is very specific, such as what happens to emergency room use when a particular payment method is introduced. Sometimes it is very general, such as how applications for food stamps fluctuate with shifts in the economy. The social worker who serves as an advisor to policymakers needs to be alert to methods of dealing with such questions.

Evaluation, when competently done, measures the extent to which a program attains its goals. The evaluative process helps the practitioner specify, from the multiplicity of objectives, the set of objectives by which the program will be judged; declare that some observable phenomenon will be the basis for judging the program successful, and explain how the favorable outcome, if there is one, is the result of the policy action or program under consideration. In evaluative research the practitioner seeks to use the scientific method as the basic analytic tool in determining the program's impact. Because real-world conditions do not have the experimental purity of controlled laboratory conditions, specific research designs are used to maximize the likelihood of determining what the results of a program were. Because of the difficulties inherent in each phase of the process, the results are "known" only within a range of certainty. The principal task of the policy evaluator is not only to show success or failure but to indicate the range of certainty with which that judgment is made.

In addition to evaluating the effectiveness of social work programs, social workers also evaluate the effectiveness of their direct work with clients. **Single-subject designs,** research designs that evaluate the impact of interventions or policy changes on a single client or case, are often used by social workers in clinical settings.

IDENTIFICATION OF GOALS

The evaluative process begins with an identification of the goals to be evaluated. This seems obvious, but in fact is an inordinately value-laden undertaking. Initially, there is the problem of ranking goals in an effort to indicate which ones are intended, and their order of importance, and which are desirable but unintended consequences of the policy action or program. Second, the evaluator needs to state clearly the goals that will be measured. Sometimes there is confusion and conflict—possibly political—over goals. Social work research needs to be precise about which goals are being evaluated. Third, the evaluator must frankly and honestly deal with the dysfunctional or undesirable consequences that occur because of the policy action or program. Social science methodology often is overwhelmed by attempts to measure many goals simultaneously, yet the false specification of a program to a too-small set of objectives may mask the good points of a program and expose the bad points. Care in goal identification is a critical first step in devising a policy-relevant evaluation plan.

FORMULATION OF OPERATIONAL DEFINITIONS

The second critical step is the selection of valid and reliable measures of the positive and negative outcomes of programs. To be evaluated objectively, such outcomes must be defined in measurable terms; that is, operational definitions which define specific concepts and terms to be studied, for example, work effort, must be formulated. Once that is done, appropriate measures must be identified. A valid measure is one that does in fact measure what it is supposed to; for example, the number of hours worked in a week is thought to be one valid measure of work effort. Reliable measures are dependable and not subject to memory loss or other distortions in observation and reporting. In the example of measuring work effort, timekeeper's job records typically are more valid and reliable indicators than a worker's memory, although clearly this is not always the case. In social work programs the evaluator has the responsibility of demonstrating that the "observed" changes are valid and reliable estimates of the object of the policy action or program. The test of program success must stand up to criticism from the scientific and political communities. Thus, attention must be paid to the permanency of the impact, the reproducibility of the observation of success, and the reliability of the observation.

DEMONSTRATING A CAUSAL CONNECTION

It is insufficient to report that a favorable outcome occurred while a program was in place. The evaluator has to demonstrate that the outcome reasonably can be attributed to the policy action or program. The basic argument of causal connection was developed by the nineteenth-century philosopher and economist John Stuart Mill and remains the foundation of social science theories of causation. His approach rests on two methods, known as the positive and negative canons. The positive canon, called the sufficient condition, states that for a result, X, to occur, there has been an element, Y, prior in time. That is to say, whenever Y is observed, X always follows. Y thus is a sufficient condition of X.

Elements of Situation 1

$A,B,Y \rightarrow$ Produce $\rightarrow X$

Elements of Situation 2

$D,E,Y \rightarrow$ Produce $\rightarrow X$

Elements of Situation N

$M,N,Y \rightarrow$ Produce $\rightarrow X$

To say that Y is a sufficient condition is not to say, however, that it is a cause. The negative canon, or necessary condition, states that the absence of Y always is associated with the absence of X.

Elements of Situation 3

$F,G,$ non-Y $\rightarrow$ Produce $\rightarrow$ non-X

Elements of Situation 4

$H,I,$ non-Y $\rightarrow$ Produce $\rightarrow$ non-X

Elements of Situation M

$M,N,$ non-Y $\rightarrow$ Produce $\rightarrow$ non-X

Thus, if we observed all theoretically possible connections and then found that when Y was present X followed and that whenever Y was absent X did not occur, we could say that Y causes X. Now try to think of an example. Whenever we find a broken optic nerve, we find blindness. Broken optic nerves are a sufficient condition for blindness, but not necessarily a cause, since we find blindness occurring as a result of other factors. When there are unbroken optic nerves, we sometimes observe blindness. When we find fire, we find oxygen; when we remove oxygen, we never find fire. Therefore, oxygen is a necessary condition of fire, but not a cause, for we find oxygen and the absence of fire. Social science evaluation uses both the positive and negative canons. This is the classical experimental design and is called the "method of difference." The inference is then made that Y causes X. This inference is subject to criticism, however, on the grounds that both Y and X could result from some more fundamental but unobserved factor or that Y is associated with X only when some other factor is present (that is, Y and X were observed in the fashion noted, but this was a fortuitous occurrence).

Elements of Situation 5

$A, B, Y \rightarrow$ Produce $\rightarrow X$

and

Elements of Situation 6

$A, B,$ non-$Y \rightarrow$ Produce $\rightarrow$ non-X

In the classical design, the evaluator uses both theory and probability to increase the likelihood that the observed relationship, in fact, is a causal relationship. Theory is used to select the observations to be made. We observe A, B, on through N cases when there are compelling, logical reasons to believe that there is a causal connection. We exclude observations where there is no particular reason for investigations. Theories thus guide observations and lead investigators closer to a realistic understanding of the relationship between observed outcome and the program or policy action. The real understanding depends on the adequacy of the theory.

Second, we trust to the rules of chance. If we note an occurrence, by resorting to various statistical manipulations, we can calculate the probability that the observation would occur merely because of random factors. If we give one set of parents a course in child nutrition and, as far as we know, withhold that information from a second set of parents, then test the nutrition adequacy of their children's packed lunch both before and after the course on a score of 1 to 100, we find results such as those in Table 16–1. We can calculate the experimental impact as $(B-A)$ minus $(D-C)$, with $D-C$ being the change attributable to nonexperimental factors that occurred. Of course, we don't know what in the program caused the change, but if $(B-A)$ minus $(D-C)$ is significantly different from what we would expect to occur by any random process, it certainly is reasonable to behave as if nutritional education and nutritional performance are casually connected. If the goal is better nutritional performance, nutritional education appears to be one way of achieving it.

Table 16–1   Nutrition Scores of Parents

	Nutrition Score Before	Nutrition Score After
Parents given course	A	B
Parents not given course	C	D

Obviously, an evaluator who clearly identified the most relevant goal, selected the most appropriate units of evaluation, structured the relationship with the most finely tuned of theories, and tested the results with the most sophisticated statistical test still could not prove that program Y is the best way of achieving goal X. He or she could show only that Y is a reasonable way. Thus, social science evaluation can be used to help decision makers reject bad policy, but it cannot help them select with certainty the "best policy." Causal relationships that seem clear on the basis of logic are often difficult to test in the real world.

In this section we have used the term *experimental* impact in a technical way but not strictly in regards to the rigorous rules of formal experimental design. Also, we have not tried to deal with the many complex problems associated with the choice of research methods—surveys, field observations, field experiments, classical laboratory experiments, intensive case studies and single-subject designs, and so on. All of these might be used to establish causal connections. The important point here is that social workers need to back their beliefs about a program's success or failure with both theory and valid, reliable observations. In the following section we explore the fact that connections between cause and effect—between program interventions and policy results or between social work interventions and clinical observations—are made at many levels of abstraction and scientific rigor.

PRACTICE RESEARCH

The practitioner-researcher problem-solving process consists of four phases, or levels, of research activity. Each level of inquiry builds on the levels that precede it, as illustrated in Table 16–2.

Level 1

Level 1 research is undertaken to provide familiarity with a topic. This may be necessary because the investigator is exploring either an old topic for the first time or a new interest, or exploratory research may be required because the subject itself is new or unstudied. The purpose of level 1 research is to seek out the facts and provide a structure for thinking about the various aspects of the problem.

As an example, let's suppose there is an interest in the topic of family violence. The newly interested student would want to know several things: How is family violence to be defined? How extensive is the problem? Is there an increase in the actual incidence of family violence, or is the increase only apparent because of better reporting of incidents? Do any important subcategories of family violence need to be studied separately? The student would want to read the contemporary and classic literature on the topic, check the figures being reported, interview social workers and volunteers working at crisis centers, and perhaps talk with survivors of incidents of family violence and even perpetrators. In exploratory research the procedures of inquiry are relatively unsystematic. It is a first effort to see what is going on.

We might find, for example, that low-income families are treated in clinics, whereas other groups are treated by private physicians; and clinic doctors, for

Table 16–2   Forms of Research by Level of Research and Intent of Inquiry

Level of Research	Intent of Inquiry			
	Distinguish Concepts and Identify Significant Variables	**Describe and Measure Interaction of Variables**	**Establish Logically Connected and Verifiable Causal Paths among Variables**	**Locate and Isolate Manageable Variables to Alter Outcome**
Level 1: Exploratory	Case Studies X			
Level 2: Descriptive	X	Cross-Case Comparisons and Surveys X		
Level 3: Explanatory	X	X	Field Experiments and Statistical Tests X	
Level 4: Perspective	X	X	X	Practice Research X

whatever reason, are more likely to report suspicious injuries. If such is the case, the relationship between socioeconomic status and family violence is apparent, but not necessarily real. We might find that class is linked to verbal skills, and verbal skills are inversely linked to family violence. This tells us that the real association between class and violence is only indicative of a more fundamental (yet harder to observe) association.

After the initial review of the literature, exploratory studies tend to become somewhat more focused. Essentially, the purpose of exploratory study is to focus attention, to learn what the important questions are. Exploratory studies most typically are done for one of two interrelated purposes: (1) to satisfy an initial curiosity or a desire for a better understanding or (2) to lay groundwork for more careful inquiry at levels 2, 3, or 4.

In this first level of study an effort is made to define the central concepts of inquiry. Take, for example, the concept "intrafamily violence." A researcher would have considerable difficulty using the same conceptual definition for legal, educational, practice, and policy purposes. Also, investigators disagree on points such as whether to include spanking in the concept of family violence. In fact, it is more appropriate to recognize that the inclusion or exclusion of spanking as a category of family violence depends on the conceptual level and the purpose of the specific inquiry.

Level 2

Inquiry at this level seeks to establish the presence or absence of empirical regularities in the problem area. How is socioeconomic class associated with family violence? Are shifts observed in the reported incidence of family violence from one social class to the next? Is the observed change an artifact of the reporting of incidents, or does the actual rate of incidents shift? An evaluator's first general question is: Does the appearance of an association reflect a real association? Do people who differ from one another on social class lines, differ from one another in regard to the dependent problem—in this example, the incidence of violence within the family?

Level 3

Once a relationship has been established, level 3 research commences, and the researcher seeks to show not only an empirical regularity but a causal connection. At this point, a formal logical model is required. A causal connection requires a causal chain of events, such as the association between education and communication skills and family violence. A formal theory is stated that links educational attainment to communication skills and communication skills to family violence. If this were established, there would be not only an explanation of why family and educational levels are connected but also of what could change the situation. The practitioner cannot easily change educational level. However, it is possible to provide instruction and information on communication skills and thus break the links between education and family violence.

Level 4

The goal of practice research is the assessment and redirection of practice. Knowledge is gained not for its own sake but for direct use in the day-to-day activities of the social worker. Practice research has been criticized as being too subservient to theory, yet insufficiently based in theory. On one side is the assertion that practice models have developed from very highly specialized theoretical frameworks that are of limited use. They are distorted when applied to the range of client problems encountered by the social worker (Muller 1979). Others assert that practice is eclectic and that models of intervention are chosen intuitively and thus are not sufficiently based in theory to allow broad guidelines for action (Brier 1979). A third critique is that practice models are fixed and closed, unchanged from one generation of users to the next.

These three very diverse critiques appear to be true simultaneously. This occurs because, until very recently, practice wisdom and social work research developed as separate spheres. Only a narrow overlap existed between research and practice. In recent years, social workers in practice have begun to expand that overlap, particularly with evaluative research (Rubin & Babbie 1989).

SUMMARY

This chapter introduces the student to the wide range of activities that constitute social work research. The specific steps in the research process are reviewed, and it is shown how each step builds on previous ones. If there is one message of this chapter, it is that research and practice are not separate spheres but interrelated domains, each fundamentally dependent on the other. All social workers need to be involved in evaluating their efforts and continuing to generate new knowledge that can be used to strengthen social welfare policies and services.

KEY TERMS

disciplinary research
evaluation
evaluative research
hypothesis

policy research
single-subject designs
theory

DISCUSSION QUESTIONS

1. To what extent do you think the practice of social work research helps efforts to assist a client?
2. Can you think of an example where the research process and the practice process actually reinforce one another?

REFERENCES

Brier, Scott. 1979. Toward the integration of theory and practice. Paper read at the Conference on Social Work Research, San Antonio, Texas, October.

Haveman, Robert. 1987. *Poverty policy and policy research*. Madison: Univ. of Wisconsin Press.

Kuhn, Thomas S. 1962. *The structure of scientific revolutions*. Chicago: Univ. of Chicago Press.

Majchrzak, Ann. 1984. *Methods for policy research*. Beverly Hills, CA: Sage Publications.

Melanson, P. H. 1978. *Knowledge, politics and public policy*. Cambridge: Winthrop.

Muller, Edward H. 1979. Evaluating the empirical base of clinical circles. Paper read at the Conference on Social Work Research, San Antonio, Texas, October.

Rubin, Allen, and Earl Babbie. 1989. *Research methods for social workers*. Belmont, CA: Wadsworth.

SUGGESTED FURTHER READINGS

Rubin, Allen, and Earl Babbie. 1989. *Research methods for social workers*. Belmont, CA: Wadsworth.

Schoor, Lisbeth. 1988. *Within our reach: Breaking the cycle of dependency*. New York: Doubleday.

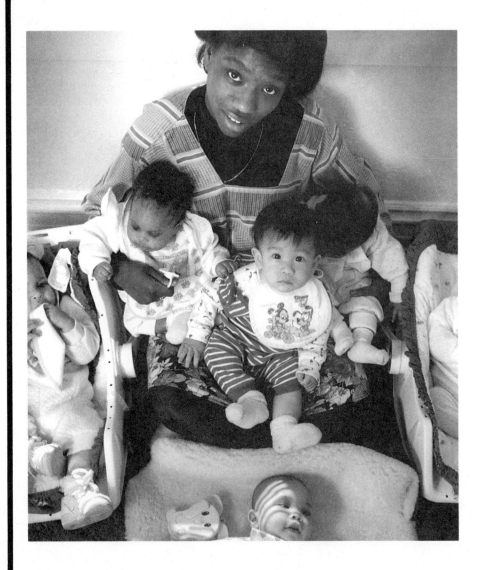

Part
IV

Special Issues

This section examines areas of special concern for the social welfare system and the social work profession. Chapter 17, "Sexism, Racism, and Homophobia: Issues and Problems in Achieving Social Equality," provides an analysis of how racism and sexism disenfranchise women and minority group members. Attention also is given to homosexuality and gender identity issues that result in differential treatment and discrimination. The roles of the social work profession in working toward the elimination of discrimination at the societal level, as well as in assisting individuals and groups experiencing problems due to discrimination and prejudice, also are addressed.

Chapter 18, "Social Work and the Other Helping Professions," identifies and describes the activities of other professionals who are involved in providing human services. This chapter also explores ways that these related professionals are used as resources in helping clients from the generalist social work perspective. This chapter is predicated upon the premise that generalist social work practitioners must be aware of and skilled at negotiating resources available for clients in the community that will enhance the resolution of problems.

Chapter 19, "The Voluntary Sector," examines the role of the private sector as a critical agent in helping individuals, groups, and communities in meeting needs and the interdependence between the private and public sectors in providing social welfare services. With continuing budgetary reductions at the federal, state, and local levels for social services, the role of nonpublic agencies has been viewed as critical in assuring that resources are available to help public service agencies accomplish their missions. This chapter explores private sector—public sector relationships and examines special issues faced by voluntary social service programs.

Chapter 20, "The Future of Social Work and Social Welfare," reviews the history of changes that characterize the social work profession and the field of social welfare, emphasizing the impact of technological and economic changes on the individual, family, and community. This chapter also attempts to forecast the probable character of the profession and of social welfare as they are influenced by future changes at the broader societal level.

These chapters seek to explore issues that are both contemporary and central to the social work profession's continual effort to anticipate and respond to social change and to assist individuals, families, and communities in adapting as these changes occur. As a growing profession, social work continually must be sensitive to social change and its implications for practice. Because social work will remain on the cutting edge in meeting human needs as we move into the twenty-first century, the profession will remain a challenging one with diverse opportunities.

Chapter 17

Sexism, Racism, and Homophobia: Issues and Problems in Achieving Social Equality

Mildred Johnson, one of three children of Frank and Leona Johnson, had always aspired to become a petroleum engineer. Frank, a maintenance man for an automobile dealer, and Leona, a cook at a local restaurant, had encouraged her to pursue her dream. Her parents contributed as much of their resources as possible in helping her complete high school and enroll in a college that offered a petroleum engineering degree. Officials at the college were not too encouraging, but her persistence finally resulted in her admittance to the program. She was an outstanding student and graduated with highest honors. Thrilled with her accomplishments, she was eager to locate a job with a major oil company and begin her career.

Mildred completed applications for several large companies. Of the seven applications that she completed, only one company responded and wanted to interview her. Officials at the company were impressed with her credentials, but they indicated that the nature of field exploration would make it difficult for her to perform her duties. They did, however, offer her a clerk's position with the company. Mildred was a twenty-five-year-old black female.

Like Mildred, many individuals seek fulfillment and opportunity, only to find that social barriers hamper the achievement of those goals. Mildred may well exemplify such a case. The evidence suggests that she was an excellent candidate for the position, having graduated with honors from a top petroleum engineering program. Why, then, was she passed over for the position? Could it have been that she was a woman? Or that she was black? The limited information provided in the short case history provides little basis for conjecture. If we are confident that Mildred was at least as well qualified as other applicants, however, it may be plausible to consider that her gender, her race, or both underlay the decision not to offer her the position. The fact that the company officials offered her a more menial position, in spite of her superior qualifications, suggests that they are not willing to advance women (and black women, in particular) to significant professional roles with the company. Even if Mildred suspected that gender or race (or both) were factors in the company's decisions, that would have been difficult to prove.

Unfortunately, Mildred represents only one of millions of Americans who find that social and economic justice is not necessarily achieved through hard work. All too often, social mobility and opportunity are not available equally to all who aspire to achieve the American dream. Women and minority group members long have been denied opportunities in business and social life that white men have come to expect and take for granted. Under the subtle guise of institutional sexism and racism, the rights to free and full participation in our social and economic institutions are denied to individuals who fail to meet dominant group criteria. In reviewing Mildred's case, it is possible that company officials' justification for not offering the job to Mildred was a tradition of having white men in petroleum engineering positions. Rationalizing their position, the officials may have felt that male engineers are more suited to the arduous fieldwork required, or they may have believed that women should not do that type of work. Whatever their rationale, their decision effectively excluded Mildred from securing the position.

In this chapter we examine the characteristics of social inequality implicit in racism and sexism in more detail. The effects of social inequality are not always equal between minorities and women. It is somewhat ironic that white women, the targets of gender inequality, often discriminate against minority group members. In order to understand better the differential effects of institutional racism and sexism, each is reviewed separately. The reader needs to keep in mind that both lead to a life of second-class citizenship in our society. The ways that prejudice and discrimination are directed toward gays and lesbians are also discussed.

PREJUDICE AND DISCRIMINATION

Social inequality is partly a result of prejudice and discrimination. **Prejudice** is a value learned through the process of socialization. Prejudices are internalized and become a dimension of an individual's value system. People who are prejudiced generally do not consider themselves so. The objects of prejudice are presumed to possess behavioral characteristics that the holders of prejudice find objectionable. Through the process of **stereotyping,** women and minority group members all are assumed to hold behavior traits that justify their exclusion from free and full participation in the social roles of society. Stereotypes are beliefs that members of certain groups always or generally behave in specific ways. Hence, the belief that women are not as intelligent as men, lack decision-making ability, are prone to be emotional, and are better nurturers; that blacks are lazy and lack initiative; that Mexican-Americans prefer the slower pace of an agrarian life; or that Jews are elitist and money hungry—these are among many of the stereotypes associated with groups. Dominant group members often behave toward members of minorities as though the stereotypes were true. To illustrate better how prejudice affects decision making, consider this example paraphrased from the work of Gordon Allport in *The Nature of Prejudice* (1958, 5):

*Applications for hotel reservations were sent to a number of resort hotels in
Canada. The name of Lockwood and Greenwood was affixed to separate letters
both sent to the same hotels and mailed separately on the same date. Lockwood received an acknowledgment of his inquiries from over 90 percent of
the hotels with most of them confirming his reservation. Less than 10 percent
responded to Greenwood's request and only 5 percent offered accommodations.*

Considering that it is highly unlikely that Lockwood's letter was always the
first opened and that he was allotted the very last room available, how does
one account for this differential outcome? Discrimination—namely, anti-Semitism
in this instance—is the only viable answer.

Prejudice is the presumption, without the benefit of factual information,
that certain behaviors are characteristic of all members of a minority group. As
a consequence, members of the dominant group may demean minorities by
assuming that assigned behaviors in fact are true, and then relate to individual
members through the filter of prejudice. In the case of Mr. Lockwood and Mr.
Greenwood, it is clear that Greenwood was perceived as Jewish and therefore
undesirable as a guest. Lockwood, on the other hand, was presumed to be
white Protestant and acceptable. The hotel's decision was made without any
specific information or facts about either.

Prejudice is a psychological construct that may result in discrimination.
Although prejudice can exist without discrimination (and discrimination without
prejudice, for that matter), they usually coexist (Yinger 1970). Prejudice fuels
the fires and provides the justification for discrimination. If it is falsely believed

*Major tenets of
the social work
profession accept
the uniqueness of
each individual
and the diversity
of groups of peo-
ple in an effort to
overcome injus-
tice and
inequality.*

(an axiom for prejudice) that people of certain groups are less intelligent, incapable of equal participation, or would threaten traditional practices, differential treatment (an axiom for discrimination) may occur, thereby placing the erroneously feared threat at some distance. Denying women, minorities, the elderly, gays, and other social groups the right to equal social participation limits the opportunity structures through which the desired behavioral characteristics could be acquired. A viscious, self-perpetuating cycle is then set in motion. Discrimination is the action that maintains and supports prejudice. Zastrow (1986, 379) observes that

> individuals who are targets of discrimination are excluded from certain types of employment, educational and recreational opportunities, certain residential housing areas, membership in certain religious and social organizations, certain political activities, access to community services, and so on.

Institutional discrimination and the resultant differential treatment have been codified in administrative rules and regulations and are thereby "intrinsic" to the mores of a society. Discrimination is reinforced through the social practices of dominant group members, who may be oblivious to the effects of their actions. Institutionalized racism is based on minority group membership, whereas institutionalized sexism results in the denial of rights or opportunities for participation on the basis of gender. In both instances, free and full participation is denied on the basis of group membership.

In the book *The Compleat Chauvinist*, Edgar Bergman, a physician in Maryland, (1982, 185) raises the question, "What would our Neanderthal forefathers have thought of our succumbing to the outrageous myth of sexual equality?" In buttressing his antiegalitarian views, he refers to comments made by Marvin Harris, a professor of anthropology at Columbia University, who is quoted as saying:

> Feminists are wailing in the wind if they think they're (sic) going to abolish sexism by raising consciousness. There is not a shred of evidence—historical or contemporary—to support the existence of a single society in which women controlled the political and economic lives of men.

Bergman offers a number of illustrations in defense of the position that men are clearly superior to women in decision making. To the detriment of social equality, Bergman's views and arguments are not new. Women have experienced social inequality throughout recorded history. Invariably, inequality was—and is—justified on the basis of the biological superiority of men, despite no evidence to support that premise. In the social sciences, social inequality is viewed as a product of human interaction and social organization (Perrucci & Knudsen 1983).

WOMEN AND SOCIAL INEQUALITY

In spite of advances made during the past several decades, women in our society experience discrimination. Perhaps sex-biased discrimination is more visible in the occupational market and economic areas than in other aspects of social participation. Zastrow (1986, 392) has identified a few of the more salient roles played by women as follows:

> Women tend to be concentrated in the lower paying, lower status positions of secretaries, child care workers, receptionists, typists, nurses, hairdressers, bank tellers, cashiers, and file clerks. Men tend to be concentrated in higher paying positions: lawyers, judges, engineers, accountants, college teachers, physicians, dentists, and sales managers.

Although some progress has been made, male-dominated job positions have remained virtually unobtainable to qualified women. Management and administrative positions at the upper levels continue to be held mostly by men.

Income

From 1890 to 1986, the proportion of all white women who were in the labor force increased from 14.9 percent to 66.3 percent, and the proportion of non-white women who were in the labor force increased from 38.4 percent to 66.4 percent (Presser 1987). These increases ushered in a number of conflicts and issues related to women's participation in the labor market. Chief among the issues was the concept of "comparable worth."

> Comparable worth has radical implications because it initiates an end to women's economic dependency and questions the market basis of wages. In doing so, it exposes the way gender hierarchy is incorporated into the organization of the economy, the traditional strategies of the labor movement, and the ideologies of gender in the United States; it provides the basis for an attack on the sexual division of labor and gender hierarchy; and it lays the foundation for reordering of gender relations throughout social life (Feldberg 1984, 312–13).

Comparable worth is a concept often best understood by the phrase "equal pay for equal work." Much of the income disparity between men and women, however, is largely attributable to differences in occupational positions, which have changed little over the past decade. As Matthews and Rodin note, "Although women have entered the labor force in tremendous numbers since 1970, they are still by and large entering occupations that are dominated by women" (1989, 1391). Income differences exist primarily because men are employed in positions of leadership or in technical fields, whereas women are disproportionately employed in the lower-paying clerical and service fields. Even when women hold positions similar to those of men, their income is less. Seniority or related factors do not always account for these differences, and employers generally concede that, for a given type of position, men get a higher income than do women. Overall, women earn only approximately 60 percent of what men do in the labor force (Johnson & Packer 1987).

Notwithstanding traditional notions that incomes produced by women are less essential for family maintenance than those generated by men, the practice of channeling women into lower-level positions, with the resultant limited career choices and lower incomes, represents an institutionalized policy of sex-based discrimination. Although efforts recently have been made to provide equal employment opportunities for women, social roles continue to be sex typed and are passed down from generation to generation through the process of socialization.

Education

Ironically, men hold leadership positions in professions that predominantly employ women, such as public education and social work. In a study of Texas public school administrators (Shuttlesworth 1978), it was found that

> administration and school leadership at all levels are dominated by males. During 1967–1977 less than 1 percent of the superintendents' positions were filled by women. In 1977, the year of the largest number of women appointed to administrative positions, women held only 7 out of 1106 superintendent positions, 607 out of 4471 principalships and 360 out of 2030 assistant principalships.

These findings suggest that a career-oriented woman entering the educational system would have greater difficulty in securing promotion to an administrative position than a similar man. As a result, women are relegated to the lower-paying, less prestigious position of classroom teacher throughout their careers. Although nondiscrimination policies exist, qualified women educators who seek promotion to administration are confronted with the task of penetrating a sex-biased tradition of assigning men to those roles in the public school system.

When comparing educational attainment, men are awarded degrees in greater numbers than women, particularly at the graduate level. In 1980, men were awarded 23,100 doctoral degrees, compared to only 9,700 awarded to women (see Table 17–1). Although larger numbers of women are now engaged in the educational process at both graduate and undergraduate levels, men continue to dominate the educational degree market (U.S. Bureau of the Census 1981). Women are less well represented in business administration, engineering, the physical sciences, law, medicine, and dentistry; and they are overrepresented in the liberal arts, fine arts, home economics, social work, and nursing, thereby limiting opportunities to achieve educational credentials necessary for entry into the male-dominated occupations and professions.

Table 17–1   College and Advanced Degrees Awarded

	Bachelors		Masters		Doctorate	
	Male	Female	Male	Female	Male	Female
1950	330,000	104,000	41,000	17,000	6,000	600
1960	256,000	139,000	51,000	24,000	8,800	1,000
1970	487,000	346,000	126,000	83,000	25,900	4,000
1980	530,000	480,000	151,000	148,000	23,100	9,700

Source: U.S. Bureau of the Census, *Statistical Abstract of the United States.* (Washington, D.C.: GPO, 1981).

Social Work

Historically, most social work professionals have been women. Dressel reported that as of 1987 two-thirds of all social work practitioners were women (1987, 297). In a field that long has championed equal rights for women (as well as one that is predominantly female), it is ironic that leadership roles are primarily held by men. Fanshel (1976) reports that men are represented disproportionately in administrative and managerial roles, and, as a group, receive higher salaries than women (448–53). To that extent, the social work profession—despite its advocacy of women's rights—reflects the tendency of other professions as well as the business community.

Religion

In organized religion, where women are more active participants, less than 5 percent are ordained to the clergy (Perrucci & Knudsen 1983). In very few instances do women hold the position of primary leadership in churches, and even less often are they employed in higher levels of administration in religious associations. Many religious groups base their male-biased pastoral leadership roles on the "holy writ," thereby effectively excluding women from appointments to significant leadership responsibilities in those bodies.

Politics

In 1991, only 29 of 435 U.S. representatives and 2 of 100 U.S. senators were women (Congressional Quarterly Weekly Report 1990). Only 3 of the 50 governors were women. These figures reflect the subordinate role that women continue to play in the legislative process. Male bias is ever present in legislative debates in those areas where laws directly affect women.

INSTITUTIONAL SEXISM

The discussion and illustrations just presented indicate the strong sexual bias in administrative and managerial positions. Women *are* treated differently in the professions and business. Their status as women negatively influences the opportunity to move into those prominent roles *regardless* of their competence or ability. In effect, women are discriminated against in the marketplace solely because they are women. This practice, called **sexism,** is a result of the values and practices embodied in our social institutions. Children are taught by their parents that boys are to be aggressive and dominant and that girls are to be nurturing and submissive. Parents model these attributes in family interaction, where father assumes the roles of rule maker, disciplinarian, and decision maker and mother assumes responsibility for the nurturing roles of caring for the children and the household.

Performance differences between men and women invariably reflect societal attitudes and values far more than any inherent physical or psychological variances in maleness or femaleness. In modern society few roles exist that could not be performed by either men or women, although throughout the life cycle sex-role distinctions are made and differences are emphasized. These distinctions become entrenched in societal values, thus hindering women from "crossing over" into roles considered masculine. Hence, an aggressive, goal-oriented, intelligent woman may be viewed as masculine and censured for departing from prescribed female role behavior.

Societal values and practices continue to result in a sex-segregated division of labor. Although some progress has been made in identifying roles as "asexual" (neither male nor female), roles in general are sex typed. Women have great difficulty gaining access to roles identified as appropriate for men only. Sex differentiation also is observed in opportunities to secure credit, purchase homes, negotiate contracts, and obtain credit cards, where men typically have the advantage.

THE ABORTION DILEMMA

One of the more emotionally charged issues that epitomizes the conflict between feminist and traditional values is abortion. In reality, abortion consists of three central concerns: (1) the legal issue, (2) the medical issue, and (3) the value issue.

The Legal Issue

The legal precedent for abortion was established in 1973 by the *Roe v. Wade* decision. In effect, the U.S. Supreme Court maintained that a woman has the constitutional right to seek an abortion, if she so desires. This decision defined abortion as a personal decision rather than one to be determined by government policy. Although the Court's interpretation was straightforward and clear, attempts were made to cut funds from family planning agencies that gave abortion counseling and references. The lack of acceptance of the Court's ruling did not, however, close the door on the controversy. More recently, states have been delegated the power to determine abortion policy. A 1989 policy established by Florida imposed strict requirements on abortions, so that legal abortions could be performed only when a pregnancy resulted from rape or when the health of the mother would be in jeopardy, should the pregnancy continue. In 1990, Louisiana sought to pass similar legislation. In spite of *Roe v. Wade,* there is no uniform code that mandates "abortion on demand" across the states. It is estimated, however, that approximately 1.5 million abortions are performed in the United States each year.

The Medical Issue

From a medical perspective, abortion, during the first trimester of a pregnancy, is a relatively simple, uncomplicated procedure. Although there is risk involved with any medical intervention, abortion is generally not considered a high-risk procedure, even during the second trimester. The majority of abortions are performed during the first trimester and very few during the last trimester. Assessing women's psychological preparedness for an abortion can be difficult. Most abortion clinics require a psychological assessment and counseling as prerequisites for an abortion. Few studies have attempted to assess postabortion adaptation, and their results have, for the most part, provided limited insight.

The Value Issue

Perhaps the most emotionally charged aspect of abortion involves values. Members of the anti-abortion (right-to-life) movement base their resistance to abortion on the conviction that life begins at conception. Consequently, they view abortion (termination of the fetus) as murder. Members of prochoice groups, on the other hand, argue that life begins at birth, and they further insist that a woman has the constitutionally granted right to decide whether she wishes to continue her pregnancy or terminate it. Anti-abortion groups seek the government's protection of the life (and rights) of the fetus in the same sense that children and adults merit the protection of the law from injury or injustice. Within each of the groups there is some variance of value positions. For example, while arguing that life begins at conception, some anti-abortion groups take the position that abortion is acceptable and justified in instances of rape or where the mother's health would be jeopardized. Other anti-abortion groups oppose abortion under any circumstance, arguing that taking the life of the fetus is not acceptable under any circumstance.

Abortion is not solely a women's problem. However, only women become pregnant and have the legal right to decide whether a pregnancy will be carried to its full term or terminated. The law remains unusually silent concerning the role of men in matters of conception and pregnancy. Fathers are referred to as "alleged fathers," and they have no legal right to affect a woman's decision to abort a pregnancy.

We have included this discussion to illustrate further the problem of differential treatment of women in our society. Social workers must be especially attuned to such treatment and to the views surrounding abortion. Although they may have personal views that would preclude their participation in abortion counseling they have a professional responsibility to assure that referrals are made in order to protect the rights of the client. Zastrow (1986) clearly outlines the profession's position as follows:

> Our premise is that social work as a profession must view abortion as a legal right of every client, should she make this choice, and must therefore sublimate personal beliefs to that end. It is the practioner's responsibility to facilitate intelligent, rational, and unanimous decision making on the part of the individual client, and to support that decision, whatever it may be.

While professional social workers may agree with the preceding statement, one must not conclude that all social workers support the prochoice position. Social workers, like other professionals, vary greatly in their personal values, and this is certainly true regarding the abortion controversy.

SOCIAL REFORM: THE FEMINIST MOVEMENT AND SOCIAL ACTION

Women have pursued equal social treatment since this nation's inception. Some of the more noteworthy leaders were Elizabeth Stanton (1815–1902), who petitioned for a property rights law for women in New York (1845); Lucretia Mott (1793–1880), who organized the first women's rights convention in New York; Susan B. Anthony (1820–1906), who helped to form the National Women's Suffrage Association in 1869; and Lucy Stone (1818–1893), who formed the National American Women's Suffrage Association. Carrie Catt (1859–1947), a political activist, founded the International Women's Suffrage Alliance and later, following World War I, the League of Women Voters, an organization that today wields significant political influence. Ms. Catt's efforts were largely responsible for the enactment of the Nineteenth Amendment to the Constitution, which extended voting rights to women in 1920 (Macksey 1976).

In more recent times, women's groups have intensified their efforts to secure equal rights. The Civil Rights Act of 1964 addressed the problems of discrimination due to gender as well as race. A major attempt to secure women's rights was embodied in the **Equal Rights Amendment (ERA).** Bitterly opposed by organized labor, the John Birch Society, the Christian Crusade, and the Moral Majority, and over the protest of Senator Sam Ervin (D–North Carolina), who castigated the proposed amendment, the bill was passed by Congress in 1972 and remanded to the states for ratification. Pro-ERA forces, including the National Organization for Women (NOW), the League of Women Voters, and the National Women's Political Caucus, lobbied the states to seek ratification for the amendment. Anti-ERA spokespersons lobbied the states against ratification and argued that all women would be sent into combat, subjected to unisex public facilities, and required to secure jobs (Deckard 1983) if the amendment passed. The Carter administration, favorable to passage of the ERA, had little influence on the states in encouraging its adoption. The Reagan administration opposed the measure. The unratified amendment died in June 1982.

SOCIAL WORK RIGHTS FOR WOMEN

Although the profession of social work has advocated for the abolition of societal barriers that deny equal treatment of women, it has not been in the forefront in providing leadership for the more significant feminist movements. During the 1960s, however, women's equality was established as a major priority for the profession. Both the National Association of Social Workers (NASW) and the Council on Social Work Education (CSWE) initiated policies committing the profession to promotion of social and economic equality for women (Zastrow 1986). Social workers were encouraged to advocate for women's rights and to treat all their clients equally. The abolition of sexism within the profession has been vigorously pursued and evidence suggests that sex-biased career opportunities are being eliminated.

GAYS, LESBIANS, AND SOCIAL INEQUALITY

According to reliable data, 10 percent of the U.S. population is homosexual. Within the past decade, considerable attention has been directed to the prejudice and discrimination that characterize societal responses toward homosexual men and women. Although one's sexual persuasion is considered to be a personal and private matter not related to free and full participation in our society, such has not been the case for homosexuals. As Dulaney and Kelly have noted, the intense negative emotional reaction to the homosexual community is a result of "deep-rooted fear and accompanying hatred of homosexual lifestyles and individuals" (1982, 178), a state of psychological conditioning known as **homophobia.** Although it is not known what percentage of the American population is homophobic, Irwin and Thompson (1977, 107–121) found that one-fourth of the respondents to a research inquiry believed that homosexuals should be banned from teaching in colleges and universities. This attitude appears to permeate the business community and carries over to other aspects of social life as well. Acquired immune deficiency syndrome (AIDS) has further promoted anxiety and fear toward homosexual relationships.

The rejection of homosexual practices, with its consequent nurturance of prejudice and discrimination, has been bolstered in fundamentalist religions as well as the more traditional psychologies. For example, the Moral Majority and Christian Voice movements, which strongly argue that homosexual practices are sinful, have condemned homosexuals along with deviants, pornographers, and athiests (Young 1982). Beiber, a psychoanalyst, in his classic work titled *Homosexuality* (1962), clearly describes traditional psychoanalysts' view that homosexuality is nonnormative and that it can be cured through psychotherapy. These (and other) "authoritative" sources reinforce the biases and prejudices that have long existed in the general population.

Twenty-five states currently have laws designed to prohibit specified sexual acts between consenting adults, with ten states classifying such behaviors as misdemeanors and the remaining fifteen, as felonies. These are laws that are generally used to restrict (or punish) homosexual behavior. Only two states (Wisconsin and Massachusetts) have passed legislation to protect the rights of gays and lesbians (Knopp 1990).

Although experts disagree as to whether sexual orientation is determined by genetics or is a product of socialization, the general public continues to view homosexuality as a matter of choice. Some gays and lesbians have become more vocal and have sought legal redress for discriminatory practices, whereas others, fearing loss of jobs, intimidation, and harassment, have opted to remain "in the closet." In 1973 the American Psychiatric Association removed "functional homosexuality" from its list of behavior disorders, and as a result, mental health professionals no longer view homosexuality as a form of mental illness. One might conclude, however, that the public maintains the perspective that gay and lesbian relationships are a form of perversion and that social contact with homosexuals should be avoided. Although some progress has been made in securing legal rights for members of the gay community, discrimination and prejudice continue to undergird public responses to them.

The homosexual life-style has not been without advocates. One of the earlier groups to support the rights of gays and lesbians was the Chicago Society for Human Rights (1924). In 1950, the Mattachine Society was founded to further rights for and acceptance of same-sex-oriented individuals. Currently, the Gay Liberation Front has established itself as a political organization promoting passage of legislation that would provide for nondiscriminatory practices against homosexuals, including recognition of same-sex marriages as well as adoption rights.

Unfortunately, in spite of the enlightenment regarding same-sex orientation, many professionals find it difficult to overcome their own biases and prejudices when helping homosexual clients. Dulaney and Kelly (1982, 178) report that

> social work is most sensitive to contemporary social pressures because of its sources of funding and orientation to community service. This sensitivity has led to a conflict in the profession regarding sexual issues and gay and lesbian clients that reflects society's dual value system, which consists of one set of values for heterosexuals and another for homosexuals.

De Crescenzo and McGill (1978) found that homophobia was far more prevalent among social workers than among psychologists and psychiatrists. Although there may be a variety of explanations as to why social workers tend to be more homophobic than other professionals, a primary reason may be that social workers' lack of skill and intense discomfort in dealing with gay and lesbian clients are largely attributable to the fact that social work students receive almost no training regarding homosexuality in their formal education (Dulaney & Kelly 1982, 179).

Since the majority of the U.S. population is heterosexually oriented, homosexuals experience prejudice and discrimination much like that faced by other minority group members. Stereotypical thinking based on erroneous information guides most heterosexuals' reactions to the gay community. Thus, same-sex-oriented individuals are often denied freedom of expression and access to an opportunity structure that is available for heterosexuals.

Clearly, social work and related professions need to address more forcefully the prejudices and biases toward homosexuality as yet pervasive within the professions. In spite of the acknowledged reticence that exists, considerable progress has been made in the preparation of social workers for engaging clients who are gay or lesbian. Accreditation standards for schools of social work require that course content address the needs of divergent populations, including gays and lesbians. Advocacy on behalf of the homosexual population directed towards the enforcement of antidiscrimination legislation has become a priority of the profession.

Unfortunately, until the fear and apprehensions concerning homosexual behavior are dispelled through public enlightenment, prejudice and discrimination will continue to remain barriers to social and economic justice for the gay and lesbian community.

SOCIAL INEQUALITY AND MINORITY GROUP MEMBERSHIP

What constitutes minority group status? According to Wirth, a **minority group** "is a category of people distinguished by special physical or cultural traits which are used to single them out for differential and unequal treatment" (Wirth 1938). The assignment to a minority status may be made on the basis of "race, nationality, religion or ethnicity" (Perrucci & Knudsen 1983). Hence, blacks, Mexican-Americans, other Hispanics, Asian-Americans, Moslems, Lithuanians, Iranians, or Vietnamese, among others, are defined by the dominant (majority) group as minorities. The concept of race suggests that marked, distinct genetic differences are present. The term, in reality, is a social definition, since few genetic differences are found to exist among homo sapiens. Race is commonly used to classify members of groups who have similar physical characteristics such as color or facial features. Behavioral traits are attributed to physical differences rather than to socialization experiences. Conversely, ethnic groups tend to be classified by language differences or cultural patterns that vary from those of the dominant group. Both racial and ethnic groups are viewed as "different" by the dominant group, and prejudice and discrimination are often the result.

PLURALISM

Complete integration of all groups in society would result in the loss of racial or ethnic identity. Many minorities find this prospect objectionable. In recent years, ethnic and racial pride has been given considerable attention by minority group members. Although complete integration (assimilation) theoretically would result in the erosion of racial and ethnic discrimination patterns, it probably will not occur. Many people argue that the contributions of our divergent ethnic and racial groups enrich our culture.

An alternative, **cultural pluralism,** the coexistence of various ethnic groups whose cultural differences are respected as equally valid (Perrucci & Knudsen 1983), is difficult to achieve without some vestige of discrimination. Dominant groups demand adherence to their values. Pluralism is difficult to achieve within the matrix of prejudice, discrimination, and cultural differences. Recently, minorities have tried to create and promote cultural pride, yet less-than-equal coexistence continues to characterize their relationship with the dominant group.

Members of minority groups invariably suffer the results of prejudice and discrimination. It is ironic that these conditions persist and are institutionalized by members of a society that values its Judeo-Christian heritage and provides equal constitutional rights and privileges to all. Progress has been made in opening avenues for social and economic participation; however, members of minorities still must cope with differential treatment and limited opportunities. The following discussion identifies issues and problems that confront minority groups and examines antidiscrimination efforts designed to neutralize racial and ethnic prejudices.

African-Americans

All minority groups have experienced discrimination, but none more visibly than our black population. Emerging from slavery, where they were considered chattel (property) and nonpersons, blacks have continually found societally imposed constraints impeding their progress toward the achievement of social equality. During the "Jim Crow" days, for example, blacks could not dine at public restaurants used by whites, could use only specially marked public restrooms and drinking fountains, had to ride in the rear of buses, had to attend segregated schools, faced expectations of subservient behavior in the presence of whites, and could get only lower-paying domestic or manual labor jobs. Few could achieve justice before the law or gain acceptance as equals to even the lowest-class whites. Although the prescribed behaviors that characterized "Jim

Crowism" represented an extreme manifestation of discrimination, all minority groups have experienced social inequality in its more subtle forms.

Today, the results of past and present discrimination are best reflected in the characteristics of blacks who represent about 11 percent of our total population. Blacks earn only 60 percent as much income as whites, unemployment is particularly high among young black adults (30 percent), and black families are three times more likely than whites to have incomes below the poverty line. Although, numerically, more whites receive public assistance in one form or another, blacks are proportionally overrepresented on welfare rolls. Educationally, whites complete high school in greater proportions than blacks, and blacks are underrepresented in the fields of law, medicine, dentistry, and business and overrepresented in occupations that require hard manual labor. These data reflect the differential opportunity structure available to the black population in this country.

Mexican-American and Other Hispanic Populations

People of Mexican descent constitute the second largest minority population in the United States. Although most live in major urban areas of the West and Southwest, many continue to reside in rural areas. The Mexican-American population is a diverse group. The urban population tends to be better educated, and the effects of acculturation are more visible among them. Those living in rural areas are less acculturated, continue to use Spanish as a primary language, and work in lower-paying jobs often related to harvesting of farm crops. This population group is rapidly growing as "undocumented aliens" continue to flow across the border into the southwestern states and California. Cultural pride is greatly emphasized and is best reflected in the retention of Spanish as a first language. Bilingual education programs have been designed to enable Mexican-American children to progress in public school systems, although dropout rates continue to be much higher than for the dominant group population. In general, people of Mexican ancestry have experienced the consequences of discrimination in that they hold lower-paying jobs and are underrepresented in politics, live in de facto segregated neighborhoods, and are viewed as being "different" by the dominant group. Upward mobility has been painfully slow in coming, although some progress has been made. Ethnic organizations such as La Raza and LULAC (League of United Latin American Citizens) have sought to unite the Spanish-speaking population to promote favorable social change and to provide greater visibility to the issues and problems that impede the achievement of social equality.

Puerto Ricans and Cubans constitute the largest other Hispanic populations. Approximately two-thirds of the Puerto Rican population reside in the New York City area, while the Cuban population has settled primarily in Florida. The social and economic progress of these groups is similar to that of the Mexican-American group. Housing is often inferior, jobs tend to be menial and lower paying, the school dropout rate is high, and access to services and support systems is difficult. Social progress has been considerably greater for the Cuban population due, in part, to its higher educational level. As has been the case with newly migrated Mexicans, other Hispanics came to the United States with

Cultural traditions are an important aspect of all cultures. Here, individuals celebrate Cinco de Mayo, a Mexican-American holiday.

the hopes of being able to achieve a higher-quality life, only to find that prejudice and discrimination presented barriers to achieving that dream. Cultural and language barriers continue to make them "different" and more visible targets for differential treatment.

Asian-Americans

The Japanese, Chinese, Vietnamese, and other Asian immigrants have divergent cultural traits and physical characteristics that separate them from the dominant group. They represent less than 2 percent of the United States population. The immigration of the Chinese dates back to the mid-nineteenth century, the Japanese to around the turn of the twentieth century, and the Vietnamese to the 1960s and 1970s. All have experienced differential treatment; however, many have been able to achieve a relatively high standard of living in spite of the social barriers. The Chinese have been noted for their ingroup living patterns;

"Chinatowns" in San Francisco, Los Angeles, New York, and other larger cities encourage the preservation of their cultural heritage. Prejudice and discrimination continue to be among the more significant obstacles for Asian-Americans in achieving social and economic progress. The Vietnamese have been the most recent target for discrimination and have had difficulty locating adequate housing, employment opportunities, and acceptance in American communities. Language barriers have intensified "differences" and have closed avenues for social and economic participation.

Native Americans

Numerically the smallest minority group, Native Americans (American Indians), have over the years, been consistently among the most oppressed. Native Americans, who, prior to colonialization were free to establish their villages and roam the countryside, lost all rights and privileges, once conquered. Considered savages (less than human), most were relegated to reservations where they found oppressive limits on their behaviors and freedom of movement. The responsibility for overseeing these reservations was given to the Bureau of Indian Affairs, a governmental agency that more often was a barrier rather than a help.

Although they were the first "Americans," Native Americans seldom have been able to experience free and full involvement in society; and, currently, large numbers continue to live on reservations, further segregating them from interaction with the dominant group and limiting their opportunity structure. Reservations represent the most overt form of purposeful discrimination. Although the plight of Native Americans has somewhat improved in recent years (with higher levels of education and commercial development on the reservations), many barriers to free and full social participation remain.

This Navajo woman is grinding corn as her young grandson looks on. Social workers working with diverse groups must provide services that understand and support the unique aspects of each group.

EFFORTS TO PRODUCE SOCIAL EQUALITY FOR MINORITY GROUPS

Bringing an end to institutional racism and discrimination is not an easy task. Prejudices have lingered over a number of generations and are difficult to extinguish, in spite of efforts to enlighten the public about the consequences of maintaining false beliefs and practices. Little progress was made in dismantling segregation until the government initiated action to do so. Until President Truman ordered the cessation of segregation in the Armed Forces (1948), most government agencies supported separation of the races (Perrucci & Knudsen 1983).

School Desegregation

The catalyst for ending separate public school education was the Supreme Court decision *Brown v. Board of Education* (1954), which mandated an end to segregation in public schools. Ruling that "separate was not equal," the Court ordered public school facilities integrated and opened to children of all races and ethnic groups. Because of de facto housing patterns, minorities lived in common neighborhoods and their children attended neighborhood schools. In order to implement the court's decision, busing became necessary, which resulted in strong resistance by the white population. White citizens' councils emerged in the South and Midwest to resist school integration. Many state governments questioned the constitutionality of the Court's decision and resisted taking appropriate action to hasten the integration process. "Evidence" was sought to support the position that integration of school facilities would have catastrophic effects on the educational achievements of children of all races. In a 1962 report entitled *The Biology of the Race Problem*, written by Wisley C. George, a biologist, and commissioned by the governor of Alabama, an attempt was made to offer scientific evidence that blacks innately were inferior to whites and would not be capable of competing with whites in the educational process. Various racist, white supremacist groups, such as the Ku Klux Klan, joined in efforts to prevent school integration. In spite of all organized resistance, school busing became commonplace and school integration a technical reality. In the 1980s a movement to return to the neighborhood school concept was supported by the Reagan administration. Although policies to eliminate busing have not been forthcoming, minority and equal rights organizations have feared such efforts.

Major Legislation

During the 1960s, significant progress was made in eliminating segregationist policies and controlling the effects of discrimination. President Johnson's Great Society programs sought to eradicate segregation entirely and to make discrimination an offense punishable under the law. In 1964, the **Civil Rights Act** was passed. This act, amended in 1965, sought to ban discrimination based on race, religion, color, or ethnicity in public facilities, government-operated programs, or employment. A similar act, passed in 1968, made the practice of discrimination in advertising and the purchase or rental of residential property or its financing illegal.

Under the new legal sanctions for desegregation, a groundswell of support mounted among disenfranchised minorities and sympathetic dominant group members. The Reverend Martin Luther King, Jr. and organized freedom marchers sought to raise the consciousness of society regarding the obscenities of segregationist policies. King's nonviolent movement provided great visibility to the injustices of discrimination and served to stimulate and influence policies for change. Other significant minority organizations, such as the Southern Christian Leadership Conference (SCLC), the National Urban League, the National Association for the Advancement of Colored People (NAACP), La Raza, and the League of United Latin American Citizens, were actively pursuing social and economic justice for minorities during this period. As the new civil rights legislation was implemented, an air of hope prevailed that discrimination would soon become a matter of history. School busing facilitated public school integration, public facilities were opened to minorities, and the employment market became more accepting of minority applicants. Further advances were made under the influence of the Economic Opportunities Act of 1964. Neighborhoods were organized, and their residents registered to vote. This movement was furthered by the Voting Rights Act of 1965, which prohibited the imposition of voting qualification requirements based on race, color, age, or minority status. The impact of the civil rights movement was far reaching in securing a toehold in the struggle for full and equal participation by minorities in the social and economic areas of our society.

Erosion of Progress

The rapid pace of the change effort was short lived. By the late 1970s, racial polarization had increased with a new wave of conservatism. Whites were much more prone to attribute the "lack of progress" among the black population to the blacks themselves, rather than to discrimination, thus supporting the position that discrimination was no longer a problem for "motivated" blacks. By the late 1970s, it was clear that racial and minority issues were not among the top priorities for the white majority. Instead,

> national defense, energy supplies, and inflation have readily replaced minority concerns as priority issues during the last decade, and that shift in attention has been accompanied by a shift of resources away from minorities. Fostered by this contraction of resources the most intense overt conflicts over resources now occur not between the majority and minority groups, but among minority groups. (Walters 1982, 26)

The outlook for a well articulated and implemented program to eliminate prejudice and discrimination during the 1990's appears bleak. The effort to creatively and forcefully address this issue has waned since the mid-70's and continues to receive only a token effort from the current administration. Issues which have emerged as priorities during the early 90's are concerns relating to budget deficits and the Persian Gulf war. These issues, along with concerns over a potential economic recession, have resulted in obscuring efforts to eradicate the social inequalities that result from racism and sexism.

Although efforts to achieve minority equality are still intact, the strong, active, government commitment has waned. **Affirmative action programs,** which once mandated the selection of qualified minority group members for publicly operated business, appear to have been down-graded. Affirmative action efforts were directed at breaking institutional discrimination in employment. Challenged as creating a **reverse discrimination** employment market, conservatives have squelched efforts to promote opportunities for minorities through this program. The Federal Civil Rights Commission has become noticeably silent and inactive since 1981. The gains achieved in the quest for social equality during the 1960s and 1970s were gradually eroded by apathetic leadership in the 1980s.

Social Work and the Civil Rights Movement

Inherent in social work's identity is its commitment to social action directed toward the elimination of barriers that deny equal rights and full participation to all members of society. Since the early days, when social workers assisted in assimilating new immigrants into our culture and sought to improve social conditions for them, the profession has engaged the citizenry in working toward social equality and an equal opportunity structure. The National Association of Social Workers, as well as the Council on Social Work Education, has given high priority to incorporating minority content into professional social work practice and social work education. Social work practitioners strive to be mindful of the consequences of minority status and familiar with the racial and cultural backgrounds of their clients when assisting them in achieving solutions to problems. Through social action, efforts are made to change community attitudes, policies, and practices that disadvantage minorities. As advocates, social workers seek to modify rules and regulations that deny equal treatment to those assigned to a minority status. As organizers, they work with minority leaders in identifying priorities, gaining community support, and facilitating change through the democratic process.

Social workers are active in organized public efforts to abolish discriminatory practices. As citizens (as well as professionals), they support political candidates who are openly committed to working for social equality. They are involved in public education designed to dispel prejudice and to promote productive interaction among divergent racial and ethnic groups. In a public climate where the pursuit of social and economic equality has lessened, social workers have the responsibility to maintain a vigilant pursuit of equality for minorities.

SUMMARY

Few observers would deny that the United States has experienced a major sexual revolution during the past few decades. As part of the human rights movement, many advances have been made in reducing sexism in our society. Opportunities for economic and social participation of women are greater now than they have been before in the history of this country. Although there have been reversals, such as the failure to ratify the ERA, societal pressures to assure equal treatment and opportunities for women continue. The continued efforts of groups committed to the achievement of equal rights should result in significant gains during the coming years, despite some opposition.

Social inequality also has characterized the treatment of racial and ethnic minorities and homosexuals in the United States. Although some progress has been made toward more favorable treatment, full participation rights have not yet been achieved. Discrimination and differential treatment of women, minority group members, and homosexuals continue to restrict their achievement of social and economic progress. Although legislation has served as a catalyst for removing long-standing practices that denied equal rights, in recent years, the conservative movement has lowered the priorities for attaining social equality for women and minorities. Even less attention has been given to social equality for homosexuals. Social work has a long tradition of promoting social equality, and the commitment of the profession to continue pressing for this will be greater as the societal thrust to do so declines.

In this chapter we did not seek to provide an in-depth analysis of the parameters of disenfranchised and oppressed minorities in America. Rather, it was designed to sensitize the reader to the fact that institutional discrimination has long existed, and its victims continue to suffer the consequences of differential treatment and limited opportunity. Although advocacy groups have been able to effect positive political changes, and public attitudes have improved markedly, much has yet to be accomplished to establish social equality for all groups in America. Prejudice and discrimination are the products of social interaction. As social constructs, they can be replaced by values that respect the dignity and worth of all human beings and result in a society that promotes equal treatment for all.

KEY TERMS

affirmative action programs
Civil Rights Act
comparable worth
cultural pluralism
Equal Rights Amendment (ERA)
homophobia

minority group
prejudice
reverse discrimination
sexism
social inequality
stereotyping

DISCUSSION QUESTIONS

1. What is prejudice? Discrimination? Institutional sexism? Racism?

2. What impact has the feminist movement had on producing social equity for women?

3. Why is homophobia more prevalent among social workers than psychologists and psychiatrists?

4. Compare and contrast the differences between *cultural pluralism* and *co-existence*. What are the implications for minority groups within each?

5. What efforts have been made to produce social equality for minority groups?

How successful have they been? What suggestions would you make to alleviate the problems of prejudice and discrimination?

6. Identify the role of social work in the civil rights movement.

REFERENCES

Allport, Gordon. 1954. *The nature of prejudice.* Reading, Mass: Addison-Wesley.

Beiber, Irving, ed. 1962. *Homosexuality.* New York: Basic Books.

Bergman, Edgar. 1982. *The compleat chauvinist.* New York: Macmillan.

Deckard, Barbara S. 1983. *The women's movement: Political and psychological issues.* New York: Harper & Row.

De Crescenzo, Teresa, and Christine McGill. 1978. Homophobia: A study of the attitudes of mental health professionals toward homosexuality. Master's thesis, University of Southern California, School of Social Work.

Dressel, P. 1987. Patriarchy and social welfare work. *Social Problems* 34: 294–309.

Dulaney, Diane D., and James Kelly. 1982. Improving services to gay and lesbian clients. *Social Work* 27(2): 178–83.

Fanshel, David. 1976. Status differentials: Men and women in social work. *Social Work* 21(6): 448–53.

Feldberg, R. C. 1984. Comparable worth: Toward theory and practice in the United States. *Signs* 10: 311–28.

George, Wesley C. 1962. *The biology of the race problem.* Report prepared by Commission of the Governor of Alabama.

Irwin, Patrick, and Norman C. Thompson. 1977. Acceptance of the rights of homosexuals: A social profile. *Journal of Homosexuality* 3 (Winter): 107–21.

Knopp, L. 1990. Social consequences of homosexuality. *Geographical Magazine* (May) 20–25.

Macksey, Joan. 1976. *The book of women's achievements.* New York: Stein & Day.

Matthews, Karen A., and Judith Rodin. 1989. Women's changing work roles. *Journal of the American Psychological Association* 11(44): 1389–93.

Perrucci, Robert, and Dean D. Knudsen. 1983. *Sociology.* St. Paul, Minn.: West.

Presser, H. B. 1987. Recent changes in women's employment. Paper presented at the John D. and Catherine T. McArthur Foundation Workshop, Women, Work and Health: The Impact of Changing Roles in Women's Health and the Family. Hilton Head, South Carolina.

Schatz, Eunice, Barbara L. Simon, and Arnold Nemore. 1987. Women and work: A conceptual framework. *Journal of Women and Social Work* 2(3): 21–31.

Shuttlesworth, Verla. 1978. Women in administration in public schools of Texas. Ph.D. diss., Baylor University.

U.S. Bureau of the Census. 1981. *Statistical abstract of the United States.* Washington, D.C.: GPO.

U.S. Government. 1990. *Congressional Quarterly Weekly Report.* (Nov. 10): 36–38. Washington, D.C.: GPO.

Walters, Ronald W. 1982. Race, resources, conflict. *Social Work* 27(1): 24–29.

Wirth, Louis. 1938. Urbanism as a way of life. *American Journal of Sociology* 44 (July): 3–24.

Yinger, J. Milton, 1970. *The scientific study of religion.* New York: Macmillan.

Young, P. 1982. *God's bullies.* New York: Holt, Rinehart & Winston.

Zastrow, Charles. 1986. *Introduction to social welfare institutions.* 3d ed. Homewood, Ill.: Dorsey.

SUGGESTED FURTHER READINGS

Berger, Raymond. 1983. What is a homosexual: A definitional model. *Social Work* 28: 312–16.

Brown, Caree R., and Marilyn L. Hellinger. 1975. Therapists' attitudes toward women. *Social Work* 20 (July): 266.

Cass, Bettina, and Cora V. Baldock. 1983. *Women, social welfare and the state.* Winchester, Mass.: Allyn & Bacon.

Davis, Angela. 1983. *Women, race and class.* New York: Vintage Books.

Feagin, R. 1984. *Racial and ethnic relations.* 2d ed. Englewood Cliffs, N.J.: Prentice-Hall.

Goodman, James, ed. 1973. *The dynamics of racism in social work.* Washington, D.C.: National Association of Social Work.

Szymanski, Albert. 1976. Racial discrimination and white gain. *American Sociological Review* 41 (June): 403–14.

Weinberg, Martin S., and Colin J. Williams. 1976. *Male homosexuals: Their problems and adaptations.* New York: Penguin.

Chapter 18

Social Work and the Other Helping Professions

*C*harles and Sarah have been married for fifteen years. They have two children, Oscar, age fourteen, and Cheree, age eight. Sarah is two months pregnant. Neither Charles nor Sarah wanted additional children. Charles has been urging Sarah to have an abortion, yet she has refused steadfastly. Sarah is a devout Catholic and feels that an abortion would be a grave sin. Charles argues that they cannot afford to have another child because Cheree has chronic health problems and Oscar has become a behavior problem in school. They suspect that he is using drugs but have not been able to prove that.

Both Charles and Sarah have difficulty facing problems head-on and hope that the problems will eventually go away. The marital relationship between Charles and Sarah has become tense, and the conflict between them has intensified. Charles has resorted to staying out later after work and is away from home more frequently during the evening. Sarah has accused Charles of losing his love for her, but he denies that he has. Sarah is experiencing headaches regularly, feels faint often, and has difficulty in handling her chores.

Sarah and Charles have not been willing to seek outside assistance with their problems, primarily because Charles feels that a man should be able to take care of his family's problems, and Sarah is reluctant to seek counseling without him. Recently, their discussions have centered around separation, which both say they do not want. Both Charles and Sarah want to be happy again but find that their situation continues to deteriorate. Sarah has finally convinced Charles that they should see a counselor to help them sort out their problems and work toward improving their relationship.

Assume that you are a friend of Charles and Sarah and they turn to you for assistance in finding a specialist to help with their problems. To whom would you refer them? A psychiatrist? A family counselor? A social worker? A pastoral counselor? A clinical psychologist? The school guidance counselor? Helping Charles and Sarah locate the appropriate professional help is not always an easy task, since there are many professionals who work within the human services. Most are trained to assist people with a variety of problems. Unfortunately, there also are individuals who lack the essential professional education to engage in human problem solving. In this chapter we describe briefly those professional helping disciplines that are most likely to be found in the human services network. Social workers often find that the unique skills of other professionals are helpful in resolving problems that are less appropriate for the social work approach. At the conclusion of the chapter we attempt to identify which of the professional helping fields might be appropriate to assist Charles and Sarah with their problems.

PSYCHIATRY

Psychiatry is a specialized field of medical practice that focuses on mental and emotional dysfunction. While psychiatrists typically treat patients experiencing some form of psychopathology, many help with other problems of social dysfunction and interpersonal relationships. For example, a psychiatrist may counsel couples experiencing marital discord, assist adolescents with problems in adaptation, use play therapy with children whose social development has been retarded, counsel individuals and couples who experience sexual dysfunctions, and so on. Unlike other professionals who assist with psychological and emotional problems as well as those of social dysfunction, psychiatrists can provide medications where physiological symptoms indicate the need for them. Because psychiatrists are physicians (with a medical degree), they have at their disposal a wide array of medical interventions as well as their expertise in treating problems of a mental and emotional nature.

Psychiatrists practice in a variety of settings. Hospitals established for the treatment of the mentally ill constitute the most frequent employment sites. Many psychiatrists establish private practices in major metropolitan areas. Others are either employed full-time or serve as treatment consultants in residential treatment centers, children's agencies, centers designed for the treatment of specialized problems such as family violence or alcohol or substance abuse, or suicide prevention centers. Some also assist other agencies that provide specialized services to the emotionally disturbed.

Like other helping professionals, psychiatrists are educated in various programs that emphasize different theoretical and methodological approaches to problem solving. Some embrace Freudian psychology, others Adlerian or Jungian, while still others incorporate Sullivanian theories into their practice, all of which are "insight therapies." In recent times, many psychiatrists have adopted learning theory approaches (behavior modification) as well as reality therapy, rational emotive therapy, transactional analysis, and related approaches. Psychiatrists typically are well educated within their speciality and constitute a significant and important resource for treating problems of the mentally ill and emotionally disturbed.

PSYCHOLOGY

Coon (1982) has identified thirty-four subspecialties in the field of **psychology.** The majority of these specialties do not involve special preparation in counseling or psychotherapy. According to Coon, over one-half of all psychologists are employed by educational institutions, another 15 percent work in hospitals or clinics, 10 percent are in government service or research, 7 percent are in private practice, and 6 percent are employed by public or private schools. In terms of the focus of their employment, 29 percent engage in clinical practice; 10 percent are experimental psychologists; 19 percent are educational or school psychologists; 9 percent are developmental, social, and personality psychologists; 8 percent are general, engineering, and other industrial specialists; 3 percent are involved in testing as a subspecialty; and 1 percent are environmental psychologists (Coon 1982, 18).

Without some awareness of the differences in specialty areas, one might find it difficult to identify the appropriate resource for problem solving! Unlike psychiatrists, professional psychologists are not physicians. Those who engage in practice designed to assist with psychological and emotional problems generally are referred to as *clinical* or *counseling* psychologists. Like psychiatrists, psychologists are educated in universities and professional schools that emphasize a wide variety of theoretical and methodological approaches to practice. Again, like psychiatrists, many have developed skills in psychotherapy and psychoanalysis. Others prefer methodological approaches that reflect a behavior modification, cognitive therapy, Gestalt therapy, or related practice modality. Psychologists treat clients with deep-rooted emotional conflict, faulty personality development, interpersonal problems represented in marriage and family conflict, substance abuse, and various psychological and behavioral disorders. Psychologists typically use various forms of **psychometric instruments** (testing) in diagnosing a problem. These instruments are designed to provide information about clients and their functioning that often is not readily observable during a client interview. Tests also may be used as a basis for establishing a personality profile for clients. Tests can be useful in providing insights into the client's abilities to handle stress and areas where the client is vulnerable. Tests, however, are only one of many sources of evidence needed to assess clients' problems.

Many psychologists are skilled in group therapy as well as individualized practice. In recent years group psychotherapy and group treatment have emerged as significant treatment techniques in helping clients with similar problems resolve those problems through the use of group dynamics and the skillful intervention of the group therapist.

Psychologists engaging in psychometry are often called on as consultants to test clients in social service agencies and educational institutions. This service is often very helpful in gaining better insights into clients and establishing appropriate treatment and intervention plans.

SOCIOLOGY

Sociologists are experts in the study of society, its organization, and the phenomena arising out of the group relations of human beings. As such, professionals in this area contribute much to our awareness of human interaction, including the establishment of norms, values, social organization, patterns of behavior, and social institutions. Sociologists are skilled in research techniques and methodologies. Like other professionals, they may focus on a subspecialty such as the family, deviancy, industrial sociology, symbolic interaction, bureaucracy and related forms of social organization, and the sociology of knowl-edge and social problems.

The majority of sociologists are employed at institutions of higher education and related educational institutions, although a growing number are entering the field of clinical, or applied, sociology. Professionals engaging in clinical sociology seek to apply the knowledge and principles gleaned from sociological theory to identify or enrich the understanding of organizational or interactional relationships, with the goal of resolving problems. Sociologists using this ap-proach may function as family counselors, group therapists, industrial consul-tants, problem analysts, or program planners. The contribution of sociology to the understanding of the impact of environment and group membership on behavior has proven immeasurable.

PASTORAL COUNSELORS

Perhaps no other single source of contact by persons experiencing problems is sought out more often than religious leaders. Priests, pastors, ministers, rabbis, and other persons in positions of spiritual leadership are called on readily by members of their congregations and others in trouble. Religious leaders are placed in a unique and valued position by the laity. As spiritual leaders, they are presumed to have an extraordinary understanding of human frailty and a special ability to communicate with supernatural powers. Just as congregations vary in size and sophistication, so do the educational background and expe-rience of religious leaders as problem solvers. Many receive extensive theo-logical education coupled with a subspecialty in counseling. Others become counselors by demand, with little academic and supervised practical instruction to do so. Still others are relatively uneducated and hold their positions by what they perceive as a unique calling from God. In most instances, they are com-mitted to helping their parishioners find solutions to problems within the context of a religious belief system.

Professional **pastoral counselors** are most often educated at schools of theology offering specializations in counseling. Typically, these programs offer classroom theory and a practicum that utilizes various psychological approaches to intervention and problem solving. Many religious leaders complete their theological education and enter graduate schools in clinical or counseling psy-chology, social work, or guidance and counseling programs. Larger congre-gations frequently employ a pastoral counselor to supplement the overall pas-toral ministry.

Pastoral counselors may assist parishioners with marriage and family prob-lems, developmental problems, social problems, difficulties with interpersonal relationships, and a myriad of other problems. Individuals experiencing inner conflict with respect to spiritual problems are frequently given assistance and support by the pastoral counselor. Skilled practitioners also may form groups to work on specific problems. Pastoral counselors also are engaged in various educational activities designed either to enrich the awareness and understanding of the congregation or to prevent problems. Like other human service profes-sionals, pastoral counselors must develop an awareness of the limits of their professional skills and make referrals, where necessary, to assure that the best interests of the client are served.

GUIDANCE COUNSELORS

Most guidance counselors are educated in public school–teacher educational programs and certified by state educational agencies. They are generally required to have classroom teaching experience before they are eligible for certification as guidance counselors. Guidance counselors specialize in assisting students with educationally related problems and in locating educational resources best suited to meet their individual interests. Students with behavioral problems, as well as those with academic difficulties, often are referred to the guidance counselor for assistance. Although guidance counselors focus on academically related concerns, they often become engaged in a therapeutic relationship with students who are experiencing adaptive or emotionally related problems. Guidance counselors also may assist the school psychologist in administering tests to students and, in smaller school systems, may assume primary responsibility for the testing program. They are called on to provide essential information to classroom teachers about the performance of students and, in collaboration with them, to develop an educational plan for students experiencing difficulty with their academic progression. Guidance counselors occasionally find themselves in the role of **ombudsman** as they seek to assist students and teachers or administrators in resolving conflicts in their interaction. They may work with the school social worker where truancy or family-related problems are related significantly to the student's academic performance. The guidance counselor's specialized awareness of educational processes and resource alternatives can be of value to students needing information or an awareness of options available to them.

Guidance counselors are not all assigned to public school systems, however. Many are employed in correctional systems, where they help inmates assess attitudes and skills needed to obtain productive employment after release from prison. This type of intervention generally requires collaboration with other members of the correctional team, for example, with specialists in vocational education and/or related areas. Correctional counselors also often network with the inmates' families as well as community social service agencies. Experience has demonstrated that many prisoners have never had an adequate opportunity structure within which productive learning and job opportunities were available. The correctional counselor attempts to equip inmates with personal, social, and job-related skills that will enable them to use their time more creatively while in prison and to make a smoother, better-prepared transition back into society when discharged. Under most circumstances, each released inmate is assigned to a parole officer, who will continue to provide counseling and assistance with job opportunities and family-related problems.

Rehabilitation counseling is yet another form of guidance counseling. Most states have established agencies to help individuals with physical or mental handicaps identify competencies and secure academic or vocational training that will enable them to find employment. These counselors may also help clients get specialized medical treatment for enhancement of physical, mental, and social capacities. Rehabilitation counselors are, by the nature of their specialization, heavily involved in teamwork and networking with other human and vocational service workers in securing resources that will assist their clients in achieving their productive potential. If successful, the client's level of independence will increase along with greater self-esteem and employability.

Guidance counselors usually are required to have an advanced degree as well as specialized coursework. In general, required coursework does not prepare the counselor for psychotherapy or long-term counseling.

EMPLOYMENT COUNSELORS

Professionals who focus on assisting clients in locating employment, assessing their skill levels, and enrolling in educational courses designed to prepare them for skill development and ultimate employment often are identified as "employment counselors." Their specialized knowledge of the employment market and unique skills in matching clients seeking work with the needs of employers are designed to improve the probabilities of securing satisfaction with a job as well as competence in performance on the job. Employment counselors are skilled at interpreting various tests used to determine a client's aptitude for various positions. Not only do employment counselors assist persons needing a position or those maladapted in the positions they hold to find employment of the most suitable nature, they also are available to assist them with locating the essential supports to maintain involvement on the job. For example, transportation or child care could represent barriers for an individual who otherwise needs work. Locating and referring the client to an appropriate resource may resolve those problems and produce a more favorable arrangement for meeting the demands of the job.

Employment counselors work with the business community in identifying employment needs and the skill requirements that will be necessary to provide optimum benefit for the business as well as the worker. Feedback and monitoring systems may be established as mechanisms for fine-tuning the job referral process.

Vocational education programs abound in the United States and provide instruction in a variety of areas: cosmetology, aircraft maintenance, welding, carpentry, computer technology, auto mechanics, heavy machine operations, office management, hotel administration, and many other specialty areas. Workers who are dissatisfied in their current employment or whose jobs have disappeared because of changing technology, persons reentering the job market, or new workers entering employment often find vocational education beneficial in learning and strengthening skills. Disabled persons also find vocational education an invaluable resource in adapting their abilities to marketable skills. Employment counselors typically are influential in helping clients use vocational educational programs that enhance development of job-related skills.

NURSES

In recent years the role of nurses has changed dramatically. Traditionally viewed as "doctors' helpers" or as pseudo-professionals whose primary responsibility was to see that the doctor's orders were dutifully carried out, contemporary nurses have emerged as professionals in their own right. Schools of nursing now focus on the psychosocial aspects of services to debilitated or hospitalized clients as well as mastery of the basic skills related to patient care. Like other professionals, nurses may specialize in a variety of areas such as pediatrics, gerontolgy, psychiatry and mental health, oncology, and a variety of related areas. The body of knowledge required to be a professional nurse today is far different than in past decades. Emphasis on the therapeutic use of relationships and psychosocial adaptation has enhanced the nurse's ability to engage the client in the healing process. Nurses are involved in counseling roles ranging from handling stress-related illnesses to counseling with families of ill patients and collaborating with other specialists in seeking the best therapeutic treatment approaches for their clients.

Professional nurses typically receive their education from colleges or universities that have accredited schools of nursing. They earn a bachelor's degree in nursing and, after successfully passing the state board examinations, become registered nurses, or RNs. Many pursue a master's degree in nursing, and larger numbers are enrolling in PhD programs.

Other nurses may opt to pursue the licensed vocational nurses (LVN) certification. Nurses, at whatever level, play a vital role in the delivery of physical care as well as human services.

ATTORNEYS-AT-LAW

Lawyers are professionals who engage in both criminal and civil matters to assist individuals in securing their rights under the law. Most communities, large or small, have practicing attorneys. Law, like other professional areas, has many subspecialties. Many lawyers are employed by large corporations and deal with contracts and their interpretation, assessing legal specifications relative to business practices and providing legal expertise essential for corporate ventures. Others are in private practice, with many handling primarily civil matters such as lawsuits, divorces, property settlements, deeds, estate management, wills, and similar civil matters. Lawyers are educated in graduate schools of law throughout the country. As professionals, they encounter a myriad of problems that have legal consequences. In some cases, such as that of divorce or child custody, the lawyer often becomes involved in a counseling role. Although many lawyers lack the appropriate educational background and expertise, clients often seek their assistance with emotional as well as legal problems. Lawyers also make referrals to appropriate agencies or other professionals when indicated.

Many of the larger communities have established legal aid clinics, which specialize in offering legal counsel to the poor or near poor. The poor, as well as the nonpoor, encounter many problems that need the attention of a legal expert, such as divorce, child custody, property settlements, and adequate defense in a court of law. Legal aid clinics are an invaluable resource for the poor. Many lawyers are employed as full-time legal counselors at the clinics, while others work part-time or volunteer their time. Legal aid clinics seek to promote justice for the poor as well as for those in better financial circumstances. Typically, law firms assign a portion of their staff time to *pro bono* ("for the public good") efforts, often representing indigent clients.

Lawyers constitute a valuable resource to the problem-solving process. Matters that need legal attention often are a source of stress and are responsive to the skillful intervention of the legal profession.

THE NEED FOR PROFESSIONAL DIVERSITY

Although the brief discussion of selected professions is by no means complete, it does encompass the primary disciplinary areas in the human service field. Social workers and others in the helping professions need to develop an awareness of the expertise available in their practice arena. Many problems require the attention of experts from diverse areas of practice in order to move toward resolution. It also is requisite that all professionals develop an awareness of their limitations as well as strengths, if clients are to receive the maximum benefit in the problem-solving effort.

In our complex, highly technological society, the emergence of a variety of specialists is a necessity. With the explosion of knowledge and our understanding of human needs, it would be impossible for any one person to master it all! Just as our society is complex, so, we have learned, are human beings. Values vary, as do the many diverse groups with whom we hold an identity. Specialty areas have emerged in response to both such diverse needs and the understanding of the theoretical explanations of behavior. Life is a problem-solving process, and our ability to respond appropriately to those problems involves not only our personality makeup but knowledge, awareness, resources, and sensitivities as well. Invariably, all of us will at times encounter problems for which there appear no ready solutions. Often, the friendly advice of a neighbor, spouse, or confidant is sufficient in providing the perspective that will lead to an acceptable solution. At other times, professional assistance is essential in achieving a satisfactory resolution of the problem.

A question often raised relates to the likenesses and differences among the professions. What, for example, does a psychiatrist do with clients that is different from what a psychologist would do? Or a social worker? Or a pastoral counselor? And so on. All, for example, might engage in marital counseling or

Social workers and other helping professionals often work as a team in assisting clients. Here, a social worker and a physician make a home visit to a client.

provide assistance to a family struggling with the behavioral problems of an adolescent. To an uninformed observer, the professional response to those problems may appear to be approximately the same. Clients see the professional for an hour or so per week, the content of the interaction consists primarily of verbal interaction, and generally the client is given specific tasks to work on until the next visit. The professionals may contact other social systems related to the client's functioning, such as the school system or employment system. What, then, constitutes the difference? In part, although not exclusively, the differences may lie in the theoretical perspective that the professional brings to bear on the problem. The specialized emphasis on individual psychodynamics as reflected in psychiatry and psychology often varies with social work's emphasis on the systems/ecological framework and the relationship between the person and the environment within which the person functions. Also, social work's mastery of and emphasis on utilizing community resources are distinct from the typical approaches used in psychiatry and psychology.

Social work emphasizes the problem-solving approach. Recognizing that stress may be generated by the lack of resources as well as intrapsychic conflict, social workers also may help their clients with concrete resources, such as locating a job, adequate housing, health care services, child care, or other needed services. The various roles that the social worker plays, such as advocate, broker, enabler, case manager, and intervener, often are essential to creating an environment in which clients may move toward problem solution.

The cooperative relationship and respect that exist among the helping professions are necessary if the optimum helping environment is to be attained. Social workers have clients who need psychiatric treatment, or the special services provided by a clinical or counseling psychologist or pastoral counselor. Many clients are assisted by referrals to the employment counselor, and students experiencing difficulty in school adaptation benefit by referrals to the school guidance counselor. Positive interaction and collaboration among these professionals enrich the service systems and increase the probabilities of securing a better quality of intervention for clients in need. Each profession has its own distinct professional culture, and an awareness of these varying cultures should promote more appropriate referrals.

A CASE REVISITED

Let us return now to the case with which we opened this chapter. It might be of value for the reader to review the problems of Charles, Sarah, and their children. Assume that you are a friend of the family and Charles and Sarah turn to you for assistance. Where would you refer them? To a psychiatrist? A clinical psychologist? A social worker? A pastoral counselor? The school guidance counselor? All of these professions might provide some assistance with the problems. Because of the multiple problems that are evidenced in this family, a social worker might serve as a case manager in assuring that appropriate resources are secured. The social worker might engage Charles and Sarah in marriage counseling, refer Oscar to the school guidance counselor, secure medical attention for Cheree and Sarah, and coordinate the efforts of professionals providing assistance to the family.

The nature of the problems at this stage of development does not appear to call for psychiatric attention. Oscar's behavioral problems may indicate a need for psychological testing, which could be performed by a clinical psychologist and made available to the guidance counselor, social worker, pastoral counselor, and others involved in the intervention process. Because of the nature of the family's problems, it is doubtful whether only one professional discipline could manage the variety of problems indicated. Sarah's guilt over the abortion issue may be addressed by a pastoral counselor sensitive to the spiritual issues involved. Alternatives may be indicated, and if so, both Charles and Sarah must commit themselves to whatever option appears to be mutually agreeable for them. Families similar to that of Charles and Sarah are commonplace throughout our society. They merit the best professional effort that we can supply in assisting them toward life satisfaction.

As just indicated, the complexities of the issues and problems that confront Charles, Sarah, Oscar, and Cheree are probably best addressed through a **multidisciplinary approach.** In many larger communities, treatment-oriented agencies employ professionals from a variety of disciplines—social workers, psychiatrists, psychologists, psychiatric nurses, guidance counselors, and others. Under such circumstances, a multidisciplinary team may be formed to provide services for families such as Charles's. This type of intervention effort requires that each member of the team work in harmony with other team members in establishing goals designed to strengthen individual and family functioning. Periodic case reviews are held, with each of the professionals sharing information and receiving feedback from other team members as it relates to treatment progress. Through clear goal setting and the coordinated effort of the treatment team, a unified approach to practice will assure that team members' efforts are reinforced.

THE BACCALAUREATE SOCIAL WORKER AND OTHER PROFESSIONS

The baccalaureate social worker (BSW) typically functions as a generalist practitioner and holds a unique position in the professional community. Their attention to a great variety of human problems demands skills as counselors, resource finders, case managers, evaluators, advocates, brokers, enablers, and problem solvers. The BSW's awareness of community resources and the ability to use them skillfully in the problem-solving process are particularly valuable in securing the needed assistance for distressed clients. BSWs work in varied social service agencies and community settings.

In cases representing the myriad of problems such as those typified by Sarah, Charles, and their children, the BSW social worker may become engaged as a case manager, with a focus on securing referrals to appropriate treatment resources. The worker may also become involved in providing the necessary supports to insure that the clients use the services. In this role, the BSW would continue to monitor and coordinate the treatment effort, with all of the intervention system components cooperating.

The BSW may serve as a vital link between community professionals. The special knowledge related to individual, family, and community functioning within the systems/ecological framework helps the BSW identify the appropriate referral resources, engage them, and become an essential component of the helping process.

SUMMARY

In this chapter we have identified some of the more prominent human service professionals who help clients with problems of adaptation. An attempt also was made to identify similarities and differences among the professional areas. The need for interprofessional collaboration was examined in relation to obtaining the greatest expertise for clients in the intervention process.

KEY TERMS

multidisciplinary approach   psychiatry
ombudsman   psychology
pastoral counselor   psychometric instruments

DISCUSSION QUESTIONS

1. Identify the similarities and differences among the professions discussed in this chapter.
2. Describe the differences in the social work approach to problem solving and those used by other helping professions.
3. After reviewing the case of Charles and Sarah, how would you approach the case? To whom would you make referrals? Why?
4. What is the baccalaureate social worker's role in working with other professions in the problem-solving process?

REFERENCES

Coon, Dennis. 1982. *Essentials of psychology*, 2d ed. New York: West.

SUGGESTED FURTHER READINGS

Basic psychiatry for the primary care physician. 1976. Boston: Little, Brown.

Berkowitz, Morton I. 1975. *A primer on school mental health consultation*. Springfield, Ill.: Thomas.

Caplan, Gerald. 1970. *The theory and practice of mental health consultation*. New York: Basic Books.

Hayes, Richard, and Roger Aubrey. 1988. *New directions for counseling and human development*. Denver: Love.

Health, 1984. 1984. Career Information Center, no. 7. Irving, Calif.: Glencoe/Macmillan.

Hensen, Michael, Alan E. Kazdin, and Alan S. Bellack. 1983. *The clinical psychology handbook*. New York: Pergamon.

Kalkman, Marion E. 1974. *New dimensions in mental health: Psychiatric nursing.* 4th ed. New York: McGraw–Hill.

Lawrence, Margaret M. 1971. *The mental health team in the schools.* New York: Behavioral Publications.

Lubin, Bernard. 1967. *The clinical psychologist: Background, roles, and functions.* Chicago: Aldine.

Norback, Craig. 1980. *Careers encyclopedia.* Homewood, Ill.: Dow Jones–Irwin.

Marziller, John S., and John Hall. 1987. *What is clinical psychology?* New York: Oxford Univ. Press.

Smith, Audrey D. 1968. *A study of the lawyer–social worker professional relationship.* Chicago: American Bar Foundation.

The Voluntary Sector

Chapter

19

Alice Longworth does not think of herself as a social worker. With a Master of Business Administration degree (MBA), she went to work in the corporate sector and soon found herself as the principal executive officer for the employment assistance program for RJR Corporation. Her basic responsibility involves working with union members, corporate officers, and community leaders to establish a wide range of programs for RJR workers and their families. Her principal work tasks include overseeing the security of the investments for the company pension fund, identifying programs to be included in the employee benefits package, helping each worker select the types of investments that best fit his or her needs, and establishing and maintaining the on-site child care program.

Carl Elders is a social worker for Lutheran Social Services of Minnesota, a voluntary social services agency funded primarily by the Lutheran church. Carl works at an outreach center in a rural community, providing a variety of services to individuals and families who live in the surrounding area. Although many of Carl's clients are not Lutherans, he works closely with church congregations in the area, providing information about his agency's services and educational programs on topics such as stress management and teenage pregnancy.

Tom Beasley founded the Corrections Corporation of America. His firm offers to build, lease, and operate minimum security prisons for cities, counties, and even states. The idea behind the lease is that private, for-profit firms can operate prisons more efficiently than public entities. Beasley believes this is due to the advantages of old-style entrepreneurship. Critics complain that the "private" public corporations skim the least costly prisoners for their facilities, leaving the high-cost prisoners in the public facilities. Since the government does not have to sell bonds for construction costs and instead signs long-term contracts, there is only an illusion of public saving.

When Jane Owen's children reached college age, Jane left her position at the family service agency and joined with a psychologist and a psychiatrist to form their own for-profit agency. With changes in the state law that allow social workers to receive directly insurance-directed payments for a wide range of services, Jane believes she is just as effective and is much better compensated than when she was not in private practice.

437

All four of the people just described are performing public social services; all, except Alice, are paid partially or indirectly from public funds; but none works for any level of the government. The old division between **public sector,** or government agencies, and **voluntary sector,** or nongovernment not-for-profit agencies, has been replaced by a patchwork in which public and private, profit and nonprofit, sectarian and nonsectarian agencies coexist and overlap as avenues for social welfare service delivery. Nonpublic social workers tend to be found in one of four types of settings: (1) traditional voluntary agencies, (2) human services programs within the corporate sector, (3) human service corporations (as employees, stockholders, or directors), or (4) private practice. Today, public agencies often contract with private agencies to perform essential services, which means that private agencies often receive the majority of their funding from government contracts. The private practice programs may charge either public or private insurance companies for client services. Add to that the many profit-oriented human service corporations which directly run hospitals, prisons, and nursing homes. The days when there was a strict separation of public agencies (funded by taxes) and nonprofit private agencies (funded by foundations and charitable contributions) have long since become history.

SOCIAL WELFARE SERVICES: A HISTORICAL OVERVIEW

Since early in American history, responsibility for the provision of social welfare services has been split between government and the **private sector,** nongovernment agencies that may be either not-for-profit or for-profit agencies. The government was not expected, indeed not able, to deal with the diverse circumstances associated with human needs. As discussed in Chapter 2, the Poor Law inherited from England provided that the government should supply meager help as a last resort. The historian Daniel Boorstin notes that in the new nation "communities existed before governments were there to care for public needs" (1985, 121). Without a tradition of centralized religious or public responsibility for welfare, the responsibility fell to ad hoc sources of assistance and to local churches' organized efforts.

In Chapter 2 we described in detail the history of American social welfare institutions. An overview at the turn of the century would have revealed a neat compartmentalization of social welfare and social service responsibilities (see Table 19–1). The public sector, or the government, accepted the responsibility for addressing long-term dependency through poor houses, which were funded and administered at the local level. The government, typically at the state level, also accepted responsibility for those social services that intrinsically required the use of sovereign authority, such as child welfare programs, the criminal justice system, and the confinement of mentally ill persons. Even today such services would be in violation of civil liberties were it not for the courts granting to the state the "right" to treat children, the insane, and the criminal as dependent persons. Sometimes, however, the state oversteps this line by treating the aged and the widowed as if they, too, have somehow lost their civil rights.

Private sector agencies generally were administered at the local level and often by sectarian, or church-related, groups. They provided the more intensely

Table 19–1 Welfare Responsibilities Dated About 1900

Public	Private
State	Sectarian
Chronically mentally ill	Moral supervision
Prisoners	Orphan homes
Child welfare	Nonsectarian
Aged	Advocacy
Local	Settlement houses
Outdoor relief to widows and half orphans	

personal social services, such as those in orphanages, nursing homes, adoption agencies, and family counseling centers. The churches very jealously protected their right to provide these personal social services, and social workers as a professional group vigorously defended the notion that the government should stay out of the private social service sector. The division of responsibilities is indicated in Table 19–1. In the twentieth century, this neat compartmentalization of responsibilities disappeared.

The Linking of Public and Private Efforts

A historical summary of the relationship between voluntary and public welfare shows that the single constant is that the two exist in a kind of dynamic tension. A good part of voluntary welfare has been an organized effort to force governments to act. Sometimes public and private agencies have been rivals, sometimes unwilling partners. The historical constant is that the shape and structure of one at any point in time cannot be understood without reference to the other. The primacy of the voluntary effort in the nineteenth century was challenged by the social reform movement of the progressive era (1890 to 1920). The reform effort was split irrevocably following Woodrow Wilson's administration. State responsibility was for cash aid to the deserving poor, and the provision of social services was the responsibility of voluntary efforts. A significant strain of thought in the first third of this century held that cash public aid was less risky and less humiliating than private charity. Following the Great Depression, government public assistance and social insurance programs replaced the previously-provided cash aid function. The voluntary sector jealously guarded its independence from government.

The spirit of earlier cooperation resumed on a small scale in the 1950s, when voluntary agencies began to accept grants and contracts to deliver highly specific child welfare services. This relationship mushroomed in the mid-1960s, when Great Society programs funded "old" social work agencies to provide many of their "new" activities. Not so gradually, public funds began to play the dominant role in the total budget for private voluntary agencies. Some social workers in the private sector raised questions about whether the heavy reliance on public dollars would affect the autonomy and integrity of the private agency. Paradoxically, this period (1965 to 1980) saw the growth of advocacy organizations engaged in monitoring the performance of public actions and working to influence the quantity and quality of publicly funded social service expenditures by direct lobbying, grassroots organizing, electioneering, and particularly litigation. No doubt, these activities contributed to the significant rise in public spending for social services.

The tables have now turned nearly 180 degrees: there is debate over the proper function of the voluntary sector. The Reagan administration eliminated much federal support for legal aid, social services, and organizing activities. The Bush administration, with its "Thousand Points of Light" programs, is encouraging returning direct social service functions to private charity. Both conservative administrations have argued that private charity can and should meet the needs for service assistance that are being created by the curtailment of publicly funded social programs.

CONTEMPORARY STRUCTURE

Today, organized social service activities clearly are not limited to those provided directly by governments or sectarian agencies. A significant share of social service expenditures (a precise estimate is dependent on the assumptions made) comes from and/or is spent by the little-understood **private nonprofit social agency.** The private nonprofit sector of the social services system employs a majority of the social workers engaged in direct practice to individuals, groups, neighborhoods, and communities. The private nonprofit agency is private in charter and organization but public in function. Neither the economic model of the private firm nor the public finance constructs of the public enterprises quite catches the essence of its operations. The nonprofit social services agencies are a diverse lot of 40,000 entities, which employ 675,000 persons and collectively spend $15 billion to accomplish rather imprecise goals. The nonprofit agencies provide a host of services ranging from prenatal to bereavement programs for individuals, groups, neighborhoods, and communities. They also serve as an organizing entity and conduit for charitable funds and voluntary efforts, with tax dollars commingled and channeled to specific projects.

Three interdependent parts comprise the social services portion of nonprofit agencies. A specific agency can represent one or all three parts, which are

1. agencies that serve public and charitable purposes but serve principally for fund raising and planning, such as the United Way agencies;
2. advocacy organizations, which bring together a group of like-minded persons who seek to generate government funding or promote public understanding and support of a specific social problem area or a specific class of persons deemed to be in need, such as retarded persons, aged persons, or disabled persons. Advocacy organizations are in essence political interest groups that attempt to garner support, including public spending, for their causes;
3. direct service agencies that deal with particular clients with specific or multiple problems of social functioning.

Despite the importance, relevance, and resources of the private sector social agency, there is no uniform explanation for its very existence, much less an

Volunteers are a vital part of many social services programs operated by both voluntary and public agencies. Here, volunteers assist with a Meals on Wheels program, which delivers meals to the homes of elderly persons unable to leave their homes easily or to prepare meals themselves. Elderly participants enjoy the contact with volunteers as much as they enjoy the meals they are brought.

agreed-upon explanation of its vitality and durability. Nevertheless, three main explanations exist, namely, historical, administrative, and economic perspectives of private sector social agencies.

Historical Explanation

The first of these three explanations, most completely developed by historian John Leiby, stresses simple historical antecedents. American society, particularly on the frontier, developed in a context of almost nonexistent government. Lacking public institutions to address the problems of collective needs, the frontier society turned to formal and informal voluntary associations, which took roots and maintained their own integrity once governments were vibrant. Even then, according to this explanation, people on the frontier maintained a healthy distrust of government. The famed French social philosopher Alexis de Tocqueville, writing in the mid-1800s, described this tendency of Americans to form nonprofit, nongovernmental associations to accomplish public tasks as characteristic of the new nation:

> Americans of all ages, all stations of life, and all types of disposition are forever forming associations . . . to give fetes, found seminaries, build churches, distribute books and send missionaries to the Antipodes. . . . In every case, at the head of any new undertaking, where in France you would find the government or in England some territorial magnate, in the United States you are sure to find a voluntary association.

(Alexis de Tocqueville, *Democracy in America,* as quoted in Palmer & Sawhill 1978, 263).

Administrative Explanation

The second explanation, the administrative one, is considerably more prosaic, although it builds on the first and adds a contemporary focus. The argument is made that during periods of expansion, public officials can more quickly provide a newly mandated service by contracting with private vendors than by launching a full-scale public program. Equally important in the mind of public officials is that a service highly sought today may be seen as an encumbrance or luxury tomorrow. It is far easier administratively and politically to cancel a contract with a vendor than it is to dismantle a fully operative program. Thus, during periods of expansion and contraction of social service spending, public officials have an incentive to purchase service contracts with nonpublic entities. The private nonprofit agencies, in turn, find their fund-raising and maintenance requirements more easily met by offering to contract to provide a particular social service.

Economic Explanation

The third explanation focuses attention on the interaction between economic and political factors in the social service marketplace. This can be visualized by assuming an oversimplified world. Suppose that only three groups competed for spending on a social work service. One group wanted to spend $6 billion, another $8 billion, and the third $10 billion. The $8 billion group, by threatening to form a coalition with either of the other groups, can get the remaining group to agree to its preference. The $8 billion dollar amount is between the two extremes. Where the compromise actually is reached depends on many factors; the critical point is that the group that wants the most certainly will be dissatisfied. If the public institutions spend only $8 billion on, say, AIDS research, and a group wants society to spend $10 billion, money for that program can be collected from the marketplace through donations. This happens all the time. Social workers convince concerned citizens to give money to do things the government ought to do but isn't doing. The voluntary sector is a kind of private voluntary government. The situation has been compounded by the fact that the majority of American citizens believed, rightly or not, that government programs were inherently inefficient. In the late 1980s and the early 1990s these dissatisfactions prompted a renewed interest in the privatization of social services (Gummer 1990).

To understand the organizational auspices of a social service delivery system we can no longer usefully think in terms of the public–private dichotomy. Instead, we need to look at the funding sources and charter of the delivery agency. We thus find many types of public, private, and voluntary agencies, as indicated in Table 19–2. From pure publicly funded and publicly run child protective services agencies, represented in cell 1, to profit-seeking child-care centers with all their users paying their own way represented in cell 11 of the table, social service programs come in many forms. Most agencies would be classed as one of the types represented by the numbered cells in bold type (i.e., cells 1, 6, 7, and 11). In practice, all combinations can be found. The critical point is that agencies need to be classified on the basis of both their charter and their principal source of funding.

BASIC CHARACTERISTICS OF TRADITIONAL VOLUNTARY AGENCIES

First, voluntary agencies represent special interest groups' concern for specific problems. This is expressed in (1) a commitment to deliver a specialized service to a client or constituent group, (2) a commitment to try to influence public policy on behalf of that specialized client population, and (3) a desire to educate a nonattentive public about the service needs, potential, and special attributes of the group of clients to be served.

Second, voluntary agencies have a considerable degree of discretion in their allocation of agency resources, since, unlike a public entity, they do not have

Table 19–2 Types of Social Service Delivery Models

Charter	Source of Funds			
	Taxes	Gifts and Grants	Payments for Service	Mixed
Public	**1**	2	3	4
Private, nonprofit	5	**6**	**7**	8
Private, for-profit	9	10	**11**	12

1- An example of a public agency funded by taxes would be a prison or a child protective services agency.

6- An example of a private, non-profit agency funded by gifts and grants is a child and family services agency or a child guidance center.

7- An example of a private, non-profit agency funded by payments for service is a church-operated child care program.

11- An example of a private, for-profit agency funded by payments for service is the Kindercare Childcare Corporation's centers located throughout the United States.

Note that public agencies, except hospitals, seldom receive payments for services from persons served.

Community United Way programs fund many local social services program, such as this county rape crisis center, where a social worker provides services to a client who was recently raped.

narrow legislative mandates, nor do their clients have specific legal claims on agency resources. Consequently, voluntary agencies have the freedom to choose which clients to serve and how to serve them. This provides maximum freedom to professional social workers, who often see employment in the voluntary agency as a way to escape bureaucratic constraints. However, serving a particular group in a particular way becomes institutionalized over time. Voluntary agencies acquire traditions and obligations that limit their freedom. This often leads to splinter agencies spinning off from the older agencies, which can become as ossified as public ones.

Third, because of their small size, unique history, discretionary power, and freedom (in the short run) from bureaucratic and legal constraints, voluntary agencies depend heavily on the quality of their executive leadership, a point that was explored in Chapter 15.

Voluntary agencies play a special role in the three-sector (i.e., public, private nonprofit, private for-profit) social service economy. They are bounded on both sides—on the one side by the private profit-oriented approach of the free market, and on the other side, by a politically driven public sector. Governed by neither marketplace nor voting booth, voluntary agencies can be creative and innovative. However, they also are vulnerable to their own excesses and to the expansionary drive of both profit and public enterprises. Thus, any agency may exist only briefly. Much like business firms, there are the few—very few— old venerables (i.e., those that have existed for about 100 years or more) a small number of agencies in their middle years, and a whole rash of new agencies, (i.e., those less than ten years old). A survey conducted by Lester Solomon (1986) found that only 40 percent of the agencies in place that year had existed ten years earlier.

There is a great deal of romantic fantasy about the voluntary approach. Conservative administrations pledged to restore the American spirit of voluntary service and of cooperation between private and community initiatives. President

Reagan lauded the spirit of the free and vigorous voluntary way, where communities, out of love, rebuilt the barn and cared for the victims of disaster in a warm, heartfelt, caring way. Conservatives listened to his message and feared the loss of a world that never was. Liberals listened to his message and recognized it for what it was—a historical inaccuracy. We cannot return to a voluntary way, not only because today the world is more complex, but principally because the voluntary spirit, then as now, responded only to a small section of the total problem.

The voluntary agency, in fact, has expanded as the public sector has expanded. Today, only a small part of our social welfare problems are responded to by the voluntary sector. Firms historically have given about 1 percent of their pretax profits to all of the voluntary sector agencies. Families have contributed about 2 percent of their pretax income to "churches and charities." Between 1969 and 1979, private family giving as a share of the GNP dropped from 2.1 percent to 1.8 percent. The decline continued although less dramatically, throughout the 1980s. Tax law changes may accelerate this decline. An increasing share of the voluntary budget now comes from grants, contracts, and purchases of service agreements from the public sector.

Social service agencies with voluntary charters spent an estimated $13.2 billion in 1980. Of this, it is estimated that $7.3 billion came from the federal government, with an additional $2.5 billion from state and local public budgets. One estimate of the flow of funds to an "average" nonprofit service agency is given in Table 19–3.

THE SOCIAL AGENCY AS INTEREST GROUP

The mother of a disabled child hopes that government will structure educational and health agencies in such a way that the life chances of her child are improved.

Table 19–3 Changes in Revenue for the Average Nonprofit Agency, 1981–1982, by Source (1981 dollars)

Source	Income in Fiscal Year 1981	Change in Income 1981–1982	
		Amount	Percentage
Government	295,665	− 18,530	− 6.3
Corporations	21,639	+ 261	+ 5.8
Foundations	24,253	+ 1,262	+ 5.2
United Way	38,165	+ 712	+ 1.9
Religious and other federated funders	19,317	+ 703	+ 3.6
Direct individual giving	42,747	+ 3,387	+ 7.9
Fees, charges	200,001	+ 13,251	+ 6.6
Endowment, investments	32,097	+ 1,323	+ 4.1
Other	40,134	+ 891	+ 2.2
Unallocated	3,595	− 599	NA
Total	717,613	+ 3,661	+ 0.5

Source: Solomon, Lester F. and M F. Gutowski. 1986. *The invisible sector.* Washington, D.C.: Urban Institute.

A physical therapist with special skills in developmental disabilities will want help in educational institutions structured so that children in need can benefit from his skills. A health, welfare, and education planner in state government wants to utilize her skills so that scarce educational dollars can be utilized more effectively to aid all medically impaired children. Soon various associations are formed to address their joint aims, and the care and maintenance of the new associations become central. Soon, however, the mother of the disabled child must consult a mosaic of organizations that shape health and welfare policy. Each is committed to the public good, but each has a limited focus.

We can think of the evolving associations, both formal and informal, as having two forms: one form is within government and the other outside. However, informal associations of paid professionals who have a common set of goals also exist. Social workers typically employed in both the public bureaucracies and private agencies are affiliated with the informal associations. These associations outside of government are called **interest groups.** These groups, which may be formal or informal, typically are loose confederations of individually oriented policy associations. Such associations often have paid staff, but they also have a membership of dues-paying persons. These members may be either potential clients or professional providers. Formal organizations such as the National Association for Retarded Citizens, the American Public Welfare Association, the North American Council on Adoptable Children, or the American Association for Retired Persons often work with ad hoc groups of interested persons around specific issues.

Together, agencies and interest groups form two parts of a political community. The third part of the political community is the staff members of the relevant legislative subcommittees (at local, state, and national levels) who write the legislation and initiate the authorization of public funding for the mission at hand. Policy-making in a particular substantive area (e.g., services for mentally disabled persons) is thus a function of the close cooperation, conflicts, and interactions of these parts of a political community.

SUMMARY

A majority of Americans view voluntary agencies as innovative and flexible vanguards of social service technology and delivery patterns. In point of fact, in recent years it is the public sector that has often been the vanguard. Essentially, voluntary and public agencies are created in particular historical circumstances. The mixture of public, voluntary, and private agency practices and the way they are funded may once have made sense, but adaptation to current needs has been slow. Often the patterns of practice do not fit well with current realities and problems.

A number of hypotheses have been advanced concerning the origins, growth, and functions of voluntary agencies. They have been studied extensively by social psychologists, sociologists, economists, and political scientists. In fact, all of the explanations about the voluntary sector are flawed in one way or another, and more research needs to be done. Basically, the public, voluntary, and even profit-oriented agencies are rapidly becoming more similar to one another.

KEY TERMS

interest group
private nonprofit social agency
private sector

public sector
voluntary sector

DISCUSSION QUESTIONS

1. How many social services agencies in your community are public? How many are voluntary? Are there ones for which you are not sure?
2. Discuss the differences between the public and the voluntary social service agencies in your community.
3. Which of the local agencies do you think ought to be voluntary and which ought to be public? Explain why for each one.
4. What principle of separation into public and voluntary would you use as an ideal for social services agencies in the United States? What principle of separation appears to operate in practice?

REFERENCES

Boorstin, D. J. 1985. *The Americans: The national experience.* New York: Random House.

Leiby, John. 1978. *A history of social welfare and social work in the United States.* New York: Columbia University Press.

Palmer, John, and Isabel Sawhill. 1984. *The Reagan record.* Cambridge: Ballinger.

SUGGESTED FURTHER READINGS

Grummer, Bernard. 1990. *Social policy administration.* Englewood Cliffs, N.J.: Prentice Hall.

Solomon, Lester M., and M. F. Gutowski. 1986. *The invisible sector.* Washington, D.C.: Urban Institute.

Wellford, W. Harrison. 1987. *The role of the nonprofit human service organizations.* Washington, D.C.: National Association of Health and Social Welfare organizations.

The Future of Social Work and Social Welfare

20

George Swain recently retired after forty-five years as a social worker in a variety of settings. His first job was as a caseworker in a settlement house, where he earned a yearly salary of $2,000. An active member of the state and local chapters of the National Association of Social Workers, George has been involved in many changes in the social work profession over the years. "In those early years, we did everything for our clients, since there were very few social service agencies," George stated in a recent interview. "In my first job, I led groups of teenagers, ran programs for senior citizens, set up a child care center, set up a rat control program in the neighborhood, transported people's belongings when they moved, and took kids into my house when they had nowhere else to go. When I retired as the director of a family services agency, there were forty-seven other social service agencies in the community, and most of my time and my staff's time was spent coordinating and linking resources for our clients with those other agencies."

"Today," George continued, "services are much more specialized—and we are more aware of human problems. I'm sure, for example, when I look back, that lots of kids I worked with when I was younger were sexually abused, but social workers in those days were relatively unaware of how extensive a problem that was."

George is especially excited because his granddaughter Jessica is a senior in the Bachelor of Social Work program at the state university and will graduate as a social worker this year. Jessica is completing her field internship at the local rape crisis center and hopes to work for the state human services agency providing services to help families on public assistance become self-sufficient when she graduates. Both grandfather and granddaughter agree that social work has grown as a profession and that many challenging opportunities are ahead for Jessica.

As we move toward the twenty-first century, the United States faces a serious domestic crisis. As more attention is given nationally to our social welfare system—and the roles various segments of society should play in meeting ever-increasing unmet human needs—increased recognition is being given to the importance of the social work profession in the process. The future of social work is a challenging one with numerous opportunities for the profession.

Social work has a historical commitment to help people cope with change, and the challenges of the 1990s and the next century suggest that our society will face major changes. The national ambiguity and strain that have existed in the United States since its founding regarding how the unmet needs of our society should be addressed have intensified during recent years. Most Americans are content with the way things are and uneasy about the future direction of the United States and the implications for them. We continue to be generous and compassionate when it comes to helping an individual in need, but limiting and suspicious when it comes to helping large numbers of individuals systematically. How our country balances individual freedom versus collective responsibility will be a major theme during the 1990s and the next century.

Any attempt to forecast future trends must be tentative. Technological and social change does not always progress at an even rate, nor is the direction of change always predictable. Nevertheless, some trends can be identified that enable us to suggest what factors will have an impact on the profession of social work and the social welfare system within the near future. In this chapter we briefly identify the major issues relating to the future of social welfare in our country and probable directions that the profession of social work will take in addressing these issues.

THE RELATIONSHIP BETWEEN PAST AND PRESENT

In order for us to comprehend the difficulty of predicting the effects of social change upon social work and social welfare, it is helpful to review the earlier chapters of this book. The history of the social work profession is related integrally to the unpredictable nature of the world in which we live. The social work profession is called to respond as social change alters the economic base of society, as well as other basic social institutions such as the family, education, religion, and political and related social organizations. The rapid growth and development of the social work profession in the latter part of the nineteenth century were related directly to the emergence of large urban communities and the accompanying problems associated with increased numbers of displaced persons, detachment from means of production, high rates of unemployment, migration, slums, the rise of a subculture of poverty, increasing health-related problems, and other conditions associated with urban blight. To remediate or eliminate the sources of these problems and to provide support for these displaced persons and their families, "trained" helpers had to become an integral part of the societal solution. Thus, the profession of social work was born from the need to ensure that a cadre of professionals armed with an understanding of human behavior, awareness of how social organizations function, and sensitivity to the effects of the environment as a determinant of individual growth and development would emerge as society's first line of remediation.

As the technological and industrial revolution erupted, the stability inherent in a primarily agrarian society began to disintegrate rapidly. The structure and function of the family, once stable and secure, were affected by the stresses and tensions produced by the economic marketplace, which called for greater mobility, division of labor outside of the home, and, consequently, a restructuring of family priorities. As a result, families have become less stable, the divorce rate has increased dramatically, multiple marriages are more common, and child abuse, spouse abuse, and various forms of neglect at all levels of society have emerged as more visible problems.

As the economy has become more unpredictable, the long-sought-after goal of financial security has become more difficult to achieve for many people. The poor have continued to be victimized by the lack of opportunity and often blamed for their condition. Increasingly, health and mental health needs of individuals have not been met. The spread of the AIDS virus has had a far-reaching effect on all segments of our society. As our population has grown older, greater numbers of older adults have become detached from means of production, and they often lack sufficient supports to provide for their maintenance and health-related needs. In addition, crime, delinquency, substance abuse, homelessness, and a variety of related problems have become sources of constant societal concern.

The organization of social welfare services is far different today from that of the Poor Law days. Gone are the almshouses, the poor houses, and "indoor" relief as a solution of first choice. The social welfare system has expanded dramatically to meet the proliferation and magnitude of new needs, and it now requires substantial societal resources to maintain.

Social workers and others within the social welfare system have responded with diversification in order to meet a variety of needs expressed by individuals whose personal resources cannot provide an adequate level of social functioning and life satisfaction. This diversification has emerged as essential in the delivery of social welfare services (See Box 20–1). Today, social workers are skilled in working not only with the displaced, the poor, substance abusers, single parents, and criminal offenders but also with persons experiencing marital conflict, family violence, mental illness, problems associated with later life, and a myriad of other related personal and social problems. In addition, the role of social workers as advocates for disenfranchised populations—the poor, women, ethnic minorities, gays and lesbians, and related groups—has become more important, as society increasingly becomes more complex and tends to overlook these groups. As new problems have emerged, the capacity of the social work profession to incorporate the knowledge and skills essential to providing assistance always has been forthcoming.

SOCIAL WELFARE AND THE FUTURE

Increased world competition and politics, changing family roles and structure, our expanding older population, gaps in health insurance, changing needs of the workplace, and the need for long-term care have serious implications that have left or will leave large numbers of individuals unable to care for themselves without assistance. Unfortunately, our current social welfare system has not

Box 20–1   Professional Levels of Practice

The National Association of Social Workers has developed a hierarchy which delineates four levels of professional social work practice and their respective job responsibilities. The hierarchy also identifies the knowledge, skills and values that social workers are expected to demonstrate at each level:

Basic Professional Level represents practice requiring professional practice skills, theoretical knowledge, and values that are not normally obtainable in day to day work experience but that are obtainable through formal professional social work education. Formal social work education is distinguished from experiential learning by being based on conceptual and theoretical knowledge of personal and social interaction and by training in the disciplined use of self in relationship with clients.

Specialized (Expert) Professional Level represents the specific and demonstrated mastery of therapeutic technique in at least one knowledge and skill method, as well as a general knowledge of human personality as influenced by social factors, and the disciplined use of self in treatment relationships with individuals or groups, or a broad conceptual knowledge of research, administration, or planning methods and social problems.

Independent Professional Level represents achievement by the practitioner of practice, based on the appropriate special training, developed and demonstrated under professional supervision, which is sufficient to ensure the dependable, regular use of professional skills in independent or autonomous practice. A minimum of two years is required for this experiential learning and demonstration period following the master of social work program.

This level applies both to solo or autonomous practice as an independent practitioner or consultant and to practice within an organization where the social worker has primary responsibility for representing the profession or for the training or administration of professional staff.

Advanced Professional Level represents practice in which the practitioner carries major social or organizational responsibility for professional development, analysis, research, or policy implementation, or that is achieved by personal professional growth demonstrated through advanced conceptual contributions to professional knowledge.

The educational standards for the four levels of Social Work Practice are:

Basic Professional Level: Requires a bachelor's degree (BSW) from a social work program accredited by the Council on Social Work Education (CSWE).

Specialized (Expert) Professional Level: Requires a master's degree (MSW) from a social work program accredited by the CSWE.

Independent Professional Level: Requires an accredited MSW and at least two years of postmaster's experience under appropriate professional supervision.

Advanced Professional Level: Requires proficiency in special theoretical, practice, administration or policy or the ability to conduct advanced research studies in social welfare; usually demonstrated through a doctoral degree in social work or a closely related social science discipline.

Source: Copyright 1981, National Association of Social Workers, Inc. *NASW Standards for the Classification of Social Work Practice.* (Silver Springs, Md.: NASW, 1981), p. 9. Reprinted with permission.

The future of social welfare programs remains uncertain as funds diminish and needs grow.

adapted to address these changes. Today's system is fragmented, with one group in need pitted against other equally needy ones, all vying for resources often insufficient to address the needs of even one group. Our social welfare system is fast approaching a crisis state and needs serious refinement and rethinking.

Our short-sightedness only results in a society of persons increasingly unable to provide for themselves or others, which has serious implications for all of us. We cannot expect people to take responsibility for themselves if they have no opportunities to escape from inadequate living situations that promote failure. The poorly prepared student of today is the marginal or unemployed worker of tomorrow. The neglected preschoolers of today are those on whom we will depend to maintain the U.S. position in the world economy, keep our Social Security system intact and pay for our care when we are old, and run our society. If unmet needs are addressed effectively, we all benefit. If unmet needs are not addressed, we all pay.

Our social welfare system must be one that focuses on our strengths and on individual diversity. It must be one that encourages self-sufficiency, yet provides humane services for those who are unable to be self-sufficient or those who need help from the system in order to function independently. It must be a system that invests in our nation's children—focusing on the preservation of the family but protecting and nurturing children when this is not possible, as well as providing prenatal care, adequate nutrition, preschool programs, and child care. It must be a system that works with other systems to provide increased opportunities for adolescents and young adults—reducing school dropout rates, increasing literacy, providing employment training, reducing teen pregnancy, and providing comprehensive health and mental health services. It must be a system that helps adults achieve and maintain self-sufficiency—

reducing poverty, providing adequate housing and employment, assuring coverage for health and mental health care. It must be a system that provides for the needs of the elderly—providing housing, as well as health and long-term care (Ford Foundation 1989).

For most individuals in our society, personal needs can no longer be met throughout the life cycle by family alone. Government participation is essential to assist those in need. Participation from non-government sources, including the private sector and all citizens, is also essential. The issue should not be whether the public or the private sector should meet human needs, but how they can work cooperatively to support each other. Both sectors are interconnected and interdependent parts of the social welfare system. Although the question of the most effective ways to provide social welfare to meet individual unmet needs requires substantial debate, most Americans agree that our society is a caring one and that the nation's future rests on how well it responds to the needs of its members. Each of us, private citizens with public responsibility, needs to examine what roles we can play in strengthening our social welfare system and providing a supportive society for ourselves and future generations.

CURRENT ISSUES IN SOCIAL WORK PRACTICE

The positions members of society take toward social problems and the resolution of those problems invariably relate to the resources available. Unfortunately, members of society do not always take an unequivocally progressive stance. For example, fiscal concerns currently are paramount in society. Federal indebtedness has resulted in massive reductions in funds available for solving social problems. As a result, monies for social welfare services have been reduced significantly, and populations at risk have not received the assistance essential for even the most minimal level of functioning.

In response to the reduction of public monies for social welfare services, considerable emphasis has been directed to encouraging the private sector to "take up the slack" and to provide both funds and extend assistance through volunteerism. Although noble, private efforts have fallen far short of success because of the magnitude of the need. As indicated earlier, a society inevitably must take a position relative to its commitment to those in need. The position and its expression are influenced by values, morality, and the availability of resources. In a materialistically oriented society such as ours, it is paradoxical that the definition of *need* is invariably related to the "amount" of resources that society is willing to allocate. Thus, in times of monetary scarcity, or when demands are made upon individuals to share (through the taxing process) more of their earned incomes, the tendency to redefine need levels is inevitable. This redefinition, of course, does not always address the "real" need that is apparent. Today, as a society, we stand at the crossroads of either continuing to reduce allocations for the resolution of problems for our members at risk or reorganizing our priorities to assume that all of our members are guaranteed access to the best of our problem-solving abilities and hope that at least their minimal needs will be met.

Related challenges facing future social work professionals include determining which of the myriad of societal and individual problems fall within the domain of the social welfare system. A traditional view of the social welfare institution holds that its services should be residual—that is, incorporating those areas that cannot be served by other societal institutions. Increasingly, however, the social welfare system is seen as a panacea to address all needs not being met by other systems—that is, a system that should be all things to all people. There is a need to define and limit the boundaries that encompass the social welfare system so that its services can be effective and retained with available resources. At the same time, however, social workers are faced with serious value conflicts over not addressing human needs that fall beyond social welfare boundaries when no one else is meeting them and they are critical for individual and societal survival.

As technology continues to generate new knowledge, the social work profession will also have to grapple with ethical issues relating to genetic engineering and surrogate parenting. Euthanasia, environmental concerns and pollution, and technological measures to prolong life will also be ethical issues of concern that will need to be addressed by many professions, including social work.

With scarce resources, ethical decisions about what types of services to provide and who should get them will increasingly fall to the social worker. How do you say no to a woman applying for AFDC benefits who has four children under age six with no housing, no food, and a temporary part-time job, who makes five dollars more each month than the income eligibility guidelines for receiving AFDC allow? How do you determine whether limited funding should be allocated to the elderly, to children, or to the disabled? How do you decide who should have first priority for heart and other organ transplants, whether limited dollars should be spent on neonatology care for premature infants who may live only a limited time, or at what point resources should no longer be provided to families with little potential to be rehabilitated and the children placed in foster care or adoption?

If limited resources do not allow for a full range of preventive and remedial/ rehabilitative services, how do you prevent problems such as child maltreatment, knowing that this may limit your resources for those already abused in the short run but prevent more abuse in the long run? Or, instead, do you help those in immediate crisis, knowing that the lack of preventive services will mean even more crises for families in the future? One social welfare advocate told his state governor and legislature that social workers were being asked to take positions similar to the one exemplified in the popular novel *Sophie's Choice,* where a mother in occupied Poland under Hitler's regime was forced to decide which of her two children would be spared the gas chamber and which would be sent to death.

Limited resources, rapid social change, the influx of additional social problems such as AIDS, the increase in an underclass of ethnic minorities and women, the health care crisis, and the shift to a technocratic society suggest new opportunities for social work professionals willing to accept these challenges. A recent survey of professional social workers (NASW, 1990) suggested that the most critical issues facing the profession in the near future include health care, substance abuse, AIDS, the aging of our society, homelessness, and persistent poverty. The social work profession and the issues it faces are challenging at all levels of society—whether one works with individuals, families, groups, the community, or at the state or national level. Social work practitioners need to increase their involvement at the legislative and policy levels and become more involved in the political arena where key social welfare decisions are made. As society becomes increasingly complex, the number of social workers will continue to grow and their roles will broaden at all levels of practice.

TRENDS IN SOCIAL WORK CAREERS

As indicated in earlier chapters, social workers today function in a variety of job settings and fields of practice and hold degrees at the undergraduate (BSW), masters (MSW), and doctoral (PhD or DSW) levels. From 1974 (when BSW programs were first accredited by CSWE) to 1984, 86,751 BSW degrees were awarded. This represents 46 percent of the social work degrees awarded by CSWE-accredited schools during that time period, with 54 percent of degrees awarded to graduate students (Hardcastle 1987). From 1958 (when MSW programs were first accredited by the Council on Social Work Education) to 1984, 250,339 social work degrees were granted by CSWE-accredited institutions. Since the late 1980s, enrollment in schools of social work throughout the United States has increased substantially as more young people have committed themselves to helping others.

A valid question asked by social work students is whether the supply of social workers will exceed the demand, particularly during fiscal cutbacks. A 1982 survey of social work practitioners found that 83 percent were employed in social work jobs, 4 percent were employed in non–social work jobs, 6 percent were retired, and 8 percent were unemployed, with over half of those unemployed at their own choosing (they were in school, raising families, etc.). Even with funding cutbacks, funding for social welfare programs has increased: from 1960 to 1979, public expenditures in social welfare rose from 10.5 percent of the U.S. gross national product to 18.5 percent, and private philanthropy in social welfare increased 214 percent during that same time period (Hardcastle 1987). This trend is expected to continue, with the number of social work jobs projected to increase. As the population continues to age, fewer younger social workers will be available to replace retirees. Additionally, more social work jobs will become available, particularly in the areas of child protective services, public assistance and welfare reform, substance abuse, health care, mental health, and gerontology.

Although social workers currently are employed in a variety of settings, most work for government or voluntary agencies (88 percent), with approximately 12 percent working for private proprietary organizations. With the privatization of health care, however, large numbers of for-profit hospitals, alcohol and drug treatment programs, psychiatric residential treatment programs, and gerontology facilities have been developed and hire social workers. Also, as states have passed licensing requirements for social workers and insurance companies include social workers under third-party reimbursement agreements, an increasing number of social workers are establishing private practices and seeing clients for psychotherapy, marriage and family counseling, and other types of clinical services. An increase in the number of social workers in private or proprietary settings is expected during the coming years.

At the same time as social work services in the private sector are increasing, new attention is being given to the need to encourage social workers to seek jobs in public social service settings, particularly state social service agencies. NASW and other organizations such as the American Public Welfare Association are working together to increase awareness about the challenges of public social services and the commitment that social work as a profession has to the indigent, who are most likely to come to the attention of a public agency. The welfare reform legislation passed in 1988 provides a number of exciting opportunities for social workers to assist families in becoming self-sufficient. The emphasis on family preservation and the national attention given to child maltreatment have also resulted in the increased professionalism of child and family services workers employed within public human services agencies.

Social workers are employed primarily in social agencies, hospitals, and outpatient facilities. A recent study (Hardcastle 1987) indicates that 57 percent of all social workers—63 percent of all BSW social workers—are employed in these types of settings (see Table 20–1). According to the study, most social workers are employed in the mental health field, a trend that has held for over a decade. When looking at BSW graduates only, the largest numbers are working with children and youth, followed by mental health. Sixty percent of all social workers, no matter what degree they have, are employed in the fields of mental health, health, or children and youth services (see Table 20–2).

The study also found that the social work profession is expanding in alcohol and drug programs, occupational/industrial social work, developmental disabilities programs, school social work, and gerontology/health problems (Hard-

Table 20–1 Employment Setting of Primary Employment for Social Work Labor Force by Degree Level (1982)

Employment Setting	Percentage				
	BSW	MSW	Doctorate	All	Rank
Social Service Agency/Organization	34.2	27.7	10.8	27.2	1
Private Practice/Self-Employed or Solo	3.7	7.2	9.9	7.1	6
Private Practice/Partnership	1.9	3.1	2.4	2.9	7
Membership Organization	1.4	0.9	0.7	0.9	13
Hospital	17.9	19.6	9.6	19.0	2
Institution (non-hospital)	4.2	3.1	1.5	3.1	8
Outpatient Facility (Clinic, Health, Mental Health Center)	10.8	16.7	7.8	15.9	3
Group Home/Residence	4.8	2.3	0.5	2.3	10
Nursing Home/Hospice	6.4	1.7	0.5	1.8	10
Court/Criminal Justice System	1.8	1.4	0.7	1.4	12
College/University	5.7	6.5	49.1	8.5	4
Elementary/Secondary School System	4.9	8.2	3.8	7.7	5
Non-Social Serv. Employment	1.8	1.6	2.0	1.5	10

Source: David Hardcastle, *The Social Work Labor Force*, (Austin: University of Texas at Austin School of Social Work, 1987), p. 16.

Table 20–2 Practice Area of Primary Employment of Labor Force by Degree Level (1982)

Practice Area of Primary Employment	Percentage				
	BSW	MSW	Doctorate	Total	Rank
Children and Youth	15.8	15.8	10.5	15.6	2.5
Community Organization/Planning	2.2	1.6	3.4	1.7	11.5
Family Services	8.4	11.9	7.5	11.5	4.0
Corrections/Criminal Justice	1.7	1.6	1.9	1.6	11.5
Group Services	0.5	0.4	0.5	0.3	16.0
Medical/Health Care	18.4	15.8	9.3	15.7	2.5
Mental Health	16.3	28.9	26.5	28.1	1.0
Public Assistance/Welfare	2.2	0.8	1.0	0.8	13.0
School Social Work	2.8	3.4	2.5	3.3	9.0
Services to Aged	11.0	4.2	4.2	4.5	5.5
Alcohol/Drug and Substance Abuse	2.6	3.2	2.9	3.1	9.0
Developmental Disabilities	5.8	3.2	2.0	3.3	9.0
Other Disabilities	0.4	0.5	0.5	0.5	14.0
Occupational	0.5	0.4	0.7	0.4	15.0
Combined Areas	6.0	4.4	11.7	4.7	5.5
Other	5.0	3.8	14.2	4.1	7.0

Source: David Hardcastle, *The Social Work Labor Force,* (Austin: University of Texas at Austin School of Social Work, 1987), p. 17.

castle 1987). Job opportunities for social workers are expected to increase faster than the average for all occupations through the year 2000 (Bureau of Labor Statistics 1990). The U.S. Bureau of Labor Statistics has forecasted 16,000 new social services positions annually for the next several years (U.S. Bureau of the Census 1983). Several popular magazines recently have cited social work in health care and gerontology as rapidly growing fields that those seeking careers should consider. Job opportunities in case management, mental health counseling, private practice and employee assistance programs, and school social work are also expected to increase (Bureau of Labor Statistics 1990).

Whatever the field of practice or the setting, social workers today and in the future face many challenges—and many opportunities for professional and personal growth. We hope that you will consider joining us as members of the social work profession.

SUMMARY

This book addresses the current state of the art in social work and social welfare. Throughout each chapter, the effects of social problems on various segments of our population are identified and the societal responses through the social welfare system are described. The many roles social workers play in addressing social welfare problems are also explored. The significant and dramatic modifications in both the social welfare system and the social work profession since the early days of organized helping efforts are apparent. Armed with knowledge about and an understanding of human behavior and complex organizations, and bringing a systems/ecological perspective to bear, the contemporary professional social worker is uniquely capable of skillful intervention in the resolution of problems. The social worker of the future will have many challenging opportunities to make major contributions to society.

KEY TERMS

advanced professional level of
    social work practice
basic professional level of social
    work practice

independent professional level of
    social work practice
specialized (expert) professional
    level of social work practice

DISCUSSION QUESTIONS

1. Identify at least three societal trends that have an impact on the future of social welfare and social work. Show how these trends will shape social welfare as an institution and social work as a profession.

2. Briefly describe at least three issues that current and future social workers must address as practicing professionals. What suggestions do you have in dealing with these issues?

3. Identify the four levels of social work practice and describe each briefly.

4. In which settings are social workers employed most often? In which fields of practice are social workers employed most often? Where are most BSW social workers employed?

5. Discuss some of the future employment opportunities for social work professionals. Which career areas interest you most and why?

REFERENCES

Bureau of Labor Statistics, U.S. Dept. of Labor. 1990. Social workers. *Education and social service occupations and clergy.* Reprinted from the Occupational Outlook Handbook, 1990–91 ed., Bulletin 2350-6: 24–27.

Hardcastle, D. 1987. *The social work labor force.* Austin: School of Social Work, University of Texas at Austin.

Task Force on Sector Force Classification. National Association of Social Workers (NASW). 1981. *NASW standards for the classification of social work practice: Policy statement 4.* Silver Spring, Md.: Author.

The common good: Social welfare and the American future. 1989. New York: Ford Foundation.

U.S. Bureau of the Census. 1983. *Statistical abstract of the United States, 1982–83.* Washington, D.C.: GPO.

SUGGESTED FURTHER READINGS

Atkinson, Z., and E. Glassberg. 1983. After graduation, what? Employment and educational experience of BSW programs. *Journal of Education for Social Work* 19(1): 5–13.

Bell, Daniel. 1974. *The coming of the post-industrial society.* New York: Basic Books.

Krager, H. J. 1983. Reclassification: Is there a future in public welfare for the trained social workers? *Social work* 28(6): 427–33.

Minahan, A. 1981. Social workers and the future. *Social Work* 5(26): 363–64.

Professional social work practice in public child welfare: An agenda for action. 1987. Portland: Center for Research and Advanced Study, University of Southern Maine.

Theobold, R. 1968. *An alternative future for America II.* Chicago: Swallow Press.

_____. 1972. *Futures conditional.* Indianapolis: Bobbs-Merrill.

Glossary

Acquired Immune Deficiency Syndrome (AIDS) a fatal disease that attacks the body's natural immune system.

Action system a system which includes all persons or groups involved in bringing about planned change of a client system (e.g. clients), such as the client system (e.g. clients), the change agent system (e.g. social worker) and the target system (e.g. client and school).

Addiction a physical and/or psychological dependence upon mood-altering substances or activities, including but not limited to alcohol, drugs, pills, food, sex, or gambling.

Adoption a process by which a child whose birth parents choose not to or cannot care for is provided with a permanent home and parents who are able to provide for the child; legal adoptions can take place only when the court terminates the parental rights of the birth parents, but many adoptions, particularly in minority communities, are informal and do not involve the court.

Advanced professional level of social work practice a level of practice in which the practitioner carries major social or organizational responsibility for professional development, analysis, research, or policy implementation; usually requires a doctoral degree in social work or a closely-related discipline.

Affirmative Action programs usually legally-mandated programs established within education, business, and industry.

Ageism discrimination against the elderly because of their age.

Aging the process of growing old.

Aid to Families with Dependent Children (AFDC) a public assistance program which provides cash assistance to families with children in need because of the loss of financial support as a result of death, disability, or the continued absence of a parent from the home.

Aid to Families with Dependent Children—Unemployed Parent (AFDC-UP) a supplemental AFDC program for two-parent families where financial need is due to specific unemployment conditions.

AIDS-related complex (ARC) second stage of the AIDS virus which moderately damages the body's immune system; at least two of the following symptoms must be present for at least 3 months for a person to be diagnosed with ARC: fever, weight loss, swollen lymph nodes, diarrhea, fatigue, or night sweats and at least one of the following signs: low white blood cell count, lowered blood cell count, low platelet count, or elevated levels of serum globulins; persons with ARC also exhibit a low number of T-helper cells and a low ratio of T-helper to T-suppressor cells.

Alcoholics Anonymous self-help group for alcoholics based on abstinence and a 12-step philosophy of living. Similar programs exist for family members of alcoholics and addicts and for persons with other types of addictions.

Alcoholism a use of alcohol that interferes with personal life, including family, friends, school, job, health, spiritual life, or the law.

Apathy-futility syndrome term used to describe a set of behaviors exhibited by a neglecting parent who is severely depressed and apathetic toward his/her immediate environment, including his/her children.

Arraignment a stage of a court case where the defendant is able to enter a plea of guilty or not guilty.

Association a relationship between two or more factors that occur together but are not necessarily causative, e.g., alcoholism and child abuse.

Basic professional level of social work practice a level of practice representing professional practice skills, theoretical knowledge, and values; requires a bachelor's degree (BSW) from a social work program accredited by the Council on Social Work Education.

Battered child syndrome a medical term used to describe a child in various stages of healing, indicating the child has been physically abused on a number of occasions.

Behavior modification an action intervention, based on the assumption that all behaviors are learned and can be changed, which focuses on reinforcing present positive behaviors to eliminate inappropriate behaviors.

Best interests of child a standard of decision-making used by courts and child welfare agencies which places emphasis on what is best for a specific child as opposed to what is best for other family members or persons.

Bioethics moral and ethical decisions associated with advanced technology in the health-care field.

Blended family a family formed by marriage or long-term relationship between partners where at least one partner or both brings children from a previous relationship into the new family system.

Boundary the limit or extent of a system; the point where one system ends and another begins.

Broker a social worker who assists clients in locating appropriate resources.

Casework services provided to individuals, groups, and families to strengthen social functioning, based on assessment of client situation, identification of problem areas, determination of appropriate interventions to address problem areas, and monitoring and evaluation of the process to ensure that outcomes address problems identified.

Catastrophic illness a chronic and severely debilitating illness that results in high medical costs and long-term dependence on the health care system.

Categorial assistance cash assistance programs given to individuals and families under the provision of the Social Security Act, which established specific categories of persons in need of cash assistance, including the aged, blind and permanently disabled (Supplemental Security Income) and children (Aid to Families with Dependent Children).

Cause/effect relationship a relationship between factors where one or more factors can be shown to directly cause a change in an additional factor or set of factors.

Change agent system the person, persons, or groups who facilitate a planned intervention: for example, the social worker and others involved in helping a client or client system.

Charity Organization Society (COS) the first relief organization in the U.S. that developed a systematic program to help the needy, promoting "scientific philanthropy" which incorporated individual assessment and development of coordinated service plans prior to providing services.

Child neglect a condition in which a caretaker responsible for a child either deliberately or by extraordinary inattentiveness fails to meet a child's basic needs, including failure to provide adequate food, clothing, shelter, medical assistance, education, and/or to supervise a child appropriately.

Child protective services mandated services provided by state social services agencies to families who abuse or neglect their children, for the purpose of protecting children whose safety is seriously endangered by the actions or inactions of their caretakers.

Child welfare delivery system a network of agencies and programs that provide social services to children, youth, and families.

Child Welfare League of America (CWLA) a national organization consisting of agencies, professionals, and citizens interested in the well-being of children and families which promotes standards for services, advocates child welfare policies and programs, conducts research, and provides publications related to child welfare issues.

Child welfare services social services which supplement or substitute for parental care and supervision when parents are unable to fulfill parental responsibilities and which improve conditions for children and their families.

Civil Rights Act federal legislation passed in 1964 and amended in 1965 which prohibits discrimination based on race, religion, color, or ethnicity in public facilities, government programs or those operated or funded by the federal government, and employment.

Client system individuals, families, groups, organizations or communities at whom intervention is directed in order to enhance social functioning.

Clinical social worker a person whose major focus is the provision of clinical social work services, usually individual, group or family counseling, often in a psychiatric, hospital, residential treatment, or mental health facility. An MSW is usually required (also termed "psychiatric social worker" in some settings).

Closed system a system with a boundary that is difficult to permeate; such systems are usually unreceptive to outsiders.

Community a group of individuals who usually live within close proximity of each other, who share a common environment, including public and private resources, and who identify themselves with that community.

Community development a social work approach to working with communities which considers and respects the diversity of a community's population and uses those differences to achieve community betterment for all of its citizens.

Community organization a method of social work practice which involves the development of community resources to meet human needs.

Comparable worth the concept that persons should receive measurably equal pay for the same type of work, regardless of their gender.

Competencies skills that are essential to perform certain functions; social workers must have competencies in a number of areas to be effective professionals.

Council on Social Work Education (CSWE) the national organization of schools of social work that focuses on social work education and serves as the accrediting body for professional social work undergraduate (BSW) and masters (MSW) programs.

Crisis intervention intervention provided when a crisis exists to the extent that one's usual coping resources threaten individual or family functioning.

Cultural pluralism the existence of two or more diverse cultures within a given society where each maintains its own traditions and special interests within the confines of the total society.

Custody legal charge given to a person requiring him/her to provide certain types of care and to exercise certain controls in regard to another individual, as in parent-child custody.

Defense attorney an attorney who represents the individual being charged by the state (the defendant) in a court case.

Deinstitutionalization a philosophy which advocates care of individuals with mental health problems and developmental disabilities in local community out-patient programs, whenever appropriate to the client's needs, as opposed to hospitalization in an institution.

Developmental disability severe, chronic disability resulting from physical or mental impairment, usually prior to age 21, which results in substantial limitations of the individual's social, emotional, intellectual, and/or physical functioning; 75 percent of those with developmental disabilities are mentally retarded.

Diagnostic and Statistical Manual of Mental Disorders (DSM) a classification system of types of mental disorders, which incorporates both organic and environmental factors, developed by the American Psychiatric Association for assessment and intervention purposes.

Direct practice a method of social work involving face-to-face contact with individuals, families, groups or actual provision of services by the social worker for the purpose of resolving problems; also referred to as casework or social casework.

Disciplinary research research designed to expand the body of knowledge of a particular discipline; also called pure or basic research.

Diversion a process where persons coming to the attention of the criminal justice system are diverted to other programs such as social services, community services, or educational (defensive driving) programs, rather than going through the court process.

Downshifting the voluntary limiting of job demands which allows a person to devote more time to family or to himself or herself.

Dual-career family a family where both spouses have careers outside of the family.

Dysfunctional impaired or abnormal functioning.

Educational group a group formed for the purpose of transmitting knowledge and enabling participants to acquire more complex skills, such as parenting.

Ego psychology a theoretical perspective which emphasizes ego growth and development.

Emotional abuse acting out against a person emotionally, such as verbally belittling or attacking a person constantly.

Emotional neglect a failure to meet emotional needs through acts of omission, such as not providing love, attention, and/or emotional support to a person.

Employee Assistance Program (EAP) workplace-sponsored program providing mental health and social services to employees and their families; services may be provided directly at the workplace, or through a contractual arrangement, by a social services agency.

Enabler a person whose behavior facilitates another person's behavior to continue; term is used most often to describe situations in families where alcoholism is a problem and other family members enable the alcoholism to continue by their reinforcing behaviors.

Encounter group a group oriented toward assisting individuals in developing more self-awareness and interpersonal skills through in-depth experiential activities nd extensive group sharing.

Entropy unavailable energy in a closed system which creates dysfunction within that system and eventually results in the system's inability to function.

Equal Rights Amendment (ERA) a proposed amendment to the U.S. Constitution to assure the complete and equal rights of all citizens without regard to race, color, creed, or gender; the amendment has not been ratified by the number of states necessary for its adoption and its future remains uncertain.

Equifinality the idea that the final state of a system can be achieved in many different ways.

Etiology of crime theories relating to the origins or causes of crime, including physiological, psychological, and sociological perspectives.

Evaluative research research undertaken to show how a program achieves (or fails to achieve) its goals.

Exosystem level the level of social environment that incorporates community factors in which an individual does not participate directly, but that affects the individual's functioning, such as school board and city council actions.

Family a group of individuals bonded together through marriage, kinship, adoption, or mutual agreement.

Family violence use of force, or threatened use of force, by one family member against another, usually by a family member who is more powerful against a member who is less powerful.

Farm crisis economic crisis experienced by farm owners, workers and rural communities from the late 1970s to the present which has resulted in serious emotional problems for many rural adults and their families.

Feminization of poverty a term used to describe the result of the increasing numbers of single-parent women being classified as poor.

Flexiplace a system that allows employees to work at alternate work sites as opposed to a standard workplace, e.g. working in their own homes.

Flextime a system that allows employees to have varied work hours as opposed to standard work hours, e.g. working one day from 6 A. M. to 3 P. M. and the next day from 7 A. M. to 4 P. M.

Food stamps in kind assistance program funded by the U.S. Department of Agriculture designed to supplement the food-purchasing power of eligible low-income households in order to allow families to maintain nutritious diets and to expand the market for agricultural goods.

Foster care a form of temporary substitute care where children live with a family other than their birth family until they are able to be returned to their birth family or adopted.

General assistance (GA) public assistance programs that provide financial aid to persons who are in need but do not qualify for federally-authorized programs; such programs are usually administered by county and local governments and are also referred to as "relief" programs.

General deterrent deterrent toward committing inappropriate/illegal acts targeted at the total population by specifically punishing those who commit such acts; imprisoning persons who commit crimes deters others from committing the same crimes.

Generalist practitioner a social worker who applies intervention methods within a systems/ecological framework to assist client systems with problem-solving.

Generalizable the ability of a theory to use what happens in one situation to explain what happens in other situations.

Gerontology the study of aging and the aging process.

Great Society a social reform program proposed by the Johnson administration in the 1960s to improve the quality of life for all Americans, with emphasis on the poor and disenfranchised; the War on Poverty was one of the major Great Society programs.

Group a social unit which consists of individuals who define status and role relationships to one another. A group possesses its own set of values and norms and regulates the behavior of its members.

Group work a process that seeks to stimulate and support more adaptive personal functioning and social skills of individuals through structured group interaction.

Head Start a comprehensive early childhood education program initially established as a Great Society Program that provides developmental learning for preschool children with health care, social services, and parent education components.

Health a state of complete physical, mental, and social well-being which is not merely the absence of disease or infirmity.

Health and welfare services programs providing services that facilitate individual health and welfare, such as maternal health and child care, public health, family planning, and child welfare services.

Health care services provided to individuals to prevent or promote recovery from illness or disease.

Health maintenance organization (HMO) pre-paid medical group practice where individuals pay monthly fees and receive specific types of health care at no cost or minimum costs per visit.

Health risk factors factors that affect a person's health and pace him/her at risk for serious health problems, e.g. smoking.

HIV-positive the first stage of acquired immune deficiency syndrome (AIDS), also called the seropositive state, that occurs when a person has tested positively for AIDS and has HIV (human immune deficiency virus) antibodies in his or her blood.

Home-based family-centered services services delivered to children and families in their own homes, with a focus on preserving the family system and strengthening the family to bring about needed change.

Home health care health care provided in a person's home as opposed to a hospital or other institutional health care setting; made available through outreach visits by social workers, nurses, physicians, and other health practitioners.

Homophobia a fear of homosexuals and homosexuality.

Hospices programs for terminally-ill individuals and their families that enable them to die with dignity and support, often away from a hospital setting.

Hypothesis a tentative assumption derived from theory that is capable of empirical verification.

Implementation carrying out the steps required to put a program or plan into practice.

Impulse-ridden behavior behavior exhibited by a neglecting parent with low impulse control, including inconsistency, leaving a child alone or in an unsafe situation without realizing the consequences to the child, or because a new activity is given a higher priority.

Incest sexual abuse between family members.

Inclusive the ability of a theory to consistently explain events in the same way each time they occur.

Independent professional level of social work practice a level of practice based on academic training and professional supervision which ensures the regular use of professional skills in independent or autonomous practice; requires a masters degree from an accredited social work program and at least two years of post-master's experience under appropriate professional supervision.

Indoor relief assistance given to the poor and the needy through placement in institutions, such as poorhouses, orphanages, and prisons.

Infant mortality rate the number of infants who die at birth or before they reach a certain age or, compared to the total number of infants, both living and not living, within that age range, within a specified geographic location and a specified time frame.

Institutional programs traditional, firstline efforts designed to meet the expected needs of individuals and families, such as the family or retirement programs.

Interest group a group of individuals organized to focus on a special interest, e.g., the homeless, the mentally ill, usually for the purpose of advocacy within the political system.

Intervention planned activities that are designed to improve the social functioning of a client or client system.

Job-sharing the sharing of one full-time job by two or more individuals; this practice is increasingly being allowed by employers and is advantageous to women with young children who do not want to work outside the home on a full-time basis.

Laissez faire an economic theory developed by Adam Smith which places emphasis on persons taking care of themselves and limits government intervention.

Least detrimental alternative a decision-making premise that places priority on making decisions regarding children based on which decision will be least damaging or upsetting to the child.

Least restrictive environment selecting a living environment for an individual that maintains the greatest degree of freedom, self-determination, autonomy, dignity, and integrity for the individual while he or she participates in treatment or receives services.

Life-span model a framework that focuses on relationships between individuals and their environments with major emphasis on where persons are developmentally and what transitional life processes they are experiencing (e.g., marriage, retirement).

Long-term care facility a program that provides long-term care to individuals, including the elderly and the disabled; state and federal regulations have established specific requirements facilities must meet to be classified as long-term care facilities.

Macrosystem level the level of social environment that incorporates societal factors that affect an individual, including cultural ideologies, assumptions, and social policies that define and organize a given society.

Mediation intervention between a divorcing or divorced couple to promote settlement of child custody and property issues in order to reconcile differences and reach compromises; mediation teams usually include an attorney and a social worker.

Medicaid federal grant-in-aid program to states to allow them to provide comprehensive medical care to low-income individuals and families.

Medical model a model which considers those with emotional problems as sick and thus not responsible for their behavior. This model also focuses on deficits and dysfunction of the client and family rather than the person's strengths. Little attention is given to environmental aspects.

Medicare federal health insurance program for the elderly.

Mental retardation a type of developmental disability attributable to mental or physical impairment which results in sub-average intellectual functioning.

Mesosystem level the level of social environment that incorporates interactions and interrelations among those persons, groups, and settings which comprise an individual's microsystem.

Microsystem level the level of social environment that includes the individual, including intrapsychic characteristics and past life experiences, and all the persons and groups in his or her day-to-day environment.

Minority group a category of people distinguished by physical or cultural traits which are used to single them out for differential and unequal treatment.

Moral treatment a philosophy among professionals and advocates working with the mentally ill in the late 1700s and early 1800s that advocated a caring, humane approach, as opposed to a punitive, repressive environment.

Multidisciplinary team approach an approach to working with clients which involves the shared expertise of professionals from a variety of different disciplines, such as social workers, health professionals, educators, attorneys, and psychologists.

National Association of Mental Health a national association of professionals and organizations concerned about mental health issues and care of persons with mental health problems; provides education, advocacy, and research.

National Association of Social Workers (NASW) the major national professional organization for social workers which promotes ethics and quality in social work practice; stimulates political participation and social action; and maintains eligibility standards for membership.

National Institute of Mental Health federal agency created by Congress in 1949 to address mental health concerns; now a part of the U.S. Department of Health and Human Services.

Natural group a group in which members participate as a result of common interests, shared experiences, similar backgrounds and values, and personal satisfactions derived from interaction with other group members (e.g. a street gang).

Natural support system resources available within a person's immediate environment to provide support without the person having to rely on formal community support systems; natural support systems include family members, neighbors, friends, and co-workers, as opposed to community agencies and programs.

Nonorganic failure to thrive a medical condition that results when a child is three percentiles or more below the normal range for height and weight and no organic reason can be determined; placing a child in a hospital and providing an adequate diet and nurturing will cause the child to gain height and weight, suggesting parental deprivation as the cause.

Nonprofit agency an agency that spends all of its funding to meet the goals of the agency with no financial profit earned by agency owners, directors, or employees.

Occupational social work social work services provided through the workplace; also termed industrial social work. Such services allow for focus on the relationships between work stresses and other systems within which individuals function.

Official poverty a way of measuring poverty that provides a set of income thresholds adjusted for household size, age of household head, and number of children under 18 years old.

Old Age Survivors and Disability Insurance (OASDI) a Social Security insurance program established as part of the Social Security Act of 1935 which provides limited payments to those eligible elderly and/or disabled persons and/or their dependents who have been employed and have had taxes deducted from their wages matched by their employers paid into a funding pool.

Ombudsman a public or private official whose function is to assist citizens in dealing with a bureaucracy.

Open system a system in which the boundaries are permeated easily.

Opportunity structure the accessibility of opportunities for an individual within that individual's environment, including personal and environmental factors such as physical traits, intelligence, family, availability of employment.

Outdoor relief cash or in kind assistance given to persons in need, allowing them to remain in their own homes; public assistance payments for food and fuel, for example.

Outsourcing the practice by U.S. businesses of having portions or all of their production carried out outside of the U.S. and its territories.

Parole a condition given to an imprisoned person to serve the remainder of the sentence outside of the detention facility, in a supervised situation, monitored by a parole officer.

Pastoral counselor a person who provides counseling services under the auspices of a religious organization, which usually includes an emphasis on spiritual well-being; usually members of the clergy.

Pedophile a person who is physically and sexually attracted to children as opposed to persons of his or her own age.

Permanency planning idea which states that all child welfare services provided should be centered around a plan directed toward a permanent, nurturing home for that child.

Physical child abuse a physical act of harm or threatened harm against a child by a caretaker which results in physical or mental injury to a child, including beating, hitting, slapping, burning, shaking, or throwing.

Planning outline of a design which incorporates the strategic use of resources in problem-solving.

Policy research research that focuses upon evaluating the effects of proposed or existing social policy on constituent populations.

Poor Law legislation passed in England in 1601 which established categories of the poor, including the deserving poor (orphans, widows, etc.) and the nondeserving poor (able-bodied males) and the treatment they were to receive from national and local governments. This law established precedents for policies toward the poor in the United States.

Poverty a determination that a household's income is inadequate judged by a specific standard.

Prejudice an irrational attitude of hostility directed against an individual, a group, a race, or their supposed characteristics.

Primary prevention targeted at the total population to prevent a problem from occurring.

Primary setting a setting where the types of services a professional provides match the primary goals of the setting; e.g., a hospital is a primary setting for a nurse but a secondary setting for a social worker.

Private insurance insurance programs available to individuals and families through the workplace or through purchase of policies with private insurance companies.

Private sector includes programs and agencies funded and operated by non-public entities, e.g., voluntary and proprietary agencies, and private businesses.

Probation an official option in which the offender has an opportunity to remain free from detention, or have a fine held in abeyance, if he/she follows the conditions of probation set by the court which are monitored by a probation officer.

Problem-solving approach a common intervention used by social workers which is based on client's motivation and capacity for change and opportunities available to the client to facilitate the change. Client and worker assess needs, identify problems and needs to be addressed, develop a plan to address problems and needs, and implement and monitor the plan, revising as needed.

Prosecutor public official (who is also an attorney) within the criminal justice system charged with presenting the evidence the state has against a defendant.

Psychiatry a branch of medicine that deals with mental, emotional, or behavioral disorders.

Psychoanalysis a method of dealing with emotional problems which focuses on intra-psychic functioning (internal conflicts within the individual).

Psychological parent a person viewed by a child as being his/her parental figure from a psychological or emotional standpoint as opposed to a birth relationship; if a boy were being raised by his grandparents and rarely sees his mother, they would be his psychological parents. Many court decisions are being made based on the concept of psychological as opposed to biological parent.

Psychology a science based on the study of mind and behavior which involves many subspecialties.

Psychometric instruments tests used to measure psychological functioning.

Psychotropic drugs types of drugs used in the treatment of severe mental health problems, including depression and psychoses, which have resulted in major reductions in numbers of individuals with emotional problems needing long-term hospitalization.

Public (social) assistance programs that provide income, medical care, and social services to individuals and families based on economic need, paid from state and local taxes, to provide a socially established minimum standard usually set by the state; Aid to Families with Dependent Children (AFDC), food stamps, and Medicaid are public assistance programs.

Public insurance insurance programs provided by the public sector to those in need who are not covered by private insurance programs and meet eligibility requirements, such as Medicaid.

Public sector includes programs and agencies funded and operated by government entities, including public schools, agencies, and hospitals.

Reality therapy an intervention, based on the assumption that people are responsible for their own behavior, which affects change by confronting individuals about irresponsible behaviors and encouraging them to accept responsibility for their behaviors and to develop positive self-worth through positive behavior.

Recreation group a group established to provide for the entertainment, enjoyment, and experience of participants through activities such as athletic or table games.

Residential treatment center a facility that provides 24-hour care with a treatment component for persons with mental health problems or developmental disabilities such as alcoholism; such programs are usually considered to be less restrictive than psychiatric hospitals.

Residual programs temporary programs established when first-line institutions fail to meet the expected needs of individuals and families; e.g., federal relief programs established during the Depression.

Reverse discrimination acts that result in unequal treatment of majority group members.

Rural a social, occupational, and cultural way of life for persons living in the country or in rural communities with less than 2500 persons.

School social work a social work approach which involves working with children, youth, and their families within a school setting: school social workers deal directly with children, youth, and their families as well as teachers, school administrators, and other community resources.

Secondary prevention targeted at subpopulations determined to be "at risk," or more likely to experience a specific problem, to prevent the problem from occurring.

Secondary setting a setting in which the types of services a professional provides differ from the primary focus of the setting; e.g. a social worker in a hospital works in a secondary setting, while a social worker in a social services agency works in a primary setting.

Self-concept the image that one has of one's self in relation to appearance, ability, skills, motivation, and capacity to react to the environment; derived primarily from feedback from others.

Self-help group a group of individuals with similar problems that meets for the purpose of providing support and information to each other and for mutual problem-solving; Parents Anonymous and Alcoholics

Anonymous are examples of self-help groups.

Sexism discrimination against an individual because of gender.

Sexual abuse the use of a child by an adult for sexual or emotional gratification in a sexual way, such as fondling, exposure, sexual intercourse, and exploitation, including child pornography.

Single-parent family a family headed by one parent, usually a female.

Single-subject designs research designs that evaluate the impact of interventions or policy changes on a single client or case.

Social action a social work approach to working with communities that stresses organization and group cohesion in confrontational approaches geared to modify or eliminate institutional power bases that negatively impact the community.

Social agencies organizations whose primary focus is to address social problems.

Social casework a social work method involving face-to-face contact with individuals, families, or groups where the social worker provides services directly to clients for the purpose of resolving problems; also referred to as direct practice.

Social group work a social work method involving intervention with groups of individuals that uses structured interaction to promote individual and group functioning and well-being.

Social inequality unequal treatment of social groups based on factors such as economic and social status, age, ethnicity, sexual preference, or gender.

Social insurance financial assistance for those whose income has been curtailed due to retirement, death or long-term disability of the family breadwinner; paid to former working persons or their dependents through a tax on earned income.

Social planning a social work approach to working with communities that emphasizes modification of institutional practices through the application of knowledge, values, and theory; a practical, rational approach.

Social Security an insurance program established as part of the Social Security Act which provides limited payments to eligible elderly persons or their dependents who have been employed and have had taxes deducted from their wages matched by their employers paid into a funding pool.

Social Security Act major social welfare legislation passed by Congress in 1935 which established social insurance programs based on taxes paid by working persons; public assistance programs to provide for those who do not qualify for social insurance programs and cannot provide for themselves or their families financially; and health and welfare services for children, families, the disabled, and the aged such as child welfare services, maternal and child health services, and services for the disabled.

Social welfare efforts organized by societies to facilitate the well-being of their members, usually focused on activities that seek to prevent, alleviate, or contribute to the solution of a selected set of social problems.

Social work the major profession that implements planned change activities prescribed by social welfare institutions through intervention with individuals, families and groups or at community,

organizational, and societal levels to enhance or restore social functioning.

Social worker a member of the social work profession who works with individuals, families, groups, organizations, communities, or societies to improve social functioning.

Socialization the process of learning to become a social being; the acquisition of knowledge, values, abilities, and skills that are essential to function as a member of the society within which the individual lives.

Socialization group a group established to stimulate behavior change, increase social skills, self-confidence and encourage motivation. The group members help participants develop socially acceptable behavior.

Specialized (expert) professional level of social work practice a level of practice which includes mastery in at least one knowledge and skill area (e.g., child and family or aging) as well as general social work knowledge; requires a MSW degree from an accredited social work program.

Special needs child a child who is available for adoption but is considered difficult to place because of special needs; special needs children are older, members of minority groups, members of large sibling groups, and/or have physical and emotional disabilities.

Specific deterrent a program or sentence targeted at an individual to discourage him/her from repeating inappropriate/illegal behavior.

Spillover effect occurs when feelings, attitudes and behaviors from one domain in a person's life have a positive or a negative impact on other domains; e.g., from the workplace to the family.

Steady state the constant adjustment of a system moving toward its goal while maintaining order and stability within.

Stereotyping holding a standardized mental picture of a group and attributing that mental picture to all group members.

Strategy a broad, long-range plan for implementing a program or policy.

Substance abuse improper use of mood-altering substances such as drugs that results in detrimental effects on an individual's personal life, including school, job, family, friends, health, spiritual life, or the law.

Substitute care out-of-home care provided for children when parents are unwilling or unable to provide care in their own homes; types of substitute care include foster care, group home care, and residential treatment, and are determined based on the needs of the child.

Supplemental Security Income (SSI) a program administered in conjunction with the Social Security Program to provide cash assistance to needy aged, blind, and/or permanently and totally disabled persons who meet certain eligibility standards established by state and federal regulations.

Synergy the combined energy of smaller parts of a larger system that is greater than the sum of the energy of those parts.

Systems/ecological framework a major framework used to understand individual, family, community, organizational, and societal events and behaviors which emphasizes the interactions and interdependence between individuals and their environments.

Tactics specific, often day-to-day, plan for implementing a program of policy.

Target system the person, persons or groups who need to change or be influenced in order to assist the client system. This may include the client system as well as others, such as school or employer.

Task-centered casework a short-term therapeutic approach to problem-solving which stresses the selection of specific tasks to be worked on within a limited time frame to address a client's problems and needs.

Tertiary prevention efforts targeted at individuals who have already experienced a specific problem to prevent that problem from re-occurring.

Testable the ability of a theory to be measured accurately and validly.

Theory a way of organizing facts or sets of facts to describe, explain or predict events.

Therapeutic group a group requiring skilled professional leaders who assist group members in addressing intensive personal and emotional problems.

Unemployment insurance (UI) an insurance program established by the Social Security Act which is funded by taxes assessed to employers and is available to eligible unemployed workers.

U.S. Children's Bureau the first federal department established by the federal government (1912) to address the needs of children and families; programs addressing problems of child abuse and neglect, runaway youth, adoption and foster care, and other child welfare services are currently operated by the Children's Bureau, which is part of the U.S. Department of Health and Human Services.

U.S. Department of Agriculture federal department that oversees the food stamp program and houses the Agricultural Extension Service, which provides services targeted to rural areas.

U.S. Department of Health and Human Services federal department that oversees the implementation of legislation relating to health and human services, including public assistance programs, child welfare services, and services for the elderly.

Values assumptions, convictions, or beliefs about the manner in which people should behave and the principles that should govern behavior.

Voluntary sector third sector of society, along with the public and for-profit proprietary sectors; the voluntary sector includes private, nonprofit social agencies.

Workers' compensation (WC) an insurance program which is funded by taxes assessed to employers and is available to eligible workers who are injured on the job or experience job-related injuries or illnesses.

Index